Vote Gun

Vote Gun

How Gun Rights
Became Politicized
in the United States

PATRICK J. CHARLES

Columbia

University

Press

New York

Columbia University Press
Publishers Since 1893
New York   Chichester, West Sussex
cup.columbia.edu

Library of Congress Cataloging-in-Publication Data
Names: Charles, Patrick J., author.
Title: Vote gun : how gun rights became politicized in the United States /
    Patrick J. Charles.
Description: New York, NY : Columbia University Press, [2023] | Includes
    bibliographical references and index.
Identifiers: LCCN 2022034767 (print) | LCCN 2022034768 (ebook) |
    ISBN 9780231208840 (hardback) | ISBN 9780231557658 (ebook)
Subjects: LCSH: Gun control—United States. | Gun control—Political
    aspects—United States. | Gun control—United States—Public opinion. |
    Firearms—Government policy—United States.
Classification: LCC HV7436 .C49 2023 (print) | LCC HV7436 (ebook) |
    DDC 363.330973—dc23/eng/20221123
LC record available at https://lccn.loc.gov/2022034767
LC ebook record available at https://lccn.loc.gov/2022034768

Cover design: Elliott S. Cairns

For my daughter Sophie Olivia Charles, named after my late friend Sophie Miller, PhD Cambridge University, and in memory of George Gusich, my father figure and friend.

Contents

Preface

I originally intended *Vote Gun* to be completed in conjunction with my book *Armed in America: A History of Gun Rights from Colonial Militias to Concealed Carry* (2018). *Vote Gun* was to be a macro history on the politicization of gun rights up through the elections in 2016. Yet in conducting my research, I quickly learned that much, if not most, of the story had yet to be told, and a microhistory was warranted. Indeed, several academics and writers have written on the politicization of gun rights in the twentieth century. What virtually all these academics and writers got wrong, however, was the historical timeline of events, particularly the point in time when firearms owners were effectively organized into a political force. The politicization of gun rights did not begin in the late 1960s or early 1970s as these authors contended. Rather, it began five decades earlier, after the passage of the New York Sullivan Act in 1911, which my book *Armed in America* definitively proves. Recently, Matthew Lacombe, in his book *Firepower: How the NRA Turned Gun Owners Into a Political Force*, has shed additional light on this historical fallacy—one that *Vote Gun* seeks to dispel.

As for why *Vote Gun* stops its historical examination at 1980, the reason is twofold. First, the history of gun rights post-1980 is so rich with historical research material that every decade will ultimately require its own volume. Second, and more important from a historiography standpoint, as it stands today, most post-1980 political collections and congressional papers are either heavily redacted or not yet open to researchers, which makes it extremely difficult for historians and academics to reconstruct any post-1980 political history with sufficient accuracy. The papers of former president Ronald Reagan are a principal case in point. But it is not just Reagan's papers. The same holds true for the papers of former president George H. W. Bush, to include items going as far back as the 1960s. Then there are the political papers of late Michigan representative John D. Dingell, Jr.—the longest-serving member in congressional history and a principal National Rifle Association (NRA) surrogate going back to the late 1950s. Although Dingell donated his political papers to the University of Michigan in 2015, and university archivists have cataloged said papers since as early as 2018, the Dingell estate has yet to formally approve their release. And when the papers are eventually released for public consumption, given that Dingell's spouse, Debbie Dingell, is a current member of Congress, researchers will almost assuredly find many items either partially redacted or withheld from public viewing altogether. Fortunately, the delayed release of Dingell's papers, although disappointing for researchers, including myself, did not negatively affect the historical content and findings in *Vote Gun*. The papers of three other NRA surrogates—Florida representative Robert F. Sikes, Iowa senator Bourke B. Hickenlooper, and Nebraska senator Roman L. Hruska—as well as several letters from Dingell that appeared in other political collections provided more than sufficient material to historically reconstruct the machinations of gun rights advocacy through 1980.

Vote Gun would not have been possible but for the help and assistance of many friends and family, colleagues, academics, and institutions. Beginning with the institutions, the staff at several archives and libraries proved invaluable. This includes the staff at the Alabama Department of Archives and History, Abraham Lincoln Presidential Library, Bob Dole Archives and Special Collections, Arizona State University, Herbert Hoover Presidential Library, Library of Congress, National Archives and Records Administration, Minnesota Historical Society, Rauner Special Collections Library, California State Archives, Hagley Archives, Wyoming American Heritage Center, Dirksen Center, Wesleyan University Special Collections and Archives, Edmund S. Muskie Archives and Special Collections, J. Willard Marriott Library Special Collections, Gerald R. Ford Presidential Library, University of Vermont Special Collections, Seeley G. Mudd Manuscript

Library, Tulane University Howard-Tilton Memorial Library, University of Virginia Special Collections, Vermont Historical Society, Harry S. Truman Presidential Library, Richard B. Russell Library for Political Research and Studies, University of Idaho Special Collections, Jimmy Carter Presidential Library, Richard Nixon Presidential Library, Ohio State University Congressional Papers Archive, John F. Kennedy Presidential Library, Stony Brook University Special Collections and Archives, University of Maryland Special Collections, Lyndon B. Johnson Presidential Library, Briscoe Center of American History, Montana Historical Society, Arizona Historical Society, University of Montana Mansfield Library, University of West Florida Special Collections, Nebraska State Historical Society, University of North Carolina Louis Round Wilson Special Collections Library, Pennsylvania Historical Society, Pennsylvania State University Special Collections, Willamette University Archives and Special Collections, University of Massachusetts Amherst Special Collections, Clemson University Special Collections, University of Connecticut Thomas J. Dodd Research Center, University of Pittsburgh Special Collections, University of Oregon Special Collections, and University of Washington Special Collections. The staff at most of these institutions took on the job of scanning and transmitting their respective collections for this project, albeit at a substantial personal financial cost.

Five institutions were particularly gracious during the research phase of *Vote Gun*. The Dwight D. Eisenhower Presidential Library ($575), University of Oklahoma Carl Albert Congressional Research and Studies Center ($1,000), and University of Michigan Bentley Historical Library ($2,000) each provided travel grants, and their staff were extremely helpful in locating materials within their collections. Everytown for Gun Safety kindly provided a $5,000 research grant, which covered roughly one-fifth of all archival scanning costs. Last, the Second Amendment Foundation (SAF) generously provided copyright permission to reprint any *Gun Week* political cartoon in *Vote Gun* at no expense. Generally, obtaining copyright permission for just one political cartoon in a book can cost upward of hundreds of dollars. Thankfully, SAF understood the broader, academic benefit of republishing these cartoons.

In addition to the assistance provided by several institutions and their staff, I am indebted to several professionals for their mentorship, guidance, and support over many years, particularly Joseph Blocher, Jake Charles,

Mark Frassetto, Jordan Gusich, Matthew Lacombe (who was kind to share his research throughout the project), Carrie Lewine McCready, Alex McCready, Darrell A. H. Miller, Robert J. Spitzer, and Jennifer Tucker.

Special thanks are due to my literary agent, Alexa Stark, and Trident Media Group for taking on this project, the late U.S. senator Joseph D. Tydings for taking time to participate in a phone interview, my former colleagues in U.S. Senate, particularly Senator Martin Heinrich's office, for showing me how our political process operates behinds the scenes, and my fellow United States Air Force (USAF) legislative fellows for providing similar insights from their respective experiences. And, of course, a special thanks to Stephen Wesley and Columbia University Press for seeing *Vote Gun* for what it is—a groundbreaking, historical deep dive into the rise of gun rights in American politics.

Finally, I want to thank my family, close friends, and colleagues and coworkers, especially within United States Special Operations Command (USSOCOM) and the wider special operations community, for their continued help and support, as well my late canine writing companions—AJ (2003–2018), TJ (2004–2020), and Benny (2007–2021, adopted 2015)—for listening to me write and think out loud for many years.

Vote Gun

Introduction

T he anti-gun law can be intelligently viewed only from the standpoint of a public menace," wrote National Rifle Association (NRA)
official C. B. Lister in 1924.[1] It would be another two years before
the NRA formally announced it was entering the fight against "anti-gun"
laws, yet Lister's quote succinctly summarizes how the NRA would characterize gun control for the rest of the century and to this day remains a
key talking point among gun rights advocates.[2] To say the politics involving
firearms is deeply emotional and polarizing would be an understatement.
Much like the issues of immigration, abortion, and crime, the politics
involving firearms are largely tribal. In one tribe are the proponents of
gun rights. According to polling over the past quarter century, the prototypical member of the gun rights tribe is likely to be a non-college-
educated, rural, white male. In another tribe are the proponents of gun
control. Based on the same polling and surveys, the prototypical member
of the gun control tribe is likely to be a college-educated, urban, nonwhite
female.[3] This is not to say that there are not non-college-educated, rural,
white males who support gun control and college-educated, urban, nonwhite females who support gun rights. There most certainly are. But what
the prototypical member of each tribe underscores is how much one's identity has come to define whether one supports gun rights or gun control.

Just consider that non-college-educated, rural, white males are almost twice as likely to politically identify with conservatism and the Republican Party as with liberalism and the Democratic Party. The reverse is true of college-educated, urban, nonwhite females, who are twice as likely to politically identify with liberalism and the Democratic Party as with conservatism and the Republican Party.[4] Needless to say, those who support gun rights are typically conservative and Republicans, and those who support gun control are typically liberal and Democrats.[5] Supporters of either gun rights or gun control, of course, are not a political monolith. Far from it, as seen in recent years with the rise of all-Black armed groups advocating for civil rights and legal reforms typically associated with today's liberals and the Democratic Party.[6] But when one looks at the subject from a wider, macro viewpoint, the political polarization is quite stark. As a recent Pew Research Center survey indicates, roughly 75 percent of self-identifying conservatives and Republicans place more importance on gun rights than on gun control. The exact opposite is true of self-identifying liberals and Democrats, roughly 75 percent of whom place more importance on gun control than on gun rights.[7]

The political polarization among proponents of gun rights and gun control, although commonplace today, is relatively recent. Throughout the 1960s and most of the 1970s, one's political party affiliation was in no way indicative of whether one favored gun rights over gun control or vice versa.[8] This is not to say that there have not been any indicators as to whether a person was more likely to support gun rights over gun control and vice versa. In the early to mid-nineteenth century, for instance, one's understanding of what the Second Amendment right to "keep and bear arms" constitutionally embodied, what were its limits, and how the right was understood to function in society was largely regional. While those living in the northeastern United States were more likely than not to view the Second Amendment in strictly "well-regulated militia" terms, those living in the deep South and rural West were more likely than not to view that amendment as being a bit more individualistic. As the United States entered the twentieth century, however, these regional differences began to diminish as the concept of *firearms localism* became normalized and accepted across the country. Firearms localism is simply another way of saying that the proper way to balance the competing political interests of gun rights and gun control is to keep the issue localized. Essentially, firearms localism provided local government officials—who were believed to have a better understanding of the needs and concerns of their constituents than did state or federal officials—the discretion to properly weigh an individual's right to keep and bear arms with the wider public health and safety concerns of the community.

Firearms localism first grew to prominence in the mid- to late nineteenth century. During that time, the country was rapidly expanding westward, and as new urban and trading centers arose, firearms localism grew in popularity. Whether it was in a frontier gateway town like Dodge City, Kansas, the mining metropolis of San Francisco, California, or the burgeoning trading center of Dallas, Texas, there was little pushback among residents whenever lawmakers enacted ordinances restricting the ownership, use, sale, and carriage of firearms. Firearms restrictions that went beyond the city limits, however, were often criticized, and understandably so given the general absence of law enforcement in those areas.[9]

Firearms localism was in fact so generally accepted that even the first gun rights movement endorsed the concept. Led by the efforts of the United States Revolver Association (USRA), a small organization dedicated to pistol marksmanship, and the editors of sporting, hunting, and shooting magazines, the first gun rights movement viewed firearms localism as the key to a "sane" approach to firearms regulation.[10] "Sane" firearms regulation, according to the USRA, included laws requiring that all firearms purchases be recorded and registered, prohibiting criminals from owning or using firearms, prohibiting minors from purchasing firearms, and requiring enhanced mandatory sentencing for anyone using a firearm in the commission of a crime.[11]

Additionally, the first gun rights movement denounced with force the promiscuous carrying of firearms, particularly in public places, or what was otherwise referred to as "gun-toting." The first gun rights movement did, however, support laws that permitted a person to obtain "license to carry a firearm" if that individual could "show cause" as to why they "should go armed."[12] Known more generally as "may issue" concealed carry laws, today, due to the Supreme Court's recent opinion in *New York State Rifle & Pistol Association v. Bruen*, such laws are inviolate of the Second Amendment. But this was not the case from the early to mid-twentieth century. If anything, both the courts and gun rights proponents saw "may issue" concealed-carry laws as an acceptable compromise to the legislative alternative of outright prohibition.[13] There was also general agreement among early to mid-twentieth-century sportsmen, hunters, and firearms owners that only persons who were adequately trained in handling firearms and could demonstrate a justifiable need to be publicly armed should do so.[14]

Support for firearms localism became even more prevalent after the NRA commandeered the gun rights movement in the late 1920s. Firearms localism was in fact one of the chief political talking points that the NRA used to fight against federal firearms controls from the early 1930s through the mid-1970s.[15] Over that time, the NRA regularly argued that the regulating of firearms was a matter best reserved to the respective states, and, constitutionally speaking, that any federal firearms regulatory power was limited in scope.[16] In the mid- to late 1960s, the NRA's argument became particularly appealing to conservatives and states' rights proponents, who generally opposed Congress's foray into civil rights legislation.[17] Given the wide political appeal to this constituency, it is not surprising that conservative Republican Richard M. Nixon co-opted the concept of firearms localism for his presidential campaign in 1968.[18] From that point on, albeit gradually, the cause of gun rights became increasingly tied to conservativism, the "moral majority," and the Republican Party.[19] This forever changed gun rights politics. For once the cause of gun rights became partisan, the concept of firearms localism was forced to gradually give way to the concept of gun rights nationalism—that is, the belief that Second Amendment rights are greater than or equal to other constitutional rights,[20] and that such rights need uniform protection across the United States.

Vote Gun examines this transformation primarily by exploring the rise, growth, and evolution of the gun rights movement. In doing so, it investigates the historical "how" and "why" gun rights politics entered American discourse, with a particular focus on the timeframe 1968 to 1980. There are indeed other historical aspects of the gun rights movement explored throughout this book. Perhaps one of the most relevant—at least for today's increasingly politically polarized atmosphere and its interconnection with organized disinformation campaigns—is the frequency with which hyperboles and myths have consumed historical facts and scientific truths. This has long been the hallmark of the gun rights movement's ability to rouse sportsmen, hunters, shooters, and firearms owners to fight against firearms controls and to influence lawmakers to support gun rights over gun control. The point to be made is that political perception is often more important than the political reality. Whatever people politically perceive to be true will often end up overriding what is in fact true.

1

"A Shot Sure to Be Heard Around Congress"

On November 6, 1968, with most of the Election Day ballots counted, the dust was settling on the composition of the 91st Congress. For the state of Pennsylvania, the results virtually mirrored those of the 90th Congress. All twenty-four of Pennsylvania's incumbents in the House of Representatives were reelected. And from the three remaining open seats, each was won by the incumbent party. Only Pennsylvania's Senate seat, held by incumbent Democrat Joseph S. Clark, ended up flipping political parties. At first glance, considering the results of the presidential race in 1968, in which Republican Richard M. Nixon handily defeated Democrat Hubert H. Humphrey in the Electoral College, the defeat of Clark may not appear all that surprising. A closer look at the election tallies, however, uncovers an anomaly of sorts. For in Pennsylvania, not only did the total votes received by Democrat House candidates outnumber those for their Republican counterparts, but also in the presidential tally it was Humphrey who handily beat Nixon by nearly 170,000 votes. Yet, in the Senate, Clark failed to ride his fellow Democrats' political coattails and lost to Republican Richard S. Schweiker by more than 282,000 votes.[1] Clark was in fact the only Democrat running for statewide office in Pennsylvania to lose that year.

There are several reasons why Clark lost his Senate seat. One was his poor likeability, even within the Democratic Party. It was no secret that

Clark clashed with the long-term party patriarch, President Lyndon B. Johnson.[2] This included Clark vocally opposing Johnson's foreign policy in Vietnam. There was also the problem of Clark's relatability among rural Pennsylvania voters. Even in the suburbs and urban areas, despite posting a positive voting record on workers' rights and civil liberties, Clark was not perceived to be the epitome of the typical, blue-collar, Pennsylvanian worker he professed to be fighting for. Rather, Clark was more commonly known for being financially well-off, and he was not shy in boasting about this fact.[3] Conversely, Clark's opponent Schweiker came from the working middle-class.[4] Schweiker, at forty-two, was widely viewed as the young, vibrant, and up-and-coming candidate with fresh political ideas. Clark was not. At sixty-seven, Clark was unflatteringly referred to by Schweiker on the campaign trail as the "Model-T" candidate—a reference to the first mass-manufactured automobile by Ford Motor Company from 1908 to 1927. And in a televised debate, Schweiker wisecracked that Clark was trying to sell "the programs of the '30s to solve the problems of the '70s."[5]

There are other reasons that help explain Clark's election defeat, but there is one that would affect the politics of both the state of Pennsylvania and the entire country for decades to come: Clark's unabashed support for firearms controls. And the sportsmen, hunters, shooters, and firearms owners who were active in Clark's defeat made sure to hold it up as proof positive that they were a powerful one-issue voting bloc, and that supporting firearms controls was a losing campaign issue. For instance, in one Pennsylvania county newspaper, outdoor columnist and gun rights supporter Del Kerr touted Clark's defeat as a "vanquished victory not only for those who cherish the right to bear arms, but for all people who believe in American freedoms." Kerr added, "Never again will sportsmen be considered a minority group. In the future, many hopeful politicians will visit gun clubs as an important part of their campaign."[6] Similarly, in an opinion editorial published in the *Philadelphia Inquirer*, another gun rights supporter noted that Clark's defeat "will come as a warning to candidates in future state elections, when they confront the carefully built-up animosity of the 998,000 licensed hunters in Pennsylvania."[7]

Although these election forecasts were embellished, they were not technically wrong. For from that point onward, whispers of the powerful "gun lobby" in elections became the norm. This is a significant historical development because up to that point in American politics, whether a political candidate supported or opposed firearms controls was generally a nonissue, at least in campaign advertisements, speeches, and policy positions. In fact, it was not until 1966 that firearms control was recognized as a potential election cycle issue, albeit in a limited capacity.[8] This changed in the wake of the 1968 elections. Certainly, Congress having recently passed the Gun Control Act—the first major federal firearms laws in over thirty years—was also an important factor in bringing about this political change. It should be noted, however, that for decades sportsmen, hunting, conservation, and shooting organizations had been calling on members to oust from office any politicians who supported firearms control, regardless of party affiliation.[9] But until 1968 these calls for political action had not borne any fruit. Clark's defeat changed that perception, and, in its wake, gun rights advocacy was able to politically morph and take on a new purpose—affecting election outcomes.

For Pennsylvania sportsmen, hunters, and firearms owners, Clark's defeat was not merely some flash-in-the-pan, grassroots political advocacy effort. The politics of firearms controls was something that Pennsylvania's

FIGURE 1.1 Campaign advertisement in 1960 for David S. Lister, of Avis, Pennsylvania. Lister ran as a Democratic candidate for the Pennsylvania Assembly. A central plank of his campaign was his opposition to "any restrictive firearms legislation" because crime cannot be "outlawed by legislating against firearms." Ultimately, he lost in the Democratic primary to Chauncey F. Royer.

representatives, senators, and governors had wrestled with for many years. Since 1931, when the Pennsylvania Assembly joined several other states in passing the Uniform Firearms Act—which was model state legislation drafted by both the National Conference of Commissioners (NCC) and the National Rifle Association (NRA)—the firearms control issue was known to be a political lightening rod.[10] Whenever a Pennsylvania lawmaker proposed restrictive firearms legislation, sporting, hunting, conservation, and shooting organizations, such as the Pennsylvania Federation of Sportsmen's Clubs (PFSC), the Pennsylvania Rifle and Pistol Association (PRPA), and even the state-run Pennsylvania Game Commission (PGC), through the print medium of newsletters, membership magazines, and journals, urged their respective members to take the necessary political action to defeat its passage.[11]

Hyperboles, half-truths, and even conspiracy theories about anyone who supported firearms controls were a regular occurrence. Consider the July 1963 edition of the PGC's *Pennsylvania Game News*. In it was an article by Jim Varner titled "Sportsmen, Help Crush Anti-Firearms Propaganda," where Varner called on PGC members to "ERADICATE the double-crossers in our society who seek to eliminate the American heritage and prevent red-blooded youngsters . . . from learning how to use a firearm." In delivering his call to political action, he claimed that the "subversive trend" of firearms control propaganda was becoming more pervasive than ever—propaganda that was "formulated by dangerous un-American groups." He went on to assert that the groups were orchestrating a three-pronged attack on Americans' Second Amendment rights. The first prong was infiltrating leading publications' editorial staffs with the primary purpose of writing favorably about firearms controls. The second was encouraging TV affiliates to frequently report on homicides committed with firearms, which in turn was intended to foster an antifirearms bias among TV viewers. The third prong was encouraging lawmakers to take up the mantle of firearms controls and in the process "ignore the American's constitutional rights in every way." Although Varner firmly believed that "dangerous un-American groups" were the ones responsible for conjuring up this antifirearms propaganda, he placed the principal blame on the media for its dissemination: "It is strikingly peculiar that certain segments of our national press appear intent on abridging any of these freedoms. One would think that members of the Fourth Estate—considering their long battle to preserve their own freedom from censorship and government control—would realize that any restriction imposed on any of the articles of the Bill of Rights is a two-edged sword that might also be applied to others."[12]

For more than three decades, in Pennsylvania as well as across the country, the practice of sporting, hunting, conservation, and shooting organizations urging their membership to take political action against firearms controls continued largely unabated—that is, until the assassination of President John F. Kennedy, on November 22, 1963, brought the American public's attention to the practice. The reason for this was twofold. First, until Kennedy's assassination, the public was generally unaware as to how these organizations were exerting political influence within state and local assemblies. While certainly the political actions of these groups were reported in local newspapers from time to time, and those lawmakers who introduced restrictive firearms legislation were aware of said actions, no one in the national media was reporting on it. Second, because the national media was not covering the issue, there was no counter, pro-firearms-control organization or movement in place to politically fight back. In fact, from the turn of the twentieth century until the assassination of President Kennedy, there had been only one such organization chartered in the United States. That organization, the National Anti-Weapon Association (NAWA), had existed for only a brief period—from 1931 to 1933.[13]

Even after the Kennedy assassination, a time when Pennsylvanians were increasingly pressuring state lawmakers to enact more restrictive amendments to the Uniform Firearms Act, sporting, hunting, conservation, and shooting organizations remained a potent political force. For five years, from 1963 to 1968, these groups successfully fought off the passage of any additional restrictive firearms legislation in the Pennsylvania Assembly. Additionally, over that time, the organizations were extremely effective in defeating restrictive firearms legislation proposed at the local and municipal level. Only the city of Philadelphia was able to buck the trend and pass a firearms registration ordinance, much to the dismay of the gun rights community (figure 1.2).[14] Its passage only increased the political stakes for what was already contentious fight in the Pennsylvania Assembly over whether to amend the Uniform Firearms Act.

During this fight, perhaps no Pennsylvania lawmaker was more aware of the contentious nature of the firearms control issue than Republican governor Raymond P. Shafer. Not long after Philadelphia enacted its

FIREARMS REGISTRATION?

The Pennsylvania State Fish & Game Protective Association, a non-political organization, urges sportsmen and the general public to join in opposing enactment of City Council Bill No. 560, which would compel the registration of all firearms, including those used for home and family protection —at a public hearing to be held in Room 400, City Hall, on Tuesday, February 9, 1965, at 10 A.M.

The record is clear—firearms registration laws on a national and state basis have had no effect in reducing crime. Only the law-abiding citizen will register his gun. No one believes that criminals will register their weapons. Actually, as in the case with automobiles, most weapons used by criminals are stolen.

Basically, the only reason for registering privately owned firearms is to make it possible for the governing authorities, through the police whom they control, to seize such weapons when, in the opinion of those authorities, such seizure is desirable. Proponents of firearms registration always deny any such intention. Usually their denial is sincere. "All we want to know is who has guns and what kind." In the next breath, they admit that they do not expect criminals to register their guns.

1. Statistics prove that criminals, representing 2% of the total population, do not purchase or acquire their guns from licensed firearms dealers.

2. Police cannot solve crime with a list of guns owned by law-abiding citizens who compose 98% of the population.

3. In spite of the present state laws requiring registration of pistols at time of purchase, practically all of the guns taken from criminals in Philadelphia by police are not registered.

4. .22 caliber rifles and shotguns, which would make up the major portion of weapons to be registered under this bill, are not, with few exceptions, used by criminals; criminals use the elements of surprise via the concealability of the weapons ie. pistols and revolvers.

5. At present, most firearms cases are not punished at the judicial level in Philadelphia. They are severely punished outside of Philadelphia. The present state and federal laws are adequate, if the penalties are enforced.

6. Cases involving sawed off shotguns, home made guns, pistols with the serial numbers removed, etc., are covered by both state and federal laws—but in Philadelphia these cases are rarely turned over to federal authorities, being dismissed by the local judiciary.

7. Zip guns are easily made, and never registered. The criminal has an advantage over the honest citizen.

8. In spite of the "switchblade" ordinance enacted in Philadelphia in 1953 prohibiting the sale or carrying of knives, this ordinance has been ineffective in preventing a fast increase in the number of knifings in Philadelphia.

9. The illusion is created by those supporting Bill 560 that if Bill 560 is passed, crimes committed by use of firearms will be nonexistent ie. a utopia.

10. Criminals who enter the City are required without paying any fee to register their presence with the Police Department. Bill 560 provides that law-abiding citizens must pay a $5.00 fee to register their firearms.

11. Art. 1, Sec. 21 of the Pennsylvania Constitution provides: "The right of the citizens to bear arms in defense of themselves and the state shall not be questioned."

The only correct solution to crimes committed with firearms is to punish the criminal and not penalize the law-abiding gun owner. If crimes committed while armed with a gun received an additional severe penalty, and this punishment were made mandatory and not left up to the discretion of the courts, criminal use of guns would be effectively stopped. Such a law would receive the full support of sportsmen and all responsible citizens.

Regardless of the good intention of some proponents, the only practical effect of a firearms registration law could be an INCREASE in the crime rate by disarming reputable citizens and thereby encouraging the activities of the criminal element, thus adding to the work of the police.

PENNSYLVANIA STATE FISH & GAME PROTECTION ASSOCIATION

1505 Race Street, Philadelphia, Pa.   Frederick H. Starling, III, President

FIGURE 1.2 Advertisement in the *Philadelphia Inquirer*, February 7, 1965, by the Pennsylvania State Fish and Game Protection Association opposing Philadelphia's firearms registration ordinance. The advertisement outlined eleven reasons why Philadelphians should oppose the ordinance, including the "only reason for registering privately owned firearms is to make it possible for the governing authorities ... to seize such weapons when ... such seizure is desirable."

firearms registration ordinance, then lieutenant governor Shafer riled up the Pennsylvania gun rights community when he summarily dismissed their political objections to firearms controls on the grounds that there really wasn't any "hunting, and fishing or sportsmen's efforts" in the Philadelphia area.[15] What Shafer unknowingly overlooked was that over 90,000 of the 820,000 state hunting licenses were from the Philadelphia metropolitan area—a fact that his personal aide and assistant press secretary, Robert McCormick, made sure to remind him of the next time he was interviewed on the matter. McCormick knew that if Shafer was ever going to succeed Governor William Scranton, it was best not to marginalize either side of the gun debate. Thus, for his next media interview, McCormick advised Shafer "NOT [to] get into [any] details" nor "alienate the sportsman or the do-gooders" should he be asked any firearms control-related questions.[16] This way Shafer could politically straddle both sides of the issue until the gubernatorial election in 1966.

Ultimately, McCormick's strategy worked. Not only did Shafer end up receiving the political endorsement of the PFSC, but he also went on to win the governorship.[17] And in the months that immediately followed, the sporting, hunting, conservation, and shooting organizations that made up bulk of the Pennsylvania gun rights community made sure to remind Shafer that it was their endorsement that helped seal the victory. In a confidential memorandum to McCormick, it was advised that Shafer once and for all cement his "love affair" with sportsmen by openly denouncing all firearms controls. What the Pennsylvania gun rights community wanted was an anti-firearms-control statement from Shafer "with real guts in it." They felt that such a statement would help curtail further legislative attempts at firearms control. Simply put, Shafer's statement denouncing firearms controls needed to be "STRONG" and his words "direct, folksy, no double talk, double meaning, etc."[18]

Shafer obliged the request in a March 17, 1967, speech before the PFSC in Harrisburg.[19] Although he stated that some additional federal legislation governing the mail-order sale of firearms was necessary to keep them out of the hands of "known criminals, minors, and the mentally-disturbed," he unequivocally denounced the enactment of any overly restrictive state or local firearms controls, including Philadelphia's firearms registration ordinance.[20] Moreover, should an overly restrictive firearms bill somehow pass the Pennsylvania Assembly, Shafer pledged to veto it.[21] "I think that we should be working to get rid of the abuses of our present gun law and not hurt the lawful users of guns in Pennsylvania," he stated.[22] In return for his anti-firearms-control statement, Shafer received the gratitude and praise of the Pennsylvania gun rights community.[23]

The gratitude and praise quickly shifted to anger and criticism, however, when it was reported that Pennsylvania attorney general William C. Sennett was considering proposing restrictive firearms controls analogous to New Jersey's. Two of the state's principal newspapers ran headlines that read "Shafer Backing Stronger Law to Control Guns" and "Shafer Seeks Tough State Gun Law," sending the Pennsylvania gun rights community into a frenzy.[24] PFSC vice president Leonard A. Green frantically wrote to Shafer: "My telephone rang a hundred times . . . from sportsmen and friends whom I helped influence to support you and your program. Needless to say, I was without any defense and my only answer was 'I have sent a telegram and Monday I'll write to see what is going on.' Please get me an answer as to why anyone would be authorized to commit your administration to such low-down proposals."[25] A telegram, sent a day earlier, noted, "Today's press release regarding proposed gun legislation was both shocking and revolting for a state that stands number one in sales of non-resident hunting license and boasts it's [number] two industry is hunting and fishing and outdoor recreation. Your administration has dealt the sportsmen of Pennsylvania an unforgiveable blow."[26]

The PRPA also expressed shock and dismay.[27] Alan S. Krug, PRPA's legislative director, wrote to Attorney General Sennett that the PRPA was "under the distinct impression that governor Shafer supported their position on firearms legislation." But should Shafer request that the Pennsylvania Assembly take up new firearms legislation, Krug enclosed copies of bills that the PRPA, National Shooting Sports Foundation (NSSF), and NRA were willing to endorse. Any other proposed firearms legislation was deemed unacceptable. Krug closed his letter with a warning: "One thing is sure, and that is, if you press for the New Jersey type firearms legislation in this state, you will institute a direct confrontation between the sportsmen of Pennsylvania and the Administration. We are completely opposed to the New Jersey anti-sportsmen firearms law."[28]

Over the next week, the Pennsylvania gun rights community bombarded Shafer's office with angry letters, telegrams, and phone calls—that is, until March 22, 1967, when Shafer issued a resounding rebuke of firearms controls at a PFSC meeting.[29] While Shafer admitted that he and Sennett were in talks with New Jersey government officials about strengthening Pennsylvania's firearms laws, they were just that—talks, i.e., a professional courtesy from one state government to another. "I don't support the New Jersey gun law and my stand is the same as last year when I talked to you," Shafer told the PFSC meeting attendees, adding, "I think that we should be working to get rid of the abuses of our present gun law and not hurt the lawful users of guns in Pennsylvania."[30] Shafer's rebuke could not have been better timed. The editors of both *Gun Week* and *Field and Stream*, two sporting, hunting, and shooting publications that frequently lamented against firearms controls, were in the process of publishing pieces highly critical of Shafer. But word of Shafer's anti-firearms-control speech effectively quashed them.[31]

With Shafer having affirmed his opposition to firearms control, the gun rights community took solace that he was assuredly one of them. Shafer made sure to imply as much whenever he responded to firearms control-related constituent letters. Time and time again, he wrote to his Pennsylvania constituents that he did "not favor any [firearms control] legislation at either the local, State or Federal level which would be restrictive to sportsmen and other law-abiding citizens who wish to purchase firearms for legitimate purposes."[32]

For the time being, the gun rights community could not have been happier with Shafer. They knew that they had Shafer's ear whenever the firearms control issue reared its ugly head in the Pennsylvania Assembly. This was particularly true for the officers of the PFSC and PRPA, who were in frequent contact with Shafer's staff.[33] From the spring of 1967 to the spring of 1968, Shafer remained firmly opposed to firearms controls. Neither the assassination of Martin Luther King, Jr., nor the riots that immediately followed, nor public opinion polls showing overwhelming support for firearms controls remotely altered his position.[34] In fact, without Shafer's support, not even the Pennsylvanian Republican leadership was willing to endorse any type of restrictive firearms legislation.[35] The initial push for controls following the assassination of New York senator Robert F. Kennedy on June 5, 1968, did not alter Shafer's position either. The very next day, echoing the political talking points of gun rights proponents, he stated that only law-abiding citizens are ever disadvantaged by firearms controls. Criminals were not, and in most cases they would continue to break the law. Simply put, to Shafer, the solution to firearms-related violence was not more controls, it was the strict, unyielding enforcement of existing laws. Only then would criminals think twice before reaching for a gun.[36]

But within a week of Senator Kennedy's death, Shafer suddenly reversed course.[37] At a press conference, he stated he was now "very much in favor of strong gun control legislation," to include firearms registration, and directed State Attorney General Sennett to advance whatever legislation deemed necessary to protect Pennsylvanians from firearms-related violence.[38] Shafer suddenly transformed into such a strong firearms control proponent that he even took to advocating for firearms controls nationally. This included advocating for a strong firearms control plank at the annual meetings of the Republican Governors Association and the Republican Platform Committee.[39]

What caused Shafer to suddenly back firearms controls? Publicly, he said it was a telegram from President Lyndon B. Johnson requesting that every governor do their utmost to strengthen their state's firearms laws.[40] The truth was that public opinion in support of firearms controls had become too vocal to ignore, even for Shafer. Thomas L. Kimball, the National Wildlife Federation's (NWF) executive director, summarized the general public's sentiment perfectly in an internal memorandum: "It is apparent . . . that the national mood following the tragic assassination of Sen. Robert F. Kennedy is to 'do something.' Unfortunately, the concrete expression of this mood is to press for tighter gun controls. . . . I am convinced that a majority of Americans probably would prohibit [the] private ownership of guns if a vote was taken today."[41]

Shafer's political flip-flop on firearms controls immediately drew the ire of the gun rights community. The same sportsmen, hunters, shooters, and firearms owners who once proudly backed Shafer were now accusing him of everything from being blinded by a "well financed propaganda campaign . . . created by liberals" to working with Communists and anarchists to disarm the country.[42] Even those within the gun rights community who once sang Shafer's praises took turns at publicly criticizing him.[43] But behind the scenes, these same individuals were pleading with Shafer to back only firearms legislation that they endorsed, and some even proposed drafting the legislation.[44]

Shafer ultimately declined their overtures.[45] Instead, he instructed Sennett to draft a firearms bill alongside Democratic state representative

Herbert Fineman, who for almost a year had been calling for the Pennsylvania Assembly to enact strict firearms controls.[46] Together, Sennett and Fineman produced what Shafer believed to be a "workable" firearms bill—one that was "designed to keep guns out of the hands of irresponsible persons" yet respected the rights of citizens to own weapons for lawful purposes. Overall, Shafer's firearms bill included six reforms, each of which centered on the establishment of a firearms identification card. To obtain the card a person would have to pass a background check, demonstrate "minimal knowledge, skill or familiarity" with firearms, and pay a five-dollar fee. Only upon obtaining a card would a person be able to purchase firearms and ammunition within the state. And, as it pertained specifically to handguns, Shafer's bill required that each purchase be registered and undergo a five-day cooling-off period.[47]

In the weeks leading up to the Pennsylvania Assembly vote on Shafer's firearms bill, the gun rights community organized several meetings and rallies condemning it. At one rally near Pittsburgh more than 1,000 people attended, many of who were wearing campaign buttons supporting the presidential campaign of Alabama governor George C. Wallace.[48] At another rally held in Hollidaysburg, more than 900 people attended, including several state and local lawmakers who promised attendees that they would work to defeat any firearms control legislation.[49] Meanwhile, at a rally held in Johnstown, more than 3,500 people attended.[50] Speaking before the rally was retired army colonel John Lee, an NRA field representative, who told the crowd: "We're not going to let some city dude who doesn't know one end of a gun from another take our guns away from us. Are we going to submit to the *traitors, enemies, and criminals* in our midst? I say no."[51]

The rallies, meetings, and overall organized opposition of the gun rights community proved effective.[52] For when Shafer's firearms control bill was laid before the Pennsylvania Assembly, it was handily defeated.[53] In its place, the assembly adopted a bill that added a mandatory five-to-ten-year prison sentence for anyone found guilty of committing a crime with a firearm.[54] Additionally, although the Pennsylvania Assembly initially voted the measure down, a bill severely restricting the carrying of firearms on public streets without a permit was enacted.[55] The passage of these two bills was undoubtedly a win for gun rights proponents, which for decades had touted the mantra "Guns don't kill people, people do." Meanwhile, Shafer, despite being "very disappointed" with the defeat of his firearms bill, thought the passage of the other two firearms measures was a "step in the right direction."[56] Still hopeful, Shafer urged the Pennsylvania Assembly to reconsider his firearms bill at the next legislative session.[57]

Fortunately for Shafer, he was not up for reelection in 1968. He was therefore able to set aside the threats from gun rights proponents that they would vote him out of office, as well any lawmaker who supported firearms controls.[58] One such gun rights proponent was Roger M. Latham, the outdoor editor for the Pittsburgh Press. In a letter to Shafer, Latham defined the firearms control issue in Pennsylvania as a political "hot potato." "I believe that politicians who favor registration or licensing will find this out next election," wrote Latham, adding, "I predict that this may be the undoing of Senator Clark this fall."[59] Shafer thanked Latham for his letter but ultimately doubled down on his desire for some form of firearms registration, particularly for handguns.[60]

Senator Clark, however, could not ignore such political threats. Ever since the PFSC passed a resolution denouncing his reelection—a PFSC first—he had been fighting for his political life on the firearms control issue.[61] Initially, Clark was not too concerned with the PFSC's resolution. If anything, he was confident that any political differences over firearms controls could be worked out. At the same time, as a matter of political due diligence, he thought it important to at least get his Republican challenger, Representative Richard S. Schweiker, "on the record."[62]

The way Clark saw it, whether the PFSC decided to back down was insignificant, nor did it really matter what Schweiker's firearms control position was. Supporting firearms controls was, in Clark's mind, a political win-win. All the reputable polls confirmed it. Thus, should the PFSC refuse to back down and Schweiker decide to take a stand against firearms controls, Clark was more than comfortable with staying the political course.[63] Furthermore, as a political calculation, he (and every political strategist, for that matter) was doubtful that firearms controls would ever become a bona fide campaign issue. There was no historical precedent for it—not in the entire history of state or federal elections. Unbeknownst to Clark, the political sands on the firearms control issue were shifting, and quite rapidly.

Clark and his staff first began noticing this shift near the end of February 1968, when two interrelated moves by the gun rights community caught the attention of the press.[64] The first move occurred when several local sporting, hunting, conservation, and shooting clubs, in solidarity with the

PFSC, adopted their own anti-Clark resolutions.[65] The second was the very same clubs issuing press releases endorsing Clark's Democratic primary challenger, Representative John H. Dent, for having come out in opposition to firearms controls.[66] Although the actual reason for Dent challenging Clark in the Democratic primary was the latter's supposed "pussy-footing" on the Vietnam War,[67] if Dent could lure more votes by making firearms controls a wedge voting issue, he was happy to do it and embrace the anti-firearms control politics of the Pennsylvania gun rights community.[68] In a statement written for the PRPA, Dent pledged to only support those firearms bills that had received the backing of the NRA. He added: "Like you, I am an avid gun enthusiast and I believe I am very responsible in my conduct with weapons—as are the vast majority of Americans. I, too, am opposed to any indiscriminate gun legislation which, in my opinion, runs the risk of disarming the law-abiding citizen but fails to deter the criminal from obtaining firearms through sources already illegal, but nevertheless available to those outside the law."[69]

It was at this juncture, with Dent's pledge to fight "indiscriminate" firearms legislation, that, for the first time in American history, firearms control was front and center in a statewide election. With it now clear to the Clark campaign that the issue was going to be relevant, the campaign staff began preparing a policy statement—one that informed the public on the need for restrictive firearms laws and highlighted how several prominent politicians, including President Lyndon B. Johnson and former president Dwight D. Eisenhower, backed them. At the same time, Clark's campaign staff wanted to make sure to not completely marginalize the sporting and hunting fraternities. Indeed, his campaign staff thought it important that any firearms control policy statement highlight how an extremist "minority" was "throttling the will of the majority" but also contain a "paragraph pointing out how the rights of hunters and sportsmen are protected." Additionally, Clark's campaign staff wanted to make sure that the policy statement did not lump together sportsmen and hunters "with the hoods and the addicts."[70]

It was amid drafting this firearms policy statement that Clark's campaign staff learned that the PFSC intended on inviting each of the senatorial candidates to speak before its annual convention. But while Dent and Schweiker received invitations, Clark did not. The stated reason the PFSC excluded Clark was that the group wanted to invite only those senatorial candidates willing to "cooperate" with sporting, hunting, conservation, and shooting organizations and who maintained a "similar interest" in opposing strict firearms controls. From the PFSC's perspective, Clark did not meet this criterion, given that his "position on [firearms controls] is a matter of public record, and is so well-known that nothing could have been gained by [Clark's] appearance."[71]

Clark tried to politically seize on the PFSC's decision to exclude him by holding a press conference, and it was there that he read the letter that he wrote to PFSC president Edward T. Balderson.[72] In doing so, Clark hoped to appeal to the sensible nature of both gun rights and firearms control proponents.[73] In the letter, he outlined why the firearms controls he supported were "reasonable, moderate and modest" and therefore would not "prevent any hunter and sportsman from buying a gun, using it for a lawful purpose, or carrying it from state to state."[74] Such controls included outlawing the mail-order sale of firearms except to licensed dealers, establishing a firearms identification card, licensing all firearms dealers, manufacturers, and importers, strictly regulating the importation of military surplus firearms, and stringently controlling destructive devices.[75] Intentionally excluded, however, was firearms registration. Nine months earlier, on his weekly radio program, Clark had touted firearms registration as necessary for the "national interest."[76] But now, realizing that the gun rights community vehemently opposed firearms registration, he reversed course. He stated he would never back any law that required sportsmen and hunters "to register [their] gun, nor infringe [on their] right to keep it anywhere [they] wanted, or to sell it."[77]

Days later, Clark reiterated his new, moderate position on firearms controls directly to the gun rights community. In a prepared statement for the editors of the popular sporting and hunting publication *Outdoor People*, he wrote:

> I am fully committed to protecting the interests of the sportsmen of Pennsylvania. I have never failed to protect the rights of hunters and sportsmen of the State. Indeed, only last week, I voted against gun control legislation which would have left the sportsmen with virtually no rights—the long gun control amendment to the Civil Rights bill. . . . The rights of sportsmen must be protected and will always be protected by me. My position has been clear and consistent from the beginning.

> We need gun control legislation, but the legislation must protect the
> rights and interests of all the people.[78]

For the time being, it appeared as if Clark had neutralized the gun rights
opposition. Not only was he beginning to receive positive press coverage
on the firearms control issue, but his moderate position was not all that
distinguishable from Dent's or Schweiker's. The only thing separating the
three senatorial candidates was the extent to which each thought the federal government should regulate the interstate mail-order sale of firearms.
While Clark preferred limiting all mail-order firearms sales to federally
licensed dealers, both Dent and Schweiker supported continuing individual mail-order firearms sales so long as prospective purchasers signed an
affidavit attesting to the fact that they were not a juvenile, criminal,
vagrant, drug addict, nor adjudged mentally ill.[79] And although Clark presented himself as a moderate, he did not shy away from calling out those
"gun sellers and their allies" who were trying to defeat him. "I know the
people of this State care far more about the public's safety, as I do, than
they care about the so-called right of the mail-order gun merchants to
put deadly weapons in the hands of criminals, juveniles and dope
addicts," he stated.[80]

It was not long after the Democratic primary that Clark came to the
abrupt realization that—despite his best efforts—the firearms control issue
was not going away.[81] Dent was not defeated by the 2-to-1 ratio that Clark
predicted. Rather, Clark won by 7 percentage points (58,189 votes), and
there were whispers that it was his previous support for firearms registration that was politically holding him back.[82] Nevertheless, he maintained
steadfast in his support for firearms controls. In a press release the day
after the primary, Clark stated he would never "knuckle under the gun
lobby" and invited his Republican opponent in the general election, Schweiker, to debate him on the issue. "If Dick Schweiker wants the support
of the gun lobby he is welcome to it," Clark stated, adding, "I intend to take
my stance [with law enforcement]."[83] Schweiker effectively sidestepped
Clark's invitation by issuing a generic, noncommittal firearms control policy statement.[84]

Schweiker's decision to not engage in a firearms control policy debate
was frustrating to Clark's campaign staff. To defend Clark's position, the
staff knew it needed to get Schweiker on the record as early as possible.

The question was how. What staff ultimately came up with was a two-pronged strategy, which they believed would compel Schweiker to take a stand on firearms controls and possibly expose him as politically vulnerable on the issue. The first prong involved Clark baselessly accusing Schweiker of working in concert with the "gun lobby."[85] Such an accusation, it was believed, would force Schweiker's political hand. The way Clark's staff saw it, Schweiker would either have remain silent, and therefore concede that he was indeed working with the "gun lobby," or outline a more detailed position on firearms controls. And regardless of how Schweiker responded, Clark's staff felt it would ultimately prove to be a political win. Herein entered the second prong of attack, which involved writing two different constituent letters to Schweiker. One letter would appear to be from a firearms control proponent, and the other from a gun rights proponent. It was hoped Schweiker's response to the letters would not only give the Clark campaign a further indication as to Schweiker's position but also, if lucky, show that Schweiker was engaged in political double-talk—telling firearms control proponents one thing and gun rights proponents another.[86]

To the consternation of Clark's campaign staff, Schweiker's response on all fronts remained generic and noncommittal. And in response to Clark's "gun lobby" charge, Schweiker simply dismissed it as "nonsense" and reiterated the importance of ensuring that any federal firearms legislation was not "unduly restrictive" on sportsmen and hunters.[87] Meanwhile, his responses to the two fake constituent letters were identical. In them, he noted he would happily support any "firearms legislation which would help prevent deadly weapons from being easily placed in the hands of maniacs and criminals," but only so long as it did not interfere "with the legitimate interests of sportsmen and firearms collectors."[88]

It was not until June 4 that Schweiker unveiled a more detailed policy position. In contrast to Clark's firearms control position, and in line with the gun rights community, Schweiker expressed support for "mandatory stiffer penalties for those convicted of using a firearm to commit a crime." While he admitted that he had previously expressed support for a federal law banning the interstate sale of handguns, he now felt that "imposing mandatory stiffer penalties" was the better solution.[89]

But the very next day Senator Robert F. Kennedy was assassinated, and Schweiker was confronted with a tough decision. Should he stick with his current, gun rights–friendly position or succumb to overwhelming public pressure and support enacting strict firearms controls?[90] Given that several prominent Pennsylvania Republicans, including Governor Shafer and Senator Hugh Scott, decided to come out in support of strict firearms controls, Schweiker followed suit and backed federal legislation that would ban the mail order of handguns.[91]

On July 2, at the second of four scheduled debates between Clark and Schweiker, the former called out the latter as having flip-flopped on firearms controls.[92] "I believed in gun controls [before the assassinations of Martin Luther King, Jr., and Senator Kennedy] and I believe in gun controls now," stated Clark, adding, "My opponent has only reversed his position of strong opposition to adequate legislation after the assassination[s] . . . after the polls have shown a great majority of the American people favor strong gun controls." Schweiker fired back that his previous position and current position were really not all that different. Both were based on the principle that "when we pass a law in Washington, we not only regulate the law-abiding citizen, [but also] the fellow that's going to violate the law." He then urged Clark to support federal legislation that would impose stiff mandatory penalties "whenever a criminal is convicted of a crime using a gun."[93]

Clark complimented Schweiker's proposal as a "sound one" that he could support. And for a moment, with both senatorial candidates appearing to support the same firearms control policies, the issue seemed to be neutralized. Clark, however, decided to take it a step further and advocate for the licensing and registration of all firearms—a policy position that he had abandoned months earlier to appear as a political moderate.[94] Now Clark, who just minutes earlier accused Schweiker of politically flip-flopping on firearms controls, was the flip-flopper.[95]

From that point onward, Clark's support for the licensing and registration of all firearms dogged his reelection campaign. There was no taking it back, even if Clark wanted to. And almost immediately the PFSC, PGC, and other sporting, hunting, conservation, and shooting organizations seized the opportunity to make the election of 1968 a statewide referendum on the licensing and registration of firearms. In newspapers across the state appeared editorials and advertisements paid for by the gun rights community—many of which were promulgated with the express purpose of spreading fear. In one editorial, it was claimed that the registration of firearms was part of a larger communist scheme to confiscate all firearms. This in turn, so the editorial claimed, would eventually set the stage for a communist invasion.[96] In an advertisement sponsored by the Citizens Opposed to Further Firearms Legislation, readers of the Stroudsburg-based *Pocono Record* were asked to write in opposition to firearms registration to stop the spread of tyranny before they were "denied the right to write!"[97] Meanwhile, in an advertisement sponsored by the Venango County Federation of Sportsmen's Clubs, the readers of the Franklin-based *News-Herald* were provided with a series of selective quotations on the registration of firearms. One was allegedly from Adolf Hitler and read: "The most foolish mistake we could possibly make would be to allow the subject races to possess arms. History shows that all conquerors who have allowed their subject races to carry arms have prepared their own downfall by doing."[98]

The political point the gun rights community wanted to drive home to voters was that firearm ownership was a positive good. Conversely, firearms controls, particularly licensing and registration, were the tools of despots. Additionally, the gun rights community hoped to convince voters that licensing and registration laws were ineffective at curbing crime. This message was conveyed to voters by simply asking whether the registration of vehicles had stopped vehicular-related hijackings, thefts, or killings. A newspaper advertisement sponsored by the Citizens Committee for Sane Gun Legislation made this point rather succinctly. In all-capitalized letters surrounding the image of a deadly car wreck, it read, "Has registration stopped this killing?" And within the fine print of the advertisement, the argument was made that no firearms law, no matter how well crafted, would stop a "lunatic" from killing with a firearm. The advertisement then went on to encourage all citizens to "protect your birthright instead of the criminal" by writing their representatives.[99]

Although these editorials and advertisements proved effective in persuading many sportsmen, hunters, shooters, and firearms owners to oppose any candidate who supported firearms controls, they were extremely misleading. For one, throughout the 1960s, the chief proponents of firearms controls were not seeking to implement a communist agenda, nor were they seeking to confiscate firearms. Such claims were nothing more than propaganda. More important, though, despite what many in the gun rights community believed, none of the chief proponents of firearms controls were claiming that restrictive firearms legislation was a panacea for crime, nor that it was a panacea for all firearm-related deaths. Rather, the principal argument in favor of firearms controls, including the licensing and registration, was that existing state and local firearms laws were too easily circumvented. For instance, if a person lived in a state or locality that maintained strict controls and wanted to avoid them, the person could simply purchase firearms in the adjoining state or locality or, in some cases, purchase the firearm through the mail.

Although Clark often articulated these more nuanced arguments and did so quite eloquently, it did nothing to stop the barrage of attacks from state and local sporting, hunting, conservation, and shooting organizations.[100] And these organizations did not shy away from letting their real intentions known. "We will get Clark this time and then go after [Hugh] Scott when he comes up for election again," stated Edward F. Boden, president of the Shamokin-based Keystone Fish and Game Association, to a news reporter, adding, "If the lawmakers want to curb violence let them go to the fundamental sources; TV and movies, and let them stop harassing the law-abiding sportsmen."[101] Similarly, the Coudersport-based Black Forest Conservation Association published the following statement in a newspaper advertisement:

When you see Senator Joseph Clark's name on the ballot November 5 THINK and ACT!! Remember that he voted for gun registration as well as registration for the individual and is doing everything in his power to promote and enact stronger gun legislation with complete disregard for the wishes of the sportsmen of Pennsylvania. Clark must go! We will take care of Senator Hugh Scott when he comes up for re-election next term. He, too, must go![102]

In the hopes of defusing the situation, Clark's campaign staff devised another two-pronged strategy. For the first prong, Clark would save political face by continuing to call for the passage of federal firearms controls as part of a larger anticrime initiative and make sure to emphasize that the controls would in no way deny law abiding citizens the right to own and acquire firearms.[103] This stance, it was believed, would frame Clark as the experienced anticrime candidate. At the same time, by pushing a policy that was meant to blur the line between Clark's and Schweiker's positions, Clark's campaign staff believed it would help mitigate the criticism of the gun rights community. The second prong involved Clark outlining why Schweiker's position was not all that different from his. On September 13 Clark called a press conference and explained why Schweiker's voting record on

WHEN GUNS ARE OUTLAWED ONLY OUTLAWS WILL HAVE GUNS!

U.S. Senator Joseph S. Clark Supports Legislation to Outlaw Guns

If You Wish to Own a Firearm, "Outlaw" JOE CLARK at the Polls in November

Firearm Licensing and Registration Lead to Firearm Confiscation

JOSEPH S. CLARK PROPOSES IT RICHARD S. SCHWEIKER OPPOSES IT

Preserve Shooting Sports — — DON'T FORGET TO VOTE

AD SPONSORED BY:
KEYSTONE FISH & GAME ASSOCIATION NORRY GUN CLUB VALLEY GUN and COUNTRY CLUB

FIGURE 1.3 Political advertisement by the Keystone Fish and Game Association in the *Shamokin (Pa.) News-Dispatch*, September 28, 1968. The ad falsely claimed that firearms registration laws ultimately lead to firearms confiscation and that Senator Joseph S. Clark wanted to "outlaw guns."

firearms control was "virtually identical" to his. From there, Clark argued that the only thing that really separated him from Schweiker was the latter's willingness to "zig-zag" on political issues to lure more votes:

> After promising the gun lobby that he would vote against a mail order ban on guns, he turned around and voted for it—but not until the assassination of Senator Robert Kennedy had stirred a national outcry for gun control. Then when the tide of public support died down, he kissed and made up with the gun lobby by announcing his opposition to registration and licensing. That has been the Schweiker pattern, and he has been rigidly consistent in adhering to it—ear to the ground, finger in the air to see which way the wind is blowing.[104]

Ultimately, Clark's two-pronged strategy was a failure. Not only did Pennsylvania sporting, hunting, conservation, and shooting organizations find Clark's "zig-zag" line of argument unappealing. They were also keenly aware that Clark's press conference omitted the one key firearms control policy that separated the two candidates—Clark supported firearms licensing and registration, and Schweiker did not.[105] Schweiker made sure to seize on this point by calling out Clark for "trying to cover up his extreme anti-sportsmen attitudes in an effort to get their vote in November."[106] "In the past [Clark] has repudiated the views of a group of Pennsylvanians," stated Schweiker, "and now he is soliciting their votes by clouding issues."[107]

With a month until Election Day, Clark's campaign staff was running out of ideas to diffuse the firearms control issue. They ultimately concluded that the best course of action was to stay the political course and hope that the polls were correct on the popularity of firearms controls. Thus, in the closing weeks of the campaign, Clark repeatedly emphasized how Schweiker, like him, had voted for two federal firearms control bills, including the Gun Control Act (GCA) of 1968. Clark also made a point to vilify the "gun lobby" as leading a misinformation campaign to defeat him. To drive this point home, Clark's staff put together an advertisement that read: "John F. Kennedy . . . Martin Luther King . . . Robert F. Kennedy . . . All of them dead by the gun. And now the gun lobby is gunning for Senator Clark, because he supports strong gun controls."[108] Last, with the hope of convincing some within the gun rights community to vote for Clark, his campaign staff tried to minimize the senator's record of supporting firearms licensing and registration.[109]

In the days leading up to Election Day, firearms control–focused advertisements, both for and against Clark, appeared in newspapers across Pennsylvania. Several sporting, hunting, conservation, and shooting organizations published an ad with the title "Prevent Gun Registration." Below it read, "Election Day, be set aside as a Special Hunting Day with an OPEN SEASON on Joe Clark, the candidate whose so-called gun control is aimed at the law-abiding citizen and would include the registration of all shotguns and hunting rifles." The advertisement then proceeded to list Election Day "hunting hours" or polling times, the "daily bag limit" or the "number of voters that any hunter may bring in for Dick Schweiker," the "suggested hunting method," and the "grand prize," which was "a lock of hair from Joe Clark's political scalp."[110] Clark countered by publishing several advertisements of his own. The most widely distributed of the bunch contained the headline "The Truth About the Gun Control Law" and outlined how the GCA was enacted with the support of both Republicans and Democrats, chief law enforcement officials, and, of course, Schweiker (fig. 1.5). The

FIGURE 1.4 Political advertisement in the *Elizabethtown (Pa.) Chronicle*, October 31, 1968. The ad urged sportsmen, hunters, and gun owners to protect their "right to own firearms" by voting for Richard Schweiker and to vote for those Pennsylvania lawmakers who opposed the Shafer-Fineman Gun Bill.

advertisement then questioned whether Schweiker, if elected, would work to repeal the GCA: "Congressman Schweiker has not been willing to stand up and tell the people in this State whether or not he will work to repeal or basic change in this law. He owed it to all of us and especially the sportsman whom he has confused and misled, to have told us where he stands on repeal of Gun Control."[111] Another advertisement published by Clark simply highlighted the fact that Schweiker had also supported firearms controls and inquired, "Why then should this be an issue in this campaign?" The advertisement then closed with: "If you're a real sportsman, you'll give Senator Clark a sporting chance."[112]

On Election Day, hours before the polls opened, Clark was beaming with confidence and went on record predicting a 100,000-vote margin of victory. When asked whether he was at all worried about the firearms control issue affecting the outcome, Clark admitted that he would undoubtedly lose some voters in the rural areas but felt it was overall a "phony issue."[113] But within just twenty-four hours, after it was reported that Schweiker had defeated Clark by more than 282,000 votes, some political commentators and members of the press arrived at the opposite conclusion. The way they saw it, the combination of Clark's support for firearms controls and the organized opposition by sporting, hunting, conservation, and shooting organizations was a principal factor in his election defeat.[114] It was an assessment that many gun rights proponents, both inside and outside Pennsylvania, embraced and amplified. Some went so far as to write Clark "I told you so" letters. One letter, penned by Waynard Stahl, queried, "Why did Schweiker . . . win in Pennsylvania when the Democrats swept the state?" Stahl answered his own question, writing, "Check the stand of these men on un-American gun laws then tell your friends who are running for public office."[115] Another letter, penned by Richard Zawacki, stated, "Make no mistake, the sportsmen vote upset your election."[116]

But despite the self-laudatory claims of gun rights proponents, the reality was that Clark's loss to Schweiker was primarily the result of other factors, not firearms controls. Yes, for the first time in Pennsylvania history, the firearms control issue was front-and-center in a statewide election. Yes, for the first time in Pennsylvania history, sporting, hunting, conservation, and shooting organizations joined forces with the explicit purpose of removing a statewide elected government official from political office. And yes, for the first time in Pennsylvania history, the campaign of a state

United States Senator Joseph S. Clark

THE TRUTH ABOUT THE GUN CONTROL LAW!

The Congress has passed and the President has signed a Gun Control Bill. It is now law. I voted for it; so did my opponent, Congressman Schweiker. And so did Republican Senator Hugh Scott. The Association of Pennsylvania District Attorneys and the Association of Pennsylvania Police Chiefs also recommended it.

It is for the protection of all citizens. It does not hurt in any way the bona fide sportsman, gun collector or hunter.

It will help us fight crime and win respect for law and order.

Now that it is law, there is only one question to be asked about Gun Control so far as this Election is concerned: will either candidate support repeal of this Bill?

I will not.

Congressman Schweiker has not been willing to stand up and tell the people in this State whether or not he will work for repeal or basic change in this law. He owed it to all of us and especially the sportsman whom he has confused and misled, to have told us where he stands on repeal of Gun Control.

There was time for him to speak the truth on this issue as I have done from the beginning.

Senator Joseph Clark

The Committee to Re-Elect Senator Joseph Clark
Chairman: James A. Michener

FIGURE 1.5 Political advertisement by the Joseph Clark campaign in newspapers across Pennsylvania in the week leading up to the election in 1968.

FIGURE 1.6 Political advertisement by the Federation of Sportsmen's Clubs in Lehigh County in the *Allentown (Pa.) Morning Call*, November 2, 1968.

elected government official dedicated significant resources to the firearms control issue. What the gun rights proponents overlooked, however, is that Democratic presidential candidate Hubert H. Humphrey, who was also vehemently opposed by many sportsmen, hunters, and firearms owners for vocally supporting firearms licensing and registration, won Pennsylvania handily by more than 170,000 votes.[117] Thus, if the firearms control issue was indeed the key factor in Clark's defeat, how could it be that Humphrey won the same state by such a wide margin?

The answer is simple—the firearms control issue was not a considerable factor in Clark's defeat. Certainly, many sportsmen, hunters, shooters, and firearms owners voted against Clark solely because of his position. It is historically suspect, however, to assume that his support for firearms controls was a considerable factor, let alone the deciding factor. While there are several facts that show this to be true, two particularly stand out. First, out of the four public debates held between Clark and Schweiker, the issue

FIGURE 1.7 Political advertisement by the United Firearms Owners and the Schuylkill County Sportsmen's Association in the *Pottsville (Pa.) Republican*, November 1, 1968. The ad showed that sportsmen understood that Democratic presidential candidate Hubert H. Humphrey also supported firearms licensing and registration.

came up only in the first.[118] The remaining three debates focused on more pressing national issues that resonated with the larger body politic, such as the Vietnam War, national security, foreign policy, the federal budget, entitlement programs like social security and food stamps, and civil rights.[119] Second, the opposition by sporting, hunting, conservation, and shooting organizations was often times exaggerated, both in the press and by gun rights supporters. For instance, several pieces of literature distributed by the gun rights community contained the mantra "one million sportsmen say defeat Joe Clark."[120] The mantra was even made into a bumper sticker. Yet the actual number of sportsmen, hunters, shooters, and firearms owners that either joined organizations to oppose Clark or signed petitions denouncing Clark was in the ballpark of 50,000.[121] Even assuming that all 50,000 voted against Clark, this accounts for only 18 percent of the more than 282,000 votes Clark lost by. Thus, as a matter of empirical evidence, the issue of firearms control was far from a considerable factor in Clark's defeat.

But what is often the reality is not the perception, especially among those that witnessed or experienced a historical event firsthand. The fact is that Clark's defeat generated whispers that the "gun lobby" was an electoral force not to be reckoned with. These whispers were heard not only within the legislative halls of Pennsylvania but also in the halls of Congress. Equally important is the fact that Clark's defeat politically galvanized the gun rights community in a new way. For decades, sporting, hunting, conservation, and shooting organizations had urged their members to vote only for those candidates who supported gun rights, yet they were unable to produce any concrete results. Clark's defeat changed that, and from it was born a new form of gun rights grassroots advocacy—affecting election outcomes.

The impact of Clark's defeat on the politics of firearms controls was immediate.[122] It was accurately foreshadowed in an editorial cartoon that appeared in the November 14, 1968, edition of the *Los Angeles Times*, where the door of the Clark's campaign headquarters was shot up by a shadowy armed figure labeled as the "gun lobby." On the bottom of the cartoon read the caption, "A Shot Sure to Be Heard Around Congress." But who was this so-called gun lobby? Was it some shadowy, behind-the-scenes operation, as the cartoon suggested? Was it the political arm of the chief gun rights advocacy organization—the NRA—as the news media often suggested?

When did this "gun lobby" first come into existence, and how did it operate? These questions, as well as others, are answered in the next chapter.

It is also worth noting that the political fight over firearms control in Pennsylvania was merely a microcosm of a fight that was taking place all over the country. Indeed, at the close of 1968, the politics of firearms controls was complex, and those who supported and opposed firearms controls came from a variety of political stripes and backgrounds. At the same time, however, the political battle lines over firearms control—at least as they are widely understood today—were beginning to crystalize, with firearms owners pitted against non-firearms owners, conservatives pitted against liberals, rural areas pitted against urban areas, and so on, and so forth.

2

The Rise of the "Gun Lobby"

Throughout the mid- and late 1960s, whenever lawmakers, political commentators, the news media, or anyone for that matter referred to the National Rifle Association (NRA) as the "gun lobby," NRA officials vehemently denounced it.[1] Time and time again, the organization countered with two arguments. The first was to tout its record of supporting "reasonable" firearms controls, particularly how it had worked with Congress to ensure the passage of the Federal Firearms Act of 1938 and the National Firearms Act of 1934.[2] The second argument was that the bulk of its annual operating budget did not come from firearms manufacturers, nor the sporting, hunting, and shooting industry. Rather, it came from NRA membership dues. Given this fact, the NRA proudly called itself the "Paul Revere Organization" because it served to rally the political interests of firearms-owning, liberty-loving Americans.[3]

Certainly, the NRA was within its rights to denounce the gun lobby label. Imprinted on its headquarters for most of the twentieth century was "Firearms Safety Education, Marksmanship Training, and Shooting for Recreation." This was the mission statement that the NRA was most prominently known for, not promoting the interests of firearms manufacturers or the sporting, hunting, and shooting industry. Behind the scenes, however, the gun lobby label was accurate. For decades, unbeknownst to the public, NRA officials lobbied lawmakers and government officials to adopt policies that principally benefited the NRA, firearms manufacturers, and the sporting, hunting, and shooting industry, whether it be enacting legislation that the NRA endorsed, foregoing legislation that it opposed, appointing the organization's officials to influential government posts, or maintaining government subsidies, such as how the federal government exclusively supplied military surplus firearms and ammunition to NRA members and affiliated clubs at a discounted rate, or how state governments often subsidized the construction and maintenance costs of NRA-affiliated shooting ranges.[4] Also, ever since the NRA first published its flagship magazine *American Rifleman*, the group received a substantial amount of advertising revenue from firearms manufacturers and dealers (figure 2.1), spent a portion of said revenue on legislative affairs, and regularly encouraged its members to write letters opposing any legislation that would restrict the purchase or ownership of firearms.[5] There is also evidence to suggest that at times it leveraged its role in fighting firearms controls to convince firearms manufacturers to enter into annual advertising contracts.[6]

The NRA's role as the "gun lobby" did not develop over the course of a week, month, or even a year. It was something the organization kind of fell into. Initially, the proverbial gun lobby was what one might expect— firearms manufacturers, working together behind the scenes to convince lawmakers and government officials to forgo enacting legislation that negatively affected their economic bottom line.[7] Of course, given the poor optics of this arrangement, firearms manufacturers did not publicly advertise their involvement. But prior to the NRA's rise as the preeminent defender of gun rights, manufacturers were very much involved in firearms legislation, whether it be at the federal, state, or local level.[8] Assisting firearms manufacturers in their efforts was the first gun rights movement, which was born in response to the passage of New York's Sullivan Law in 1911.[9] Established through loose collaboration of the United States Revolver Association (USRA) and the editors of sporting, hunting, and shooting magazines, this early gun rights movement was successful in rousing sportsmen, hunters, shooters, and firearms owners to politically rail against what they referred to as "anti-firearm" and "anti-pistol" legislation.[10]

Undoubtedly the principal achievement of the early gun rights movement was influencing lawmakers to enact what was historically the first model firearms legislation.[11] Drafted by USRA official and Olympic

FIGURE 2.1 Political advertisement by Smith & Wesson in *American Rifleman*, April 1927. The ad put forward an argument about why the "revolver is an effective instrument in the promotion of law and order" but also suggested that the best way to reduce criminal activity was the "swift, sure punishment" of the offender. In making these points, it recited the operative clause of the Second Amendment.

shooting gold medalist Karl T. Frederick, who would later go on to become NRA president, the first legislation was intended to accomplish four objectives:[12] First, it would replace any existing firearms regulations that the gun rights community felt hindered the nation's ability to produce "citizen soldiers" through firearms training and familiarity.[13] Second, it would prevent well-intentioned sportsmen, hunters, and firearms owners from falling victim to the myriad of local firearms restrictions.[14] Third, it would ensure that law-abiding citizens were able to "procure weapons for house protection," as well as publicly arm themselves "when necessary," yet deny the criminal element the ability to own and use firearms.[15] Finally, it was postulated that model firearms legislation would be less susceptible to harmful amendments from anti-gun "propagandists."[16]

Frederick's model firearms legislation sought to achieve this last objective by proposing the following reforms (figure 2.2):

None but citizens, personally known, or properly identified to a licensed dealer in firearms, are permitted to purchase pistols or revolvers. A record of sale must be filed with the police.

No pistol or revolver may be delivered to the purchaser until the day after the sale.

Owners of such firearms are not permitted to carry them on their persons or in a vehicle without a license from the police.

Dealers are not permitted to display pistols or revolvers, or limitations thereof, where they can be seen from outside of the store.

Possession of a pocket firearm by a person committing or attempting to commit a felony, is regarded as prima facie evidence of criminal intent, and *is punishable by a mandatory sentence of five years' extra imprisonment.*

Heavy penalties are prescribed for second and third offenders. Fourth offenders may be sentenced to life imprisonment.

Manufacturers' serial numbers or other identifying marks on pistols or revolvers must not be altered or erased.

Aliens and persons who have been convicted of a felony are not permitted to possess a pistol or revolver.[17]

In the pantheon of history, virtually all the USRA's proposed reforms were unoriginal. For instance, laws requiring dealers to register firearms sales had been on the statute and ordinance book for decades. The same was true of laws requiring a license to carry deadly weapons in public

SANE REGULATION
OF REVOLVER SALES

BULLETIN No. 2	NEW YORK CITY	JANUARY 24, 1923

Regulation of the sale of pistols and revolvers is a matter for the States to deal with.	ISSUED BY THE UNITED STATES REVOLVER ASSOCIATION 14 West Forty-eighth Street New York City
Unduly restrictive laws favor the criminal to the disadvantage of the honest citizen.	IN THE INTERESTS OF THE UNIFORM REVOLVER LAW

Why Revolver Laws Should Be Uniform

Not for Congress Laws governing the sale and ownership of pistols and revolvers should be uniform in all of the States.

Otherwise effective enforcement will be impossible.

Such regulation is not a matter with which Congress can properly deal. It comes within the police powers of the various States.

If one State has strict laws and another has not, criminals in the one will go to the other to supply their requirements. The criminal will always see to it that he is armed.

But the law-abiding citizens of the State where the sale and ownership of arms is unduly restricted are placed at a disadvantage. Such restriction operates entirely in the criminal's favor.

By having the laws dealing with this matter uniform in all States, with reasonable restriction on the sale of weapons, the honest citizen would be able to arm himself for the defence of his life and property, and the criminal would find it increasingly difficult to obtain one of the important tools of his trade.

Here is a Model Law Most of the States have revolver laws of one kind or another. Practically no two of these laws are alike.

To overcome this defect, the United States Revolver Association is recommending the enactment by all State Legislatures of a Uniform Law, based on the bill introduced in the United States Senate by Senator Capper of Kansas, for operation in the District of Columbia.

Briefly, the Uniform Law provides that:

None but citizens, personally known, or properly identified to a licensed dealer in firearms, are permitted to purchase pistols or revolvers. A record of sale must be filed with the police.

No pistol or revolver may be delivered to the purchaser until the day after the sale.

Owners of such firearms are not permitted to carry them on their persons or in a vehicle without a license from the police.

Dealers are not permitted to display pistols or revolvers, or imitations thereof, where they can be seen from the outside of the store.

Possession of a pocket firearm by a person committing or attempting to commit a felony, is regarded as prima facie evidence of criminal intent, and is punishable by a mandatory sentence of five years' extra imprisonment.

Heavy penalties are prescribed for second and third offenders. Fourth offenders may be sentenced to life imprisonment.

Manufacturers' serial numbers or other identifying marks on pistols or revolvers must not be altered or erased.

Aliens and persons who have been convicted of a felony are not permitted to possess a pistol or revolver.

FIGURE 2.2 USRA bulletin, the second in a series meant to educate sportsmen, hunters, firearms owners, and lawmakers on the benefits of the Capper bill. Although the USRA supported the concept of model firearms legislation, it opposed federal intervention.

places, including the USRA's recommendation that applicants show "proof of necessity" or "good reason to fear an injury to [their] person or property" before obtaining a license.[18] It was the USRA's call for model legislation that was forward thinking. Up to this point, opponents of firearms legislation had not considered model legislation to stem the tide of additional, more restrictive legislation.[19] The USRA's was notably the first, and its officers were quite convincing when pitching it to lawmakers. Although the USRA willingly conceded that "no law" would "prevent criminals from obtaining pistols and revolvers," it did promise lawmakers that stiff penalties would make the criminal acquisition of firearms more difficult and ensure that criminals would be unable to cross state lines to avoid this difficulty.[20] As the organization put it, "Pass laws which permit law-abiding citizens to arm themselves and at the same time provide severe penalties for the use of pistols or revolvers in the commission of crimes, or for the unauthorized carrying of weapons of this character on the person or in vehicles and you provide a strong deterrent to the criminal use of these weapons."[21]

The USRA's efforts gave rise to what was at the time the largest overhaul in firearms laws in U.S. history.[22] It was on the heels of the group's success that the NRA entered the political fray.[23] Initially, with the help of Frederick, the NRA worked alongside the USRA.[24] But by the close of 1932, the NRA had commandeered the gun rights movement as its very own.[25] As it pertained to things like advocating for model legislation, determining whether firearms legislation was "sane" or "reasonable," and the meaning and scope of the Second Amendment right to "keep and bear arms," the gun rights movement was not all that different under the NRA's tutelage.[26] Where the movement was changing was the manner in which it advocated for and against firearms controls. While the USRA focused primarily on forming partnerships to accomplish its objectives, the NRA utilized a variety of tactics, each designed to rouse sportsmen, hunters, and firearms owners to take political action. One tactic was to characterize anyone who advocated for or supported firearms controls, often referred to as "reformers" or "do-gooders," in a negative light.[27] The NRA was not the first to utilize this gun rights political tactic.[28] The NRA was, however, instrumental in normalizing it.

"Reformers" or "do-gooders" were often cast as weak, unpatriotic, and purely ignorant of firearms.[29] In some instances, misogyny loomed, and

STOP THE SALE OF PISTOLS!

Even Justice Herself Is Not Safe as Long as Deadly Weapons Are Within Easy Reach.

FIGURE 2.3 Political cartoon in the *Washington, D.C., Evening Star,* June 24, 1913. The cartoon reflected the view of a small, early twentieth-century movement to ban the sale of all handguns except to law enforcement officers and the military. This movement, along with the passage of New York's Sullivan Law, prompted the USRA to become politically active in firearms legislation.

reformers or do-gooders were characterized as feminine, near-women, or petticoated.[30] The NRA's disparaging of these people was at times so pervasive that it led many within the gun rights movement to believe that anyone who advanced firearms controls was a traitor to their country.[31] Such was the case for Colonel Harold P. Sheldon, a World War I veteran who went on to work as an editor for several sporting, hunting, and shooting magazines, and who firmly believed in the virtue of compulsory military training.[32] The way Sheldon saw it, not only did compulsory military training aid in the national defense, but it also helped combat crime. In his writings, he often chastised firearms-control proponents as being misguided, cowards, and even un-American. In one instance, he wrote, "Any law, bill or proposal to interfere with the American right to possess and use arms is suspect and often intentionally traitorous." In another, he lumped fire-arms control supporting "reformers' with Nazis: "There is a quality of sticky-footed obsequious, Nazi-like tenacity about the professional reformer in the early stages of his campaign that shouldn't blind us to the fact that the slimy fellow can be outrageously arrogant later on." Sheldon went so far as to hypothesize that attempts at controlling firearms were part of a larger, covert and insidious foreign scheme. "Anti-firearms cam-paigns seldom originate in the organizations that appear to sponsor them," he wrote, adding, "The real leaders cannily stay under cover while sincere but misguided enthusiasts bent on interfering with other people's business carry the banner and make the speeches."[33]

While attacking the character of so-called reformers and do-gooders, the NRA made sure to cast the cause of gun rights as a positive social good. This effectively shaped a cultural divide, with many in the gun rights movement adopting the mentality of "us versus them," "good versus bad," and "right versus wrong." Misogyny loomed, but in a manner that depicted the sportsman, hunter, and firearms owner as the "good guy" or "hero."[34] The NRA's weapon of choice in fostering this cultural divide was histori-cism. This involved framing the past in a way that made sportsmen, hunters, and firearms owners believe that they were the patriotic defend-ers of the nation. And the NRA made sure to reinforce this narrative whenever possible by asserting that sportsmen, hunters, and firearms owners were carrying forth the arms-bearing tradition of the American Revolution era Minutemen. At times, to punctuate this message, it adopted the motto "Make America Once Again a Nation of Rifleman."[35] Essentially, what the NRA wanted was to socialize sportsmen, hunters, and firearms owners into believing was that they, with their personal admira-tion of American firearms culture and the Second Amendment, were the true, patriotic citizens of the nation. "Reformers," "do-gooders," or any-one for that matter who supported firearms controls were not.[36]

Another gun rights tactic to become normalized by the NRA was the sensationalizing of firearms controls as a slippery slope to complete dis-armament. The NRA would claim that one firearms control would lead to another, and then another, until somehow the private ownership of firearms was eliminated. The group used New York's Sullivan Law, which required individuals to obtain a permit before being able to purchase a handgun, most often as a straw man when making this argument.[37] And the argument, although disingenuous, proved quite effective in convincing many in the gun rights community to become politically active.

In fact, to this day, the slippery-slope argument remains a staple of the NRA's political messaging strategy. The reason for this is simple: the argument is a self-fulfilling prophecy of sorts. Anyone who practices or studies the law knows that it is fluid and constantly changing. This is how the law has functioned since its inception and will continue to function for as long as governments exist. In most, if not all, instances, what drives legal change are changes in society, whether in politics, culture, technology, demography, or other elements. Just consider that the issues and problems of the late nineteenth century are not one and same with those of the twenty-first century, or even the early twentieth century. For this reason, the laws of the late nineteenth century are often quite different from the laws of today. The same is true for firearms laws. The availability, firing rate, firing distance, lethality, and portability of modern firearms are significantly greater than in the late nineteenth century. Thus, not surprisingly, today's firearms laws are radically different from their late nineteenth-century predecessors. Indeed, the regulatory categories—ownership, use, carriage, transport, and commerce—and the principal driving force behind regulation—preventing firearms-related crimes, homicides, and needless death—remain largely the same. However, the provisions contained in today's firearms laws are far more extensive and detailed.

Yet, ever since it commandeered the gun rights movement, the NRA consistently asserted that this legal change is not what it appears to be. Rather, it was alleged to be part of a large, insidious scheme to undermine all constitutional freedoms and eventually disarm every patriotic, firearms-loving American. And to convincingly sell this disarmament scheme narrative, the NRA took to scapegoating either a small group of organized anti-gun "fanatics"—a group that the NRA was never able to pinpoint and therefore fabricated to arouse the gun rights movement to action—or broad-based political ideological beliefs, such as pacifism, socialism, and communism.[38]

But perhaps the NRA's most utilized tactic in defeating firearms controls was to espouse a form of firearms libertarianism, that is, to claim that virtually every individual firearms control was ineffective at both stopping crime and preventing firearms-related injuries or death. The less firearms controls there were, the better. This was the "American way," or, in the NRA's words in 1931, "When those professional viewers-with-alarm who are so concerned with *lawless* American set about to create an America with *less law*, another great American paradox will become evident—a lawful America is an America with less law."[39] In advancing this libertarian line of argument, the NRA resorted to several gun rights mantras that remain prevalent to this day, such as punishing the criminal, not the law-abiding citizen, enforcing the laws on the books before enacting others, advocating firearms education over firearms legislation, and asserting that firearm controls only lead to an increase in crime. Conversely, in those jurisdictions where people were encouraged to own and use firearms, the NRA claimed that there was far less criminal activity, as well as far fewer firearms-related injuries and deaths.[40] Yet despite the NRA's assurances, there was (and to this day remains) no substantiated scientific evidence to support such claims.[41] Still, just by floating the claim of "more guns equals less crime," the NRA effectively convinced its supporters that society benefited significantly from having more firearms per capita than less.[42]

The editors of the NRA's flagship magazine *American Rifleman* especially pushed the "more guns equals less crime" mantra when it came to the topic of thwarting armed criminals.[43] At times, with this objective in mind, the editors went so far as to sanction vigilantism.[44] "The vigilante method is short and very much to the point," wrote the editors in 1928, adding, "and it leaves 'no work for the jury.' "[45] Similarly, in 1934 the editors claimed that crime could be effectively "stamped out by an aroused *armed* citizenry, either called to the aid of the police as posse men, or, as in the days of the Old West, disgusted with corrupt police officials and organized into their own law-enforcement groups—the Vigilantes."[46]

In 1932 the editors of the *American Rifleman* transformed the "more guns, less crime" mantra into a reoccurring column titled "Guns vs. Bandits," which provided NRA members with real-world examples of armed citizens thwarting criminal activity. Later the editors noted that the principal purpose of the column was to counter the "shortsighted, or rather, misinformed" newspaper coverage that favors "laws prohibiting the possession of firearms by Mr. John Citizen," as well as to debunk the "fallacy of an unarmed citizenry."[47] The column was discontinued in 1941.[48] But in 1958 it was revived and renamed "The Armed Citizen." The editors felt the revived column showed that "law enforcement officers cannot at all times be where they are needed to protect life or property in danger of serious violation," and thus there are "many instances" where "the citizen has no choice but to defend himself with a gun."[49] Years later the editors slightly modified their justification for the column by noting that there are "instances in which the mere presence of a firearm in the hands of a reso-lute citizen prevented crime without bloodshed."[50]

Although the editors of the American Rifleman touted the idea of arming more citizens to stop and deter criminals, the NRA, as both a matter of pub-lic policy and longstanding constitutional doctrine, did not support the idea of citizens going indiscriminately or habitually armed.[51] Rather, it was on record stating that citizens should go armed only in those instances where it was absolutely necessary and they were properly trained to do so.[52] What the NRA adamantly opposed were laws where state or local authori-ties exercised unbound discretion to grant or deny armed carriage licenses, or those instances where a license was deemed necessary to transport firearms for lawful purposes, such as to one's place of business, a shooting range, or hunting grounds.[53] In many state and local jurisdictions, the NRA protested against such undesirable laws and ordinances by lobbying for the enactment of its model firearms legislation. Otherwise known as the Uni-form Firearms Act (UFA), the legislation contained a provision that exempted "the regularly enrolled members" of the NRA from "going to or from their places of assembly or target practice" without an armed car-riage license.[54]

The NRA's moderate stance on armed carriage was largely a reflection of its core mission of firearms education. It would have been hypocritical for the NRA to advance itself as a professional marksmanship and safety organization yet advocate for people going indiscriminately armed. Addi-tionally, the NRA leadership understood that legislative compromise was necessary to advance the organization's long-term objectives. Most law-makers, as well as most Americans, abhorred the concept of needless pre-paratory armed carriage, and therefore the NRA knew it was best to not press the matter.[55] The NRA's moderate stance can also be attributed to its theory as to how restrictive laws came to be. The organization perceived restrictive laws, including firearms laws, to be the result of an accident or unfortunate event—the after-the-fact, "there ought to be a law" mental-ity of lawmaking.[56] The more accidents or unfortunate events of a similar nature that occurred, the more likely it was that a restrictive law would be passed. Applying this theoretical construct to preparatory armed carriage, it is understandable why the NRA supported armed carriage licensing laws. If citizens were given the opportunity to indiscriminately carry firearms without proper training, the NRA knew it was more likely that "gun-toting" accidents and unfortunate events would occur, which would therefore give the so-called reformers and do-gooders all the evidence they needed to argue that "there ought to be a law." Armed carriage licensing laws hedged against this. They allowed the NRA to dismiss accidents and unfortunate events as just that, which in turn afforded it a credible platform to emphasize its key message—the importance of firearms ownership, training, and safety.

Perhaps the best way to characterize the NRA's early foray into influencing firearms legislation is that it was a constant balancing act of sorts, with the end goal being the combined preservation of the organization, firearms manufacturing, as well as the wider sporting, hunting, and shooting industry. Certainly, to achieve desired legislative outcomes, the NRA's leadership knew that it needed to distribute a message that would effectively arouse the gun rights movement to political action. Often this meant sensationalizing facts, advancing political propaganda, and floating what can best be described as conspiracy theories. Such theories included the NRA one time going so far as to erroneously claim that antifirearms laws were being secretly financed by "gangsters."[57] In another instance, the group made several unrelated historical assertions before positing the unsupported theory that the most "sinister" actors were pushing the nation's restrictive firearms laws and bills. Although the NRA admitted it could not prove this sinister-actors theory, the organization nevertheless posited the following question to its members: "Can such a collection of incidents be reviewed without raising a question in any sane man's mind as to how deep-rooted and far-flung may be the sinister influence behind the continuing agitation for that type of firearms regulation which would place the honest citizen at the mercy of the armed criminal, the crooked politician, and the petty bureaucrat?"[58]

Yet to maintain respectability among lawmakers, the NRA's leadership knew they would need show a willingness to legislatively compromise. And whenever coming to a compromise, the NRA almost always made sure to advance whatever legislation would minimally impact the sportsman, hunter, and firearms owner. To help ensure such beneficial outcomes, it made sure to put together detailed political talking points, articles, and bulletins, each of which served to educate the gun rights community about which legislative proposals were "sane" or "reasonable" and which were not.

From the moment that the NRA entered the political fray, it proved to be much more effective than the USRA at influencing lawmakers. The reason for this was threefold. First, upon commandeering the gun rights movement, the NRA's membership enrollment was roughly ten times that of the USRA. Second, unlike the USRA, the NRA maintained shooting and rifle clubs in every state in the union, totaling more than 1,700. These clubs were already serving as the NRA's proxies when it came to federal, state, and local legislation involving the subsidizing of shooting ranges and conservation. Why not also utilize them to serve as the NRA's eyes and ears in combatting restrictive firearms controls? Third, unlike the USRA, the NRA maintained a nationally circulated publication—*American Rifleman*—through which it was able to effectively relay its political message. Conversely, the USRA's publications achieved only modest circulation and were far less informative than virtually all other contemporary sporting, hunting, conservation, and shooting publications.[59]

It was in 1932—on the heels of failing to repeal and replace New York's much-maligned Sullivan Law with the UFA—that the NRA made the decision to ramp up its lobbying efforts.[60] This decision was immediately reflected in the pages of the *American Rifleman*.[61] For instance, on the title page, the NRA began holding itself out as a lobby.[62] The same held true for NRA advertisements.[63] In one such advertisement, the group asked its members to enlist others to help it in stopping the "attempted dictation of anti-gun cranks and pacifists who are 'out to outlaw firearms.' "[64] In another, the NRA touted its lobbying activities, writing, *"No anti-firearms legislation opposed by the N.R.A. has been passed by any of the State Legislatures which have been in session this year.* Perhaps there are other N.R.A. membership benefits of more tangible value than this. But the Association's organized systematic fight against bad firearms laws, we believe, is the *one* outstanding N.R.A. service."[65]

In addition to the presenting itself as a lobby, the NRA issued monthly editorials in *American Rifleman* that were becoming much more politically charged and increasingly exhibited a "Chicken Little"—the "sky is falling"—quality. For instance, near the close of 1932 the NRA warned its members that the country was "entering one of those legislative years when anything can happen" and a "united front on the part of sportsmen through their established National Association" will be "more important this year than has been the case during the entire past generation."[66] The next year the NRA warned, "Unless the sentiment of sportsmen, dealers, editors, and manufacturers can be . . . crystalized so as to present a united front in opposition to the desire of the [anti-gun] fanatics, the actual disarmament of America will be a matter quickly accomplished."[67]

The hub of the NRA's lobbying efforts was its legislative division. Established in 1933, the division's objectives included monitoring the "interests of the shooters in Congress and State Legislatures," carrying forward the "organized fight against unsound anti-gun laws," encouraging "legislation for the aid of civilian rifle practice," and assisting NRA members in obtaining "permits to carry firearms to and from a range in states requiring such permits."[68] The legislative division accomplished each of these objectives by harnessing the power of the NRA's existing social network. NRA field representatives, affiliated rifle and shooting clubs, and members would relay pending state and local firearms bills to the legislative division. From there, the legislative division would determine whether the bills were detrimental to the interests of the NRA, the firearms industry, or individual firearms ownership. If a bill were deemed detrimental, the legislative division would take one of three actions, or some combination of the three. One was notifying NRA supporters of the pending bill through the *American Rifleman*.[69] Another was directly communicating with affected NRA-affiliated clubs to formulate a political response. The last was drafting a legislative bulletin to affected NRA members and calling on them to write their lawmakers opposing the bill.[70] The legislative division's ability to communicate directly to sportsmen, hunters, and firearms owners was further amplified through the collaborative reporting of local newspaper columnists who opposed restrictive firearms controls. These columnists served as the NRA's bullhorn, particularly in rural communities where newspapers were the primary, if not the only, means of widely distributing information.

The purpose behind the legislative division arousing sportsmen, hunters, and firearms owners to political action was not solely preventing the enactment of firearms controls. It was to also open opportunities for the

NRA to shape state and local firearms policy.[71] Essentially, the NRA's strategy was to politically straddle both sides of the firearms control issue. The organization would tout itself to lawmakers and government officials as a supporter of reasonable firearms controls, but at the same time, it would inform sportsmen, hunters, and firearms owners that virtually all firearms controls would either make firearms ownership a crime or eventually lead to disarmament, and that they, with the assistance of the NRA, were the only ones who could stop it. Sportsmen, hunters, and firearms owners would then pressure lawmakers and government officials to vote against the laws the NRA opposed and instead vote in favor of laws the NRA supported.

The NRA's political straddling strategy was on full display in 1934, when Congress for the first time took up the mantle of comprehensive federal firearms legislation.[72] Up to that point, except for the passage of a 1927 law prohibiting the private mailing of any concealable firearm through the U.S. Postal Service (law enforcement excluded), Congress had not seriously considered legislation that would limit criminal access and use of firearms.[73] This would all change following the election of Franklin D. Roosevelt as president.[74] The earliest indication that the Roosevelt administration would actually take up the firearms control issue was in August 1933, when the Department of Justice, led by Attorney General Homer Cummings, announced it would be ramping up efforts to stop organized crime. Over the next couple of months, meetings between President Roosevelt, Attorney General Cummings, Assistant Attorney General Joseph B. Keenan, and several members of Congress were held on the subject. What everyone involved in these meetings agreed on was that a series of anticrime bills would be submitted to Congress, the first of which would be a firearms bill.[75]

From the very outset, even before a bill was drafted, the NRA worked to undermine the Department of Justice's efforts. In a January 1934 American Rifleman editorial, the NRA argued that any attempt by Congress to curtail the sale of deadly weapons to criminals would ultimately prove ineffective. To buttress this argument, the editorial advanced two talking points. The first was that instead of seeking to pass firearms legislation—legislation that the NRA claimed would affect only law-abiding citizens—Congress should be proactive in encouraging more people to be armed. To the NRA, the principal lessons of history showed that a trained armed citizenry was the true "weapon of democracy." The second talking point was that if Congress was going to legislate on firearms, its efforts should not be directed at the firearm itself, but at the criminal abuser. With this thought in mind, the NRA urged Congress to instead take up legislation that reformed the entire federal justice system in a way that punished criminals severely, including the imposition of strict mandatory penalties for anyone found committing a crime with a firearm.[76]

In was in early 1934 that the first firearms bills were introduced before Congress. The most popular among them were S. 885 and S. 2285, both sponsored by New York senator Royal S. Copeland, who chaired the Senate Subcommittee on Racketeering on Crime, and who had been advocating for federal firearms controls for nearly a decade.[77] Copeland was confident that his two bills offered the most practical approach to controlling the type of firearms most commonly used by criminals—handguns.[78] The NRA was of opposite opinion and, if possible, hoped to convince Congress to forgo adopting any firearms legislation. The underlying reason for the NRA's opposition is not historically difficult to ascertain—it was organizational self-interest and self-preservation. It had taken the NRA years to garner political influence among state and local assemblies, and the passage of any federal firearms legislation would almost certainly override it. Moreover, the NRA was aware that leveraging political influence in the halls of Congress was far more difficult to achieve. Indeed, the organization had lobbied members of Congress many times before to obtain federal tax dollars for NRA-sponsored rifle matches and other marksmanship-related programs. However, it knew that its track record on Capitol Hill was mixed.[79]

It was not long after Copeland introduced S. 885 and S. 2285 that the NRA began an all-out campaign to derail both bills. In one press release, the group stated it was prepared "to fight *any legislation* proposed during the present session of Congress which might impose unreasonable restrictions upon the right of an honest citizen to possess any kind of gun, excepting a machine gun, for his protection or for sporting purposes."[80] In another, the NRA noted how the "sportsmen of the country are literally up in arms against the Copeland firearms bill," and that the NRA would be there leading the "fight."[81]

Within the NRA's press releases were a wide array of arguments. One was that federal firearms legislation would only exasperate the crime problem. And if Congress must pass some type of firearms legislation, the NRA advocated that it be mandatory penalties for "the use of the gun in com-mission of a crime."[82] Another argument it advanced was that if federal anticrime legislation was to be directed toward any tangible object, it was the automobile and the airplane, not firearms. The way the NRA put it, it was the "progressive development of the automobile and the airplane" that exasperated the "growth of criminal aggressiveness and criminal power." Therefore, the NRA recommended that Congress pass a law "against the driving of automobiles or airplanes across interstate boundaries by known criminals, with a penitentiary sentence." Such a law would be "far more reasonable and would be a far more popular and effective law than one affecting the interstate transportation of firearms."[83]

Through its expansive social network of magazine editors, newspaper columnists, state game commissions, and state and local chapters of the American Legion and the Izaak Walton League, the NRA was able to widely distribute its press releases railing against federal firearms legislation.[84] The same political message was distributed on the pages of the NRA's *American Rifleman*.[85] Sportsmen, hunters, and firearms owners were instructed there to write their members of Congress and make two requests: First, both Copeland bills must be rejected. Second, if members of Congress truly wanted effective and "reasonable" firearms legislation, they must work with NRA officials. Essentially, what the NRA wanted its members, affili-ated clubs, and the wider gun-rights community to convey was that the NRA was "on the side of law and order," maintained "no sympathy for the crook or gangster," and would gladly assist in preparing legislation that did not negatively impact the "honest citizen."[86]

The NRA's political call to arms proved effective. Capitol Hill was besieged with letters and telegrams from sportsmen, hunters, shooters, and fire-arms owners echoing the NRA's talking points. In some cases, affiliated clubs submitted formal resolutions denouncing any form of federal fire-arms legislation as in violation of the Second Amendment. This outpour-ing produced the political result that the NRA wanted—a chance to formally present its objections at a congressional hearing.

Surprisingly, the first hearing on firearms legislation involved neither of the highly publicized Copeland bills before the Senate, but a bill pend-ing before the House of Representatives, H.R. 9066. Authored by the Roos-evelt administration's Department of Justice, the bill was primarily a tax measure, which stipulated that a federal tax would be levied on every pistol, revolver, sawed-off shotgun, or machine gun sold, assigned, or transferred in interstate commerce. H.R. 9066 also prescribed strict measures regarding the importation, manufacturing, and interstate transportation of said firearms. These measures included requiring new purchasers to provide the Internal Revenue Service (IRS) with personal information, fingerprints, and a photograph. Additionally, in order for any purchaser to transport a firearm, they would have to first obtain a permit.[87]

On April 16, 1934, Attorney General Cummings testified before the House Committee on Ways and Means that H.R. 9066 was necessary because the crime problem had grown "beyond the power of control of merely local authorities." In the same breath, he conceded that the bill was just a proposal, and that the Department of Justice was open to amending it however Congress saw fit.[88] Two days later Milton A. Reckord outlined the NRA's objections. In doing so, Reckord gave an account of events where officials in the Department of Justice led him to believe that the NRA would have a hand in drafting H.R. 9066. However, according to Reckord, the department reneged on its promise, and it was not until just days before the hearings that the NRA was given its first opportunity to review the bill. Reckord then informed the committee that the NRA was "absolutely favorable to reasonable legislation" and "not obstructionists in any way."[89]

But Reckord's account of events was far from truthful. The Department of Justice never offered the NRA such a promise, nor was Reckord being honest with the committee on NRA obstruction. Assistant Attorney General Keenan, when given his chance to testify, informed the committee as much by providing a vastly different account of events—one in which NRA officials stated they would cooperate with the Department of Justice only on the condition that handguns were excluded from the bill.[90]

Prior to Keenan's testimony, NRA officials testifying before the committee were unwavering in their opposition to H.R. 9066, as well as any federal legislation directed at handguns. NRA president Karl T. Frederick was especially outspoken. Throughout his testimony, not only did Frederick criticize virtually every provision within H.R. 9066 as an attempt to disarm all of rural America, but he bemoaned even the notion of Congress enacting restrictive firearms controls: "In my opinion, the useful results which can be accomplished by firearms legislation are extremely limited," he stated.[91] Therein Frederick showed himself to be both an artful political tactician and the foremost pro-gun expert on firearms law.[92] For every point a member of the committee made in favor of federal firearms control, Frederick provided a thought-provoking counterpoint.[93]

For a time, it appeared that the NRA had gained the political upper hand and the committee would be forced to table H.R. 9066—that is, until Keenan's testimony refuted much of the NRA's story. It was Keenen's testimony, along with the evidence showing that the NRA was in fact responsible for flooding Capitol Hill with ill-informed telegrams and letters, that caused the NRA to suddenly reverse course and request an opportunity to cooperate with the Department of Justice. The committee obliged the NRA's request.[94]

From the moment the House Committee on Ways and Means adjourned on April 19 until it reconvened on May 14, despite the Department of Justice having made several changes to H.R. 9066 to accommodate the NRA's objections, the principal issue of dispute—the bill's inclusion of handguns—remained unresolved. While the NRA was adamant that handguns be left out of the bill, the Department of Justice was just as adamant that they be left in. The reason that the Department of Justice was unwilling to budge on the issue was that every statistical study showed that three-quarters of all firearms-related crimes and homicides were committed with handguns. Therefore, from the department's perspective, any firearms bill that excluded handguns would make it useless in the war on crime. In the hopes of convincing the NRA to change its position, the Department of Justice offered a concession—one that would exempt NRA members and a few other classes of persons from the law's permit provisions. The NRA rejected it.[95]

By the time the House Committee on Ways and Means reconvened to hear testimony on the revised draft of H.R. 9066, the relationship between the Department of Justice and the NRA had completely soured. The NRA blamed the Department of Justice for acting in bad faith.[96] Conversely, from the department's standpoint, it was the NRA through the organization's dissemination of misleading literate urging sportsmen, hunters, shooters, and firearms owners to oppose H.R. 9066—that was the problem. The rift was apparent at the hearing as each side delivered their testimony. Neither showed any willingness to concede.[97] NRA executive vice president Reckord became frustrated to the point that after the hearing he confronted Keenan and accused the Department of Justice of trying to place "onerous restrictions on 120,000,000 honest Americans" just to "catch a few crooks." "Limit your bill to machine guns, submachine guns and sawed-off shotguns and we'll have no objection," he shouted at Keenan. Reckord then took his dissatisfaction to the press gallery, which had just witnessed the confrontation. "If Keenan wants to be rough, I can be rough, too," he stated, adding, "Ordinarily I'm a peace-loving citizen, but not now."[98]

Two weeks later, on May 28, the Senate Subcommittee on Commerce opened its hearings on both the Copeland bills, and a third bill submitted by the Department of Justice, S. 3680, that was almost identical to H.R. 9066.[99] It was over this two-week period that the House Committee on Ways and Means, by the slim vote margin of 13 to 12, decided to move forward with a stripped-down version of H.R. 9066—one that met all the NRA's objections. The final bill, H.R. 9741, in many ways resembled H.R. 9066 except for the fact that handguns were omitted. Considering this develop-ment, the NRA urged the Senate Subcommittee on Commerce to place aside all three bills before them and take up H.R. 9741. The subcommittee's chair-man, Senator Copeland, rejected the idea. The way he saw it, the House of Representatives' business was their business. The Senate would conduct its own hearing and make its own recommendations on Senate bills, and, if the Senate and House arrived at two different conclusions as to how fire-arms should be regulated, the matter would be handled in due course by a joint conference committee.

The NRA's lobbying against Copeland's bills certainly did not help their case. Copeland in fact opened the subcommittee's hearing by discussing the "great deal of misinformation" the NRA had "sent out over the coun-try." "One would think from reading the records printed that it is the desire of the Senate to disarm good men and to furnish arms only to men who are bad," stated Copeland, adding, "nothing could be further from the truth."[100]

Reckord was the first to testify before the Copeland- chaired subcom-mittee, and the New York senator made sure to extensively question Reck-ord on the NRA's lobbying activities.[101] At one point Copeland inquired whether the NRA had made any "attacks" on any subcommittee mem-bers.[102] Reckord responded in the negative, to which Copeland inquired again. Copeland knew that Reckord either was lying or had fortuitously for-gotten what the NRA had been claiming in its literature.[103] It was not until after Copeland pressed the issue nearly a dozen more times that Reckord finally conceded that the NRA had distributed literature overly critical of

Copeland.[104] With that admission out of the way, Copeland decided to extend an olive branch to better understand the NRA's objections:

> COPELAND: Now, I want to get on common ground with you, General. You are the most influential man in this country in opposition to firearms legislation. Do you believe that any bill would be satisfactory which would permit any Federal control over pistols and revolvers?
> RECKORD: Yes, sir.
> COPELAND: You do not oppose, then, some Federal regulation?
> RECKORD: If it is reasonable and proper, and not a subterfuge, I believe it can be worked out?[105]

After more political back and forth between Copeland and Reckord as to what "reasonable" handgun legislation looked like, Reckord proffered a bill that the NRA would most assuredly back—one that prohibited anyone convicted of a "crime of violence" from possessing and transporting a firearm in interstate commerce. Reckord felt that such a bill, accompanied with "a machine gun bill," was all that was necessary for law enforcement to stop armed criminals. Copeland responded, "Well, yet, a little while ago, you told me that you were willing to have Federal control over pistols and revolvers?" Reckord answered this by offering up another bill that the NRA was willing to back—one that would make any handgun shipped in interstate commerce "amendable to the law of the state into which it is shipped."[106] Copeland could not believe what he was hearing. In addition to asking Congress to altogether forego regulating handguns, Reckord was arguing that best federal response was to enact a legal redundancy. State laws regulating the interstate shipment of firearms were already constitutionally valid. Thus, if Congress accepted Reckord's suggestion and enacted a bill recognizing the legitimacy of such laws, Copeland knew it would be hardly worth the paper it was printed on. This frustrated him immensely. The entire purpose of the subcommittee hearing was to produce a firearms bill that was tangible—a bill that would make it harder for criminals to obtain firearms. Reckord's proposals did nothing in the way of achieving that purpose. What also frustrated Copeland was that Reckord was politically sidestepping the key problem facing state and local law enforcement—laws governing the sale and purchase of handguns were not uniform, and therefore a criminal could easily circumvent a restrictive state or local law by simply purchasing a firearm in an adjoining jurisdiction that maintained minimal restrictions.[107]

The NRA was now facing an uphill battle to get the subcommittee onboard with its position. Still, undeterred, the NRA stayed the course by outlining each of its objections to the three bills before the subcommittee. At the same time, it once again pleaded with the subcommittee to abandon the three bills and instead take up H.R. 9741. In one heated exchange, Copeland rebuked Reckord for continuing to push H.R. 9741. "If I did not believe in firearms legislation, I would think this is the best bill in the world," he stated, adding, "This [bill with its omission of handguns] would not give the American people the slightest protection at least, the protection would be so slight it would be negligible." Copeland pointed to the Department of Justice's bill, S. 3680, as a "real bill" that the subcommittee should accept. He then called out the NRA for mischaracterizing the intent behind the three bills. "It has been made to appear to the American people we are a dreadful lot of folks on this crime committee," he said to Reckord, adding that the truth of the matter was that the subcommittee merely wanted to "protect the men and women and children of America, and one of the ways to do it is to make it more difficult to get pistols."[108]

Near the close of the day's testimony, it appeared as if nothing was going to stop Copeland from advancing a bill that included handguns. Copeland informed Reckord of as much in his final statement for the day: "General, there isn't any question at all—and I want you to take this page out of my experience of the past year—there isn't any question at all but that this country is demanding a firearms bill, a small-arms bill, and we have gone far enough today to discover that we could write such a bill."[109] Yet, by conclusion of the second and final day of testimony, Copeland decidedly reversed course. The reason for his reversal was the compelling and convincing testimony of the NRA's foremost legal expert and president, Karl T. Frederick. Much like before the House Committee on Ways and Means, Frederick persuasively laid out each NRA talking point against restrictive firearms controls: criminals will obtain firearms regardless of how restrictive the law is; punish the criminal, not the law-abiding citizen; mandatory penalties for the commission of a crime while armed are preferred to regulating firearms; and firearms regulation is a matter best left to state and local governments. Additionally, he outlined how several provisions contained each of the three bills before the subcommittee were either use-less or unworkable.[110]

Once the hearing adjourned, Copeland met privately with Frederick and Reckord for over an hour. It was there that the three men came to an agree-ment. Copeland would drop handguns (for now), as well as permit the NRA to make constructive changes to any bill of their choosing.[111] In exchange, he received the NRA's assurance that it would work with the Sen-ate Subcommittee on Racketeering and Crime in producing agreeable leg-islation to aid the Department of Justice in preventing criminals from obtaining firearms through interstate commerce.[112] Subsequently, Cope-land proceeded forward with the NRA-approved bill, and President Roos-evelt signed it into law as the National Firearms Act.[113]

The NRA celebrated its political victory by publishing a scaremonger-ing editorial that depicted Assistant Attorney General Keenan as dishon-est, and the federal agents responsible for enforcing the National Firearms Act as coldblooded killers. The editorial also suggested that sportsmen, hunters, and firearms owners should thank the NRA for successfully removing handguns from the bill. For, if not for the NRA, federal "snoop-ing squads" would most certainly be "going around from house to house to see who does and who does not possess arms."[114]

In the months that followed, as Reckord and Frederick worked behind scenes to draft legislation that was agreeable with the Senate Subcommit-tee on Racketeering and Crime, the NRA focused its lobbying efforts at the state level, particularly westward, where restrictive handgun legislation was pending before the California Assembly.[115] It was not until the start of 1935 that the NRA began urging sportsmen, hunters, and firearms owners to back a federal compromise.[116] The way the NRA sold it was that sports-men, hunters, shooters, and firearms owners had one of two choices: The first was to give up and let the Department of Justice persuade Congress to pass legislation that would "make it possible for Federal officers to arrest any citizen who possesses a pistol or revolver (perhaps any gun) without having complied with regulations issued by some Secretary, or Bureau Chief, in Washington—on the theory that by so doing a few crooks . . . may be arrested." The second and preferred NRA choice was to get behind a bill, S. 3, drafted by senator Copeland—one drafted "in the name of the repu-table citizens and sportsmen of this country, and [that] will make it possible for Federal officers to arrest a crook who runs about the country with a firearm of any description, but will let the reputable citizen alone."[117]

But in espousing support for S. 3, what the NRA failed to disclose to the gun rights community was that Reckord and Frederick had worked with the Senate Subcommittee on Racketeering and Crime in drafting it.[118] This was undoubtedly intentional, for it allowed the NRA to politically straddle both sides. To lawmakers and the American people who wanted something to be done about the unimpeded traffic in firearms, the organization was able to present itself as a sensible voice.[119] But to the sportsmen, hunters, shooters, and firearms owners who made up the gun rights community, the NRA continued to be perceived as an ardent defender of the Second Amendment. This straddling approach by the NRA accomplished two objectives: First, it ensured that the gun rights community would continue to contest every piece of firearms legislation unless it was legislation that the NRA already endorsed. Second, it sent a message to lawmakers that working with the NRA was crucial if they wanted to get any firearms legislation passed.[120] The approach proved effective. Once again, at the NRA's urging, the gun rights community flooded Congress with letters and telegrams, but this time urging S. 3's adoption.[121] There were, however, some letters from the gun rights community outright opposing any additional federal firearms legislation, regardless of the NRA's endorsement.[122]

By the time the Senate Committee on Commerce held its hearing on S. 3 in April 1935, the Department of Justice had introduced its own, alternate bill. It was essentially the same bill that Congress was provided with a year earlier—that is the National Firearms Act with handguns included.[123] In the hearing, officials from the Department of Justice and the NRA once again squared off. But this time the political deck was substantially stacked in the NRA's favor. Not only were three NRA officials allowed to testify in favor of S. 3, but so were several gun rights proponents, such as Calvin C. Goddard, Northwestern University professor, ballistic expert, and NRA member, and Seth Gordon, president of the American Game Association and NRA member. Conversely, only two witnesses testified on behalf of the Department of Justice's bill—Assistant Attorney General Keenan and John L. Whitehurst, who represented the General Federation of Women's Clubs.

Yet despite the NRA having the political upper hand, Keenan was successful in derailing one S. 3 provision that was included at the request of the NRA—a provision that would have negated altogether the National Firearms Act and a 1927 federal law prohibiting the private mailing of any concealable firearm through the U.S. Postal Service.[124] However, other than the Department of Justice convincing Congress to remove this provision, the hearing proved to be a total victory for the NRA. This was because the NRA was able to persuade the members of the committee to make the remaining provisions in S. 3 even less burdensome than they already were.[125]

This time the members of the committee did not care that the NRA was continuing to distribute misleading literature—literature that Keenan found to be offensive. "The Department of Justice, notwithstanding the printed leaflets of the National Rifle Association, at no time has attempted to be allied with the gangsters of this country, or to favor them with any legislation, or to punish or discourage the lawful activities of any citizens," stated Keenan before the committee, adding, "To say that [the Department of Justice] is working in the interest of the criminal is to confess that we

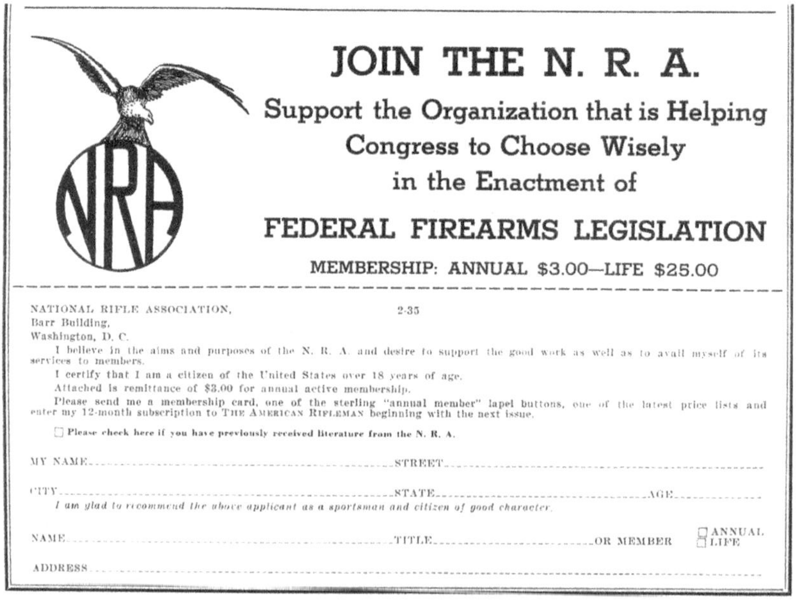

FIGURE 2.4 Membership advertisement in *American Rifleman*, 1935. The ad urged sportsmen, hunters, and firearms owners to join the NRA in helping Congress "wisely" pass federal firearms legislation.

are a Nation of lawbreakers, and that we are so selfish in our purpose and our desires that we are unwilling to comply with some honorable formalities of the law." All that mattered to the members of the committee, particularly its chairman, Senator Copeland, was that Congress advance legislation that the "sportsmen" would cease opposing. This was made abundantly clear in the following statement by Copeland to Keenan: "You cannot pass laws, without great effort, unless they appeal strongly to certain groups in this country. . . . I believe, speaking for myself, that this bill is as far as we can go with any hope of passing the legislation. If the Department of Justice can put over a more drastic law, God bless them. I am glad. But I feel that it is my duty to say . . . that no more stringent law than this can be enacted."[126]

Upon conclusion of the hearing, the Department of Justice and NRA retreated to their political corners to advocate for their respective bills, each assailing the other's bill as the wrong approach. In early 1936, when the Senate voted in favor of S. 3, it appeared that the NRA would achieve a swift political victory. To the NRA's disappointment, however, the Department of Justice, with the assistance of North Carolina representative Robert L. Doughton, chairman of the House Ways and Means Committee, was able to stall the legislation in the House of Representatives for more than a year. It was during this time that the Department of Justice—with the hopes of bringing the NRA onboard with the registration of handguns—advanced an even more sweeping firearms control proposal, one that would register virtually every firearm in the country. In an October 5, 1937, speech before the Annual Convention of the International Association of Chiefs of Police, Attorney General Cummings outlined why he believed the law was necessary. Although he acknowledged that firearms ownership and use were longstanding American traditions—traditions that should be adequately considered whenever crafting firearms legislation—he outlined why he felt that some legislative "red tape" was necessary to curb the illegal, criminal use and traffic of firearms.[127] To Cummings, such necessary "red tape" included the "registration of *all* firearms." Indeed, in making this pitch, Cummings acknowledged that firearms registration would not immediately disarm criminals. Firearms registration would, however, at least according to Cummings, be an important "first step" in making the criminal acquisition of firearms more difficult.[128] This in turn would lower firearms-related crimes and homicides.

The NRA responded by publishing several full-page membership recruitment advertisements in the *American Rifleman*.[129] One advertisement recited the Second Amendment verbatim and urged NRA members to recruit "another good American to join . . . [and] take an active, intelligent part in [the] campaign to save the guns of honest citizens from registration, confiscation or further taxation."[130] Another lambasted Cummings for insinuating that the objections of the NRA members were orchestrated by the "mythical, non-existent pistol-manufacturers' lobby." The advertisement went on to encourage NRA members and affiliated rifle clubs to recruit others who would stand up and say, "The right of the American Citizen to bear Arms shall not be infringed."[131]

On top of organizing a membership drive, the NRA put together several talking points as to why firearms registration was ill-advised. One was that firearms registration would make even the most law-abiding citizen a criminal suspect:

> Suppose the registered owner of a weapons is away; his home is burglarized; it is ten days or two weeks before he returns. Meanwhile a murder is committed and the police find the murder weapon, which is registered in the name of the man who is out of town! It has not been reported stolen (because the owner does not yet know his home has been burglarized). The perfectly natural thing for the police to do is to broadcast a "look-out" for the missing owner of the gun. An honest man thereby becomes a "fugitive from justice" without knowing it, and faces the ignominy of arrest at his vacation hotel, and the notoriety in his home town papers of having been called upon to prove an alibi in a murder case. Far fetched? Not at all to anyone who knows the methods of operation employed in most American police departments. And the pathetic part of the picture is the fact that while the police are following the obvious "lead" to the innocent man, the real trail to the actual murderer is growing dimmer—and the registration of the gun has harmed rather than helped the apprehension of the criminal.[132]

Another NRA talking point was that firearms registration would not disarm the criminal. It would, however, "provide a lot of unnecessary red tape for honest citizens and sportsmen across the country."[133] And to the NRA, the imposition of any red tape was unacceptable.

The NRA also advanced hyperbolic talking points, such as claiming Attorney General Cummings and his assistants were deceitful and unethical.[134] Here, the key message that the NRA hoped sportsmen, hunters, and firearms owners would take away was that the Department of Justice was on the side of criminals, not law-abiding citizens. And to ensure that this message was spread far and wide, the NRA sent officials to speak anywhere and everywhere they would be heard.[135] This included taking part in a National Broadcasting Company (NBC) radio debate with Assistant United States Attorney General Brien McMahon on the merits of federal firearms registration. It was there that Reckord condemned the Department of Justice's different firearms registration proposals as "unreasonable and unnecessary" and added it was "for that reason and that reason alone" that the NRA opposed them.[136]

Certainly, the NRA was within its right to criticize Cummings and the Department of Justice for proposing firearms registration. The real driving force behind the NRA's opposition, however, was not the registering of firearms per se.[137] It was ensuring that state and local governments did not follow the federal government's lead. The way the NRA saw it, if Congress passed even the skinniest of firearms registration laws, it would open the firearms-control floodgates. One state or local government would follow Congress's lead, and another, and another until firearms ownership was thing of the past. The passage of S. 3—at least from the NRA's perspective—would stop such a doomsday scenario from ever happening.[138]

But in contrast to what the NRA was telling the gun rights community, there is nothing in the historical record to suggest that Cummings or the Department of Justice maintained any improper motives for pushing federal firearms registration. Their motive was rather straightforward—to shore up what Cummings, the Department of Justice, and many other law enforcement officials believed to be considerable shortfalls within the National Firearms Act. The correspondence between the heads of the Department of Justice and the Federal Bureau of Investigation (FBI) weigh this out. What the heads of both agencies were concerned with was the myriad of ways in which criminals were able to circumvent existing federal laws.[139] Equally concerning were advancements in firearms technology, particularly manufacturing improvements to the powerful .357 Magnum revolver and the development of zinc alloy ammunition, which increased the penetrability of bullets.[140]

What the historical record also informs is that Cummings and the Department of Justice were becoming increasingly frustrated with the NRA's opposition tactics, particularly the spreading of false and misleading information.[141] To counter the NRA, the Department of Justice did what it could to garner public support. This included it developing its own set of talking points that expressly refuted the NRA's; asking certain nonprofit organizations to provide legislative endorsements; issuing press releases and radio broadcasts on the need for additional federal firearms legislation; writing proregulation editorials in newspapers and sporting magazines; and even taking part in a broadcast debate on the need for federal firearms registration.[142]

Entering the spring of 1938, the Department of Justice was growing confident that Congress would at least agree to the registration of handguns, especially after the Institute of Public Opinion released its national survey on the subject.[143] Headed by Dr. George Gallup, the survey's findings were reprinted across the country despite repeated attempts by the NRA to stop its publication. The NRA additionally requested that the American Psychological Association oust Dr. Gallup from their ranks for "unethical behavior."[144] Dr. Gallup's survey asked respondents: "Do you think all owners of pistols and revolvers should be required to register with the government?" Overall, 84 percent of respondents favored registration and 16 percent opposed. The largest approval numbers came from the New England states (90 percent) and from cities (86 percent). What was most promising to Department of Justice officials was the survey's finding that even in those geographic areas of the country that were "fondly known to generations of . . . Americans as 'the Wild West,'" an overwhelming 82 percent of respondents supported registration.[145]

But to the disappointment of Department of Justice officials, the NRA was far more politically shrewd than they were. No matter how the officials modified their proposal or pleaded their case for firearms registration, it did nothing to stop the NRA's barrage of letters and telegrams—and it was this barrage that was the deciding factor in convincing members of Congress to vote in favor of S. 3. This cannot be historically overstated. The fact is that until the late 1950s it was quite rare for Capitol Hill to receive a steady flow of constituent mail on any issue. Therefore, when members of Congress received a constant barrage of letters, telegrams, and even formal resolutions by sportsmen, hunting, conservation, and shooting organizations favoring S. 3 over the Department of Justice's bill, it was political common sense for members of Congress to vote for the former over the latter. It did not matter that the polls supported firearms registration.[146] What mattered to members of Congress was what their constituents were writing. The NRA understood this better than anyone else, and it is why the organization always made sure to include the names and addressed of lawmakers when calling the gun rights community to action.

In June 1938, when President Roosevelt signed S. 3 into law as the Federal Firearms Act, the NRA declared it a "sportsmen's victory" for "sane, reasonable, and effective" firearms legislation. "In this law we have a reasonable approach to the solution of a difficult problem, for the control of firearms in the hands of the underworld," claimed the NRA.[147] And it had every reason to celebrate the passage of S. 3, for the bill did nothing to interfere with individual access to firearms. It only imposed regulatory burdens, albeit very minimal ones, on firearms manufacturers, importers, and dealers.[148] S. 3 indeed made it a crime for felons and fugitives from justice to receive a firearm in interstate commerce. In line with the NRA's mantra of "punish the criminal, not the law-abiding citizen," however, the bill did not place any bureaucratic red tape in the way of an individual purchasing a firearm.[149]

Yet despite having every reason to celebrate its political outmaneuvering of the Department of Justice, S. 3 was not the total victory that the NRA hoped it would be. Recall that one of the motives for the NRA endorsing the bill was to cut off future attempts at firearms registration, whether at the federal, state, or local level. This did not happen.[150] Instead, over the nine-year period from 1939 to 1947, the Department of Justice introduced to Congress one federal firearms registration proposal after another.[151]

The NRA's playbook for defeating the Department of Justice's firearms registration proposals over this nine-year period was not all that different from how the NRA handled the National Firearms Act and Federal Firearms Act.[152] The group's principal weapon continued to be its ability to rouse sportsmen, hunters, and firearms owners to political action. It was able to accomplish this feat by having socialized the gun rights community to view any attempt at firearms registration as a battle of "good" versus "evil"—what it means to be an American, with the gun rights community being told they were on the side of "patriotism."[153] In the same breath, the NRA surmised far-fetched scenarios should firearms registration ever become a reality—scenarios where the law-abiding, firearms-loving citizen became the criminal. Finally, the NRA made sure to characterize the consequences of firearms registration in simple, all-or-nothing terms—that is, as the first step toward complete disarmament.

There was one technique, however, that the NRA began relying on more and more to rouse the gun rights community to political action—sensationalism and fearmongering. The historical event that helped the organization to achieve this effect was the outbreak of World War II. It significantly heightened Americans' fears over the spread of fascism, both as an ideology and as a military incursion. It is worth noting that the NRA did not immediately resort to sensationalism and fearmongering.[154] In fact, it initially assumed a more cautious, level-headed approach to the global conflict—one that urged NRA members to exercise restraint when determining whether a reported fascist danger was real or fictional.[155] It was not until after the War Department suspended a little-known federal program that benefited only NRA members and affiliated rifle clubs that this cautious, level-headed approach was discarded in favor of fearmongering and sensationalism.[156]

The federal program affected was one where NRA members and affiliated rifle clubs could purchase surplus military rifles and ammunition directly from federal armories at discounted prices.[157] Although the War Department told the NRA that it was only temporarily suspending the program to shore up the country's military preparedness, the real reason was intelligence reports indicating that Nazi sympathizers living in the United States—otherwise known as fifth columnists—were planning to join the NRA with the sole purpose of using the federal program to stockpile firearms and ammunition.[158] What also prompted the War Department to temporarily suspend the sale of surplus military rifles and ammunition was that the FBI had recently arrested seventeen members of the anti-Semitic Christian Front, three of whom turned out to be NRA members.[160]

Hoping to pressure the War Department to lift the suspension, the NRA published a special bulletin that called on the gun rights community to write their congressional representatives and educate them on the real "facts" about the NRA. Although the NRA meant for the bulletin to be a line-by-line defense of those who would dare question "one of the country's best known, most praised practical-patriotic organizations," at several points the bulletin reads like a series of lame excuses for the NRA's lax membership enrollment practices. For instance, in response to the reports that three of the arrested Christian Fronters were NRA members, rather than admit any responsibility, the NRA sidestepped the issue by arguing that a higher percentage of the arrested Christian Fronters were New York National Guardsmen and New York City policemen. Similarly, in response to news reports that twelve Nazi sympathizers, who were also NRA members and had purchased surplus military rifles, the NRA sidestepped the issue by arguing that this was only a tiny fraction of the its overall membership.[160]

Only when it became apparent that the NRA's proven tactic of bombarding Congress with telegrams and letters was not going to persuade the War Department to lift the suspension did the NRA's leadership decide to take a corrective approach—one that involved the NRA committing to several institutional reforms.[161] This was accomplished by the NRA Executive Committee adopting two resolutions. The first resolution recommitted the NRA to the mission statement outlined within its by-laws, that is, "to educate the youth of the nation in marksmanship, to encourage marksmanship throughout the United States, particularly among civilians, both as a sport and for the purposes of qualifying as finished marksmen those individuals who may be called upon to serve in time of war." The second resolution revamped the NRA's membership recruitment practices. For decades, all that was required for an individual applicant to obtain NRA membership was that any current member in good standing vouch for the applicant's moral fitness. But now, to dispel any "uncertainties" regarding the NRA's commitment to national security, the NRA Executive Committee took the additional step of requiring every applicant to take an oath of allegiance to the United States, as well as formally denounce any "organization or group pledged to, or working for, a program aimed at the destruction of our present system of government as established by the Constitution of the United States."[162]

While the NRA was preoccupied with the politics of restoring its access to surplus military rifles and ammunition, calls for firearms registration by the Department of Justice, state attorneys general, and lawmakers were gaining political steam. But this time the calls for firearms registration had less to do with criminal access to firearms. Rather, they were driven by the very same concern that had caused the NRA to lose access to surplus military rifles and ammunition—the perceived threat of a fifth column. At all

FIGURE 2.5 World War II propaganda poster produced by Appreciate America, a Chicago-based organization that published pamphlets, literature, and posters designed to encourage unity among all Americans despite racial, ethnic, and religious differences. The poster depicted how fifth columnists—through their use of "bigotry" and "foreign propaganda," meant to politically divide Americans—were trying to knock down the pillars of "liberty," "unity," "justice," and "equality" that unite Americans.

levels of government, proponents of firearms registration began pointing to the dangers of having armed fifth columnists inside the United States (figure 2.5). Firearms registration, it was argued, would mitigate this threat.[163]

The NRA responded to this new firearms registration justification by advancing three principal talking points. The first was that the so-called fifth column threat was more nominal than real.[164] According to the NRA, the threat was nothing more than an attempt by the "anti-firearms campaign" to substitute "hysteria for reason."[165] The second point somewhat undermined the first but was used to counter any lawmaker who remained deeply concerned with the fifth column threat. It involved the NRA conceding the dangerousness of the fifth column yet at the same time arguing that the *real* danger was not armed fifth columnists but the fifth column's ability to undermine American institutions. The threat to American democracy was what lawmakers needed to focus on, not firearms registration, the organization argued.[166] The third talking point the NRA advanced was built on the second and was referred to as the "fifth column trap." In advancing this point, the group imaginatively claimed that many, if not all, firearms registration proposals were an insidious fifth column scheme meant to undermine the national defense. According to the NRA, immediately following firearms registration, fifth columnists would acquire the lists and subsequently target, burglarize, and seize the firearms of individual citizens (figure 2.6).[167] The "fifth column trap" was also, according to the NRA, the means through which the German Nazis, should

FIGURE 2.6 Political cartoon in *Outdoor Life*, April 1941. An insidious wolf in the cartoon advocated for firearms registration to protect the country from fifth columnists. The wolf licked his lips in preparation for the sheep—the American people—having their firearms confiscated because of registering them. Below the cartoon appeared the caption: "Don't delay a moment—or it may be too late! Write or wire your representative and senator to be on guard against this brazen movement (made in the guise of patriotism) to hamper and disarm millions of loyal American sportsmen."

they invade the United States, would locate citizens' firearms, confiscate them, and subsequently defeat the United States.[168]

By the close of 1940, with several fifth column investigations in the House Committee on Un-American Activities underway,[169] groups like the American Legion's Department of Americanism calling on its members to report on the "subversive activities" of the "dangerous menace of the Fifth Column,"[170] and the American people becoming increasingly concerned with the national security threat posed by fifth columnists, it did not take long for the NRA to abandon its moderate position and replace it with an all-out sensationalist one.[171] In doing so, it fashioned a narrative where supporters of antifirearms legislation and fifth columnists were working together, or, at the very least, the rank-and-file of the "anti-gunners" had been infiltrated and coerced by fifth columnists.[172] Either way, the NRA wanted to harness the fear of the fifth column to convince NRA members, affiliated rifle clubs, the wider gun rights community, and hopefully lawmakers and the American people that any firearms registration proposal was something that the fifth columnists most assuredly wanted.[173]

The NRA first unveiled its sensationalist position in a special bulletin titled *Let's Fight the Fifth Column Trap*, which sought to answer the question: "Does [firearms registration] promise defense for the American form of Government and American homes against the 'Fifth Column' or does it promise [a] happy hunting ground for the foreign agent and the political buccaneer?"[174] The bulletin begins by claiming that fifth columnists were secretly undermining American institutions through "smooth propaganda"—that is, "plausible arguments backed with half-truths and distorted facts." And the supposed impetus of this "smooth propaganda" was undermining the country's military preparedness. The NRA claimed that the passage of firearms registration laws would all but ensure this outcome, given that it was common knowledge that firearms registration inevitably leads to the firearms confiscation. "All the old familiar sugar-coating appears in the current [fifth column] propaganda [such as] 'no inconvenience,' 'no registration fee,' 'no danger to those who have a good reason to possess a gun,' [and] 'important to the national defense,'" cautioned the NRA, adding, "Sweet nothings!"[175]

The NRA bulletin concluded by calling on the "Sportsmen of America" to "fight this Fifth Column trap," watch for propagandist legislation at the local level, and be active in educating others of the pending danger:

Bills introduced into State or National Legislatures attract attention and hearings are allowed before action is taken. But in more cities and towns comparatively little attention is paid to administrative changes in police regulations. Hence there is a much better change of putting the scheme over the form of a city police ordinance than to attempt it in the form of a State law. . . .

. . . Point out the true facts to every red-blooded American you can reach. This is not time to pull punches. If someone in your own city Government has not already introduced an ordinance requiring firearms registration it is most probably that someone will, because the propaganda has apparently been spread from coast to coast.

Check with your own Councilman and arrange to be immediately notified if such a proposal appears. . . .

. . . This will be a hard, unremitting fight against a skillful, well-organized, powerfully backed machine. We must guard every town and city council in America. That means that every individual member of the National Rifle Association is an outpost on a far-flung, thin picket line. It means that every sportsmen's club, trap and skeet club, veteran's organization and patriotic society must be attuned to their danger, and their active support secured. Your national association will, as always, do its part to co-ordinate, to advise, and to act as a message center for warnings, but with thousands of points to be watched, with hundreds of thousands of local citizens to be educated to the danger inherent in this plausible theory; the major portion of the "spade work" must of necessity be done by individual sportsmen and local groups.[176]

From the publication of *Let's Fight the Fifth Column Trap* to the close of World War II, the NRA held up the threat of the fifth column as *the* principal reason for Americans to oppose firearms registration. For instance, in an *American Rifleman* editorial in 1942, the NRA audaciously claimed that several firearms registration proposals proffered by local National Defense Councils were part of an insidious fifth column scheme. Although the NRA acknowledged that local National Defense Councils were "patriotic" groups, it also suggested it was more than plausible that the councils were being misled by fifth column "elements" on firearms registration. "The only *practical* use for such 'defense' registration lists will be to make available to Fifth Column groups information as to where *they* can acquire additional

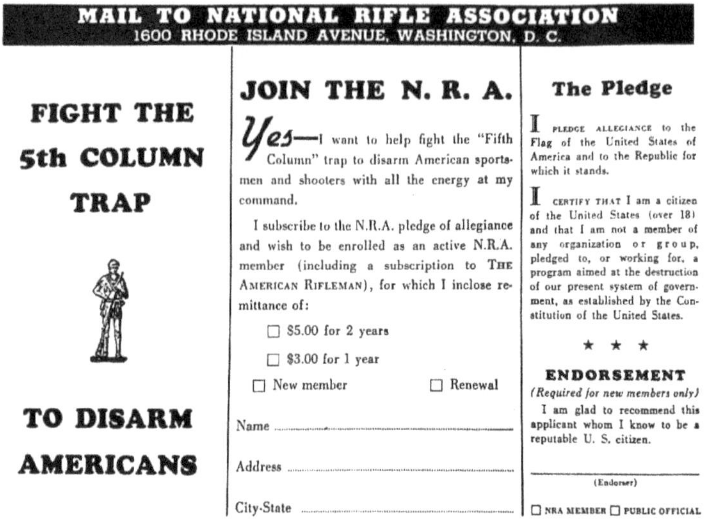

MAIL TO NATIONAL RIFLE ASSOCIATION
1600 RHODE ISLAND AVENUE, WASHINGTON, D. C.

FIGHT THE
5th COLUMN
TRAP

TO DISARM
AMERICANS

JOIN THE N. R. A.

Yes—I want to help fight the "Fifth Column" trap to disarm American sportsmen and shooters with all the energy at my command.

I subscribe to the N.R.A. pledge of allegiance and wish to be enrolled as an active N.R.A. member (including a subscription to THE AMERICAN RIFLEMAN), for which I inclose remittance of:

☐ $5.00 for 2 years
☐ $3.00 for 1 year
☐ New member   ☐ Renewal

Name ....

Address ....

City-State ....

The Pledge

I PLEDGE ALLEGIANCE to the Flag of the United States of America and to the Republic for which it stands.

I CERTIFY THAT I am a citizen of the United States (over 18) and that I am not a member of any organization or group, pledged to, or working for, a program aimed at the destruction of our present system of government, as established by the Constitution of the United States.

★ ★ ★

ENDORSEMENT
(Required for new members only)
I am glad to recommend this applicant whom I know to be a reputable U. S. citizen.

_____
(Endorser)

☐ NRA MEMBER ☐ PUBLIC OFFICIAL

FIGURE 2.7 NRA recruitment advertisement to "Fight the Fifth Column Trap," published in *American Rifleman* beginning with the February 1941 edition. The ad included the new NRA membership requirements of reciting the Pledge of Allegiance and an oath of allegiance, as well as being a U.S. citizen.

arms and what homes they should descend on *first* when outbreaks of local violence are called for by the enemy plan," claimed the NRA, adding, "*Our own Defense Councils are taking the first step to help establish that old-familiar Nazi Deadline—'all guns must be surrendered under penalty of death.'*"[177]

The NRA's strategy of lumping firearms registration with the fifth column proved effective in rousing many in the gun rights community to political action. Retired army colonel and World War I veteran Harold P. Sheldon, for one, bought the manufactured fifth column, "specialists in treason" narrative wholesale, writing: "Anti-firearms campaigns seldom originate in the organizations that appear to sponsor them. The real leaders cannily stay under cover while sincere but misguided enthusiasts bent on interfering with other people's business carry the banner and make the speeches. Under cover of the confusion incident to the national defense program, fresh attempts are being made to compel the registration of firearms. They should be watched."[178] A similarly inspired letter to Oklahoma lawmakers warned that firearms registration law would only disarm the "honest American citizen" and place them "at the mercy of

the well-armed criminal, gangster or fifth columnist." The letter went on
to state, "Now we are told that we must disarm to keep guns out of the
hands of the fifth columnists. I say without any reservation that this is
plain idiocy. Do you think for a minute that the fifth columnists will register or surrender his guns? Yeah—if and when Hitler tells them to."[179]

No matter where in the United States a firearms registration proposal
reared its head, the NRA and its supporters railed against it as a fifth column trap. Such was the case in Los Angeles, California, where even before
the fear of fifth columnists gripped the American psyche, the Board of
Police Commissioners requested the city council enact an ordinance requiring the registration of "any pistol, revolver or other firearm capable of
being concealed upon the person" in the hopes of thwarting the "perpe-
tration of vicious crimes."[180] Although the ordinance was unanimously
adopted by the Los Angeles City Council's Police and Fire Committee and
initially voted on favorably by the entire council, it was subsequently
defeated via the NRA's organized opposition.[181] At that time, the NRA had
not yet embraced the idea of fifth column sensationalism. Rather, it was
able to defeat the proposed ordinance on the grounds that it would do nothing to stop criminals from acquiring firearms. The NRA also claimed—
with the scantest of statistical evidence—that there was "no relationship
whatsoever between the crime rate and the existence of a firearms registration law in . . . large cities of the United States." It urged the city council to conduct a "study which might determine the actual reasons for the
unusually high crime rate" in Los Angeles.[182]

Undeterred by the NRA's organized opposition, the Police and Fire Committee moved forward with a slightly different firearms registration ordinance.[183] It did not take long, however, before the NRA once again politically outmaneuvered the committee, this time by convincing the majority
of the Los Angeles City Council that firearms registration was not a local
issue but a state one.[184] At that time the NRA had already switched its anti-
firearms registration messaging by embracing fifth column sensationalism. Thus, when the California legislature finally took up the issue of firearms registration in early 1941, the NRA and the gun rights community
responded in kind with claims of fifth column propaganda and eventually
won the political fight.[185]

Over the next two years, the issue of firearms registration remained
largely dormant in Los Angeles politics—that is, until the summer of 1943,

following the events of the Zoot Suit Riots. The riots began on June 3, 1943, after some sailors claimed that they had been attacked by a group of Mexican American zoot suiters. The accusations escalated what were already deep racial tensions among the city's residents, and over the next several days Los Angeles experienced full-scale rioting.[186] It was not long after the riots had been quelled that Los Angeles chief of police C. B. Horrall wrote a letter urging the Board of Police Commissioners to once again take up the issue of firearms registration. Although the letter never mentioned the Zoot Suit Riots, they were almost assuredly a contributing factor. Horrall cited several reasons why firearms registration was necessary, including an unprecedented increase in firearms being stolen, the Los Angeles Police Department's inability to properly track firearms that were either stolen or found at the scene of a crime, and the ever-growing "black-market" in firearms.[187]

It did take long for the Board of Police Commissioners to oblige Horrall's request, and the issue of firearms registration was once more before the Los Angeles City Council.[188] It also did not take long before the NRA delivered several counterpoints. One of them was that firearms registration was a fifth column trap.

On September 15, at the urging of the NRA and its allies, the Los Angeles City Council agreed to hold a public hearing on the matter. Therein both proponents and opponents of firearms registration were provided an opportunity to present their case. Only two of the more than a hundred hearing attendees were proponents of firearms registration—one of whom was Horrall.[189] All other hearing attendees—who mainly comprised NRA members, including Judge Hillard Comstock of Sonoma County, the sitting NRA president, who provided testimony—were opposed.[190]

The fact that the opponents of firearms registration outnumbered proponents by roughly fifty to one was more than enough to persuade the council to vote down Horrall's firearms registration proposal. But what made the decision even easier for the council was that the only other person to testify in support of the proposal was Jane Wilson, chair of the Legislative Committee for the Los Angeles Communist Party.[191] What makes Wilson's testimony noteworthy was the prevalence of anticommunist sentiment at the time, both in Los Angeles and across the country. To those attending and reading about the hearing, it wasn't relevant that the United States was fighting Nazi fascism along with several communist allies, for at that point anticommunist sentiment was so deeply ingrained in the American psyche. Not to mention, as it pertained to Los Angeles specifically, due largely to inaccurate reporting and ideological prejudices, many, if not most, of the city's residents blamed communists for the Zoot Suit Riots. It did not matter that there was no bona fide evidence connecting the two.[192]

Aware of the rampant anticommunist sentiment, as well as the claims of the riots being communist-driven, the Los Angeles Communist Party decided to decisively back Horrall's firearms registration proposal. The reason for this was twofold: First, party members were living in a state of fear. Threats of violence from overzealous, far-right wing political supporters were commonplace. Second, the party wanted to show that it was innocent of any wrongdoing in the riots and therefore maintained no reservations about complying with firearms registration requirements. "Fascist-inclined groups or other anti-democratic bodies," however, argued the party would "have good cause to fear making public through police registration, their possession of arms."[193]

Yet, despite the Los Angeles Communist Party's well-intentioned support for Horrall's firearms registration ordinance, it was disingenuously cast by the NRA as being part of a larger, insidious, communist scheme to disarm the country.[194] In 1948, when New Jersey attorney general Walter Van Riper proposed firearms registration to state lawmakers, the NRA recalled the events of the 1943 Los Angeles hearing to characterize the proposal as a clear "Communistic move."[195] Similarly, in the NRA's *Annual Report* for 1947, the hearing was cast in sensationalist, ahistorical terms: "History was made in 1943 when the Communist Party for the first time publicly supported a gun registration ordinance in the city of Los Angeles. The ordinance was promptly killed. Although 'disarming the Bourgeoise' is a prominent part of the Communist operations plan they apparently realized their technical blunder in openly supporting such legislation and have not repeated the performance since."[196]

It is worth noting that firearms registration was not the only firearms control measure to be defeated at the hands of the NRA's sensationalized fifth column rhetoric. Other, far less intrusive proposals were also labeled insidious, fifth column traps. For instance, in the summer of 1940, when Vermont attorney general Lawrence C. Jones put forward an amendment to the Vermont Constitution that would have provided the State Assembly with the power to "regulate or restrict" the right to bear arms "for the purpose of preventing crime," there was little push back from the Vermont gun rights community.[197] But in the matter of a few months, after the NRA began espousing its sensationalist, fifth column rhetoric, editorials and letters to Vermont lawmakers opposing the Jones's amendment arrived in droves. Jones's amendment was labeled everything from a "fifth column trap," to a "subversive proposition," to an attempt to "disarm the populace."[198] This outpouring of anti–firearms control sentiment, coupled with the Vermont assembly being flooded with sportsmen the day the proposed amendment was scheduled for a vote, prompted the state's senators to unanimously reject Jones's amendment.[199]

Throughout World War II, in addition to persuading many in the gun rights community to perceive all firearms control proposals as an insidious fifth column trap, the NRA often relied on its tried and tested political playbook. And the NRA's primary go-to was to highlight something else—anything but firearms—that needed to be regulated. In the 1920s and 1930s, often that "something else" was automobiles and airplanes.[200] But now, with the threat of the fifth column ever looming, the NRA's "something else" became migrants.[201] There were two types of migrant regulations that the organization put forward in lieu of firearms controls. The first was a federal law requiring the registration of all migrants. The second was state laws prohibiting the possession of firearms by someone who was not a U.S. citizen. Such legislative measures, the NRA argued, would impose a "direct blow at the 'fifth columnist.' "[202] The NRA made sure to practice what it preached by immediately excluding all noncitizens from its membership ranks.[203] The NRA even went so far as to urge its members to be vigilant in monitoring the nation's borders for unlawful immigrant crossings and report them to the proper authorities.[204]

By the close of World War II, the NRA's lobbying tactics led to the defeat or tabling of virtually every firearms control proposal in the country.[205] The key to achieving this feat was the group's legislative division, which was tasked with formulating and relaying a message that resonated with NRA members, affiliated clubs, and the wider gun rights community, who then spread the message through both word-of-mouth and a variety of news media outlets. The legislative division's ability to achieve this effect is what made the NRA the early twentieth-century gold standard in grassroots lobbying. And immediately following World War II, due largely to the NRA's decision to offer free marksmanship training to the U.S. military, as well as encourage members to be proactive in the war effort (whether it be volunteering to join the military, home guard, or their local defense council), the NRA became an even more formidable lobbying organization. For it was through wartime volunteering that the group was able to develop an even closer partnership with the War Department—a partnership that aided the NRA in lobbying for government subsidies and appropriations, getting service members to join the NRA, and coproducing educational films with the Department of Army.[206]

The exponential impact the partnership with the War Department had on the NRA's success can be seen by examining the increase in membership and *American Rifleman* circulation after World War II. In 1941, at the start of the war, NRA membership totaled 44,951, and *American Rifleman* circulation stood at 64,147. Yet by 1947, two years following the war's armistice, NRA membership and *American Rifleman* circulation quintupled to 253,692 and 281,800, respectively.[207] The effect that this quintupling had on the NRA's ability to defeat or table firearms control proposals was immediate, as was seen from 1946 to 1947, when the Department of Justice once again presented Congress with several firearm registration proposals. What primarily distinguished these proposals from the Department of Justice's previous ones was the reason behind it—the flooding of foreign military-grade firearms and explosives into the United States.

The post–World War II surge of foreign military-grade firearms and explosives was largely a self-inflicted problem. Beginning in late 1945, after the war's conclusion, as millions of military service members left the battlefield and returned home, often accompanying them were war trophies. Common among these were foreign military-grade firearms and explosives.[208] And it did not take long before these weapons of war made their way onto American streets and contributed to thousands of crimes, homicides, and injuries.[209] The problem was so acute that President Harry S. Truman was compelled to acknowledge it, and he assured the American public that the federal government would be taking the "necessary steps" to prevent these military "implements of destruction from getting into the wrong hands."[210]

But before Truman acknowledged the severity of the problem, the Department of Justice, FBI, Department of Treasury, and state and local law enforcement officials were doing everything within their power to find a solution. This included urging returning military service members to register their foreign military-grade firearms and explosives, as well as

seizing any war trophies found to be noncompliant with the National Firearms Act.[211] With the intent of further assisting law enforcement officials
in locating, finding, tracking, and possibly removing any illegal firearms
from the streets, Attorney General Tom C. Clark asked New Jersey senator
Albert W. Hawkes to sponsor a bill to require the registration of most nonsporting firearms.[212]

The NRA responded, as the Department of Justice expected, by charac-
terizing firearms registration as a "Gestapo idea" on par with Mussolini
and Hitler.[213] According to the NRA, Hawkes's firearms registration bill was
nothing more than another insidious attempt by government officials "to
disarm the reputable American citizen" with "masses of half-truths, lies,
innuendo, and hysteria." The NRA even opposed the provision in Hawkes's
bill that expressly acknowledged the Second Amendment "right of any
individual to keep and bear arms." "Indeed, let no one say that [Hawkes]
intends to have his bill used as a vehicle to assist in the government in
legally repossessing any arms which are presently illegally possessed by
some citizen," exclaimed the NRA.[214]

Given the quintupling of NRA membership, as well as legislative warnings issued by the firearms industry, the response from the gun rights community was more forceful than ever. Letters and telegrams parroting the
NRA's talking points against firearms registration flooded Congress and
newspaper editorial boards. The letters and telegrams espoused everything
from firearms registration would "classify sportsmen as criminals," to firearms registration is the "first step towards confiscation," to Hawkes's bill
"reeks to high heaven [of] the same Gestapo methods that were employed
by Hitler and Mussolini before their downfall," was "designed with the evident intent to catch the unwary off guard, and . . . put every owner of
sporting firearms at the mercy of the F.B.I," and was the " 'Pearl Harbor'
bill of the anti-gun cranks."[215] The response on Capitol Hill was in fact so
forceful that not only was Hawkes's bill swiftly defeated—even after under-
going several weakening amendments—but also several members of Congress took to echoing some of the NRA's talking points.[216]

Undeterred by the NRA-led opposition, and citing the "vast unaccounted
amounts of firearms" being used by criminals, the Department of Justice
once again urged Congress to take up a firearms registration bill.[217] This
time it was Wisconsin senator Alexander Wiley, chairman of the Senate
Judiciary Committee, who agreed to sponsor it.[218] And much like Hawkes's
before him, through the organized opposition of the NRA and its allies,

Wiley's bill was handily defeated.[219] The volume of mail and telegrams Wiley received was so overwhelming that he issued a press release offering a formal apology for having ever sponsored it.[220] "I am opposed to needless controls on outdoor sports, which are, of course, so wholesome and well loved by countless Americans, and particularly the scores of thousands of sportsmen in my own state—a hunting paradise," he stated in withdrawing the bill.[221]

And Wiley's bill was not the only thing targeted by the NRA in its anti-firearms registration messaging campaign. The NRA also took aim at Attorney General Clark's manhood. In an *American Rifleman* editorial titled "A Gun-Shy Texan," it painted Clark as a coward for having "turned to the law," instead of joining the military after graduating from the Virginia Military Institute. "Probably nobody in Texas would have cared very much about Tom Clark's being gun-shy if he had just gone on politicking and chasing Big Business one way, then chasing Big Labor the other way," noted the NRA, adding, "but everyone in Texas had known for a long time that there was a little bunch of termites in the Department of Justice . . . who had been trying to get honest Americans' guns away from them since about the time Tom has supposedly been learning something about guns on the range at V.M.I."[222]

The swift, sure-handed defeat of the Department of Justice's post–World War II attempts at federal firearms registration were a resounding victory for the NRA and a testament to the organization's lobbying prowess. It brought about—at least what seemed at the time—a golden age of gun rights. For from the time Wiley's firearms registration bill was defeated until the assassination of President John F. Kennedy in late 1963, the NRA maintained what can best be described as a monopoly on influencing firearms legislation.[223] It did not shy away from this fact. In 1958 NRA executive director Floyd L. Parks bragged that whenever a firearms bill was proposed that "nibbl[ed] away at the constitutional right to bear arms," the NRA would know about it in "three to four hours" and subsequently alert "the people in that state" so that they could "take care of the situation themselves."[224]

The NRA had become so politically influential and connected that it was able to convince the Truman administration to forgo pursuing any other attempts at regulating war trophies.[225] In its place, under the rationale that war veterans were "entitled to possess trophies of war and should exhibit them proudly," the NRA persuaded the administration to establish the

National War Trophy Safety Program (NWTSP), which was an ad hoc special committee made up of officials from the Department of the Treasury, War Department, Department of Navy, and the NRA.[226] With the exception of war trophies found to be in violation of the National Firearms Act, the NWTSP offered no opinions on restricting the importation, sale, or transfer of any foreign military-grade firearms and explosives. Rather, its primary mission was to provide educational services on the dangers of war trophies and rendering them safe.[227]

Essentially, what the NRA forced the Truman administration to accept was the gun rights mantra of "education over legislation."[228] As fate would have it, however, the NRA's political victory over the Truman administration was also in part the undoing of the first gun rights golden age. For the rifle that Lee Harvey Oswald used to assassinate President Kennedy—*the event that led to the NRA being publicly outed as the "gun lobby" and ended its quasi-governmental status*—was none other than a foreign military-grade, World War II era firearm—the Italian Carcano M91/38 rifle.[229]

3

The Great "Gun Lobby" Awakening

On November 21, 1963, the New York State Rifle and Pistol Association (NYRPA), a state club affiliate of the National Rifle Association (NRA), hosted a dinner for the New York Joint Legislative Committee on Firearms and Ammunition with the hopes of convincing the committee to dismantle the state's longstanding pistol licensing law. Time and time again gun rights advocates had held up the law, otherwise known as the Sullivan Law, as a prime example of legislative overreach. At the dinner, lawyer and future NRA president Woodson D. Scott told the press, "Make no mistake about it. We're out to get the Sullivan law changed and we will. It's like climbing a mountain; we're taking one step at a time."[1]

Before that day, and for several years that preceded it, the NRA openly voiced its opposition to firearms controls with little, if any, pushback from either the public or the press.[2] But on November 22, 1963, at 12:30 CST, everything pertaining to the politics of firearms controls would change forever. On that day President John F. Kennedy was shot by Lee Harvey Oswald with an Italian Carcano M91/38 rifle. Kennedy died within the hour, and so too did the NRA's aspiration of dismantling the Sullivan Law. For within hours of Kennedy's death, rather than the New York Joint Legislative Committee on Firearms and Ammunition considering multiple NRA-backed amendments that would have systematically dismantled the law, it approved several amendments to strengthen it, including one amendment that would have made the public carrying of a loaded firearm a felony, whether carried concealed or not.[3] Although the NRA and its supporters were able to mitigate the damage before any of the strengthening amendments could overcome all the legislative hurdles, Kennedy's death would forever change how Americans viewed the organization. A seismic shift in the politics of firearms controls was underway.[4]

Today, if one performs an internet search with the terms *NRA* and *gun control*, several articles, blog posts, and other publication mediums historically characterize the NRA as once being a chief proponent of firearms controls.[5] These same entities also advance the notion that the NRA was mainly a sporting, hunting, and marksmanship organization before the Cincinnati Revolt in 1977, when its voting members reformed the organization to oppose any and all firearms controls. While there is indeed some truth to this historical narrative—particularly that the NRA was mainly a sporting, hunting, and marksmanship organization—it is a narrative based more on myth than on substance.[6]

As outlined in the preceding chapter, beginning in the late 1920s—more than four decades before the Cincinnati Revolt—the NRA had commandeered the political fight against firearms controls from the United States Revolver Association (USRA). It is a narrative that virtually every late twentieth- and early twenty-first-century scholar to examine the history of firearms controls has overlooked.[7] This includes the recently published and well-received book *Misfire: Inside the Downfall of the NRA*, written by National Public Radio (NPR) correspondent Tim Mak.[8] Why do so many scholars, writers, and members of the media continue to overlook the NRA's lobbying activities prior to the 1970s? The answer is quite remarkable. In the decades leading up to the Cincinnati Revolt, and especially in the aftermath of President Kennedy's assassination, a time when the national press first began exposing the NRA's involvement in opposing firearms controls, it is a historical narrative that the NRA itself advanced to project a positive persona. In fact, it is fair to say, except for the NRA and other gun rights advocates convincing the Supreme Court to accept their broad individual rights view of Second Amendment history, convincing so many scholars that the NRA was once the chief proponent of firearms controls is perhaps the NRA's greatest historical sleight of hand.

Certainly, from the 1930s through the 1960s, if one peruses gun rights literature, as well as congressional testimony, there is an abundance of instances where the NRA professed support for "reasonable" firearms controls.[9] If one looks closer at the evidence and reads the fine print, however, it becomes evident that the NRA's first and foremost firearms control policy was to oppose any law that imposed even incidental burdens on law-abiding citizens' access to firearms.[10] As the NRA board of directors resolved in 1946, "We will fight, with every means in our power, the adoption of municipal, state or federal legislation embodying those principles of bureaucratic or autocratic control of the citizen's private arms which throughout history have been a necessary forerunner of the establishment of dictatorship by individuals or minority groups."[11] What laws qualified as "bureaucratic" or "autocratic" fluctuated because they were subject to ever-changing interpretation, but the overarching presumption that the NRA wanted sportsmen, hunters, and the wider gun rights community to take away was that any legislative "red tape" that burdened law-abiding citizens' access to firearms was "bad" and "unreasonable."

To ensure that sportsmen, hunters, and the broader gun rights community arrived at this conclusion, the NRA formulated what it described as a "commonsense," five-part test to determine whether one should oppose a prospective firearms law. And not one of the NRA's five parts included anything relative to whether a prospective firearms law would aid in the reduction of firearms-related crime, death, or injury:

1. Is it an enforceable law?
2. For what purpose is the law intended, and will it actually achieve that purpose?
3. Could the law be used by an unscrupulous person or party to extend or perpetuate its own power?
4. Is the law really necessary or does it merely contribute to a network of technical restrictions which can trip you or some other conscientious sportsman into being an unintentional violator?
5. Is the law an attempt to accomplish by prohibition by what can be accomplished only by education and training?[12]

Whether the prospective law was "enforceable," was "necessary," would achieve its "purpose," would hurt sportsmen, or would be better served through "education and training," was subject to every reader's personal interpretation.[13] But given that the NRA consistently messaged that firearms controls were useless, resulted in higher crime rates, and need-lessly burdened law-abiding citizens,[14] if any sportsmen, hunter, or firearms owner faithfully applied the NRA's five-part test to any prospective fire-arms law, the result was almost always a failed grade.[15] Ultimately, what the NRA wanted sportsmen, hunters, and the wider gun rights community to accept was that "anti-gun legislation" was not a *disease* but a *symptom*." To the NRA, the disease was public ignorance. And if sportsmen, hunters, and firearms owners wanted to cure it, much like any disease, they needed to attack it with "real facts" whenever the first symptom of antifirearms legislation reared its ugly head.[16]

The NRA's five-part test was just one of many ways in which the group exploited the power of division politics to motivate sportsmen, hunters, and firearms owners to fight against firearms controls.[17] Regardless of the prospective firearms control, the NRA was able to reframe it in simple "good versus evil" and "right versus wrong" terms.[18] Those who supported firearms controls were cast as the enemy or wrongheaded.[19] As one NRA congressional surrogate put it, "Let us create the climate where those attacking [the] cherished right [to keep and bear arms] will be properly viewed as eccentrics and cranks who are a threat to our antient liberties."[20] Conversely, those who stood with the NRA in fighting firearms controls were cast as virtuous and rightminded. And to amplify the power of divi-sion politics, the NRA almost always made sure to associate firearms con-trols with communism, Nazism, and the potential for disarmament and confiscation. In doing so, sportsmen, hunters, and firearms owners increas-ingly came to view firearms controls as a slippery slope toward the United States becoming a totalitarian police state.[21]

The historical takeaway is that the NRA projected different personas depending on the intended audience. To lawmakers and the public, it presented itself as an organization that supported "reasonable" firearms controls. Meanwhile, to sportsmen, hunters, and firearms owners, it pro-jected an organization that ardently defended gun rights.[22] There were indeed other personas that the NRA sought to project, but none more so than that of being one of the country's foremost patriotic organizations. This was what the NRA wanted the public to associate the organization with.[23] And from the late 1930s until the assassination of President Kennedy, the NRA unquestionably succeeded in its effort. There are two reasons for this: First, from the late 1930s to the mid-1960s, except for the short-lived National Anti-Weapons Association (1931–1933), there were no pro-firearms-control organizations. In other words, for nearly three decades, the NRA was able to lobby against prospective firearms legislation with little, if any, pro-firearms-control opposition, and therefore it experienced little, if any, scrutiny for its lobbying activities or use of misleading propaganda.[24] Second, until the growth of investigative journalism in the early 1960s, the NRA maintained what can best be described as a monopoly on its persona. Through its public relations division, the NRA was able to influence a vast media network of sporting, hunting, and conversation magazine editors, newspaper columnists, and radio personalities.[25] Without ever questioning the NRA's intentions or motives, this media network effectively relayed the group's political messaging, including reprinting its talking points verbatim.

And even in those instances where the NRA did not maintain a connection with a respective newspaper, journal, magazine, or wider media market, it was still able to project a positive image. This was because it periodically educated its affiliated clubs and members on the importance of utilizing the media to convey a positive image of firearms and the shooting sports. Not to mention, the NRA understood that the media was the key to influencing Americans to oppose restrictive firearms controls. Here is an example of how the organization sold it to affiliated clubs and members:

> [Through the press] it is not only proper but wise to link the right to bear arms with the other great freedoms—freedom of speech, of the press, of assembly, and of religion. In our history the right to bear and the ability to use arms has been an important factor in maintaining the other four, and the interdependence of one upon the other cannot help but impress all thinking persons.
>
> The invention of the printing press set the state to free man's mind form the dogmas of the past and gave him the tool by which he could lift himself spiritually, educationally, and economically.
>
> And the invention of the hand firearm for the first time gave the poor man in olden times a chance to snap the shackles of political and personal servitude imposed by armor-clad barons and their retainers.

These two things, the printing press and hand firearms, invented five to six centuries ago, are the anchors of democracy and the founding for the other freedoms.

When you tell your fellow townspeople these facts, when you've made them aware of the great role of firearms in American history directly and the history of man in general, you will have struck an important blow not only for the sport we all love, but for our country as well.

Tyranny and restrictions on firearms and a free press go hand and hand, abetted by ignorance and indifference.

Let each of us "shoot the breeze" wherever and whenever we can, but most of all to those who known the least about it. When we do, we'll find a ready audience and unbelievable support.[26]

What also helped the NRA project a positive persona was the organization's longstanding affiliation with the military, especially during World War II.[27] This special relationship first blossomed at the turn of the twentieth century, a time when the NRA had just been reestablished and reconstituted its annual shooting matches at military firing ranges. The relationship developed even further following the passage of the National Defense Act (NDA) in 1916.[28] The act is noteworthy because it afforded sportsmen, hunters, and shooters certain benefits that could be obtained only by joining the NRA. For instance, the NDA affirmed that the War Department could distribute surplus rifles, ammunition, and military equipment only to NRA-affiliated rifle clubs and members. Moreover, it established the Office of the Director of Civilian Marksmanship (DCM), which was governed by the National Board for the Promotion of Rifle Practice (NBPRP) and in part comprised NRA officials.[29]

The NRA made sure to take advantage of its influence on the NBPRP to lobby for both federal and state tax dollars that benefited the NRA's goals and objectives, to include increasing membership rolls.[30] For instance, in October 1942, a time when the United States was mobilizing for World War II following the attack on Pearl Harbor, the NRA lobbied both Congress and state assemblies to provide funding for the establishment of an NRA-led internal security force of "Minute Men."[31] The organization claimed that such a force would provide an effective counterpoise to the threat of communist cells seeking to attack the United States from within. Two decades later, with virtually zero pushback, the NRA once again used the threat of communism to pitch to members of Congress on the need for a million-dollar grant. According to the NRA, the grant would accomplish two objectives: First, it would assist state and local rifle clubs in building much needed shooting ranges. Second, it would fund rifle and marksmanship training in public schools. Additionally, the NRA claimed that should Congress provide the grant it would "foster a revival of marksmanship," much like the "frontier ancestors once did."[32]

Before the assassination of President Kennedy, the relationship with the military services was in fact so special that the NRA held itself out as a "quasi-governmental institution."[33] Consider that in 1961 the Department of the Army coproduced a pro-gun film with the NRA titled *The Right to Keep and Bear Arms*. The film played on 350 television stations within the United States and another 44 stations overseas. Additionally, 130 prints of the film were made readily available for public viewings through Army Signal Corps libraries located across the country.[34] The film opens with people staring apprehensively as a man places a Kentucky rifle against a war monument near Capitol Hill.[35] From there, the Kentucky rifle narrates the film and romanticizes about a period in American history when firearms were not "curiosity's end" but "part of the family, provided food, solved some problems, and brought law and order where there wasn't any." The film then shifts to television actor Craig Stevens, prominently known at the time for his role in the detective drama *Peter Gunn*, who warns that the registration of firearms and other "undesirable" firearms controls will ultimately lead to the end of all firearms recreation and shooting. But Stevens assures the audience that the NRA is working to protect against this scenario through its firearms education and safety programs, or, in the words of Stevens, "a program that emphasizes safety procedures, rather than firearms control, makes it possible for a growing number of sportsmen and women to enjoy the recreation and healthful benefits of good sport and good shooting."[36]

And it was not just coproducing films in which the NRA benefited from its special relationship with the military services.[37] Obtaining laudatory messages from high-ranking military officers was another perk, including from several commanders-in-chief, that is, presidents of the United States. From the late 1930s through the early 1960s, the NRA presented these laudatory messages as proof of the organization's preeminent quasi-governmental status.[38] A closer look reveals, however, that most if not all the laudatory messages were not what the NRA portrayed them to be—that is, organizational praise initiated and written by the respective senders. Rather, most laudatory messages were initiated and principally authored by NRA officials for self-publicity purposes. While the NRA was not always successful in getting high-ranking officers to approve and sign off on their self-authored laudatory messages, often, with the help of the NRA's military connections, the effort bore fruit.

Consider the NRA's laudatory messages from Presidents Franklin D. Roosevelt, Harry S. Truman, and Dwight D. Eisenhower. Each of these laudatory messages was not of the sender's own volition but of the NRA's, through close connections within the military services.[39] In 1938, in the case of Roosevelt, it was NRA executive vice-president Milton A. Reckord who submitted a request through Colonel James Roosevelt, who was both the president's personal assistant and his son.[40] The younger Roosevelt then routed the request to fellow personal assistant William D. Hassett, who reached out to the War Department to inquire whether "such a message is justified."[41] Within a matter of days, the War Department sent a note to the younger Roosevelt recommending that the president oblige the request. Included in the note were minor edits to the NRA's self-written laudatory message.[42] Days later, President Roosevelt signed it, and in the March 1938 edition of the *American Rifleman* read the headline, "President Commends Association at Annual Meeting."[43]

In 1945, in the case of President Truman, it was Jim Berryman, editor of the *American Rifleman*, who reached out to the White House. Berryman requested that the White House do the NRA a "favor" by drafting a letter of commendation signed by Truman, or what Berryman otherwise referred to as a "brief 'pat-on-the-back.' "[44] Ultimately, it was not anyone in the White House who drafted the letter, but the NRA. The final letter of commendation signed by Truman, except for a few deletions, was virtually the same as the NRA's.[45]

The same can almost be said of Truman's statement regarding the formation of the National War Trophy Safety Program (NWTSP). The statement came about following the NRA having thwarted the Truman administration's attempt to pass federal firearms registration legislation. At that time, the country was being flooded with surplus foreign firearms and explosives from the battlefields of World War II. These weapons subsequently turned up at crime scenes and were involved in thousands of accidental deaths across the country. The Truman administration responded by introducing legislation to expand the types of firearms requiring registration under the National Firearms Act—that is, until the NRA handily defeated it in Congress and convinced the War Department to accept an "education over legislation" approach with the formation of the NWTSP.

Therein the NRA assisted the War Department in drafting a statement for Truman to sign endorsing the NWSTP. Truman agreed with most of what was in the NRA's draft statement except for one notable deletion. The draft statement had Truman saying: "In my opinion, legislation *cannot eliminate or reduce the existing hazard.* The problem is one of education." Truman's staff deleted the first sentence in its entirety and modified the second sentence to read: "The problem is one primarily of education."[46]

Perhaps no president—that is, until after the overt politicization of gun rights in the late 1970s—signed more laudatory messages to the NRA than Dwight D. Eisenhower. From 1953 through 1960, except for 1959, Eisenhower sent a laudatory message to the organization for every annual convention. Given this fact, one might assume that he was a true-blue NRA supporter. It turns out, however, that Eisenhower's praise was not so much his personal thoughts, but what the NRA wanted him to publicly project. For one, it was the NRA, not Eisenhower, that initiated and drafted each message. Eisenhower's staff did edit several of them substantially. The fact remains, however, that it was the NRA that initiated and drafted them all.[47]

Second, although it is true that Eisenhower became an NRA life member in 1956, it was not of his own volition.[48] Rather, much like John F. Kennedy and Richard M. Nixon, the membership was bestowed on Eisenhower for being president, and it was one of hundreds of honorary memberships so bestowed while he was in office.[49] Other honorary memberships accepted by Eisenhower include the Sapsscam Amateur Chefs Club and the American Society of Mechanical Engineers, to name just two.[50] But what is particularly telling as to why Eisenhower was an NRA member in name only was an administrative edit to the NRA's draft laudatory message for the annual convention in 1960. In it, the NRA asked Eisenhower to state, "I am proud to be a Life Member of the NRA," but the sentence was deleted, with no mention of Eisenhower's honorary membership included anywhere in the final message.[51]

Yet much like the NRA's self-written laudatory messages by high-ranking military officers, the organization projected—and to this day continues to project—the misleading narrative that Eisenhower, as well as other presidents and prominent government officials, were true-blue NRA members.[52] A noteworthy example of the NRA's sleight of hand in this regard is that of Supreme Court Chief Justice Earl Warren, whom the NRA touted for several years as being a "very enthusiastic Life Member."[53] While the NRA would have been correct in stating that Warren graciously accepted an honorary NRA life membership, it was quite another thing for the NRA to mislead the public into believing that Warren was personally invested in the organization.[54]

The NRA's misleading narrative regarding prominent government officials being true-blue NRA members, as well as failing to disclose the backstory behind the messages, was just one part of the its broader strategic messaging campaign—that is, the NRA willfully put forward a narrative that was meant to advance the organization's political objectives. This was particularly the case for prospective firearms legislation. Despite the lack of any organized firearms control effort, the NRA consistently put forward the false narrative that such an effort was constantly afoot. And when possible, to further advance this false narrative, it singled out individuals—whether they be journalists, lawmakers, or public figures—who supported firearms controls as being nothing more than antifirearms political strawmen.[55] In turn, NRA-affiliated clubs and members, as well as the wider gun rights community, flooded these individuals with letters, telegrams, and phone calls. The NRA in fact encouraged its affiliated clubs and members to stand up against anyone who would subvert the Second Amendment. From the NRA's perspective, this was not only in the gun rights community's best interest; it was also their civic duty. For those firearms control supporters who were seemingly unaware of the societal benefits afforded by firearms, the NRA directed its affiliated clubs and members to take a positive, tempered approach.[56] "We are all to blame, all of us—all shooters—if this ignorance continues to breed prejudice and fear and opposition to guns and shooting," wrote the NRA.[57] But in those instances in which firearms control supporters were thought to have intentionally disseminated "vicious propaganda aimed at disarming the American citizen," the NRA urged its members to take "aggressive action."[58] In either case, whether the situation called for a positive or an aggressive response, the NRA provided its affiliated clubs and members the necessary tools and talking points to stall, amend, or defeat the passage of firearms controls.[59] It was for this reason that it proudly called itself the "Paul Revere Organization," because at any time it could rally the gun rights community to political action.[60]

The Paul Revere capability of the NRA was in high gear from 1957 through 1963, a time when the federal government was seriously considering new firearms controls for the first time in more than a decade. No matter the type of control, whether it involved limiting foreign imports, requiring the federal registration of all handguns, requiring licensed manufacturers and importers to impress serial numbers on firearms, or implementing new administrative requirements on the interstate sale and shipment of firearms, the NRA opposed and defeated it. In fact, from 1957 to 1963, the only two federal firearms proposals to overcome all the required bureaucratic and legislative hurdles were those that the NRA took part in drafting.[61] They were the kinds of laws that the NRA had long championed—laws that only punished the offending criminal and did not impose any administrative red tape on the law-abiding citizen (figure 3.1).

In August 1963 the NRA signaled it was willing to accept another change to federal law. As early as 1956, state and local government officials had urged Congress to do something, anything, to halt the unscrupulous sale of mail-order firearms. In the years that followed, once the news media began reporting on how gangs and criminals were taking advantage of the situation, public calls for Congress to pass legislation restricting the mail-order of firearms became commonplace. There was the additional problem of minors being able to purchase mail-order firearms with little, if any, difficulty.[62] These scenarios were particularly worrisome to lawmakers because both criminals and minors were already prohibited by state and local laws from purchasing firearms from licensed dealers, yet the laws did very little to stop them from acquiring firearms through the mail.[63] The political writing on the wall was that Congress was going to do something to remedy the problem. The only question was how it was going to do it. It was for this reason that the NRA began working with Connecticut senator Thomas J. Dodd and the Senate Subcommittee on Juvenile Delinquency that he chaired in drafting federal firearms legislation.

Initially, before the problems surrounding the unregulated mail-order firearms market were made available to the public, the NRA did everything

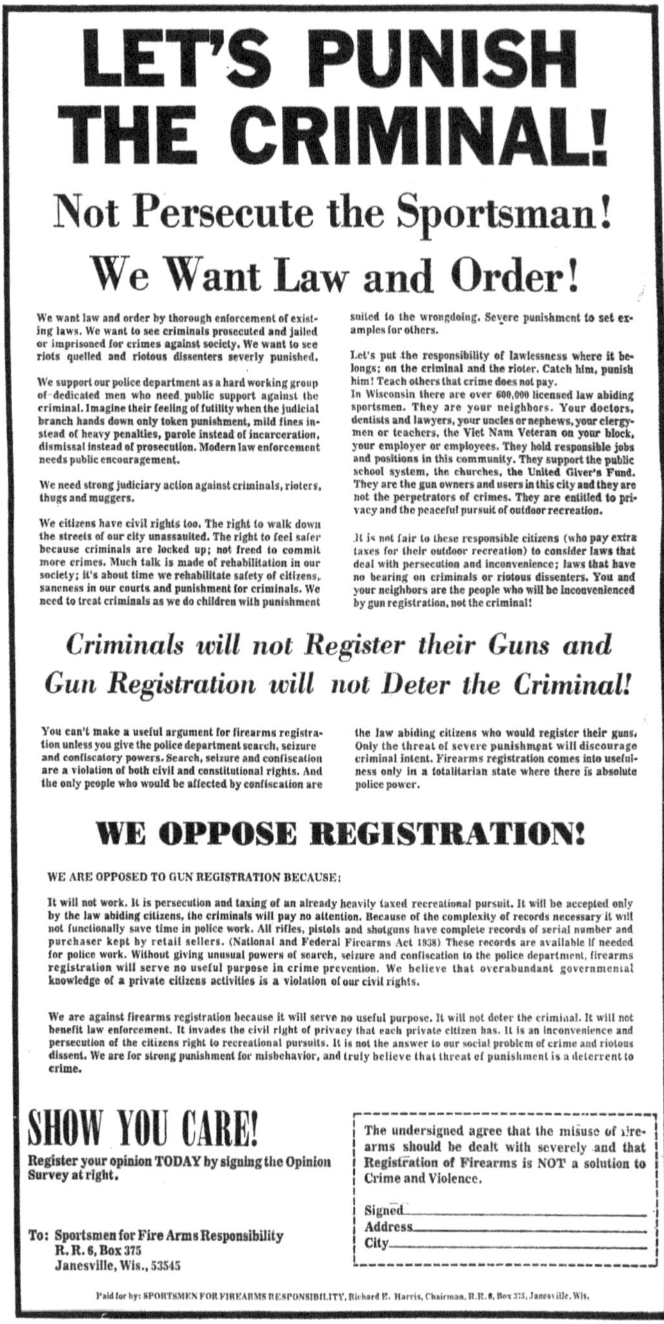

LET'S PUNISH THE CRIMINAL!

Not Persecute the Sportsman!

We Want Law and Order!

We want law and order by thorough enforcement of existing laws. We want to see criminals prosecuted and jailed or imprisoned for crimes against society. We want to see riots quelled and riotous dissenters severly punished.

We support our police department as a hard working group of dedicated men who need public support against the criminal. Imagine their feeling of futility when the judicial branch hands down only token punishment, mild fines instead of heavy penalties, parole instead of incarceration, dismissal instead of prosecution. Modern law enforcement needs public encouragement.

We need strong judiciary action against criminals, rioters, thugs and muggers.

We citizens have civil rights too. The right to walk down the streets of our city unassaulted. The right to feel safer because criminals are locked up; not freed to commit more crimes. Much talk is made of rehabilitation in our society; it's about time we rehabilitate safety of citizens, saneness in our courts and punishment for criminals. We need to treat criminals as we do children with punishment suited to the wrongdoing. Severe punishment to set examples for others.

Let's put the responsibility of lawlessness where it belongs; on the criminal and the rioter. Catch him, punish him! Teach others that crime does not pay.

In Wisconsin there are over 600,000 licensed law abiding sportsmen. They are your neighbors. Your doctors, dentists and lawyers, your uncles or nephews, your clergymen or teachers, the Viet Nam Veteran on your block, your employer or employees. They hold responsible jobs and positions in this community. They support the public school system, the churches, the United Giver's Fund. They are the gun owners and users in this city and they are not the perpetrators of crimes. They are entitled to privacy and the peaceful pursuit of outdoor recreation.

It is not fair to these responsible citizens (who pay extra taxes for their outdoor recreation) to consider laws that deal with persecution and inconvenience; laws that have no bearing on criminals or riotous dissenters. You and your neighbors are the people who will be inconvenienced by gun registration, not the criminal!

Criminals will not Register their Guns and Gun Registration will not Deter the Criminal!

You can't make a useful argument for firearms registration unless you give the police department search, seizure and confiscatory powers. Search, seizure and confiscation are a violation of both civil and constitutional rights. And the only people who would be affected by confiscation are the law abiding citizens who would register their guns. Only the threat of severe punishment will discourage criminal intent. Firearms registration comes into usefulness only in a totalitarian state where there is absolute police power.

WE OPPOSE REGISTRATION!

WE ARE OPPOSED TO GUN REGISTRATION BECAUSE:

It will not work. It is persecution and taxing of an already heavily taxed recreational pursuit. It will be accepted only by the law abiding citizens, the criminals will pay no attention. Because of the complexity of records necessary it will not functionally save time in police work. All rifles, pistols and shotguns have complete records of serial number and purchaser kept by retail sellers. (National and Federal Firearms Act 1938) These records are available if needed for police work. Without giving unusual powers of search, seizure and confiscation to the police department, firearms registration will serve no useful purpose in crime prevention. We believe that overabundant governmental knowledge of a private citizens activities is a violation of our civil rights.

We are against firearms registration because it will serve no useful purpose. It will not deter the criminal. It will not benefit law enforcement. It invades the civil right of privacy that each private citizen has. It is an inconvenience and persecution of the citizens right to recreational pursuits. It is not the answer to our social problem of crime and riotous dissent. We are for strong punishment for misbehavior, and truly believe that threat of punishment is a deterrent to crime.

SHOW YOU CARE!

Register your opinion TODAY by signing the Opinion Survey at right.

The undersigned agree that the misuse of firearms should be dealt with severely and that Registration of Firearms is NOT a solution to Crime and Violence.

Signed__________
Address__________
City__________

To: Sportsmen for Fire Arms Responsibility
R. R. 6, Box 375
Janesville, Wis., 53545

Paid for by: SPORTSMEN FOR FIREARMS RESPONSIBILITY, Richard E. Harris, Chairman, R.R. 6, Box 375, Janesville, Wis.

FIGURE 3.1 Advertisement in the *Janesville (Wis.) Daily Gazette*, July 11, 1968. Paid for by the Sportsmen for Firearms Responsibility, the ad promoted several long-standing gun rights mantras, including "punish the criminal not the law-abiding citizen" and "firearms registration leads to firearms confiscation."

possible to defeat any prospective legislation that placed even an incidental burden on the interstate sale and purchase of mail-order firearms.[64] However, upon learning that Congress was going to legislate mail-order firearms in some capacity, the NRA shifted its strategy by advocating for a de minimis bill.[65] The bill that Dodd and the NRA ultimately agreed to was intended to keep the federal government out of state and local affairs and impose minimal burdens on firearms manufacturers, federally licensed dealers, and firearms purchasers. As it pertained to the last group, the bill required that every mail-order firearms purchaser submit a signed affidavit attesting that they were (a) eighteen years or more of age; (b) not a person already prohibited by federal law from receiving a firearm in interstate or foreign commerce; and (c) not subject to any state or local laws, regulations, or ordinances that would be violated by said purchase. Meanwhile, for licensed firearms dealers and firearms manufacturers, the only burden the bill would impose was that they receive the firearms purchaser's affidavit.[66]

This proposed legislation was unquestionably the best that the NRA and its allies could have hoped for.[67] The assassination of President Kennedy, however, quickly changed the political status quo. For it was not long after that Dodd, at the behest of the Department of Justice, reneged on his agreement with the NRA and began advocating for a new, more restrictive mail-order firearms bill.[68] Initially, the NRA responded with a tempered, positive approach.[69] But by the middle of 1964 the NRA was agitated to the point that it began messaging that national calls for new, restrictive firearms controls were based on nothing more than "hysteria."[70] The reason the NRA suddenly shifted its messaging strategy was the continuous clamoring among the news media to find out why the United States maintained the world's most lax firearms laws.[71] And what the news media quickly came to find out, in virtually every instance where the push for firearms controls was stalled or defeated, whether at the local, state, or federal level, the NRA was responsible.[72] It did not help the organization's image that the very rifle used to kill Kennedy was purchased through a mail-order advertisement in the NRA's flagship magazine, *American Rifleman*. Needless to say, in the wake of the assassination, the NRA was facing intense scrutiny unlike ever before. It eventually reached a point where the public no longer predominantly saw the group as a patriotic, sportsmen organization, but as the "gun lobby."[73]

The NRA vehemently denounced the "gun lobby" label by touting its history of supporting "reasonable" firearms controls.[74] On the one hand, the NRA was correct to denounce its new label. The mission statement imprinted on the NRA's headquarters was "Firearms Safety Education, Marksmanship Training, and Shooting for Recreation." On the other hand, the "gun lobby" label bore truth.[75] It was in the early 1930s that the NRA began touting its role in fighting restrictive firearms legislation.[76] In fact, within the table of contents of *American Rifleman*, it advertised this fact. For instance, in 1932 the NRA listed as one of its ten organizational objectives the prevention of "the passage of legislation unnecessarily restricting the use of firearms by honest citizens."[77]

From 1932 onward the NRA did not shy away from publicizing its role in fighting firearms controls.[78] In a 1941 mass mailing, NRA

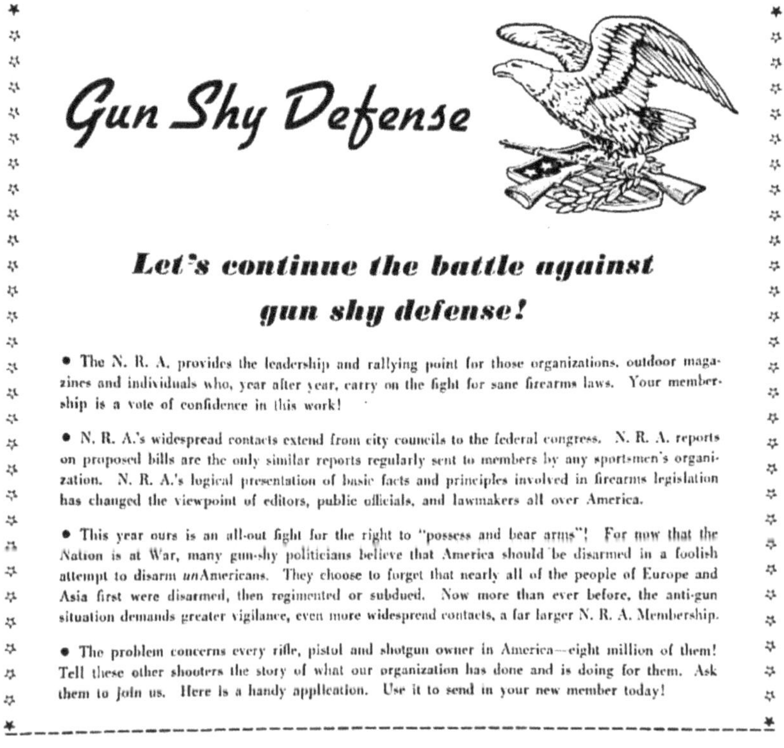

Gun Shy Defense

Let's continue the battle against gun shy defense!

- The N. R. A. provides the leadership and rallying point for those organizations, outdoor magazines and individuals who, year after year, carry on the fight for sane firearms laws. Your membership is a vote of confidence in this work!

- N. R. A.'s widespread contacts extend from city councils to the federal congress. N. R. A. reports on proposed bills are the only similar reports regularly sent to members by any sportsmen's organization. N. R. A.'s logical presentation of basic facts and principles involved in firearms legislation has changed the viewpoint of editors, public officials, and lawmakers all over America.

- This year ours is an all-out fight for the right to "possess and bear arms"! For now that the Nation is at War, many gun-shy politicians believe that America should be disarmed in a foolish attempt to disarm unAmericans. They choose to forget that nearly all of the people of Europe and Asia first were disarmed, then regimented or subdued. Now more than ever before, the anti-gun situation demands greater vigilance, even more widespread contacts, a far larger N. R. A. Membership.

- The problem concerns every rifle, pistol and shotgun owner in America—eight million of them! Tell these other shooters the story of what our organization has done and is doing for them. Ask them to join us. Here is a handy application. Use it to send in your new member today!

FIGURE 3.2 NRA membership advertisement in *American Rifleman*, April 1942. It highlighted the NRA's "leadership," "widespread contacts," and role in fighting attempts to disarm Americans.

secretary-treasurer C. B. Lister claimed that the NRA was the "one, and only one organization" that was fighting "anti-firearms laws." The NRA "has provided the leadership and rallying point for the ever-increasing number of organizations, outdoor magazines and individuals who are now waging an effective campaign against unwise anti-firearms laws," bragged Lister.[79] Likewise, within several shooting, marksmanship, and hunting materials, the NRA advertised that it was *the* "group that protects ["gun-owning American citizens"] from misguided anti-gun legislation, [and] protects [the] right to own and use firearms."[80] There are indeed other examples abound, whether it be editorials, advertisements, or some other print medium, where the NRA marketed itself as *the* organization standing up for the Second Amendment and fighting against firearms controls.[81] One notable example is an NRA membership application from 1959, which reads: "For more than thirty years, your NRA Legislative Service has kept constant watch over the nation's gun laws. The results of this round the clock vigilance can be measured in the thousands of restrictive bills which were *never passed*."[82] Also, one cannot ignore that during every one of NRA's conventions and meetings from 1948 to 1963, legislative sessions were convened that publicized the organization's fight against firearms controls.

In fact, seven months prior to President Kennedy's assassination, at the NRA's 92nd annual meetings held in Washington, D.C., NRA president John M. Schooley noted that the organization's "policy on firearms legislation" was to oppose every law, "regardless of its stated objective," because firearms legislation always resulted in "nothing more than the harassment of law-abiding citizens." Schooley added, "We fight anti-firearms legislation, not only because of our regard for firearms and our desire to use them in our lawful sport and for our national defense, but because of the *sinister motive* behind so much anti firearms legislation" and the "ever growing effort to *destroy our way of life* and substitute therefor a *police state*."[83]

Despite the historical evidence showing that from the 1930s to the early 1960s the NRA played a prominent role in lobbying against firearms controls,[84] there is a nuanced legal argument to be made that it was not at this time technically a lobby, at least not as defined by the Federal Regulation of Lobbying Act (FRLA) of 1946.[85] For in the FRLA's accompanying Senate report it states that any organization "formed for other purposes whose efforts to influence legislation are *merely incidental* to the purposes for which formed" is exempt from registering as a lobby.[86] And given that the

NRA's charter of 1871 stated that the organization's principle purpose was to "educate the youth of the nation in marksmanship," "to encourage marksmanship . . . both as a sport and for the purpose of qualifying as finished marksman," and "to encourage competition in marksmanship between teams and individuals in all parts of the United States," it is fair to argue—and NRA officials did argue—that the NRA was not technically a lobby.[87]

The holding in the Supreme Court case *United States v. Harriss* (1954) appears to strengthen this argument. In that case, in an opinion written by Chief Justice Earl Warren, the Court held that organizations that receive contributions with "only an 'incidental' purpose of influencing legislation" were exempt from the FRLA's lobbying registration requirements. A closer look at *Harriss* reveals, however, that the Court left federal officials with some leeway in determining whether an organization was subject to the provisions of the FRLA. As Warren noted in his opinion, just because an organization's "principal purpose" was not lobbying did not mean that the organization was exempt from the FRLA's registration requirement. To determine whether to classify an organization as a lobby, federal officials needed to answer the following question in the affirmative: "Are any of the organization's 'main activities' lobbying?" And to help federal officials in answering this question, Warren outlined "three prerequisites" that the organization must meet to be classified as a lobby. These included (1) the organization "solicited, collected, or received contributions"; (2) one of the "main purposes" of said contributions was to "influence the passage or defeat of legislation by Congress"; and (3) the "intended method of accomplishing this purpose" must be "through direct communication with members of Congress."[88]

As to whether these three prerequisites were applicable to the NRA's legislative activities, the totality of the historical evidence suggests that the NRA was in fact a lobby. Beginning with the first two *Harriss* prerequisites—that the NRA "solicited, collected, or received contributions" to "influence the passage or defeat of legislation by Congress"—one does not have to look further than the NRA's own marketing and advertising.[89] Not only did the NRA publicize its leading role and influence in defeating unwanted firearms legislation, whether it be at the local, state, or federal level, but it also often marketed its legislative service as the most essential benefit of being an NRA member.[90] This included a January 1964 letter to all members informing them that the NRA was *"strengthen[ing] its firearms*

legislative staff, thus broadening its capacity to evaluate firearms legislation and increasing its ability to help NRA affiliated organizations and
members deal with proposed gun laws."[91] Indeed, if one examines the
NRA's operating budget from the 1930s through the 1960s, only a small
portion of its total annual revenue went directly to its legislative service
and staff.[92] However, the NRA's line-item accounting in this regard is misleading, for it excludes just how involved the group's other divisions
were in the fight against firearms controls.[93] Not to mention, the NRA
openly held out its legislative service as providing two key lobbying services: The first was the "drafting of intelligent laws which prove effective
against the criminal, yet do not hinder the right of reputable citizens to
possess and use firearms for legitimate purposes." The second was providing assistance in "combatting unwise gun control measures which would
impost severe restrictions or prohibitions on the law-abiding member of
the community."[94]

As it pertains to the third and last *Harriss* prerequisite required for an
organization to qualify as a lobby under the FRLA—that the NRA sought
to influence the outcome of federal legislation "through direct communication with members of Congress"—at first glance it appears that the NRA's
legislative activities fall short. Recall earlier how the NRA took pride in presenting itself as a "Paul Revere Organization"—an organization that
merely utilized its First Amendment freedoms to provide sportsmen, hunters, and the wider gun rights community with the necessary educational
materials to oppose anti-firearms legislation.[95] Presuming that the NRA
only furnished educational materials and left it up to every individual
sportsmen, hunter, and firearms owner to determine for themselves
whether to take political action, it is difficult to claim that it was seeking
to influence members of Congress via "direct communication."

Until 1969 the NRA in fact advanced this very line of argument to shield
itself from being labeled a lobby.[96] Its reason for this is not difficult to
ascertain—the legal consequences for a 501(c)(4) engaging in illegal lobbying were virtually unknown at the time. The NRA's concerns were exacer-
bated by the fact that several lawmakers and prominent public figures were
urging the Department of Justice and Internal Revenue Service to punish
the organization for illegal lobbying.

For these reasons, NRA officials were rather outspoken that their fight
against firearms controls legally constituted a "principal purpose" under

the FLRA. As Executive Vice President Franklin L. Orth explained before the Senate Subcommittee on Juvenile Delinquency in 1967:

> The key word . . . is "principal," "the principal." [Lobbying] is certainly not the principal or even a principal job of this organization. As I have said, our principal effort is in public service activities in respect to firearms users and owners. And they are competitors nationally, internationally; they are hunters, they are collectors, they are a fine group of cross section of American people, and we service them.
>
> Now, in recent years, there has been this problem which has sprung up relative to restrictive legislation relative to firearms. For that reason, in order to protect, we added this as another service to the membership.[97]

There was a problem, however, with the Orth's nonlobbying claim. It was a bold-faced lie, as was his claim that the NRA's legislative service only came about in "recent years." While Orth would have been correct to note that the NRA did not require its members to write their representatives in Congress, it did disseminate highly embellished, factually questionable information to motivate its members to action.[98] So much so in fact that it was common for Capitol Hill to receive a barrage of constituent letters from NRA supporters that were conspiratorial in nature. And the most often restated conspiracy that made its way to Capitol Hill was that communists were the secret driving force behind restrictive firearms legislation.[99]

This was particularly the case in 1957, when the Internal Revenue Service (IRS) proposed several new administrative regulations on firearms and ammunition. Consider a letter from NRA member Robert H. Kirkwood to Oregon senator Wayne Morse. Kirkwood wrote, "For years, I have heard that the communists have been trying to accomplish just such an effect [of preventing citizens from being familiarized with firearms]. . . . Now [the IRS's] proposal would oblige them by opening the back door for it."[100] Similarly, NRA member D. C. Besly wrote to Montana representative Lee Metcalf that the IRS's proposal was a "Communist inspired and backed initial step . . . long range program designed eventually to disarm the American public." Besly then demanded that Congress conduct a "thorough investigation" into anyone, including those working for the IRS, who proposed firearms restrictions in the future, or in Besly's words, "All resources [should be] brought to bear upon their prevention with incidental investigation of the authors of such restrictions."[101]

Four years later, in 1961, when New York representative Victor L. Anfuso put forward a federal bill to require the registration of all handguns, the communist conspiracy letters once again flooded Congress.[102] In a letter to Florida representative Robert F. Sikes, one gun rights supporter postulated the origins of the Anfuso bill as follows: "Communists and the Underworld are very well organized in the U.S., neither has to come to the front and boldly express their aims and desires. It is much easier and safer to have some front organization to bid for their desires and do all the work in carrying them thru into the long process of becoming law."[103] Likewise, in a letter a to Iowa senator Bourke B. Hickenlooper, NRA member Virgil Tapps wrote, "I sincerely believe that a great majority of these so-called citizens, who bring forth anti-firearm bills, are either communists or communist sympathizers. . . . They realize that the first step in seizing control of a nation is by bringing forth anti-firearms legislation, and trying to have their stooges, politicians already in office, doing their utmost to get it passed into law." He added, "There is one name, whose name seems to be consistently popping up in our *American Rifleman Magazine*, *Guns & Ammo Magazine*, and others, as being our utmost opponent, and his name is Rep. Victor Anfuso, as he seems to be bound and determined that he's going to get the American people disarmed, or have all of our firearms, at least, registered with the police."[104]

It is worth noting that the NRA never expressly claimed that Anfuso was a communist. But it did not have to for those within the gun rights community to make the association.[105] This was because for over a decade the NRA had claimed that firearms registration was an insidious communist scheme, devised with the sole purpose of disarming the nation.[106] For instance, in the pamphlet titled *The Pro and Con of Firearms Registration*, the NRA argued that the "only reason for registering privately owned firearms is to make it possible for the political authorities . . . to seize such weapons when . . . such seizure is necessary or desirable," and the "only practical effect of firearms registration is to play into the hands of unscrupulous seekers for political power."[107] The pamphlet closed with the following claim: *"No dictatorship has ever been imposed on a nation of free men who have not been first required to register their privately owned weapons."*[108]

For many years, those within the gun rights community restated the NRA's firearms registration claim as historically true. Yet when the Library of Congress was asked to weigh in on its accuracy, the reply was there was "no positive correlation between [restrictive] gun laws and dictatorships."[109] The same holds true of another fallacy that the NRA had long held up as historically true—the "Communist Rules for Revolution." To the gun rights community, chief among the "Communist Rules" was the insidious desire to "cause the registration of all firearms on some pretext, with a view of confiscating them later and leaving the population helpless." Although the NRA and the gun rights community came to associate the "Communist Rules" with communism—a viewpoint that was widely believed throughout the Cold War[110]—the "Communist Rules" first appeared in American newspapers in early 1942 and were not attributed as being communist in origin, but as a Nazi blueprint to destroy the United States from within.[111] Not long after World War II, however, amid the fervor of the communist "red scare," the rules were reinvented with a new communist background story.[112]

That the "Communist Rules" were nothing more than anticommunist propaganda was seemingly unknown to the gun rights community. It was not until 1969, when Congress asked the Federal Bureau of Investigation (FBI) to weigh in, that the "scrupulous" origins of the "Communist Rules" became public knowledge.[113] Whether the NRA had personal knowledge of this history up to 1969 appears unlikely.[114] What is known is that as late as 1973 the NRA seized on the "Communist Rules" and other anticommunist propaganda to rail against firearms registration as a communist plot.[115] The same was true of other gun rights advocates, including the editors of *Guns & Ammo* and *Guns Magazine*, who at times held up the "Communist Rules" as proof positive that firearms confiscation would most certainly follow registration.[116] Eventually, the gun rights community's belief in the "Communist Rules" as being historically true gave rise to the popular anti-firearms registration mantra "register communists, not firearms."[117]

The gun rights community's belief that communism was the principal driving force behind restrictive firearms controls was so pervasive that it was in-part responsible for some rather far-flung conspiracy theories.[118] One was that Senator Dodd was a communist agent and sympathizer, and his firearms control bill was the beginning of an organized communist effort to disarm all Americans.[119] Another far-flung conspiracy theory involved President Kennedy's assassination. The conspiracy theory went as follows: President Kennedy was assassinated at the direction of communist leaders to convince Congress to pass a law requiring the federal registration of all firearms.[120] Subsequently, upon militarily invading the United States, the communists would leverage the federal government's "list" to locate, confiscate, and destroy all privately owned firearms. As far-flung as these conspiracy theories may seem, gun rights supporters of all regions and backgrounds believed them to be true. This included prominent Kansas businessman Fred C. Koch, the founder of Koch Industries and founding member of the John Birch Society. In a form letter sent to several members of Congress, Koch warned that federal firearms controls were exactly what the communists wanted. The communists' first step was the registration of all firearms. This would be followed by their confiscation and the murder of all "anti-Communists." "By decreeing registration of firearms or regulations of them, you will make it just that much easier for the Communists to take over the United States," wrote Koch, adding, "This is not a fairy tale and not a myth, but a stark, grim reality."[121]

The evidence linking the NRA to lobbying is not limited to the organization's proliferation of highly embellished and often factually questionable information to motivate the gun rights community to political action. The NRA's lobbying was often far more deliberate and coordinated. The fact is that for nearly two decades before Kennedy's assassination, unbeknownst to federal officials, the news media, and the public, the NRA was lobbying members of Congress with the purpose of influencing legislative outcomes. For instance, in the immediate aftermath of World War II, it directly lobbied members of Congress to oppose federal firearms registration. Also, up through the assassination, the NRA directly lobbied members of Congress for appropriations that benefited the NRA's objectives.[122] Last, from 1957 to the assassination of President Kennedy, the NRA lobbied members of Congress to advance several pieces of firearms legislation that it authored in part or in whole.[123]

Now, it was not NRA policy to send its officials to Capitol Hill and lobby from one congressional office to another. The NRA did not have to.[124] The reason for this was the NRA maintained a number of congressional surrogates in both the House of Representatives and the Senate, who were more than willing to advance the NRA's legislative agenda.[125] In the House, the NRA's congressional surrogates included California representative Cecil R. King (Democrat), Michigan representative John D. Dingell, Jr. (Democrat), and Florida representative Robert F. Sikes (Democrat), with both

King and Sikes concurrently serving on the NRA's board of directors. Meanwhile, in the Senate, the NRA's congressional surrogates included Arizona senator Carl T. Hayden (Democrat), Iowa senator Bourke B. Hickenlooper (Republican), and Nebraska senator Roman Hruska (Republican). The way the NRA utilized its congressional surrogates was simple. The NRA would communicate its legislative objectives to the surrogates, who would then take whatever steps were necessary to achieve them, whether it be introducing legislation at the behest of the NRA, lobbying other members of Congress to accept the NRA's position on a particular piece of legislation, or fostering other congressional relationships on behalf of the NRA. It is important to note that the NRA never monetarily compensated its congressional surrogates for any assistance rendered (at least not that I could find). The NRA did, however, provide its congressional surrogates with other benefits, such as honorary membership, a variety of firearms services, paid trips to NRA-sponsored events, and free and open access to the NRA's indoor shooting range in Washington, D.C. This latter NRA perk was sometimes extended to other members of Congress, their personal staff, and even their children, with the intent of fostering new relationships on Capitol Hill.[126]

In addition to receiving these perks, congressional surrogates politically benefited from the connections within the NRA's "official family," which was an internal NRA term used to denote the organization's extended network of political contacts, firearm industry leaders, and social influencers.[127] The official family consisted of other sporting, hunting, and shooting organizations, such as the Sierra Club, National Wildlife Federation (NWF), and state game commissions; other national organizations, such as the Izaak Walton League, American Legion, and Boy Scouts of America; firearms and shooting organizations, such as the National Shooting Sports Foundation (NSSF) and Automatic Weapons Association (AWA); and the editors of sporting, hunting and shooting magazines and newspaper columns across the country. Both before and after President Kennedy's assassination, the existence of the official family was crucial to the NRA's lobbying success, whether it be at the local, state, or federal level. Not only did the official family amplify whatever political message the NRA wanted to convey, but it also effectively shielded the NRA from most lobbying exposure. Not to mention, whenever lawmakers held public hearings on prospective firearms legislation, the official family always came through in providing several witnesses and experts to make the NRA's case either for or against the legislation (all without said witnesses and experts ever identifying themselves as being affiliated with the NRA). This allowed the NRA to stack the political deck in its favor without politicians, the news media, or the public being wise to what was going on. Such was the case in the 1930s, when Congress convened several hearings on federal firearms legislation. The same held true in 1965, when the Senate Subcommittee to Investigate Juvenile Delinquency held hearings on the Dodd bill, and every witness to testify against the bill was not so coincidentally a member of the official family.[128]

In historical retrospect, given the copious amount of evidence showing that the NRA lobbied lawmakers for decades, it is remarkable that so many late twentieth-century and early twenty-first-century writers came to the conclusion that the NRA did not become the "gun lobby" until the mid-1970s. Certainly, these writers would be correct in stating that the NRA's current lobbying arm—the Institute for Legislative Action (ILA), which was originally named the Office of Legislative Affairs (OLA)—was not formed and registered until 1974.[129] However, to historically equate the formation of the ILA with the NRA becoming the "gun lobby" is like saying the movement for American independence began upon the publication of the Declaration of Independence on July 4, 1776. While there is some truth to both statements, they are serious oversimplifications of the past. Moreover, it cannot be emphasized enough that it was the NRA who was principally pushing the narrative that it was not engaged in lobbying. It was a self-serving, propagandic narrative that was meant to benefit the NRA's bottom line, whether it be in terms of maintaining the NRA's positive image, continuing the receipt of federal appropriations and military assistance for NRA sponsored shooting matches, or legally shielding the NRA from prosecution under the FRLA by the Department of Justice.

By 1966 the political, public, and legal consequences of being designated a lobby were in fact viewed so negatively that an emergency NRA committee was assembled to address the problem. What the committee ultimately decided was to hire the "largest" public relations firm on "Madison Avenue" that money could buy.[130] The firm's responsibilities were threefold: First, it was to expand the NRA's media opportunities. Second, it was to vet all the NRA's messaging to ensure it would not be construed as lobbying. Third, the firm was to put forward the narrative that the NRA was a highly patriotic organization that only intended to interject reason in the debate over firearms controls.[131] Additionally, the firm was hired to assist the NRA in crafting a narrative that depicted firearms control proponents as hysterical, extremist, and political opportunists.[132]

The NRA's decision to hire a public relations firm—although a sensible decision at the time—proved to be a terrible waste of money. For despite the firm's best efforts at reforming the NRA's image, it could not simply erase the decades of NRA lobbying activity, stop the news media from reporting on it, nor stop the public from perceiving the NRA as the "gun lobby." Certainly, not all NRA news media coverage in the wake of President Kennedy's assassination was fair and balanced. Attempts by some members of the news media to blame the NRA for the actions of others, such as when extremist groups utilized the NRA's shooting programs to obtain firearms and ammunition, or when anticommunist Cubans attempted to fire a bazooka rocket at the United Nations from the other side of New York City's East River, leaned more toward sensationalist than objective news reporting.[133] However, the overwhelmingly majority of post-Kennedy assassination media coverage was properly researched and sourced. The NRA just did not like it.[134]

From the NRA's dislike of media coverage grew animosity toward the press—animosity that led to the NRA frequently scapegoating the press as having a liberal, anti-gun bias.[135] In 1967, before the NRA board of directors, Harold W. Glassen lamented what he felt was a constitutional double standard by members of the press. "Most papers minimize or even ridicule the Second Amendment but scream to high heaven if ever any law or any regulation is suggested which they feel might infringe the rights of freedom of the press," stated Glassen, adding that the "Second Amendment might well have been and probably was placed immediately following the First Amendment with the idea of making enforcement of the first possible."[136] Some within the NRA's "official family" went so far as to postulate that most of the critical press coverage was part of larger, well-financed, anti-gun conspiracy. For instance, writing in 1964, NRA surrogate and *Wood, Field and Stream* columnist Oscar Godbout postulated that the press was targeting the NRA so that its ability "to inform its members of unreasonably restrictive legislation will be impaired with a greater chance for such legislation to pass unnoticed before shooters can make their views known to their legislators."[137]

Another reason the decision to hire a public relations firm turned out to be a waste of NRA's financial resources is that in 1968 the NRA was ultimately forced to concede to the lobbying label.[138] On the advice of outside legal counsel, the NRA brokered a deal with the Department of Justice in which Executive Vice President Orth would register as a lobbyist.[139] While the NRA's lobbying concession was indeed a moral defeat, the deal with the Department of Justice ensured that the NRA would not be punished for any prior illegal lobbying activity.[140]

Just because Orth formally registered as a lobbyist did not mean that the NRA was suddenly active on Capitol Hill. It was in fact the opposite. For several years the NRA remained cautious in how it publicly messaged for or against firearms legislation. As will be discussed later, the NRA's cautious approach became an issue of great frustration among the organization's newest members—members who had expressly joined under the auspices that the NRA was in fact the "gun lobby." But before delving into how many of its newest members perceived the NRA's cautious approach, as well as the secondhand effect this had on the gun rights movement politically splintering, it is important to examine how the assassination of President Kennedy and the outing of the NRA as the "gun lobby" affected the politics of firearms controls.

4

A Political Synopsis of the Great "Gun Lobby" Awakening

From June 30, 1938, when President Franklin D. Roosevelt signed the Federal Firearms Act into law, until the assassination of President John F. Kennedy on November 22, 1963, the National Rifle Association (NRA), its "official family," and the wider gun rights community were able to shape firearms policy across the United States with little scrutiny. Over that twenty-five year span, while there were certainly instances where the NRA's motives were called into question or where individuals highlighted the implications of not adequately regulating firearms, neither the public nor the average lawmaker was fully aware of how deliberate and orchestrated the NRA-led fight against firearms controls truly was. As outlined in the preceding chapter, the immense scrutiny that the NRA faced in the wake of President Kennedy's assassination forever changed the political status quo. There was now a public face as to why the United States was internationally known, in the words of late Massachusetts senator Edward Kennedy, for being "first in guns, last in controls."[1]

On the one hand, given that the NRA was at the forefront in the fight against firearms controls, it is understandable why the organization became widely known as the "gun lobby," and many scapegoated the organization for the nation's lack of firearms laws. On the other hand, one might say that the NRA was a victim of its own political success. It was not the NRA's fault that lawmakers, time and time again, made the conscious decision to vote down firearms controls. The NRA indeed utilized every lobbying tool at its disposal. But at the end of the day, it was lawmakers—not the NRA—who cast the decisive votes, and they did so without the hyperpoliticization of gun rights that exists today. In fact, many of the lobbying tools that the NRA and other gun rights advocacy groups use today to persuade lawmakers were nonexistent prior to the Kennedy assassination. This includes "grading" lawmakers' votes, donating to lawmakers' campaigns, and officially endorsing political candidates.

The point to be made is that prior to the close of 1963—other than perhaps disappointing the gun rights community at times—there was nothing politically consequential standing in the way of lawmakers enacting firearms controls. Lawmakers simply chose not to, and this was largely due to the lack of any organized firearms control movement. For without a political counterpoise to the lobbying efforts of the NRA, the decision to forgo enacting firearms controls was a relatively easy one for most lawmakers. The political reality was that whenever a restrictive firearms bill was up for consideration, it was almost always a one-sided affair. If a public hearing was held on a firearms control bill, the NRA and its "official family" were there ready to provide lawmakers with "expert" testimony, and therefore amplify the gun rights position. Even if there was not a public hearing, and the bill somehow made it to the legislative floor for a vote, the NRA could influence the outcome by simply packing the legislative chamber with gun rights supporters. This sent a clear message to lawmakers that the gun rights community was a political force to be reckoned with.

It was rare, however, that a firearms control bill even made it the legislative floor for a vote. This was because the NRA—through its legislative reporting service—successfully defeated most bills at the committee stage. The way it worked was that NRA field representatives, affiliated rifle and shooting clubs, and members would relay pending firearms control bills to the NRA's legislative reporting service.[2] From there, the legislative reporting service would alert the wider gun rights community of the bill's dangers, whether it be in the pages of the *American Rifleman*, in a special legislative bulletin, or through its extended network of hunting, sporting, and outdoor newspaper columnists, who would then broadcast the NRA's talking points against it (figure 4.1). This triggered a letter-writing campaign against the bill, effectively killing it at the committee level.

WARNING
New Gun Laws Ahead

Look Out! Hundreds of laws concerning the ownership and use of guns will be proposed this year. Every other year a big majority of state lawmaking bodies meet. 1953 is one of these big years . . . 45 legislatures will be in session.

In 1951 (the last big year) 240 firearms control bills were introduced into state legislatures. Fifty of these were bills which discriminated against law-abiding, gun-owning sportsmen like yourself . . . definitely *not* the sort of laws you want to see "on the books" in your state.* *You can expect 1953 to outdo that record.*

Let's face it. Anti-gun legislation *can* take away your guns. Laws, even well-intentioned laws, *can* destroy your enjoyment in the use of guns. Congress, your state legislature, your game commission, or your local lawmaking body *can* restrict your ownership and use of guns by requiring registration, license fees, police permits, and "red tape" to the point that all your pleasure is killed.

Your NRA is your first line of defense against bad gun laws. Through the NRA Legislative Service you receive prompt notice of bills that affect you and your sport. As citizens, it's up to you to judge each such bill . . . support the good ones, vigorously oppose the bad ones.

Certainly this is one of the most important services the NRA gives its members. This is a vital matter to every American who owns a gun and enjoys any legitimate form of shooting. Continue to support, with your own membership, the organization which leads the fight for sensible gun laws—your NRA. Enlist every other gun-owning sportsman you know as a fellow member. It's his fight, too.

*   *Because of the opposition of NRA members, not a single one of these 50 un-wise gun bills became law.*

FIGURE 4.1 NRA recruitment advertisement in *American Rifleman*, February 1953. The ad highlighted the importance of the NRA's legislative reporting service, which served as the "first line of defense against bad gun laws."

It cannot be emphasized enough just how effective the NRA-led writing campaign was in influencing legislative outcomes. Much like at public hearings, the level of support for the NRA's position was always a one-sided affair.[3] No matter the region, state, or locality, virtually every piece of constituent mail on any firearms bill came down in favor of the NRA's position. It was even common for those doing the writing to directly refer lawmakers to the NRA for legislative guidance, which would then afford NRA officials the opportunity to politically intervene and craft legislation that the NRA supported.

The letters from gun rights supporters opposing firearms controls came in several forms. Some parroted the NRA's talking points verbatim. Other letters were more personal or in some cases conspiratorial. Some were part of a chain in which the contents of each were virtually the same.[4] Others were organized as petitions and came from a variety of organizations, whether it be NRA-affiliated rifle clubs,[5] sporting, shooting, or game associations,[6] or some other organization, such as state and local chapters of the Isaak Walton League or American Legion.[7]

While the gun rights supporters who took part in letter-writing campaigns were virtually unanimous in opposing firearms controls, they came from a variety of backgrounds. Indeed, it is fair to assume that up through the 1960s most gun rights supporters were firearms-owning white males. This was undoubtedly the target audience of the editors of the NRA's flagship magazine *American Rifleman*, as well as the editors of other sporting, hunting, and shooting publications, such as *Sports Afield*, *Field & Stream*, *Outdoor Life*, and *Guns Magazine*. However, other than being overwhelming white and male, gun rights supporters were a professional and socioeconomically diverse group.[8] As one lawmaker aptly stated in 1966, gun rights supporters "range from bus drivers to bank presidents, from Minutemen to four-star generals, and from morons to geniuses, but they have one thing in common: they don't want anyone to tell them anything about what to do with their guns, and they mean it."[9]

From the late 1920s through the mid-1950s, despite the lobbying success of the NRA's letter-writing campaign, it did little to convince lawmakers that firearms control was a voting issue from which to politically benefit. Lawmakers' responses to the letters during this period bear this out. The most common type of response lawmakers gave was to sidestep the issue of firearms control entirely. They accomplished this in one of two ways: The first was to respond to the letter with merely the procedural status of the firearms control bill in question.[10] The second was to acknowledge receipt of the letter and then promise to give the matter "close" or "careful" attention should the firearms control bill ever be brought to the floor for a vote.[11] There were exceptions of course, such as Oklahoma representative Carl Albert, who, given the predominantly rural makeup of his district, sometimes responded with a more definitive pro-gun assurance. "You may be assured that I agree with you one hundred percent in your opposition to legislation which will limit ownership of firearms and require finger printing and further restrictions upon American citizens," wrote Albert to a constituent in 1947, adding, "I feel that it is high-time that we recognize that it is one thing to curtail criminal activity and another thing to tie the hands of every good citizen of our country by more laws and regulation."[12] Another exception is a letter written in 1957 by the entire Montana congressional delegation, in response to the Internal Revenue Service (IRS) proposing a series of new administrative regulations on firearms and ammunition—regulations that drew the ire of the NRA and its allies. The proposed regulations were particularly contentious in western rural states, and therefore the Montana congressional delegation came together to condemn the IRS for invading the "rights and privileges of the sportsmen in our States as well as those throughout the nation."[13]

The earliest indication that firearms controls may become a voting issue was in the fall of 1959. Therein, for the first time in two decades, a study was conducted on the public's desire for firearms controls, and the results were rather alarming to the NRA.[14] According to the study, an overwhelming majority of Americans (75 percent) supported laws requiring individuals to obtain a police-issued permit before acquiring a handgun. An even larger majority supported laws that either completely forbade (34 percent) or strictly regulated (51 percent) the use of firearms by minors (85 percent in total). Meanwhile, simple majorities supported laws requiring owners to unload firearms stored in the home (53 percent) and a permit to purchase ammunition (54 percent).[15]

For the most part, the NRA accepted the study's findings as true. It did note, however, that the findings were illustrative of how easy it was for antifirearms reformers to spread misinformation.[16] "We, as a people, must not be deceived by public opinion polls and others aimed at destroying our basic right to keep and bear arms," wrote NRA executive director Louis F. Lucas.[17] Additionally, the NRA thought that the findings underscored what the organization had been saying for two decades: that the gun rights community needed to use "every opportunity to publicize the fact that firearms are used by millions of fine people for sport, for hunting, and in defense of their life and property," and that the answer to crime was never additional firearm controls, but a society that deals "quickly and effectively with the criminal."[18]

The gun rights community responded by voicing their displeasure with the study's findings. Some invoked the Second Amendment as an affirmative defense. Some criticized the study's methodology. Meanwhile, others

FIGURE 4.2 Advertisement in the *Quad-City Times* (Davenport, Iowa), July 7, 1968. Echoing NRA talking points, the ad urged sportsmen, hunters, and gun owners to write their representatives to protect the Second Amendment.

condemned the "unthinking public" or labeled the study's findings as fraudulent.[19] Lawmakers took notice, and coincidentally *Guns Magazine* had just begun publishing a reoccurring column titled "Know Your Lawmakers," where the magazine's editors sent letters to governors and members of Congress requesting that they share their thoughts on the Second Amendment and firearms controls.[20] Specifically, the editors asked governors and members of Congress the following questions: "Do you believe that this amendment is of significant importance in today's world? How do you view the Founding Fathers' meaning of the word 'militia' in terms of today's people and circumstances? What is your view of the purpose and proper effect of the statement that the right to keep and bear arms shall not be infringed?"[21]

The "Know Your Lawmakers" column was first published in June 1959 and appeared regularly in *Guns Magazine* through February 1962, when the column was abruptly discontinued without reason. However, in September 1963—a time when the NRA was working with Senator Thomas J. Dodd and the Senate Subcommittee on Juvenile Delinquency in drafting legislation regulating mail-order firearms—it was revived for a second iteration, and it continued through May 1966. In total, *Guns Magazine* published 268 responses from lawmakers: 149 were published during the column's first iteration from June 1959 through February 1962.[22] Out of these 149 responses, 27 were from governors and 122 from members of Congress (90 representatives and 32 senators). The remaining 119 lawmaker responses appeared in the column's second iteration from September 1963 through May 1966. Out of these 119 responses, 13 were from governors and 106 from members of Congress (84 representatives and 22 senators).

There is much that can be historically deduced from the responses. For one, they provide a useful historical snapshot of lawmakers' perceptions on the Second Amendment and firearms controls. Indeed, the responses are far from comprehensive. Moreover, one needs to consider that the editors of *Guns Magazine* might have given publication preference to those responses that were more politically appealing to its readership, or that certain lawmakers might have consciously decided not to provide a response to a magazine known for vocally opposing firearms controls.[23] Still, despite these evidentiary biases and shortcomings, the "Know Your Lawmakers" column historically provides the largest and most far-reaching collection of lawmaker opinions on the Second Amendment and firearms controls from the late 1950s through the mid-1960s. What also makes the column a useful historical tool is that its two iterations of publication are almost perfectly divided by the assassination of President Kennedy. This is relevant because it provides historians with useful data on how, if at all, state and federal lawmakers' views on firearms controls were affected by the NRA's post-Kennedy assassination maximum pressure campaign.

As outlined in tables 4.1–4.4, the first iteration of the column shows that 64 percent of lawmakers from across the political spectrum viewed the Second Amendment as protecting an individual right to keep and bear arms in some form. If one excludes those responses where the respective lawmaker chose not to comment on the Second Amendment, the percentage rises to nearly 80 percent. As it pertains to firearms controls, lawmaker support for broad governmental regulation or additional firearms legislation was 33 percent, with another 25 percent expressing the opinion that existing firearms controls were sufficient. If one excludes those responses where a respective lawmaker chose not to comment on firearms controls, the percentage of lawmakers supporting broad governmental regulation or additional firearms legislation increases to 53 percent. Meanwhile, the percentage of lawmakers espousing support for the status quo increases to 39 percent.[24]

The second iteration of "Know Your Lawmakers" shows just how effective the NRA's post-Kennedy assassination maximum pressure campaign was at influencing lawmakers' views on firearms controls. For instance, the percentage of lawmakers who viewed the Second Amendment as protecting an individual right to keep and bear arms, in some form, increased from 64 to 80 percent. If one excludes those responses where the respective lawmaker chose not to comment on the Second Amendment, the percentage increased from roughly 80 percent in the first iteration to 90 percent in the second. What is more telling are the changes in lawmakers' views on firearms controls. While lawmaker support for broad governmental regulation or additional firearms legislation remained stagnant, the view that existing firearms controls were adequate jumped up from 25 percent in the first iteration to 43 percent in the second. Additionally, given the increase in news media exposure on the subject, the percentage of lawmakers deciding not to comment of firearms controls fell precipitously, from 38 percent to 23 percent. The percentage of lawmakers deciding not to

TABLE 4.1

Lawmaker Categories	Second Amendment Interpretation Categories					
	NC	B	I	MI	C	SC
Governors (27)	11	1	14	0	0	1
	40.7%	3.7%	51.9%	0%	0%	3.7%
U.S. Representatives (90)	11	12	46	15	5	1
	12.2%	13.3%	51.1%	16.7%	5.6%	1.1%
U.S. Senators (32)	6	4	16	5	0	1
	18.8%	12.5%	50.0%	15.6%	0%	3.1%
U.S. Congress (122)	17	16	62	20	5	2
	13.9%	13.1%	50.8%	16.4%	4.2%	1.6%
All Lawmakers (149)	28	17	76	20	5	3
	18.8%	11.4%	51.0%	13.4%	3.4%	2.0%
Democrats (88)	12	12	45	15	3	1
	13.6%	13.6%	51.1%	17.0%	3.4%	1.3%
Republicans (61)	16	5	31	5	2	2
	26.2%	8.2%	50.8%	8.2%	3.3%	3.3%

Source: "Know Your Lawmakers," Guns Magazine, Second Amendment Interpretation Analysis, June 1959–February 1962.

Note: Categories: NC (no comment); B (broad statement/unclear); I (individual right); MI (modified individual or national defense understanding); C (collective right); SC (Supreme Court's interpretation).

comment on the Second Amendment also fell, but only a modest 7 percentage points.[25]

It is worth noting that of the 119 responses published during the second iteration of "Know Your Lawmakers," 32 were from lawmakers who had given a response during the first iteration.[26] This subset of responses also indicates just how effective the NRA's maximum pressure campaign was at influencing lawmakers. As it pertains to the meaning of the Second Amendment, 13 of the 32 lawmakers changed their position, of which 6 changed in support of an individual rights interpretation. Meanwhile, not one of the 32 lawmakers who supported an individual rights interpretation of the Second Amendment during the first iteration changed their position for the second. As it pertains what constituted adequate firearms controls, 16 of the 32 changed their position from the first iteration to the second, 8 of whom changed their answers to state that existing firearms

TABLE 4.2

Lawmaker Categories	Firearms Control Categories			
	NC	D	A	GC
Governors (27)	5	7	0	15
	18.5%	25.9%	0%	55.6%
U.S. Representatives (90)	37	24	5	24
	41.1%	26.7%	5.5%	26.7%
U.S. Senators (32)	16	5	1	10
	50.0%	15.6%	3.1%	31.3%
U.S. Congress (122)	53	29	6	34
	43.4%	23.8%	4.9%	27.9%
All Lawmakers (149)	58	36	6	49
	38.9%	24.2%	4.0%	32.9%
Democrats (88)	34	21	6	27
	38.6%	23.9%	6.8%	30.7%
Republicans (61)	24	15	0	22
	39.3%	24.6%	0%	36.1%

Source: "Know Your Lawmakers," Guns Magazine, Firearms Control Analysis, June 1959–February 1962.

Note: Categories: NC (no comment); D (did not think further legislation was necessary or discouraged additional legislation); A (absolutist or opposed most controls); GC (supported some general firearms control or additional regulations).

controls were adequate. Only 4 lawmakers changed their answer to state support for either broad governmental regulation or additional firearms legislation.

Another distinguishing characteristic between the lawmaker responses for the first and second iterations of "Know Your Lawmakers" was the level of detail in which they discussed firearms controls. During the first iteration, lawmakers who expressed support for either broad governmental regulation or additional firearms legislation often did so in general terms. For the second iteration, however, given the increased news media coverage and the wide range of firearms controls proposals being offered, it was now commonplace for lawmakers to outline specific firearms controls policies they supported and why.[27] Conversely, for those lawmakers who felt that additional federal firearms controls were unnecessary, they took to more frequently repeating the NRA's talking points, whether it was

TABLE 4.3

Lawmaker Categories	Second Amendment Interpretation Categories					
	NC	B	I	MI	C	SC
Governors (13)	0	1	11	0	0	1
	0%	7.7%	84.6%	0%	0%	7.7%
U.S. Representatives (84)	8	5	70	0	1	0
	9.5%	6.0%	83.3%	0%	1.2%	0%
U.S. Senators (22)	6	1	15	0	0	0
	27.3%	4.5%	68.2%	0%	0%	0%
U.S. Congress (106)	14	6	85	0	1	0
	13.2%	5.7%	80.2%	0%	0.9%	0%
All Lawmakers (119)	14	7	96	0	1	1
	11.8%	5.9%	80.7%	0%	0.8%	0.8%
Democrats (57)	5	3	48	0	1	0
	8.7%	5.3%	84.2%	0	1.8%	0%
Republicans (62)	9	4	48	0	0	1
	14.5%	6.5%	77.4%	0%	0%	1.6%

Source: "Know Your Lawmakers," *Guns Magazine*, Second Amendment Interpretation Analysis, September 1963–May 1966.

Note: Categories: NC (no comment); B (broad statement/unclear); I (individual right); MI (modified individual or national defense understanding); C (collective right); SC (Supreme Court's interpretation).

arguing for states' rights, outlining the importance of firearms localism, or pushing what can best be described as gun rights propaganda.[28] Needless to say, in the aftermath of the Kennedy assassination, regardless of whether a lawmaker was for or against firearms control, the political issue was becoming increasingly relevant.

While comparing the first and second iterations of responses in the column is useful in ascertaining lawmakers' collective opinions on the public meaning of the Second Amendment and the overall desirability of firearms controls, they are far less useful in determining each lawmaker's personal views. There are several instances where the column outlined a lawmaker's position succinctly, as is the case for those members of Congress who in part made up the NRA's "official family," which included Florida representative Robert F. Sikes, Michigan representative John D. Dingell, and Arizona senator Paul Fannin.[29] For almost all other lawmakers,

TABLE 4.4

Lawmaker Categories	Firearms Control Categories			
	NC	D	A	GC
Governors (13)	3	4	0	6
	23.1%	30.8%	0%	46.1%
U.S. House Reps. (84)	20	41	0	23
	23.8%	48.8%	0%	27.4%
U.S. Senators (22)	5	7	0	10
	22.7%	31.8%	0%	45.5%
U.S. Congress (106)	25	48	0	33
	23.6%	45.2%	0%	31.2%
All Lawmakers (119)	28	52	0	39
	23.5%	43.7%	0%	32.8%
Democrats (57)	12	23	0	22
	21.1%	40.4%	0%	38.5%
Republicans (62)	16	29	0	17
	25.8%	46.8%	0%	27.4%

Source: "Know Your Lawmakers," Guns Magazine, Firearms Control Analysis, September 1963–May 1966.

Note: Categories: NC (no comment); D (did not think further legislation was necessary or discouraged additional legislation); A (absolutist or opposed most controls); GC (supported some general firearms control or additional regulations).

however, outlining their respective firearms control position requires a more thorough examination. Consider the example of President Kennedy, whose response to "Know Your Lawmakers" in 1960 is still used today by the gun rights community to advocate for broad Second Amendment rights.[30] The use of Kennedy's response began almost immediately after his assassination in 1963 —a time when the public and the news media were urging Congress and state assemblies to enact new firearms controls. To counter these legislative calls to action, the gun rights community took to quoting Kennedy's response as evidence that the late president was a staunch supporter of the Second Amendment and therefore would have opposed the very firearms controls being proposed in his name. For instance, E. B. Mann, who served as an editor for Guns Magazine, as well as on the board of several shooting organizations, could not understand "how anyone who believed in, or respected" the idea that President Kennedy could support firearms controls.[31] Another gun rights supporter anonymously wrote: "The logic of Mr. Kennedy's [1960] statement is precise and clear. It should serve to bring into focus the real issues hidden in the well-meaning but ill-conceived campaign now being conducted against all firearms and their owners."[32]

There is a problem, however, with associating Kennedy's "Know Your Lawmakers" response with standing firmly against firearms controls. At no point did Kennedy raise the issue. Here is what he wrote:

> By calling attention to "a well regulated militia," the "security" of the nation, and the right of each citizen "to keep and bear arms," our founding fathers recognized the essentially civilian nature of our economy. Although it is extremely unlikely that the fear of governmental tyranny which gave rise to the Second Amendment will ever be a major danger to our nation, the Amendment still remains an important declaration of our basic civilian-military relationships, in which every citizen must be ready to participate in the defense of his country. For that reason I believe the Second Amendment will always be important.[33]

Kennedy's response clearly falls within the confines of an individual, but national defense–centric interpretation of the Second Amendment. It was an interpretation that Kennedy echoed upon politically ascending to the White House. On March 7, 1961, in a speech celebrating the leadership of late President Franklin D. Roosevelt, he called on Americans to embrace the "cause of liberty," much like the Massachusetts Minutemen of the American Revolution, who took up arms for the "preservation of freedom as a basic purpose of their daily life."[34] Kennedy's remarks quickly garnered the attention of NRA executive vice president Franklin L. Orth, who used them as an opening to offer the thirty-fifth president honorary NRA life membership. Orth's offer noted that the NRA embodied the "spirit of the Minutemen of 1776" and was "dedicated to the promotion of the social welfare and public safety, law and order, and the national defense; and to the education and training of citizens of good repute in the safe and efficient handling of small arms."[35] No mention was made of the NRA's policy of opposing most firearms controls.

Kennedy's secretaries responded as they did to most organizations that offered honorary membership. It was graciously accepted in a letter signed by the president, which unsurprisingly mentioned nothing pertaining to firearms controls.[36] In a reply letter dated April 19, 1961, NRA secretary Frank C. Daniel formally welcomed Kennedy as a life member. Daniel noted that the key "purposes and objects" of the NRA were "to educate the youth of the nation in good citizenship, in safe and proper gun handling and in marksmanship, to promote shooting as a sport and for the purposes of qualifying as finished marksmen those individuals who may be called upon to defend our country or its citizens," and to "create public sentiment for the encouragement of rifle practice for all these purposes."[37] No mention was made of the NRA's policy of opposing most firearms controls.

From the time that Kennedy accepted honorary NRA life membership until his assassination, there is not one instance to be found where the late president espoused even the slightest disfavor of firearms controls, nor a broad individual rights conception of the Second Amendment. The same is true of Kennedy's personal papers, which, if anything, convey that his position on firearms controls was in line with that of most other lawmakers before the NRA was publicly outed as the "gun lobby." This position was that Kennedy had not given the firearms control issue much thought and was willing to agree with whatever opinion his constituents were relaying to his office, which at that time was predominantly the opinion of the NRA.[38] Yet despite the lack of any evidence showing President Kennedy opposed firearms controls, to this day the gun rights community continues to cite his "Know Your Lawmakers" response, as well as his letter accepting honorary NRA life membership, as definitive proof that the late president was an ardent defender of gun rights.[39] This is a historical bridge too far.

Ultimately, what the example of President Kennedy informs is the problem of historically inferring too much from the individual lawmaker responses to the "Know Your Lawmakers" column. The responses should not be construed as providing a full, contextual understanding of a respective lawmaker's position. Rather, each response merely serves to provide a small window into a much larger historical inquiry. Consider the example of Illinois senator and minority leader Everett M. Dirksen, who in 1963 provided the editors of *Guns Magazine* with the following cryptic response: "I know of no movement or effort to impair the right of a citizen to keep and bear arms and I am quite sure in view of the attention which this matter received years ago in the House of Representatives that any endeavor in this direction has been pretty well laid to rest."[40] Other than seemingly endorsing the individual rights interpretation of the Second Amendment and acknowledging that previous attempts by Congress to further regulate firearms were summarily defeated, Dirksen's response tells us nothing about his overall firearms control policy, nor whether the Second Amendment impedes or restricts federal action. It is only upon examining Dirksen's personal papers and the accompanying public record that one learns his firearms control position: that Dirksen was a supporter of moderate firearms controls and did not view them as being inviolate of the Second Amendment.[41] Conversely, Dirksen viewed strict firearms controls—such as federal registration of all firearms—with political disdain. This was because he believed that firearms registration would be a federal intrusion into state and local governmental authority.[42]

Montana senator Lee Metcalf is another example where a lawmaker's "Know Your Lawmakers" response fails to tell the whole story. Over the course of the column's seven-year publication, Metcalf provided a total of three responses. The first, published in December 1960, was an endorsement of the individual, national defense–centric interpretation of the Second Amendment.[43] The second, published less than a year later, balanced the individual right to "keep and bear arms" against the government's role in imposing "reasonable controls in the public interest."[44] The same was true of Metcalf's third and final response, which was published in February 1965.[45] As to what qualified as "reasonable controls," or how to properly weigh the government's interest in regulating firearms with the Second Amendment, was never answered in any of Metcalf's three responses. But if one examines his personal papers and the accompanying public record, a much more distinct firearms policy is outlined. While Metcalf vehemently opposed the idea of firearms registration at all levels of government for most of his tenure in the Senate, he was politically supportive of other forms of firearms controls, such as prohibiting the sale of firearms to criminals and dangerous persons, first requiring parental consent before a minor may purchase or operate a firearm, licensing of the carrying of firearms in public places with the exception of unloaded and cased transport for lawful purposes such as hunting and target shooting, and regulating—but not prohibiting—the mail-order sale of firearms.[46]

It is worth noting that Metcalf's position on firearms registration and mail-order purchases was largely influenced by the NRA's letter-writing campaign—a fact that Metcalf himself acknowledged.[47] This is not to say that he accepted the views of every NRA member or the wider gun rights community carte blanche. In fact, on several occasions, when Metcalf received a letter containing a conspiratorial, outlandish, or mistaken view of a pending firearms control bill, he made sure to correct the author with the facts.[48] But for generally standing with the cause of gun rights, Metcalf received the NRA's praise. "For a number of reasons you have not always received the recognition from the news media that your support of the shooter-sportsmen across the country has merited," wrote NRA vice president Franklin L. Orth to Metcalf in October 1965, adding, "I assure you our members know that you have been in the forefront of the struggle in the Congress to prevent this onerous and unwise legislation from becoming a statutory reality."[49]

Not long after the June 6, 1968, assassination of New York senator Robert F. Kennedy, however, the NRA's and wider gun rights community's support for Metcalf shifted to contempt. The reason was Metcalf's stunning political about-face on firearms controls. For in the immediate aftermath of Senator Kennedy's assassination, public outcry for firearms controls was at an all-time high, and Metcalf was now of the opinion that strict firearms control measures were indeed necessary. "I think we should have a complete prohibition on the sale of handguns. . . . I would have that my State of Montana through its legislature would pass the kind of registration law that would be operative on that State to control long guns and that the State of Montana would prohibit the use of handguns except under very unusual situations in gun clubs, and so forth," stated Metcalf on the floor of the House of Representatives.[50] That Metcalf was advocating only for state, not federal, firearms registration did little to mitigate the subsequent gun rights criticism. For Metcalf's support for firearms registration— although brief given that he would change his position again—became the basis from which many within the Montana gun rights community would call for his ouster.[51]

Metcalf was not the only lawmaker to do a political about-face on firearms controls in the wake of Senator Kennedy's assassination. Several members of Congress made the transition. Consider fellow Montana senator Mike Mansfield, who went from being a cautious moderate on firearms controls to a staunch supporter. Like Metcalf, Mansfield made the political calculation to endorse firearms registration.[52] "I do not expect that [firearms registration] is any sort of cure-all to the problem [of firearms violence]," wrote Mansfield to a constituent, adding, "Nevertheless, I have taken this course in the hope and belief that there can be some mitigation in the rise level of violence of the gun which has come to plague our land,

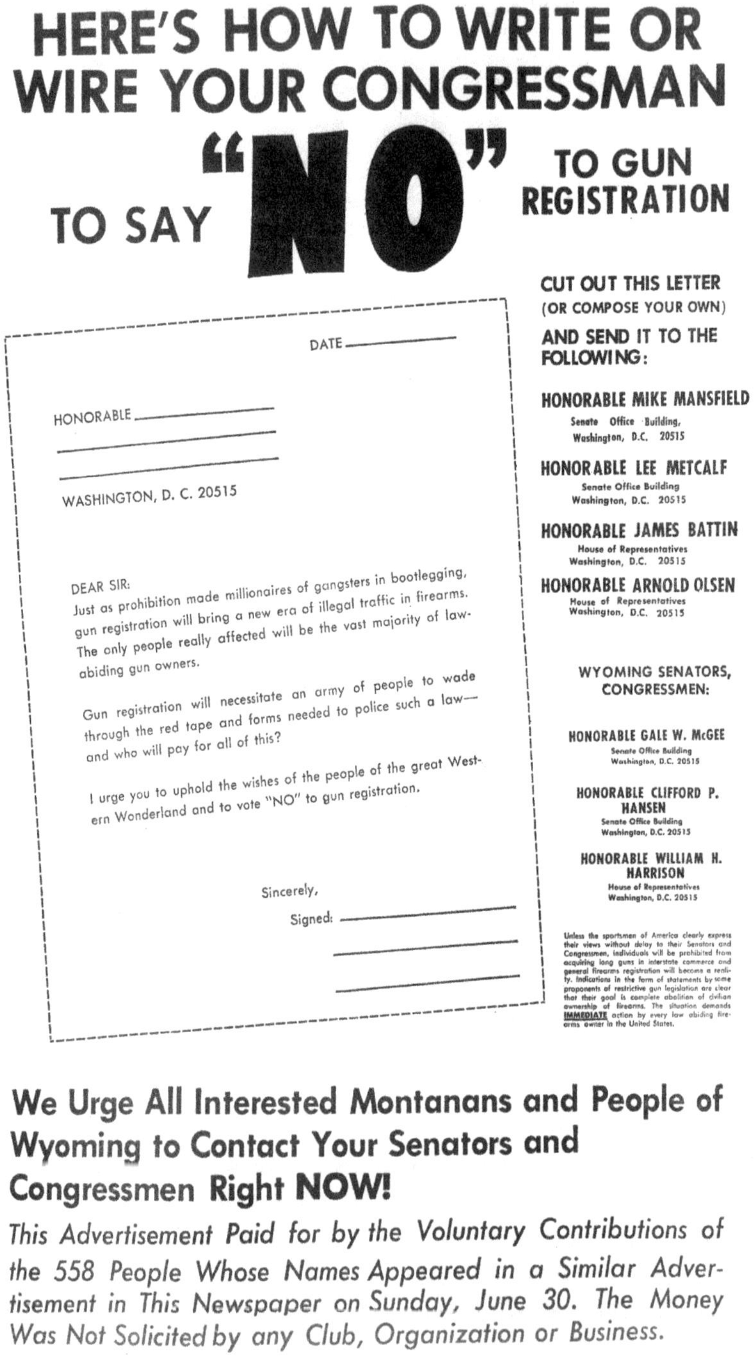

HERE'S HOW TO WRITE OR WIRE YOUR CONGRESSMAN

TO SAY "NO" TO GUN REGISTRATION

CUT OUT THIS LETTER
(OR COMPOSE YOUR OWN)

AND SEND IT TO THE FOLLOWING:

DATE _____

HONORABLE _____

WASHINGTON, D. C. 20515

DEAR SIR:

Just as prohibition made millionaires of gangsters in bootlegging, gun registration will bring a new era of illegal traffic in firearms. The only people really affected will be the vast majority of law-abiding gun owners.

Gun registration will necessitate an army of people to wade through the red tape and forms needed to police such a law— and who will pay for all of this?

I urge you to uphold the wishes of the people of the great Western Wonderland and to vote "NO" to gun registration.

Sincerely,

Signed: _____

HONORABLE MIKE MANSFIELD
Senate Office Building,
Washington, D.C. 20515

HONORABLE LEE METCALF
Senate Office Building
Washington, D.C. 20515

HONORABLE JAMES BATTIN
House of Representatives
Washington, D.C. 20515

HONORABLE ARNOLD OLSEN
House of Representatives
Washington, D.C. 20515

WYOMING SENATORS, CONGRESSMEN:

HONORABLE GALE W. McGEE
Senate Office Building
Washington, D.C. 20515

HONORABLE CLIFFORD P. HANSEN
Senate Office Building
Washington, D.C. 20515

HONORABLE WILLIAM H. HARRISON
House of Representatives
Washington, D.C. 20515

Unless the sportsmen of America clearly express their views without delay to their Senators and Congressmen, individuals will be prohibited from acquiring long guns in interstate commerce and general firearms registration will become a reality. Indications in the form of statements by some proponents of restrictive gun legislation are clear that their goal is complete abolition of civilian ownership of firearms. The situation demands IMMEDIATE action by every law abiding fire-arms owner in the United States.

We Urge All Interested Montanans and People of Wyoming to Contact Your Senators and Congressmen Right NOW!

This Advertisement Paid for by the Voluntary Contributions of the 558 People Whose Names Appeared in a Similar Advertisement in This Newspaper on Sunday, June 30. The Money Was Not Solicited by any Club, Organization or Business.

FIGURE 4.3 Advertisement in the *Billings (Mont.) Gazette*, July 2, 1968. The ad urged both the Montana and the Wyoming gun rights communities to write their congressman in opposition to firearms registration.

especially the cities of our nation."[53] Another example is that of Michigan senator Philip. A Hart. Like Metcalf and Mansfield, Hart had rejected the idea of the federal government further interfering with what was traditionally a state and local matter. While Hart was amenable to supporting a few minor, interstate restrictions on handguns under the constitutional umbrella of Congress's Article II power to regulate interstate commerce,[54] he adamantly opposed any federal legislation that touched on rifles and shotguns.[55] For his firm stance against most federal firearms controls, Hart received the praise of both the NRA and the Michigan gun rights community.[56] Yet the assassination of Senator Kennedy was a political inflection point for Hart, and the Michigan senator suddenly became one of Congress's most vocal firearms control proponents. Hart admitted as much in a September 10, 1968, letter to a constituent:

> My position on gun control has, indeed, changed. Originally, I felt that when the only proposal was to provide mail order control of long guns it was a useless gesture, since such action would in no way provide adequate controls but would simply provide an inconvenience to the catalogue buyers. Since proposals for registration and licensing of shoulder arms have now been made, it seems to me that this, coupled with a mail-order ban, represents a real answer and I am supporting such legislation.[57]

Another example of a member of Congress changing their position on firearms controls is that of South Dakota senator George McGovern.[58] For years, McGovern felt that any additional federal firearms controls would not adequately "account for the differences among the states in the relationship between the proper, beneficial use and misuse of firearms." "Those who call for increased controls," stated McGovern, "would do well to concentrate on state legislatures and city councils where the fundamental power to deal with firearms and their misuse resides."[59] On top of opposing additional federal firearms controls, McGovern was on record in *Guns Magazine* as supporting a robust right to arms: "The Second Amendment guaranteeing 'the right of the people to keep and bear arms' is an essential part of the American tradition. It has stood us well in both peace and war. I think it would be a serious mistake for the Congress to pass legislation that would in any way jeopardize this time-honored and time-tested freedom of the American people."[60]

But after the assassination of Senator Kennedy, McGovern changed his positions on both the Second Amendment and federal firearms controls. As it pertained to the Second Amendment, he went from endorsing an individual right interpretation to a states' rights interpretation.[61] And as it pertained to firearms controls, although McGovern continued to acknowledge the legitimate interest of sportsmen and hunters in using firearms for lawful purposes, he was now adamant that the federal government needed to do something:

> I have in the past opposed measures to extend Federal controls on the sale of rifles and shotguns. The hearings on this issue include a statement by me, which you may have seen, objecting to the Administration's proposal on the grounds that it would interfere with the opportunities of people who own firearms for worthwhile purposes, and that we have no proof that it would substantially reduce crime.
>
> My position has accurately reflected what I feel is the consensus of South Dakota people, where firearms for sporting purposes are an important part of our lives and our economy. It has also been based upon my own background as an enthusiastic hunter, in a part of the country where shotguns and rifles are owned by virtually every family as a matter of course.
>
> I am asking that you joint me now, however, in an honest reappraisal of this position, based on a full understanding of what the most seriously considered [Dodd] bill [regulating mail order firearms sales] would and would not do from the standpoint of individual sportsmen and hunters . . .
>
> This legislation would unquestionably create some inconvenience for sportsmen in some parts of the country. Its sponsors . . . believe, however, that it would be helpful in preventing the purchase of firearms by people who are likely to misuse them.[62]

Of course, not every member of Congress who made the post–Senator Kennedy assassination transformation to support federal firearms controls did so from a position of opposition. Several members of Congress had chosen to remain neutral or silent until that point. Michigan representative James G. O'Hara,[63] Louisiana representative Hale Boggs,[64] and Maine senator Edmund S. Muskie are all examples in this respect. Focusing on Muskie, for years the Maine senator had politically straddled both sides of the firearms control issue. For instance, to appeal to those on the gun rights political spectrum, a picture of Muskie hunting fowl was included as part of his *Guns Magazine* "Know Your Lawmakers" response. At the same time, to shield himself from the criticism of firearms control proponents, Muskie put forward a noncommittal answer when asked whether additional federal firearms legislation was necessary:

> It is clear to me that some degree of firearms control is necessary in order to prevent irresponsible individuals from acquiring weapons. The basic question to be considered is what constitutes effective control, and who should exercise that control. In considering this issue, we must be reasonable and realistic. It is my intention to thoroughly study every aspect of this problem in an effort to reach a solution which will protect the rights of all American citizens.[65]

From December 1964 to early June 1968, Muskie continued to politically straddle both sides. But after the assassination of Senator Kennedy, he decisively threw his support behind firearms controls.[66] And over time, Muskie gradually became one of Congress's most vocal firearms control advocates.[67] For instance, at a news conference in 1970, Muskie lambasted anyone who discussed the issue in simple "no control at all or confiscate guns" terms. The subject was much more complex than that, and Muskie dismissed the idea that the only sure-fire way to stop firearms violence was to impose mandatory sentencing minimums:

> What good is [a mandatory minimum for a crime committed with a firearm] going to do when you have been shot by a mental defective, who has the defense of insanity anyway, to have imposed a *stricter penalty* for his having committed a crime with a gun? What good does it do you with respect to these other categories to have a stricter penalty when the *deed has been done*—someone is dead? . . . Is anyone really willing to say that society should take a complete hands off attitude about guns in the hands of all kinds of people? Is that really a responsible attitude to take? . . . I know those who are fighting this issue simplify it by saying, "This guy is for gun control and is for confiscating your guns." *That is a phony issue.*[68]

In political contrast to Muskie was Utah senator Wallace F. Bennett, who at the time of Senator Kennedy's assassination was *the* chief proponent of mandatory sentencing minimums. Initially, in the aftermath of the assassination, Bennett could be best described as a moderate on firearms controls. Although he consistently held up the Second Amendment as an individual right, he generally conceded that several types of firearms controls were indeed necessary, including "tighter control over the use of firearms by juveniles" and the "mail order purchase of weapons," as well as the need for stricter firearms laws in the populated urban centers.[69] To Bennett, the key difficulty in this legislative area was finding the proper balance between reducing "the accessibility of arms for criminal purposes without depriving our people the right to have firearms for recreation, including hunting."[70]

It was in early 1966, after having attended the grand opening of the NRA's Firearms Museum, that Bennett suddenly went from being a moderate on firearms control to the Senate's chief proponent of mandatory sentencing minimums.[71] The way he sold it, and the way the NRA wanted him to sell it, was that firearms violence was not a rural issue but an urban one. It made little sense, therefore, for Congress to pass extensive firearms controls. Rather, according to Bennett, it was best if the federal government treaded lightly in what were historically matters for state and local governments, and instead provide stiff mandatory sentencing minimums.[72] Even after the assassination of Robert Kennedy, Bennett remained adamant that mandatory sentencing minimums was the proper approach for Congress in stopping firearms-related violence.[73]

The key historical takeaway is that from the great "gun lobby" awakening in late 1963 to the assassination of Senator Kennedy in 1968, the politics of firearms controls cannot, and should not, be categorized in simple pro-gun and anti-gun terms. The subject is far more complex, and lawmakers' viewpoints often varied. Certainly, there are instances in which historical data, such as the collective responses to Guns Magazine's "Know Your Lawmakers" column, can be used to make a few broad based conclusions. Yet is important to note that such conclusions fail to tell whole story. As it pertains to the politics of firearms controls in the 1960s, such broad-based conclusions fail to inform that there was a plurality of views among lawmakers. Moreover, as will be outlined in the next chapter, they fail to properly contextualize how exactly the politics of firearms controls evolved in the 1960s, and how ultimately, in the wake of Senator Kennedy's assassination, the politics changed forever.

5

The Evolution of the NRA and Firearms Control Politics

Although being outed as the "gun lobby" was in many ways consequential for the National Rifle Association (NRA), sustaining membership rolls was not. The same was true for circulation of the NRA's flagship magazine *American Rifleman*. Both increased exponentially in the years following the assassination of President John F. Kennedy. As it pertains to membership rolls, from the start of 1964 to the close of 1967, membership increased from roughly 620,000 to just over 900,000.[1] And with it came a 67 percent increase in nontaxable annual income for the NRA, from $3,900,000 to $6,500,000.[2] Over the same period, the circulation of *American Rifleman* increased from 682,000 to 985,000.[3] NRA executive vice president Franklin L. Orth boasted that these increases were proof of organization's righteous cause: "Never before has the NRA or any other sportsmen's organization been more assailed and misrepresented. Yet never before has the NRA grown at a faster rate or strengthened its membership or structure more. It would appear that our opposition is such that it brings friends flocking to our cause."[4]

While publicly Orth and other NRA officials displayed an aura of confidence, it was a much different story behind the scenes. Many of the NRA's newest members joined under the auspices that the organization was in fact the "gun lobby," and therefore wanted its officials to fervently oppose every firearms control bill without compromise. This was rather problematic for the NRA because the organization's political success was built on straddling both sides of the issue. The way it worked was that the NRA would tout itself to lawmakers and government officials as a supporter of reasonable firearms regulations.[5] At the same time, the NRA informed sportsmen, hunters, and gun owners that virtually all firearms controls would either make gun ownership a crime or somehow lead to disarmament, and that they, with the assistance of the NRA, were the only ones who could stop it.[6] Sportsmen, hunters, shooters, and firearms owners—especially those within NRA-affiliated clubs—would then pressure lawmakers and government officials to vote against the firearms control bills that the NRA opposed, and, in its place, vote in favor of bill the NRA endorsed—bills that typically had little to no impact on an individual's ability to acquire, purchase, or sell firearms.[7]

The earliest indication that the NRA's newest members would not go along with a political straddling approach was in late 1964, a time when the NRA's leadership was negotiating a backdoor legislative compromise with Connecticut senator Thomas J. Dodd regarding the interstate purchase and sale of mail-order firearms.[8] And all the while the NRA was secretly working with Dodd, the NRA was portraying itself to membership as the preeminent defender of the Second Amendment.[9] The NRA also made sure to characterize the push for firearms controls as nothing more than hysteria and emotionalism.[10] Ideally, by politically straddling both sides, the NRA's leadership thought they would be able to minimize the regulatory burden on mail-order firearms and subsequently convince members to back it. But in this instance, many new members were unwilling to follow the organization's lead. Rather, they voiced their dissatisfaction by flooding the NRA with the very antagonistic letters, telegrams, and phone calls that were typically reserved for firearms control–supporting lawmakers. Some members went so far to issue death threats to the NRA's leadership.[11]

Yet despite this resistance, in the hopes of blocking the more restrictive firearms control bills from the 89th Congress's liberal wing, the NRA's leadership pressed forward in compromising with Dodd.[12] Eventually it succeeded. In conjunction with Dodd and the Senate Subcommittee on Juvenile Delinquency that Dodd chaired, the NRA put forward an amendment to the Federal Firearms Act that required every purchaser of a mail-order firearm to enclose a notarized affidavit certifying their age, name, address, and felony convictions, and that they were acting in compliance with state and local firearms regulations. The firearms dealer was then required to forward a copy of the affidavit and a description of the firearm to the purchaser's local law enforcement agency. Although the Dodd-NRA compromise bill imposed a new affidavit requirement on the purchasing of mail-order handguns, it effectively did nothing in the way of stopping minors, criminals, or other prohibited classes from ultimately receiving the handgun. The affidavit requirement's underlying deficiency—at least from an enforcement and control perspective—was that the handgun was shipped regardless of whether the respective local law enforcement agency investigated the purchaser's background.[13]

Yet despite this glaring legal loophole, Dodd was so pleased in having reached a legislative compromise that he immediately took to defending the NRA. Just months earlier, he had criticized the organization for asserting that his original bill, S. 1975, violated the Second Amendment. It was what he referred to as the NRA's "big lie technique."[14] But with a legislative compromise now in hand, Dodd took to defending the NRA and placed the blame on an "unreasonably and unjustly opposed small, vocal, and well organized hard core minority" for stalling much-needed federal firearms reforms.[15] Likewise, the NRA defended Dodd by informing its membership and the wider gun rights community that "under today's conditions *some guidelines* must be established for the *control of firearms*."[16]

The legislative compromise between Dodd and the NRA turned out to be short-lived, for on March 8, 1965, President Lyndon B. Johnson requested Congress to take up a much more restrictive firearms control bill than the one agreed on by Dodd and the NRA.[17] Not long thereafter, both Dodd and the NRA politically retreated to their respective corners.[18] While it is unclear which side retreated first, what is known is that both sides quickly devised new political strategies. Dodd's was simple and straightforward—do whatever was necessary to make President Johnson's firearms control bill a reality.[19] Thus, on March 22 he unveiled a new bill, filed as S. 1592, that contained seven reforms, to include (1) prohibiting the mail-order sales of firearms except between importers, manufacturers, and dealers; (2) prohibiting the sale of all firearms to persons under twenty-one, with the exception of sporting rifles and shotguns to those over eighteen; (3) placing curbs on the importation of surplus military firearms into the United States; (4) placing under federal control the interstate shipment and disposal of large-caliber weapons such as bazookas and antitank weapons; (5)

increasing existing dealer licensing fees and individual registration fees; (6) prohibiting the sale of firearms, other than rifles and shotguns, to any person not a resident of the state in which they seek to purchase; and (7) implementing other measures designed to make it easier for the states to control interstate firearms traffic.[20]

Just days earlier, with the assistance of Texas representative Robert Casey, the NRA also introduced a new bill. In accord with the gun rights mantra "punish the criminal, not the law-abiding citizen," the NRA proposed a mandatory sentence of ten years for anyone found guilty of using or carrying a firearm in the commission of a crime.[21] The sentence increased to twenty-five years for a second offense.[22] "At long last a bill has been introduced into Congress aimed at the proper target—the criminal use of firearms—instead of the legitimate gun owner," stated the NRA in a press release.[23] The National Shooting Sports Foundation (NSSF), the unofficial lobbying arm of the gun rights community, also praised Casey's bill: "The American public, especially in our metropolitan centers, is tired of being pushed around by criminals. Tough laws aimed at the criminal, with vigorous prosecution and mandatory sentences; are needed to help our overworked police departments."[24] What Casey, the NRA, and the NSSF failed to disclose, however, was that seemingly every state in the union already maintained mandatory sentencing laws for anyone found guilty of using a firearm in the commission of a crime.

Mandatory sentencing was in fact a key provision of the NRA-sponsored Uniform Firearms Act (UFA) of the late 1920s and early 1930s.[25] The same was true of the UFA's predecessor—the United States Revolver Association's (USRA) model firearms legislation—in which the USRA claimed that if the criminal "knows that the use of a weapon in the commission of crime means the certainty of an added term of imprisonment, he will hesitate to use one."[26] At the NRA's annual convention in 1965, officials praised the Casey bill as the "right approach" to "gun laws." Conversely, S. 1592 was portrayed as infringing on Americans' constitutional right to "bear arms" and opening the door to firearms registration. Additionally, NRA officials urged membership to "pour one million letters into the White House" in protest of President Johnson's call for strict firearms controls.[27]

All the while the NRA was rallying its membership to political action, Dodd took to lambasting the group—and the "twentieth-century Daniel Boones" that backed the organization—for opposing S. 1592, particularly on Second Amendment grounds. Although he conceded that firearms had long served as an "integral part" of American freedom from the "first shot fired at Concord in April 1775, to the present conflict in Vietnam," he considerably diverged from the NRA and its members on the constitutional meaning and applicability of the Second Amendment. Citing Supreme Court precedent, Dodd felt that the "only prohibition" imposed by the Second Amendment on Congress was "interfer[ing] with the maintenance of State Militia forces."[28]

It was not long after the NRA and Dodd exchanged political salvos that the organization would once more gain the upper hand. It began when the NRA pressed forward with its own mail-order firearms control bill. Introduced in the House in mid-April by California representative Cecil R. King, who also served on the NRA board of directors, and in the Senate by Iowa senator Bourke Hickenlooper, the bill was aptly described by one gun rights advocate as a "mild" version of the NRA-Dodd legislative compromise.[29] What made the bill "mild" was that it only governed the mail-order purchase of handguns. Rifles, shotguns, and all other long guns would be unaffected. To prevent the mail-order purchase of handguns by minors, criminals, and other prohibited classes, the King-Hickenlooper bill provided that every mail-order purchaser must submit a sworn statement to the selling firearms manufacturer or dealer. Each statement had to include that the purchaser (1) was at least eighteen years of age, (2) was not prohibited by federal, state, or local law from receiving or possessing a firearm, and (3) provided the name and address of their principal law enforcement office. Upon the firearms manufacturer or dealer receiving the mail-order purchaser's sworn statement, a copy was forwarded by registered mail to the purchaser's principal law enforcement office. Once confirmation of the letter's receipt arrived or should the law enforcement office refuse to accept the letter, the firearms manufacturer or dealer could then proceed with mailing the firearm to the purchaser.

Much like the failed NRA-Dodd legislative compromise, the King-Hickenlooper bill affidavit requirement did nothing in the way of effectively delaying or controlling the mail-order sale of handguns. This was what the NRA wanted—a law that effectively did nothing to impede the acquisition, sale, or purchase of firearms. And whether the bill was ever enacted into law was inconsequential. For if past was prologue, the principal purpose of the bill was twofold: First, by presenting an alternative mail-order firearms control bill, the NRA ensured that Dodd's S. 1592 would never even make its way out of committee throughout the 89th Congress. Second and equally important, the King-Hickenlooper bill allowed the NRA to counter the "gun lobby" label bestowed on it in the wake of President Kennedy's assassination. NRA officials could now point to the King-Hickenlooper bill as proof that the organization did in fact support "reasonable controls."[30] In the same breath, as a means to keep the gun rights community engaged in political action, NRA officials alleged that Dodd's S. 1592 would provide the secretary of the treasury with unlimited powers to impose "arbitrary and burdensome restrictions," and these restrictions would place "such a burden on the sale, possession and use of firearms for legitimate purposes as to totally discourage, and thus to eliminate the private ownership of all guns."[31]

There was a problem, however, with the NRA's claims. They were patently false and, in May 1965, before a hearing of the Senate Subcommittee on Juvenile Delinquency that Dodd chaired, the Connecticut senator made sure to address the matter. Ideally, he wanted to pressure the NRA into admitting that S. 1592 was not as burdensome, nor unconstitutional, as the organization was professing. Appearing on behalf of the NRA was Executive Vice President Franklin L. Orth, who began his testimony by highlighting the NRA's involvement in providing for the national defense, training law enforcement, and supporting reasonable firearms controls, such as the National Firearms Act of 1934 and the Federal Firearms Act of 1938.[32] He then proceeded to expound why—from the NRA's perspective—most of the provisions within S. 1592 would only burden law-abiding citizens.[33] He concluded by assuring the subcommittee that the NRA would do everything "within its power to assist the Congress in the development of proper legislation aimed at the specific problem areas in the President's war on crime."[34]

It was during Orth's question-and-answer period that Dodd went to the heart of the dispute—the NRA's mischaracterization of S. 1592:

> DODD: Well, as you know, there have been many major difficulties arise, I feel, from a [April 9, 1965] newsletter that the NRA circulated . . . to some 675,000 members, and affiliated clubs throughout the United States, and that newsletter purports . . . to be an analysis of the provisions of S. 1592. It urged members to write their Senators and Congressmen with respect

to their opinion. I have read it and reread it many times. And I must say it is not an accurate presentation of the provisions of the bill. . . .

ORTH: Well, the NRA policy on the content of S. 1592 . . . was prepared by a committee of the NRA board of directors. Serving on that committee were two presiding superior court judges and four prominent practicing attorneys. They studied S. 1592 conscientiously and earnestly, and in light of what the bill says, and what interpretations could be placed upon it, and found the broad administrative powers delegated to the Secretary of the Treasury. . . . If this committee of ours is guilty of an error as you charge, I would say that—very definitely, that it was not with any intent to mislead.[35]

After several back-and-forth exchanges as to what prompted the NRA to claim that S. 1592 would lead to firearms confiscation, Dodd eventually accepted Orth's explanation but made sure to note that it was not the only "untrue statement" the NRA had disseminated. Dodd then proceeded to go through each one of the NRA's claims and compare it to the actual language in S. 1592.[36] In the end, his interrogation approach won the political day by outlining how many, if not most, of the NRA's talking points against S. 1592 were unsubstantiated. However, given that the end goal was to compel Congress to enact S. 1592 into law, Dodd was still losing the political war, and losing badly. What he failed to realize was it really did not matter how many times he, or anyone for that matter, outed the NRA's talking points as propaganda. So long as the NRA kept its membership and the wider gun rights community politically engaged in the fight against firearms controls, and lawmakers continued to receive letters, telegrams, and phone calls opposing firearms controls, neither S. 1592 nor any restrictive firearms control bill was going to make its way through the 89th Congress.[37]

The key political hurdle that Dodd needed to overcome was getting S. 1592 approved by the Senate Commerce Committee. This was no easy feat. It required convincing the committee's chair, Washington senator Warren G. Magnuson, to present the bill for a committee vote. But Magnuson was adamant that firearms controls was a state issue, not a federal one, and therefore refused to let the committee act on S. 1592.[38] He was not alone in viewing the issue of firearms controls in this way. The view was common among members of Congress who represented rural constituencies.

Another common view was that of firearms localism over firearms federalism. Members of Congress supportive of this view claimed that because each state's and locality's relationship with firearms and crime was different, it made little sense to enact uniform federal firearms controls. While supporters of firearms localism generally acknowledged the need for some types of restrictive firearms controls, they felt that said controls would be needed only in densely populated urban areas, not lightly populated rural ones. Whether the reason for opposing additional federal firearms controls was "firearms control is a state issue," "firearms localism over firearms federalism," "enforce the firearms laws already on the books," or some other mantra, the NRA not only supported it but also made sure to disseminate it far and wide.[39] The more reasons for Congress to politically oppose restrictive firearms controls, such as S. 1592, the better.

In early 1966, in addition to disseminating talking points against S. 1592, the NRA rolled out a three-point legislative package.[40] Two of the points related to firearms control bills that the NRA was already endorsing—Texas representative Casey's mandatory sentencing bill and a bill banning all "destructive devices," such as bazookas, grenades, bombs, and the like. The third point, however, built on the states' rights and firearms localism lines of argument. It involved Congress enacting a law that made it illegal for any firearms manufacturer or dealer to "ship or transport . . . any firearms in interstate or foreign commerce, to any person . . . in any state where the receipt by such person of such firearm . . . would be in violation of any statute of such state." However, the proposed law would absolve any firearms manufacturer or dealer from federal criminal liability so long as they made "reasonable efforts . . . to ascertain whether such shipment would be in violation of state law."[41] Seemingly unbeknownst to everyone but NRA leadership, this was not the first time that the NRA proposed this type of law to Congress. In 1934, before the Senate Subcommittee on Commerce, NRA executive vice-president Milton Reckord proffered a similar law as an alternative to New York senator Royal S. Copeland's pistol registration bill.[42] And much like in 1934, the version of the NRA law in 1966 was nothing more than a legal redundancy, meant to deceive members of Congress into thinking that the proposed law was new and effective, when in fact it was not worth the paper it was written on.[43]

In the late summer of 1966, despite the NRA's shrewd political tactics, as well as facing considerable opposition from NRA membership, the NRA's extended "official family," NRA congressional surrogates, and the wider gun rights community, Dodd eventually succeeded in getting S. 1592 before the Senate Judiciary Committee. What propelled its consideration was not a change of heart by the committee's chairman, Mississippi senator James O. Eastland, who, given the rural and conservative makeup of his state, had opposed virtually every firearms control bill.[44] Rather, it was the shocking August 1, 1966 mass shooting at the University of Texas, where Charles Whitman killed fifteen people and injured thirty-one others with a rifle from the observation deck atop the university's central tower.[45] The shooting enhanced the public's outcry for additional firearms controls. As a result, Eastland felt obliged to hold a hearing.[46] Even Senator Magnuson, who had opposed the various Dodd bills over the years, reversed course and promised that the Senate Commerce Committee would fully consider whatever firearms control bill made it out of the Senate Judiciary Committee.[47]

With the assurances of Senators Eastland and Magnuson in hand, Dodd was hopeful that S. 1592, or at least some amended version, would make it to the Senate floor by the year's end. Unfortunately for Dodd, consideration of the bill was being stalled by the likes of Illinois senator Everett Dirksen and the other members of the Senate Judiciary Committee who continued to oppose any new federal firearms controls.[48] For over a month, Dodd pleaded with his fellow committee members to take up consideration of the bill.[49] Yet at every scheduled hearing there was either a procedural snafu or a lack of quorum to hold a vote. This provided NRA officials with more than enough time to mount their political response.

The House of Representatives was already seemingly in the NRA's pocket, for in an August 5 letter, NRA president Harlon B. Carter had contacted Majority Leader Carl Albert about the prospects of a Dodd-like bill making it to the House floor. Carter praised Albert's "strong and steady" demeanor thus far in opposing "firearms restrictions." Carter went on to write how the NRA deplored the mass shooting in Austin, Texas, but felt strongly that no firearms law would have prevented it. He closed his letter by outlining the various NRA-sponsored firearms control bills before Congress.[50] Albert replied by thanking Carter for his letter and noting that there was not a concurrent House bill to Dodd's S. 1592. He assured him that he would fully consider the "needs of sportsmen and law-abiding citizens" should a firearms bill make its way to the House floor.[51]

With the NRA confident that the House of Representatives would not advance a firearms control bill before the end of the 89th Congress, the organization focused its attention on the Senate. The NRA's strategy was to have its congressional surrogate on the Senate Judiciary Committee, Nebraska senator Roman L. Hruska, submit an alternative mail-order firearms control bill for the committee's consideration. Filed as S. 3767, Hruska's bill was almost synonymous with the King-Hickenlooper bill, albeit with a few minor differences. One difference was that the Hruska bill increased the minimum age to purchase a handgun in interstate commerce from eighteen to twenty-one. Another was that the bill included a requirement that all out-of-state handgun purchasers—not just mail-order purchasers—submit a sworn statement attesting that they were at least twenty-one years of age and were not prohibited by federal, state, or local law from purchasing a handgun, and that disclosed the name and address of their local law enforcement office.[52]

With the Hruska bill now a viable political option for the Senate Judiciary Committee, there was conveniently a quorum for the committee's August 31 hearing. Therein the committee's members voted down both the Dodd and Hruska bills. Dodd stormed out of the hearing furious. "It is now obvious that the opponents of gun laws now before this Congress, and particularly to my proposed amendment to the Federal Firearms Act, do not really want any gun law at all," he exclaimed.[53] Over the next few weeks, Dodd pleaded with his fellow committee members for a second round of voting. This time, however, he was going to ensure that one of the two bills made it out of committee. While he was hopeful that he would acquire enough votes to advance his bill, S. 1592, he devised a contingency plan if it did not—a plan where his bill's supporters would all vote in favor of the Hruska bill. This would ensure that a mail-order firearms control bill would move out of committee, and hopefully to the Senate floor. It was there that Dodd would offer his bill as a substitute for the Hruska bill [54]

At the Senate Judiciary Committee hearing held on September 22, Dodd's plan went into motion. After failing to secure enough votes for S. 1592, Dodd and his supporters successfully advanced Hruska's bill out of committee by a vote of 9 to 4. For a time, it appeared that the Senate was finally poised to take up firearms control. But Hruska upended Dodd's plan by first stalling publication of the committee report, followed by leveraging the Rules of the Senate to run out the remaining legislative calendar leading into the long election recess. The political riff between Dodd and Hruska became so divisive that Senate Majority Leader Mike Mansfield was asked to intervene. What everyone ultimately agreed to was that Hruska would allow Dodd to obtain unanimous consent on the Senate floor to refer S. 1592 back to the Senate Commerce Committee for consideration before the 90th Congress.

Iowa senator and NRA congressional surrogate Bourke B. Hickenlooper relished in the outcome, writing, "The Dodd gun bill is dead as a prehistoric Indian for this Congress, at least, and if they have a gun bill in the next Congress, which I assume they will have, it nevertheless will have to be refiled, re-referred to committee and go through the committee process. Probably there will be less steam behind it [than] there was behind the Dodd bill because of the emotions of the Kennedy death."[55] Unbeknownst to Hickenlooper, the political weight of President Johnson was once more about to be brought to bear on the firearms control issue.

On January 10, 1967, in delivering the State of the Union, President Johnson promised that his administration would work with Congress to enact "strict controls on the sale of firearms."[56] Weeks later, in his crime message, Johnson unveiled just how "strict" the firearms controls would be. His proposed measures included (1) prohibiting "certain mail order sales and shipments of firearms, except between federal licensees'" (2) prohibiting "over-the-counter sales of firearms . . . to any person who does not reside in the state in which the federal licensee does business"; (3) prohibiting the sale of handguns to anyone under twenty-one, as well as prohibiting the sale of rifles and shotguns to anyone under eighteen; and (4) curbing the importation of surplus military firearms. While Johnson acknowledged that his measures were "no panacea for the danger of human irrationality and violence in our society," he also felt that they would ultimately help "keep lethal weapons out of the wrong hands." To those concerned sportsmen, hunters, shooters, and firearms owners, he offered the assurance that his proposed measures would "not curtail ownership of firearms used for sport or self-protection." But then he made a reference to the very law that heightened the gun rights community's worst fears—that his proposed measures would be strengthened once the states "pass firearms laws legislation and licensing laws similar to the Sullivan Law in New York."[57]

Dodd quickly obliged President Johnson's request by refiling his bill, which for the 90th Congress was S. 1. And for the first time, with the full political weight of President Johnson behind that bill, there was a companion bill filed in the House of Representatives, H.R. 5384. Sponsored by New York representative Emanuel Celler, this bill was scheduled to be fast-tracked through the House Judiciary Committee, which Celler chaired. The NRA and its allies were now suddenly faced with what they saw as a full-blown assault on the Second Amendment, or what they referred to as the "recurring fever" of "anti-gun legislation."[58]

To counter the unified efforts of Dodd, Celler, and President Johnson, the NRA stuck with its tried-and-true playbook for defeating firearms controls. First, with the help of its congressional surrogates, the NRA refiled the same firearms bills that it had sponsored during the 89th Congress. Second, it made sure to cast the Dodd-Celler bill as making criminals out of law-abiding gun owners.[59] In one American Rifleman editorial, the NRA went so far to falsely claim that the "so-called 'crime control' bills [introduced by Dodd and Celler] would saddle millions of law-abiding Americans who buy guns with the possibility of being jailed on the basis of supposed intent or 'knowledge or reason cause to believe' that a firearms crime is being committed." The NRA closed out the editorial by noting that the passage of the Dodd-Celler bill would reverse "American justice back to the days of the witchcraft trials."[60] Finally, the NRA played to the gun rights community's fear that organized anti-gun forces were responsible for the assault on the Second Amendment: "The inescapable conclusion, in the opinion of NRA officials, is that the American public is being misled by one of the biggest propaganda campaigns in human history."[61] But contrary to the NRA's claim, there were no such organized anti-gun propaganda campaign afoot. Not to mention, not a single firearms control advocacy group had yet to be established.

The belief that there was an organized anti-gun conspiracy to disarm the country had long been a fixture within gun rights literature.[62] Claims of communist plots or influence were commonplace. For instance, the editors of Guns & Ammo surmised that "certain elements such as the Communists" were the ones pushing anti-gun bills on the American people. "It is high time that the average citizen ask himself if there could be other deeper and more insidious motives behind the anti-gun campaigns than the high-sounding but illogical purpose of 'helping to prevent the criminal use of firearms,'" claimed the editors.[63] Meanwhile, the Association to Preserve

Our Right to Keep and Bear Arms (APORKBA) warned in one of its newsletters that Celler had to be "aiding the Communist Conspiracy." As evidence of Celler's alleged treason, APORKBA supplied a list of political organizations, or, in its words, alleged "Communist fronts and enterprises," in which Celler was personally affiliated.[64] A separate APORKBA newsletter advanced an even more outlandish claim—political "liberals" were being influenced by the Soviet Union. According to the newsletter, the Soviet Union was working behind the scenes with liberals to manipulate "working class" labor unions, minorities, and even the civil rights movement, all in effort to usurp longstanding conservative American values through the spreading of communist propaganda. And with the United States military fighting in Vietnam, the "only defense left" for Americans from this alleged Soviet threat was the "local police and the armed citizens defending their own homes and families." But should the Soviets succeed in implementing their anti–gun law strategy, Americans would lose their last line of defense and subsequently pave the way for a "Soviet America."[65]

Alongside the alleged communist plots were gun rights claims of lawmakers being compromised by secret anti-gun lobbyists, who of course did not exist except in the minds of several gun rights supporters.[66] These gun rights supporters firmly believed that anti-gun lobbyists were funding a propaganda campaign to deprive Americans of their Second Amendment rights. And once President Johnson became a leading proponent of firearms controls, some gun rights supporters came to believe that anti-gun lobbyists had infiltrated the highest echelons of government, or that President Johnson was in fact the secret head of the anti-gun lobby. Certainly, most within the gun rights community viewed Dodd as "the Number One Enemy of gun-minded people."[67] The editors of Guns Magazine, however, decided to float the conspiracy theory that Dodd was merely a political puppet of President Johnson. They created the false persona that Johnson was doing everything within his "well organized" and "well financed" power to make criminals of law-abiding firearms owners. This allegedly included Johnson manipulating the print media, ensuring "one-sided coverage by national broadcasting networks," and making up new rules "under the auspices of the government."[68] Some of the NRA's congressional surrogates even entertained some of this conspiratorial gun rights nonsense.[69] Senator Hickenlooper, for one, postulated that officials within the Johnson administration were behind a "concentrated movement in the country to disarm the public."[70]

The NRA did little to dispel these and other conspiracy theories. Whatever motivated gun rights supporters to political action did not matter so long as the NRA remained the influencer-in-chief. Nothing irritated the NRA's leadership more than when political upstarts attempted to interfere with their political monopoly. Neal Knox, who served as the editor of *Gun Week*—a burgeoning Midwest gun rights publication—was one such upstart. Generally, Knox and the other editors of *Gun Week* carried forward the NRA's message with little pushback.[71] But every now and then, when deemed necessary, they criticized the NRA for being politically soft, thus irritating the NRA's leadership.[72] One such instance occurred in April 1967, when Massachusetts senator Ted Kennedy met with the NRA board of directors behind closed doors.[73] Kennedy, a leading proponent of firearms controls, had requested to speak before the NRA's annual meeting attendees.[74] The NRA's leadership declined the request and instead invited Kennedy to privately meet with the NRA board of directors, in an "atmosphere not conditioned by publicity."[75] Kennedy obliged.[76] The day the two sides met, Kennedy, in a prepared speech, assured the NRA board of directors that Congress would pass a firearms control bill "with the assistance of your members or in spite of them."[77] Afterward, he distributed copies of his speech to the media, and the follow-on news coverage was overwhelmingly supportive of Kennedy's message.

Knox and the other *Gun Week* editors blasted the NRA's leadership for the handling of the affair as the first "in a series of tactical retreats." Even worse, according to Knox, was that Kennedy emerged "as a victorious anti-gun gladiator in the eyes of the press and public." What Knox and the other editors at *Gun Week* did not understand is why the NRA did not allow Kennedy to speak before the entire 1967 NRA convention, particularly in a debate-like format against an "articulate, knowledgeable NRA spokesman":

> Since Sen. Kennedy is not an authority upon gun control legislation, we doubt seriously that he would have been willing to participate in a debate. This would have put Sen. Kennedy in a "hot spot," politically. He would have been faced with the choice of being ridiculed for his failure to accept the debate or taking the risk of getting his ears pinned back in public

while allowing the arguments against prohibitive gun control legislation to be publicized.[78]

In a private letter to Knox, NRA president Harold W. Glassen outlined why the NRA decided to meet with Kennedy privately. Glassen took particular issue with Knox labeling the Kennedy meeting a "fiasco" and claiming that "N.R.A. leadership need[ed] education." Glassen closed his letter by writing, "I do not object to criticism and say again it is your privilege, but it does our cause no good to undermine the confidence of our membership and others who look to us for leadership."[79]

The dissention created by Knox, *Gun Week*, and the Kennedy "fiasco" did not last long.[80] For in the May 1967 issue of *American Rifleman*, the NRA published an editorial that quickly changed the national conversation on gun rights. Titled "Who Guards America's Homes?," the editorial cast a dystopian picture of "unsettled times" where "courts pamper criminals," "too many Americans revel in all sorts of law-breaking," "law enforcement officers are only popular on television," and the National Guard is being called upon to "quell riots and preserve order." America's cultural fabric, according to the NRA, was tearing at the seams. And should the National Guard suddenly deploy overseas to fight a war, the NRA queried, "Who then guards the doors of American homes from senseless savagery and pillaging?" The NRA's answer to its self-imposed question was armed citizens. It was armed citizens' support of "law and order, whether as a civilian member of the *posse comitatus* or as one of the unorganized militia" that would serve as a "community stabilizer." But firearms controls, such as those proposed in the Dodd-Celler bill, would end up "seriously reduc[ing] the possession and availability of firearms for home protection."[81] Therefore, according to the NRA, it was imperative that every sportsman, hunter, gun owner, and liberty-loving citizen oppose firearms controls at all costs.

Several news outlets seized on the "Who Guards America's Homes" editorial as evidence that the NRA was promoting vigilantism and extremism. The NRA had already been linked to the Minutemen, a heavily armed extremist group that believed communism would soon take over the United States. Indeed, the reporting that many Minutemen were also NRA members was correct. What several news outlets either forgot or willfully ignored, however, was that the NRA had already rejected any Minutemen affiliation two years earlier, as well as any affiliation with known extremist groups. "If we catch any of our members belonging to the Minutemen, Ku Klux Klan, Black Muslims or any vigilante organization they are put out immediately," stated NRA executive vice-president Franklin L. Orth in a press release in 1965.[82] In fact, opposing political extremism had been a requirement to join the NRA since 1940. Additionally, the NRA was on record supporting legislation that prohibited the sale or transfer of firearms to any "member of a subversive organization."[83] And while it was rare within the pages of American Rifleman to see anyone pictured who was not white or Caucasian, at no point did the NRA ever take the position of excluding any American citizen from the organization on the basis of race, color, or creed.[84]

Yet extremists, like the militantly anticommunist Minutemen, used American Rifleman editorials like "Who Guards America's Homes?" to spread their political message.[85] The same was true for many segregationists and white supremacists.[86] As Ben A. Franklin, a widely circulated New York Times columnist, noted at the time, out of the "11 urban disasters" cited in the editorial as "mob action on a scale unprecedented in the modern United States," coincidentally nine were "clashes" involving predominantly Black communities.[87] This type of racial cause-and-effect was music to the ears of segregationists and white supremacists.[88]

Interestingly, while Franklin and others saw a hint of racism in "Who Guards America's Homes?," at least one newspaper columnist read the editorial as promoting the Black Panthers' creed of going publicly armed anywhere and everywhere.[89] A Black Panther document titled "What We Want Now! What We Believe" included the following: "We believe we can end policy brutality in our black community by organizing black self-defense groups that are dedicated to defending our black community from racist police oppression and brutality. The Second Amendment of the Constitution of the United States gives us a right to bear arms. We therefore believe that all black people should arm themselves for self-defense."[90] However, to link any of the NRA's literature with the Black Panthers' belief on the necessity of going publicly armed is misguided.[91] Indeed, the NRA was of the opinion that having more armed citizens was preferred to having less as a criminal deterrent.[92] This policy preference was frequently conveyed in the pages of American Rifleman.[93] The NRA, however, made sure to hedge its preference of having more citizens armed on the conditions that the person be law-abiding, properly trained in the use and handling of firearms, and

FIGURE 5.1 At a December 10, 1967, Ku Klux Klan rally in Montgomery, Alabama, a Klan member held a sign containing several political mantras. Included were gun rights mantras—"Register Communists Not Firearms" and "Don't Worry, a Disarmed U.S. Will Protect You"—showing how gun rights advocacy sometimes intersected with extremist ideology. The sign was one of several anti-firearms-control signs Klansmen carried at the rally. Reproduced with permission of the Alabama Department of Archives and History.

have a justifiable reason for doing so.[94] Up until 1985, the NRA denounced, with particular force, the promiscuous or habitual toting of firearms.[95]

What further undermines any link between the Black Panthers' belief in habitually going armed and the NRA is the fact that the latter helped draft the legislation responsible for disarming—that is, in public places—the former. On May 2, 1967, a group of thirty Black Panthers appeared visibly armed at the California State Capitol Building to protest a firearms control bill, A.B. 1591, aimed at prohibiting the carrying of loaded firearms in public places. The bold political action of the Black Panthers that day all but ensured the bill's enactment, as well as the enactment of other amendments to California's firearms laws.[96] Given this fact, in recent years several writers have either stated or implied that A.B. 1591 is inherently racist.[97] This includes historian Carol Anderson, who claims that the push for firearms controls in the 1960s was in large part driven by white fears of armed Blacks, and that A.B. 1591 was specifically "designed to ensure" that the Black Panthers would no longer be "law-abiding citizens." What substantiated historical evidence does she provide to support her claim? A newspaper article, which reported how Willie L. Brown, Jr., a Black California assemblyman, surmised that A.B. 1591 "*might* be racially inspired."[98] However, what Anderson leaves out is that Brown also noted in the same newspaper article that A.B. 1591 did not have any "racial implications." Fellow Black California assemblyman Leon Ralph concurred with Brown, noting, "I think [this bill] is aimed at Nazis, the KKK, the Minutemen, and others, and that is should be applied equally to all, black or white."[99]

As for Anderson's broader claim that the push for firearms controls in the 1960s was in part driven by white fears of armed Blacks, so far there is not enough in the historical record to lend it academic credibility.[100] Certainly, racism in the United States was rampant in the 1960s. Additionally, it is fair to conclude that there were whites and white communities (some racist at that) who were fearful of armed Blacks, just as many Blacks and Black communities were fearful of armed whites. The fears of Blacks and Black communities were particularly justified given the long, tragic U.S. history of white violence toward people of color. However, for Anderson or any other writer to historically tie either group's fear as a principal or key motivation for the legislative push for additional firearms controls in the 1960s is an evidentiary bridge too far. There just is not any evidence in the legislative record that gives it credence, nor any evidence in constituent correspondence to lawmakers that supports such a claim.[101]

This is even true for California A.B. 1591. What Black assemblymen such as Brown and Ralph knew was the Black Panthers were not the only group A.B. 1591 was aimed at.[102] It was well-known that in addition to the Black Panthers, several white suburban communities had formed their own armed patrols in contravention to the requests of local law enforcement.[103] As Don Mulford, the California assemblyman who drafted A.B. 1591 with the support of the NRA, noted, "Let me assure you . . . that there are no racial overtones in this measure. There are many groups that have been active in Californian with loaded weapons in public places and this bill is directed against all of them."[104]

Of course, it is historically indisputable that but for the actions of the Black Panthers on May 2, 1967, it is unlikely that A.B. 1591 would have been enacted as quickly as it was.[105] Yet the fact remains that it is was the NRA that helped draft the bill and subsequently endorsed its passage.[106] "This legislation was specifically designed with the help of the National Rifle Association to protect our constitutional right to bear arms and yet to assist the law enforcement people who asked for this bill do to something about the armed bands of citizens who are walking our public streets and in public places with loaded weapons," stated Mulford in a letter defending the bill's passage.[107] In addition to the NRA, California governor Ronald Reagan, who in part ran his gubernatorial campaign on a gun rights platform, expressed support for Mulford's bill by echoing the NRA's position on transporting firearms.[108] "I don't know of any sportsman who leaves his home with a gun to go out into the field to hunt or for target shooting who carries their guns loaded," stated Reagan, adding, "The first thing any real sportsman learns is to carry an empty gun until he gets to the place where he's going to do the shooting."[109]

In addition to stirring media controversy, the "Who Guards America's Homes?" editorial resulted in several NRA members writing letters to the organization venting their frustration. Some members expressed unease over the NRA's membership-screening process, or lack of process, which was nothing more than requiring an applicant to sign an oath of allegiance to the U.S. government.[110] Other members took to criticizing the NRA for publishing the editorial and threatened to leave. But rather than heed these members' concerns and politically tone down the anti-firearms-control rhetoric, the NRA's leadership decided to stay the course. Indeed, although the NRA received an uptick in criticism from its members for the "Who Guards America's Homes?" editorial, most letters—those from the newer, more ardent anti-firearms-control members—were supportive.[111] And so long as overall membership and *American Rifleman* circulation continued to increase, there was no discernable reason for the NRA to change its political calculation.[112] Moreover, the NRA's leadership was well experienced in turning any public relations negative into a political positive. For instance, in response to the negative publicity received for the "Who Guards America's Homes?" editorial, the NRA resorted to its tried-and-true tactic of exploiting political division. The way the NRA's leadership sold it, the organization's legislative policies, ardent belief in the Second Amendment, and support from the "most law-abiding group" of American citizens were not the problem.[113] The problem was the "anti-gun element" seeking to disparage the NRA as a ploy to pass firearms control legislation. They were the *real* "fanatics" and "extremists determined to destroy what we know and treasure as the American way of life."[114] "What really disturbs us . . . is that the proponents of strict gun control legislation believe that the way to pass their bill is to attack those who believe otherwise," stated NRA president Harold W. Glassen in a speech before the National Press Club, adding, "This is not the American way, and we will fight these tactics even harder than the Bill itself."[115]

It was at the NRA's 96th annual meeting, held in early April 1967 that Glassen formally assumed the NRA presidency from Harlon B. Carter.[116] In doing so, Glassen blasted all the major newspaper writers for having "thrown in with the anti-gun lobby." What particularly irked him was how the writers "minimize[d] or even ridicule[d] the Second Amendment but scream[ed] to high heaven if ever any law or any regulation is suggested which they feel might infringe the rights of freedom of the press." "I have never seen any of the big papers mention that the Second Amendment might well have been and probably was placed immediately following the First Amendment with the idea of making enforcement of the first possible," he stated. Glassen was well aware that he could do little to stop the newspapers from reporting the facts or expressing their opinions.[117] It was their constitutional right. Glassen could, however, shore up the NRA's "war" posture. With this goal in mind, he reassured membership that the NRA would not "whistle in the dark":

We have faced great odds before. The greatest danger in my opinion is l'ennui, fatigue of our members, the feeling among some that "something is going to be passed." Let us be sure, let us be confident and let us see to it that that "something" is not something that carries the seeds of destruction of the National Rifle Association. . . .

. . . It has been said by I know not whom "that he who makes no mistakes does too little of tasks too simple." I know that the tasks in front of me are not simple and I know that I intend not to do too little. Therefore you may anticipate and I know there will be mistakes made. Much that faces us her has no simple answer and will require calculated risks. I feel that I have your confidence so that we may aggressively proceed knowing that you will understand that chances must be taken.[118]

Despite Glassen's promise of an "aggressive" approach, the NRA's political playbook initially did not change all that much. The organization continued to advance its slippery-slope argument that one firearms control was one too many. According to the NRA, history was ripe with examples where one firearms control led to another, and another, until the anti-gun forces achieved their ultimate objective of firearms confiscation. Additionally, it continued to advance the argument that the strict enforcement of existing firearms laws was the best solution to stopping firearms-related violence and crime. The NRA and its "official family" claimed that as of 1965 there were twenty thousand firearms laws spanning across the country.[119] Yet the estimate was something that the NRA seemingly created out of thin air. This is because for that number to hold true, in 1965 every state would have had to maintain an improbable four hundred firearms laws.[120] Even if every state subdivision's laws were included in the twenty thousand estimate, an estimate of four hundred firearms laws per state was the highest of estimates. And it falls apart when one considers how smaller states—for example, New Hampshire, Delaware, and Connecticut—would not come anywhere close to four hundred firearms laws, thus requiring larger states—for example, California, Texas, and Alaska—to have substantially more than four hundred such laws.[121]

Under Glassen's leadership, there were indeed other longstanding gun rights mantras that the NRA advanced to stall and defeat the passage of unwanted firearms controls. But ever since the wave of negative publicity the organization received following President Kennedy's assassination, its leadership knew it was equally important that the NRA take a "positive approach"—that is, put forward firearms legislation that was agreeable to the sporting, hunting, and shooting sports. Thus, for the newly elected 90th Congress, its legislative plan was not all that different from that of the 89th Congress. Yet for the purpose of political fanfare, in a press release Glassen touted the plan for the 90th Congress as going "far beyond any previous legislation that has had the NRA support."[122] Another NRA official described the plan as a "moderate, middle-of-the-road approach, one that provides for legislation that is sensible, designed to curb the misuse of firearms, and that will be effective, without interfering with the rights of the capable American citizen to keep and bear arms."[123] What Glassen and other officials omitted was that the only distinguishing feature between the NRA's plan for the 90th Congress and that of the 89th Congress was the former put forward a four-point plan rather than a three-point plan. Still, both plans advanced the exact same legislative agenda of (1) amending the NFA by banning "destructive devices" such as antitank guns, bazookas, and rockets; (2) federalizing state mail-order firearms laws; (3) enacting federal mandatory minimums for felonies committed with firearms; and (4) banning all handgun sales to minors and requiring a sworn statement for every mail-order and over-the-counter out-of-state handgun purchase.[124]

Given that the legislative substance of the NRA's plans for the 90th and 89th Congresses were virtually identical, both maintained the same deficiencies. Neither succeeded in imposing even modest burdens on criminals, minors, or other prohibited classes in their attempts to illegally obtain mail-order firearms. The only striking impact that either of the NRA's legislative plans would have imposed was the federalizing of existing state firearms laws. And for those members of Congress who were politically moderate on the firearms control issue, this was a nonstarter. As Oregon senator Wayne L. Morse wrote in a letter to constituents: "I am very much in disagreement with proposals that the commission of a crime with a gun be made a federal crime. Such a statute would bring federal law enforcement into every community of the nation, and the federal police would soon replace state, county, and city police."[125]

The fact that political moderates did not embrace the NRA's four-point plan was not all that important. What mattered most to the NRA was that unwanted federal firearms controls, such as the Dodd-Celler bill, languished in committee.[126] The four-point plan helped ensure this outcome. And should any of the four points of the NRA's legislative plan make their way out of a committee, the NRA was confident that one of its loyal congressional surrogates would alter or amend the bill as instructed. The organization was particularly confident of bills S. 1854 and S. 1853, both of which were introduced by Senator Hruska on the NRA's behalf.[127] S. 1854 sought to amend the NFA by banning certain "destructive devices.[128] Meanwhile, S. 1853 was almost identical to S. 3767, which Hruska had introduced during the 89th Congress. S. 1853 stipulated that every mail-order hand-gun purchaser must fill out an affidavit to be filed with their local law enforcement agency prior to the handgun being shipped. The NRA applauded S. 1853 as a "practical attempt to give the federal government authority to control or regulate the interstate commerce in handguns and to aid the states by prohibiting shipments in violation of their own laws."[129]

From the time the NRA's four-point plan was unveiled until the close of 1967, it is fair to say that the gun rights movement was winning the "war" on firearms controls. As the year went on, more and more senators expressed support for Hruska's S. 1853 over Dodd's S. 1, including both the Senate majority and minority leader. This turn of events compelled Dodd to amend S. 1 in a way that would allow the states to individually exempt the interstate sale of rifles and shotguns. The interstate sale of handguns, however, would still be prohibited under federal law except among licensed manufacturers, distributors, and dealers. While Dodd's amendment proved to be enough to get S. 1 out of the Senate Judiciary Subcommittee he chaired, there was broad consensus on Capitol Hill that it would never make it out of full committee.[130] Celler's companion bill in the House of Repre-sentatives was not doing much better. While that bill, like Dodd's, was able to make it out of subcommittee, the odds of it being voted out of full com-mittee were slim to none.[131]

Entering 1968 the NRA's four-point plan, and overall political playbook for that matter, continued to be effective in beating back the Dodd-Celler bill and any other undesired firearms controls. The NRA was also making significant political headway at the state and local levels. The NRA had become so politically confident that it took to questioning whether the national polls indicating strong support for firearms controls were in fact valid. If, the NRA queried, the national polls were indeed accurate, then why were the American people not urging their representatives to act? The NRA then urged the proponents of firearms controls to stop hiding behind the polls—which the NRA thought were severely misleading and poorly conducted—and inform the American people of the truth. It was time, it said, that the proponents of firearms controls "recognize that the demand . . ., if there is one, has decreased as fast as people realize that the harassment of law-abiding gun owners will not reduce crime."[132]

Although the NRA publicly expressed confidence in its fight against fire-arms controls, behind the scenes its leadership was wary of how the

THE LONG ARMS OF THE LAWS

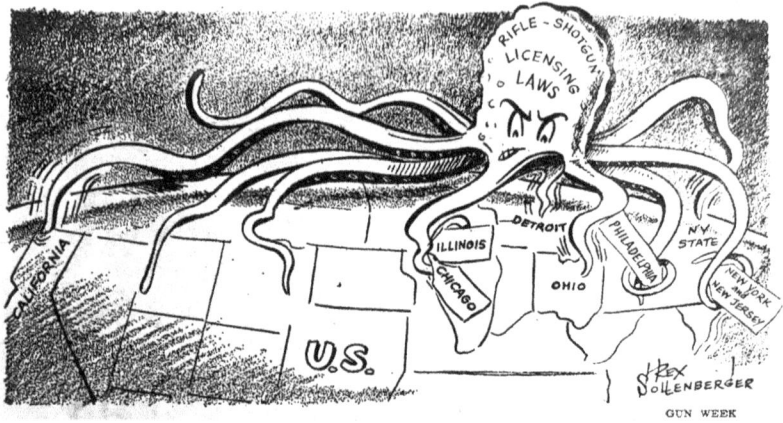

FIGURE 5.2 Political cartoon in *Gun Week*, February 23, 1968. In early 1968, although the NRA and its allies were winning the "war" on firearms controls, it was important to keep the gun rights community engaged. Here, that community was reminded of how unwanted firearms controls in certain states and cities could serve as models for others. Reprinted with permission from the Second Amendment Foundation.

organization was losing its ideological hold on the gun rights movement. It was becoming increasingly common for the NRA to receive mail criticizing the organization for being too defensive or not aggressive enough. Moreover, new, non-NRA-affiliated gun rights organizations were increasingly chipping away at the NRA's prestige. These new organizations were not supportive of the NRA's politically nuanced, "positive" approach to gun rights advocacy. Rather, they supported what is referred to today as Second Amendment absolutism—the belief that any regulation, no matter how minor, on the ownership, use, or availability of firearms is a constitutional infringement on the right to arms. This absolutist interpretation of the Second Amendment was a far cry from the NRA's longstanding "reasonable restrictions" and "right as a responsibility" interpretation.[133] Thus, while the NRA was performing its political balancing act between gun rights advocacy and its shooting and conservation programs, these new organizations were full-blown, unrelenting gun rights advocates. Moreover, they made sure to distinguish themselves from the NRA by constantly feeding their supporters the hyperpoliticized, political gun rights "red meat" they craved, particularly the claim that proponents of firearms controls were secretly colluding to deny Americans their right to keep and bear arms.[134]

The NRA responded to its new competition by stepping up its own political rhetoric. NRA members and the gun rights movement were now being increasingly told things like there was a "concentrated campaign being carried on these days to deprive Americans of . . . the right to keep and bear arms,"[135] or that members of Congress and the press were intentionally making false statements about the NRA simply to "discredit the association and the hundreds of thousands and dedicated and patriotic members,"[136] or that the "Kennedys and Dodd" were outright liars and the only thing standing in the way of real, sensible firearms legislation.[137] On April 6, 1968, before the NRA's ninety-seventh annual meetings held in Boston, Massachusetts, NRA president Glassen delivered a speech highlighting these very themes. He informed the attendees that not only was the NRA blossoming despite being "under attack from many quarters," but also its position on firearms controls was increasingly being seen by the public, lawmakers, and the media as the only one with any "merit":

> We [the NRA] are winning the fight through reason. We are regaining our respect as one of the nation's most patriotic organizations . . . as law-abiding sportsmen who are vitally concerned with the criminal use of firearms.
>
> We are and always have been advocates of proper firearms legislation which would be effective in keeping guns out of the hands of those who should not have them. We have proposed such a program, and we have the support in the Congress to see that it is carried into law. . . . As I see it, we have but only one way to go. Up.[138]

But little did Glassen know, both the NRA's public persona and the politics of firearms control were about to change forever.

6

1968

Firearms Control Becomes an Election Issue

At the start of 1968, it appeared that the National Rifle Association (NRA) was on the cusp of having a banner year.[1] The organization recorded its best one-year membership increase, as well as its best one-year increase in circulation for *American Rifleman*.[2] It was also winning the fight against firearms controls, whether it be in Congress or in state and local assemblies. Four straight years of critical news media coverage had tarnished much of the NRA's longstanding positive image, but the fact remained that the group's political strategy on firearms controls was achieving the desired result. The NRA had grown so confident in its political strategy that its messaging was becoming more and more bold. For instance, in late January, after New York senator Robert F. Kennedy delivered a speech before the University of Buffalo criticizing the organization for opposing reasonable firearms controls, NRA executive vice president Franklin L. Orth fired back and accused the senator of having a personal "vendetta" against the NRA. Orth decried Kennedy for orchestrating a "smear" campaign against a "great American organization aimed at supporting the national defense and law enforcement posture of this nation."[3] Months later, he again called out the New York senator as well as his brother, Massachusetts senator Edward M. Kennedy. This time, Orth alleged that it was not the NRA but the "Kennedy brothers" who were responsible for blocking sensible firearms controls.[4]

In addition to criticizing the Kennedys, the NRA called out the entire television industry for what it saw as blatant hypocrisy. In an *American Rifleman* article titled "Are We Really So Violent?," the NRA argued that it was not firearms, nor their ready availability, that was to blame for the precipitous increase in firearms-related crimes and deaths. Rather, it was the violent programming choices of television executives:

> The upswing in violence in recent years coincides with . . . television's growing incitement to murder and mayhem by abnormal, exaggerated emphasis on the misuse of firearms and all matter of diabolical attacks. Ironically, some of the same networks that have smeared legitimate firearms ownership under the guise of protecting the American public from guns have televised gun play, gore and horror galore. This bombardment, if we may use the word, approaches a 7-day, 24-hour saturation of the American mind with the nation that gunplay is good clean fun.[5]

The "blame the television executives for violence" argument quickly became a staple in the NRA's "blame everything but guns" messaging arsenal (and remains a staple to this day). For in a separate *American Rifleman* article published later that year, the NRA alleged that "never before in the long history of mankind has the human mind been subjected to the explosive effect of such much violence, viciousness and depravity before its eyes" or have the "goriest crimes been projected into the American home in gruesome detail as news, and then warmed over to regale as 'entertainment' in fiction form." The NRA then called on television executives to "make an immediate contribution . . . toward reducing violence" by "refraining from sensationalism."[6]

While the NRA was accusing television executives of causing an increase in national violence, the political winds continued to fortuitously blow in the organization's favor. In late January 1968 the National Advisory Commission on Civil Disorders (NACCD), which had been formed in response to the urban riots of 1967, determined that the instances of gunfire during said riots were "highly exaggerated" and that most of the reported gunfire appeared to come at the behest of law enforcement officials and National Guardsmen, not armed civilians.[7] It was a finding that severely undercut the arguments of firearms control proponents, who had claimed there was an undoubted link between the riot gunfire and lax firearms laws.[8] But undoubtedly the most fortuitous turn of events was the news that President Lyndon B. Johnson was open to compromising on firearms controls in his Omnibus Crime Control and Safe Streets Act. The NRA surmised that if Johnson was indeed willing to back a compromise, it was only a matter of time before Connecticut senator Thomas J. Dodd, Maryland senator Joseph D. Tydings, New York representative Emanuel Celler, and the other firearms control–supporting Democrats would have to follow suit. The NRA capitalized on the news by touting its record of supporting "reasonable" firearms controls. "The NRA consistently has taken a responsible position on gun control legislation," stated Executive Vice President Orth, adding, "We have actively sought to reach agreement with those who have been critical of our position, but unfortunately they seem more anxious to continue their irresponsible attacks than to enact an effective bill."[9]

Come April, as the Senate Judiciary Committee was deliberating the Omnibus Crime Control and Safe Streets Act, Nebraska senator Roman Hruska was laying the groundwork for his NRA-backed S. 1853 to be offered as an amendment. On April 2, before the Senate floor, several cosponsors of Hruska's S. 1853 took turns lambasting Dodd's S. 1 as the wrong approach to regulating firearms. Utah senator Frank E. Moss, for one, issued lengthy remarks as to how S. 1 disproportionately burdened rural firearms owners. South Carolina senator Strom Thurmond followed by highlighting the "legitimate" uses of firearms. Meanwhile, Iowa senator Bourke B. Hickenlooper submitted for the congressional record a study by the National Shooting Sports Foundation (NSSF) as proof that firearms were used in only "3 percent of . . . serious crimes, and in perhaps one-half percent of our total crime picture." As for Hruska himself, the Nebraska senator attacked S. 1 as a prohibition on the mail-order purchase of all firearms. He then held up his amendment as a better solution: "[S. 1853] is a strict bill. It is a proper bill. It is capable of effective enforcement. It goes as far as any such measure can go without ceasing to be realistic, and without unduly burdening or interfering with law-abiding owners and users of firearms."[10]

Two days later, on April 4, the Senate Judiciary Committee convened a hearing on the Omnibus Crime Control and Safe Streets Act. Therein Dodd tried offering S. 1 as an amendment. The committee voted 9 to 4 against it. He then offered a modified version of S. 1, which provided every state legislature the discretion to exempt itself from any of the bill's long gun mail-order restrictions. This too was defeated, by an 8 to 5 vote. Finally,

Dodd offered a severely water-downed version of S. 1, which removed every mention of long guns. This resulted in a 6 to 6 tie, allowing the amendment to be reconsidered at a subsequent hearing.[11]

But within a matter of hours of the Senate Judiciary Committee adjourning, a groundswell of support for strict firearms controls was unleashed following the assassination of civil rights leader Martin Luther King, Jr. While standing on the second-floor balcony of the Lorraine Motel in Memphis, Tennessee, King was struck in the neck by a sniper's bullet. He was immediately rushed to the hospital, where he was pronounced dead. Shock and rage over King's death sparked urban rioting across the country. Much like after the assassination of President Kennedy in 1963, there were increased public calls for Congress to enact firearms controls.[12] Dodd and other firearms control proponents politically seized on the moment by holding up King's assassination as another example of unchecked, readily available firearms gone wrong.[13] "There are too many guns too easily available to too many people who are ready to use them," stated Dodd upon hearing the news of King's assassination, adding, "I warned the committee of the disaster that is coming if something is not done."[14] Days later, after having personally toured the damage caused by the riots in the District of Columbia, he issued another statement that singled out the NRA as the reason for congressional inaction on firearms control:

> [The NRA] tells its members to: "Arm themselves to prepare for the coming riots." And the sale of guns rose 25% last year. Meanwhile, back in the Senate, the firearms legislation that I have been fighting for was stalled for 5 years while racists and extremist groups on both sides of the civil rights issue have divided the country into two armed camps. I feel that the assassination of Dr. King will mark the beginning of a new level of civil warfare. We are facing an internal disaster of horrifying proportions. I can only hope that this tragedy has jarred the Congress into a state of awareness that it must disarm the bigots, the racists, the extremists and the criminals before it is too late.[15]

The NRA's immediate response to the King assassination and the follow-on calls for firearms controls was to stay the political course.[16] Much like after the assassination of President Kennedy, the NRA cast the King assassination as one of those events that "no law . . . could have prevented,"[17] the follow-on outcry for firearms controls as nothing more than misguided emotionalism,[18] and the national polls showing large majorities of Americans supporting firearms controls as "bought-and-paid-for" by anti-gun television executives. Additionally, the NRA pointed to the chief proponents of firearms controls as the ones really responsible for Congress failing to pass "realistic and practical" firearms legislation—and by "realistic and practical" the NRA meant the provisions within Hruska's S. 1853.[19]

It is fair to say that the NRA was in both political and public relations crisis mode. Just days before King was assassinated, the NRA had boasted how public support for firearms controls was dissipating.[20] Yet now, following the Senate Judiciary Committee's decision to reconvene and approve Dodd's water-downed, no long gun restrictions version of S. 1 as an amendment to the Omnibus Crime Control and Safe Streets Act, the NRA was scrambling to defeat a vote on the Senate floor.[21]

Fortunately, the group's officials had prepared for such a scenario. The NRA's plan was rather simple—bolster political support for Hruska's S. 1853. The plan was executed on the very last day of its ninety-seventh annual convention.[22] Therein, NRA president Harold W. Glassen called for "solidarity among hunters, target shooters, conservationists, sportsmen and gun owners to obtain passage of sensible and practical gun legislation" like Hruska's S. 1853. He went on to state that those who "pay lip service to [the] NRA but criticize us for our stand on gun control legislation" are the "political gun bearers for the Kennedys and the Dodds regardless of their political affiliation." He closed his remarks by urging the gun rights community to form a "solid block of opposition" to Dodd's S.1.[23]

For the rest of April, the NRA and its allies worked diligently to bolster the political prospects of Hruska's S. 1853. This included reaching out to congressional surrogates about opposing Dodd's S. 1. At the same time, the NRA was forthright in casting Dodd as a political "demagogue" who relied on "emotional tragedies" and "parliamentary trick[s]" to advance legislation, including taking "advantage of the feelings of his colleagues in some tragedy like the assassination or killing of Dr. King."[24] The editors of *Gun Week* were equally dismissive of Dodd, accusing the Connecticut senator of peddling "distorted figures and outright lies" to advance S. 1.[25] Then there was NRA president Glassen, who in a series of speeches outlined several reasons why gun rights supporters must oppose Dodd's S.1. For instance, in a speech before the Comstock Rifle Club in Sacramento,

California, he likened Congress enacting S. 1 to "burning down a building because someone in there might be a criminal."[26] Days later in San Francisco, he dismissed the notion that additional firearms controls would have even the slightest effect on reducing violent crime: "A sick-minded assassin . . . is not likely to pause or be deterred by any manmade law," stated Glassen.[27]

While the NRA and its political allies worked hard to bolster Hruska's S. 1853, Dodd was preparing for the possibility that he might need to make further concessions to get S. 1 passed as an amendment to the Omnibus Crime Control and Safe Streets Act.[28] But Dodd's staff was against the idea. They warned Dodd not to make any more concessions on S. 1 or it would present the "disastrous" risk of losing the political support of not only President Johnson, but also many firearms control–supporting senators. Dodd was also warned not to fall for any of Hruska's overtures for legislative compromise, to include meriting any of Hruska's "frivolous and overly technical objections."[29] Dodd ultimately followed his staff's advice.

Entering May, both Dodd and the NRA stepped up their political rhetoric, each blaming the other for congressional inaction on firearms controls. Dodd urged the public to write their representatives and asked his colleagues to "stop cowering before the gun lobbies."[30] The NRA did the same by urging its nearly one million members to barrage Capitol Hill with angry letters. Over a period of two weeks, from May 3 to May 15, the issue of firearms control was intensely debated between members of Congress, newspaper editors, and the public.

It was on May 16 that the Senate scheduled its vote on the Omnibus Crime Control and Safe Streets Act. Both proponents and opponents of firearms controls were ready with their amendments. The initial series of amendments came from the proponents. The first, sponsored by Senators Edward M. Kennedy and Joseph D. Tydings, sought to ban the sale of all mail-order firearms. It failed by a vote of 53 to 29. The next amendment, sponsored by New York senator Jacob K. Javits, sought to regulate the mail-order sale of long guns through a presale affidavit procedure. It failed by a vote of 52 to 28. This was followed by sweeping amendment to ban the private purchase of all destructive devices. By a vote of 47 to 30 it too failed. Then came two amendments by firearms control opponents. The first was a proposal by Utah senator Wallace F. Bennett to require a mandatory federal sentence for anyone convicted of federal crimes of violence with a firearm. It failed by a voice vote. Then came the highly anticipated Hruska amendment, which would substitute S. 1583 for Dodd's S. 1. To the NRA's disappointment, the amendment failed by a vote of 45 to 37.[31]

On May 23, after all the procedural motions were settled, the Senate passed the Omnibus Crime Control and Safe Streets Act by a 72 to 4 vote.[32] Among those voting for the act were several NRA congressional surrogates, including Hruska. In a letter, Dodd thanked Hruska, writing, "Now that the gun fight at the Senate 'OK Corral' is about over, I want to tell you that I greatly respect and admire you for the way that you conducted yourself and, particularly, for the way you so courteously treated me in the course of the debate. I hope the next time we will be on the same side."[33]

Although Dodd and other firearms control proponents had reason to celebrate, it was uncertain whether the Omnibus Crime Control and Safe Streets Act would ever become law. This was because the House had passed an alternate version of the same act a year prior, and the differences between the House and Senate versions were not minor. The Senate version included several controversial items, such as reversing Supreme Court precedent on the admissibility of confessions as evidence and providing state and local police with sweeping wiretapping authorities.[34] Even President Johnson was on record warning that the Senate's version raised "grave constitutional questions."[35] This prompted speculation that should Congress ultimately proceed with the Senate's version of the Omnibus Crime Control and Safe Streets Act, Johnson would veto it. What further complicated matters was that the 1968 elections were rapidly approaching, and members of Congress in competitive districts were hoping to postpone voting on any hotly contested issues, to include firearms controls.

While the Senate and House leadership pondered the next political step, the presidential campaign to be Johnson's successor was in full swing. Vying for the Democratic nomination were Vice President Hubert H. Humphrey, Senator Eugene J. McCarthy of Minnesota, and Senator Robert F. Kennedy of New York.[36] As it pertained to the firearms control issue, neither Humphrey nor McCarthy had staked out a firm position. Indeed, given that Humphrey was the vice president, he was already on record supporting President Johnson's position on mail-order firearms controls— that is, so long as the controls did "not deny law-abiding citizens the use of firearms for their protection or pleasure."[37] As of late May, however, Humphrey's position had yet to be set in stone.[38] In fact, when the editors of *Gun Week* inquired about it, Humphrey's campaign staff drafted a largely noncommittal, middle-of-the-road response that acknowledged the legislative necessity of mail-order firearms controls but left the matter of any additional controls up to the wisdom of state and local governments. "What form [firearms controls] might take would depend upon the needs identified by officials of the jurisdiction concerned," the draft response stated, adding, "Since localities differ in population characteristics, some jurisdictions might want to adopt fairly stringent requirements for gun ownership whereas, in stable areas of low population density, the need for strong legislation might be warranted."[39] For some unknown reason, the draft response was never sent. It was not until July 9, amid the public fervor for additional firearms controls in the wake of Senator Robert F. Kennedy's assassination, that Humphrey's campaign finally provided the editors of *Gun Week* with a response that formally endorsed the concept of firearms registration.[40]

Prior to Senator Kennedy's assassination, the only Democrat vying for the presidency to stake out a firm campaign position was in fact Kennedy himself—his position being that strict firearms controls were necessary to reduce firearms-related crime and violence. On May 25, while campaigning in Roseburg, Oregon, for the state's primary, Kennedy brought up the firearms control issue after noticing a dozen or more anti–firearms registration signs where he was speaking. He stated to the attending crowd, "I understand a local radio station is saying Bobby Kennedy will take away your guns." A local gun rights advocate, S. J. Schoon, then made his way to the microphone and outlined why he believed the Omnibus Crime Control and Safe Streets Act would ultimately lead to federal firearms registration, followed by confiscation. Kennedy asked Schoon, "Does anything in the legislation say you can't have firearms?" "No," Schoon replied, to which Kennedy asked, "Do you think it makes sense for a 6-year-old or a criminal or an insane person to purchase firearms?" "No," Schoon again replied. Kennedy then quipped, "I'm very pleased to be here," followed by a sardonic laugh.[41]

Kennedy ended up losing the Oregon primary to McCarthy but went on to win both California and North Dakota six days later. On June 4, at the Ambassador Hotel in Los Angeles, two minutes before midnight, Kennedy delivered his victory speech. As he walked away from the podium and passed through the hotel kitchen to shake hands, applause erupted, and chants of "We want Bobby" rang throughout the hotel. Suddenly, several shots from an Iver Johnson .22 caliber revolver transformed the applause and chants to gasps and screams. Kennedy was mortally wounded, and roughly twenty-four hours later, at 1:44 a.m. on June 6, he died.[42]

The assassination of Robert F. Kennedy was one of those events that people remember where they were upon learning of it. To say that Kennedy's death "shocked the nation" would be an understatement. As it pertained to the politics of firearms control, the assassination proved to be the proverbial straw that broke the camel's back. Many Americans had become fed up with what they perceived to be congressional malfeasance and began taking matters into their own hands.[43] This included many businesses immediately curtailing their mail-order and over-the-phone sales of firearms and ammunition (figures 6.1 and 6.2).[44] Such was the case for the country's two largest mail-order houses, Montgomery Ward and Sears-Roebuck.[45] Meanwhile, many Americans directed their shock and anger at the NRA. From these Americans' perspective, it was the NRA that was stalling Congress from enacting the necessary firearms controls. It did not help the NRA's image that Senator Kennedy was known for being one of its most vocal critics since the assassination of his brother five years earlier. The senator's death quickly became *the* political lightning rod for strict firearms controls.

As expected, the NRA put out several statements as to how "no law" could have stopped Kennedy's assassination. Conversely, also as expected, proponents of firearms controls invoked the tragedy to advance their political cause. Kennedy had not even been pronounced dead before Maryland senator Tydings issued a statement calling for an all-out prohibition on the mail-order sale of firearms.[46] Dodd, too, quickly issued a statement urging Congress "to follow the examples of other countries and make registration of all guns compulsory."[47] Indeed, such calls to action from Tydings, Dodd, and other proponents of firearms controls were expected. What was noticeably different this time around was that similar calls were coming from lawmakers of both political parties and all ideological backgrounds. The calls to action were so intense that the House fast tracked consideration of the Senate's version of the Omnibus Crime Control and Safe Streets Act for a vote the following day, June 6.[48]

The day of the vote, and just hours after Kennedy succumbed to his wounds, President Johnson delivered a message to Congress on the need

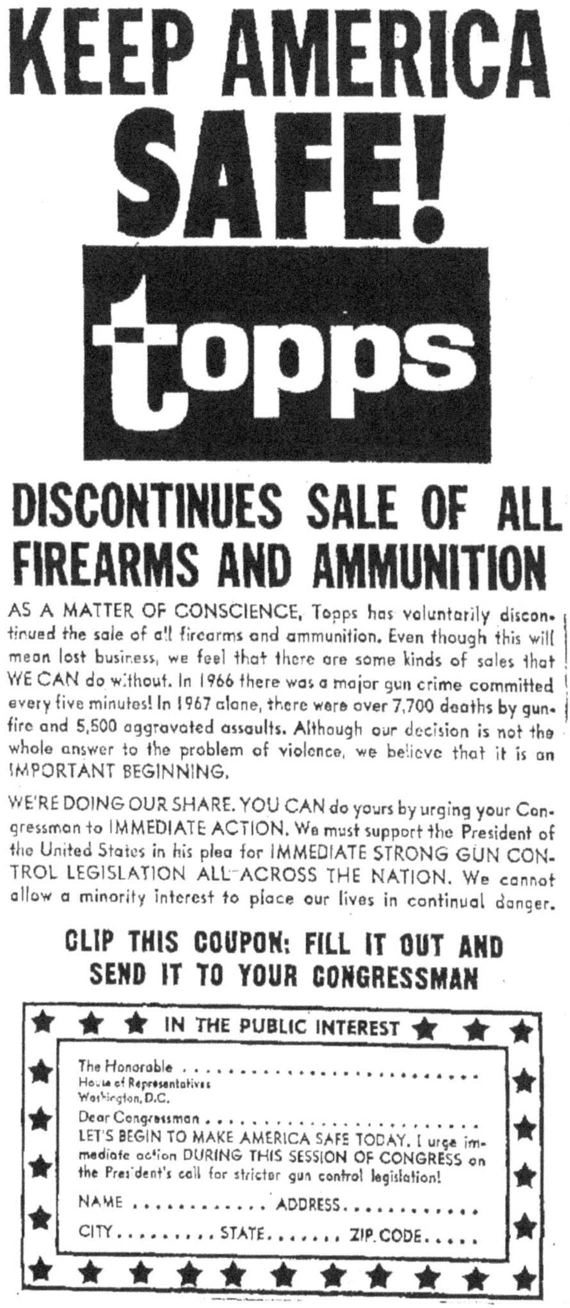

FIGURE 6.1 Commercial advertisement by Topps Department Stores in the *Bridgeport (Conn.) Post*, July 19, 1968. Topps was one of many small companies to publicly take a side either for or against firearms controls in the wake of Senator Robert F. Kennedy's assassination.

FIGURE 6.2 Commercial advertisement by Lloyd's Appliance in the *Spokane (Wash.) Chronicle*, August 5, 1968. In contrast to the small companies that published ads either for or against firearms controls in the wake of Senator Kennedy's assassination, Lloyd's took a humorous approach, which was intended to poke fun at the debate over mail-order firearms controls and firearms registration.

for strong firearms controls. While he expressed support for the firearms provisions included in the Senate's version of the bill, he felt they were "not enough" given that they left the "deadly commerce in lethal shotguns and rifles without effective control—fifty-five long months after the mail-order murder of President John F. Kennedy." Johnson then called on Congress "in the name of sanity, in the name of safety—and in the name of an aroused nation—to give America the Gun Control Law it needs."[49]

At around the time the president delivered his message, the Columbia Broadcasting Service (CBS) was airing a special report on Congress possibly passing the first federal firearms controls in thirty years. The broadcast began by noting the irony of the situation—that Congress was fast tracking legislation that Robert F. Kennedy did not support. Not only did the Senate version of Omnibus Crime Control and Safe Streets Act contain constitutionally questionable provisions that Kennedy opposed, but even the bill's firearms controls had been viewed by the late senator as woefully inadequate, particularly the omission of any long gun controls. The broadcast then cut to NRA president Glassen, who labeled the firearms provisions within the bill as embodying a "complete prohibition rather than regulation" of firearms. CBS news correspondent Steve Rowen pressed Glassen on whether the mail-order firearms control provisions that the NRA supported—Hruska's S. 1853—would have "stopped the sale of guns" to either the King or Kennedy assassin. "Neither the law that we recommended, nor any law that the mind of man can conceive would have stopped that," responded Glassen.[50]

Glassen's argument ultimately fell upon deaf ears. Unlike previous tragedies involving firearms, there was nothing left in the NRA's political bag of tricks to stall a floor vote. And on June 6, when the final votes were tallied, the Omnibus Crime Control and Safe Streets Act overwhelmingly passed the House by a whopping 369 to 17 margin.[51]

The passage of the act was just one of many concerns facing the NRA in the wake of Robert Kennedy's assassination. For nearly a week, the NRA's headquarters was picketed and received bomb threats. Additionally, by executive order, President Johnson created the National Commission on the Causes and Prevention of Violence, which would advise Congress on the way ahead for any additional federal firearms controls.[52] At the same time, he was doing his utmost to pressure lawmakers at all levels of government to take up the matter. Johnson even pressured the U.S. Postal Service to require that all firearm shipments be visibly labeled as such and that the local "chief law enforcement officer be made aware [to whom] that delivery will be made."[53]

While these developments were taking place, given that public support for firearms controls was at its zenith, firearms control bills, whether at the federal, state, or local level, were being filed at a record pace. An internal National Wildlife Federation (NWF) memorandum from Executive Director Thomas L. Kimball, written six days after the House passed the Omnibus Crime Control and Safe Streets Act, captured the prevailing mood of the gun rights community succinctly: "It is apparent to those of us here in Washington, DC, that the national mood following the tragic assassination of Sen. Robert F. Kennedy is to 'do something.' Unfortunately, the concrete expression of this mood is to press for tighter gun controls. . . . I am convinced that a majority of Americans probably would prohibit [the] private ownership of guns if a vote was taken today."[54]

The NRA's response to the flood of new firearms control bills was twofold: First, the organization remained steadfast in its opposition to most firearms controls. Second, it began peddling the idea of a government-sponsored, anti-gun conspiracy. In an editorial for the *New York Times*, NRA president Glassen shockingly labeled the firearms control "phenomenon" as being reminiscent of what "the German people did in the 1930's as the Goebel's propaganda mill drilled lies into their into their subconsciousness and dictated their every move."[55] Glassen went on to claim the existence of a "syndicated attempt" to "deceive the American population into believing it should abrogate the Second Amendment"—that is, a "step-by-step move afoot to accomplish the ultimate deprivation of the American right to keep and bear arms."[56]

While the NRA was working to rally the gun rights community to political action, a new, unforeseen threat was forming. For decades, the NRA was able to lobby for or against firearms legislation without any considerable opposition supporting firearms control. This changed with the formation of the Emergency Committee for Gun Control (ECGC).[57] Led by former astronaut John H. Glenn, the ECGC was central in rallying the public to write their representatives and urge the enactment of strict firearms controls. What made the ECGC so effective was its ability to counter virtually every longstanding NRA talking point. For example, as it pertained to the NRA's assertion that firearms controls do not prevent criminals from obtaining weapons illegally, the ECGC responded: "It is self-evident that a criminal . . . will have a harder time obtaining guns if he has to apply for a license than if he can purchase one at will. . . . No one claims gun laws will end crime or even end gun crime. But they will make guns less available to people who should not have them." And as it pertained to the often-stated gun rights talking point that firearms registration was the first step toward disarmament, the ECGC responded: "The use of autos, drugs and passports have not been diminished by laws regulating their use. . . . Only if the crescendo of slaughter and injury from guns continues unabated will there be pressure for general restrictions on gun usage, but right now no one has proposed any such measure or expressed an intention to do so."[58]

In addition to formulating talking points that countered the NRA's, the ECGC employed many of the NRA's grassroots tactics.[59] For instance, to better mobilize public support, it initiated letter- and telegram-writing campaigns, held marches and protests, and organized public events with the purpose of educating the public on the problems associated with gun

★ ★

"THE RIGHT OF THE PEOPLE TO KEEP AND BEAR ARMS SHALL NOT BE INFRINGED"

THE SECOND AMENDMENT TO THE
CONSTITUTION OF THE UNITED STATES

(1) Registration of firearms is unrelated to the problems of crime since such laws will be completely ignored by the criminal.

(2) Registration of firearms will result in increases in governmental spending; the price to be paid by the public. Such expense will only result in increased red tape and harassment of the law-abiding-citizen.

(3) Registration of firearms will give certain persons the power to determine who is qualified to own a firearm. Such power to discriminate on the basis of vague rules and "judgment" is dangerous and is an infringement upon the freedom of American people.

(4) History teaches that registration can lead to confiscation and dictatorship.

(5) We wonder how the enemies of our country feel about these bills, especially gun registration, which we know is the first step to disarming the United States? We wonder how many gangsters, rioters, and Communists will step forward and register their firearms?

Wire or Write Your Senator and Congressman

TODAY Opposing Restrictive Firearms Legislation

SENATOR BIRCH BAYH
SENATE OFFICE BUILDING
WASHINGTON, D. C. 20510
"I Oppose Restrictive
Firearms Legislation"
NAME
ADDRESS
CITY   STATE

SENATOR VANCE HARTKE
SENATE OFFICE BUILDING
WASHINGTON, D. C. 20510
"I Oppose Restrictive
Firearms Legislation"
NAME
ADDRESS
CITY   STATE

Do It TODAY ... TOMORROW
MAY BE TOO LATE!

CONGRESSMAN J. T. MYERS
HOUSE OFFICE BUILDING
WASHINGTON, D. C. 20515
"I Oppose Restrictive
Firearms Legislation"
NAME
ADDRESS
CITY   STATE

CONGRESSMAN RICHARD ROUDEBUSH
HOUSE OFFICE BUILDING
WASHINGTON, D. C. 20515
"I Oppose Restrictive
Firearms Legislation"
NAME
ADDRESS
CITY   STATE

PAID ADVERTISEMENT

★ ★ ★ ★ ★ ★★ ★

FIGURE 6.3 Political advertisement in the *Terre Haute (Ind.) Tribune*, July 11, 1968. The ad sought to encourage firearms owners to write their Indiana members of Congress to vote against firearms registration. Its talking points against firearms registration mirrored those of the NRA.

violence. Strategic messaging was particularly important to the ECGC's grassroots efforts. Full-page newspapers advertisements were published in those states where members of Congress were either opposed to or undecided on new federal firearms controls (figure 6.3). One advertisement read, "You say you want stronger gun control laws. But have you said it to your Senators?"[60] Another full-page ad published in the *New York Times* contained a picture of the late Senator Kennedy walking his dog, with the caption, "Where is the public outcry for more effective gun laws?" Below the caption were the names of nearly four hundred government officials, actors, musicians, authors, and entrepreneurs, calling for Congress to act.[61]

The arrival of the ECGC could not have come at a better time for President Johnson, who, with the help of Dodd, had successfully fast-tracked a firearms control bill that would become the Gun Control Act of 1968. Docketed as S. 3633 and titled the State Firearms Control Assistance Act, the bill sought to extend the interstate handgun sale provisions of the Omnibus Crime Control and Safe Streets Act to long guns, as well as institute controls over the interstate sale of ammunition.[62] On June 12 Dodd formally introduced the bill, and within less than a week it was reported out of the Senate Subcommittee on Juvenile Delinquency that he chaired.[63] It was anticipated that the full Senate Judiciary Committee would vote on S. 3633 by June 20. The timing aligned perfectly with the scheduled House Judiciary Committee's vote on the companion bill, H.R. 17735.[64] However, while the House Judiciary Committee voted 29 to 6 in favor of H.R. 17735, the vote on S. 3633 was postponed by the Senate Judiciary Committee.[65]

There are several reasons why the Senate Judiciary Committee postponed the vote, including the unforeseen absence of several committee members. But the reason that was most consequential was Maryland senator Tydings's desire to combine S. 3633 with the firearms registration provisions in his own bill, S. 3634. Neither Dodd nor the Johnson administration maintained any qualms about the concept of firearms registration. Dodd was already on record stating that he would introduce his own firearms registration bill to the Senate—a bill drafted and touted by the Johnson administration—on the very same day that he had announced the introduction of S. 3633.[66] What concerned Dodd and the Johnson administration was pushing for a firearms registration bill in conjunction with S. 3633. And even if they wanted to simultaneously push both bills,

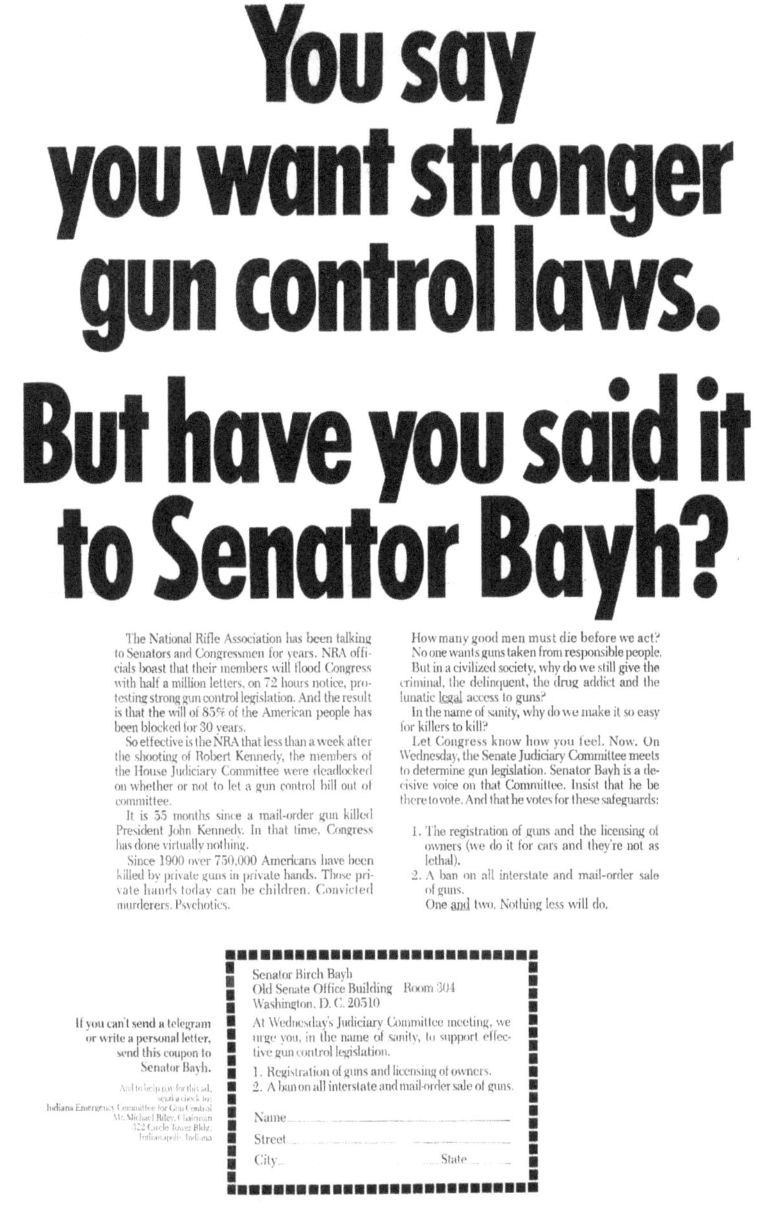

You say you want stronger gun control laws. But have you said it to Senator Bayh?

The National Rifle Association has been talking to Senators and Congressmen for years. NRA officials boast that their members will flood Congress with half a million letters, on 72 hours notice, protesting strong gun control legislation. And the result is that the will of 85% of the American people has been blocked for 30 years.

So effective is the NRA that less than a week after the shooting of Robert Kennedy, the members of the House Judiciary Committee were deadlocked on whether or not to let a gun control bill out of committee.

It is 55 months since a mail-order gun killed President John Kennedy. In that time, Congress has done virtually nothing.

Since 1900 over 750,000 Americans have been killed by private guns in private hands. Those private hands today can be children. Convicted murderers. Psychotics.

How many good men must die before we act? No one wants guns taken from responsible people. But in a civilized society, why do we still give the criminal, the delinquent, the drug addict and the lunatic legal access to guns?

In the name of sanity, why do we make it so easy for killers to kill?

Let Congress know how you feel. Now. On Wednesday, the Senate Judiciary Committee meets to determine gun legislation. Senator Bayh is a decisive voice on that Committee. Insist that he be there to vote. And that he votes for these safeguards:

1. The registration of guns and the licensing of owners (we do it for cars and they're not as lethal).
2. A ban on all interstate and mail-order sale of guns.

One and two. Nothing less will do.

If you can't send a telegram or write a personal letter, send this coupon to Senator Bayh.

And to help pay for this ad, send a check to: Indiana Emergency Committee for Gun Control Mr. Michael Riley, Chairman 322 Circle Tower Bldg. Indianapolis, Indiana

Senator Birch Bayh
Old Senate Office Building Room 304
Washington, D. C. 20510

At Wednesday's Judiciary Committee meeting, we urge you, in the name of sanity, to support effective gun control legislation.

1. Registration of guns and licensing of owners.
2. A ban on all interstate and mail-order sale of guns.

Name_____

Street_____

City_____ State_____

FIGURE 6.4 Advertisement by the Emergency Committee for Gun Control (ECGC) in the *Muncie (Ind.) Evening Press*, July 8, 1968. The ECGC ran several newspapers ads urging the public to write their senators in support of firearms controls. This one encouraged Hoosiers to write Indiana senator Birch Bayh to vote in favor firearms registration and licensing, as well as a ban on the interstate and mail-order sale of firearms.

there was concern that Tydings's bill—which was being labeled the "most extreme" firearms registration bill out there—was the wrong approach.[67]

As of mid-June, after several senators suddenly decided to politically back additional firearms controls, Dodd and the Johnson administration were confident that there were more than enough votes to get S. 3633 passed on the Senate floor. But adding Tydings's amendment to the bill changed the voting dynamic.[68] Moreover, as a procedural matter, given that the Senate had yet to hold any hearings on firearms registration, combining Tydings's bill with S. 3633 would require postponing a Senate vote until at least one hearing on the subject was concluded.

It was on June 19 that Tydings decided to take political matters into his own hands by having his assistant schedule a meeting with President Johnson to discuss the necessity of firearms registration. But due to a mix-up with the White House operator, Tydings's assistant was connected directly with the president. Tydings quickly got on the line and asked for Johnson's support. "There is an opportunity here Mr. President . . . to not only do the minimum of mail order [controls], but to do the whole job of gun registration and licensing," he stated. Johnson, after realizing there was a call mix-up, asked Tydings to call back the next day.[69] As it turned out, however, Tydings did not have to call Johnson back. For later that day Tydings received a phone call from Attorney General Ramsey Clark, who informed him that Johnson would be putting forward his own firearms registration proposal.[70]

On June 24 Johnson formally unveiled his firearms registration proposal, which Dodd filed in the Senate.[71] At the same time, Dodd scheduled a hearing for the bill for two days later. But despite Dodd's urgency, Johnson's decision to simultaneously push two firearms bills all but ensured that the Senate Judiciary Committee would not take up either one until after the summer recess. This afforded the NRA and its allies enough time to mount a response.[72]

During the first two weeks following Senator Kennedy's assassination, and for the first time since the firearms control issue was brought to the political forefront following President Kennedy's assassination, the constituent mail on Capitol Hill was tilting in favor of firearms controls, and overwhelmingly so. By the third week, however, once the NRA had organized the gun rights community to political action, the constituent mail quickly shifted back to being overwhelmingly in opposition. In a letter to all NRA members, President Glassen wrote how the "right of sportsmen in

the United States to obtain, own and use firearms for proper lawful purposes [was] in the greatest jeopardy in the history of our country." He closed
the letter by writing that unless every firearms owner "clearly expresses
their views without delay," the goal of "some proponents of restrictive gun
legislation" to completely abolish the "civilian ownership of firearms" was
all but certain.[73] President Johnson's formal urging of firearms registration only amplified the NRA's key anti-firearms control message—that is,
the passage of one unduly restrictive firearms control leads to another, and
another, until all firearms are confiscated.[74] For decades, the NRA had
prophesized such "slippery-slope to disarmament" scenarios as a means
to rouse sportsmen, hunters, and firearms owners to political action, and
now many within the gun rights community believed the prophecy was
about to come true.[75] And if anyone in community had somehow forgot the
prophecy, the NRA made sure to remind them of it.[76]

The NRA also made sure to play up the communist angle. Recall that
during World War II the organization had claimed—without any substantiated evidence to support it—that firearms registration was a part of
an insidious communist plot to disarm Americans. In the years following
the war, the NRA continued to utilize this and other communist-centric
arguments to rouse the gun rights community against firearms controls.
Therefore, in late 1963, when the public learned that President Kennedy's
assassin, Lee Harvey Oswald, was a communist sympathizer, many in the
gun rights community surmised that the postassassination calls for firearms controls were part of an insidious communist scheme. Calls for
firearms controls in the wake of Senator Kennedy's assassination were
cast in a similar light. Knowing this, the NRA put forth the argument that
firearms registration would play right into communist hands.[77]

The NRA's communist angle was tempered in comparison to that of
other, more extreme gun rights advocates.[78] Consider, for instance, the
pamphlet *Wake Up America! Before the "Liberals" Take Away Your Guns!*, which
claimed that firearms control–supporting liberals were either working
with or unknowingly appeasing communists.[79] The literature and newsletters from the Association to Preserve Our Right to Keep and Bear Arms
(APORKBA) are another example. APORKBA took to promoting the conspiracy that the assassinations of Senator Kennedy, Martin Luther King, Jr.,
and President Kennedy were all interconnected and part of a communist
plot to disarm America. "Does it follow that communists, while refraining
from assassinating their enemies for fear of martyring them, might

arrange assassination that would create sympathy for something communists want?," queried APORKBA director Earl Sherwood in an editorial. Sherwood then answered his own question:

> The murder of Senator Robert Kennedy is being used as fuel in a stupen-
> dous propaganda drive for rigid gun-control laws. . . . Anti-communists
> have been warning us for years that gun-control laws are part of the com-
> munist program for imposing dictatorship on the United States: ram-
> paging crime and mob violence are incited and encouraged until life and
> property of everyone is endangered; the police are discredited and hand-
> icapped so that they cannot adequately protect law-abiding citizens,
> who are disarmed by gun-control laws so that they cannot protect them-
> selves; the people are then ready to accept dictatorship to restore law
> and order.[80]

By early July, within just two weeks of President Johnson requesting
Congress to pass his firearms registration bill, the momentum for firearms
controls quickly began to lose steam.[81] Dodd was concerned to the point
that he wrote to Johnson that although the "licensing and registration
bill which the Administration submitted to Congress represents the ideal
for which we must strive," it was not within the political "art of the possible." Tydings's attempt to attach his firearms registration bill as an amendment to the State Firearms Control Assistance Act was certainly not helping
matters. "Now, the possibility exists that, by reaching for too much at one
time, we may lose everything," cautioned Dodd.[82]

Despite privately doubting the prospects of Congress passing a firearms
registration law by the end of the year, publicly Dodd advocated that state
and local governments should enact their own firearms registration laws.
He even made time to promote a firearms registration bill in his home state
of Connecticut. On July 16, Dodd attended a town hall meeting to explain
why the Connecticut Assembly should pass such a law. Over a period of
seven hours, he was heckled with boos, catcalls, and insults from the nearly
seven hundred sportsmen, hunters, and firearms owners in attendance.
When it was finally the Dodd's turn to speak, the crowd became so loud
that he had to shout into the microphone. Eventually, he became so frustrated that he referred to the attending sportsmen, hunters, shooters, and
firearms owners as "rabid," "unreasonable," and "gun nuts."[83]

FIGURE 6.5 Flyer-poster from 1968 linking the assassinations of President John F. Kennedy and Senator Robert F. Kennedy with an alleged communist plot to disarm American citizens.

Dodd's town hall experience made it abundantly clear to him that a firearms registration bill was not going to pass Congress.[84] And he was not the only member of Congress that saw the proverbial writing on the wall. The NRA's ability to rouse the gun rights community to political action also prompted Montana senator and majority leader Mike Mansfield to pull his support for Tydings's firearms registration bill.[85] Initially, Mansfield's decision to back the bill made political sense.[86] Constituent mail in many congressional districts was running upwards of 40 to 1 in support of firearms controls.[87] Additionally, eight senators who had once opposed most firearms control bills prior to Senator Kennedy's assassination—Washington senator Warren G. Magnuson, Oklahoma senators Fred R. Harris and Mike Monroney, Maine senator Edmund S. Muskie, Wisconsin senators Gaylord A. Nelson and William Proxmire, Michigan senator Philip A. Hart, and Pennsylvania senator Hugh Scott—were now either supporting a total ban on mail-order firearms or some type of firearms registration. The push back from firearms-owning Montanans was so intense, however, that Mansfield would ultimately withdraw his support for Tydings's bill.[88]

When Mansfield announced that he was backing Tydings's bill, he provided two principal reasons for doing so. First, although most Montanans had never witnessed or felt the personal pain of firearms-related violence or death, it was an issue that Mansfield believed to be plaguing many of the nation's urban areas. Indeed, he knew that the "problem of violence" could not be solely blamed on the "uncontrolled gun." However, he thought that firearms were a key "element" through which violence was carried out.[89] Therefore, from his perspective, regulating firearms was necessary in the interests of public safety. The second reason Mansfield backed Tydings's bill was that it respected every state's police power to regulate firearms.[90] This was important to Mansfield because it would allow Montanans the opportunity to craft a firearms registration bill in a way that respected their way of life.[91] This was also the reason why Mansfield "overwhelmingly rejected" President Johnson's "one size fits all" firearms registration proposal.[92]

In late June Mansfield outlined a third reason why he was backing Tydings's bill—the death of Marine second lieutenant Thaddeus R. Lesnik, a Montanan who was killed by a handgun in the District of Columbia on the very same day as Senator Kennedy.[93] Mansfield told Lesnik's parents that their son's death was "decisive in bringing me to a soul-searching reexamination of the question of gun-control." He wrote:

> May I say that I am not unaware of traditional Montanan attitudes on guns. Controls have been generally repugnant to those who, like your family, and many others in Montana, have been taught and adhere to the responsible use of firearms. Nor was I unaware of the adverse reactions which were to be anticipated if I took a position in support of controls. After your son was killed, however, I reached the conviction that my duty to the people of the State, as Montanans and as Americans, impelled me, in good conscience, to support the Tydings bill.
>
> I say, frankly, I do not expect that [firearms control] is any sort of cure-all of the problem. Nevertheless, I have taken this course in the hope and belief that there can be some mitigation in the rising level of violence of the gun which has come to plague our land, especially the cities of the nation.[94]

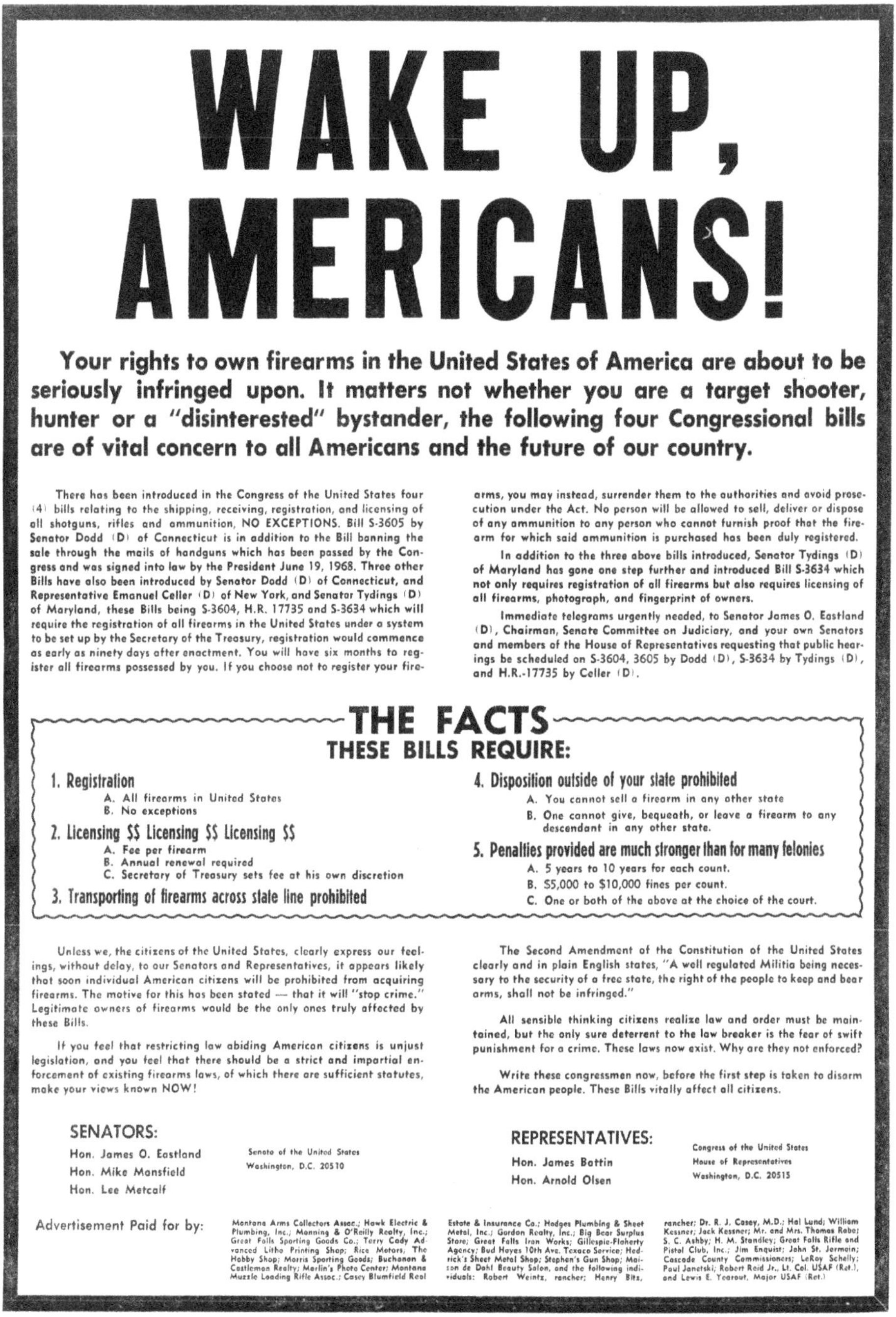

WAKE UP, AMERICANS!

Your rights to own firearms in the United States of America are about to be seriously infringed upon. It matters not whether you are a target shooter, hunter or a "disinterested" bystander, the following four Congressional bills are of vital concern to all Americans and the future of our country.

There has been introduced in the Congress of the United States four (4) bills relating to the shipping, receiving, registration, and licensing of all shotguns, rifles and ammunition, NO EXCEPTIONS. Bill S-3605 by Senator Dodd (D) of Connecticut is in addition to the Bill banning the sale through the mails of handguns which has been passed by the Congress and was signed into law by the President June 19, 1968. Three other Bills have also been introduced by Senator Dodd (D) of Connecticut, and Representative Emanuel Celler (D) of New York, and Senator Tydings (D) of Maryland, these Bills being S-3604, H.R. 17735 and S-3634 which will require the registration of all firearms in the United States under a system to be set up by the Secretary of the Treasury, registration would commence as early as ninety days after enactment. You will have six months to register all firearms possessed by you. If you choose not to register your firearms, you may instead, surrender them to the authorities and avoid prosecution under the Act. No person will be allowed to sell, deliver or dispose of any ammunition to any person who cannot furnish proof that the firearm for which said ammunition is purchased has been duly registered.

In addition to the three above bills introduced, Senator Tydings (D) of Maryland has gone one step further and introduced Bill S-3634 which not only requires registration of all firearms but also requires licensing of all firearms, photograph, and fingerprint of owners.

Immediate telegrams urgently needed, to Senator James O. Eastland (D), Chairman, Senate Committee on Judiciary, and your own Senators and members of the House of Representatives requesting that public hearings be scheduled on S-3604, 3605 by Dodd (D), S-3634 by Tydings (D), and H.R.-17735 by Celler (D).

THE FACTS

THESE BILLS REQUIRE:

1. **Registration**
   - A. All firearms in United States
   - B. No exceptions
2. **Licensing $$ Licensing $$ Licensing $$**
   - A. Fee per firearm
   - B. Annual renewal required
   - C. Secretary of Treasury sets fee at his own discretion
3. **Transporting of firearms across state line prohibited**
4. **Disposition outside of your state prohibited**
   - A. You cannot sell a firearm in any other state
   - B. One cannot give, bequeath, or leave a firearm to any descendant in any other state.
5. **Penalties provided are much stronger than for many felonies**
   - A. 5 years to 10 years for each count.
   - B. $5,000 to $10,000 fines per count.
   - C. One or both of the above at the choice of the court.

Unless we, the citizens of the United States, clearly express our feelings, without delay, to our Senators and Representatives, it appears likely that soon individual American citizens will be prohibited from acquiring firearms. The motive for this has been stated — that it will "stop crime." Legitimate owners of firearms would be the only ones truly affected by these Bills.

If you feel that restricting law abiding American citizens is unjust legislation, and you feel that there should be a strict and impartial enforcement of existing firearms laws, of which there are sufficient statutes, make your views known NOW!

The Second Amendment of the Constitution of the United States clearly and in plain English states, "A well regulated Militia being necessary to the security of a free state, the right of the people to keep and bear arms, shall not be infringed."

All sensible thinking citizens realize law and order must be maintained, but the only sure deterrent to the law breaker is the fear of swift punishment for a crime. These laws now exist. Why are they not enforced?

Write these congressmen now, before the first step is taken to disarm the American people. These Bills vitally affect all citizens.

SENATORS:

Hon. James O. Eastland
Hon. Mike Mansfield
Hon. Lee Metcalf

Senate of the United States
Washington, D.C. 20510

REPRESENTATIVES:

Hon. James Battin
Hon. Arnold Olsen

Congress of the United States
House of Representatives
Washington, D.C. 20515

Advertisement Paid for by: Montana Arms Collectors Assoc.; Hawk Electric & Plumbing, Inc.; Manning & O'Reilly Realty, Inc.; Great Falls Sporting Goods Co.; Terry Cady Advanced Litho Printing Shop; Rice Motors; The Hobby Shop; Morris Sporting Goods; Buchanan & Castleman Realty; Merlin's Photo Center; Montana Muzzle Loading Rifle Assoc.; Casey Blumfield Real Estate & Insurance Co.; Hodges Plumbing & Sheet Metal, Inc.; Gordon Realty, Inc.; Big Bear Surplus Store; Great Falls Iron Works; Gillespie-Flaherty Agency; Bud Hayes 10th Ave. Texaco Service; Hedrick's Sheet Metal Shop; Stephen's Gun Shop; Maison de Dahl Beauty Salon, and the following individuals: Robert Weintz, rancher; Henry Bitz, rancher; Dr. R. J. Casey, M.D.; Hal Lund; William Kessner; Jack Kessner; Mr. and Mrs. Thomas Rabe; S. C. Ashby; H. M. Standley; Great Falls Rifle and Pistol Club, Inc.; Jim Enquist; John St. Jermain; Cascade County Commissioners; LeRoy Schelly; Paul Janetski; Robert Reid Jr., Lt. Col. USAF (Ret.), and Lewis E. Yearout, Major USAF (Ret.)

FIGURE 6.6 Full-page advertisement appeared in the *Great Falls (Mont.) Tribune*, July 7, 1968. The ad was one of several that urged Montanans to write their members of Congress in opposition to any additional federal firearms controls, particularly firearms registration and licensing.

Yet come August, Mansfield's constituent mail was running overwhelmingly against firearms controls. Mansfield's office received only 1,221 constituent letters in support of firearms controls and 16,477 constituent letters against—many of which were fervently opposed to firearms registration.[95] This prompted Mansfield to withdraw his support for Tydings's bill, albeit quietly and without political fanfare.

What also prompted Mansfield to reverse political course on Tydings's bill was the fact that Montana's other congressional Democrats had decried the passing of any additional federal firearms controls. Arnold Olsen, who represented the western half of the state, was especially vocal. For years, Olsen had cultivated his political image alongside Mansfield. However, Mansfield's support for firearms registration required Olsen to politically distance himself for the election in 1968. Olsen was cognizant that he had won reelection in 1966 by the slim margin of just 2,800 votes.[96] Thus, as a matter of political self-preservation, he needed to be on the "right side" of Montana politics when it came to contentious issues. This was particularly true for the firearms control issue, where Olsen's constituent mail was running nearly 10 to 1 against.[97] For this reason, he borrowed the NRA's tried-and-true "slippery-slope to disarmament" argument in announcing his opposition to any additional federal firearms controls. "I say this legislation will not work and gun control proponents will want more next year, or the next year, and they will not be satisfied and anything less than confiscation," he stated.[98] By adopting this position, Olsen effectively nullified the firearms position of his election opponent, Dick Smiley, who often recited gun rights talking points on the campaign trail, such as "punish the criminal, not the law-abiding citizen," "there are enough firearms controls on the books already," and "criminals do not obey firearms controls."[99] Olsen convincingly won reelection over Smiley by a more than ten thousand votes, 74,974 to 64,862.[100]

The politics of firearms control played out similarly in Montana's other House race, where incumbent Republican James F. Battin won reelection by a staggering 83,888 to 39,752 vote over Democrat Robert L. Kelleher.[101] The firearms control issue was effectively nullified in this race given that both Battin and Kelleher opposed any additional federal firearms controls.[102] Battin was in fact already well versed on the issue given its relevance during his reelection campaign in 1966. That experience prompted him to write Richard M. Nixon's headquarters in fall of 1967—five months before the former vice president declared his candidacy for the Republican presidential nomination. The way Battin saw it, it would be a "good idea" if Nixon "stayed away from the gun legislation issue" altogether. "There are millions of people who will never be convinced that we should regulate guns any more than they are now," wrote Battin. "When you travel west of the Mississippi River the question is unthinkable and arouses the most indignation." Battin closed his letter by urging Nixon to take a "careful and studied approach, for in any close election this could make a great deal of difference."[103]

The Nixon campaign followed Battin's advice.[104] Through the first half of 1968, Nixon remained noncommittal on firearms controls.[105] But the assassination of Senator Kennedy changed everything. The pressure was on Nixon to take a position, and his campaign began formulating several courses of action. One proposed course was that Nixon would highlight the Johnson administration's failure "to enforce the gun control laws now on the books," which would further complement Nixon's "law and order" message.[106] Another proposed course was that Nixon would come out in support the State Firearms Control Assistance Act. Not only was public opinion strongly in favor of "tighter gun control legislation," but also the "arguments in support of such legislation" were "much more compelling than those opposed to it." Not to mention, by coming out strongly in favor of mail-order firearms controls, Nixon could "eliminate a key issue" from the 1968 election.[107] Federal firearms registration, however, was viewed much differently by Nixon's campaign staff. Although Nixon personally supported the idea, the campaign thought it best to adopt a middle-of-the-road approach. This meant that Nixon would express support for the principal of firearms registration, but with the caveat that it was a matter best left to the states to explore and "each state should base its standards and requirements on its particular problems and needs." Adopting this political course of action would not diminish Nixon as the "law and order" candidate and, more important, not draw the ire of "responsible hunters and sportsmen."[108]

On June 17 Nixon issued his first formal firearms control policy statement. He expressed support for the firearms control provisions within the Omnibus Crime Control and Safe Streets Act and urged President Johnson to "cease dragging his feet" on signing it into law. Additionally, he expressed support for restrictions on the "interstate mail order shipment of shotguns and rifles ... to prevent their falling into the hands of minors, convicted criminals, those with a history of mental illness and others not qualified to have a gun in their possession," as well as restrictions that "prevent the mail order circumvention of state and local gun control laws." Nixon then went on note that any new firearms control laws should in no way "interfere with the legitimate right of sportsmen and hunters to buy and own weapons they are licensed to buy and own in their states." "But let us keep this in mind," he stated, "there is no gun legislation at the Federal, state and local level that by itself will bring us the solution to the crime crisis spawned in America in recent years."[109]

Nixon's firearms control policy was politically effective in two respects. First, it nullified firearms control as an issue between Nixon and his chief rival for the Republican presidential nomination, New York governor Nelson A. Rockefeller, who had a long track record of supporting firearms controls. Second, should Nixon end up receiving the Republican nomination, the policy afforded the campaign sufficient leeway to modify his position depending on the political state of play. And ultimately, when the NRA and its allies roused the gun rights community to political action in early July, this is exactly what the Nixon campaign did by reframing its firearms control policy in more gun rights–friendly terms. For in the campaign's July 9 statement on firearms controls, Nixon blasted the "gun control legislation now being considered by Congress" as failing to adequately deal with the "armed criminal." While he continued to express support for legislation that would keep firearms out of the hands of minors, criminals, alcoholics, addicts, and the "mentally incompetent," the former vice president was emphatic that strict controls, such as those in New York City and Great Britain, did nothing in the way of keeping "firearms out of the hands of criminals of all kinds, from assassins to common thugs." Rather, strict controls only disarmed "law-abiding citizens," to include the "merchants, cab drivers, and bus drivers who ... because they have obeyed the gun law become the easy prey of the criminals who have evaded it." Nixon then offered up the popular gun rights alternative to strict firearms controls—mandatory minimums for "any person convicted using a gun in the commission of a major crime." This meant Congress passing "immediate legislation providing for a mandatory prison term of substantial duration for any fellow who uses a firearms in the commission of a serious Federal crime."[110]

The Nixon campaign was aided in crafting its firearms control policy through the advice and counsel of William L. Wallace, who was concurrently serving as a lobbyist for firearms manufacturers Remington Arms Company, Marlin Firearms Company, and Sturm Ruger & Company. It was Wallace who first introduced the Nixon campaign to the political demographics of firearms control. He highlighted how "real activist hunters, shooters, gun owners, and their organizations . . . cuts across party lines and other normal political groupings," and that generally a "broader group can be counted on to support the ultimate right to bear arms, [when] they begin to feel that this is really threatened." Wallace also educated the Nixon campaign on how more than half of all American households owned firearms, on how the previous year's firearms sales were somewhere between 3.5 to 4.5 million firearms, and on how nearly 30 million people self-identify as hunters and shooters. Basically, the political quandary that Wallace helped the Nixon campaign navigate was how best to frame the firearms control issue in a way that stayed on the right side of public opinion yet at the same time garnered the support of the gun rights community. Or, as Wallace put it, "If there were a way to win these people to all out support of a particular presidential candidate, without direct confrontation with the powerful anti-gun forces [of 'prominent do gooder groups,' and 'many women'], and the media, this issue alone could swing the presidential election and could have significant impact on the Congressional election."[111]

Wallace ultimately answered his own question by suggesting that the Nixon campaign identify and maintain a "constructive, middle position between the emotional extremes of the current debate."[112] This would stop the large groups of "pro-gun militants" from either voting for the American Independent Party's (AIP) presidential nominee, George Wallace, who unequivocally opposed all restrictive firearms controls,[113] or "skip[ping] the presidential line on the ballot."[114] The key to accomplishing this, according to Wallace, was that Nixon embrace the NRA's political straddling approach. This meant that Nixon would express support for reasonable firearms controls yet in the same breath state several well-known gun rights talking points. These points included: firearms controls will have no noticeable effect on overall crime; punish criminals with enhanced mandatory penalties; responsible and properly trained armed citizens help reduce crime; there are several "legitimate uses of privately owned firearms," to include hunting, target shooting, self-defense, and "community and national defense"; and "anti-gun propaganda is a blatant effort to make guns a scapegoat for the total ineffectiveness of [the Johnson] administration in dealing with runaway crime rates."[115]

As can be seen in Nixon's July 9 policy statement, as well as Nixon's follow-on "law and order" campaign brochure, Wallace's firearms control advice was largely followed. Yet but for Nixon having established a firm hold on the Republican presidential nomination at the start of July, it is unlikely that his campaign would have pivoted on the firearms control issue when it did. And Nixon was not alone. Many other candidates running for election in 1968 also pivoted on firearm controls, depending on the political state of play. Consider the Pennsylvania Senate race between Democratic incumbent Joseph S. Clark and Republican challenger Richard S. Schweiker. Both candidates modified their respective firearms control positions before and after Senator Kennedy's assassination—Clark more so than Schweiker.[116] The same was true in Maryland. In the immediate aftermath of the assassination, all ten of Maryland's members of Congress expressed support for strict controls.[117] Once the bulk of constituent mail switched from overwhelming support for firearms controls to overwhelming opposition, however, several Maryland congressmen either modified their policy position or conveniently forgot that they ever supported firearms controls. This was particularly true in the case of Senator Daniel B. Brewster, who issued several contradictory firearms control statements in a period of three months.[118]

What makes these political pivots or adjustments noteworthy is that they represent the first instances in U.S. history where congressional candidates began devising election strategies based on the firearms control issue. And often political candidates based their strategy on public opinion. Consider the case of Senator Gaylord A. Nelson, who represented the largely rural and hunting-friendly state of Wisconsin. Not long after the assassination of Senator Kennedy, Nelson decided to back firearms registration.[119] But by late June the bulk of his constituent mail was outright opposed to any additional federal firearms controls. This factor alone prompted many candidates running for reelection in 1968 to pivot or modify their firearms control position, but not Nelson.[120] His campaign viewed the dispute over firearms controls as being waged between political "amateurs and professionals." In this case, the "amateurs" were the public and the "professionals" the gun rights advocates. And what ultimately compelled the Nelson campaign to side with the "amateurs" was the under-standing that—as with many political issues—the "professionals often win simply because they are in the fight to stay." To the campaign, this was not reason enough to change political course on firearms controls. For it would improperly illustrate that a "well-organized, determined, and artic-ulate minority can ... wield an influence far greater than its numbers would seem to justify."[121]

The sudden rise of firearms control as a political issue can also be seen among the different governors' conferences and party platform commit-tees that started in mid-June 1968. By that time, it was increasingly clear to lawmakers and political pundits that firearms control would be a vot-ing issue for the upcoming elections. The question that governors' confer-ences and party platform committees needed to answer was how to prop-erly address the issue in a way that eased the public's concerns yet did not ignore the beliefs and culture of firearm-owning Americans.

The Republican Governors' Conference was the first to take up the issue. Urging the adoption of a strong firearms control resolution was Pennsyl-vania governor Raymond P. Shafer, who had mostly catered to the politi-cal preferences of gun rights advocates ever since assuming office in 1967.[122] Yet, as it did for many lawmakers, the assassination of Senator Kennedy shook Shafer's conscience to its core, and the Pennsylvania governor sud-denly became a vocal firearms control proponent. His urging of a strong firearms control plank was disfavored by fellow Republican governors Ron-ald Reagan and Tim Babcock,[123] both of whom had been outspoken against restrictive firearms controls.[124] Reagan and Babcock were particularly opposed to a resolution that included any mention of firearms registra-tion on the grounds that registration was the tool by which communists removed the "people's ability to fight back" against totalitarianism.[125] In the end, to Shafer's disappointment, the conference agreed only to sup-port the "adoption of such gun control legislation *as is needed* to restrict the criminal, psychopath, narcotics addict, and mentally incompetent from having access to guns, while avoiding interference with the legitimate citi-zen's right to possess arms."[126] Days later, the Southern Governors' Confer-ence approved a firearms control resolution that signaled the importance of states' rights. The resolution stated that the "challenge and responsibil-ity of promoting and enacting appropriate [firearms] legislation [lies] within each state."[127] In late July the National Governors' Conference followed suit by noting that the control of firearms "lies primarily within each of the several states."[128] It was a resounding rebuke to Vermont governor Phillip H. Hoff, who had proposed to the conference much stronger language.

Since assuming office in 1963, Hoff had neither advocated for nor against firearms controls in a state well-known for having some of the most lenient firearm laws in the nation. But after Senator Kennedy's assassination, Hoff felt Vermont needed to shore up its firearms laws and ordered state attorney general James L. Oaks to explore legislative possibilities.[129] In a letter to Hoff, Oaks explained how Vermont's laws were the result of our "past history of being a rural state with no centers of urban concentration."[130] And while the firearms-related crime rate in Vermont remained low compared to other parts of the country, Oaks noted that "criminal elements" were taking advantage of Vermont's laws to circumvent the firearms controls of neighboring states, including New York and Massachusetts. Given this fact, Oaks encouraged Hoff to back a series of legislative proposals, to include firearms registration, firearms licensing, and a seventy-two-hour "cooling-off period" between the time of purchase and the delivery of the firearm.[131] Hoff concurred with each of Oaks's legislative proposals and even supported a strict firearms control resolution before the New England Governors' Conference held in late June.[132] Convincing the National Governors' Conference to support such a resolution, however, proved to be a political bridge too far. Hoff expressed his indignation by calling the resolution "the most weak-kneed possible" and felt the conference "could do a while of a lot more." "What we really are saying is that we are ducking our responsibility," he Hoff.[133]

The resolutions of the Republican Governors' Conference, Southern Governors' Conference, and National Governors' Conference set the stage for the Republican Party Platform Committee when it took up the issue. The committee was chaired by Illinois senator Everett Dirksen, who for several years had been outspoken against strict firearms controls. Like many members of Congress, the call for firearms controls in the wake of Senator Kennedy's assassination forced Dirksen to soften his stance.[134] For a brief time, Dirksen was even open to supporting federal firearms registration so long as states with strict firearms licensing laws, such as Illinois, were exempt from any additional federal requirements.[135] But by the time the Republican Party Platform Committee convened in early August, the political state

FIGURE 6.7 Advertisement in the *Chicago Tribune* by radio station 97.9 WSDM, August 5, 1968. The ad encouraged readers to write Illinois senator Everett Dirksen in supporting a "strong gun registration law." With the word "protest" appearing from the flames of a burning NRA membership card, it adequately depicts how many Americans blamed the NRA for stalling effective federal firearms controls.

of play had shifted considerably in favor of gun rights proponents. Moreover, Nixon, the presumptive Republican presidential nominee, had already staked out a gun rights position. These factors ultimately convinced Dirksen and the Platform Committee to reject the calls for a strong firearms control plank. They instead agreed on following: "We pledge an all-out, federal-state-local crusade against crime, including enactment of legislation to control indiscriminate availability of firearms, safeguarding the right of responsible citizens to collect, own and use firearms for legitimate purposes, retaining primary responsibility at the state level with such federal laws as necessary to better enable the states meet their responsibilities."[136]

Like the firearms control resolutions of the Republican Governors' Conference and National Governors' Conference, the Platform Committee's plank was music to the ears of gun rights advocates. Not only did it recognize that the Second Amendment protected an individual right to arms—something that many firearms control proponents dismissed—but it also promised that the federal government would intrude lightly into a legislative area that was historically reserved to state and local governments—governments where the NRA and its allies maintained considerable political influence. The NRA was especially pleased with the outcome. Although its policy at the time was to never endorse or elevate one political party over another, the NRA was encouraged by what had transpired. Still, it was eager to know how the Democratic Party Convention would come out on the firearms control issue. As NRA president Glassen noted in private correspondence, if Senator Eugene McCarthy won the Democratic presidential nomination, the NRA anticipated that the Democratic Party's firearms control plank "would not be essentially different than the Republican" one. However, if Vice President Humphrey won the nomination, Glassen predicted that the Democratic Party would align its firearms control plank with the policies of the Johnson administration. Glassen closed his letter with, "I have always hoped that the N.R.A. would never become involved in any party politics but fifteen to thirty million sportsmen may have to make themselves appropriately heard in the coming election."[137]

Ultimately, Glassen's prediction turned out to be wrong. Certainly, given that President Johnson was the face of the Democratic Party, and the principal proponents for strict firearms controls were also of the same party, it was fair for Glassen to assume that the Democratic Party Platform Committee would come out in favor of strict firearms controls. Such an outcome was bolstered by the fact that everyone who provided or submitted testimony on the issue to the Democratic Party Platform Committee endorsed strict firearms controls.[138] Senator Tydings, for one, urged the committee to adopt a "strong endorsement of gun control legislation." "We Democrats must speak the truth," he stated before the committee, adding, "Those who cry, 'Law and order,' but oppose gun control and correctional reform are accomplices to the murder of police officers and innocent citizens." Tydings went on to note how he believed the Republican Party's calls for "law and order" were nothing more than "code words for race."[139] Dr. J. Elliott Corbett of the National Council for a Responsible Firearms Policy (NCRFP) also urged the Democratic Party Platform Committee adopt a plank that supported "strict gun controls." "Those who oppose such controls ought to recognize that continued neglect of what so urgently needs to be done in this field, and the resulting rise in the irresponsible use of guns that is sure to follow, will increase the changes of the gun confiscation they fear," stated Corbett.[140] Last, there was Senator Dodd, who was adamant not only that the Platform Committee be forthright in its support for firearms controls, but also that it outline specific firearms policies.[141] Dodd went so far as to propose the following language:

> We endorse legislation regulating the interstate commerce in mail-order firearms and ammunition and in the over-the-counter, non-resident commerce in firearms, and;
>
> We endorse Federal controls over the sale of firearms to juveniles and minors.
>
> We urge the states and their political subdivisions to take affirmative action, under their responsibility for policing their states, to enact effective legislation to control the sale of firearms and ammunition within their borders.
>
> We urge a continuing study of this entire problem, and if the States do not accept their responsibilities, then the Federal Government should move to enact licensing and registration laws that are necessary and proper to protect the general welfare of all of our citizens.[142]

In the end, the Democratic Party Platform Committee rejected Dodd's proposed language, as well as the other proposals for a strong firearms control plank. Rather, with the goal of appealing to all political sides of the issue, the committee issued a short and simple plank—one that not only highlighted the party's leadership in passing the first federal firearms controls in thirty years but also provided Democrats vying for political office sufficient leeway to take several stances. The plank simply stated that the Democratic Party would continue to promote "the passage and enforcement of effective federal, state and local gun control legislation."[143]

Yet the selection of Vice President Hubert H. Humphrey as the presidential nominee all but ensured that gun rights supporters would interpret the Democratic Party's firearms control plank as being averse to the Second Amendment. The failure to even acknowledge an individual right to arms on par with the Republican Party did not help the Democratic Party's position. Certainly, prior to the assassination of Senator Kennedy, this strategy may have worked. For at that time the Humphrey campaign, like the Nixon campaign, was doing its utmost to portray a middle-of-the-road position.[144] In the wake of the assassination, however, Humphrey was obliged to go along with President Johnson's position and therefore express unequivocal support for firearms registration and licensing.[145] In light of Humphrey's support for firearms controls, gun rights voters overwhelmingly began to back Nixon. Even prior to the Democratic Party Convention, there were concerns within the gun rights community should Humphrey be nominated.[146] The Right to Bear Arms, Inc., a Michigan-based gun rights advocacy group, was particularly outspoken against Humphrey's nomination, or that of any other firearms control–supporting candidate. The group warned that "if the delegates [to the convention] . . . nominate Hubert Humphrey or any other anti-gun candidate for president, they will have an up-hill battle all the way." It added, "When the votes are counted next November all the anti-gun senators and representatives will wake up to the 50,000,000 gun owners who believe that the right of the people to keep and bear arms shall not be infringed."[147]

The NRA was not outspoken like The Right to Bear Arms. Internally, however, the NRA was leaning Republican. For after the Democratic Party Convention, the presumption was that the Democratic Party was effectively endorsing the Johnson's administration's position—a position the NRA vehemently opposed. "The N.R.A. has avoided party politics like the plague but it seems to me that the Democratic Party is deliberating making an issue of gun control and if this becomes a party issue I do not know of anything that our members and people who think like our members can do but vote accordingly," wrote NRA President Glassen. By "vote accordingly," he meant vote for the "satisfactory" firearms control policy positions of Nixon and the Republican Party.[148] E. B. Mann, who had served as editor-in-chief of multiple shooting magazines, arrived at a similar conclusion in an article for *Shooting Industry*. The way Mann saw it, the 1968 election was a referendum on whether the private ownership of firearms would be abolished. Mann forewarned that millions of Americans will simply vote "yes" for candidates that support firearms controls because they were "brainwashed by the hysteria . . . and the emotional disinformation dispensed by the sensation-seeking majority of the news media." Therefore it was the responsibility of firearms owners to save the Second Amendment by voting for the "realistic" position of Nixon and the Republican Party. Mann closed his article by urging firearms owners to vote not simply for the party or candidate that their "grand daddy" supported, but rather for those candidates who stood with the right to arms.[149]

Yet despite the preference among many gun rights advocates for the Republican Party over the Democratic Party, the political reality was that individual Republican and Democratic members of Congress maintained a variety of opinions on firearms controls. Throughout the 1960s a Democratic member of Congress was no more likely to support firearms controls was than a Republican one, and vice-versa. Even after the assassination of Senator Kennedy, Republican and Democratic candidates alike based their respective firearms control policy positions on local rather than national politics. There were, of course, exceptions, particularly in the Senate, given that senators must be reelected every six years. Conversely, the entire House of Representatives was up for reelection every two years. The same held true for many state and local officials. In the summer of 1968, therefore, it was common for candidates from both political parties to instruct their campaigns to monitor the pulse of their constituency on the firearms control issue. Essentially, a political war on the necessity and usefulness of firearms controls was being waged across the country—a war that was pitting candidates running for office with largely urban constituencies against those running for office with largely rural constituencies.

A political war was also being waged inside state party conventions, where debates over including firearms controls in party planks were becoming commonplace. And those state party conventions that decided to include a firearms control plank did not necessarily follow their national party convention's lead. For instance, given the unpopularity of firearms controls in Texas, the Texas Democratic Party rejected the national Democratic Party's plank and instead embraced Nixon's "law and order" message by endorsing firearms laws that provided "heavier penalties for criminal acts involving the use of guns."[150] Conversely, the Delaware Democratic Party decided to take the national Democratic Party's plank a step further by endorsing firearms registration, but only so long as it was "at no cost and minimal inconvenience to gun owners."[151] The same was true of the Iowa Democratic Party, which also decided to endorse firearms registration, as well as a prohibition on "mail order retail sales and over-the-counter sales [of firearms] to out-of-state residents."[152] As for Vermont, both the Democratic and Republican state platforms expressed support for firearms controls.[153] What separated the two was the former's support for the registration of handguns.[154] Meanwhile, in Wisconsin, the Democratic and Republican state platforms came out with opposite firearms control planks. While the Wisconsin Democratic Party expressed support for certain firearms controls, the Wisconsin Republican Party decided to come out even more supportive of gun rights than the national Republican party: "[We] hereby uphold[] the right of individual law-abiding and responsible citizens to own and use firearms without costly and ineffective nuisance of gun registration as well as the licensing of the gun."[155]

The political war over firearms controls taking place at the state party conventions paled in comparison to what was taking place on Capitol Hill. There a political phenomenon known as the "shooting cycle" was in full-swing—a phenomenon that dominated the politics of firearms controls for most of the twentieth century. The "shooting cycle" takes place whenever a tragedy involving firearms occurs. Strict firearms controls initially receive the support of the public. After enough time elapses, however, public support becomes less enthusiastic, and the cycle of outrage, action, and reaction eventually fades away. And while the public's support fades, the opposition of the gun rights community gains momentum, which ultimately leads to limited, if any, legislative action on firearms controls.[156]

The "shooting cycle" phenomenon is what happened in the case of President Johnson's proposed firearms controls following the assassination of Senator Kennedy. If the 90th Congress would have acted quickly, as Johnson wanted, it is likely that the strict firearms controls within the State Firearms Control Assistance Act would have been enacted into law. It is also likely that 90th Congress would have passed a federal firearms registration bill. Neither happened. Instead, due to a combination of the NRA's grassroots advocacy, the political shrewdness of firearms control opponents, and a series of self-inflicted political wounds by firearms control proponents, what ultimately became the Gun Control Act was a shell of what it could have been.

What principally doomed the prospects of federal firearms registration was the political posturing of Mississippi representative William Colmer, who chaired the House Rules Committee.[157] According to Colmer, it was ill-advised to advance any "legislation on the basis of hysteria and emotion," especially firearms controls.[158] But what Colmer really wanted was an assurance from House Judiciary chairman Emanuel Celler that he would oppose any attempt to attach firearms registration to the bill on the House floor. Celler obliged, stating, "I will state here that I will oppose any amendment offered on the floor for registration and licensing, and I will oppose any Senate amendment for registration and licensing in a conference."[159] It was not until July 9 that the House Rules Committee approved the State Firearms Control Assistance Act. But Colmer allowed this to happen on only two conditions—conditions that effectively weakened the final bill. The first was the inclusion of the "open rule," a procedural move that not only allowed an unlimited number of weakening amendments on the House floor but also ensured that House proceedings and amendments would be time consuming. The second condition was meant to be a legislative poison pill—the inclusion of a mandatory sentencing minimum in the bill for anyone convicted of a felony with a firearm.[160] Colmer knew that the provision was a nonstarter for many firearms control proponents and therefore could derail the final passage of the State Firearms Control Assistance Act.[161]

On July 24, by a vote of 305 to 118, the bill finally passed the House, but not before the NRA's congressional surrogates were successful in passing several weakening amendments.[162] One amendment was particularly concerning to firearms control proponents. Introduced by Florida representative Robert F. Sikes—who, due to a conflict of interest on the House Appropriations Committee, was forced to vacate his seat on the NRA's board of directors a year earlier[163]—the amendment exempted from the law all military surplus firearms and ammunition purchased or acquired from the army through the National Board for the Promotion of Rifle Practice (NBPRP).[164] And seeing that only NRA members and NRA-affiliated rifle clubs were eligible to purchase or acquire these items from the NBPRP, the amendment was viewed as proof positive of the NRA's role as the "gun lobby." Celler was particularly incensed by the amendment's passage and threatened an investigation into the NRA if it survived the Senate.[165] "The National Rifle Association is so insidious, so insistent, that they seem to prevail," stated Celler, adding, "But they won't prevail for long."[166] The NRA responded by informing its membership that Celler made the threat only because the House had voted down firearms registration and licensing.[167] It was a bald-faced lie. Celler had already agreed to oppose firearms registration and licensing if the House Rules Committee allowed the bill to proceed to the House floor.[168] What upset Celler was that he made the agreement with the understanding that the bill's provisions would apply uniformly. Yet Sikes's amendment assured that would not be the case.[169]

While the House version of the State Firearms Control Assistance Act was being finalized, Senator Tydings was pleading with the Senate Judiciary Committee to advance his firearms registration bill, S. 3634. The plea fell on deaf ears. Tydings was told that unless he formally withdrew S. 3634 from consideration, the committee would not advance the Johnson administration's mail-order firearms bill, S. 3633.[170] Tydings reluctantly agreed, but on the condition that S. 3634 could be offered as an amendment on the Senate floor.[171] On July 24 the Senate Judiciary Committee cleared S. 3633, albeit not before several conditions and limiting amendments were imposed on the bill, much like had been done in the House. Senator Dodd celebrated the committee's action, stating, "My seven-year-long struggle for strict gun control appears to be nearing final realization. . . . I am confident that the Senate will pass this strict and sensible gun control bill without any further delay."[172] But there was a delay—of over a month—given the Senate's scheduled August recess, and therefore it was not until September that the Senate formally took up S. 3633.[173]

The Senate's scheduled recess provided the NRA and its allies with more than enough time to voice their dissatisfaction and hopefully convince the Senate to not pass any additional firearms controls before Election Day. The organization and its allies provided the gun rights community with answers and talking points on everything pertaining to firearms controls. Firearms registration was criticized with particular force. The gun rights mantras "punish the criminal, not the law-abiding citizen" and "enforce the firearms laws already on the books" were repeated often. As for opinion polls showing large American majorities supporting firearms controls, the NRA and its allies dismissed them as being "wrong," "open to question," and containing "half-truths," and the Americans being polled were characterized as misinformed and uneducated on the issue.[174] As for why President Johnson was urging Congress to pass strict firearms controls, the NRA and its allies alleged that it was a political "smokescreen," that is, part of a larger "cover up to take the public's mind off assassinations, Vietnam and crime."[175] And as for who was really peddling the conspiracies and lies, the NRA and its allies stated that it was not them. Rather, it was firearms control proponents. They were, in the words of *Guns Magazine* editor E. B. Mann, the "real tilters at windmills," for it was "they, most of all, who aim lances of ignorance at Gibraltors of violence."[176]

By the time the Senate reconvened for business in early September, the anger among the gun rights community was considerably high.[177] The number of petitions, flyers, and advertisements opposing firearms controls was insurmountable, and it was abundantly clear that firearms controls were going to be an Election Day issue. What particularly concerned members of Congress was the groundswell of gun rights opposition. Indeed, the national polls showed large majorities of Americans supporting strict firearms control measures such as licensing and registration. The sheer volume of mail from the gun rights community, however, accompanied by news media reports of fervent opposition from sportsmen, shooters, and hunters at legislative and assembly meetings, was telling a much different story—a story of an electorally energized gun rights opposition.

It was in mid-September that the Senate reconvened for business on S. 3633. As anticipated, given the organized gun rights opposition, several amendments to strengthen S. 3633 were rejected. This included Tydings's and other senators' amendments to tack on firearms registration. Additionally, much like in the House, the Senate agreed to several weakening amendments to politically appease the NRA and its allies. On September 18, upon completion of the amendment process, the Senate version of the State Firearms Control Assistance Act passed by a vote of 70 to 17.[178]

There were three principal areas where the Senate bill turned out notably different from the House bill. The first was regarding the interstate sale of ammunition between firearms licensed dealers. While the House bill restricted the sale of only handgun ammunition, the Senate bill restricted all firearm ammunition, whether it be from a handgun, a rifle, or a shotgun. The second area of difference was that the Senate bill failed to include the controversial Sikes amendment, which exempted all military surplus firearms and ammunition purchased or acquired through the NBPRP. The final area difference between the two bills pertained to mandatory minimums. While the House bill included a provision that would subject a person convicted of a crime while in possession of a firearm to a fixed sentence, the Senate bill provided judges with the discretion to impose an indeterminate sentence of up to life imprisonment for various federal "crimes of violence."

Given that the Senate's version differed from that of the House, the bills went to a joint conference committee.[179] On October 10 the joint committee agreed on a compromise bill that both the House and Senate approved the same day.[180] The bill expanded federal control over the interstate shipment of all firearms and ammunition, created additional penalties for using a firearm while committing certain federal crimes, imposed a series of new regulations on all federally licensed dealers, and expanded the categories of persons to whom sales of firearms would be barred. In addition to these new measures, several concessions were included to appease gun rights proponents. These included providing several legal exceptions for firearms collectors, exempting anyone purchasing or acquiring firearms and ammunition through the NBPRP from the law's mail-order restrictions, and authorizing state governments to individually opt out from the law's prohibition on out-of-state firearms and ammunition purchases, so long as said purchases were from residents of contiguous states.[181]

From September 18, when the Senate passed its version of the State Firearms Control Assistance Act, through October 10, when House and Senate adopted the joint conference committee's version, the NRA remained adamant that Congress was taking the wrong approach.[182] The way the NRA saw it, the answer to firearms-related violence should never be "stricter gun regulation," but "simply law enforcement."[183] On the day that the Senate passed its version of the act, NRA president Glassen was adamant that "no one can say a law is going to save a life" and there was not one "indication that the availability of firearms has anything to do with crimes."[184] And while the joint conference committee was hammering out the differences between the House and Senate versions, Glassen repeatedly called on the gun rights community to let their fifty million "minority" votes be heard come Election Day by voting out firearms control–supporting lawmakers.[185] He was not alone in issuing this electoral plea. As early as March— that is, three months before Congress enacted the Omnibus Crime Control and Safe Streets Act—gun rights advocates from across the country were urging sportsmen, hunters, shooters, and firearms owners to vote for only those candidates that supported the Second Amendment. "A vote for the wrong man can and will deprive your CHILDREN from THE RIGHT to OWN a FIREARM!," read one gun rights newsletter.[186]

Of course, it was nothing new for the NRA and its allies to call on gun rights supporters to vote out firearms control–supporting lawmakers. In 1952, for instance, the organization published an advertisement in the *American Rifleman* that read, "Even with us—It's Ballots Before Bullets." The advertisement sought to remind NRA members that the right to vote was the "most precious privilege of American citizenship." It stated: "We often talk about the right to own and bear arms. The future of that right, and many others we enjoy, depends on the representatives your vote elects. So be sure you vote next month."[187] Similarly, in 1932, at a time when the NRA was trying to stop Congress from passing what would become the National Firearms Act, the *American Rifleman* contained an editorial reminding NRA members of the "basic principles of Americanism, the principle of government by elected representatives of the people." The editorial called on "the American shooter who has always borne the brunt on the field of battle in fighting with bullets" to "take the offensive in a bloodless battle of ballots."[188]

What was unique in 1968 was that for the first time congressional candidates and the news media were beginning to take notice. Congressional candidates were suddenly jockeying for the votes of gun rights supporters. Such vote jockeying was far more common among House races than Senate races, and particularly common for races involving largely rural congressional districts. The earlier examples of Montana representatives James F. Battin and Arnold Olsen bear this out, but there are indeed others. Take, for instance, Washington District 3, where Democrat incumbent Julia B. Hansen faced off against Republican challenger Wayne M. Adams. On July 24, Hansen voted in favor of the State Firearms Control Assistance Act. However, after receiving considerable opposition from the gun rights supporters, when it was time for the House to consider the joint conference committee's bill, she voted against it. Yet despite Hansen changing her vote, several political advertisements seized on the fact that she had previously voted for firearms controls. One ad claimed: "IF YOU WANT TO LOSE YOUR GUNS RE-ELECT Your Active Congresswoman Julia Butler Hansen."[189] The day before Election Day, Hansen's campaign fired back with its own advertisement touting the representative's vote against the joint conference committee's bill. Hansen won reelection by 13 percentage points.

The House race for Utah District 1 is another example where congressional candidates running in largely rural districts politically jockeyed for the votes of gun rights supporters. In several political advertisements, Republican incumbent Laurence J. Burton touted his status as a sportsman, hunter, and opponent of firearms controls. One advertisement highlighted how Burton was outspoken "against federal gun control bills" and believed that "the people who misuse guns, not sportsmen should be punished."[190] Burton won reelection by 37 percentage points.

There are other examples where candidates vying for a seat in the House of Representatives jockeyed for the votes of gun rights supporters, but while this is significant in the pantheon of electoral history, there is no evidence to suggest that such political jockeying was a deciding factor in any House election outcome. Certainly, in largely rural districts where there was a high proportion of firearms-owning households, it would have been politically unwise for a congressional candidate to support strict firearms controls. In largely suburban and urban districts, however, whether a congressional candidate supported firearms controls proved to be a nonissue come Election Day. This can be seen through an election analysis of incumbents who voted for the House version of the State Firearms Control Assistance Act. Of the 305 representatives who voted for firearms controls on July 24, only four incumbents seeking reelection lost.[191] That number is cut in half to just two if the October 10 vote on the joint conference committee version of the State Firearms Control Assistance Act is the benchmark.[192] What is even more telling is that only one of the firearms control-supporting incumbents to lose reelection did so from a challenger who opposed firearms controls—and from one no less who failed to make firearms controls a key issue.[193]

The Election Day impact that firearms controls had in the Senate races was much like that of the House—minimal. Yet according to gun rights advocates the exact opposite was true. The way advocates saw it, sportsmen, hunters, shooters, and firearms owners were instrumental in voting out several "anti-gun" senators.[194] For instance, in the January 1969 edition of *American Rifleman*, the NRA identified six Senate races where "sportsmen and conservationists ... weighed the gun control issue and acted according to their conclusions."[195] The editors of *Gun Week* were more tempered in their praise and identified only three such races.[196] The same was true for the editors of *Guns Magazine*.[197] As for the news media's take, there was only once such Senate race—Pennsylvania's, where Republican challenger Richard S. Schweiker handily defeated Democrat incumbent Joseph S. Clark by 282,100 votes. What made the race so newsworthy was Clark's outspoken support for firearms registration, as well as Clark's disdain for the "gun lobby." The postelection issue of *Pennsylvania's Outdoor People*—the official publication of the Pennsylvania Federation of

Sportsmen's Clubs (PFSC)—ran the headline "Sportsmen Boot Clark Out."[198] Similarly, another Pennsylvania outdoors newspaper column ran the headline "Sportsmen Zapped Clark."[199]

While few people, if anyone, will disagree that many, if not thousands of, Pennsylvania sportsmen voted against Clark solely because of his outspoken support for firearms controls, there is no evidence to suggest that this was a considerable factor, let alone the deciding one in Clark's defeat. As outlined in chapter 1, there are several reasons why Schweiker defeated Clark. The firearms control issue does not appear to one of them. The most glaring evidence of this can be found by looking at the corresponding Pennsylvanian vote in the presidential election, where Vice President Humphrey handily defeated Nixon by 169,388 votes. Like Clark, Humphrey was on record having supported President Johnson's strict firearms control legislation, including firearms registration. Thus if the "sportsmen" vote or Clark's outspoken support for firearms controls was indeed a considerable factor in the race outcome, how could it be that Humphrey won the same state over Nixon by such a wide margin?

The fact that the "sportsmen's vote" was not a considerable factor in Clark's defeat does not mean that the issue of firearms controls was not relevant in several Senate races in 1968. Across the country, senatorial candidates from both political parties, incumbents and challengers alike, sought to make firearms controls a voting issue. In the case of Western states, it was common for senatorial candidates to openly advertise their opposition to firearms controls. In the Idaho Senate race, Democrat incumbent Frank Church ran several "pro-gun" advertisements after Republican challenger George V. Hansen ran an advertisement claiming that he was the "first in Idaho" to oppose federal firearms controls. One Church advertisement called out Hansen for "trying to distort the record" and even included news snippets showing how Church was well-known for leading the fight against firearms registration.

A similar "pro-gun" faceoff was taking place in the Oklahoma Senate race, where Democrat incumbent Mike Monroney was pitted against Republican challenger Henry Bellmon. Throughout his time in the Senate, Monroney had opposed even the idea of firearms registration.[200] Yet after Robert F. Kennedy was assassinated and Monroney's office began receiving a flood of constituent mail supporting strict firearms controls, Monroney shifted course and came out supportive.[201] Less than three weeks

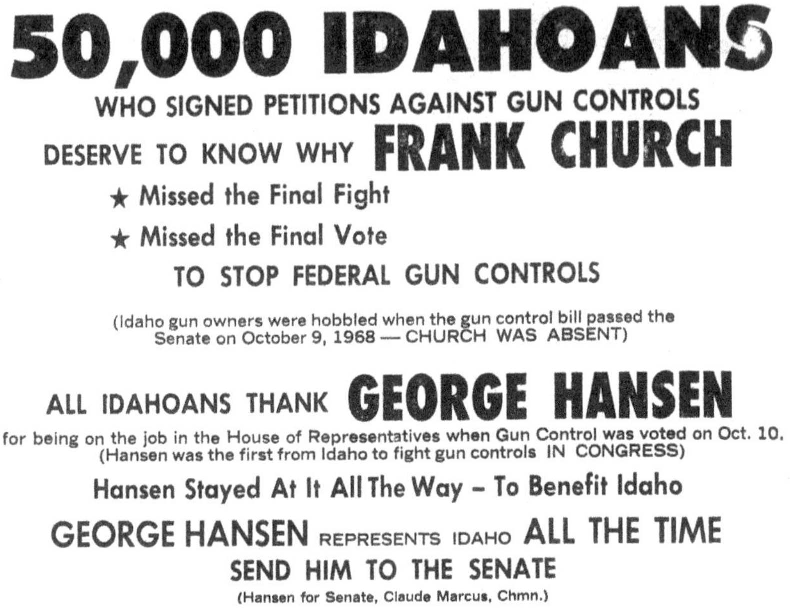

50,000 IDAHOANS

WHO SIGNED PETITIONS AGAINST GUN CONTROLS

DESERVE TO KNOW WHY FRANK CHURCH

★ Missed the Final Fight

★ Missed the Final Vote

TO STOP FEDERAL GUN CONTROLS

(Idaho gun owners were hobbled when the gun control bill passed the
Senate on October 9, 1968 — CHURCH WAS ABSENT)

ALL IDAHOANS THANK GEORGE HANSEN

for being on the job in the House of Representatives when Gun Control was voted on Oct. 10.
(Hansen was the first from Idaho to fight gun controls IN CONGRESS)

Hansen Stayed At It All The Way – To Benefit Idaho

GEORGE HANSEN REPRESENTS IDAHO ALL THE TIME

SEND HIM TO THE SENATE

(Hansen for Senate, Claude Marcus, Chmn.)

FIGURE 6.8 Political advertisement that appeared in several Idaho-based newspapers in 1968. The ad, paid for by Republican George Hansen during the Idaho Senate race, sought to capitalize on Democratic incumbent Frank Church's absence on the Senate floor when what eventually became the Gun Control Act of 1968 was first voted on.

later—that is, once the NRA had roused the gun rights community to political action and flipped the constituent mail back in opposition to firearms controls—Monroney went back to opposing firearms registration.[202] Therein Bellmon tried making Monroney's brief support for firearms registration a campaign issue. But time and time again, Monroney was adamant that he had opposed to the idea, which led to Monroney and Bellmon running competing advertisements, each claiming that they would fight against any additional firearms controls.[203] In line with the expert predictions, by riding Nixon's political coattails, Bellmon ultimately beat out Monroney.

But the most closely watched "pro-gun" faceoff for a Senate seat took place in Oregon, where four-time Democrat incumbent Wayne Morse and Republican challenger Robert W. Packwood were in a tight race. Morse was adamantly opposed to all firearms controls, including the water-downed

provisions within the Omnibus Crime Control and Safe Streets Act.[204] Packwood also opposed firearms controls. But after Senator Kennedy's assassination, Packwood conceded that if he were a sitting senator, he would
have voted for the Omnibus Crime Control and Safe Streets Act given all
the other good provisions in the bill.[205] It was a concession directly at odds
with Packwood's previous statements. Just months prior, in an interview
with APROKBA, he had stated, "If gun control legislation is passed by this
Congress, the greatest fraud in political history of the U.S. will have been
perpetrated on the citizens of Oregon and this country."[206] At election's end,
the challenger Packwood squeaked out a victory over incumbent Morse by
less than half a point.[207]

Of course, not every Senate race was a competition over who disliked
firearms controls the most. Several races pitted firearms control opponents
against proponents, with the former seeking exploit firearms controls as
a wedge voting issue. The earlier example of Democratic senator Gaylord A.
Nelson of Wisconsin bears this out. Therein Nelson, who supported firearms controls, to include firearms registration, was pitted against Republican challenger Jerris Leonard, who opposed them.[208] The same was true
in North Carolina, where Democratic incumbent Sam J. Ervin, who voted
in favor of the firearms control provisions in both the Omnibus Crime Control and Safe Streets Act and the Gun Control Act,[209] was being challenged
by Republican Robert V. Somers, who was "unalterably opposed to gun control legislation of any kind" (figure 6.9).[210] Also, in Vermont, Democrat
incumbent senator George D. Aiken was often criticized by Republican
challenger William K. Tufts on the issue. While Aiken had repeatedly backed
firearms controls, including at one point firearms registration,[211] Tufts was
somewhat of a Second Amendment absolutist—that is, someone who
believes any and all firearms controls are in violation of the right to keep
and bear arms.[212] A similar situation was playing out in Missouri, where,
following incumbent Edward V. Long's loss to Tom Eagleton in the Democratic primary, the race for the Senate was now between two political
newcomers. While Eagleton openly supported federal firearms controls,
including federal firearms registration, Republican challenger Tom Curtis
believed that firearms control was a state and local matter, and that federal law should punish only firearms abusers, not law-abiding citizens.[213]
"I favor stronger enforcement on the use of guns by the criminal element,
but I believe federal controls on all guns are not the American way," stated

GUN CONTROL

Bob Somers is against Gun Control of any kind, against Registering Firearms.

Sam Ervin Voted for Gun Control—twice.

PRAYER IN THE PUBLIC SCHOOLS

Bob Somers is for Prayer in the Public Schools.

Sam Ervin Voted against Prayer in the Public Schools.

STAND UP FOR AMERICA

ROBERT VANCE SOMERS
Republican For
UNITED STATES SENATE

Friends of Somers . . . Stephen H. Conger, Chairman

FIGURE 6.9 Political advertisement that ran in newspapers across North Carolina in the weeks leading up to the 1968 election. Paid for by Friends of [Robert Vance] Somers, the ad sought to use North Carolina senator Sam J. Ervin's votes for both the Omnibus Crime Control and Safe Streets Act and the Gun Control Act against him.

Curtis in an interview, adding, "The right to bear arms is a constitutional guarantee which I believe Congress cannot change."[214] Meanwhile, in the South Dakota Senate race, Republican challenger Archie Gubbrud called out Democratic incumbent George McGovern for having come out in support of firearms controls in the wake of Senator Kennedy's assassination.[215] "I won't vote to remove the gun from the back of the farms pickup," stated Gubbrud, adding, "If the man my opponent supports and urges we elect—Hubert Humphrey—has his way, there are going to be a lot less hunters in South Dakota in coming years."[216]

It is worth noting that in all five of these Senate races, the winning candidate proved to be the one who expressed support for firearms controls on the campaign trail—that is, Nelson, Ervin, Aiken, Eagleton, and McGovern—and did so despite running in a largely rural state. Also notable is the fact that they were all Democrats, yet the presidential race in each of their respective states came out for Republican Richard Nixon. The opposite was true in Pennsylvania, where Clark, an incumbent Democrat, handily lost to Schweiker, yet the state's presidential race swung overwhelmingly for

Democrat Humphrey. Considering these facts, it would be rather far-fetched to conclude—much like the editors of Guns & Ammo did in their postelection issue—that the elections of 1968 were a national referendum on gun rights over gun controls.[217]

Even if one historically accepts that the Clark-Schweiker race outcome was principally due to the organized opposition of Pennsylvania sportsmen—and that is a big if—it was a one-off for the 1968 elections and in no way indicated that organized gun rights opposition could principally sway the outcome of statewide elections, let alone any national election. The New York senate race between Republican incumbent Jacob K. Javits and Democratic challenger Paul O'Dwyer bears this out. Until June 4, 1968, Javits was largely noncommittal on the firearms control issue.[218] As with many other senators, however, the assassination of Robert F. Kennedy compelled Javits to become a strong firearms control proponent, including going so far as to advocate for firearms registration.[219] Javits had in fact transformed into such a firearms control proponent that he attended firearms control rallies, advocated that the Republican Party Platform Committee adopt a strong firearms control plank, defended the Sullivan law maligned by gun rights supporters, and delivered speeches urging Americans to use the "power of the pen" to convince Congress on the need to pass strict federal firearms controls.[220] Javits quickly drew the ire of New York sportsmen, who organized a "Dump Javits" campaign (fig. 6.10).[221] The core purpose of the campaign was to ensure that "gun owners everywhere," from "every race, every religion, every social group . . . every occupation and every economic status," to include "Republicans, Democrats, liberals, Conservatives, [and] independents," were "heard loud and clear at the ballot box."[222] Javits did not back down one iota to the "Dump Javits" campaign. "I intend to remain as they call me 'a political tiger' who will relentlessly seek effective gun control laws—laws that are also fully compatible with the needs of the people and do not unduly hamper hunters and sportsmen," he Javits.[223]

Javits went so far as to defend his firearms control policy position before the thirty-fifth annual conference of the New York State Conservation Council. He was in fact the only firearms control–supporting politician who agreed to speak before the gun rights–friendly audience.[224] Javits was heckled and booed before sportsmen holding bumper stickers and signs reading "If Guns are Outlawed, Only Outlaws Will Have Guns" and "Help

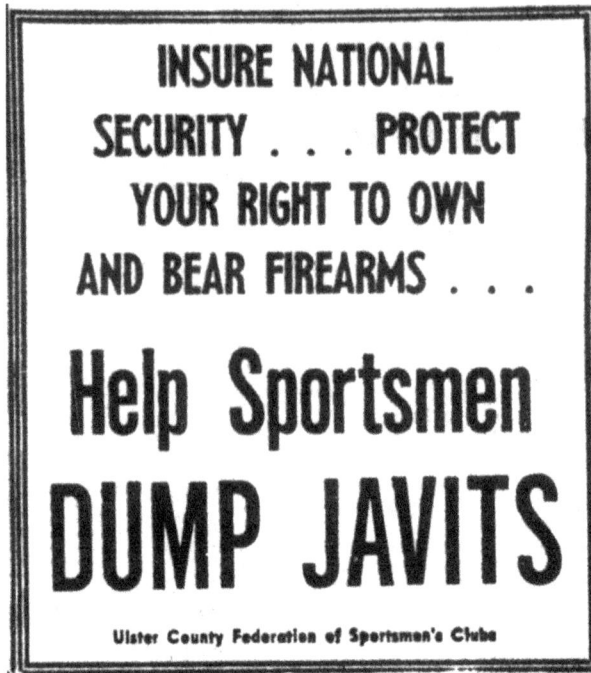

FIGURE 6.10 Political advertisement in the *Kingston (N.Y.) Daily Freeman*, November 2, 1968. Paid for by the Ulster County Federation of Sportsmen's Clubs, the ad was one of several urging sportsmen to "Dump Javits."

Sportsmen Dump Javits."[225] Yet he kept his composure, held his political ground, and defended the Senate's passage of the State Firearms Control Assistance Act. In doing so, he made almost every political misstep possible to turn the gun rights–friendly audience against him, including calling out the "Dump Javits" campaign for thinking "misguidedly," defending federal firearms registration as an effective criminal deterrent, and asserting that the Second Amendment only "protect[s] the right of a state to raise a militia *but not the right of an individual to possess a gun.*"[226] Needless to say, Javits's speech did little to assuage gun rights supporters' firearms confiscation fears. It did not help Javits's campaign that NRA president Glassen delivered an address later in the day, urging New York sportsmen to vote out any firearms control–supporting candidate from office.[227] Ultimately, however, Javits won reelection over O'Dwyer by 17 percentage points.

That Javits and other firearms control–supporting incumbents won their respective Senate races in the face of organized gun rights opposition is not to say that every such candidate running for the Senate won on Election Day. The defeat of Clark by Schweiker is a case in point, but there was also another—the Ohio Senate race between two newcomers, Democrat John J. Gilligan and Republican William B. Saxbe. Saxbe, who firmly stood by the gun rights mantra "punish the criminal, not the law-abiding citizen," narrowly defeated Gilligan, who expressed support for strict firearms controls, including registration. The Ohio Senate race was in fact so close that it is plausible that any one-issue voting bloc—including the sportsmen's vote—may have affected the election outcome. Unlike the Clark-Schweiker race, however, there is no evidence to suggest that the Gilligan-Saxbe race was affected by the votes of Ohio sportsmen or the wider Ohio gun rights community. This is because, unlike Pennsylvania or even New York, the Gilligan-Saxbe race lacked the organized involvement of gun rights groups, whether it be organized opposition toward Gilligan or organized support for Saxbe.

Yet despite the lack of any organized gun rights involvement in that race, gun rights advocates insisted otherwise. The question is: Why? The evidentiary record does not provide a clear answer. If past is prologue, however, history informs two reasons. First, by insisting sportsmen had a hand in Gilligan's defeat, gun rights advocates were sending a message to lawmakers that they too could be voted out of office if they did not support gun rights over firearms controls. Second and equally important, by publicizing how sportsmen were victorious at the ballot box, gun rights advocates were keeping the gun rights community politically motivated.[228] For if gun rights advocates had signaled anything but victory on Election Day, many of the sportsmen, hunters, shooters, and firearms owners who made up the gun rights community would have politically disengaged themselves, thus harming gun rights advocates' bottom line, both financially and politically.

And it was not only the Gilligan-Saxbe race in which sportsmen, hunters, shooters, and firearms owners were misled by gun rights advocates. In the race for the Florida Senate seat vacated by George Smathers, the NRA touted the victory of Republican Edward J. Gurney over Democrat Leroy Collins. "Gurney voted for a number of NRA-favored provisions including the mandatory penalty for misuse of firearms in crime and to exclude .22

rimfire and shotshell ammunition," stated the NRA.[229] What the NRA conveniently omitted was the fact that Gurney also voted for the Gun Control Act, and before Senator Kennedy's assassination he was on record supporting mail-order restrictions on long guns.[230] Another misleading claim of victory by gun rights advocates involved the Maryland Senate race, where Democratic incumbent Daniel B. Brewster lost reelection to Republican challenger Charles Mathias.[231] Brewster's defeat was far from a victory for gun rights supporters. Indeed, advocates were correct to note that Brewster initially cosponsored fellow Maryland senator Tydings's firearms registration bill after Senator Kennedy's assassination. Brewster later dropped his support, however, after he was unable to convince Tydings to amend the bill in a way that recognized a "basic right" to own firearms and use them for legitimate purposes.[232] Additionally, gun rights advocates conveniently omitted the fact that Brewster's opponent, Mathias, was also on record supporting firearms controls, including a federal ban on mail-order purchases.[233]

The fact that gun rights advocates grasped at straws to make the elections of 1968 appear to be something that they were not is not to say that gun rights political action was not overall impactful. The historical evidence is clear and convincing that the 1968 elections forever changed the political landscape on firearms controls. As will be discussed in ensuing chapters, these elections gave lawmakers the perception of a politically powerful "gun lobby"—a lobby that could easily influence the vote of sportsmen, hunters, shooters, and firearms owners. Although this perception was far from the reality, it was a reality nonetheless to lawmakers going forward.

7

1969–1970

The "No Compromise" Gun Rights
Movement Arrives

To kick off 1969, the National Rifle Association (NRA) published an *American Rifleman* editorial titled "An NRA Life Member in the White House," which highlighted how Richard M. Nixon was the sixth president of the United States to hold NRA life membership. The editorial noted how the organization looked forward to continuing its "close and cordial relationship" with the White House, as it had before President Lyndon B. Johnson.[1] NRA executive vice president Franklin L. Orth penned a similar sentiment in a letter to every life member. "With the new [Nixon] administration taking over in Washington, something is in the air," he wrote, adding, "Call it expectancy, hopefulness, enthusiasm, or just plain newness, everybody recognizes its presence." Orth concluded his letter by noting, "NRA wholeheartedly subscribes to President Nixon's aim of 'Forward Together.'"[2]

The NRA was not alone in celebrating a Nixon White House. The editors of the magazine *Shooting Industry* started off the new year by proclaiming "Nixon's the One!"[3] Similarly, the editors of *Guns & Ammo* wrote how Nixon was a "refreshing departure from the philosophy of the last administration which believed in the Federal Government playing Big Brother and preempting the field of firearms legislation."[4] But not everyone in the gun rights community was enthusiastic about what Nixon might bring in the way of firearms policy. S. J. Schoon, president of the gun rights extremist organization Association to Preserve Our Right to Keep and Bear Arms (APORKBA), was a bit more hesitant. While Schoon conceded that Nixon was far better than Hubert H. Humphrey, the fact remained that on the campaign trail Nixon had expressed support for several firearms controls. This, coupled with the "ever-increasing number of Anti-Gun bills" being filed in the 91st Congress, suggested to Schoon that it was best to "keep a watchful eye" on Nixon before gun rights supporters threw their full support behind him.[5]

What gun rights extremists like Schoon wanted was for Nixon to embrace the policy position of the American Independent Party (AIP)—the only political party that was forthright in declaring that firearms control was an issue best left to the state governments, and that firearms registration "would do little or nothing to deter criminal activity."[6] AIP's presidential nominee in 1968, former Alabama governor George C. Wallace, was even more direct in opposing firearms controls. While on the campaign trail, Wallace actively touted gun rights mantras such as "register communists, not firearms," "crime control, not firearms control," and "enforce the firearms laws already on the books." But having Nixon in the White House was undoubtedly the next best thing for gun rights extremists like Schoon.[7] Nixon's statements on firearms controls were very much in line with the NRA's political straddling approach—that is, expressing support for firearms controls, but only on the condition that said controls are "reasonable" and seek to punish the criminal misuse of firearms.[8]

It was not long after the NRA published its *American Rifleman* editorial celebrating a Nixon White House that gun rights advocates began questioning whether the thirty-seventh president was truly on their side. This was because the editorial immediately prompted firearms control proponents to request that Nixon resign his NRA life membership.[9] He ultimately did so, but not at the behest of firearms controls proponents. Rather, according to a White House spokesman, because Nixon could not recall having ever accepted his life membership, he decided to resign it, as well as resign all other organizational memberships in which he was not an active participant.[10] The following White House statement accompanied Nixon's decision: "Some years ago, when [Nixon] was Vice President of the United States, apparently the National Rifle Association bestowed upon him an honorary life membership. Since that time, the President has had no occasion to take notice of this honorary membership. It may be of interest that the President owns no guns."[11]

What the NRA failed to disclose when it published "An NRA Life Member in the White House" is that Nixon's life membership was much like that of President John F. Kennedy—more ceremonial than real. It was one of hundreds of honorary memberships bestowed on Nixon while he was serving as vice president. The same was true of President Kennedy, as well as President Dwight D. Eisenhower. Not to mention, ever since accepting the NRA's offer of life membership in 1957, Nixon had never attended nor taken part in any NRA events, nor had he ever provided the NRA with any political favors such as Eisenhower had done with his congratulatory messages. In 1954, however, while serving as vice president, Nixon did attend the NRA's annual meeting.[12] Therein, contrary to his NRA membership resignation statement, Nixon personally received four handguns from firearms manufacturers Colt, Ruger, and Smith & Wesson.[13] He also signed a congratulatory letter for the NRA, acknowledging the organization for its "great contribution . . . in teaching skill and safety in the handling of firearms."[14] Nonetheless, the fact the Nixon attended the NRA's 1954 annual meeting speaks little to whether the thirty-seventh president was truly a NRA supporter, or for that matter an opponent of firearms controls.

While there was understandably much apprehension within the gun rights community when Nixon resigned his NRA life membership—with some going so far to accuse Nixon of being a "double-crosser"—the NRA and other gun rights advocates made sure to provide the president with political cover by blaming the entire fiasco on "anti-gun" zealots.[15] It was in the summer of 1969, following a hearing by the Senate Subcommittee on Juvenile Delinquency on the necessity of additional firearms controls, that any lingering nervousness over Nixon resigning his NRA life membership quickly died out. Therein Deputy Attorney General Donald E. Santarelli sent the gun rights community a surefire political signal that the White House fully intended to deliver on Nixon's firearms control campaign promises.[16] In particular, Santarelli testified that the Gun Control Act would need time to go into effect before the Department of Justice would even consider supporting any additional federal firearms controls. And should another tragedy involving firearms occur prompting the country to once more cry out for firearms controls, Santarelli urged Congress to defer the matter to state and local officials. For Congress to do otherwise, he warned, would be an "unwarranted invasion into the province of State and local governments."[17]

So Far,
A Memory Like An Elephant!

FIGURE 7.1 Political cartoon in *Gun Week*, September 5, 1969. The cartoon sought to assure readers that President Richard M. Nixon was following through on his firearms control campaign promises. Image reprinted with the express permission of the Second Amendment Foundation.

This is not the say that the Department of Justice was unwilling to support any new federal firearms laws. As Santarelli noted in his testimony, the department would gladly consider prospective amendments to existing laws, but only so long as said amendments made the laws "more equitable" in application." He then proceeded to provide the subcommittee with several prospective amendments—amendments that were clearly lifted from the NRA and other gun rights advocates' political playbook, such as increasing the mandatory minimum sentencing for armed felonies and stopping the "proliferation of cheap, small caliber handguns, known commonly as Saturday Night' Specials." In addition to these prospective amendments, Santarelli proffered one more that quickly garnered the backing of the NRA and other gun rights advocates—repealing the Gun Control Act's ammunition record keeping requirements for licensed firearms dealers.[18] Ever since the Gun Control Act became law, the NRA and other gun rights advocates had singled out the record-keeping requirement as both unduly burdensome and unnecessary, with some going so far as to decry it as "backdoor registration."[19]

Indeed, there was nothing in the Gun Control Act that remotely con-
doned federal firearms registration in any form. According to gun rights
advocates, however, given that the Gun Control Act stipulated that every
ammunition purchaser needed to fill out personal information such as
their name, age, address, date, make of firearm, ammunition caliber or
gauge, and ammunition quantity, the act was seemingly imposing ipso
facto registration on firearms owners.[20] But this gun rights perception of
the Gun Control Act was not the reality. No one knew this more than the
Nixon White House, which, at the request of the NRA and other gun rights
advocates, agreed to fully investigate the matter. And what the White House
ultimately concluded was that the "registration allegation" was "without
merit in law or fact." The NRA and other gun rights advocates conveniently
omitted from their accusation of "backdoor registration" that the ammunition purchase records never came into the custody of any federal government official, nor was the Department of Treasury ever intending on
copying the records and storing them "at any central location." Rather, the
records were maintained and kept by individual licensed firearms dealers.
In addition to the "backdoor registration" complaint being "without merit,"
the White House investigation concluded that if federal, state, or local
governments genuinely wanted to gather information on individual firearms owners, there were far more efficient avenues to do so. These more
efficient avenues included obtaining lists of "those who have been issued
hunting licenses, the membership of hunting, shooting and other sporting clubs, and those who have joined such organizations as the National
Rifle Association."[21]

Yet despite the NRA and gun rights advocates having no factual basis for
their "backdoor registration" complaint, repealing the Gun Control Act's
record-keeping requirement for long gun ammunition quickly garnered
support on Capitol Hill. This was particularly true among members of Congress representing western states.[22] Leading the effort was Utah senator
Wallace C. Bennett, who for many years was one of the Senate's staunchest
opponents of firearms controls. He was in fact the first member of Congress
to formally agree with the NRA and other gun rights advocates in character-
izing the Gun Control Act's ammunition record keeping requirement as
ipso facto firearms registration.[23] From that point onward, the false characterization gained political traction.[24] So, too, did Bennett's bill S. 845,
which sought to repeal the record-keeping requirements for all long gun

ammunition. When initially filed, S. 845 maintained twenty-four senator cosponsors, twenty of whom represented states west of the Mississippi River.[25] Yet by the end of July, the number of senator cosponsors increased to thirty-seven, eight of whom had opposed an amendment to the Gun Control Act the year prior that would have exempted all long gun ammunition.[26] And by September, S. 845 had amassed forty-six senator cosponsors.[27]

One of the cosponsors was Senate majority leader Mike Mansfield of Montana. A year earlier, in the wake of Senator Robert F. Kennedy's assassination, Mansfield had proved to be a key congressional voice in passing the first comprehensive federal firearms controls in thirty years. For a brief time, he even cosponsored Maryland senator Joseph D. Tydings's federal firearms registration bill. But that was before Mansfield faced overwhelming opposition from Montana sportsmen.[28] Nevertheless, because he had briefly lent his voice to the political cause of firearms controls, many in the Montana gun rights community were marking November 3, 1970, on their calendar.[29] Mansfield was keenly aware of this gun rights opposition, which caused him to politically pivot on the firearms control issue at the start of the 91st Congress. He went so far as to back mischaracterizing the Gun Control Act's ammunition record keeping requirement as "deceptive" back-door registration.[30] And Mansfield's pivot on the firearms control issue did not stop there. Recall that following Senator Kennedy's assassination, Mansfield had thrown his support behind firearms controls "in the hope and belief that they [would provide] some mitigation in the rising level of the violence of the gun which has come to plague our land, especially the cities of our nation."[31] Yet come the 91st Congress, he was of the opposite opinion.[32] Now, according to Mansfield, firearms controls imposed a "clear" disproportionate burden on law-abiding Montanans. While he indeed continued to acknowledge that "large metropolitan centers" were being "wracked" by firearms-related violence, he now felt that Montanans should not have to endure any federal firearms control burdens. "What we stand to benefit from its hoped-for objective—a reduction in gun crime—is greatly disproportionate when viewed solely within the geographical confines of Montana," he stated.[33] And to even further endear himself to gun rights supporters, Mansfield introduced the type of bill that the NRA and other gun rights advocates had long promoted as the only way to curtail firearms-related violence—punish the criminal misuse of firearms with mandatory minimums.

Filed as S. 849, Mansfield's bill sought to impose a ten-year mandatory sentence for any person having committed a felony with a firearm, and a twenty-five year mandatory sentence for a second.[34] He touted the bill as necessary to "assist Federal, State and local law enforcement agencies in their fight against crime and violence." Mansfield also touted S. 849 as being more justiciable than other forms of firearms control given that the bill imposed "no burden," "no sacrifice" on the part of "law-abiding gun owners."[35] He went so far as to name S. 849 the "Lesnik Mandatory Sentencing Bill" after Marine second lieutenant Thaddeus R. Lesnik. Recall that it was Lesnik who was tragically killed by a handgun in the Georgetown district of Washington, D.C., on the same day as Robert Kennedy. And it was Lesnik's death that compelled Mansfield to throw his support behind federal firearms controls.[36] Yet come the 91st Congress, Mansfield was invoking Lesnik's death to decisively flip on the firearms control issue.[37] "A little more than a year ago, Thaddeus Lesnik . . . was shot down in a restaurant here in the District," he stated, adding, "That tragic act of violence, like so many others, caused me to reassess my thinking on gun legislation."[38]

FIGURE 7.2 Political cartoon in *Gun Week*, October 24, 1969. The cartoon showed an "anti-gun" politician ready to be beheaded in the guillotine of sportsmen's "future votes." It sought to remind the gun rights community to be politically active in the 1970 elections, as well as to convey that anti-gun politicians needed to be voted out of office. Image reprinted with the express permission of the Second Amendment Foundation.

Mansfield was not the only one in the Senate to do a political about-face on firearms controls. Newly appointed Senate minority leader Hugh Scott of Pennsylvania was also quick to change political course. In late 1963, in the wake of President John F. Kennedy's assassination, it was Scott who coalesced his fellow Republicans around stopping the indiscriminate mail-order sale of firearms.[39] Likewise, in the wake of Senator Kennedy's assassination, it was Scott who urged his fellow Republicans to back several firearms control proposals. This included Tydings's firearms registration bill, which Scott ended up voting for.[40] Last, it was Scott who urged his fellow Republicans to reject several restricting amendments to the Gun Control Act.[41]

Yet come the 91st Congress, Scott decisively flipped on the firearms-control issue. He claimed he experienced a change of heart after hearing how "law-abiding citizens" were "suffering inconveniences and burdens" under the Gun Control Act.[42] This, according to Scott, propelled him to cosponsor Bennett's S. 845 and Mansfield's S. 849.[43] But Scott's professed reason for flipping on firearms controls was not the reality. Like Mansfield, Scott's key interest was political self-preservation. Scott did not want end up like Pennsylvania senator Joseph S. Clark, who was defeated in the elections in 1968, allegedly at the hands of Pennsylvania sportsmen.[44] But before decisively flipping on firearms controls, Scott reached out to Clark's 1968 election opponent, now junior Republican Pennsylvania senator, Richard S. Schweiker, for information regarding whether there really was "anything such as a hunter-conservationist" or "sportsman's bloc" vote. The answer Scott received from Schweiker was that "the hunters and the gun control issue are out there and they exerted tremendous clout" in defeating Clark.[45] With that assurance, Scott began working closely with Schweiker to remold his political image as an ally of Pennsylvania sportsmen.[46] However, those who had followed the events leading up to the enactment of the Gun Control Act were not so naïve as to buy into Scott's professed reason for flipping on firearms controls.

This included the editors of *Gun Week*, who sounded off against Scott's record of supporting firearms controls. They then posited the following question to *Gun Week*'s readers: "If Sen. Scott is re-elected, will he, being bolstered by a new six-year term, revert to the anti-gun stand he held for so many years under the tutelage of Sen. Dodd?" Although the editors decided to leave it up to each reader whether to "forgive and forget" Scott for his "former sins," they did urge them to hold Scott politically accountable.[47] And Scott did not make it easy on Pennsylvania sportsmen. Consider his October 4, 1969, speech before the annual meeting of the Pennsylvania Rifle and Pistol Association (PRPA). Therein, to the surprise of attendees, he claimed that in 1968 he was "strongly opposed to the Tydings bill to establish a national system of firearms registration," when in fact he had voted for it.[48] Scott's political altering of the truth did not end there. In subsequent speeches, statements, and press releases, he self-servingly renamed Bennett's S. 849 the "Bennett-Scott bill." Additionally, he oddly claimed he was one of the original cosponsors to Bennett's S. 849.[49] He was not.[50]

With many now publicly questioning Scott's motives for flipping on firearms controls, the Senate minority leader made a bold decision. He would tell the *truth*—that is, of course, a politically expedient version of the truth—in two letters addressed to the gun rights community. The first, written in November 1969, was printed in *Gun Week*.[51] The second, written in February 1970, was printed in *Guns & Ammo*.[52] Although the two letters were structured differently and contained distinct verbiage, the overall political objective was the same—convince the gun rights community to forgive him. And the *truth* that Scott tried to confess was one of personal mistake and mistrust. What he wanted the gun rights community to take away was that he was simply swept up in the highly emotional rhetoric in favor of firearms control following the assassinations of Senator Kennedy and Martin Luther King, Jr. But now, according to Scott, after having been enlightened to the true facts of firearms controls—that firearms controls were unduly burdensome and did nothing but create a bureaucratic nightmare for "law-biding sportsmen" who were "being treated like criminals instead of the real criminals roaming the streets"—he was on their side.[53]

The fact that both Mansfield and Scott decidedly flipped on the firearms control issue speaks volumes to how they viewed sportsmen, hunters, shooters, and firearms owners as an important one-issue sportsmen's voting bloc that could tilt the scales of any election.[54] And Mansfield and Scott were not the only members of Congress fearful of the power of this voting bloc. Across Capitol Hill were whispers of the "gun lobby" being an electoral force not to be reckoned with.[55] As Florida representative and NRA congressional surrogate Robert F. Sikes stated before the NRA's annual meetings in 1969: "The last election produced some upsets in

Trying To 'Switch' His Way Out!

FIGURE 7.3 Political cartoon in *Gun Week*, January 30, 1970. The cartoon showed Pennsylvania senator Hugh Scott trying to bash a snake that represents the Gun Control Act's .22 caliber ammunition record-keeping requirement yet doing so with a skinny branch rather than a large "definite policy" club. It was an attempt to criticize Scott's perceived half-hearted approach to remedying problems with the act and therefore to question his sincerity with regard to the gun rights cause. Image reprinted with the express permission of the Second Amendment Foundation.

which anti-gun partisans were defeated through the efforts of sportsmen to bring the facts to the voters. The word is out that it was not the rank and file of the people who wanted anti-gun laws, and already there have been some converts to the cause of sane legislation. Some of last year's zealous proponents of anti-gun legislation now are piously asserting their belief in the rights of law-abiding citizens to own and use weapons."[56]

Gun rights advocates were naturally thrilled with the political turn of events. It was a far cry from the doomsday scenario they had prophesied a year earlier. From the moment President Lyndon B. Johnson signed the Gun Control Act into law, gun rights advocates had insisted that the law would be the "anti-gunners" first step toward achieving total firearms registration, followed by total firearms confiscation. It did not matter to gun rights advocates that even the most modest firearms confiscation bill did not stand a chance of making it out of a congressional subcommittee, let alone passing both chambers of Congress. What mattered was that gun rights supporters believed firearms confiscation was possible and therefore stayed politically engaged. It was equally important to advocates that

gun rights supporters believed that the enactment of new firearms controls always led to an increase in crime. The way these advocates sold it,
through the enactment of just one firearms control law, crime would
increase, which would in turn afford "anti-gunners" the opportunity to
call for additional firearms controls under the political ruse of crime control.[57] "The first recommendations [by firearms control proponents] are
always reasonable and mild, but these are immediately followed by less reasonable suggestions," stated NRA president Harold W. Glassen at Duke
University, adding, "There is no waiting period to see if that which has
passed will accomplish the task set for it, but immediately further and
greater restrictions are recommended." Then, over time, according to
Glassen, the "private ownership of firearms" would be no more.[58]

Although gun rights advocates knew that these firearms confiscation
scenarios were far-fetched, behind the scenes the NRA and National Shooting Sports Foundation (NSSF) were preparing model firearms owner identification card legislation should any registration or licensing proposals
gain political momentum at the state or local level. It is unknown which
organization was the first to legislatively explore the feasibility of a firearms owner identification card. What is known is that on April 9, 1968, days
after the assassination of Martin Luther King, Jr., the NRA approved explor-
atory consideration of a "Data Retrieval System," which would have insti-
tuted a background check system capable of distinguishing law-abiding
citizens from "criminals and irresponsibles."[59] Similarly, after the killing
of Senator Kennedy, the NSSF issued a memorandum to governors asking
them to reject any firearms registration and licensing proposals. It urged
them instead to work with sportsmen's groups in creating a firearms "ID
system" where purchasers would undergo a "police clearance," that is,
background check, to obtain an "ID card which entitles [them] to own certain categories of firearms."[60]

Despite the uncertainty over which organization was the first to legislatively explore the idea of a firearms owner identification card, what is
known is that while the NRA ultimately decided against the idea, the NSSF
proceeded forward with it as a "middle-of-the-road, happy medium
approach" to firearms control—a decision, when made publicly known,
that was greeted with gun rights hostility.[61] While several of the older, more
moderate gun rights supporters took to defending the NSSF, the newer,
more extreme supporters claimed that by just proffering the idea of a

firearms owner identification card, the NSSF had committed an utter "betrayal of the right to keep and bear arms."[62] The gun rights backlash was so intense that the NSSF published an apology in *Gun Week* defending its decision. "The NSSF believes that the states now have all of the federal controls necessary to enforce their own laws . . . [and] if additional controls are needed [the NSSF believes] they should be passed at the state level," read the advertisement. As it pertained specifically to model firearms owner identification legislation, the NSSF apology noted that that any identification card concept was "preferable" to the alternatives of firearms registration and licensing. It went on to state that the NSSF's policy was to never "introduce" or "campaign for" any of its model firearms legislation. Rather, the NSSF "simply developed" model legislation for "anyone interested."[63] But these claims were patently false. Campaigning and lobbying for model legislation that benefitted sporting, shooting, and hunting was one of the principal purposes for which the group was founded. Not to mention, at the time the apology was published, the NSSF was actively campaigning and lobbying regarding several other model firearms bills.[64]

The apology ultimately fell on deaf ears and resulted in the NSSF removing its proposed firearms owner identification card legislation from its portfolio.[65] Its actions sent the surefire signal that the new, "no compromise" gun rights movement was increasingly gaining influence. And the way this movement saw it, any attempts at political nuance or political straddling by gun rights advocacy groups were no longer accepted.[66] As a result, the voices of the older, more moderate gun rights advocates of years past were beginning to be drowned out. In other words, the days of gun rights advocates compromising on firearms controls were effectively over, and, in the interest of political self-preservation, the advocates of old generally got onboard. This included former NRA president Harlon B. Carter, who in March 1969 delivered the following remarks on sportsmen needing to reject calls for political compromise in the future:

> We, the sportsmen, have yielded much. We have yielded too much and yet there are those among us who seek to find some accommodation by giving in still further. There are some among us who would not take the fatal step, which we don't have to take—licensing and ID cards. We yielded a little bit—we kind of played possum—on mail order control of pistols,

and we obtained the so-called Omnibus Crime Bill—complete prohibition on shipment of handguns in interstate commerce. . . .

. . . We said we could live with that and I suppose we could live with it. But, as it never will, it did not stop there either. Now we have received under the Gun Control Act of 1968 a complete prohibition of interstate mail order of rifles and shotguns. But our opponents did not stop at that. By issuing regulations the government has now obtained what the Congress denied it, national registration of all firearms and registration of all individuals by name and by description who buy ammunition or components. . . .

Where is the compromise? Where is the concession which those people made for us? No, they have conceded nothing. We are being led down a one-way street to the confiscation of our guns.[67]

Although Carter was quick to embrace the new "no compromise" movement, the same could not be said of the NRA that he formerly led. From the fall of 1963 through the summer of 1968, the NRA had benefitted substantially—both politically and economically—from its notoriety in opposing firearms controls. During that time, it was the undisputed gold standard in gun rights advocacy. Indeed, there were times when some of its newer, more extreme members expressed frustration with the NRA's political straddling approach, or when burgeoning gun rights advocates questioned its political strategy. In the end, however, the gun rights community, as a whole, always agreed that the NRA was *the* organization best positioned to lead and carry the fight against firearms controls. But the passage of the Omnibus Crime Control and Safe Streets Act and the Gun Control Act led many to cast doubt on the organization's political influence.[68] Supporters of newer, more extreme gun rights movement were cognizant that it was not the NRA nor its state and local club affiliates that organized the Election Day defeat of "anti-gun" lawmakers in 1968. It was local, organizationally independent political action groups formed with the purpose of removing firearms control–supporting lawmakers from office.[69]

When the 91st Congress convened, not only were these local, organizationally independent political action groups starting to gain more members, but they were also forming at an unprecedented rate.[70] In Minnesota there was the Committee for Effective Crime Control.[71] In Virginia there was the Fairfax County Citizens Opposing Gun Registration & Licensing

Association and Virginia Gun Owners and Sportsman Alliance.[72] In Ohio there was the Sportsmen and Firearms Council, Citizens Committee for Sensible Firearms Legislation, and Ohio Sportsmen's Alliance.[73] Come early 1970 there were roughly thirty local, organizationally independent political action groups formed with the sole purpose of defeating firearms control supporting lawmakers.[74] And while these groups were flourishing, the NRA was experiencing its first noticeable membership decline in its history. By the close of 1969, the organization had lost nearly 43,000 members.[75] The circulation of American Rifleman also experienced a substantial decline for the first time in its history, from 1,159,000 to 1,092,000, while the annual cost of publishing the magazine increased by nearly $100,000.[76]

To offset its financial losses, the NRA sent a letter to every one of its members asking them to enroll at least one new member.[77] Additionally, members were instructed on how the NRA could principally help the gun rights political action groups forming across the country. For decades, the NRA's state and local club affiliates had led the fight against firearms controls. In doing so, these club affiliates accepted and understood their place in the gun rights advocacy hierarchy. The NRA was the proverbial brains of the operation, providing the club affiliates with useful messaging and guidance in the fight against firearms controls. Meanwhile, the club affiliates were the proverbial muscle, providing the NRA with boots-on-the-ground grassroots advocacy. The problem—at least for the NRA—was that many of the new political action groups refused to accept this dynamic. The new groups were particularly frustrated with the NRA's inability to provide them any financial assistance. The NRA responded: "Neither [our] charter nor [our] master plan, nor [our] financial structure contemplated financing major legislative campaigns or brush-fire battles against State and local anti-gun measures. Furthermore, [we are] non-political and non-partisan. That, too, does not leave [us] exactly free to pursue anti-gun politicians with a broad axe on election day."[78]

Yet despite being unable to legally provide the new political action groups with any financial assistance, the NRA tried extending an olive branch. What the NRA hoped the new groups would at least appreciate and respect was that it wholeheartedly supported their advocacy efforts—that is, so long as the groups were not being infiltrated "by militant extremists from any direction."[79] For the time being, the NRA's olive branch did little to garner the support of the new political action groups, nor was it effective in recruiting new members.[80] To help remedy this, the NRA formulated a two-pronged response—step up advertising on its role in fighting firearms controls and start parroting the political message of a "no compromise" gun rights movement. In addition to paying for advertisements in well-established hunting and sporting magazines, for the first time the NRA bought ads in the pages of *Gun Week*. Since *Gun Week*'s inception, its editors and the NRA had had what can best be described as a love-hate relationship.[81] The two sides loved each another when they agreed on an issue and hated each other when they did not. But the NRA could no longer ignore that while the circulation of *American Rifleman* was declining, that of *Gun Week* was increasing.[82] The first NRA advertisement to appear in *Gun Week* contained the headline "Mr. Gun Owner—<u>Right now</u> is your minute of decision." The ad highlighted how the NRA needed "one new member every minute" in order to save the "interests of America's responsible gun owners." It claimed, "Never before in history has the threat to the rights and privileges or responsible gun owners been so great as today."[83] The second NRA advertisement contained the headline, "Shooters Beware! If ever there was a time when you needed the NRA to help protect your present and future rights . . . That Time is Now!" Like the first ad, the second noted how the NRA needed to recruit "one new member every minute" to sustain its fight against firearms controls. Additionally, it audaciously claimed that there was an "insidious war" afoot "against the rights of *you* and every responsible law-abiding sports shooter and hunter!"[84]

Alleging that there was some sinister, behind-the-scenes effort to destroy the Second Amendment and confiscate firearms was nothing new for the NRA. In the late 1920s and 1930s, it had alleged that "gangsters" were secretly funneling money in support of the "anti-gun" campaign.[85] Come World War II, the blame was shifted toward fifth columnists and Nazi operatives.[86] This was followed by the Communist Party, and after the passage of the Gun Control Act the NRA alleged there was a secret, "well-organized and well-financed campaign" involving "movie stars, prominent figures and other public relations devices."[87] What was different come the close of 1969 was the NRA's willingness to embrace the "no compromise" gun rights movement's views on the need to repeal the Gun Control Act. This was a stark contrast to the NRA's political straddling approach, where the organization criticized several Gun Control Act provisions as being "unduly restrictive and unjustified" yet also acknowledged that the law "as a whole appears to be one that the sportsmen of America can live with."[88] But with the precipitous rise of new gun rights political action groups—each urging outright repeal of the Gun Control Act—the NRA was eventually forced to follow suit. Ideally, it would have preferred to continue to politically back a piecemeal approach to fixing any burdensome Gun Control Act provisions. The NRA knew that the Nixon administration would never support repealing the entire Gun Control Act, and therefore urging as much could undermine the NRA's other legislative initiatives or, even worse, hinder its working relationship with the Nixon administration. At the same time, however, the NRA could no longer ignore that the newer, more extreme gun rights movement wanted repeal. This prompted the organization to write every member of Congress inquiring whether they would support repealing the Gun Control Act, replace it with a "more practical and workable anti-crime measure," or, at the very least, "eliminate [those] features [of the law] which are of little use in crime control and apparently serve principally to harass law-abiding sportsmen."[89]

The NRA's embrace of the "no compromise" gun rights movement did not mean that the organization was suddenly endorsing the concept of Second Amendment absolutism—that is, the belief that any regulation, no matter how minor, on the ownership, use, or availability of firearms is a constitutional infringement on the right to arms.[90] The NRA's response to the Illinois Constitutional Convention decision in 1970 to include a right to arms amendment in the Illinois Bill of Rights bears this out. Illinois voters ultimately approved the amendment (and several others in conjunction with it) by a 2 to 1 vote.[91] The amendment provided that "subject only to the police power, the right of the individual citizen to keep and bear arms shall not be infringed." Leading up to the vote, many in the "no compromise" gun rights movement urged the Illinois gun rights community to vote "no" unless the amendment's "police power" language was removed. The way they saw it, that language essentially "negated" the "right to keep and bear arms" language.[92] In other words, according to the "no compromise" movement, if the "police power" constitutional language were adopted, Illinois lawmakers could legislatively outlaw or confiscate everyone's private firearms by simply claiming it "will help safeguard the welfare of the community."[93] But the NRA and its Illinois affiliated clubs outright dismissed this interpretation.[94] Illinois State Rifle Association president Raymond F. Hamel for one responded rather bluntly to the "no compromise" movement's interpretation by exclaiming, "Nothing could be further from the truth!" Hamel went on to note that the principal purpose of the amendment was to ensure that the "right to 'keep' as well as to 'bear' arms" in Illinois was understood to be an "individual right rather than a collective one, and . . . that the 'arms' involved are not limited by the needs of the state militia." As for the amendment's "police power" language, Hamel explained that it was a tacit acknowledgment of the state's "broad authority to provide for the health and safety of their citizens." "The [police] power has existed without regard to any constitutional provision from the earliest days of our republic and its inclusion here serves only to assure concerned voters that present [firearms control] statutes will not be invalidated," he added. But, according to Hamel, if Illinois lawmakers attempted to "ban possession or use" of any firearms which "law-abiding persons commonly employ for purposes of recreation or the protection of person and property," or try to impose "regulations or taxes so onerous as to produced that result," the amendment provided a constitutional safeguard.[95]

Attorney Robert J. Kukla, a member of the NRA board of directors who was well-known to be outspoken against firearms controls, also dismissed the "no compromise" gun rights movement's interpretation of the "police power" language. He argued that such a broad and sweeping interpretation of the "police power" language was based on "unfounded apprehension" and a clear misunderstanding of how governmental police powers worked—powers that were "inherent in any sovereign body, and in the case of the United States they have been reserved by the Federal Constitution to the individual states." Kukla then went on to explain why the "police power" language was included in the amendment:

> [There was] fear that in the absence of that language it might be construed that the Illinois Licensing Law or the Chicago Registration Ordinance would be held invalid. They . . . wanted to differentiate between confiscation per se and laws which would tend to have the effect of indirect confiscation, or as for example taxation or regulatory provisions that would be impossible to be met. The language represented a compromise to satisfy the necessary number of people on the Bill of Rights Committee and delegates to the Constitutional Convention to secure their adaption of the thing.[96]

The NRA's embrace of the "no compromise" gun rights movement's campaign to repeal the Gun Control Act also did not mean that it was suddenly as politically extreme as many of the newer political action groups. The NRA remained dedicated to its principal mission of promoting marksmanship, hunting, and the shooting sports. And to achieve this principal mission, the NRA understood the importance of remaining nonpartisan, as well as conveying the image of an organization that supported "reasonable" firearms controls.[97] Although the categories of firearms controls that the NRA deemed "reasonable" were always a moving target, by pointing to any category of firearm control, even the least restrictive, the group was able to use this evidence as proof that it did not oppose all firearms controls.[98] More important, the NRA's professed support for "reasonable" firearms controls served as a political shield of sorts whenever extremists copied and amplified its anti-firearms-control messaging. For ever since the NRA commandeered the gun rights movement in the early twentieth century, it had become common for conservative action groups to copy its anti-firearms-control message as their own. The NRA generally did not take issue with this so long as said groups supported and defended the U.S. Constitution. But every now and then, a conservative action group or a subset of individuals within the group would amplify the NRA's message in an extremist way.

Such was the case for the late 1968 film produced by Publius & Associates, titled *Firearms and Freedom*. For several years, in affiliation with the ultraconservative John Birch Society, Publius & Associates produced films such as *Education or Indoctrination* and *The Hippies*, both of which audaciously claimed there was an insidious leftist effort afoot to indoctrinate America's youth to support communism, whether it be through textbooks, music, or political demonstrations. *Firearms and Freedom* was produced in the same spirit. For the most part, it parroted several NRA anti-firearms-control mantras, such as punish the criminal not the law-abiding citizen, firearms registration only leads to firearm confiscation, and enforce the estimated twenty thousand firearms laws already on the books. At several points, however, the ultraconservative bent of the film is obvious. At one point the film's narrator claims that "bleeding heart" liberals are seeking to confiscate firearms. At another point the narrator claims that liberals view criminals as a "natural resource to be protected in every way possible." There are several instances where the film resorts to what can best be described as propaganda. The most glaring example is its historical account of the San Francisco earthquake in 1906: "The city was under martial law, and orders were issued that looters were to be shot on sight," stated the film's narrator, adding, *"No one thought this was unusual and there was remarkably little looting."* This historical account was then juxtaposed with the urban riots in 1968, which the narrator described as follows:

> When looting, burning, and rioting erupted in April 1968, police were ordered by their politician superiors not to interfere, and the violence raged on for several days. Halfway across the nation in Chicago, arsonists and rioters set the torch to large portions of the city. When [Chicago] mayor [Richard J. Daley] suggested that police be permitted to shoot arsonists and looters, if necessary, to stop the holocaust, the wailing and weeping of the bleeding hearts over such inhumanity was heard across the land. The bleeding hearts shed no tears for the victims. . . . The cry was, "No matter what suffering they inflict, no harm must come to the criminals." This attitude makes it nice and cozy for the criminals, but just a little hard on the honest citizens who are the victims.[99]

The film was correct to note that Daley had issued an emergency order authorizing Chicago law enforcement to "shoot to kill any arsonist" and "shoot to maim or cripple anyone looting."[100] It was also right that Daley had been widely criticized for issuing the order, as were many other mid-to-late 1960s lawmakers that expressed support for the "get tough . . . when the looting starts the shooting starts" approach to riot control.[101] What it got wrong, however, was its historical account of the 1906 San Francisco earthquake. While there was indeed an emergency order authorizing federal and local law enforcement to "KILL any and all persons found engaged in Looting or in the Commission of Any Other Crime," the order was both unusual and ineffective at stopping the looting.[102] It also led to several unnecessary armed conflicts and deaths.[103] In one instance, the very militia that was called into San Francisco to restore order ended up taking part in the looting.[104]

Firearms and Freedom's use of faux history to shore up its propagandistic message did not end there. It also applies to the film's historical account of the origins, meaning, and purpose behind the Second Amendment. The film both begins and ends with the historical fallacy that the Second

Amendment was included in the Bill of Rights to constitutionally enshrine an armed citizenry.[105] Not true. Ultimately, for any historian to accept this conclusion would require deleting the Second Amendment's "well-regulated militia" language and replacing it with what the eighteenth-century militia commentators often referred to as an "unregulated" or "ill-regulated" militia. To be clear, there is no substantiated historical evidence that suggests that the Founding Fathers understood the two concepts of a well-regulated militia and an armed citizenry to be one and the same.[106] Yet the belief that the Second Amendment protects an armed citizenry had permeated gun rights literature throughout the early to mid-twentieth century.[107] The post–World War II fear of communism, coupled with the civil unrest of the 1960s, only strengthened this gun rights belief. It also amplified how gun rights supporters viewed armed citizens as being necessary to counter and deter criminal activity.

The belief that everyday armed citizens would effectively deter crime is one of the ideological pillars on which the early twentieth-century gun rights movement was built. As the first gun rights advocacy organization, the United States Revolver Association (USRA), put it in 1923, if criminals know "that all citizens have the right to possess weapons and presumably have availed themselves of that right and are therefore in a position to defend themselves, [criminals] will hesitate to attack."[108] The NRA carried forward this criminological viewpoint upon commandeering the gun rights movement from the USRA. It began with a reoccurring *American Rifleman* column titled "Guns vs. Bandits," which sought to debunk the "fallacy of an unarmed citizenry."[109] The column was discontinued in 1941 and revived in 1958 as "The Armed Citizen."[110] By the mid-to-late 1960s the belief in armed citizens serving as an effective criminal deterrent became almost synonymous with the conservative calls for "law and order."[111] As William Loeb, publisher of the conservative-leaning *Manchester Union Leader*, put it, "If the good guys were all armed the minority of bad guys wouldn't have a chance."[112]

Where right-wing extremists diverged from the NRA and the mainstream gun rights movement was the role armed citizens could serve in countering any perceived domestic threats. While the NRA and the mainstream gun rights movement indeed supported arming citizens, especially for homebound self-defense, they generally drew a line when it came to everyday citizens performing the role of law enforcement.[113] Right-wing extremists viewed it much differently. They saw armed citizens as a resource that state and local law enforcement could utilize to stamp out riots, looting, crime, and other societal problems.[114] But they knew this would require both changing state and local laws in a way that liberalized armed self-defense for average citizens and changing American perceptions on the utility of having armed citizens serving as law enforcement auxiliaries.[115]

Yet despite gun rights supporters maintaining varying opinions on a range of issues, what always brought them together was their utter disdain for the Gun Control Act—a disdain that rivaled that of the much maligned Sullivan Law of 1911. This was evident when the Department of Treasury's Alcohol, Tobacco & Firearms Division (ATFD) of the Internal Revenue Service (IRS) decided to produce an educational film on how the Gun Control Act assisted federal, state, and local law enforcement agencies in solving firearms-related crimes.[116] To make the film, titled *That's What It's All About*, as appealing as possible to modern audiences, the producers gave it the appearance of a television crime drama. The film begins with several quick depictions of armed crimes and criminals before cutting to three hunters returning from the field, each complaining about the "lousy new gun law." They stop off at a tavern before three armed criminals drop in, rob the place, shoot the bartender, and steal the hunters' vehicle. But during the commotion, one of the criminals leaves behind a handgun, which turns out to be the only clue the ATFD investigators are left with. With the help of the Gun Control Act's record-keeping requirements for licensed firearms dealers, the investigators were able to trace the handgun, and a fifteen-minute dramatized story unfolds where they succeed in catching an international gunrunner who operates from a yacht full of bikini-clad young women. The film then suddenly cuts back to the same three hunters in the field. One states how he just bought a gun and did not feel unnecessarily inconvenienced by the form he had to fill out, nor by having to show his driver's license.[117]

Given that more than half of *That's What It's All About* is centered on a dramatized crime story unrelated to the workings of the Gun Control Act, criticism of the film was indeed warranted. However, gun rights advocates decided to take their criticism a step further by chastising what they perceived to be the film's "sexy" and "violent" content.[118] "There was too much sex and violence and too little information about the new law," stated

This Time He's Right!

FIGURE 7.4 Political cartoon in *Gun Week*, March 20, 1970. The cartoon conveyed the gun rights community's negative perception of the film *That's What It's All About*. Connecticut senator Thomas J. Dodd, who fought to have the film reinstated, is shown holding an award for the film in the categories of "Anti-Gun Propaganda" and "Waste of Taxpayers Money." Image reprinted with the express permission of the Second Amendment Foundation.

Michigan representative and NRA congressional surrogate John D. Dingell after watching the film. He demanded that the film be immediately pulled. ATFD responded to the criticism by noting how the film's dramatized storyline was included to keep modern audiences interested while providing them with useful information as to how the Gun Control Act worked. "There was less sex and violence than you see on television," stated one Department of Treasury official in defending the film.[119]

The "sexy" and "violent" criticism of *That's What It's All About* paralleled what many contemporary gun rights advocates were claiming to be the root cause of firearms-related violence—morally repugnant television programming.[120] But the "blame the television industry for violence" argument was nothing more than a distraction for the real reason gun rights advocates wanted the film pulled—that it might "orient the public . . . toward an automatic crime-firearms relationship."[121] When news of the "sexy, violent movie" reached the White House, the Department of Treasury was instructed to cease and desist any further showings pending the film's review. "Firearms control is an exceedingly important issue for us, and [we would] appreciate being kept informed of all public efforts to depict this Administration's position," wrote one Nixon official to the Department of Treasury.[122] Therein the department provided the Nixon White House with a private screening of the film. Not long thereafter, ATFD officials went from defending the film to issuing a public apology and canceling any further showings.[123]

Firearms control proponents did their utmost to salvage the film. Investigative journalists with the Columbia Broadcasting Station's (CBS) television program *60 Minutes* even ran a segment on the film.[124] In the end, however, gun rights advocates succeeded in having *That's What It's All About* pulled.[125] And canceling it was just one of many gun rights victories leading into the spring of 1970, perhaps the most notable being Nixon signing into law a slightly modified version of Senator Bennett's S. 845, which nullified the Gun Control Act's record-keeping requirements for long gun ammunition with the exception of the .22 caliber rimfire. Another notable gun rights victory was the rapid spread of contiguous state firearms bills. Adopted state by state, the bills effectively superseded a provision in the Gun Control Act that restricted out-of-state purchases of long guns, but only so long as the purchase was done in a contiguous or neighboring state.[126] As of May 1970, largely through the lobbying efforts of the NSSF and NRA, thirty-six states had adopted contiguous state firearms bills.

And the gun rights victories did not end there. In state legislatures across the country, gun rights advocates succeeded in mobilizing supporters to defeat virtually every firearms control bill that would have imposed some form of registration, licensing, or a purchaser identification card requirement. In the cases of San Francisco and Beverly Hills, California, two cities that had passed firearms registration ordinances in 1968, gun rights advocates were able to effectively nullify them by lobbying California lawmakers to enact a state firearms preemption law.[127]

Each of these gun rights victories, while impressive, politically paled in comparison to the influence that gun rights advocacy would have on the elections of 1970. Much like in 1968, the firearms control issue during the 1970 elections was a reflection of the urban-rural divide over such controls. Political candidates running for office in largely urban districts were more likely to support firearms controls than political candidates representing largely rural districts. What distinguished the 1968 election from the 1970 election was that the firearms control issue was far more prevalent in the latter. This was due in large part to two factors. First and foremost, the 1968 elections cultivated the perception that the sportsmen's vote could affect election outcomes. Second, come 1970 gun rights advocates had effectively amplified this perception to keep gun rights supporters politically engaged. They were often reminded that their political cause should never be construed as partisan, but "simply [as] a matter of selecting men who will support our rights under the Second Amendment and under similar clauses in the constitutions of most of our states." In other words, gun rights advocates wanted gun rights supporters to view any politician "who does not support [the rights to keep and bear arms as] our enemy, regardless of his party."[128] And to accomplish this objective, some supporters were willing to change political parties in order to vote out "anti-gun" lawmakers in

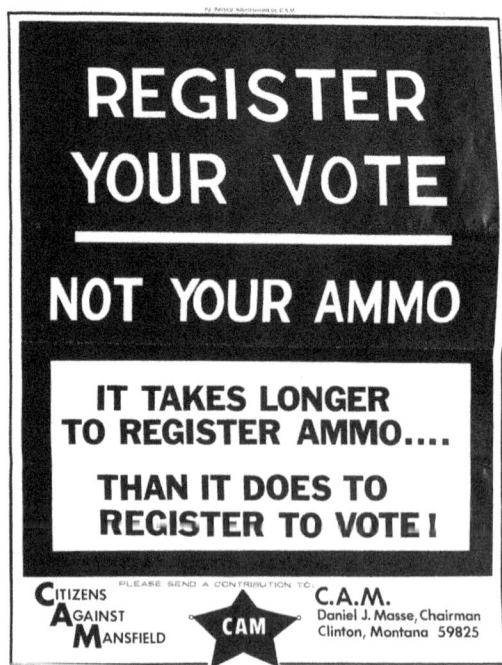

FIGURE 7.5 Poster published in several newspapers by Citizens Against Mansfield (CAM), a gun rights–centered political action group dedicated to the Election Day defeat of Montana senator Mike Mansfield in 1970.

the primaries.[129] Ultimately, it was the repeated calls to action by gun rights advocates that spurred the formation of new gun rights political action groups at an unprecedented level.[130]

The increased prevalence of firearms controls as a political issue is best gauged historically by comparing the Senate races in 1970 with those of 1968. Of the thirty-four Senate races in 1968, fourteen (41.2 percent) included the firearms control issue in some capacity. And of those fourteen races, only two (5.8 percent of all Senate races in 1968) involved organized gun rights opposition. In 1970 the number of Senate races to include the firearms-control issue increased to nineteen (57.6 percent), six (18.2 percent) of which involved organized opposition. While the increase in organized gun rights opposition is notable, what is even more notable is the political lengths that several senators up for reelection in 1970 went to garner the sportsmen's vote.

Majority leader Mike Mansfield of Montana and minority leader Hugh Scott of Pennsylvania provide two cases in point. Following the 1968 elections, both senators decisively flipped on the firearms control issue to garner the sportsmen's vote, with Scott going as far as penning an apology for having voted for the Gun Control Act. Another notable example is that of Wyoming senator Gale McGee. For much of the 1960s, McGee's firearms control policy position was not all that different from those of other members of Congress representing largely rural or western states. To McGee, the right to keep and bear arms was an essential part of America's identity, and firearms controls were nothing but a burden on law-abiding citizens.[131] Even after the assassination of Martin Luther King, Jr., McGee felt that Congress would be "kidding [itself] by thinking that because [it] might pass a bill aimed at controlling the sale of firearms somewhat more than we do today that [it is] going to have made [America's] streets safe or put a stop to crimes of violence."[132] However, following the assassination of fellow senator Robert F. Kennedy, McGee decided to back Maryland senator Joseph D. Tydings's federal firearms registration bill. He defended his decision by casting registration as a "mere inconvenience" that was necessary to keep firearms out of the hands of "derelicts" and "criminals."[133] "Any other approach other than registration is simply piecemeal and stopgap . . . and does not get at the objectives of any meaningful type of gun legislation [which are] simply to determine how many there are, who owns them, and where they are located," stated McGee.[134]

But the outpouring of constituent mail from the gun rights community that followed, coupled with the upcoming elections, propelled McGee to change political course for the 91st Congress. He did everything possible to make amends with the gun rights community. His strategy was essentially threefold: First, he cosponsored Utah senator Bennett's bill—S. 845—that sought to remove the record-keeping requirements for all long gun ammunition.[135] Second, he introduced his own pro-gun bill, S. 3417, which sought to exempt "sporting" rifles, shotguns, and ammunition from the Gun Control Act's mail-order provisions. Third, through a press release, rather than wait for some political rival to criticize his support in 1968 for federal firearms registration, McGee decided to be proactive in defending his actions. In the press release, he highlighted how he was the only Wyoming senator to vote against the Gun Control Act. Additionally, he explained that he had only supported Tydings's bill because it would have provided Wyomingites a voice in crafting their firearms registration law.[136]

As of early 1970, it appeared that McGee's political strategy was working.[137] Although not everyone in the gun rights community was willing to forgive and forget his statements and actions of 1968, McGee did obtain the endorsement of the Wyoming State Shooting Association.[138] Also, he was for a time successful in bucking any media criticism for having flip-flopped on firearms controls.[139] But when he decided to take credit for Nixon reversing a Lyndon B. Johnson rule requiring licensed firearms dealers to label all mail-order firearms packages with the word "FIREARMS" in one-inch black letters, many in the gun rights community expressed their frustration.[140] "[McGee] tried to sandbag us into believing he is friendly to the gun owners of Wyoming, but we have enough snow out here to know a 'snow-job' when we see it," stated one gun rights supporter.[141] McGee's pro-gun bona fides were also being questioned on the campaign trail by his Republican challenger in 1970, freshman Wyoming representative John S. Wold. Leading up to his House election in 1968, Wold chastised the Gun Control Act as both a waste of time and a "threat to Wyoming sportsmen and every American's right to bear arms."[142] Thus it was not surprising when Wold took political aim at McGee for having previously supported firearms registration.[143] McGee responded by introducing another pro-gun bill—one that would remove .22 caliber rimfire ammunition from the record-keeping requirements of the Gun Control Act.[144]

For his pro-gun actions, McGee received a letter of praise from NRA secretary Frank C. Daniel. Not long after, in a speech before the Rock Springs Sportsmen's Club, McGee held up Daniel's letter as an official NRA endorsement of his candidacy.[145] But Daniel's letter was not intended to be a campaign endorsement. Not only had Daniel sent virtually identical letters to other members of Congress, including McGee's opponent Wold, but it was longstanding NRA policy to never endorse or grade political candidates—a policy that the NRA would not dispense with until 1976.[146] The NRA quickly issued a press release to set the record straight.[147] Wold in turn seized on McGee's NRA endorsement blunder by publishing a series of newspaper advertisements calling into question McGee's integrity.[148]

Neither McGee nor his campaign thought it politically wise to apologize for or even explain the NRA endorsement blunder. Rather, they pivoted by pointing to another prominent sporting, hunting, and shooting endorsement—*Field & Stream* magazine. What is interesting about this endorsement is that it was neither personal nor glowing. What *Field & Stream* did was merely score 150 congressional candidates on fifteen criteria and then place each candidate into one of four categories—excellent, good, fair, or poor. McGee was in the "good" category; Wold, in the "fair" category.[149] This categorical differentiation alone is why *Field & Stream* issued a one-line endorsement of McGee over Wold. Yet to help move away from the NRA endorsement blunder, McGee and his campaign made sure to highlight the *Field & Stream* endorsement and did so in a full-page advertisement that appeared in every major Wyoming newspaper (fig. 7.6). The ad showed a picture of McGee hunting in a field, alongside of which was a detailed list of his pro-gun accomplishments. At the bottom of the picture, in large letters, read, "Take it from *Field & Stream* magazine . . . McGee is the Sportsman's Choice."[150]

Field & Stream's endorsement—if one could even call it that—was also center stage in the Vermont Senate race between Republican incumbent Winston L. Prouty and Democratic challenger Philip H. Hoff. Therein it was Hoff who received *Field & Stream*'s one-line endorsement, and the former Vermont governor made good use of it in a campaign advertisement that highlighted his having "spoken out" against firearms controls. Ironically, two years earlier, as Vermont governor, Hoff had proffered several restrictive firearms control proposals to the Vermont Assembly, including firearms

LET'S SHOOT STRAIGHT

ABOUT SENATOR
GALE McGEE'S
RECORD ON GUNS & FIREARMS LEGISLATION

Here it is...
"ON THE RECORD."

- Senator McGee voted *NO* on the Gun Control Act of 1968.
  (Congressional Record, Sept. 18, 1968, p. S10986.)
- Senator McGee voted *for* a bill to limit the record-keeping provisions of the Gun Control Act.
  (Congressional Record, Oct. 9, 1969, p. S12306.)
- Senator McGee sponsored two bills to remove shotgun shells and rifle ammunition from the restrictions of the Gun Control Act.
  (Congressional Record, Feb. ¼, 1969, p. S1182 and July 29, 1969, p. S8711.)
- Senator McGee sponsored another bill to eliminate record-keeping requirements on .22 caliber ammunition. Some 30 Senators have joined him. *
  (Congressional Record, April 16, 1970, pp. S5855-6.)
- Senator McGee sponsored another bill to permit the interstate transportation of sporting and target firearms.
  (Congressional Record, Feb. 6, 1970, pp. 1344 and 1399.)
- Senator McGee sponsored another amendment to protect the right of sportsmen to re-load their own ammunition and possess gun powder.
  (Congressional Record, July 9, 1970, p. S10855.)
- Senator McGee, as Chairman of the Post Office Committee, forced the Post Office Department to eliminate labeling requirements for firearms shipped by mail—a practice which had led to the theft of many guns.
  (Congressional Record, Jan. 22, 1970, p. S359. Federal Register, Jan. 23, 1970, p. 975.)

* The Executive Secretary of the National Rifle Association says about Senator McGee's efforts to remove record-keeping requirements from .22 caliber ammunition: "You certainly are to be commended for your untiring efforts to relieve the sportsmen of the United States from this burdensome and entirely useless provision of the Gun Control Act of 1968."

Gale McGee is pledged to support your right to keep and bear arms. A sportsman and gun collector himself, he isn't about to knuckle under to a gun registration law.

TAKE IT FROM

Field & Stream MAGAZINE
(SEPT., 1970, p. 65)

McGEE
IS THE
SPORTSMAN'S CHOICE

PAID FOR BY THE
DEMOCRATIC STATE CENTRAL COMMITTEE,
DONNA OWENS, TREASURER

FIGURE 7.6 Political advertisement in the *Casper (Wyo.) Star-Tribune*, October 21, 1970. The ad showed Wyoming senator Gale McGee hunting in a field. On the right was McGee's record on firearms legislation in the 90th and 91st Congresses. Noticeably omitted from the list was his support for Maryland senator Joseph D. Tydings's federal firearms registration bill in 1968. At the bottom the ad highlighted McGee's endorsement by *Field & Stream* over challenger John S. Wold.

registration, licensing, and a seventy-two-hour "cooling-off period" for all firearms purchases.[151] Yet come 1970, to garner the sportsmen's vote, Hoff expressed a change of heart on firearms controls. According to Hoff, it was not long after Senator Kennedy's assassination, once he had time to personally examine the firearms control issue, that he realized restricting access to firearms was ineffective at "curbing criminal activities." "Here in Vermont," he stated in an interview, "people are overwhelmingly opposed to [controlling firearms], and really at this point, it is not a rational policy nor is it needed [here]."[152]

Prouty made it a point on the campaign trail to criticize Hoff for having politically flipped on firearms controls.[153] In several Vermont newspapers, Prouty ran full-page advertisements to drive home the point. In large, bold, black letters, the advertisement read "COMPARE these statements on gun control." Below it contained a one-sentence quote from both Hoff and Prouty. While Hoff's quote underscored his support for strict firearms controls in 1968, Prouty was quoted as stating that every "law-abiding Vermont sportsman should not be harassed by unnecessary controls."[154] But what Prouty left out was that he, too, had flip-flopped on firearms controls. In fact, not long after Senator Kennedy's assassination, Prouty had joined fellow Vermont senator George D. Aiken in urging federal firearms registration.[155] Also, in accord with Aiken, Prouty had voted for the Gun Control Act. However, it appears that Hoff was unaware of Prouty having flip-flopped on the firearms control issue.[156] For rather than call Prouty out, Hoff decided the best political course of action was to issue a formal apology for being "wrong in 1968."[157]

What likely helped in suppressing Prouty's firearms control–supporting past was that come the 91st Congress, the Vermont senator had effectively created the persona of being a strong gun rights proponent.[158] Other incumbent senators were not as fortunate. Consider Indiana senator Vance Hartke, who in 1968 had voted in favor of the firearms control provisions in the Omnibus Crime Control and Safe Streets Act, Senator Tydings's federal firearms registration amendment, and the Gun Control Act.[159] By late 1969 Hartke began politically espousing a much more gun rights–friendly demeanor. In addition to cosponsoring several pro-gun bills, he began openly questioning the effectiveness of firearms controls in reducing crime.[160] Yet despite attempting to politically pivot on the firearms control issue, Hartke faced repeated criticism for having ever supported firearms controls, especially from his election challenger in 1970, Republican Richard L. Roudebush.[161] New Mexico senator Joseph Montoya was faced with a similar predicament. Not only was he criticized on the campaign trail for having voted for the Gun Control Act, but he was also accused of having supported federal firearms registration.[162] Yet the firearms registration accusation was without merit. It was based on the highly misleading "backdoor registration" claim regarding the Gun Control Act's ammunition record-keeping requirements for licensed firearms dealers.[163] Yes, Montoya's firearms control critics were correct in noting that he had voted for the Gun Control Act's record-keeping requirement. However, requiring licensed firearms dealers to maintain records of ammunition purchases was not firearms registration.[164] The two types of firearms control are quite distinct, yet Montoya's firearms control critics refused to acknowledge this. These critics also refused to acknowledge that Montoya, like Prouty, McGee, and several other senators had decisively flip-flopped on firearms controls after the 1968 elections.[165] In fact, as of late 1970, to appeal to the sportsmen's vote, Montoya had gone so far as to support repealing the Gun Control Act, an act he had voted for just two years earlier.[166]

Montoya was not the only senatorial candidate in 1970 to urge repeal of the Gun Control Act to try to garner the sportsmen's vote. In the Utah Senate race, both Democratic incumbent Frank E. Moss and his Republican challenger, House representative Laurence J. Burton, were quick to back repeal once campaign season kicked off.[167] Additionally, both candidates advertised their pro-gun bona fides early and often. In fact, repealing the Gun Control Act and opposing restrictive firearms controls were two of only a handful of issues on which the "liberal" Moss and "conservative" Burton seemed to politically agree.[168] Yet the Moss campaign came up with the more memorable anti-firearms-control slogan: "Liberal or conservative, the West wasn't won with a registered gun."[169]

Repeal of the Gun Control Act was also center stage in the Texas Senate race between Lloyd Bentsen, who defeated incumbent senator Ralph Yarborough in the Democratic primary, and Republican House representative George H. W. Bush. Both candidates were rather outspoken against firearms controls.[170] What separated the two was how to best to go about fixing the Gun Control Act. Bush supported a piecemeal amendment approach. Meanwhile, Bentsen was for all-out repeal and ran several advertisements on this very point. One ad read in bold black letters: "Help Repeal the 1968 GUN CONTROL ACT, VOTE for Lloyd Bentsen."[171] Bentsen's ads also criticized Bush for having voted in favor of the House version of the State Firearms Control Assistance Act, which, after clearing the joint conference committee, was renamed the Gun Control Act.[172] The Bush campaign fired back by claiming that Bentsen's advertisements were misleading given that Bush did not actually vote on the joint conference committee bill.[173] But Bentsen felt Bush's defense was unavailing. To Bentsen, the fact remained that Bush had voted for federal firearms controls. "[Bush] says this is really not a gun control act, but apparently he did not know what he was voting for," joked Bentsen at a press conference.[174] Bush responded in kind by running several advertisements highlighting his anti-firearms-control position (fig. 7.7).[175]

The gun rights pushback that Bush faced on the campaign trail was minor compared to that of incumbent senators Philip A. Hart of Michigan, Joseph D. Tydings of Maryland, Majority Leader Mike Mansfield of Montana, and Minority Leader Hugh Scott of Pennsylvania. This was because each of these senators faced firm, organized opposition from gun rights political action groups. Beginning with Hart, prior to the assassination of Senator Kennedy, the Michigan senator was generally opposed to the idea of the federal government interfering in what was traditionally a state and local area of regulation, though he was willing to concede to a few minor, interstate handgun restrictions.[176] He adamantly opposed any firearms control legislation that touched on rifles and shotguns.[177] For his opposition to most firearms controls, Hart received the praise of both the NRA and the Michigan gun rights community.[178] But the assassination of Senator Kennedy was a political inflection point for Hart, and he quickly became one of Congress's most vocal firearms control proponents.[179] At times, he even expressed support for firearms registration.[180] "If registration is a practical solution for the problem of establishing automobile ownership— and I hear no opposition to this—then gun registration could accomplish the same purpose," wrote Hart to a constituent.[181]

At the start of the 91st Congress, Hart stayed the political course by expressing his unabashed support for firearms controls. But this abruptly changed following an August 15 meeting with James L. Rouman, the executive director of the 102,000-member Michigan United Conservation Clubs (MUCC), an organization known for opposing most firearms controls. It was

GEORGE BUSH DOESN'T BELIEVE IN HIDING BEHIND A PARTY LABEL.

HE BELIEVES IN TELLING YOU EXACTLY WHERE HE STANDS ON THE ISSUES.

HERE'S WHERE HE STANDS ON GUN REGISTRATION.

"I am opposed to the registration, licensing or requiring of permits for firearms. I have consistently voted this way every time this question has come before the House. While I have voted for many crime control bills, I have never voted for any bill that provided for gun registration, licensing or permitting in any form. I do not think registration of shotguns, rifles, pistols or any kind of weapon will solve the crime problem, and I would unquestionably oppose any legislation which could conceivably disarm our citizens — this is a basic right under the Constitution and should not be tampered with." *George Bush*

Vote for the man, not the party. He has done more to fight gun controls.

GEORGE BUSH. HE CAN DO MORE.

Paid Political Advertisment by George Bush for U. S. Senate Committee, Mrs. Hubert Braden, Chairman

FIGURE 7.7 George H. W. Bush political advertisement that appeared in several Texas-based newspapers on November 1, 1970. The ad sought to counter Lloyd Bentsen's accusations that Bush was a supporter of firearms controls.

after the meeting that Hart's special assistant, John M. Cornman, put together a policy memorandum, which examined each of Hart's firearms control policy positions over a twenty-month period. What Cornman ultimately concluded was that over that period, Hart's policy position had become increasingly "fuzzy." He also expressed reservation over Hart having voted in favor of firearms registration and licensing. There was, however, a silver lining—Hart's various policy positions appeared to be "on fairly safe grounds" with that of public opinion. Yet with the 1970 elections looming, Cornman advised Hart to be more conscious and disciplined with his firearms control message. The way Cornman saw it, Hart needed to present himself as a firearms control moderate. This meant he needed to distance himself from any policies or bills that could be interpreted as supporting a ban on all handguns. According to Cornman, supporting such a position would only anger sportsmen "fearing long guns next," "Blacks, seeing [the] move as whitey's attempt to disarm them," and "White suburbanites, who feel safer with a pistol tucked in [a] handbag, shoulder holster or bedside table."[182] In accord with Cornman's suggestions, by the fall of 1969 Hart began espousing a vastly different tone when it came to firearms controls. He not only began referring to the Gun Control Act's ammunition record-keeping requirement as "ridiculously burdensome," but he also promised Michigan sportsmen that he would not support any additional restrictions on long guns.[183] Handguns were a different matter. Hart remained steadfast in opposing their "unrestricted purchase" and hoped that every state would "enact some sort of minimum [universal] standards."[184]

Hart's strategy of portraying himself as a moderate did little to appease the Sportsmen's Alliance of Michigan (SAM)—a new gun rights political action group based in Lansing.[185] SAM's very first political "target" was none other than the Election Day defeat of Senator Hart in 1970.[186] In the hopes of accomplishing this objective, SAM endorsed Hart's Republican challenger, political newcomer Lenore Romney, whose husband, former Michigan governor George W. Romney, had advocated for strict firearms controls in the wake of Senator Kennedy's assassination.[187] Lenore Romney openly accepted SAM's endorsement and agreed to speak before the group's monthly meeting. Therein she criticized Hart for being soft on crime and civil disobedience: "At a time when this country is being torn apart by riots, bombings and disorder, Senator Hart said he couldn't 'get up tight' about massive civil disobedience." Romney also criticized Hart for having voted for firearms controls: "I don't want to take away guns from sportsmen," she stated while citing the Second Amendment, adding, "Only if there is conclusive evidence that restricting guns is necessary to protect our police from being ambushed and our nation overrun will I change my position."[188]

As Election Day approached, SAM stepped up its opposition to Hart by distributing handouts and running newspaper advertisements urging the Michigan gun rights community to "protect your constitutional rights . . . help remove Philip A. Hart from the United States Senate."[189] In one handout, SAM labeled Hart as "the most accomplished turncoat produced in the country since 1776."[190] Another read: "WANTED Philip A. Hart removed from the U.S. Senate for supporting federal firearms registration and owner licensing and for violating the trust with the sportsmen of Michigan"[191] SAM had borrowed the idea for the handout from another gun rights political action group—Citizens Against Mansfield (CAM) (fig. 7.8).

CAM was an offshoot of the extremist organization APORKBA. Headed by Daniel J. Masse, CAM was established for the sole purpose of upending Montana senator Mansfield's 1970 reelection campaign.[192] It was one of two political action groups formed by APORKBA—the other being Citizens Against Dellenback (CAD). As early as December 1969, Mansfield became aware of CAM when Masse wrote a letter demanding that the Montana senator back outright repeal of the Gun Control Act or face the stiff opposition the Montana gun rights community.[193] The fact that Mansfield had already flip-flopped on firearms controls was irrelevant to Masse and CAM. The only thing that mattered was Mansfield's prior support. In this respect Masse and CAM reflected the political views of the newer, more extreme "no compromise" gun rights movement—a movement that embraced a "scorched earth" approach to politics.

This approach can be seen in CAM's handouts and advertisements. One handout read, "Firearms Legislation Can Disarm You, Mr. Citizen." It promised that CAM would "not yield to any manipulations or compromises by Elected or Appointed Officials *who allow infringements* on the citizens' rights of gun ownership." This included Mansfield, who, according to CAM, "consistently aligned himself with . . .'Gentlemen from the East' who are persistent in their efforts to lead us down the road towards total confiscation of our sporting arms, pistols, and target training guns." The handout also

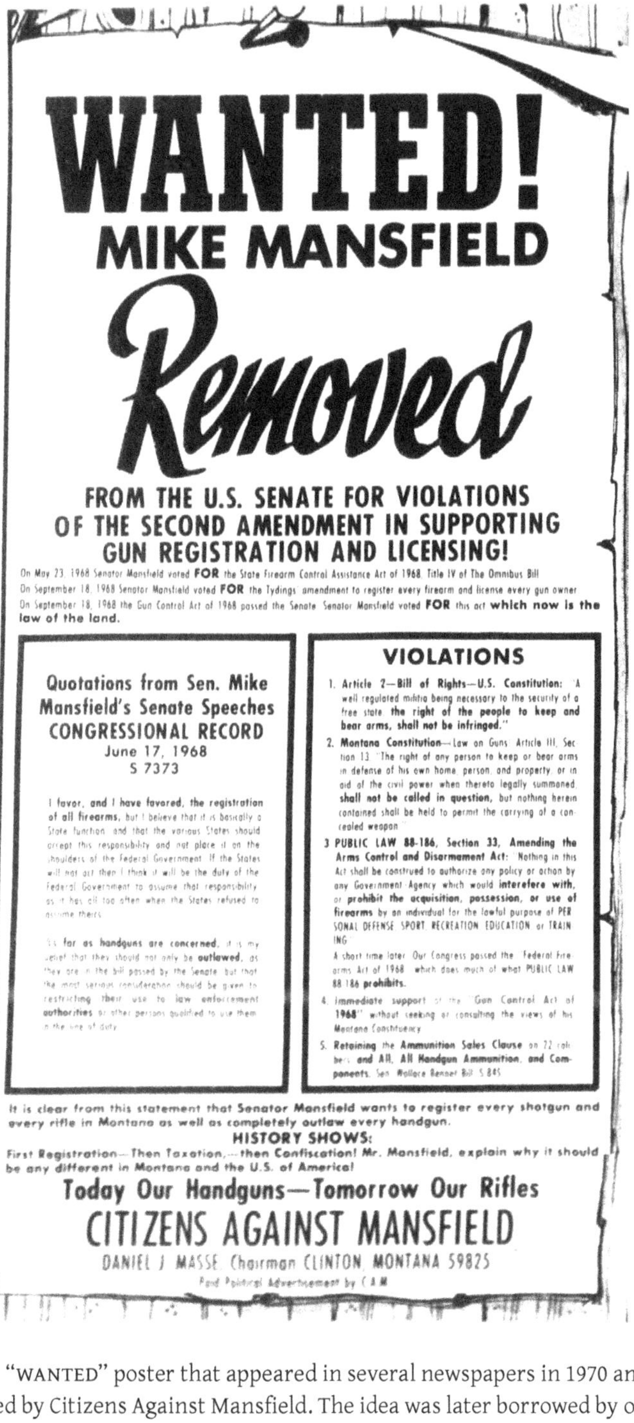

FIGURE 7.8 "WANTED" poster that appeared in several newspapers in 1970 and was distributed by Citizens Against Mansfield. The idea was later borrowed by other gun rights–centric political action groups.

accused Mansfield of having endorsed "legislation for the *withdrawal of all pistols from our citizens.*"[194] But the accusation was patently false. There was nothing in Mansfield's political record that even implied that the majority leader supported a handgun ban. And CAM's false accusations did not end there. For in other handouts, Mansfield was accused of having voted for firearms registration and licensing during the 90th Congress.[195] He had not. While CAM would have been correct in stating that Mansfield initially backed Senator Tydings's firearms registration proposal, by the time the Senate voted on it as an amendment to the Gun Control Act, he had effectively withdrawn his support.

When CAM first arrived on the political scene, Mansfield did not give the organization serious thought. As Election Day drew closer, however, CAM—through news interviews, letter-writing campaigns, and anti-Mansfield advertising—quickly became a political thorn in his side.[196] All across Montana, CAM members were distributing posters, flyers, and literature with mottos like "300,000 Sportsmen Say Defeat Mike Mansfield," "Go Ahead Sucker Register Your Firearm," and "Help Turn Mike Mansfield Out to Pasture."[197] Often included with the CAM flyers and literature were reprints of *American Rifleman* editorials. This prompted Ashley Halsey, Jr., chief editor of the magazine, to pen a cease-and-desist letter to Masse and CAM. Halsey expressed concern that by including the editorials in flyers and literature, it might lead someone to "readily conclude that the NRA actively endorses the aims of your organization and its solicitation of campaign funds," when in the fact the NRA "is a non-partisan organization which does not endorse any candidates for any office at any level anywhere." In other words, according to Halsey, CAM's political use of the editorials was not in accordance with "longstanding" NRA policy.[198]

It is unclear who alerted the NRA about CAM's use of the editorials. According to Halsey's letter it was "several" individuals, but it is more likely that the letter came at the request of someone in Mansfield's office—perhaps even Mansfield himself. Three historical observations point to this possibility. First, in addition to writing CAM, Halsey wrote Mansfield about the matter, and in doing so he enclosed a courtesy copy of the CAM cease-and-desist letter.[199] Second, until Halsey penned the cease-and-desist letter, there is no record of the NRA sending similar letters to any other person, organization, publisher, or news outlet for reprinting or distributing *American Rifleman* editorials.[200] In fact, for more than two decades, almost every edition of the magazine contained a disclaimer allowing anyone to reprint its editorials in part or in full without obtaining the NRA's express permission.[201] This includes the very editorials reprinted and distributed by CAM. The final reason why someone in Mansfield's office requested or tipped off the NRA to write the CAM cease-and-desist letter is that the "longstanding" policy Halsey cited was non-existent. Indeed, until the NRA established its Office of Legislative Affairs in 1974 (later reorganized and renamed the Institute for Legislative Action (NRA-ILA),[202] the NRA took pride in being nonpartisan. It was also NRA policy to never endorse one political candidate over another.[203] Yet neither the organization's nonpartisan status nor its no-endorsement policy was ever included or mentioned in the disclaimers authorizing anyone permission to reprint or distribute *American Rifleman* editorials. Moreover, for decades the NRA had openly encouraged its members, as well as the wider gun rights community, to be politically active in voting out antifirearms politicians.[204] This was in fact the key message in the NRA's *American Rifleman* editorial for February 1970 —one of the very editorials reprinted and distributed by CAM—in which NRA members were urged to work with local firearms dealers to obtain lists of "registered voters who might be inclined to oppose anti-gun moves" and encourage them to "vote in support of the right to bear arms."[205]

The point to be made is that the historical record strongly suggests that the CAM cease-and-desist letter was politically motivated.[206] It effectively allowed the NRA to continue cultivating a relationship with Mansfield, who, as Senate majority leader, provided the organization with a powerful political ally in its fight to undo unduly restrictive firearms controls.[207] Certainly, the NRA would have preferred Mansfield to support outright repeal of the Gun Control Act. But because he was part of the Democratic leadership—and therefore largely responsible for the passage of the Gun Control Act—he could not completely reverse course and support repeal without undercutting the Democratic Party as a whole. The NRA understood this, and it was what principally separated it from the new gun rights political action groups. The NRA was gladly willing to forgive almost any politician who flip-flopped from supporting firearms controls to supporting gun rights. Conversely, the new gun rights political action groups like

CAM embraced the "no compromise" movement to the point that they were both unforgiving and unrelenting in their opposition toward anyone who had previously supported firearms controls.

CAM's embrace of the "no compromise" movement ended up dividing the Montana gun rights community. While CAM's tactics were indeed attractive to many "local gun nuts," the older, more moderate NRA faithful were appalled. The same was true of the Mansfield campaign, which was aghast over CAM classifying the Senate majority leader as being too "liberal" and hell bent on confiscating Montanans' firearms.[208] To counter CAM's extreme messaging, the Mansfield campaign devised a two-pronged response. First, it created a gun rights–focused political action group of its own—Sportsmen for Mansfield. The group did everything from conducting outreach with sportsmen and hunting organizations, to distributing pro-Mansfield literature, to answering questions regarding Mansfield's conservation record, to writing newspaper editorials defending his position on firearms controls.[209] Second, the campaign made sure that Mansfield would neither cower nor apologize for helping pass the Gun Control Act.[210] Rather, he would display an aura of confidence and strength for having voted for the law, and at the same time express vocal support for the Second Amendment rights of sportsmen, hunters, and every firearm-owning Montanan.[211]

While Mansfield was displaying an aura of confidence and strength in the face of CAM opposition, his Senate counterpart, Minority Leader Hugh Scott of Pennsylvania, had decided to display humility. Scott believed that he stood the best chance of winning reelection if he could just make political amends for his firearms control–supporting past.[212] Scott felt that this strategy would, at a minimum, effectively splinter the sportsmen's vote. And to help make this outcome a reality, his campaign established a sportsmen political action group of their own—Outdoorsmen for Scott—to "set the record straight" on Scott's firearms control position.[213] Initially, the strategy appeared to be working. Although some in the Pennsylvania gun rights community continued to oppose Scott as a matter of principle, most were taking a wait-and-see approach.[214] This included the gun rights political action group Allied Sportsmen of Pennsylvania, which was principally formed in 1968 to defeat former Pennsylvania senator Joseph S. Clark.[215]

Yet by April 1970, following the publication of two *Gun Week* articles that detailed Scott's firearms control–supporting past, Scott's humility approach appeared to be in peril.²¹⁶ The first *Gun Week* article reprinted portions of a June 24, 1968, letter that Scott penned to Connecticut senator Thomas J. Dodd in which he wrote that he was "pleased to be a co-sponsor" of what would ultimately become the Gun Control Act. Additionally, the letter showed Scott politically boasting of his firearms control bona fides.²¹⁷ The second *Gun Week* article, written by attorney Franz O. Willenbucher, was just as critical of Scott. The article detailed how Scott intentionally pivoted on the firearms control issue to garner the sportsmen's vote. Ultimately, Willenbucher concluded that Scott's self-manufactured, pro-gun narrative was disingenuous: "Senator Scott has neither demonstrated by any action nor made any public statement that he considers any part of the 1968 gun legislation to have been a 'mistake.' "²¹⁸

Scott's challenger, Democrat William G. Sesler, seized on the *Gun Week* articles by immediately calling out Scott for having flip-flopped on firearms controls.²¹⁹ Sesler made sure to advertise Scott's record of supporting firearms registration.²²⁰ Even worse for Scott was that a new, anti-Scott, gun rights political action group had formed. Named Citizens Against Scott (CAS), the group's mottos were "Vote for Anyone but Scott" and "Don't Let Scott Go Scott Free." And if the Pennsylvania gun rights community proved successful in defeating Scott on Election Day, CAS proclaimed that their "voting power" would be known "throughout the land."²²¹

Months before there was ever CAS or CAM, there was Citizens Against Tydings (CAT). Formed in late September 1969, CAT was by far the most relentless of the "Citizens Against" political action groups.²²² Initially, neither the news media nor Tydings gave CAT serious thought.²²³ But within two months' time, the group had developed the blueprint from which all other up-and-coming gun rights political action groups would follow. The key to CAT's success was twofold: First, its officers were experienced in the field of gun rights advocacy and came from a variety of sporting, hunting, and shooting organizations, including the Maryland Wildlife Foundation, Maryland Association of Citizens and Sportsmen, Associated Gun Clubs of Baltimore, and the Maryland-D.C. Rifle and Pistol Association, to name a few.²²⁴ Second, because Tydings was one of the Senate's three principal proponents for firearms controls, CAT was provided with plenty of material to work with.²²⁵ Tydings even published an article in *Playboy* explaining why Congress should oppose the NRA-led "gun lobby" and enact a federal firearms registration bill.²²⁶ The article ended up inspiring the gun rights

FIGURE 7.9 Political cartoon on the cover of *Gun Week*, October 3, 1969, not long after Citizens Against Tydings was formed. Image reprinted with the express permission of the Second Amendment Foundation.

anti-Tydings slogan "Playboy Joe Has Got to Go."[227] But what really irked so many in the gun rights community and ultimately drove them to support CAT was that Tydings often described himself as a principled sportsmen and firearms owner.[228]

Going into the primary elections of 1970, Tydings remained adamant that his policy position on firearms control was the right one. It was not until W. B. Doner & Company provided a qualitative research report that Tydings began to reconsider his approach. According to the report, on a personal level, the public perceived Tydings as aloof, inaccessible, and far from "warm and endearing." Equally troubling was the fact that Marylanders knew little of the senator's legislative policies other than that he supported firearms controls. The report noted that this was problematic for Tydings, seeing that "even among the liberal segments . . . support on the gun control issue is not uniform." The report went on to note: "There is a strong feeling of being denied individual rights and it is surprising that even in the better educated higher, socio-economic groups, they feel that gun control legislation essentially means that certain people will be denied the privilege of having guns. They feel that criminal and radical elements will always have guns available to them whether federal legislation required them to be registered or not. Consequently, they don't feel it will be an enforceable legislation and will only adversely affect innocent people."[229]

Simply put, what the Doner report made clear—particularly in the case of Maryland—was that the political talking points of the NRA and other gun rights advocates were proving to be far more convincing than those of Tydings and firearms control proponents.[230] What the report also made clear was that it was too late in campaign season for Tydings to politically flip or modify his position. He could, however, redefine his position in crime-control terms. Tydings could also emphasize how his firearms control proposals did nothing to prevent law-abiding citizens from acquiring, owning, or using firearms for lawful purposes. And this is exactly how Tydings began portraying his position.

For a brief time, Tydings hammered home three talking points to portray himself as a principled moderate. The first was that his various firearms control proposals only sought to disarm the criminal element. The second was that the proposals did nothing to hinder the Second Amendment rights of law-abiding citizens. Rather, according to Tydings, his proposals safeguarded the right to keep and bear arms. Tydings was not the only member of Congress making this claim during the 1970 elections. In a campaign pamphlet, Connecticut senator Thomas J. Dodd, who was also up for reelection, audaciously referred to Gun Control Act as the "Dodd Gun Rights Act" and claimed the law was the "sportsmen's best friend."[231] This brings us to the final political talking point Tydings advanced to portray himself as a principled moderate on the firearms control issue. It involved dismissing the "gun lobby's" criticisms of his various firearms control proposals as false and misleading.[232] And when Tydings dismissed these criticisms, he did his utmost to not mention the NRA or any other gun rights advocacy group by name.[233]

Tydings's strategy did little in the way of curtailing CAT's opposition. All across Maryland, CAT continued to distribute advertisements and flyers with headlines such as "If Tydings Wins . . . YOU LOSE!" and "IF YOU THINK SENATOR TYDINGS IS NOT YOUR PROBLEM, YOU DESERVE TO LOSE YOUR GUNS!"[234] By the Tydings campaign's estimate, more than 130,000 flyers were mailed out, each urging firearms dealers, sportsmen, hunters, shooters, and other gun rights advocacy groups to monetarily contribute to CAT whatever they could.[235] Gun rights advocates heeded CAT's call by holding several "Help Defeat Senator Tydings" fundraisers, each involving raffling off firearms donated by firearms manufacturers.[236] This provoked Tydings to revert back to calling out the NRA by name and accusing its officials of helping fund his defeat.[237] For the remainder of the 1970 campaign, he railed against the NRA as a "powerful, special interest, profit-motivated national gun lobby" that was using "the 'big lie' technique in an attempt to purge [him] from the United States Senate."[238] Tydings also called out his Maryland Senate race opponent, Republican representative Glenn Beall, Jr., as being too politically weak to stand up to the NRA-led "gun lobby," thus ensuring that firearms controls remained a top campaign issue. Beall, seeing firearms controls as a helpful wedge voting issue, did not shy away from it.[239] Beall in fact used the firearms control issue as an opportunity to criticize Tydings for "trying to create a straw man" out of the NRA.[240] The NRA and other gun rights advocates were equally critical of Tydings's criticisms.[241] As for CAT, the gun rights political action group blasted Tydings for being "careless with his facts." "A lobbyist is one who is employed, i.e., paid to influence legislation," wrote CAT officer J. Robert Esher in an editorial, adding, "None of us are." Esher went on to criticize Tydings, writing, "As to the charge that we are raising funds out of state—that is very interesting coming from one who had to bring in Hollywood personalities to his fund-raising dinner last fall."[242]

In the days leading up to the election, CAT placed several full-page advertisements in major Maryland newspapers, each urging voters to cast a ballot for Beall on the firearms control issue alone. One advertisement headline read: "TYDINGS CALLS THIS AD 'POLITICAL PORNOGRAPHY.' HE'S WRONG. IT'S JUST THE TRUTH." Another read: "REAL CRIMINALS ARE LAUGHING AT TYDINGS' GUN REGISTRATION AND LICENSING PROPOSAL. BUT YOU WON'T BE LAUGHING WHEN IT MAKES A 'CRIMINAL' OUT OF YOU OR A MEM-BER OF YOUR FAMILY!" Provided below each CAT advertisement headline were several talking points explaining why Tydings could not be trusted on the firearms control issue. "Tydings claims his gun registration bill won't affect honest citizens," stated one CAT advertisement, adding, "But who can believe him, when he continually lies about what it would and wouldn't do, and when he already supports efforts to eventually outlaw

M-MM! DEE-LICIOUS!

FIGURE 7.10 Political cartoon in *Gun Week*, November 20, 1970. The cartoon celebrated Maryland senator Joseph D. Tydings's defeat at the hands of Citizens Against Tydings (CAT). It was a follow-up to a cartoon on October 16, 1970, that showed CAT's cat waiting to pounce on little bird "Joe Tydings." Image reprinted with the express permission of the Second Amendment Foundation.

private firearms ownership."[243] The fact that Tydings had neither stated nor implied he would support outlawing the private ownership of firearms did not matter to CAT. What did matter was that Maryland firearms owners believed it.

Come Election Day, Tydings ultimately lost to Beall by 24,538 votes, a 2.5 percent margin. In the following day's edition of the Baltimore-based newspaper *Evening Sun* appeared an editorial titled "Gun Lobby Went After, Got Tydings."[244] The editors of *Gun Week* celebrated the outcome with the headline "Sportsmen Dump Tydings, Dodd from Senate Seats."[245] Not to be outdone in celebrating the success of the sportsmen's vote, the editors of *American Rifleman* published an article titled "Anti-Gun Leaders Toppled."[246] Beall too initially credited the sportsmen's vote for his Election Day victory.[247] Weeks later, however, he claimed his victory had less to do with organized gun rights opposition than a general "dissatisfaction" among Marylanders with Tydings's legislative policies.[248] As for Tydings, the lame duck senator was certain the NRA-led "gun lobby" was to blame for his defeat. The NRA "will undoubtedly be giving seminars across the country" on how to defeat other firearms control supporting lawmakers like him, he Tydings.[249]

Whether in fact the NRA, CAT, or some other organized gun rights opposition was in part responsible for Tydings's defeat was something that he revisited from time to time until his death.[250] Certainly CAT and other gun rights advocates thought they were responsible, especially given Beall's narrow margin of victory. Several news media outlets also bought this gun rights narrative wholesale. But the historical reality was that Tydings lost reelection for several reasons: his political hubris; his lack of a positive public image among Maryland's working class; his support for progressive ideals; and his vocal opposition to the Vietnam War.[251] But perhaps what really doomed Tydings was *Life Magazine*'s exposé on how the Maryland senator allegedly used his political office to promote the growth and profits of a small Florida investment company in which he was one of the largest stockholders.[252] Unbeknownst to almost everyone at the time, the allegations against Tydings were provided to *Life Magazine* by Charles "Chuck" Colson, an advisor to Richard Nixon, with the express purpose of torpedoing Tydings's reelection.[253] Tydings was ultimately cleared of any ethics violations ten days after Election Day, but by then it was too late: he had already lost to Beall.[254]

The fact that Tydings lost reelection in 1970 for several reasons unrelated to the firearms control issue is not to say that this issue did not lose Tydings Election Day votes. It certainly did. However, the firearms control issue was far from the deciding factor in Tydings's defeat. The same held true for the other 1970 election defeats that gun rights advocates took credit for—defeats that an article in *Guns & Ammo* celebrated as being a political "mandate for repeal" of the Gun Control Act.[255] Take, for instance, the 1970 election defeat of the Senate's chief proponent of firearms controls, Thomas J. Dodd. Indeed, Dodd was highly unpopular among Connecticut's sportsmen, hunters, shooters, and firearms owners throughout his reelection campaign.[256] However, Dodd's election loss was primarily the result of several Senate ethics violations.[257] For it was the ethics violations that cost Dodd the support of the Connecticut Democratic Party, which in turn forced him to run for reelection as a political independent.[258] And by running as an independent, all Dodd ended up accomplishing was splintering the Democratic vote and thus handing over his Senate seat to Republican Lowell Weicker, who, oddly, was also a proponent of federal firearms controls.[259]

The two other Senate victories celebrated by gun rights advocates—the defeats of Tennessee senator Albert A. Gore and New York senator Charles Goodell—are equally specious.[260] Indeed, both senators had voted for the Gun Control Act and supported firearms registration.[261] However, neither faced any serious organized gun rights opposition during their respective reelection campaigns.[262] Moreover, their election defeats are easily attributable to other, more prominent factors. In the case of Gore, from the very start of his reelection campaign, the Tennessee senator was identified as one of the most politically vulnerable due to his "liberal" support for virtually every civil rights initiative while representing a predominantly conservative state.[263] Meanwhile, in the case of Goodell, the New York senator, although a Republican, did not receive Nixon's endorsement due to his anti–Vietnam War views.[264] That honor—albeit an indirect endorsement—went to Conservative Party candidate James L. Buckley, who ended up winning the three-way Senate race with less than 39 percent of the vote.[265]

The historical point to be made is that the post-1970 election claims of the sportsmen's vote being responsible for the defeat of several "anti-gun" senators were unsubstantiated. Much like after the 1968 elections, such claims were severely overblown. This was even the case for those Senate races where incumbents seeking reelection faced stiff, well-organized gun rights opposition. In the Montana Senate race, for instance, despite the efforts of CAM and an opponent that made firearms controls a wedge voting issue, Mansfield handily won reelection by 21 points. The same was true in the Michigan Senate race, where Hart won reelection by nearly 34 points despite the efforts of SAM and an opponent that also made firearms controls a wedge voting issue. Even in the Pennsylvania Senate race, where the sportsmen's vote was thought to be most prevalent, Scott comfortably won reelection by 6 percentage points. Certainly, in all three of these examples, the winning incumbent modified their policy position on firearms controls with the purpose of garnering the sportsmen's vote.[266] Nevertheless, the fact remains that in all three cases the winning incumbent senator was fiercely opposed by gun rights political action groups.[267] In fact, out of the six 1970 Senate races that involved organized gun rights opposition, only the Maryland race involving Tydings was successful. But again, the evidentiary record cuts against Tydings's defeat being primarily due to organized gun rights opposition.

This is not to say that lawmakers' perception of the sportsmen's vote did not have a profound impact on the politics of firearms controls. It most certainly did, as can be seen by the number of lawmakers once outspoken in favor of firearms controls in 1968 now backtracking or changing their position in 1970. Several examples have been outlined in this chapter. But there are two more—the Senate races in Ohio and Minnesota—worth expounding on. Beginning with Ohio, much like in other states following the defeat of Pennsylvania senator Joseph S. Clark in 1968, several gun rights political action groups were formed in the Buckeye state, including the well-organized Ohio Sportsmen's Alliance (OSA).[268] OSA's first political target was none other than former astronaut John H. Glenn, who was seeking the Democratic nomination to replace retiring senator Stephen M. Young.[269] Recall that it was Glenn who had served as the public face and chairman of the Emergency Committee for Gun Control (ECGC), the nongovernmental organization most responsible for organizing the public to write Congress to enact strict firearms controls. This, according to OSA, was reason enough for sportsmen to join the organization and "help put Glenn back in orbit."[270]

The criticism leveled by OSA and other gun rights advocates was something that Glenn thought best not to ignore.[271] Initially, Glenn approached the firearms control issue much like Tydings, by noting that his "true" firearms control policy position was being widely misinterpreted by gun rights propagandists. Also, like Tydings, Glenn presented himself as being a principled and responsible sportsman, and one who had owned firearms and actively hunted for most of his life.[272] Where Glenn distinguished himself from Tydings was that he no longer favored firearms registration, though he did support the licensing of firearms owners.[273] Glenn also separated himself from Tydings by agreeing to an interview with the editors of *Gun Week*, which published the transcript in full. Throughout the interview, the editors did their utmost to make Glenn appear ignorant of not only the firearms control issue but also firearms in general by repeatedly asking questions about the type of firearms he owned. At several points, the editors made snide comments and false accusations about Glenn. Eventually, their interview demeanor reached a breaking point, prompting

Glenn to call out *Gun Week* for covering him on the firearms control issue yet giving his Democratic primary opponent, Howard Metzenbaum, a political pass: "That's where you guys are so doggone gullible it makes me sick. If you don't mind my saying so, you don't apply the same questions to [Metzenbaum]. You let him get away with a nebulous statement [on the issue] and I'm put on the pan for the things I really stood for and have guts enough to stand up for. And [Metzenbaum] won't take a stand so you give him a clean bill of health. What a bunch of garbage."[274]

Glenn, although tactless and unthinking in criticizing *Gun Week*'s editors, was not wrong. Neither *Gun Week* nor OSA was holding Metzenbaum even remotely accountable on firearms controls. Rather, they allowed him to speak in generalities on the issue. And based on the outcome of the Democratic primary between Glenn and Metzenbaum, that strategy appeared to have paid off. "The stunning defeat of John Glenn in the Ohio Democratic primary by approximately 13,000 votes by virtually unknown Howard Metzenbaum has to be credited in a large part to the shooting and hunting sportsmen of Ohio," wrote the editors of *Gun Week*.[275] The editors of the *Armed Eagle* were just as exuberant, writing, "John Glenn is but one example of the impact of organized opposition by dedicated and concerned sportsmen in defending their belief in the Second Amendment."[276]

But much like the other sportsmen's vote election victories, the narrative being espoused by gun rights advocates was not the reality. It is important to note that Glenn was at that time a political novice, who purposely ran an underwhelming, low-key campaign.[277] Conversely, Metzenbaum, although lacking Glenn's celebrity status, was politically experienced and vocal in criticizing Glenn for trying to ride his celebrity coattails into office. Additionally, Metzenbaum's personal fortune—obtained through investing and real estate transactions—provided him with an overwhelming advertising advantage. By the end of the campaign, Metzenbaum had outspent Glenn by a ratio of more than 5 to 1.[278] But even if one places these facts aside, what ultimately undermines the gun rights narrative of the sportsmen's vote affecting the outcome of 1970 Ohio primary is that the candidate opposed by OSA for the Republican Senate primary, Representative Howard Taft, Jr., ended up defeating the more gun rights–friendly Governor James A. Rhodes.[279] Moreover, come the general election, Taft comfortably defeated Democratic candidate Metzenbaum by more than 2 percentage points.[280]

Still, if there remains any historical doubt that the collective power of the sportsmen's vote was being severely overhyped by gun rights advocates, the outcome of the Minnesota Senate race dispels it. Therein Democratic-Farmer-Labor (DFL) Party candidate and former vice president Hubert H. Humphrey squared off against Republican representative Clark MacGregor to see who would fill the Senate seat of retiring Eugene McCarthy. Recall that during the presidential race in 1968—much to ire of the gun rights community—it was Humphrey who carried the "anti-gun" mantel of the Johnson administration by campaigning for federal firearms registration.[281] This included repeatedly calling out Nixon for not supporting strict firearms controls. Yet in the 1970 election, despite the gun rights narrative of 600,000 Minnesota sportsmen standing ready to vote against firearms control–supporting lawmakers, both past and present, Humphrey was not held to account for his "anti-gun" sins.[282] Instead, by more than 220,000 votes, Humphrey was elected Minnesota's next senator. And Humphrey was not the only "anti-gun" candidate to win in Minnesota that year. Several did, including the DFL candidate for Minnesota attorney general, Warren Spannaus, who was outspoken in favor of strict handgun controls, such as registration and a handgun buyback program.[283] Spannaus ended up defeating his gun rights–friendly Republican opponent, Robert A. Forsythe.[284] There is indeed a historical argument to be made that the Minnesota sportsmen's vote was, if anything, underwhelming. For not one of the seven Minnesota congressmen up for reelection in 1970 who voted for the Gun Control Act lost reelection that year. This included Representative Donald M. Fraser, who was a strong proponent of firearms registration.[285] In fact, the only Minnesota congressman to lose reelection was the only one who voted against the Gun Control Act, Odin Langen.[286]

That the collective power of the Minnesota sportsmen's vote—and the national sportsmen's vote for that matter—was more nominal than real does not mean that candidates vying for Minnesota congressional and state offices were not fearful of it. This was no more evident than when several DFL candidates broke ranks with their party's firearms control plank. The DFL firearms control plank in 1970 declared that because the proliferation of handguns had "led to an alarming increase in the number of violent deaths," the DFL would urge that the sale of handguns "be severely restricted and *made* by permit only."[287] One of the DFL candidates to break rank was its most prominent, former vice president Humphrey, who was now unwilling to support the strict control of handguns unless it could be proved that said controls decreased the propensity for armed crime to occur. And Humphrey's rebuke of his 1968 firearms control position did not end there. For in the months leading up to Election Day, Humphrey repeatedly outlined a rather gun rights–friendly position whenever questioned on the issue. In correspondence with his former political advisor Ted Van Dyk, Humphrey explained his political change of heart as follows:

> Out here [in Minnesota], people feel a lot differently about gun control than they do back on the East coast. . . . This isn't the major issue of our lives. I don't intend to let this issue stand in the way of getting things done that need to be done that are far more significant than whether or not you register a shotgun. Frankly, I am amazed that some of the columnists are so uptight on the question of registering guns. That, at best, is a minor item in a law enforcement program or even in public safety. . . . Once you get away from Washington, the issue of whether to register .22 ammunition and a shotgun seems so dammed insignificant that you wonder how the federal government even got involved.[288]

Humphrey's political confession on the firearms control issue underscores three historical points concerning the 1970 elections: First and foremost, gun rights advocates, with the assistance of some in the news media, were undoubtedly successful in convincing many, if not most, lawmakers that the sportsmen's vote was a powerful, one-issue voting bloc not to be ignored. Second, many, if not most, of the lawmakers who came to support firearms controls in the wake the Martin Luther King, Jr., and Robert F. Kennedy assassinations, including Humphrey, did so because it was the politically expedient thing to do at the time. Finally, many, if not most, lawmakers were happily willing to modify or altogether abandon their support of firearms controls in the interest political self-preservation. As Humphrey noted to Van Dyk, he was not about to let the firearms control issue "stand in the way" of him being elected and accomplishing more important things.[289] Indeed, the collective power of the sportsmen's vote was more myth than fact. But, as is often the case in politics, what is the no-kidding reality can easily be consumed by political perception. All that is ostensibly required for this to happen is a considerable belief in whatever political perception—even a demonstrably untrue one—is being marketed.

8

1971–1974

Firearms Control Politics and the Saturday Night Special

To President Richard M. Nixon's advisors, the elections in 1970 all but confirmed the political benefits of courting the sportsmen's vote for the upcoming 1972 election.[1] At the same time, given that the national polls continued to show overwhelming support for firearms controls, Nixon's advisors believed it was important that the president come out in support of some firearms legislation. The political conundrum was: What type of legislation could he support without "impinging upon legitimate gun owners" and drawing the ire of the "gun lobby"? The answer, according to Nixon's advisors, was the Saturday Night Special—a term commonly used to describe cheap, concealable handguns that served no sporting, hunting, or marksmanship purpose.[2]

There were three reasons why Nixon's advisors decided to pursue Saturday Night Special legislation. First, these guns were already subject to federal regulation. Under the Gun Control Act of 1968, it was unlawful for anyone to import them into the United States. But nothing in the Gun Control Act impeded their domestic production and sale, which brings us to the second reason why Nixon's advisors decided to pursue Saturday Night Special legislation: the frequency with which the cheap handguns were used to commit crimes. According to the Federal Bureau of Investigation (FBI), more than half of all crimes involving firearms were committed with such guns. The final reason to pursue this legislation was undoubtedly the most important: the National Rifle Association (NRA) and other gun rights advocates were already on record supporting Saturday Night Special regulation, and therefore Nixon's advisors believed the president would not face any considerable organized gun rights opposition.[3]

As early as 1928, decades before cheap, junk handguns were referred to as Saturday Night Specials, the NRA was on record "campaign[ing] against the sale of junk revolvers and pistols by mail."[4] Thirty-five years later, in 1963, the organization lambasted the "irresponsible merchants and purchasers" of "cheap handguns" and even applauded the Senate Subcommittee to Investigate Juvenile Delinquency's efforts to regulate them.[5] Four years later, in a 1967 press release, the NRA stated it would unequivocally back a ban on the importation of "cheap, 'junk' handguns" deemed unsuitable as "sport shooting equipment, or objects of art, of historical significance, or useful for research and development."[6] Two years later, in an *American Rifleman* editorial in 1969, the NRA urged Congress to pass legislation that would "curb these cheap, concealable little handguns that local police departments blame for 40% to 60% of recent crimes involving guns."[7]

The first lawmaker to take the NRA up on its offer was none other than its political archnemesis, Connecticut senator Thomas J. Dodd. "We shut off the importation of this dreadful type of gun only to wake up and find out Americans [can still acquire Saturday Night Specials domestically]," stated Dodd, adding, "It's outrageous."[8] Dodd's firearms control bill, S. 2932, sought to close the Saturday Night Special loophole by providing the Department of Treasury with the authority to ban their domestic production, sale, and transfer. Initially, the NRA and other gun rights advocates offered nothing in the way of criticizing S. 2932. This was largely because the bill did nothing to change the criteria allotted to the Department of Treasury under the Gun Control Act in defining what constituted a Saturday Night Special. It merely sought to extend the department's international commerce and importation authority to include all domestically produced Saturday Night Specials.[9]

The other reason the NRA and other gun rights advocates were initially not critical of Dodd's S. 2932 was that their attention was intently focused on the recently published recommendations of the National Commission on the Causes and Prevention of Violence (NCCPV), particularly the recommendation that the private sale and purchase of all handguns should be outlawed. It was a recommendation that forever changed how gun rights advocates politically messaged on the firearms control issue. For decades, the NRA and others had intentionally made the distinction between sporting and nonsporting firearms. The latter were generally cast aside as not worthy of legal protection. Hence, while gun rights advocates generally supported laws restricting access to machine guns, "destructive devices," military-grade firearms, and the like, they were simultaneously messaging that one firearms control was one too many and a slippery slope to complete disarmament. Once the NCCPV recommended that lawmakers cut off the private sale and purchase of *all* handguns, not just nonsporting ones, the NRA and other gun rights advocates, largely at the behest of the "no compromise" gun rights movement, were compelled to change their political message on firearms controls.

This change in messaging did not develop in the span of a few days, weeks, or even months. It took years because, for a time, it ended up pitting the older, more moderate gun rights advocates against the newer, "no compromise" advocates. The way the more moderate advocates saw it, any "no compromise" position was politically untenable. Defending "nonsporting equipment" such as "riot guns, assault rifles, grenades, and military sidearms" under the umbrella of the Second Amendment would be committing political "sabotage" from within. "If we expect to base our right to arms on the argument of not penalizing the law-abiding sportsman, it's time we start living up to the ideals we promote," wrote one moderate gun rights advocate.[10] The "no compromise" rebuttal was that by placing a "sporting" designation on firearms, moderates were politically "selling out" their fellow gun rights supporters and the Second Amendment. "Far too many sportsmen—and some gun writers—are losing sight of the fact that there is a proper place for all types of firearms, including the cheap handguns, commonly known as 'Saturday Night Specials,'" wrote the editors of *Gun Week*.[11] From that point onward, the political talking point that public access to all firearms, not just sporting firearms, is protected under the constitutional umbrella of the Second Amendment became part of the gun rights movement.

What also sidetracked any gun rights criticism of Dodd's S. 2932 was the election cycle in 1970. Not only were gun rights advocates intently focused on defeating firearms-control-supporting lawmakers at the polls, but also, not to upend any Republicans who were riding Nixon's political coattails into the 1970 elections, there was little, if any, appetite among his advisors to take up firearms-control legislation. The upcoming presidential election of 1972, however, changed the political calculation. Inside the White House, Nixon's advisors believed that if the president backed some form of Saturday Night Special legislation, he would politically appease "the right by removing the main source of agitation for gun control legislation without affecting gun ownership and mollify the left by having the Administration propose some sort of gun legislation."[12] Simply put, Nixon's advisors viewed Saturday Night Special legislation as a political win-win. But before proceeding further, they wanted to first meet with the NRA and other key members of the gun rights community to test the political waters.[13]

The first meeting took place on January 18, 1971, as an off-the-record event at the White House attended by representatives of the Department of Treasury, Department of Justice, NRA, and several other sporting, hunting, and shooting organizations and publications. Nixon's advisors organized the meeting agenda in a way that made the president appear as friendly to and supportive of gun rights as possible.[14] This was accomplished by putting forward a sandwich meeting agenda, that is, starting and ending the meeting with positive gun rights topics and inserting the contentious firearms control topic in the middle. At the top of the agenda was an open discussion on the "strengths and weaknesses" of the Gun Control Act, including identifying the provisions deemed "most offensive to law abiding citizens" and the possibility of Nixon sponsoring legislation to "eliminate these difficulties." From there the agenda shifted to discussing the possibility of Nixon pursuing firearms control legislation, particularly for Saturday Night Specials. The agenda closed with the advisors offering attendees an assurance that Nixon would reject the NCCPV's recommendation of a handgun ban, followed by several reminders on how Nixon had always "dealt fairly" with "American sportsmen in the areas of firearms and explosives control."[15]

Afterward, Nixon's advisors convened several one-on-one engagements with the meeting attendees before bringing everyone back together for a second White House meeting on March 25. It was at this meeting that the advisors pitched the NRA and other key members of the gun rights movement on legislatively fixing the "public safety" issues with Saturday Night Specials. The way the advisors sold it was that the administration would first conduct a quality-control study on a variety of domestically produced handguns. The findings of that study would then determine what, if any, legislation was needed for regulating Saturday Night Specials.[16]

Based on the reporting from gun rights publications, the second White House meeting could not have gone any better.[17] The editors of *Gun Week*, for one, assured readers that imposing "quality-control" standards was indeed necessary, and they even applauded the Nixon administration for its gun rights–friendly approach to the problem. "The simple fact that the Administration will sit down with firearms industry and sportsmen's group leaders and that the Nixon Administration is taking a sensible approach to the crime problem in America," wrote the editors, adding, "Who could ask for more?"[18] Similarly, Neal Knox, editor-in-chief of *Handloader Magazine*, wrote, "As far as we're concerned, these positive actions [by the Nixon administration] speak much louder than words; and, though we're not trying to get involved in partisan politics, this record must not be ignored in future elections."[19] Meanwhile, the editors of *Guns Magazine* expressed their appreciation for Nixon's continued support of the "shooting sportsman," especially his efforts at "combatting registration and confiscation proposals."[20]

Contracted to perform the handgun quality-control study was H. P. White Laboratory, an independent firearms and ballistics lab located in Bel Air, Maryland. The laboratory was given 150 different handguns to test, ranging from high-priced precision-target types to small-caliber .22 rimfire types that sold for as little as ten dollars. Each handgun was broken down and measured, underwent a dye penetration test to check for invisible manufacturing defects, was fired first with high-velocity commercial cartridges, and then was fired with standard ammunition approximately a thousand times. The final test—the thousand-round standard ammunition firing test—was considered the most important in determining the "point at which the firearm will cease to function or will malfunction in a hazardous manner."[21]

From the conclusion of the March 25 White House meeting to mid-September, Nixon's advisors were intent on not doing "anything that would undermine [their positive political] position with the sportsmen and hunters."[22] Thus when the National Broadcasting Company (NBC) aired a special report on Saturday Night Specials and claimed that Nixon was seeking to impose "further gun control under the 'guise' of quality control,"

Nixon's advisors quickly prepared talking points should the president receive any gun rights criticism.[23] Likewise, when Attorney General John N. Mitchell appeared on the *David Frost Show* and stated he was "diametrically opposed to anybody having a gun, except law enforcement officers,"[24] Secretary of the Treasury special assistant G. Gordon Liddy assured gun rights supporters at the NRA's annual meeting in 1971 that Nixon, unlike former president Lyndon B. Johnson, would never "confuse the 40 million law-abiding, responsible Americans who rightly own firearms with criminals." Liddy also offered up the assurance that Nixon's primary interest in regulating Saturday Night Specials was not to control firearms but to ensure product safety.[25]

While Nixon's advisors awaited the results of White Laboratory's handgun quality-control study, public clamoring for additional handgun controls was mounting. A slew of media reports on the Saturday Night Special domestic manufacturing loophole was causing the issue to gain political steam. A Harris Poll found that two-thirds of Americans supported "strict control and registration" of all handguns. The largest support came from those living in the suburbs (75 percent favor, 24 percent oppose), followed by those living in cities (71 percent favor, 25 percent oppose) and towns (64 percent favor, 33 percent oppose). The Harris Poll also indicated a plurality of support for firearm ownership (49 percent favor, 43 percent oppose), with 51 percent of all households surveyed maintaining that they own at least one firearm.[26]

President Nixon took notice of the public clamoring for additional handgun controls and began inquiring about the status of his administration's Saturday Night Special legislation. On June 1, after being told that his advisors were still awaiting the results of White Laboratory's handgun quality control study, Nixon replied, "I wish we could outlaw this kind of thing."[27] Weeks later, as part of a larger discussion on the "war on crime," Nixon asked his advisors to maintain pressure on the NRA to produce "limited" Saturday Night Special legislation: "I think the gun lobby could make themselves a whole hell of a lot of support. They ought to come out and support that legislation. . . . Somebody should talk to the NRA. I don't know these people, but they are a very powerful lobby."[28] Nixon was then briefed that the NRA had previously supported the "outlawing" of Saturday Night Specials in the past, the organization was being "kept informed of [the] Administration's development of tests seeking objective standards for handguns, and that they will be consulted in the development of legislation if we find such legislation feasible."[29]

Little did Nixon or his advisors know that they were about to be beaten to the Saturday Night Special punch by Democratic Indiana senator Birch Bayh.[30] On August 11 Bayh announced he would be introducing S. 2507, which would bar the sale or transfer of any handgun by a federally licensed firearms dealer that the treasury secretary determined unsuitable for lawful sporting purposes. This made Bayh's S. 2507 very different from what Nixon's advisors had promised gun rights advocates. Gun rights advocates viewed S. 2507 as taking a subjective, "sporting purposes" approach to Saturday Night Specials. Conversely, Nixon's proposal was viewed as taking an objective, product safety approach. This made Nixon's proposal more palatable to gun rights advocates.[31] However, because Bayh had filed his legislation first, Nixon was suddenly placed on the political defensive, and his administration was forced to stonewall Bayh's repeated requests for information.

It was on September 14, at a hearing of the Senate Subcommittee to Investigate Juvenile Delinquency, that the Nixon administration finally responded to Bayh. Assistant to the Secretary of the Treasury Eugene Rossides stated there that the administration was drafting Saturday Night Special legislation and that Nebraska senator Roman L. Hruska was involved.[32] Both claims were nothing more than political smokescreens. The Nixon administration had yet to draft anything in the way of Saturday Night Special legislation, and as for Hruska, the long-time NRA congressional surrogate had lent his name only to provide Nixon some political cover. Noticeably absent from Rossides's testimony was how Nixon's advisors were coordinating with the NRA and other, more moderate gun rights advocates. This was intentional, for some in Nixon's inner circle were fearful of the "political ramifications" if it got out that the administration was "working hand in glove with [the 'gun lobby'] in the formulation of legislation." "This will undoubtedly leave us open to a very severe political attack," wrote White House counsel Charles Colson to Nixon advisor Egil Krogh, Jr., adding, "This could very well destroy the credibility of our legislation." Colson then recommended that Krogh quickly draft Saturday Night Special legislation without any "gun lobby" coordination to avoid any "charges of collusion."[33]

That Rossides and other Nixon administration officials conveniently left out the fact that they were working with the NRA and other, more moderate gun rights advocates initially worked to everyone's political advantage.[34] It was especially beneficial in muting any criticism from the more extreme gun rights supporters. But once Rossides testified that the Nixon administration was drafting Saturday Night Special legislation of its own, the "no compromise" wing of the gun rights movement became infuriated. What particularly incensed them was that this legislation was being drafted before the release of the White Laboratory's handgun quality control study. Even more infuriating was the fact that Nixon's advisors were proceeding with Saturday Night Special legislation without having consulted them. "Looking back on it all, it now appears that the Administration may have concocted the handgun tests as a method of justifying a position already taken," surmised the editors of *Gun Week*, adding, "If this is the case, it could mean bad news for gun owners, because such a development could mean a drastic change of thinking on gun control matters within the Administration."[35] The editors of the gun rights extremist publication *Armed Citizen News* were even more critical. "The [Nixon administration's handgun] tests appear to have been run to provide the controlled news media a propaganda club for deceiving the people and creating necessary emotionalism for our prostitute politicians to violate the Second Amendment again," wrote the editors.[36]

The Nixon administration was not alone in receiving criticism from the "no compromise" wing of the gun rights movement. The NRA too fell within the movement's crosshairs following Executive Vice President Maxwell E. Rich's testimony before the Senate Subcommittee to Investigate Juvenile Delinquency. Rich confirmed what had been the NRA's position on Saturday Night Specials for nearly a decade: that the NRA concurred "in principle with desirability of removing from the marketplace crudely made and unsafe handguns."[37] To the "no compromise" wing, the NRA's support for Saturday Night Special legislation—no matter how limited in scope—was not only a political act of betrayal but also another foolish attempt at trying to appease the ever unappeasable "anti-gun" contingent.

Behind the scenes, despite facing vocal opposition from the "no compromise" wing, Nixon administration officials, Senator Hruska, NRA executive vice president Rich, and *American Rifleman* editor Ashley Halsey, Jr., all agreed to proceed in drafting Saturday Night Special legislation. Administration officials were given two key instructions in working with their gun rights advocacy counterparts: The first was to handle negotiations "very carefully,"[38] and to "avoid the emotionalism" that allegedly surrounded the passage of the Gun Control Act.[39] The second instruction was that whatever form of legislation was ultimately agreed on, the bill itself could not read as if it were "Made and Approved by the Gun Nuts."[40] By early November, it appeared that a "middle ground" Saturday Night Special bill was ready to proceed—one that put forward objective "reliability and safety" handgun testing standards.[41] However, when Rich and Halsey presented the bill to the NRA board of directors for their approval, it was summarily rejected on the grounds it would ban dozens of handguns currently on the market. For the NRA board of directors to come onboard would require the reliability and safety standards to apply prospectively. Moreover, the authority to establish and modify the reliability and safety standards would need to be vested with the National Bureau of Standards, not the Department of Treasury's Alcohol, Tobacco & Firearms Division (ATFD).[42]

Fear of a federal agency dedicated to the enforcement of firearms controls had long permeated gun rights literature.[43] Therefore when the ATFD was formally established following the passage of the Gun Control Act, it did not take long before the agency became a chief gun rights political target. Highly exaggerated and overdramatized accusations of the ATFD intimidating firearms dealers and harassing law-abiding firearms owners were commonplace. Then came the Kenyon F. Ballew incident, which politically enraged the gun rights community as never before (fig. 8.1). The incident took place after the ATFD received information that Ballew maintained several unregistered hand grenades at his Silver Spring, Maryland, apartment. On June 7, 1971, the ATFD, accompanied by local Montgomery County police, forcefully entered Ballew's apartment. During that forced entry Ballew sustained a nonfatal gunshot to head. Subsequently, the event became most covered gun rights story line of the year. In virtually every prominent gun rights publication, what happened to Ballew was held up as proof that the Gun Control Act was usurping the constitutional rights of everyday, law-abiding Americans. Gun rights advocates cast Ballew as everything from an innocent firearms collector, to the prototypical NRA member, to a highly respected Boy Scout leader. Conversely, they criticized the ATFD's actions as being "gestapo-like."[44] One advocate went so far as to label the ATFD's actions as "Nazi-Storm Trooper like."[45]

Certainly, the ATFD's forced-entry tactics at Ballew's apartment are worthy of criticism and perhaps even condemnation.[46] However, the

FIGURE 8.1 Political cartoon in *Gun Week*, August 13, 1969. The cartoon represented how gun rights advocates depicted the ATFD raid on Kenyon F. Ballew's apartment. Image reprinted with the express permission of the Second Amendment Foundation.

reporting of the incident in gun right publications stretched the bands of historical elasticity and sometimes bordered on conspiracy. Thus when the Department of Treasury's investigation and subsequent court proceedings found the ATFD to be legally blameless for Ballew being shot in the head—seeing that it was Ballew who first pulled a firearm on the ATFD agents—and the agents had repeatedly announced themselves prior to knocking Ballew's door down—gun rights advocates took to claiming the investigation was a political "whitewash" and "coverup."[47] For months, gun rights publications cast Ballew as both a victim and a hero. The publications claimed that he was simply defending himself against unidentified assailants and that any law-abiding citizen would have reacted exactly the same. As a result, what happened to Ballew became a gun rights' rallying cry against the ATFD and the federal firearms laws the agency enforced. What gun rights advocates wanted every supporter to principally take away was that what happened to Ballew could happen to any one of them.[48] As long as the Gun Control Act remained in force, it was only a matter a time before an ATFD agent came knocking on their door looking for them.[49] To show solidarity with Ballew, some thirty sporting, hunting, and shooting organizations sold bumper stickers that read: "Ken Ballew Could Be You"—the proceeds of which helped offset Ballew's medical expenses.[50] One gun rights supporter went so far as to write a poem about the incident, which cast Ballew as a "fine young lad of good report" and the ATFD as just another law enforcement agency gone astray from American values: "In the days of old our lawmen were of loyal blood and true / Who gave their lives, and gladly, to protect both me and you, / But the standards must have changed, my friend, when a badge of any hue, / Can justify the shooting of a man like *Ken Ballew!*"[51]

Considering how gun rights publications covered the Ballew incident, the political prospects of Nixon's advisors getting the "sporting fraternity" onboard with any Saturday Night Special legislation in 1971 was slim to none. Not even the NRA—which was on record supporting such legislation—was able to offer the Nixon administration any political assurances.[52] The NRA's leadership knew that if it came out in support of any proposed Saturday Night Special legislation, the "no compromise" wing of the gun rights movement's backlash would be so swift that it would affect the NRA's economic bottom line with the loss of membership. It was a scenario that the NRA could ill afford at the time. From the moment the Gun Control Act was signed into law through the elections in 1970, while the NRA's expenditures continued to increase, there were continued difficulties in growing the membership rolls. These membership difficulties persisted throughout Nixon's presidency. From January 1971 until Nixon's resignation on August 9, 1974, membership remained largely stagnant, fluctuating from just under one million members to just over one million.[53] Similarly, circulation of *American Rifleman* was unable to reach or surpass its 1968 peak of 1,159,000.[54] Rather, circulation fluctuated from a high of 1,080,000 to a low of 1,026,000.[55]

The NRA was not alone in failing to attract new supporters. The more extreme gun rights publication *Gun Week*—which had grown substantially leading up to the 1970 elections—was also experiencing difficulties in attracting new supporters. By the end of 1973 its circulation was down 33 percent, from a high of 55,468 to a low of 37,286.[56] The post-1970 election stagnation or decline in gun rights political enthusiasm, depending on one's historical perspective, was not due to lack of effort by the NRA and other gun rights advocates. They remained dedicated to executing their tried-and-true gun rights playbook for defeating unwanted firearms controls, with particular attention focused on any proposals that would either impose firearms registration or outlaw any types of firearms. Additionally, in the hopes of attracting more of the estimated seventeen million licensed hunters to the political cause, gun rights advocates—the NRA especially—began sending alerts on the political movement to expand legal protections for endangered species, or what gun rights advocates politically cast as the "anti-hunt" movement.[57] One NRA membership advertisement went so far to assert that the sudden "huge wave of anti-hunting sentiment" would eventually make all hunting "extinct."[58] And to further entice more hunters to join the NRA and the cause of gun rights, the NRA started an entirely new magazine titled *American Hunter*, dedicated primarily to "the outdoorsman and firearms enthusiast."[59] Meanwhile, in hopes of appealing to the "no compromise" wing, the NRA and other advocates began urging gun rights supporters to oppose anyone and anything that supported restrictive firearms controls or opposed their Second Amendment right to keep and bear arms. It is a political practice that today is often referred to as "cancel culture"—that is, the act of withdrawing support for public figures and companies after they do or say something considered politically objectionable or offensive.

For whatever reason, these efforts by the NRA and other gun rights advocates failed to produce even a modest increase in gun rights political enthusiasm. New supporters were not flocking to join the political cause as they had in previous years. Not even the prospect of ousting "anti-gun" lawmakers for the upcoming elections was working.[60] And this stagnation or decline in enthusiasm was happening despite the repeated calls to political action by the NRA and other gun rights advocates—political action that was seen as necessary if the gun rights community was ever going to repeal the Gun Control Act.

Fortunately for gun rights advocates, the White House had not taken any notice. President Nixon and his advisors remained convinced that garnering the sportsmen's vote was important to the Republican Party's electoral success in 1972. It was for this reason that Nixon's advisors postponed their plans to push any Saturday Night Special bill until the start of the 93rd Congress. This is not to say, however, that they were abandoning such legislation altogether. Nixon had promised members of Congress and the news media that a bill was forthcoming, and his advisors planned

"Spiro, Let Me Make One Thing
Perfectly Clear — This Could
Hurt Our Political Careers"

FIGURE 8.2 Political cartoon in *Gun Week*, December 3, 1971. The cartoon depicted President Richard M. Nixon as being forced to retract his late 1971 push for Saturday Night Special legislation, given the firm opposition from the gun rights community. Image reprinted with the express permission of the Second Amendment Foundation.

on delivering on that promise. Nixon's advisors understood that to do otherwise—that is, not submit any Saturday Night Special legislation—would subject the president to immense political criticism.[61] As for appeasing the NRA, other gun rights advocates, and the wider gun rights community, the advisors offered the assurance that the administration would be "softening" its approach going forward.[62] The assurance effectively muted any serious gun rights criticism for a five-month period. This provided them with the necessary time to redraft the Saturday Night Special bill with minimal outside interference. Yet from mid-December 1971 to mid-May 1972, the promised bill never came to fruition—at least not for public consumption. Outside of a few Nixon administration officials, only a handful of NRA officials and congressional surrogates were provided with drafts and given the opportunity to propose changes.[63] Notable among the latter group was Democratic representative John D. Dingell of Michigan, who in private correspondence offered Nixon's advisors several suggestions.[64]

For Nixon's transparency and cooperation, the NRA provided favorable coverage in the pages of *American Rifleman*. At the same time, to seemingly bolster Nixon's reelection prospects, it provided critical coverage of Minnesota senator Hubert H. Humphrey and Oklahoma senator Fred R. Harris, both of whom were vying to be the Democratic presidential candidate in 1972 and politically backing Bayh's S. 2507.[65] Just two years earlier, Humphrey had promised that he would no longer back any new federal firearms controls, unless there was evidence showing that said controls would "reduce [the] coincidence of crime in America."[66] Yet with the Democratic Party's presidential nomination at stake, Humphrey once more flip-flopped on the firearms control issue. He was now of the opinion that more federal firearms controls were indeed necessary, including handgun registration.[67]

Harris, too, had flip-flopped on the firearms-control issue. Both prior to and after the passage of the Gun Control Act, he had politically positioned himself as a supporter of both the Second Amendment and firearms localism.[68] However, when it came to the subject of the interstate sale and shipment of firearms, he was willing to concede that some federal regulation was "necessary in order to make state and local laws effective."[69] Yet once Harris decided to run for president, the Oklahoma senator politically reshaped his position to compete with the other Democratic challengers.[70] What he ultimately decided was to put forward a new position favoring handgun controls—one that he believed would not incur the "wrath of the gun lobby, etc." Harris's new position first required "getting on the Bayh bill." This was followed by him going "one step further" by backing Michigan senator Philip Hart's bill limiting "handgun ownership to law enforcement officers and security guards." Harris believed that he could politically back both bills without undermining his longstanding position of "strongly protecting the rights of sportsmen and other to own and use firearms for *proper* purposes without unnecessary restrictions."[71] Unfortunately for Harris, his presidential campaign never got off the ground due to a lack of campaign funds.[72]

Entering the spring of 1972, support for handgun controls turned out to be a popular political position among the field of nearly a dozen Democratic presidential candidates. While the candidates disagreed on the particulars, they perfectly understood that supporting some type of handgun control was politically necessary to attract the more liberal wing of the Democratic Party. In fact, the only Democratic presidential candidate to come out against handgun controls was former Alabama governor

George C. Wallace, who, entering the Maryland primaries, had proven himself to be a rather formidable adversary among the crowded presidential field. "I'm sure I feel as you do, that restrictive gun legislation, wherever it might be—at the national level, or at the state level—really in the long run restricts the law-abiding citizen who owns a gun, but for a law violator, he doesn't pay attention to any law, whether it is gun control or any other law," stated Wallace before the April 25, 1972, Conference of Sportsmen.[73] Three weeks later, on May 15, while campaigning in Laurel, Maryland, for the state primary, Wallace was shot five times with a revolver by Arthur H. Bremer.[74] And thanks to the Gun Control Act, it took the ATFD roughly ten minutes to trace the serial number of the revolver back to a Milwaukee, Wisconsin, retail outlet where Bremer purchased it.[75] Wallace fortunately survived the shooting but was left paralyzed from the waist down and forced to resign his campaign.

Much like the assassinations of Martin Luther King, Jr., and Senator Robert F. Kennedy in 1968, the Wallace shooting set off a political firestorm on the need for additional firearms controls. Nixon administration officials were suddenly bombarded with questions on the issue, as well as questions regarding the status of the promised Saturday Night Special bill. President Nixon's initial political inclination was to come out in support of a handgun ban, but his advisors convinced him otherwise. Still, he was adamant that the administration needed to propose something in the way of handgun legislation and "do it fast."[76] His advisors responded by once more trying to drum up political support behind the scenes for their bill. In doing so, they remained cognizant of the promises that administration officials had made to gun rights advocates. Just weeks earlier, at the NRA's annual meeting in Portland, Oregon, Nixon advisor and Department of Treasury official William L. Dickey had promised that the president still felt that "the subject of firearms control ought to be left predominantly to the determination of the state and local governments." Additionally, Dickey promised that the President would continue to oppose firearms registration and licensing, as well as continue to work with sportsmen in undoing any burdensome provisions within the Gun Control Act.[77] Dickey made no mention of the Saturday Night Special bill that the Nixon administration had been working on for more than a year. This was undoubtedly intentional. Nixon's advisors preferred not to talk about even the prospects of a bill unless the situation absolutely required it. The Wallace shooting proved to be one of those situations, and the advisors did their utmost to maintain a gun rights–friendly message.

While Nixon's advisors were trying to drum up political support behind the scenes for their bill, Bayh's S. 2507 was moving in the Senate. On May 17, just two days after the Wallace shooting, that bill passed the Senate Subcommittee to Investigate Juvenile Delinquency, and a full Senate Judiciary Committee vote was forthcoming. What aided its prospects was the fact that Senator Hruska—a longtime NRA congressional surrogate—was principally onboard with advancing some type of Saturday Night Special bill. Hruska and Bayh merely disagreed on the bill's scope and content.

As for the NRA, like Hruska, the organization continued to publicly support a Saturday Night Special bill in principle.[78] Privately, however, the NRA opposed it. Yet as a political strategy, the organization and its allies knew it would be foolish to advance a purely "negative position."[79] Not only would such a position make the NRA highly susceptible to attacks from the news media, but it might also damage the organization's positive working relationship with the Nixon administration. For these reasons, the NRA decided it was best to focus any political negativity squarely on Bayh's S. 2507, which it described as a "long and dangerous step toward disarming law-abiding Americans at all levels of our society."[80] But unlike the early to mid-1960s, the NRA's criticism did little to prevent S. 2507 from receiving a Senate Judiciary Committee vote.[81] For on June 27, despite Hruska offering an alternative and far less restrictive bill, Bayh's S. 2507 sailed through the Senate Judiciary Committee by a 12 to 2 vote.[82]

With the Senate now scheduled to vote on a firearms control bill for the first time in four years, one might presume that President Nixon would be supportive. He was not. Rather, Nixon was agitated. Bayh and the Democrats had beaten him to the political punch. This prompted him to forge a new strategy so that he would receive at least some of the political credit. That strategy involved Nixon signaling that he would sign whatever Saturday Night Special bill made it to his desk but letting it be known that his administration was working closely with members of Congress on the issue.[83] It did not take long, however, before the political winds shifted, and Nixon's strategy once again had to change course. It began on July 15, following an NRA Executive Committee meeting. Therein, due to pressure from the "no compromise" wing of the gun rights movement, the NRA decided to come out in opposition to any Saturday Night Special bill, especially Bayh's S. 2507.[84] Additionally, the NRA outlined a new, five-point anticrime program. As it pertained controlling firearms, the new program provided nothing new. The NRA continued to espouse support for mandatory minimums, prohibitions on criminals, undesirables, and minors from purchasing firearms, and the licensing of firearms dealers. It also continued to oppose firearms registration and licensing laws. What was new this time around was the NRA's decision to opine on the criminal justice system. In particular, the organization weighed in on the hotly contested subjects of bail, parole, and plea bargaining. All three privileges, according to the NRA, should no longer be afforded to any criminal caught with a "deadly weapon."[85]

The NRA's change in policy on Saturday Night Specials was too late to affect the Senate vote on S. 2507. On August 9, by a bipartisan supermajority vote of 68 to 25, S. 2507 passed the Senate.[86] However, the NRA's policy change did come in time to effectively stall action in the House. The rapidly approaching 1972 elections worked in the NRA's favor.[87] Nixon in fact became so concerned about the NRA's change in policy on Saturday Night Specials and the accompanying gun rights opposition that he secretly urged his House allies to torpedo any Saturday Night Special bill until after the election.[88]

Thankfully for Nixon, the NRA's change in policy arrived prior to the Republican Party's deliberation of its platform for 1972. This effectively allowed the Platform Committee to incorporate the NRA's concerns and once again portray the party as supportive of gun rights. Nowhere in the platform was the banning of Saturday Night Specials stated or implied. Instead, the platform formally pledged that the Republican Party would only "intensify efforts to prevent access to all weapons, including special emphasis on cheap, readily-obtainable handguns, retaining primary responsibility at the State level, *with such Federal law as necessary to enable the States to meet their responsibilities.*" Additionally, the platform promised to "safeguard the right of responsible citizens to collect, own and use firearms for legitimate purposes, including hunting target shooting and self-defense."[89]

In contrast to the Republican Party's platform was that of the Democratic Party, which, much like in 1968, failed to recognize a Second Amendment right to own firearms for lawful purposes. Instead, the Democratic platform was forthright in declaring that there "must be laws to control the proper use" of handguns. Citing the recent assassination attempt on Wallace, the platform further declared that any future attempts at handgun legislation must include "a ban on the sale of . . . Saturday night specials which are unsuitable for sporting purposes."[90] There are two reasons that help explain why the Democratic Party came out in support of handgun controls in its 1972 platform. First, the party had adopted its platform prior to the NRA formally coming out against any Saturday Night Special bill. This is not to say that the Democratic Party was not provided the opportunity to include more gun rights–friendly language. On June 23, before the Democratic Party Platform Committee, NRA executive vice president Maxwell Rich requested the adoption of such language.[91] Additionally, weeks later, during the Democratic National Convention, Wallace and his supporters requested that the Platform Committee adopt language affirming that the individual right to "keep and bear arms" was "inviolate" and a "disarmed citizenry would soon lose its liberty and freedom."[92] The second reason the Democratic Party came out in support of additional handgun controls was that the two leading presidential candidates going into the Democratic National Convention—Minnesota senator Hubert H. Humphrey and South Dakota senator George McGovern—had made several campaign statements to this effect.[93] It was a position in line with the most recent Harris and Gallup polls on the issue, both of which showed upward of 70 percent supporting stricter firearms controls, to include firearms licensing and registration.[94]

Once the Democratic Party Platform was finalized and made public and the Democratic National Convention had formally nominated Senator McGovern to be the party's presidential candidate in 1972, it did not take long for gun rights advocates to throw their support behind Nixon.[95] The editors of *Guns & Ammo* published an article by former NRA president Harlon B. Carter titled "Nixon—The Shooters' Man for '72!"[96] Gun rights supporters mostly followed suit. Indeed, some in the "no compromise" wing of the gun rights movement decided to back American Independent Party (AIP) candidate John G. Schmitz—a candidate who throughout his political career had vocally supported the Second Amendment and vocally opposed firearms controls.[97] However, most gun rights supporters felt that a vote for Schmitz—or any third-party candidate for that matter—was essentially a vote wasted.[98]

That gun rights advocates backed Nixon over McGovern was not without political contradiction. Consider that Nixon admitted to never having owned or used firearms.[99] Conversely, McGovern owned several firearms throughout his life and was known to be an active sportsman, hunter, and conservationist. Leading up to Election Day, McGovern even penned an article in the popular sporting and hunting magazine *Field & Stream* outlining the positive actions he would take if elected president to "save . . . hunting and fishing for future generations."[100] As for the all-important firearms control issue, a close study reveals that Nixon's position was not all that different from McGovern's. Both had expressed support for legislation banning Saturday Night Specials. Both had expressed support for increasing penalties for anyone convicted of crime committed with a firearm. And both opposed firearms registration and licensing, as well as any further restrictions on the types of firearms used primarily for sporting purposes.[101]

What also made gun rights advocates decision to endorse Nixon over McGovern a political contradiction was the former's lackluster record on "law and order"—an issue that had politically resonated with the gun rights community since the early twentieth century.[102] Recall how Nixon ran for president in 1968 on the promise of restoring "law and order" and reducing crime. Yet for the first three years of his presidency, the crime rate continued to rise sharply: 10.3 percent in the first year, another 9.3 percent in the second year, and another 6.1 percent in the third year.[103] And it was not as if McGovern was known for being soft on crime. Throughout the 1972 presidential campaign, he put forward a remarkably similar "law and order" message and at times criticized Nixon for failing to deliver on the issue.[104]

The historical point to be made is that gun rights advocates' professed reasons for endorsing Nixon over McGovern were not tangible. Yet it was an endorsement that made political sense when viewed in the context of the Nixon administration's willingness to work with gun rights advocates. Additionally, from the perspective of advocates, the Nixon administration was a known political commodity—one that provided them with a level of direct White House access that they had never before experienced. This is not to say that gun rights advocates were provided *complete* access. As outlined earlier, Nixon's advisors provided this access—limited, need-to-know access at that—only to convince advocates to back additional firearms controls, which in turn would reinforce Nixon's "law and order" image and aid in his reelection. In other words, the Nixon administration's political embrace of gun rights advocates was simply one of many political means used to achieve the self-serving political end of the president's reelection.

And reelected Nixon was, by what was at the time the second largest Electoral College spread (520 to 17) since the popular vote became a factor in deciding state electoral votes. Nixon's reelection also provided what remains the second highest popular vote margin of victory (23.2 percent) for any presidential election. The victory was in fact so overwhelming that McGovern even lost his home state of South Dakota by nearly 9 points. As to what, if any, impact the sportsmen's vote had on Nixon's reelection, it appears to have been minimal. Not even the editors of *Gun Week* were able to characterize the election results as anything other than a mixed bag. Like most national elections, a handful of incumbent lawmakers were defeated on Election Day—some of whom happened to support firearms controls. At the same time, however, most incumbent lawmakers were ultimately reelected, including those who were on record supporting firearms controls.[105]

The reason the 1972 elections were a mixed bag for gun rights supporters was the precipitous decline in political enthusiasm across the gun rights community. Not even the fear of a Saturday Night Special ban was all that effective in moving the political enthusiasm needle. This is not to say that gun rights supporters were not politically active in many state and local campaigns, nor does it suggest that political candidates did not try to garner the sportsmen's vote. Both were commonplace leading into the 1972 elections. The Senate races in the largely rural states of Montana, Colorado, and Oklahoma bear this out.[106] What was different for the election cycle in 1972 was the noticeable decline of gun rights political advocacy groups that were so prevalent going into the 1970 elections, such as Citizens Against Mansfield (CAM) and Citizens Against Tydings (CAT).[107]

From Nixon's reelection through the first weeks of 1973, all was relatively quiet on the firearms control front. Then on January 30, 1973, Mississippi senator John C. Stennis, as he was returning to his North Cleveland Park home in the District of Columbia, was robbed and shot twice with a handgun by two assailants.[108] The next day, a reporter asked President Nixon about the shooting and whether he regretted having not spoken "out very strongly against gun controls, particularly handguns." Nixon replied that his administration had long advocated for Congress to pass Saturday Night Special legislation, but to no avail. The "problem," at least as Nixon stated it, was finding the right political "formula" to "get the [congressional] support necessary to deal with the specific problem, without, at the same time, running afoul of the rights of those who believe that they need guns for hunting and all that sort of thing." Nixon made it clear that he had "never hunted," maintained "no interest in guns" or the NRA, and would continue to support whatever Saturday Night Special bill that could "get through Congress."[109] Six weeks later, in a message to Congress on law enforcement and drug abuse prevention, he doubled down on his support for a bill, sending gun rights advocates into political frenzy.[110] Some of the more extremist advocates went so far as to accuse Nixon of violating his oath to defend the Constitution.[111]

Not even the NRA was willing to provide Nixon any political cover. The organization knew it could not renege on its July 15, 1972, decision to oppose any Saturday Night Special bill.[112] Instead, it announced a $10,000 reward for the apprehension of the assailants who shot Stennis.[113] Additionally, the NRA noted how the District of Columbia's strict firearms controls did nothing to stop the assailants from robbing and shooting Stennis. "This attack on the life of a United States senator occurred in a city that has a law which requires a license for the carrying of a handgun openly or concealed and which requires the registration of firearms," stated NRA executive vice president Maxwell E. Rich in an interview before spouting off several other District of Columbia firearms controls. He then pointed to what he and the NRA had long felt was the real root of the crime problem in the United States—the lax enforcement of criminal laws and the lack of strict mandatory sentencing minimums for armed criminals.[114]

Support for Saturday Night Special legislation was not the only thing causing a political rift between gun rights supporters and Nixon. So, too, was the Department of Justice's position on the Second Amendment before the federal courts, particularly in the Federal District Court of Indiana case *Freeman v. United States*. Therein the Department of Justice was faced with a constitutional challenge to the Gun Control Act on several grounds, one of which was that the Second Amendment outright prohibited it. Much to the dismay of gun rights supporters, the department argued that any Second Amendment challenge to the Gun Control Act must fail given that "the

Amendment applies only to the organized militia of a State and not to individuals."[115] And it was not just the Department of Justice's interpretation of the Second Amendment that gun rights supporters were upset about. There was also the Senate Judiciary Subcommittee on Constitutional Rights' most recent edition of the *Layman's Guide to Individual Rights Under the United States Constitution*, in which the Second Amendment was cast as largely an antiquated right.[116] Although the *Layman's Guide* acknowledged that the Second Amendment was ratified by the Constitution's framers to "provide the freedom of the citizen to protect himself against both disorder in the community and attack from foreign enemies," such late eighteenth-century concerns were now "much less important" given that a "well-trained military and police forces" were available "to protect the citizen." But want really angered the more extremist gun rights supporters was the guide's pronouncement that "State and Federal Governments may pass laws prohibiting the carrying of concealed weapons, requiring the registration of firearms, and limit[] the sale of firearms for other than military uses."[117] "Hogwash!" declared the editors of *Gun Week*, adding, "The right to keep and bear arms is more important today than when this country was founded . . . we're sick and tired of hearing wailing social planners and potential dictators saying otherwise, especially in pamphlets printed at government expense."[118]

Both the interpretation of the Second Amendment by Nixon's Department of Justice and the Senate Judiciary Subcommittee on Constitutional Rights set into motion what would become the most deliberate political propaganda campaign to reinterpret a constitutional provision.[119] For decades, whenever gun rights supporters cited or pointed to the Second Amendment as an affirmative defense to firearms controls, they were summarily dismissed by most jurists, scholars, and historians, as well as by many firearms-control-supporting lawmakers, as being misinformed.[120] Over that time, not even the NRA was able to counter these dismissals with anything other than textual innuendos and unsubstantiated historical inferences. It was not until 1964 that it was able to muster its first historically based justification for an individual right to "keep and bear arms"— this justification being a handful of nineteenth-century cases.[121] However, the NRA and other gun rights advocates were still without any founding era evidence, which left them open to serious criticism from firearms-control proponents. Connecticut senator Thomas J. Dodd, for one, referred to the claim that the Second Amendment protected an individual right to own firearms as one of the gun rights advocates' "big lie" techniques.[122] Officials within the administration of President Lyndon B. Johnson were equally critical of gun rights advocates' continued appeals to the Second Amendment in legal memoranda and congressional testimony.[123]

But the Nixon presidency was supposed to be different. Nixon himself had acknowledged there was a "legitimate right of sportsmen and hunters to buy and own weapons" on several occasions, yet his Department of Justice was refusing to acknowledge such a right existed.[124] The same was true for several members of the Senate Judiciary Subcommittee on Constitutional Rights. Individually, whether on the campaign trail or in correspondence, many senators on the subcommittee had espoused support for an individual Second Amendment right to arms, yet somehow collectively the subcommittee arrived at a much narrower interpretation—one that summarily dismissed the Second Amendment as an antiquated right.

Gun rights advocates knew something needed to change in order to protect the Second Amendment for future generations, and that something was convincing lawmakers, legal scholars, historians, the American people, and hopefully the federal courts that the Founding Fathers drafted, ratified, and understood the amendment as embodying a broad right to own, procure, and use firearms, divorced from government-sanctioned militias, as a means to check government through an armed citizenry, and to provide individuals with the means of armed self-defense should they be assailed in private or public.[125]

Fortunately for gun rights advocates, newly appointed 7th Circuit Court of Appeals judge Robert A. Sprecher provided them with the academic blueprint to do so in an essay for the American Bar Association's (ABA) annual Samuel Pool Weaver Constitutional Law Essay Competition in 1965. The question the ABA posed was whether the Second Amendment guaranteed a right to arms for "private purposes" or the right to arms was conditioned on service in a state militia. Sprecher ultimately won the competition with his essay "The Lost Amendment." In it, Sprecher became the first to delve into eighteenth-century history to extrapolate an individual rights interpretation of the Second Amendment. Although he conceded that the Constitution's framers indeed predicated the amendment on the fear of federal standing armies and the desire for a well-regulated militia to counter them, he thought that this history did not "warrant concluding . . . that a person has a right to bear arms solely . . . as a member of the militia." To Sprecher, history also supported an individualized self-defense interpretation. But in order for such an individual Second Amendment right to be jurisprudentially recognized, the courts would need to be convinced that armed individual self-defense served "some sound public purpose." This would require a complete reversal of the legal status quo—a return to "the bravado of the Old West," where individuals were allowed to "protect [themselves] against the ravages and depredations of organized crime through the Second Amendment." Perhaps, then, the courts would "find the lost Second Amendment, broaden its scope and determine that it affords the right to arm a state militia and also the right of the individual to keep and bear arms."[126]

For the next decade, Sprecher's essay served as the scholarly beacon for all other Second Amendment articles and books that either originated with or were commissioned by gun rights advocates. Not only was Sprecher able to breathe life into virtually every one of the unsubstantiated historical assertions made by gun rights advocates over the years, but even more important, he gave them intellectual credibility. The Second Amendment was not antiquated or obsolete, as the overwhelming majority of early to mid-twentieth century scholars contended. Rather, its history, purpose, and meaning were simply lost to time, and if the American people and the federal courts could be educated on this point, the right to keep and bear arms could be restored to its constitutional pedestal. At first, the effort to restore the Second Amendment began with the NRA and other gun rights advocates tracking scholarship and legal opinions that in one way or another buttressed their individual-rights view of the Second Amendment.[127] The NRA, however, soon distinguished itself from the other organizations by establishing a History Committee, which focused on producing and distributing literature that promoted a positive historical image of shooting, hunting, and the Second Amendment.[128]

Returning to the political rift that was developing between gun rights advocates and President Nixon, it was something that Nixon's advisors were closely monitoring. And it was ultimately because of this political rift that Nixon decided against pursuing a Saturday Night Special bill, albeit quietly. This is not to say that he did not have any other proposed political courses of action to pursue. He was in fact provided with three before deciding to forgo any Saturday Night Special legislation. The first involved

Nixon once again backing an "objective standards" safety test for handguns, which "would have no effect on the number of handguns available" but would technically satisfy Nixon's "public commitment" for Saturday Night Special legislation "without unduly aggravating the gun lobby." The second involved him backing a much stricter "combination of [firearms control] measures designed to have a cumulative effect on reducing handgun availability in future years." These stricter measures, in addition to outlawing the sale of Saturday Night Specials, included imposing new mandatory sentencing minimums on anyone found carrying a concealed firearm in the commission of a felony and creating a federal registry of persons prohibited from purchasing or possessing handguns. The final political course of action presented to Nixon was to back legislation "outlawing the sale and private possession (outside the home) of all handguns except by public and private law enforcement officers." To properly execute this course of action, Nixon would have to make a "dramatic Presidential TV address stating the time had come to end the public menace of handguns."[129] His advisors believed this would convey to the American people that the president was willing to stand up to special interests.

Ultimately, the reason Nixon quietly decided against pursuing a Saturday Night Special bill was the rapidly unfolding Watergate scandal—a scandal that led to his resignation. Nixon knew he needed all the political support he could get, and by pursuing such a bill he felt he would only end up losing even more of his shrinking political base.[130] But when Nixon arrived at this conclusion it was already too late. The appointment of then secretary of defense Elliot L. Richardson to succeed the Watergate-embattled Richard G. Kleindienst as U.S. attorney general in May 1973 turned out to be the last straw for many gun rights supporters. Richardson was well-known for having supported firearms controls while serving as Massachusetts attorney general. And at Richardson's Senate confirmation hearing, gun rights supporters' worst fears were confirmed: not only did Richardson defend his record of supporting firearms controls, but he even expressed support for the "registration of all handguns," including private transfers, and "very strict" handgun controls for "all sales across State lines."[131] Months later, after being formally confirmed by the Senate, Richardson announced that the Department of Justice would begin considering the firearms control recommendations of the National Advisory Commission on Criminal Justice Standards and Goals, one of them being the confiscation of all privately owned handguns.[132]

Gun rights supporters were livid yet some took political solace with the fact that the Watergate scandal was effectively drawing attention away from the firearms control issue altogether. This was especially true after the infamous Saturday Night Massacre on October 20, 1973, where Richardson and his deputy William D. Ruckelshaus refused to carry out Nixon's order to fire Watergate special prosecutor Archibald Cox. As a result, Richardson and Ruckelshaus were forced to resign their posts, and Cox was subsequently fired by the third-most-senior Department of Justice official, Solicitor General Robert H. Bork. Not long thereafter, the impeachment process against Nixon was fully underway. On August 8, 1974, Nixon formally resigned from office, prompting then vice president Gerald R. Ford to become the thirty-eighth president of the United States.

Ford had just been sworn in as vice president eight months earlier following the October 10, 1973, resignation of Spiro Agnew for tax evasion and money laundering. Prior to Ford's appointment as vice president, he had represented Michigan in the House of Representatives for more than two decades, eventually earning the position of House minority leader. As for firearms controls, Ford was neither adamantly for nor against them. He had embraced the delegate model approach to the firearms control issue— that is, his position was representative of his rural Michigan constituency. Thus for much of his time in Congress, he was understandably on record opposing most firearms controls.[133] There were exceptions, of course, such as his brief support for firearms controls following the assassination of Robert Kennedy and the mass shooting in 1966 at the University of Texas by Charles Whitman.[134]

Upon assuming the presidency, Ford received a mixed reception among gun rights supporters. On the one hand, they expressed relief that it was Ford succeeding Nixon, not the "anti-gun" Nelson A. Rockefeller, whom Nixon had initially considered to succeed Agnew.[135] On the other hand, given that Ford ended up selecting Rockefeller to be his vice president, the more extreme gun rights supporters expressed concern over what a Ford presidency meant for the gun rights movement moving forward.[136] The NRA, however, decided to take a positive approach by penning Ford a letter and offering him the organization's full support.[137] Not long thereafter, knowing full well that the firearms control issue would once again rear its head, Ford personally requested the policy papers on the subject prepared for Nixon a year earlier.[138]

9

1974–1980

The Gun Rights Reformation

When President Gerald R. Ford was sworn into office, the National Rifle Association (NRA) was facing an internal crisis of sorts. Many gun rights supporters no longer considered the organization the preeminent defender of the Second Amendment. Rather, the NRA was increasingly viewed as being more concerned with expanding its own stature. There were several grievances from gun rights supporters regarding the direction the organization was headed. For one, the NRA appeared much more focused on raising funds for its new National Shooting Center in New Mexico than helping gun rights political action groups. There were also whispers that the NRA might move its headquarters away from Washington, D.C. But what was most concerning to gun rights supporters was the NRA's insistence that it was not a lobby and therefore had no intention of getting politically involved.[1]

The NRA's insistence that it was not a lobby ultimately afforded other, more extreme gun rights advocacy groups the opportunity to fill the political vacuum, causing many dedicated supporters to redirect their attention and pocketbooks elsewhere. And it did not take long for the NRA to take notice. For in early 1973, at the request of Michigan representative and longtime NRA congressional surrogate John D. Dingell, the board of directors commissioned a "feasibility" study on the establishment of a separately funded "lobbying branch." The authors of the study were asked to explore three possible roles for the lobbying branch: (1) serving as a "think tank" to deal with "political and public efforts dealing with gun control"; (2) providing a "legislative drafting and analysis service" that would "scrutinize proposed firearms control legislation at Federal, State and local levels of governments"; and (3) establishing a "political activism service" that would "organize and mobilize sportsmen at the local and State level to lobby in the State capitals and municipal governments." The first two roles were old hat for the NRA. Its legislative division, its public relations division, and the editors of *American Rifleman* had long performed these functions. The third role was also arguably old hat for the NRA. Ever since commandeering the gun rights movement in the late 1920s and early 1930s, the group had effectively organized and mobilized its state and local club affiliates to political action through grassroots advocacy. The only difference between this longstanding practice and the proposed "political action service" was that the latter included direct election involvement, but only on the condition that said involvement was "nonpartisan."[2]

On September 22, 1973, after receiving the results of the feasibility study, the NRA board of directors elected to proceed with establishing a separately funded lobbying branch, officially named the Legislative Action Unit (LAU). In doing so, however, the board limited the "lobbying" role of the new branch to merely analyzing proposed firearms control legislation. The NRA urged its membership to send whatever money they could with the goal of reaching $500,000 in annual donations. NRA members were informed that the LAU's "prime responsibility" was to study and analyze "anti-gun and anti-hunter legislation and recommend what response would be appropriate."[3]

The formation of the LAU received little fanfare from gun rights supporters. This was because it was really nothing more than a reorganization of the NRA's existing legislative and public relations divisions. Moreover, the LAU offered very little in the way of enhancing, let alone complementing, the political action efforts of the other, more extremist gun rights advocacy groups, most notably the Citizens Committee for the Right to Keep and Bear Arms (CCRKBA). Established in 1970, the CCRKBA was largely meant to complement the advocacy efforts of the NRA.[4] Over time, however, the CCRKBA found its niche as the political voice of gun rights extremists. It achieved this status by playing to their attitudes, such as that liberalism and leftist politicians were to blame for firearms controls and that those who supported firearms controls were not so much misinformed as they were weak-kneed political "enemies" hell bent on destroying the Second Amendment, and promoting a cancel culture or social boycott mentality toward any organization that espoused support for firearms controls. The CCRKBA also became the first gun rights organization to tout a political action "war chest"—known as the Right to Bear Arms Political Action Fund—dedicated to helping "pro-gun candidates at the local, state, and national level."[5]

In early 1974, aware of the CCRKBA's rising status, the NRA decided to finally pull the political action trigger by formally declaring itself a lobby. As a result, the fledgling LAU was expanded, reorganized, and rebranded the Office of Legislative Affairs (OLA). In addition to assuming the LAU's principal functions of studying, analyzing, and reporting on firearms controls, the OLA assembled a team of lobbyists intent on increasing "person-to-person contact" between the NRA and lawmakers.[6] Fundraising efforts for the OLA were immediate. NRA members were told that stopping "new assaults on gun ownership" boiled down to "one inevitable word"—money. And the NRA promised that every dollar its members donated would fund not only OLA personnel, research, studies, and political outreach, but also a top-of-the-line IBM "computerization program which will improve the NRA's already efficient facilities for alerting the most involved groups . . . to gun control issues."[7]

Despite the NRA having formally declared itself a lobby with the establishment of the OLA, it would take roughly two years before the organization was able to surpass the CCRKBA's political action efforts. Thus for the elections of 1974, it was the CCRKBA, not the NRA, leading the fight to defeat "anti-gun" lawmakers at the polls. The CCRKBA put forward the audacious goal of defeating thirty such members of Congress come Election Day. This included such high-profile members as Indiana senator Birch Bayh, Michigan senator Philip A. Hart, Massachusetts senator Edward M. Kennedy, New Jersey representative Peter W. Rodino, and Michigan representative John Conyers, Jr., to name just a few. The organization accused these thirty members of Congress, collectively referred to as the "Terrible Thirty," of instituting a plan of "creeping confiscation" with the assistance of the "powerful news media" and "well-heeled anti-gun organizations."[8] Yet despite these political action efforts, when the votes were tallied, every single member of the Terrible Thirty was reelected. Even worse for the CCRKBA was the fact that twenty-seven members of Congress deemed gun rights political allies lost reelection—several of whom lost considerably to firearms control proponents.[9] And this was not counting the race for the open Ohio Senate seat vacated by recently appointed U.S. attorney general William B. Saxbe. In that race, to the disdain of the CCRKBA and other gun rights advocates, famed astronaut and former head of the Emergency Committee for Gun Control (ECGC) John H. Glenn won by more than a million votes.

The CCRKBA acknowledged the poor Election Day showing in its monthly newsletter *Point Blank*: "The results of this month's congressional elections across the United States were potentially disastrous for America's 50 million law abiding firearms owners. Every anti-gun Representative and Senator who ran for reelection was reelected. In addition, some former Representatives who ran for the House again this year were successful in their election attempts."[10] Yet despite having nothing positive to report from its "Terrible Thirty" campaign, the CCRKBA pointed to its Election Day failure as *the* reason why gun rights supporters needed to donate even more money to the organization and enroll more members. "The new, liberal anti-gun majority [in Congress] has already become very vocal," it warned, adding, "With the encouragement of the biased news media they are already touting proposed anti-gun rights legislation under the guise of crime control."[11]

The CCRKBA's postelection fundraising and membership campaign proved to be a resounding success. So much so, that members of Congress began joining the organization at an unprecedented rate. In just five months, from December 1974 to June 1975, roughly forty members of Congress decided to join the CCRKBA's National Council Advisory, bringing the overall total to fifty-three. Two months later the number grew to seventy-one. This included longtime NRA congressional surrogate and Florida representative Robert F. Sikes. The CCRKBA was also able to lure longtime *American Rifleman* editor John M. Snyder to become its director of publications and public affairs.

The precipitous rise of the CCRKBA once more prompted the NRA to reorganize its fledgling lobbying arm and rename it the Institute for Legislative Action (ILA). Operationally, the ILA was not that different from the OLA or LAU. The NRA decided that all ILA revenue would be self-generating and kept separate from any headquarters funds. Additionally, much like the OLA and LAU, the ILA's central purpose was to monitor, report, study, and fight proposed firearms control legislation. Last, like the OLA and LAU, the ILA was prohibited from participating in partisan political action. The ILA's only distinguishing factor from its predecessors was the way the NRA exercised oversight of it. The ILA would not be directly managed by the NRA headquarters' staff but instead by its own executive director—one who was chosen by the NRA board of directors and served at their behest.[12] The first ILA executive director chosen by the board was Harlon B. Carter.[13]

Ever since relinquishing the NRA presidency to Harold W. Glassen in April 1967, Carter's political rhetoric had become extremist. He was one of the first well-known gun rights advocates to come out in support of the "no compromise" gun rights movement.[14] He was also a frequent contributor to the gun rights publication *Guns & Ammo*, where he often espoused sensationalist political points of view. In one article, Carter audaciously claimed that the attempts to domestically regulate Saturday Night Specials were merely a political front to "encourage crime" and "make all handguns illegal."[15] Months later, in a separate article, he referred to firearms controls as both "government subsidized crime" and a "prelude to a police state."[16] In another article, he boldly called on the gun rights community to advocate for the repeal of all firearms controls, many of which were ironically enacted with the support of past gun rights advocates. "We cannot stand around much longer, piously pointing to thousands of laws we already have on the books and demanding that they be enforced," wrote Carter, adding, "Gun laws . . . cannot be enforced except by methods of tyranny."[17]

Carter particularly took pleasure in blaming "liberals" and their "liberal thinking" for the alleged social menace created by firearms controls. In one article, he postulated that the "ideologues of liberalism" will never be satisfied until they have upended the country's "fixed values." To Carter, the chief problem with liberals was their unwillingness to "stand for the kind of measures needed to establish a more orderly . . . law-abiding, society." Another problem with liberals, according to Carter, was their desire to placate anyone who viewed the justice system as being "racially tainted." In other words, he believed that because "poor" and "minorities" votes were at stake, liberals would never agree to what was really required to stop crime—a "rigid law-and-order society."[18]

Carter, of course, was not the first to blame "liberals" and their "liberal thinking" for firearms controls, nor was he the first to politically bootstrap the cause of gun rights to conservatism. From the mid-1960s through the early 1970s, the editors of shooting, hunting, and sporting publications frequently associated conservative and Christian values with that of gun rights. So, too, had conservative politicians.[19] Thus by 1975 the connection between conservatism and gun rights was almost inseparable. This was in part due to the political rise of Ronald Reagan on the national stage. As California governor, Reagan had frequently sided with gun rights supporters. This included backing the NRA-sponsored Mulford Act in 1967, which made it a felony to publicly carry any firearm—either openly or concealed—in public places without a governmental license to do so.[20] "I don't know of any sportsman who leaves his home with a gun to go out into the field to hunt or for target shooting who carries that guns loaded," stated Reagan in support of the Mulford Act, adding, "The first thing any real sportsman learns is to carry an empty gun until he gets to the place where he's going to do the shooting."[21]

Come the summer of 1975, Reagan was far and away the gun rights community's preferred presidential candidate—so much so in fact that the CCRKBA began selling "Reagan for President" bumper stickers a whole six months before he formally announced his candidacy.[22] Earlier that year, Reagan had published a gun rights political manifesto of sorts in *Guns & Ammo*. Therein he delivered several political talking points that appealed directly to gun rights supporters, including firearms controls aided, not hindered, armed criminals; crime control, not firearms control; liberals are soft on crime; mandatory minimums are the best means to lower crime rates; and a few others. But perhaps his most salient talking point was his emphasis on the need to preserve the right to keep and bear arms. According to Reagan, the Second Amendment was included in the Bill of Rights for a "very specific reason"—the Founding Fathers "distrusted government." This let gun rights supporters know that Reagan viewed the Second Amendment as they did—as embodying both an individual right to armed self-defense and the collective promise of "future security."[23]

Although the gun rights movement was increasingly leaning conservative and Republican, the NRA did its utmost to remain nonpartisan. It was something that even NRA-ILA executive director Carter was forced to get behind. Carter was, however, given carte blanche to politically frame all firearms controls as a slippery slope toward total firearms confiscation, label anyone who supported firearms controls as being "radical," and do anything and everything within his power to defeat the passage of firearms control legislation.[24] This included Carter painting a dystopian societal picture if strict firearms controls were ever adopted at the federal level, alleging that crime rates would rise to a point where Americans would be "forced to barricade themselves inside their homes, bolt down their belongings to protect their lives and property from criminal attack."[25]

The establishment of the NRA-ILA could not have come at a better time for the gun rights movement. The outcome of the congressional elections in 1974 all but ensured that firearms controls would once again be politically prevalent. For the upcoming 94th Congress, the Democrats had gained five seats in the Senate, thus increasing their respective majority from fifty-six to sixty-one senators. Meanwhile, in the House of Representatives, they gained a whopping forty-nine seats, increasing their respective majority from 232 to 291 representatives. These Democratic congressional gains were not from the Dixiecrats of elections past. Rather, they were from leftist echelons of the Democratic Party, thus making the 94th Congress arguably the most progressive and liberal at that point in American history.[26] Considering this fact, many political pundits speculated that new federal firearms controls would be forthcoming. What they could not predict, however, was the types of firearms control bills the 94th Congress would file and how strict they would be. Financially, the political speculation benefited the NRA-ILA substantially. For by the close of 1975, the ILA had demolished its $500,000 annual fundraising goal with more than $4,000,000 in donations.[27]

As for President Ford, the speculation that the 94th Congress would take up the firearms-control issue prompted his advisors to formulate a political strategy. What they ultimately decided was they would approach the issue much like Nixon's advisors—that is, by having Ford introduce "some sort of ["middle ground"] Saturday Night Special legislation."[28] This would effectively complement other aspects of Ford's legislative agenda. For one, it would show that Ford was for "law and order," that is, tough on crime. It would also show that he supported bipartisanship. But most important, through the simple act of introducing a Saturday Night Special bill, Ford would gain political capital no matter whether the 94th Congress passed it or any other similar bill. For if Congress indeed passed a Saturday Night Special bill, he could state it was due in large part to his leadership on the issue. Conversely, if Congress failed in its effort to pass such a bill, Ford could state that it was because the Democrats had failed to coalesce. On paper, Ford's political strategy was almost foolproof.

The only problem that his advisors foresaw was that gun rights advocates were continuing to oppose every type of Saturday Night Special bill. They were already pressuring the White House in the wake of Ford's attorney general, Edward H. Levi, testifying he would work with Congress in drafting an effective bill.[29] Yet in the face of this gun rights opposition, Ford's advisors decided to press forward with the Department of Justice in drafting what they believed to be a modest Saturday Night Special bill. At the same time, they began putting together a more polished firearms control policy position for the president. In doing so, they made sure to draft the policy position in a way that did not undermine Ford's previous statements for mandatory minimums and against firearms registration.[30]

While Ford's advisors were drafting the president's policy position, in a speech before the International Association of Chiefs of Police, Attorney General Levi unilaterally floated the idea of a "targeted," localized approach to lowering firearms-related violence. Levi proposed a plan in which federal enforcement of firearms laws, particularly as they related to handguns, would ramp up in urban areas where "the problem of handguns is most critical." "A handgun makes an individual in a city too powerful for his environment," he stated, adding:

> It is a menace because it can be so readily available. It is a mechanism that translates passion or a passing evil intent into destruction. The possibility . . . that people roam the streets with handguns in their pockets has called into question the safety of even venturing out from behind locked doors. And the fear of handgun violence has provoked people to purchase their own handgun for self-defense, causing a proliferation of arms that aggravates the basic problem. In short, handguns pose a great threat in cities beleaguered by violence.

Levi then outlined his "formula" for identifying the "critical" urban areas that Department of Justice would partner with to bring down the rate of firearms related violence. The partnership would involve the imposition of several strict federal firearms controls over a two-to-five-year period. The controls Levi recommended included a ban on Saturday Night Specials, banning the "possession of handguns outside the home" except for those who obtain a "special permit of extremely limited duration" to transport for target shooting, and restrictions on transferring handguns.[31] Gun rights advocates rejected Levi's entire list of recommended firearms controls, prompting Ford's advisors to go on the defensive. Yet to Levi's credit, Ford eventually adopted his "targeted," localized approach to lowering firearms-related violence.[32]

In a June 19, 1975, message to Congress on crime, Ford stated that the Bureau of Alcohol, Tobacco, and Firearms (BATF) would "double its [firearms control] investigative efforts in the Nation's ten largest metropolitan areas." It was one of several firearms control–related reforms proposed by Ford. The others included enhancing mandatory minimums for felonies committed with a firearm, a mandatory waiting period for all handgun purchases, banning the sale of multiple handguns during a single purchase, increasing BATF funding to expand enforcement of the Gun Control Act, and banning the domestic production of Saturday Night Specials.[33] With the exception of enhancing mandatory minimums for felonies committed with a firearm, the NRA rejected all of Ford's proposed reforms. In fact, the day before Ford delivered his crime message to Congress, the NRA requested that his advisors include "alternative," more gun rights–friendly language and talking points.[34] When the advisors rejected the request, the NRA resorted to a policy-by-policy rebuttal of each of the proposed reforms. In doing so, to maintain a positive working relationship with Ford, the NRA was cognizant not to be overly critical. While some of the more extreme gun rights advocates cast Ford's proposed reforms as a blatant attack on the Second Amendment, the NRA diplomatically described it as bureaucratically "muddled," but with "well-meaning" and "good intentions."[35]

Despite facing stiff opposition from the NRA and other gun rights advocates, Ford's advisors decided to press forward with drafting a Saturday Night Special bill. Throughout the drafting process, they periodically reached out to NRA officials and their longtime congressional surrogate, Nebraska senator Roman Hruska, on the possibility of coming to a legislative compromise. Yet neither the NRA nor Hruska expressed much willingness to do so. In the case of Hruska, not even a personal phone call from

Ford was able to persuade the senator.[36] This prompted Ford to seek other fellow Republicans to sponsor the bill. Ultimately, it was Hawaii senator Hiram L. Fong and Illinois representative Robert McClory who agreed.[37]

The NRA's initial response to Ford's Saturday Night Special bill was tempered. As expected, the group restated several tried-and-true gun rights talking points, such as "guns don't kill people, people do" and any Saturday Night Special bill was merely a political Trojan horse for the ultimate banning of all handguns.[38] Yet, to maintain a good political rapport with Ford, the NRA refrained from espousing its usual sensationalist rhetoric. But two assassination attempts on Ford's life in a span of three weeks—both by handgun—upended the NRA's preferred, tempered approach.

The firearms control issue was once again front-and-center in the news, and the NRA quickly pivoted to a sensationalist message to rouse gun rights supporters to political action.[39] The impact of the grassroots call to arms was not immediate. For the week of September 29 through October 3, the White House mail came out slightly in favor of additional firearms controls—169 letters for and 135 against.[40] Come November 21, however, the mail overwhelmingly tipped the other way, with a total of 40,591 letters against firearms controls.[41] And for the following week, the White House received a total of 6,737 letters, not a single one in support of firearms controls.[42]

In addition to rallying gun rights supporters to political action, the results of a firearms control survey commissioned and paid for by the NRA turned out better than anticipated. For years the NRA and other gun rights advocates had been unhappy with the national polls, particularly those conducted by Harris and Gallup, which consistently found that a large majority of Americans supported firearms controls such as registration and a permit to purchase a handgun. At times, the NRA and other gun rights advocates looked for a silver lining within the polling data to hang their political hats on.[43] But the silver lining always paled in comparison to the polls' overall findings. For this reason, in early 1975, while the OLA was reconstituting itself as the ILA, the NRA decided to conduct its own internal survey of sorts. Members were asked a series of four questions— questions that were purposefully worded in a way that would end up showing (a) support for the NRA's belief in arming more citizens and (b) opposition to legislative proposals that banned any type of handgun, Saturday Night Specials included:

1. Do you believe you have a right to personally defend yourself and your property against a violent criminal attack?
2. Do you believe your local police need to carry firearms to arrest and murder suspects?
3. Do you believe that by banning the ownership of firearms (including sporting and antique guns) that the number of murders and robberies would significantly be reduced in your community?
4. If a new firearms law was enacted in your state banning all ownership of guns, do you believe that hoodlums and organized criminals would volunteer their guns to your local police department?[44]

The clear, inherent bias contained in the NRA's self-conducted survey was something ILA executive director Carter was forced to admit before a House Judiciary Subcommittee hearing. The survey "was something which was in vogue before I [assumed my post]," stated Carter in an apology to the subcommittee, adding that this type of survey "has been very successful for the purposes for which it is there, and it will gradually fade, as our collection techniques become more sophisticated and more successful."[45] And "more sophisticated" the NRA's techniques became when it hired the political consulting firm Decision Making Information (DMI), based in Santa Ana, California, to conduct an independent firearms-control survey.[46]

Formed in 1970, DMI had made a name for itself as the preferred political consulting firm of California Republicans and conservatives. It had consulted the likes of President Ford, former president Richard M. Nixon, and presidential hopeful Ronald Reagan. The NRA was in good hands. As for the DMI survey findings, the NRA could not have been more pleased. The survey found that 82 percent of respondents viewed the Second Amendment as protecting an individual right, 76 percent opposed private handgun ownership bans, 71 percent opposed laws requiring a permit to purchase a firearm, and 84 percent felt that firearms registration would do nothing in the way of stopping criminals from obtaining firearms, as well as several other pro-gun findings.[47] According to NRA, the DMI survey was "carried out under the strictest scientific conditions" and cast "serious doubts on the validity of the results of certain well-publicized polls covering the same subject."[48] Indeed, the NRA was correct in noting that DMI's findings were in stark contrast to those of other "well-publicized" polls, particularly Harris and Gallup.[49] The group was wrong, however, in labeling the DMI survey as the gold standard in scientific polling. For a close examination of DMI survey reveals several methodological and objectivity concerns—most notably the existence of a heavy pro-gun bias in the comparable firearms control statements that respondents were asked to select between.[50]

Methodological and objectivity concerns aside, once the NRA unveiled the DMI survey, it did not take long before the NRA's congressional allies pointed to the survey as evidence why Congress should forgo enacting additional federal firearms controls. Thirty-nine members of Congress signed a letter stating that the survey debunked many misconceptions about the public's opinion on the Second Amendment and the effectiveness of firearms controls.[51] Perhaps most startling to these members was the survey's finding that the general public had little knowledge of existing firearms laws. It was a finding that the members described as "disappointing and disturbing, and indicat[ive that] the Federal Government needs to do much more in the field of education, as well as enforcement, with the laws already on the books."[52] It was the same finding that the NRA relied on to advance its most longstanding gun rights talking point—firearms controls were useless and ineffective at reducing violent crime. As ILA executive director Carter wrote in the ILA's *Reports from Washington*: "Surely if the general public understands little about the gun laws, in large part it is because the national media have failed to do anything but distort the facts in our case and have covered-up for the total failure of any gun laws to reduce violent crime. Gun laws don't work. They don't work and they won't work because criminals won't obey them."[53]

Between the White House mail coming in overwhelmingly in opposition to firearms controls and the findings in the DMI survey, it was clear to Ford's advisors that the political burdens of pursuing Saturday Night Special legislation outweighed the benefits. It was also clear that his chief rival for the Republican presidential nomination in 1976, Ronald Reagan, was going to make firearms controls a wedge voting issue.[54] In light of these facts, come 1976, Ford's advisors modified how the president framed the firearms control issue. Now, whenever Ford spoke on firearms controls, he generally did so in abstract terms. And when he did express support for specific firearms control policies, it was only those policies that were acceptable to the NRA and other gun rights advocates. During the State of the Union address in 1976, for instance, Ford omitted most of the firearms control polices he had outlined just seven months earlier to Congress. Instead, he signaled that the *real* threat to "every American's person and property" was not any particular handgun nor their easy availability, but rather the "criminal carrying a handgun." "The way to cut down on the criminal use of guns is not to take guns away from the law-abiding citizen, but to impose mandatory sentences for crimes in which a gun is used, make it harder to obtain cheap guns for criminal purposes, and concentrate gun control enforcement in high crime areas," stated Ford.[55]

Ford's reframing of the firearms control issue did not mean that he was also renouncing his previous support for Saturday Night Special legislation. Indeed, formally renouncing the need for such legislation would have drawn immense cheers from gun rights supporters. However, Ford knew that such a political move would also provoke severe criticism from the news media and firearms control proponents. It was best that he stay the course and, like Nixon before him, continue to cultivate the political support of the gun rights community. Ford sought to accomplish this by inviting the most prominent and influential gun rights advocates to a meeting at the White House with Treasury Department secretary William E. Simon.[56] This meeting, Ford believed, would afford gun rights advocates the opportunity to "express their feelings about proposed legislation," and him the opportunity to earn their political support. Simon was instructed to convey to the gun rights attendees that Ford viewed the firearms control issue as they did, that is, "from the standpoint that there is misuse of firearms, and it is the misuse which should be corrected rather than a program to control the use of all firearms; and further, that we should not create a new bureaucracy to police the book-keeping requirements of the Gun Control Act, but should leave the enforcement as we can to the dealer himself."[57]

From the perspective of the attendees, the White House meeting was well received. In several gun rights publications, it was cast in a positive light.[58] As for behind the scenes, some gun rights advocates used the meeting to levy their grievances against BATF's enforcement of the Gun Control Act of 1968—grievances that the Ford White House investigated and ultimately found to be unsubstantiated.[59] Other gun rights advocates used the meeting to let the Ford's advisors know that—like the Civil Rights Movement—the gun rights movement "too can influence elections and demand that we be heard." "We are not going to give up our guns and we are not going to vote for anyone who infringes on our right to keep them," wrote Harry L. Tennison, Game Conservation International president, to Ford administration official John C. Vickerman after the meeting, adding, "We are in a mild [civil war] now, concerning our civil rights, so [do not give us] another reason to be mad about some of the things that have been shoved down our throats already, or we might shove back."[60]

For a time, all appeared politically quiet on the firearms control front. But come early spring, Ford was placed in another difficult situation. It began with the Reagan campaign, which insisted on making firearms controls a wedge voting issue. In a nationally televised speech on March 31, 1976, Reagan delivered his standard conservative talking points on unemployment, growing the economy, lowering inflation, and restricting welfare benefits. He also criticized forced busing. "The concept that black children can't learn unless they are sitting with white children is utter and complete nonsense," he stated, adding that taxpayer money is "being wasted on this social experiment." He then hit Ford as being two-faced on firearms controls: "The other day, Mr. Ford came out against gun control. But, back in Washington, D.C., his Attorney General has proposed a seven-point program that amounts to just that: *gun control*."[61]

Two weeks later, by a vote of 20 to 12, the House Judiciary Committee advanced a Saturday Night Special bill (H.R. 11193) to the House floor, thus placing Ford in the precarious position of deciding whether to come out for or against it. Introduced and sponsored by Republican Illinois representative Thomas Railsback, the bill was initially perceived on Capitol Hill as an agreeable compromise. It was certainly less restrictive than Ford's. More important, H.R. 11193 did not ban all Saturday Night Specials, but rather only their future manufacture and importation. However, despite the bill's conciliatory nature, it did not take long before gun rights advocates began lambasting it as "most onerous" and imposing "even greater burdens for law-abiding firearms owners than . . . the Gun Control Act of 1968!"[62]

That gun rights advocates came out strongly against H.R. 11193 did not surprise Ford's advisors.[63] What was concerning, however, was the bill's political timing and potential impact on Ford's presidential campaign. "Earlier, the President had the best of both worlds on the issue of gun control," wrote White House associate counsel Ken Lazarus to White House chief counsel Philip Buchen, adding "His legislative initiative appeared to satisfy the anti-gun forces while the lack of any congressional action tempered the reaction of the pro-gun lobby." Yet now, with H.R. 11193 having been sent to the House floor for a vote, Ford was on his political heels with the firearms control issue. Ultimately what his advisors decided was that it would be "unwise" for the president to backtrack on his support for Saturday Night Special legislation. The best he could do was "avoid heating up the issue" by pointing to his record and stating that just like every other bill before Congress, H.R. 11193 "will be considered in due course." Such a response, Ford's advisors believed, would buy the president sufficient time "to get through the key primaries without suffering any strongly adverse consequences" on the firearms control issue.[64]

While on campaign trail, Ford indeed stuck to his firearms control record. Whenever anyone pressed him on H.R. 11193, he did not shy away from the fact that he supported further restrictions on Saturday Night Specials. But when doing so, he avoided commenting on any of H.R. 11193's specifics. "It is so early in the legislative process, until it gets further down the road we really don't have the time to take a look at this," stated Ford when one news reporter pressed him on the bill.[65] In addition to sidestepping H.R. 11193, Ford always made sure to reiterate several gun rights–friendly talking points, such as how he adamantly opposed "any gun control legislation that involves the registration of the individual gun owner or the restriction of the gun" or how he wholeheartedly supported Congress making "penalties mandatory and certain for the person who uses a gun in the commission of the crime."[66]

Ford's political straddling approach toward the firearms control issue did nothing to halt Reagan's criticism. Reagan even took to lambasting Ford in his home state of Michigan through several mailings directed at gun rights supporters, each of which claimed that Ford's Saturday Night Special bill was "the first step towards confiscation of all guns."[67] Reagan's mailings in Michigan were ultimately ineffective given that Ford easily defeated him in the primary, 690,187 votes to 364,052. But for the remaining state primaries, the electoral votes for Ford and Reagan ended up being virtually split. As a result, going into the Republican National Convention, the Republican Party was without a conclusive presidential nominee. Still, for the time being, Ford's advisors were adamant that the president stay the political course and only change his firearms control position if the Republican Party Platform in 1976 demanded it.[68]

As the convention drew closer, firearms controls were one of a handful of platform issues that Ford's advisors felt could become divisive. Abortion, busing, capital punishment, the Panama Canal, and the Equal Rights Amendment were the others. Whatever the Republican Party Platform Committee decided on each of these issues, Ford was told to just accept it as is. Otherwise, advisors feared that Ford "may lose additional delegates."[69] As it pertained to firearms controls, the Platform Committee was essentially presented with two courses of action: The first course of action, put forward by the Reagan camp, read: "The Second Amendment of the U.S. Constitution guarantees citizens the right to keep and bear arms. Any attempt to deny law-abiding citizens this right should be resisted at all levels of government."[70] The second course of action, put forward by the Ford camp, came in the way of several differently worded proposals. Each proposal, however, advanced the following firearms control policies: support for (a) banning the manufacture and importation of Saturday Night Specials; (b) enhancing mandatory minimums for persons convicted in the commission of a crime with a firearm; (c) opposing firearms registration; and (d) protecting the rights of law-abiding firearms owners.[71] Ultimately, the committee advanced a firearms control plank that reflected the middle ground between the two courses of action. In doing so, the committee not only ensured that the Republican Party remained the party of gun rights but also ensured that whoever received the party's presidential nomination was not placed in a difficult political situation. The committee accomplished this by leading its firearms control plank with a strong affirmation of gun rights: "We support the right of the citizens to keep and bear arms." This affirmation was followed by the only two firearms control policy positions that both Ford and Reagan both agreed on: "We oppose federal registration of firearms. Mandatory sentences for crimes committed with a lethal weapon are the only effective solution to this problem."[72]

To the disappointment of many gun rights supporters, Ford would go on to defeat Reagan at the Republican National Convention. This disappointment, however, was short-lived given the Democratic alternative. Not only did the 1976 Democratic Party Platform advance the idea of finding new, affective ways "to curtail the availability" of handguns,[73] but also the Democratic Party's presidential nominee, former Georgia governor Jimmy Carter, was on record supporting handgun registration.[74] For these reasons, gun rights supporters were quick to back Ford over Carter. This was particularly true for the NRA, which did its utmost to provide Ford with as much political support as possible. Indeed, at least for the time being, it was against NRA policy to formally endorse one political party or candidate over another. There was nothing in the NRA's by-laws, however, that prohibited the organization from favorably advertising a political candidate. The NRA was quick to take advantage of this by-law loophole by distributing several favorable statements and articles on Ford, as well as distributing several unfavorable statements and articles on Carter.[75] The NRA even provided Ford the opportunity to publish a letter in *American Rifleman* explaining why he was the quintessential president for gun rights supporters. At this point in the presidential campaign, Election Day was fast approaching, and it appeared that neither chamber of Congress would take up any type of firearms control legislation until after the 1976 elections.[76] Given this political state of play, in an attempt to further endear himself to gun rights supporters, Ford's *American Rifleman* letter effectively modified his position on Saturday Night Special legislation:

> I found most enlightening the arguments [the NRA] raised concerning the attempts to define the so-called "Saturday Night Special." Your discussion of the subtleties and the implications of the terms presently used shows a thorough understanding of the problems encountered in trying to establish clear legislative definitions. In addition, your statements concerning the possibilities for harassment by federal employees are interesting. I will keep these points in mind when considering the impact of any future legislation in this area.[77]

Two weeks after penning the *American Rifleman* letter, once it was clear that Congress would not take up any Saturday Night Special bill prior to Election Day, Ford became even more politically outspoken against firearms controls. In Gulfport, Mississippi, he stated, "The law-abiding citizens of this country should not be deprived of the right to have firearms for their own protection, and if you want to go hunting, you shouldn't have to go down and register your firearm with some federal official." In nearby Biloxi, Ford stated, "I think we ought to make it very clear [that] all *right-thinking people* who are law-abiding ought to have the traditional right under the Constitution to retain firearms for their own national protection, period." Meanwhile, in Pascagoula, Florida, he stated, "No law-abiding citizen should be deprived of the right to have a gun in his possession under our Constitution."[78]

As for Jimmy Carter, prior to securing the Democratic Party's presidential nomination, the Georgia governor had done little in the way of politically appeasing gun rights supporters. Although the Carter campaign had formed the group Conservationists for Carter to attract sportsmen, hunters, and conservationists to their cause, the group had yet to do any considerable political outreach.[79] But with the Democratic Party's presidential nomination now in hand, the Carter campaign began brainstorming on how to best approach the firearms-control issue. Ultimately, the campaign devised a two-pronged, divide-and-conquer strategy. The first prong involved driving a "wedge" between "gun enthusiasts" and the "sophisticated sportsman."[80] This feat was to be accomplished by targeting the latter with a conservationist and environmental message. As for attracting "gun enthusiasts," although the Carter campaign acknowledged it was a political longshot, Carter was urged to soften his firearms control message. This proved to the centerpiece of the Carter campaign's second prong in its divide-and-conquer strategy. It was premised on the belief that Carter's and Ford's firearms control policies were not all that different in substance. Other than the fact that Carter supported handgun registration, both candidates supported virtually the same policies. All that would need to change—at least in the mind of Carter's campaign—was that Carter replace his statements on handgun registration—which he was told make the "hunters go bananas"—with statements on firearms-control policies that both he and gun rights supporters opposed, such as the registration of long guns.[81] Additionally, Carter was instructed to speak more frequently on those firearms controls policies that mirrored Ford's. This would—again, in the mind of Carter's campaign—have the effect of making Carter and Ford politically indistinguishable on the firearms-control issue.[82]

The Carter campaign put together several materials to help drive its two-pronged, divide-and-conquer strategy home. One was a form letter addressed to "shooting enthusiasts" that highlighted the "many programs promoting the interests of hunters and sports shooters" that Carter sponsored as governor.[83] Another form letter stated that if Carter was elected president, he would be the "first real conservationist, outdoorsman, hunter, and gun owner [in] the White House since Theodore Roosevelt."[84] The Carter campaign also put out a sportsmen-targeted flier

FIGURE 9.1 Political cartoon in *Gun Week*, August 13, 1976. The cartoon depicted Democratic presidential candidate Jimmy Carter, a peanut farmer, as an anti-gun version of Planters's Mr. Peanut. Image reprinted with the express permission of the Second Amendment Foundation.

titled "Jimmy Carter on Guns and Hunting." The flyer, written from Carter's perspective, sought to directly address the gun rights community's "domino theory" fear of firearms control, that is, that one firearms control would lead to another and another until the private ownership of firearms was no more. To assuage this fear, Carter assured firearms owners that his only desire, if elected president, was to control "the abuse of firearms while protecting sportsman's rights." "If proponents of extreme gun control recommend misguided regulator controls, which would be contrary to the legitimate interests of sportsmen, I would do all I could to oppose them," wrote Carter. The flyer then provided "three principles for controlling the abuse of firearms while protecting the sportsmen's rights"— banning Saturday Night Specials, prohibiting criminals and mental incompetents from owning guns, and imposing handgun registration, licensing, and waiting periods.[85] And after Ford delivered several pro-gun statements while campaigning in the South, the Carter campaign responded with a press release titled "Gerald Ford's Record on Gun Control," which sought to remind the gun rights community of Ford's previous "drastic" firearms control proposals. It noted that Ford was trying to get away

Attention, Sportsmen!
Gerald Ford's Record On Gun Control

Those who heard Mr. Ford talk about gun control while campaigning along the Mississippi Gulf Coast in September might reasonably conclude that he has opposed all legislation restricting gun ownership and that his position is identical to the gun clubs and sportsmen's groups whose votes he is seeking. That is what he would like the voters to think.

But this campaign rhetoric clashes with what Mr. Ford has been doing in Washington. He seems to think that on this issue, like so many others, the American people will not bother to look at the record before they vote in November. Let's take a look.

The Ford Administration proposed legislation to this Congress (S. 2186) that included the following provisions:
(1) a ban on both commercial and private transfers (even between family members) of so-called "Saturday night specials"
(2) a definition of "Saturday night specials" that would prohibit sale of 54% of the handguns produced in the United States in 1974.
(3) minimum standards for gun dealers that would put two-thirds to three-quarters of all gun dealers out of business
(4) tighter restrictions on the number of handguns an individual can purchase and a full FBI name check on all purchasers

Not surprisingly, Mr. Ford's Attorney-General, Edward Levi, said that in his opinion the Constitutional Amendment on the right to bear arms was "very remote" from handgun controls.

Attorney-General Levi had suggested an even more radical gun control program in an April, 1975, speech to law enforcement officials. For 62 metropolitan areas, it would completely ban possession of handguns outside of private home or place of business, as well as banning all transfers of handguns and handgun ammunition in those areas. Handgun owners wishing to transport a weapon would have to obtain a special permit "of extremely limited duration" after showing "a legitimate reason". When questioned at a May news conference about this drastic proposal, Mr. Ford said he would certainly consider it, since it did not involve registration!

It is hard to imagine that the opponents of gun registration have these kinds of alternatives in mind as acceptable alternatives, but Mr. Ford has not bothered to tell them what he has actually proposed.

In spite of this record, Mr. Ford still thinks he can campaign as an opponent of all gun control, saying one thing in the North and another in the South, one thing on the campaign trail and another in Washington. The American people have been saddled with that kind of government and that kind of President for too long. They will not tolerate it for four more years.

Jimmy Carter is a hunter and an advocate of Sportsmen's Rights. The entire list of Democratic Candidates on the Ballot stand four-square against any infringement of Sportsmen's Rights and their opponents know it! Don't Be Fooled by this blatant attempt to misrepresent the views of Democratic Candidates. Vote as if your future depends on it.

It Does!
Vote Straight Democratic!
Venango County Democratic Committee, John D. Baker, Chairman

FIGURE 9.2 Political advertisement in the *Oil City (Pa.) Derrick*, November 1, 1976. The ad outlined how President Gerald Ford's pro-gun campaign statements contradicted his administration's firearms control record. It concluded by touting Democratic presidential candidate Jimmy Carter as the true supporter of "Sportsmen's Rights."

with "saying one thing in the North and another in the South." It closed with: "The American people have been saddled with that kind of [double-talking] government and that kind of president for too long. They will not tolerate it for four more years."[86]

Yet despite the Carter campaign's best efforts at managing the firearms control narrative, gun rights advocates were not having it. They remained steadfast in their criticism of Carter, with some going so far as to label him the most "anti-gun" presidential candidate ever.[87] For instance, a mass mailing from the Georgia Outdoor Sportsmen Club warned firearms owners about Carter's "anti-gun" stance and noted that "if you are not helping the fight against gun control you are helping the fight for it and an end to our Second Amendment rights."[88] Not to be out done, the NRA-ILA published an article criticizing Carter for trying to modify his firearms control position. "Carter has tried to make it look as that his position is clear of the extreme anti-gun position of most of his close associates," wrote the ILA, adding, "but his own pronouncements are not reassuring. He sounds 'moderate' only be comparison to the wild proposals of his close friends and associates." The article closed by encouraging the gun rights community to "vote carefully and thoughtfully . . . as if our right possession of firearms depended on it."[89]

Seeing firearms controls as a losing issue, the Carter campaign decided not to press it too hard. Indeed, the campaign knew that Ford was politically "waffling" on the issue, but it did not want elevate firearms controls to a "media-level issue" and therefore "distract from the [other] issues" it "really want[ed] to stress."[90] The fact that the Carter campaign took a step back on the firearms control issue is not to say that they abandoned it altogether.[91] The campaign continued to advance its conservationist and environmental message in publications like *Outdoor Life* and *Field & Stream*.[92] The former publication was far more politically friendly than the latter, which ran a special editorial touting Ford's pro-gun, anti-firearms-control stand.[93] And after seeing Ford's pro-gun letter appear in the October issue of *American Rifleman*, the Carter campaign reached out to the NRA about doing something similar for November. Ashley Halsey, Jr., *American Rifleman* editor-in-chief, responded that the NRA would not be able to honor such a request—at least not in *American Rifleman*. The organization would, however, provide the Carter campaign an opportunity to publish something in its other monthly publication, *American Hunter*.[94]

That *American Hunter*, not *American Rifleman*, was offered should have signaled to the Carter campaign that the NRA was setting them up for failure. For one, *American Hunter* maintained roughly 15 percent the circulation of *American Rifleman*.[95] Moreover, since its first publication in October 1973, the magazine's editors had yet to publish anything even remotely political.[96] This was intentional, seeing that *American Hunter* was one of several ongoing initiatives meant to attract apolitical sportsmen and hunters to join the NRA.[97] And seemingly unbeknownst to the Carter campaign, it was not as if the NRA was too close to its print deadline to publish a statement from Carter in *American Rifleman*. Ford's letter wasn't finalized for publication in the October issue until September 14.[98] Yet with nine more days in the month of October, the NRA declined the Carter campaign's request for the November issue.[99] The point to be made is that the group could have published Carter's statement in the November issue of *American Rifleman* if it wanted to. It simply chose not to provide Carter with the wider platform.

For the November issue of *American Hunter*, the Carter campaign chose to submit the content within its sportsmen-targeted flyer "Jimmy Carter on Guns and Hunting," which the NRA published in full.[100] What the Carter campaign did not anticipate was how the NRA would frame it. Rather than simply provide *American Hunter* readers with Ford's and Carter's statements as they had done in presidential elections past, the NRA made sure to hold up Ford's statement as "the strongest endorsement of legitimate firearms ownership since President John F. Kennedy." Conversely, Carter's statement was lambasted for having failed to answer any of the "12 specific questions" previously raised by the Georgia Wildlife Foundation. Additionally, the NRA audaciously claimed that if Carter were elected president, he would most assuredly surround himself with several "anti-gun leaders." It closed its criticisms of Carter (and support for Ford) with a disingenuous apolitical statement: "So there it is, laid out in the open. You can like Mr. Carter. You can like Mr. Ford. It is still a free country. Take your choice."[101]

As the November issue of *American Hunter* was being finalized, printed, and distributed, the third and final nationally televised presidential debate took place. Therein Ford and Carter were pressed on variety of issues, such as defense appropriations, tax policy, and welfare. Toward the latter half of debate, Ford was asked a question on firearms controls. The debate moderator inquired why Ford remained "so adamant in . . . opposition to substantive gun control" despite the rising national crime rate, the precipitous increase in use of handguns to commit crimes, and the fact that the president had personally experienced two assassination attempts. Ford responded exactly how gun rights supporters hoped he would, by criticizing restrictive firearms controls as unduly burdensome on law-abiding citizens and pointing to mandatory minimums as the only viable solution. Carter was prepared for Ford's answer and delivered an effective retort. He pointed out that Ford's answer at the debate was far removed from what he had pronounced earlier in the year, that is, prohibiting the "sale of so-called Saturday Night Specials, and . . . [placing] very strict control over who owned a handgun." Carter then made sure to point out how he had owned and used firearms most of his life. Finally, Carter noted that although he supported registering handguns, he opposed the registration of long guns.[102]

Although Carter's firearms control response was on point, it was Ford's overall debate performance that won the day. For following the debate, he was able to reverse his polling deficit with Carter. As of mid-August, Carter had an impressive 54-to-32-point lead over Ford. Following the third and last televised debate, however, Ford was now polling slightly ahead at 49 to 48.[103] If the sportsmen's vote was indeed as impactful as gun rights advocates and many political pundits believed, surely Ford would run away with the presidency. Yet it was Carter who was elected president, which included him winning the very southern states that Ford had campaigned using an anti-firearms-control message. The myth of the all-powerful, election-swinging sportsmen's vote was politically exposed.[104] And it was not just the outcome of the presidential election that exposed it; so, too, did the congressional elections.

Much like in 1974, the congressional elections of 1976 failed to provide gun rights advocates with any notable victories on which to hang their political hat. This failure occurred despite the dedicated and organized political fundraising efforts of several gun rights advocacy groups. The CCRKBA for one had repeatedly touted its Right to Bear Arms Political Victory Fund—the "first national political war chest to make funds available to pro-gun candidates"[105]—with the intent of removing "66 hardcore anti-gun" members of Congress, each of whom the CCRKBA alleged was backed by the "powerful news media and . . . well-heeled anti-gun organizations" intent on instituting their "program of 'creeping confiscation.' "[106]

Similarly, the newly formed gun rights advocacy group Gun Owners of America (GOA) met its lofty fundraising goal of $500,000 to vote out "anti-gun" members of Congress and replace them with "strong, moral candidates who believe in upholding our constitutional freedoms and strict and swift punishment for the criminal element."[107] And not to be outdone, by October 1976 the NRA, too, had successfully formed its own Political Action Committee (PAC).[108]

In addition to providing pro-gun candidates with monetary contributions, gun rights advocates ramped up their political grading efforts. Ever since Congress enacted the Gun Control Act in 1968, gun rights advocates had sporadically issued lawmaker grades or report cards on the firearms-control issue.[109] Come 1976, the practice was normalized to the point that every gun rights advocacy group was issuing them. This included the NRA. The 1976 elections were in fact the first in which congressional candidates touted the NRA's new rating system to appeal to the sportsmen's voting bloc. Yet for those candidates challenging congressional incumbents, their positive NRA rating had little to no bearing on Election Day. The outcome of the elections was so underwhelming for gun rights advocates that most chose to not even comment on it.[110] And those who did focused solely on the failed Massachusetts ballot initiative, which, if it had passed, would have prohibited the possession, ownership, or sale of any handgun.

That gun rights advocates underperformed for the 1976 elections is not to say that the firearms control issue was not politically impactful. As with prior election cycles, congressional candidates continued to tailor their firearms control message in the hopes of appeasing gun rights supporters. While there are many examples to point to, there is one that is more historically noteworthy than the others—the senatorial campaign of Joseph D. Tydings. Recall that from 1965 to 1970 Tydings was one of the Senate's most outspoken supporters of firearms controls. He even called out the "gun lobby" on several occasions during his failed 1970 reelection campaign, a loss that many attributed to organized Maryland gun rights opposition.[111] This included Tydings.[112]

Yet a few years later, after having studied his political defeat more closely, Tydings arrived at a much different conclusion. While he conceded that the gun rights opposition in Maryland was indeed effective in turning out the sportsmen vote, Tydings now felt that the "principal reason" for his 1970 defeat was having "misjudged" Maryland's overall "political

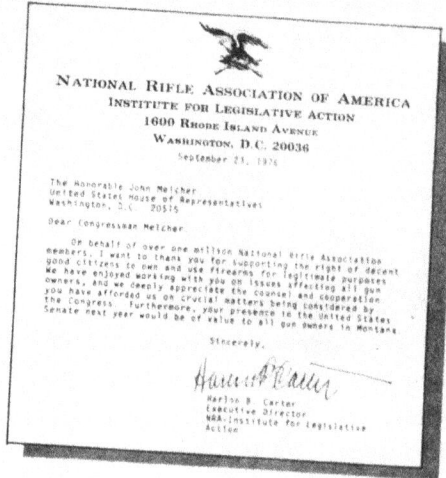

FIGURE 9.3 Political advertisement in the *Billings (Mont.) Gazette*, October 15, 1976. The ad highlighted Montana Democratic senatorial candidate John Melcher's NRA endorsement. Melcher was one of only a few congressional candidates in 1976 to advertise their NRA endorsement and win on Election Day.

climate." Tydings thought the same was true for the 1968 defeat of Pennsylvania senator Joseph S. Clark. "I don't believe the gun lobby would have
been successful if it weren't for the fact that [Clark and I] were involved in
other issues which had weakened us at the particular period when we stood
for reelection," wrote Tydings.[113] Ironically, despite concluding that the
"gun lobby" played a limited role in his 1970 defeat, come the 1976 election
cycle, Tydings began politically hedging on the firearms control issue by
issuing a moderate, more nuanced message—one that focused squarely on
restricting handgun purchases, including a ban on the domestic sale and
manufacture of Saturday Night Specials.[114]

It did not take long, however, before Citizens Against Tydings (CAT) was
reestablished and began urging sportsmen to defeat Tydings once again.[115]
This prompted Tydings to issue several speeches and press statements voicing regret for having ever supported federal restrictions on long guns, to
include firearms registration.[116] He also made sure to throw his support
behind mandatory minimums.[117] It was all to no avail. For in the Maryland
Democratic primary, Tydings was overwhelmingly defeated by Paul Sarbanes by a 3 to 1 ratio.[118] And given that Sarbanes's firearms control policy
was virtually identical to that of Tydings, the latter's defeat had nothing
to do with CAT or the sportsmen's vote.[119] This was punctuated by the fact
that Sarbanes, who was given a "D" rating by the NRA heading into Election Day, ended up defeating the Republican incumbent John Glenn
Beall, who was given an "A" rating.[120] Simply put, the Maryland Senate race
in 1976 historically underscores that the all-powerful, election-swinging
sportsmen's vote continued to be built more on myth than on fact.

Still, the fact that Tydings thought it was politically necessary to hedge
on the firearms-control issue shows the immense political clout that the
NRA and other gun rights advocates held. As the Ralph Nader Congress
Project observed in 1975:

> The actual role of the NRA [and other gun rights advocates] in the
> [1970] Tydings defeat can never be known for certain, but if the
> [election-swinging sportsmen's vote] thesis is true . . ., one might well
> conclude that the NRA [and other gun rights advocates exercise]
> influence well beyond what [their] actual ability to deliver votes would
> warrant. Members of Congress and the press believe that [NRA and
> other gun rights advocates] wrath carries more potential harm than it

does, and because they believe this, this belief becomes something of a self-fulfilling prophecy.[121]

The poor sportsmen's vote showing for the 1976 elections led to much finger pointing and infighting among gun rights advocates. This was particularly true within the NRA. For not long after the 1976 elections, NRA-ILA executive director Harlon B. Carter effectively resigned his post. What exactly transpired behind the scenes is difficult to ascertain. But according to secondhand accounts, the outcome of the elections created an internal power struggle within the NRA. Those who supported Carter's vision wanted to allocate even more financial resources to defeating anti-gun lawmakers and opposing firearms controls. Meanwhile, those who did not support Carter's vision wanted to maintain the status quo and, if possible, increase the NRA's financial commitments to marksmanship, hunting, and recreational programs. Ultimately, the latter group won out, leading the NRA board of directors to fire upward of seventy-four NRA employees who had supported Carter's vision. Although the board offered Carter the option to stay on as ILA executive director, he resigned in protest. In the next edition of *American Rifleman*, the NRA framed the firings as a necessary "reduction in force" to "streamline" operations and "enable cost savings in 1977 of well over $1 million."[122] As for Carter's resignation, the NRA stated it was Carter's plan all along. According to the NRA, Carter had "agreed, at the outset, to head NRA-ILA for 'only as long as it takes to get the Institute off the ground,' and he planned to resign after a year in Washington."[123]

In the months that followed, Carter and his allies hatched a plan to take control of the NRA at its annual convention in 1977, being held in Cincinnati, Ohio, and reform it in their own image. In executing the plan, Carter and his allies relied on the same propaganda and misinformation tactics that the NRA had utilized over the years to defeat firearms controls. The image they painted was one of NRA ineptitude, malfeasance, and betrayal. The gun rights community was sold on the idea that NRA had become soft on firearms control and was focused only on conservation, recreational shooting, and a 37,000-acre outdoor center to be opened in Raton, New Mexico. As a result, rumors spread about the NRA's lack of dedication in defending the Second Amendment, with some going so far to allege that it had been infiltrated by "members of a conspiracy to take away our guns, and then the rest of our freedom."[124] Although the NRA denounced the rumors as just that, the decisions being made at the organization's highest level were not helping its case, particularly the decision to move the NRA's headquarters from the nation's capital to Colorado Springs, Colorado.[125] The postelection optics of the decision to the move the NRA headquarters were serious enough that Gene Crum, NRA board member and associate editor of *Gun Week*, questioned "whether there will even be an organization called the National Rifle Association" by 1978.[126]

The reality, of course, was much different. The NRA was not backing away from gun rights advocacy or from defending the Second Amendment. As Carter and his allies well knew, although the NRA was planning on moving its headquarters—a decision in June 1976 that received little gun rights pushback or fanfare prior to Carter's November resignation—the ILA would remain in the nation's capital to continue the fight against firearms controls. Moreover, Carter and his allies knew that the ILA was more than adequately funded to achieve this purpose.[127] They just did not agree with the plan and sought to reverse it.

Concerned with the unrelenting criticism by Carter and his allies, the NRA commissioned an internal study, which provided an interesting, paradoxical look inside the minds of NRA members. While NRA members often described themselves "as liberals in the original sense of the word," they refused to label themselves as such and instead claimed to be "conservatives." Additionally, many members believed that the NRA's charter stipulated that the group's two principal functions were dealing with the "gun control issue" and defending "freedom . . . from government control and interference." The charter stipulated neither of those functions. Nevertheless, the way many members saw it, the NRA was failing to meet its charter obligations. These observations led the authors of the internal study to recommend that the NRA immediately institute several reforms, such as periodically expressing appreciation for member opinions, focusing on membership benefits other than "conservation," particularly legislative and political action, establishing better forms of communication and participation, taking a more aggressive attitude toward negative NRA news media stories, and full transparency by the NRA board of directors.[128]

In addition to the critical feedback from the internal study, a separate member survey found that the NRA's promotion of conservation and firearms recreation did not align with membership attitudes. Based on over 130,000 responses, the member survey was clear that fighting firearms

controls and defending the Second Amendment were of foremost importance to the membership (47.7 percent of respondents). Hunting polled a
distance second (14.7 percent), followed by firearms as a hobby (12.2 percent).[129] Thus, heading into the annual convention in 1977, the NRA's leadership knew it was not meeting its members' expectations—members who
adamantly disagreed with the decisions to move the headquarters to Colorado and keep all ILA funding separate from general headquarters
funds.[130] In the hopes of appeasing these unhappy members, the NRA
offered several assurances that it was unwavering in its support for the
right to keep and bear arms. Protecting the Second Amendment against
its "enemies," according to the May issue of American Rifleman, was the
NRA's "first job."[131] NRA executive vice president Maxwell E. Rich was also
forthright in declaring the organization's commitment to protecting the
Second Amendment. As he entered the annual convention on its first day
of scheduled events, Rich told reporters that the NRA was "the single major
force in blocking the passage of handgun laws," through the "very, very
successful" efforts of NRA lobbyists. He then decried the need for additional firearms controls and pointed to the enforcement of the existing
twenty thousand firearms laws currently "not being enforced" as a better
solution.[132] Unbeknownst to Rich and the other members of the NRA leadership, an organized coup was about to take place.

On May 22, hardline gun rights supporters flooded the NRA convention
hall and used parliamentary procedure to modify the NRA's by-laws and
oust Rich, as well as the other NRA officials who supported him. Otherwise
known as the Cincinnati Revolt, one by one, the attending gun rights supporters replaced the incumbent NRA officials with hardline anti-firearms-
control ones. Carter was voted in as NRA president. In appreciation, he
promised to strengthen the ILA to fight against firearms controls. And
strengthen the ILA Carter did, by hiring nearly fifty lobbyists, lawyers, and
researchers whose sole purpose was protecting and furthering the "rights
of law-abiding citizens to own and use firearms."[133] And with Carter's ramping up of the ILA, the NRA no longer balked at being called the "gun lobby."
Rather, with Carter at the helm, it embraced the label, as well as Carter's
unapologetic rhetoric that all firearms controls infringed on Americans'
most basic freedoms.[134] As Carter later put it: "Any national gun law, no
matter how innocent and apparent, no matter how simple it might be, pre-
supposes a still further growth in a centralized, computerized, gun

control bureaucracy in Washington, D.C. A monstrous invasion into the rights of privacy, of you law-abiding and decent people, who have never committed a crime, and concerning there is no evidence you ever will."[135]

There is virtual academic consensus that the Cincinnati Revolt was a watershed moment in gun rights history. For many academics, the revolt is seen as a gun rights revolution of sorts—one that forever transformed the NRA from a politically moderate sporting, hunting, and conservation organization into an extreme, no-compromise lobbying arm. But there are several problems with this historical conception. For one, it ignores that the NRA was already engaged in political lobbying—whether it wanted to admit it or not—for upward of five decades. Additionally, this historical conception ignores that the NRA had already adopted a "no compromise" position on firearms controls seven years earlier. This is not to say that the Cincinnati Revolt is insignificant in the pantheon of gun rights history. It most certainly is. But looking at the historical evidence in its totality, what many academics have characterized as a revolution was more of a reformation and an organizational reshuffling. Yet to attract the members and followers of other, more extreme gun rights advocacy groups such as the CCRKBA and GOA, Carter and his supporters historically framed the Cincinnati Revolt as being substantially more significant than it really was. Furthermore, to politically legitimize the actions of those who took part in the revolt, the NRA officials who were ousted from their positions of leadership were cast as incompetent and self-serving. It was a narrative that cast Carter and his hardline supporters as political saviors.[136]

Initially, the Cincinnati Revolt did not have the galvanizing impact that Carter and his allies expected. In the year that followed, instead of sportsmen, hunters, shooters, and firearms owners flocking to join the NRA, there was a 15 percent net decrease in membership.[137] As more time passed, however—two years to be exact—NRA membership began to reach new heights, prompting Carter to shoot for two million by 1982.[138]

While Carter was working to reform the NRA in his own image, President Jimmy Carter's advisors were debating the merits of pursuing handgun controls. The debate was prompted by bureaucrats within the Department of Justice, who wanted to draft a handgun control bill in line with Carter's campaign promises in 1976. Initially, Carter's advisors were optimistic about the prospects of the bill. In the words of one advisor, it was a "good first step."[139] It did not take long, however, before the contents of the bill were leaked, and gun rights advocates began making wide, speculative claims.[140] One writer alleged that Carter's handgun control bill would realign BATF from the Department of Treasury to the Department of Justice and therefore "vastly increase the power" of the latter department and that "of the President over gun control."[141] Meanwhile, relying on reporting in the *Christian Science Monitor*, the CCRKBA speculated that the bill was proof positive that anti-gun groups were working hand-in-hand with the Carter administration.[142] They were not. Yet such gun rights speculation planted the seed that President Carter was diligently working to deprive Americans of their Second Amendment rights.

Early on, at least one Carter advisor was wise to what was taking place and urged the administration to move forward with a handgun control bill while the NRA was in "disarray."[143] The advisor noted how the gun rights movement was being driven by the extremists, who were already aligned with "conservative politics rather than traditional sportsmen's attitudes." Given this fact, as well observations that "pro-control groups represent the natural constituency of the President" and firearms controls were almost impossible to pass during an election year, the advisor urged Carter to take immediate action.[144] But instead, Carter decided to tack the Department of Justice's handgun control bill onto the administration's larger crime bill.[145] It was a plan that was easily scuttled following the sudden political resurgence of the NRA.

In the February 1978 edition of *American Rifleman* appeared an article titled "Worst Firearms Bill Yet Has White House Okay." As the title implied, the article depicted the Department of Justice's handgun-control bill—which no one on Capitol Hill had yet seen—as going "far beyond any anti-gun measure drafted by any previous administration." According to the article, the bill would create a massive "registration and licensing system designed to give federal gun control agents in Washington instant access to the names of every handgun owner in the nation 'within one generation' and empower Federal agents to put out of business the majority of the 160,000 federally licensed dealers."[146]

The NRA's characterization of the bill was only part true. While the bill sought to tighten the requirements for firearms dealers that sold handguns, it did nothing in the way forcing firearms dealers out of business (except for pawnbrokers, who would be outright prohibited from selling handguns). The NRA's registration and licensing claim was equally misleading.

Indeed, the bill sought to implement a new, federal-state background check requirement for all handgun purchases. However, the NRA conveniently omitted that the bill prohibited the BATF from maintaining any individual handgun purchaser's information. The only information that it could legally maintain on file was the handgun serial numbers and the firearms dealers the handguns were purchased from.[147]

Politically, it did not matter that the NRA mischaracterized the contents of the Department of Justice's bill. All that mattered was the follow-on gun rights backlash, which again proved itself effective in halting the bill's advancement. The rapidly approaching 1978 elections did not help the bill's political prospects either, prompting Carter's advisors to abandon the issue for the time being. As one internal White House memorandum put it: "This [Department of Justice firearms control] proposal has no chance of passage by Congress and is sure to add to our negative perception in the West. At some point I think we have to stop taking these hopeless 'good government' positions and concentrate our political capital on the big issues that matter. No one will miss this if we quietly drop it."[148]

"Let's Think About This, Jimmy"

FIGURE 9.4 Political cartoon in *Gun Week* showing President Jimmy Carter hesitantly putting forward a "gun bill." Behind Carter was an individual—meant to be Congress— sweating at the prospect of taking up firearms-control legislation with the upcoming elections of 1978. Image reprinted with permission from the Second Amendment Foundation.

That the Carter White House decided to abandon the firearms control issue did not mean that they advertised it. Much like Ford and Nixon, the Carter White House decided that for the rest of the 95th Congress it was best to talk about firearms controls only in the political abstract. The less information the better. But if any congressional or media inquiries were received on the issue, Carter administration officials were instructed to state that the president fully intended to fulfill his firearms control campaign promises.[149] As to when these promises would be fulfilled, White House officials were instructed to state that no timetable had been set.[150]

At around the time that Carter White House decided to abandon the firearms-control issue, the Department of Treasury published in the *Federal Register* several proposed administrative rule changes pertaining to the BATF's enforcement of federal firearms controls, to include improving its firearms tracing program.[151] Although the Carter White House thought the proposed changes were "modest"[152]—particularly when compared to the provisions within the Department of Justice's proposed handgun-control bill—the NRA and other gun rights advocates cast them as another backdoor attempt at federal firearms registration. NRA-ILA executive director Neal Knox for one hinted that the proposed rule changes were the first step toward total firearms confiscation. "There is ... mounting evidence beyond suspicion that central record keeping or registration is a means to an end—confiscation of privately owned firearms," claimed Knox.[153] Not to be outdone, CCRKBA official and former *American Rifleman* editor John M. Snyder likened the proposed rule changes to the firearms laws of Nazi Germany.[154] In total, the Department of Justice received over 337,000 letters on the proposed rule changes, 95 percent of which were in opposition.[155]

In addition to facing overwhelming gun rights opposition to the proposed rule changes, the BATF was facing an onslaught of political criticism for its alleged abuses against law-abiding firearms owners. Hyperbolic accusations against BATF by the NRA and other gun rights advocates were already commonplace. What was new this time around was that members of Congress, eager to garner the sportsmen's vote for the upcoming elections, were increasingly acknowledging and parroting them.[156] Ultimately, the political backlash was so fierce that the House Appropriations Committee, by a vote of 38–3, decided to cut the BATF's proposed annual budget by $4.2 million—the exact amount that the Department of Treasury had requested to improve the firearms-tracing program.[157] The Senate

Appropriations Committee followed suit by including language in its appropriations bill expressly prohibiting the use of any funds for firearms registration purposes.[158] This led President Carter's outgoing domestic policy advisor, Annie Gutierrez, to pen the following to her successor Franklin White: "I think we can safely say that handgun legislation has no chance, after seeing what the NRA did with the Treasury regulations."[159]

Yet despite all the political trepidation over the firearms control issue within the Carter White House, the issue did not show itself to be all that relevant during the 1978 elections. Certainly, as with prior congressional elections, candidates vying for seats in western, southern, or largely rural constituencies advertised their pro-gun bona fides. However, without the immediate prospect of Congress taking up firearms control legislation, there was not much in the way of political angst for the NRA and other gun rights advocates to exploit. What was unique for 1978 was that it proved to be the first election cycle in which the NRA-ILA was able to aggressively assert itself in the area of political action. And assert itself the ILA did. One way was through political grading. Although the ILA decided against publishing a full list of its grades, given "the very real possibility that anti-gun organizations would use our published research to compile an 'enemies list' of our friends," it claimed its 1978 grades were the "most comprehensive firearms legislation rating of congressional office-seekers ever attempted."[160] In addition to political grading, the ILA aggressively asserted itself in field of political fundraising and spending. Its Political Victory Fund not only outraised and outspent all other gun rights advocacy PACs combined, but the fund ended up being ranked sixth among all PAC spending in the trade, membership, and health PAC category.[161] After the election, the ILA boasted that out of the 258 congressional candidates that the Political Victory Fund donated to, 213 (83 percent) were victorious on Election Day. "All and all, the whole trend of this election has been favorable for the pro-gun movement, a demonstration of the political strength sportsmen bring to the polling place," exclaimed ILA executive director Knox.[162]

Knox's upbeat assessment of the elections in 1978 was far from the reality. The fact remained that the ILA could not identify a single congressional race where a prominent firearms control–supporting incumbent was defeated. The best it could do was highlight its involvement in the "Dump Fraser" campaign, which the ILA helped organize to prevent Minnesota representative Donald M. Fraser from ascending to the Senate seat vacated following the death of Hubert H. Humphrey. Fraser ultimately lost the Democratic primary election to Bob Short—whom the ILA endorsed—by roughly 3,500 votes. But then, as fate would have it, Short lost the general election to Republican David Durenberger by more than 400,000 votes.[163]

Come the start of 1979, whether the electoral impact of the sportsmen's vote was real did not matter to the majority of the newly sworn 96th Congress. All that mattered was they believed it, so much so in fact that entering the election cycle in 1980, members of Congress flocked to cosponsor the McClure-Volkmer Firearms Control Act, which sought to repeal several unfavored firearms control provisions in the Gun Control Act. To members of Congress, it did not matter that several studies had shown a gun rights proponent was no more likely to vote against a firearms control–supporting lawmaker than a firearms control proponent was to vote against a gun rights–supporting lawmaker.[164] All that mattered was that members of Congress believed that the sportsmen voting bloc *could* be the difference between them winning and losing their next election. This was particularly true for the Indiana Senate race between Democratic incumbent Birch Bayh and Republican representative Dan Quayle. Recall that from the early to mid-1970s it was Bayh, as chairman of the Senate Judiciary Committee, who led the effort to regulate and restrict Saturday Night Specials. Yet come 1980 and facing reelection, Bayh decidedly flipped on the firearms control issue to lure the sportsmen's vote.[165] Not only did Bayh flaunt an NRA "thank you" letter as an official campaign endorsement, but he also penned an editorial expressing his unequivocal support for the Second Amendment and opposition to the BATF's enforcement of firearms controls, as well as any other "misguided, overzealous public officials who deny law abiding citizens their basic Constitutional rights."[166] The NRA, however, denied having endorsed Bayh.[167] "We have had a policy that if there is a heated contest for a seat, and two candidates are equally good on the issues, we don't go into it," stated an NRA spokesperson.[168] Bayh ended up losing to Quayle by 166,492 votes.

The belief in the power of the sportsmen's vote was particularly on display for the presidential race in 1980. This was no more evident than when the Carter White House decided once again to abandon pursuing even a modest handgun-control bill. Instead, seemingly borrowing from Ford's 1976 campaign playbook, the Carter White House's hedged on the firearms control issue by placing the political onus squarely on Congress's

FIGURE 9.5 Political advertisement in the *Twin Falls (Idaho) Times-News*, October 31, 1980. Paid for by Republican representative Steve Symms during the Idaho Senate race of 1980, the ad sought to depict incumbent Democratic senator Frank Church as being politically weak on the firearms-control issue. Twelve years earlier, during the Idaho Senate race in 1968, Republican challenger George Hansen similarly tried to make firearms control a wedge voting issue between him and Church but lost. In the 1980 election, however, Symms defeated Church by a slim 4,262-vote margin (0.97 percent).

shoulders.[169] As for Carter's Republican challenger, virtually every candidate vying for the Republican Party's presidential nomination made sure to put themselves on record opposing firearms controls.[170] "I don't know of any place that has more gun control laws than New York City and I don't know any more dangerous place," stated former California governor Ronald Reagan before those attending the Gun Owners of New Hampshire Forum. "If you compromise on Saturday Night Specials, those same bleeding hearts will come back for regular handguns," stated Illinois representative Philip M. Crane at the same forum. Meanwhile, former Central Intelligence Agency (CIA) director George H. W. Bush let the forum attendees know that he supported "strong, direct consistent opposition to registration." Only Illinois representative John Anderson came out in favor of firearms controls. "What is so wrong about telling law-abiding residents we will license gun owners?" queried Anderson. The forum crowd responded by booing and calling Anderson a "traitor."[171]

While the Republican Party's presidential nominees were vying for the sportsmen's vote, President Carter was facing a serious challenge for the Democratic presidential nomination by well-known firearms control proponent Senator Edward M. Kennedy of Massachusetts. Yet it was not at the behest of Carter that Kennedy was criticized on the presidential campaign trail for having supported strict firearms controls. That distinction went to the NRA-ILA, which, through its Political Victory Fund, spent $230,000 on a series of anti-Kennedy mailings, advertisements, and broadcasts.[172] In doing so, the ILA borrowed the CAT slogan from 1970 of "If Tydings Wins, You Lose" and replaced it with "If Kennedy Wins, You Lose."[173] For the Iowa Caucuses alone, the ILA ran several newspaper advertisements with the headline "Will the Real Kennedy Please Stand Up?" The advertisement chastised Kennedy for allegedly telling Iowans several "half-truths, distortions or lapses of memory" on the firearms control issue.[174] Later, for the Pennsylvania Democratic primary elections, the ILA ran the advertisement "Seventeen Good Reasons for Sportsmen to Vote Against Senator Ted Kennedy." As the title implies, the ad provided readers with seventeen examples of Kennedy supporting restrictive firearms controls. It closed by asking Democrats to bring "5 of your fellow sportsmen with you" to the polls.[175] In publishing these advertisements, the ILA let it be known that Kennedy was far and away the most hostile presidential candidate, Democrat or Republican, to the cause of gun rights.[176]

FIGURE 9.6 Advertisement in the *Allentown (Pa.) Morning Call*, April 13, 1980. The ad was one of several paid by the NRA-ILA Political Victory Fund for the Pennsylvania Democratic primary elections.

Kennedy eventually failed in his effort to win the Democratic nomination. Whether the ILA's "If Kennedy Wins, You Lose" campaign was a factor is unknown. But with Kennedy now out of the way, and Reagan having won the Republican Party's nomination, the ILA ramped up its anti-Carter rhetoric. According to the ILA, ever since Carter took his presidential oath of office there had been a coordinated anti-gun effort afoot "against the National Rifle Association, against the membership, and against all Americans who believe in the right to keep and bear arms." "For these [last] four years of the Jimmy Carter Administration, NRA members have spent over $13.8 million to keep the White House and the Federal bureaucracy in check," it claimed, adding, "If Jimmy Carter is not voted out of office, what future price must we pay to preserve our firearms and hunting rights?"[177] Naturally, given the NRA's unabashed opposition to Carter's reelection, it was implying that the gun rights community needed to vote for Reagan. The NRA had made a similar inference during the presidential race in 1976. What was different for 1980 was the implication was no longer necessary. For the first time in the NRA's 109-year history, it was formally endorsing one presidential candidate over another, and that candidate was Reagan:

> The combination of a belief in the people's right to keep and bear arms, and in the rights of citizens to be free from bondage of an oppressive government will be for us a new beginning.
>
> Perhaps uniquely—better than any other single class of citizens—NRA members and the nation's firearms owners—have felt the full force of government which is beyond the control of the people. Especially during the past four years we have been victimized by an arrogant Federal bureaucracy rejecting the right of individual citizens to own and use firearms for lawful purposes . . .
>
> With a Ronald Reagan Administration—those small men, those invisible bureaucrats will no longer be allowed to corrupt the law to their own ends, or to use our tax dollars against us!
>
> With a Reagan Administration, we will see the end of the abusive practices of the Federal gun police—the Bureau of Alcohol, Tobacco and Firearms. . . .
>
> With a Reagan Administration, we will see wholehearted support for the legislative effort to remove the onerous provisions of the Gun

Control Act of 1968—a law which has spawned the BATF abuses of the past four years and done nothing to limit crime. . . .

A Reagan Administration—a Reagan Presidency—is a must for the nation's firearms owners and hunters![178]

At the time the NRA issued its endorsement of Reagan, Carter was leading in the polls by 4 points.[179] Yet in the final week of polling, Reagan suddenly developed a 3-point lead over Carter. And on Election Day, Reagan won by more than 9 points, carrying forty-four of fifty states. The final Electoral College tally was 489 for Reagan and 49 for Carter. The NRA reveled in the outcome: "The election results were a clear tribute to the political clout wielded by gun owners at the polls." Although Reagan did not personally recognize the importance of the sportsmen's vote in his Election Day victory speech, the Reagan campaign later issued a statement expressing appreciation for "the support of the sportsmen across the country."[180]

Was the sportsmen's vote in part responsible for Reagan's landslide victory? Gun rights advocates certainly thought so. Although there is no substantiated evidence that confirms it, and the firearms control issue did not rear its head at any of the four presidential and vice presidential debates, the fact remains that Reagan and his vice presidential running mate George H. W. Bush did their utmost to court the sportsmen's vote. Repeatedly, both Reagan and Bush made it clear that they outright opposed any further firearms regulations.[181] At one point, the Reagan-Bush ticket went so far as to promise to "prosecute those in government who abuse citizens for the political ends of gun control," thus giving political credibility to the largely manufactured gun rights narrative of the BATF abusing the civil liberties of law-abiding firearms owners.[182] Additionally, it is worth noting that garnering the sportsmen's vote was so important to the Reagan-Bush ticket that it enlisted NRA-ILA deputy director Tanya K. Metaksa to serve as chairwoman of Sportsmen and Conservationists for Reagan-Bush.[183]

The point to be made is that the Reagan-Bush ticket saw immense political value in leveraging the firearms control issue. The same was true for President Carter. Much like in 1976, the Carter campaign tried to reassure gun rights supporters that the president would veto any overly restrictive firearms controls.[184] But Carter could not override the perception—albeit

FIGURE 9.7 NRA-ILA advertisement in support of Ronald Reagan that appeared in several Pennsylvania-based newspapers in the days leading up to Election Day in 1980. In addition to endorsing Reagan, the ad criticized President Jimmy Carter's "arrogant bureaucracy." It closed by asking readers to vote as if their "gun rights depend on it."

one manufactured by gun rights advocates—that he was in cahoots with the anti-gun lobby.[185] Conversely, Reagan was far and away the preferred presidential candidate among gun rights supporters. And it did not take long for supporters to take stock of their new president-elect. For within just month following the election, singer-songwriter and former Beatle John Lennon was shot and killed by an obsessed fan while entering his New York City apartment. As with other high-profile firearms-related deaths, the calls for firearms controls were swift.[186] Reagan, however, when asked about the political prospects of his administration supporting new legislation, remained steadfast in opposition.[187] "I've never believed you can stop it with legislation," he said, adding, "If somebody commits a crime and carries a gun while he's doing it, add five to 15 years to his prison sentence."[188]

Epilogue

Unbeknownst to most living at the time, the elections in 1980 proved to be the event that inseparably tied the gun rights movement to the Republican Party and conservatism. From its genesis in the early twentieth century through the mid-1960s, the gun rights movement was largely built on conservative ideals. Indeed, throughout that period, the National Rifle Association (NRA) and other gun rights advocates were adamant that sportsmen, hunters, shooters, and firearms owners should dispense with partisanship. Patriotism, they were told, should ultimately decide whom to vote for on Election Day. "Your ballot is a bullet fired in the battle for American constitutional government,"[1] wrote C. B. Lister in an *American Rifleman* editorial in 1944. Yet while sportsmen, hunters, shooters, and firearms owners were being instructed to set aside partisanship when casting their vote, they were also being socialized on the importance of preserving conservative ideals and longstanding American traditions. And the most important conservative ideal and longstanding American tradition worth preserving was the Second Amendment right to "keep and bear arms." Sportsmen, hunters, shooters, and firearms owners were told that if the Second Amendment was ever usurped or weakened, it would not be long before the "reformers" and "liberals" achieved their goal of erecting a totalitarian system of government.[2] In other words, to the gun rights community, the Second Amendment was viewed as the constitutional linchpin for the entire Bill of Rights.[3] As the National Association to Keep and Bear Arms (NAKBA) put it in 1971, the Second Amendment "alone" was the means through which "fellow Americans" ensured that their "God-given rights as restated in the Bill of Rights [would] never be infringed."[4]

Looking at the rise of the gun rights movement in historical retrospect, it is not all that surprising that it eventually latched itself onto a political party. As with any political issue, once the firearms control issue became nationalized in the late 1960s, it was only a matter of time before a political party tried capitalizing on it. At first, as is evidenced by the 1968 election cycle, both major political parties—Democrats and Republicans—expressed support for some types of firearms controls. As time went on, however, and Republican presidential candidates began tailoring their political message to appease gun rights supporters, it was only logical that the lower echelons of the Republican Party would soon follow. Barry Goldwater was notably the first such presidential candidate.[5] He was followed by Richard M. Nixon in 1968 and 1972 and Gerald R. Ford in 1976. But it was Ronald Reagan who inseparably tied the political cause of gun rights to the Republican Party. For it was Reagan's presidential primary challenge to Ford that ultimately pushed the Republican Party Platform Committee in 1976 to adopt what was at the time its most gun rights–friendly plank. Additionally, it was Reagan who propelled the Republican Party Platform Committee in 1980 to adopt an even friendlier gun rights message—one that supported removing any provisions within the 1968 Gun Control Act of 1968 that did not "significantly impact . . . crime" but instead "serve to restrain the law-abiding citizen in his legitimate use of firearms."[6] Finally, it was Reagan who gave the NRA and other gun rights advocates almost unimpeded White House access and influence on the firearms-control issue.

Of course, the election of President Reagan in 1980 neither prompted all Republicans to support gun rights over firearms controls nor the NRA and other gun rights advocates to support only Republican candidates over Democratic candidates. That political transformation would take another two decades to shake itself out. Reagan's election did, however, set the stage for a political shift where a prospective candidate's Republican bona fides could be gaged by their support for gun rights over firearms controls. As a result of this political shift, Republicans nationwide gradually came to accept, support, and advance the gun rights movement's legislative agenda, whether that be enacting "right to carry" firearms laws, prohibiting government agencies from researching firearms-related violence, or shielding firearms manufacturers from tort liability. Now, whatever the gun rights movement wants to legislatively achieve, it maintains the backing of the Republican Party. At the same time, whatever the gun rights movement wants to politically stall or defeat, it maintains the backing of the Republican Party.

Today there is little doubt that a Republican candidate's half-hearted or lukewarm support for gun rights could very well affect their ability to remain in political office. Those Republican candidates who vote for firearms controls or fail to expand gun rights are now often referred to as Republicans-in-Name-Only (RINOs). But prior to the Republican Party tying itself to the cause of gun rights, whether a political candidate, Republican or Democrat, supported or opposed firearms controls was largely irrelevant. This is not to say that a particular candidate's firearms-control stance could not result in their gaining or losing individual votes. It most certainly did. It is also not to say that political candidates did not fear or believe in the electoral power of the sportsmen's vote. They most certainly did. To date, however, no one has been able to provide any substantiated evidence proving that a candidate's support for firearms controls and accompanying sportsmen's vote opposing said candidate was the deciding factor on Election Day. If anything, as multiple studies from the mid-1970s and early 1980s have shown, whether a political candidate supported or opposed firearms had a minimal effect on their election or reelection campaign.

But in the hyperbolic world of politics, perception often outweighs reality. And the perception among most politicians, both past and present, is that the firearms-control issue indeed matters, especially on Capitol Hill. Firearms control is not exceptional in this respect. The issue is unique, however, given that virtually the same gun rights propaganda and political talking points used from the early to the mid-twentieth century are still in use today. Certainly, the social context and media through which gun rights advocates disseminate their propaganda and political talking points have changed over time. But the means and end goal—politically win at all costs—have not.

Notes

Information Regarding Notes and Note Abbreviations

The amount of research material accumulated for *Vote for Gun* was volumi-
nous. The note word count for the original manuscript was over 130,000
words. To meet standard print publishing guidelines, this word count was
cut in half to roughly 65,000 words. The unabridged notes, albeit in a different style and citation format, can be found at http://www.patrickjchar
les.com, where they are organized by chapter and linked to their respective page, paragraph, and sentence.

A&M	*Arms and the Man*
AGLTF	Alabama Governor Legislative Tracking Files, 1955–1979 (Montgomery: Alabama Department of Archives and History)
AH	*American Hunter*
AMP	Abner Mikva Papers (Springfield, Ill.: Abraham Lincoln Presidential Library and Museum)
APORKBA	Association to Preserve Our Right to Keep and Bear Arms
AR	*American Rifleman*
BC	Benedict Collection (Fullerton: California State University-Fullerton Archives and Special Collections)

BDP   Bob Dole Papers (Lawrence: Kansas University Dole Archives and Special Collections)

BHP   Bourke Hickenlooper Papers (West Branch, Iowa: Herbert Hoover Presidential Library)

BMGP   Barry M. Goldwater Papers (Tempe: Arizona State University)

CAP   Carl Albert Papers (Norman, Okla.: Carl Albert Congressional Research and Studies Center)

CCRKBA   Citizens Committee for the Right to Keep and Bear Arms

CEGP   Cornelius E. Gallagher Papers (Norman, Okla: Carl Albert Congressional Research and Studies Center)

CEHP   Clare E. Hoffman Papers (Ann Arbor: University of Michigan Bentley Historical Library)

CELP   Curtis E. LeMay Papers (Washington, D.C.: Library of Congress Manuscripts Division)

CLGP   Charles Lewis Gilman Papers (St. Paul: Minnesota Historical Society)

CNP   Carlton Neville Papers (Atlanta: Jimmy Carter Presidential Library)

CRCNYP   Canaan Rifle Club, New York Papers (owned by author)

CSJP   Charles S. Joelson Papers (Washington, D.C.: Library of Congress Manuscripts Division)

CTHP   Carl T. Hayden Papers (Tempe: Arizona State University Library)

CWTP   Charles W. Tobey Papers (Hanover, N.H.: Dartmouth College Rauner Special Collections Library)

DDEPP   Dwight D. Eisenhower Presidential Papers (Abilene, Kans.: Dwight D. Eisenhower Presidential Library) (hereafter Eisenhower Papers)

DMFP   Donald M. Fraser Papers (St. Paul: Minnesota Historical Society)

DMP   Don Mulford Papers (Sacramento: California State Archives)

EBMP   E. B. Mann Papers (Laramie: University of Wyoming American Heritage Center)

EDP   Ernest Dichter Papers (Wilmington, Del.: Hagley Archives)

EMDP   Everett M. Dirksen Papers (Pekin, Ill.: Dirksen Center)

EQDP	Emilio Q. Daddario Papers (Middletown, Conn.: Wesleyan University Special Collections and Archives)
ESMP	Edmund S. Muskie Papers (Lewiston, Maine: Edmund S. Muskie Archives and Special Collections Library)
F&S	*Field & Stream*
FDRPP	Franklin D. Roosevelt Presidential Papers, (Hyde Park, N.Y.: Franklin D. Roosevelt Presidential Library)
FEMP	Frank E. Moss Papers (Salt Lake City, Utah: J. Willard Marriott Library Special Collections)
FHP	Fred Harris Papers (Norman, Okla.: Carl Albert Congressional Research and Studies Center)
G&A	*Guns & Ammo*
GANP	Gaylord A. Nelson Papers (Madison: Wisconsin Historical Society)
GCSF	Geoffrey C. Shepard Files (Ann Arbor, Mich.: Gerald R. Ford Presidential Library)
GDAP	George D. Aiken Papers (Burlington: University of Vermont Special Collections)
GEMP	George E. MacKinnon Papers (St. Paul: Minnesota Historical Society)
GM	*Guns Magazine*
GMP	George McGovern Papers (Princeton, N.J.: Princeton University Seeley G. Mudd Manuscript Library)
GRFCP	Gerald R. Ford Congressional Papers (Ann Arbor, Mich.: Gerald R. Ford Presidential Library)
GRFPP	Gerald R. Ford Presidential Papers (Ann Arbor, Mich.: Gerald R. Ford Presidential Library)
GW	*Gun Week*
GWRP	George W. Romney Papers (Ann Arbor: University of Michigan Bentley Historical Library)
HBP	Hale Boggs Papers (New Orleans, La.: Tulane University Howard–Tilton Memorial Library)
HCPS4C	Homer Cummings Papers, Series 4: Correspondence of the Attorney General and Post-Attorney General, 1933–1956 (Charlottesville: University of Virginia Special Collections)

HCPS4S	Homer Cummings Papers, Series 4: Speeches, 1886–1950, and Articles, 1918–1945 (Charlottesville: University of Virginia Special Collections)
HHHP	Hubert H. Humphrey Papers (St. Paul: Minnesota Historical Society)
HPSP	Harold P. Sheldon Papers (Barre: Vermont Historical Society)
HSP	Hugh Scott Papers (Charlottesville: University of Virginia Special Collections)
HSTPF	Harry S. Truman Papers, Personal Files (Independence, Mo.: Harry S. Truman Presidential Library)
HSTP/ WHCF/PPF	Harry S. Truman Papers, White House Central Files: President's Personal File (Independence, Mo.: Harry S. Truman Presidential Library)
HTP	Henry Tallmadge Papers (Athens, Ga.: Richard B. Russell Library for Political Research and Studies)
HWGP	Harold W. Glassen Papers (Ann Arbor: University of Michigan Bentley Historical Library)
JAMP	James A. McClure Papers (Moscow: University of Idaho Special Collections)
JCP	James Cannon Papers (Ann Arbor, Mich.: Gerald R. Ford Presidential Library)
JCPP	Jimmy Carter Presidential Papers (Atlanta: Jimmy Carter Presidential Library)
JCPPP	Jimmy Carter Pre-Presidential Papers (Atlanta: Jimmy Carter Presidential Library)
JDEP	John D. Ehrlichman Papers (Yorba Linda, Calif.: Richard Nixon Presidential Library)
JFKPP	John F. Kennedy Presidential Papers (Boston: John F. Kennedy Presidential Library)
JGOP	James G. O'Hara Papers (Ann Arbor: University of Michigan Bentley Historical Library)
JHGA	John H. Glenn Archives (Columbus: Ohio State University Congressional Papers)
JJFJP	John James Flynt, Jr., Papers (Athens, Ga.: Richard B. Russell Library for Political Research and Studies)

JKJP	Jacob K. Javits Papers (Stony Brook, N.Y.: Stony Brook University Special Collections and Archives)
JMUP	Jesse M. Unruh Papers (Sacramento: California State Archives)
JNCP	John N. Camp Papers (Norman, Okla.: Carl Albert Congressional Research and Studies Center)
JSCP	Joseph S. Clark Papers (Philadelphia: Pennsylvania Historical Society)
JTP	Joseph Tydings Papers (College Park: University of Maryland Special Collections)
JVBPP	James V. Bennett Personal Papers (Boston: John F. Kennedy Presidential Library)
JWTP	John William "Elmer" Thomas Papers (Norman, Okla.: Carl Albert Congressional Research and Studies Center)
LACCMV1	Los Angeles City Council Minutes 1940–1944, vol. 1 (Los Angeles: City of Los Angeles Office of the City Clerk)
LBJPP	Lyndon B. Johnson Presidential Papers (Austin, Tex.: Lyndon B. Johnson Presidential Library)
LBP	Lloyd Bentsen Papers (Austin, Tex.: Briscoe Center of American History)
LFFP	La Follette Family Papers (Washington, D.C.: Library of Congress Manuscripts Division)
LHBP	Lyle H. Boren Papers (Norman, Okla.: Carl Albert Congressional Research and Studies Center)
LMGP	Lorraine M. Gensman Papers (Norman, Okla.: Carl Albert Congressional Research and Studies Center)
LMP	Lee Metcalf Papers (Helena: Montana Historical Society)
LPWP	Lowell P. Weicker Papers (Charlottesville: University of Virginia Special Collections)
MAEP	Merritt A. Edson Papers (Washington, D.C.: Library of Congress Manuscripts Division)
MFP	Mansfeld Family Papers (Tucson: Arizona Historical Society)
MMP	Mike Mansfield Papers (Missoula: Mansfield Library, University of Montana)
MRP	Milton Reckord Papers (College Park: University of Maryland Library)

NAKBA   National Association to Keep and Bear Arms
NRA   National Rifle Association
NYT   *New York Times*
OL   *Outdoor Life*
PAHP   Philip A. Hart Papers (Ann Arbor: University of Michigan
         Bentley Historical Library)
PB   *Point Blank*
PBP   Page Belcher Papers (Norman, Okla.: Carl Albert Congressio-
         nal Research and Studies Center)
PGN   *Pennsylvania Game News*
PHHP   Phillip H. Hoff Papers (Burlington: University of Vermont
         Silver Special Collections Library)
PJFP   Paul J. Fannin Papers (Tempe: Arizona State University)
RBAP   Robert B. Anderson Papers (Abilene, Kans.: Dwight D.
         Eisenhower Presidential Library)
RFSP   Robert F. Sikes Papers (Pensacola: University of West Florida
         Special Collections)
RHP   Roman Hruska Papers (Lincoln: Nebraska State Historical
         Society)
RLDP   Robert L. Doughton Papers (Chapel Hill: University of North
         Carolina Louis Round Wilson Special Collections Library)
RLSP   Robert L. Schultz Papers (Abilene, Kans.: Dwight D. Eisen-
         hower Presidential Library)
RNP   Richard Nixon Papers, Pre-Presidential Collection (Yorba
         Linda, Calif.: Richard Nixon Presidential Library)
RNPP   Richard Nixon Presidential Papers (Yorba Linda, Calif.:
         Richard Nixon Presidential Library and Museum)
RPSP   Raymond P. Shafer Papers (Harrisburg: Pennsylvania State
         Archives)
RRGCF   Ronald Reagan Gubernatorial Campaign Files, 1966–1975
         (Simi Valley, Calif.: Ronald Reagan Presidential Library)
RSKP   Robert S. Kerr Papers (Norman, Okla.: Carl Albert Congres-
         sional Research and Studies Center)
RSSP   Richard S. Schweiker Papers (State College: Pennsylvania
         State University Special Collections)
RTHP   Robert T. Hartman Papers (Ann Arbor, Mich.: Gerald R. Ford
         Presidential Library)

RWPP	Robert W. Packwood Papers (Salem, Ore.: Willamette University Archives and Special Collections)
S&WR	Smith & Wesson Records (Amherst, Mass.: University of Massachusetts Amherst Special Collections)
STP	Strom Thurmond Papers (Clemson, S.C.: Clemson University Special Collections)
TEWP	Thomas E. Wessel Papers (owned by author)
TJDP	Thomas J. Dodd Papers (Storrs: University of Connecticut Thomas J. Dodd Research Center)
TJSP	Thomas Jefferson Steed Papers (Norman, Okla.: Carl Albert Congressional Research and Studies Center)
TMP	Toby Morris Papers (Norman, Okla.: Carl Albert Congressional Research and Studies Center)
USRA	United States Revolver Association
WDFP	William D. Ford Papers (Ann Arbor: University of Michigan Bentley Historical Library)
WEBP	William E. Borah Papers (Washington, D.C.: Library of Congress Manuscripts Division)
WEGP	William E. Guckert Papers (Pittsburgh, Pa.: University of Pittsburgh Special Collections)
WEMP	Wayne Morse Papers (Eugene: University of Oregon Special Collections)
WETP	William E. Timmons Papers (Yorba Linda, Calif.: Richard Nixon Presidential Library)
WFBP	Wallace F. Bennett Papers, MSS20 (Salt Lake City, Utah: J. Willard Marriott Library Special Collections)
WLDPP	William L. Dunfey Personal Papers (Boston: John F. Kennedy Presidential Library)
WLPP	Winston L. Prouty Papers (Burlington: University of Vermont Special Collections)
WNMP	Warren Magnuson Papers (Seattle: University of Washington Special Collections)
WVP	Weston Vivian Papers (Ann Arbor: University of Michigan Bentley Historical Library)
WWWPP	W. Willard Wirtz Personal Papers (Boston: John F. Kennedy Presidential Library)

Introduction

1. C. B. Lister, "The Remedy," *Du Pont Magazine*, March 1924, 10, 11.
2. "All Together Fellows! Pull!," *AR*, February 1, 1926, 21.
3. See, e.g., Kim Parker et al., "America's Complex Relationship with Guns," Pew Research Center, June 22, 2017, https://www.pewresearch.org/social-trends/2017/06/22/americas-complex-relationship-with-guns/; Nate Silver, "Party Identity in a Gun Cabinet," *NYT*, December 18, 2012, https://fivethirtyeight.blogs.nytimes.com/2012/12/18/in-gun-ownership-statistics-partisan-divide-is-sharp/.
4. See "The Parties on the Eve of the 2016 Election: Two Coalitions, Moving Further Apart," Pew Research Center, September 13, 2016, https://www.pewresearch.org/politics/2016/09/13/the-parties-on-the-eve-of-the-2016-election-two-coalitions-moving-further-apart/; "A Deep Dive Into Party Affiliation: Sharp Differences by Race, Gender, Generation, Education," Pew Research Center, April 7, 2015, https://www.pewresearch.org/politics/2015/04/07/a-deep-dive-into-party-affiliation/; Frank Newport, "Democrats Racially Diverse; Republicans Mostly White," *Gallup Poll*, February 8, 2013, https://news.gallup.com/poll/160373/democrats-racially-diverse-republicans-mostly-white.aspx.
5. "Gun Policy Remains Divisive, but Several Proposals Still Draw Bipartisan Support," Pew Research Center, October 18, 2018, https://www.pewresearch.org/politics/2018/10/18/gun-policy-remains-divisive-but-several-proposals-still-draw-bipartisan-support/.
6. See, e.g., Nicole Chavez et al., "An All-Black Group Is Arming Itself and Demanding Change. They Are the NFAC," *CNN*, October 25, 2020, https://www.cnn.com/2020/10/25/us/nfac-black-armed-group/index.html; Benjamin Fearnow, "Armed Black Militia Challenges White Nationalists at Georgia's Stone Mountain Park," *Newsweek*, July 5, 2020, https://www.newsweek.com/armed-black-demonstrators-challenge-white-supremacist-militia-georgias-stone-mountain-park-1515494.
7. See "Public Views about Guns," Pew Research Center, June 22, 2017, https://www.pewresearch.org/social-trends/2017/06/22/views-on-gun-policy/.
8. See, e.g., Samuel C. Patterson and Keith R. Eakins, "Congress and Gun Control," in *The Changing Politics of Gun Control*, ed. John M. Bruce and Clyde Wilcox (New York: Rowman & Littlefield, 1998), 45–73.
9. For more on firearms localism, see Joseph Blocher, "Firearms Localism," *Yale Law Journal* 123 (2013): 82–146.
10. Patrick J. Charles, *Armed in America: A History of Gun Rights from Colonial Militias to Concealed Carry* (Amherst, N.Y.: Prometheus Books, 2018), 179–90.
11. See "The Effects of Revolver Legislation Upon Hardware Dealers," *American Artisan and Hardware Record*, May 25, 1912, 30; "The US Revolver Association to Take Hand in Law Making," *Miami (Fla.) Herald*, March 20, 1912, 9.
12. See *Handbook of the National Conference of Commissioners on Uniform State Laws and Proceedings of the Twenty-Fourth Annual Meeting* (Philadelphia: n.p., 1924), 714; "Anti-Pistol Legislation and Its Tendencies: A Bullet-Proof Revolver Law," *Hardware Reporter*, March 21, 1913, 59.

13. This compromise developed in the mid- to late nineteenth century, and subsequently "may issue" armed carriage laws expanded across the United States. See Charles, *Armed in America*, 158–61.

14. See, e.g., H. C. Ridgely, "Why Not Carry Firearms?," *OL*, December 1926, 464, 465; "Where the Sullivan Law Fails," *Binghamton (N.Y.) Press and Sun-Bulletin*, January 8, 1925, 6; "A Congressional Firearms Inquiry," *AR*, March 15, 1924, 11; "The Talk of the Day," *New-York Tribune*, July 29, 1912, 6.

15. See, e.g., NRA, *1963 Operating Report* (Washington, D.C., 1964), 8.

16. See, e.g., Remarks of Harold W. Glassen, president National Rifle Association of America, Before the Annual Meeting of the National Society of State Legislatures, Chicago, Illinois, July 27, 1967, HWGP, box 1; "Existing Federal Gun Controls," *AR*, April 1966, 16; NRA, *Basic Facts of Firearms Control* (Washington, D.C.: 1965); J. Basil, Jr., and Daniel J. Mountin, "Firearms Legislation and the Gun Owner," *AR*, July 1964, 30–31; Judge Bartlett Rummel, "To Have and Bear Arms," *AR*, June 1964, 41; "Basic Facts of Firearms Control," *AR*, February 1964, 14; NRA, *The Pro and Con of Firearms Legislation* (Washington, D.C., 1940), 4; *To Regulate Commerce of Firearms: Hearing Before the Committee on Commerce United States Senate* (Washington, D.C.: Government Printing Office, 1935), 84–104 (testimony of NRA president Karl T. Frederick).

17. See, e.g., Roman L. Hruska, press release, [undated 1967], RHP, box 39, folder 98; letter from Wallace F. Bennett to Sterling R. Bossard, October 5, 1965, WFBP, MSS 20, box 316, folder 4, Firearms 1965–1966; "Know Your Lawmakers," *GM*, December 1964, 4 (California senator Thomas H. Kuchel). See also statement of Paul J. Fannin before the Senate Subcommittee on Juvenile Delinquency, May 24, 1965, PJFP, box 27, folder 14, Firearms Legislation 1965.

18. See Richard M. Nixon, *Disarming the Criminal Class* (July 9, 1968), HHHP, 1968 Presidential Campaign Files, John G. Stewart Research Files, box 1, folder Gun Control; Statement of Richard M. Nixon, June 17, 1968, RMPP, White House Central Files, box 26, Staff Member Office Files, folder Martin Anderson, Gun Control.

19. Charles, *Armed in America*, 296–305; Barry M. Goldwater, speech before the 100th Anniversary Banquet of the National Rifle Association, April 7, 1971, BMGP, series 6, box 58, folder 36, Remarks Before 100th Anniversary Banquet of the NRA; Harlon B. Carter, "Religion and the Armed Citizen," *G&A*, March 1971, 32–33, 68.

20. See, e.g., Wayne LaPierre, "America's First Freedom," *AR*, December 1997, 8; "Freedom!," *Armed Citizen News*, January 1971, 1.

1. "A Shot Sure to Be Heard Around Congress"

1. *Statistics of the Presidential and Congressional Election of November 5, 1968* (Washington, D.C.: U.S. Government Printing Office, 1969), 38–40.

2. George R. Clark, "Joseph Sill Clark," *Proceedings of the American Philosophical Society* 135, no. 1 (1991): 92, 95–96.

3. "Clark-Schweiker Contest One of the Most Important," *Clearfield (Pa.) Progress*, November 5, 1968, 2; "Clark Deserving of Third Term," *Simpson's Leader-Times*

(Kittanning, Pa.), October 31, 1968, 24; James Helbert, "Clark v. Schweiker: A Cliff-Hanger," *Pittsburgh Press*, October 22, 1968, 22.

4. Lee Linder, "Cliffhanger Predicted in Clark-Schweiker Race," *Clearfield (Pa.) Progress*, October 15, 1968, 5.

5. "Clark and Schweiker Tangle in TV Debate," *Uniontown (Pa.) Evening Standard*, July 3, 1968, 17; Ingrid Jewell, "Dent Would Have Been Tougher He Says: Clark's Win Pleases Schweiker," *Pittsburgh Post-Gazette*, April 25, 1968, 4.

6. Del Kerr, "Outdoors in Potter County," *Potter (Pa.) Enterprise*, November 13, 1968, 6.

7. Jerry Quincy, "Gun Power," *Philadelphia Inquirer*, March 29, 1969, 16.

8. The issue of firearms controls was raised during the reelection campaigns of Montana representative James F. Battin and New Jersey senator Clifford P. Casein 1966. The issue, however, was not very prevalent given that both Battin and Case had already voiced opposition to restrictive controls. For supporting documentation, see "Sportsmen Are Opposed to Wilentz Over Gun Law," *Central New Jersey Home News* (New Brunswick), October 25, 1966, 30; "Sportsmen Recommend Vote Against Wilentz," *Vineland (N.J.) Daily Journal*, October 26, 1966, 5; "Montana Lawmakers Reply on Firearms Legislation," *Helena (Mont.) Independent-Record*, September 2, 1966, 4 (includes letter by Montana representative James F. Battin); "Melcher Offers Alternative to Legislation Against Guns," *Great Falls (Mont.) Tribune*, August 29, 1966, 12.

9. See Patrick J. Charles, *Armed in America: A History of Gun Rights from Colonial Militias to Concealed Carry* (Amherst, N.Y.: Prometheus Books, 2018), 296.

10. Charles, 194–230.

11. See, e.g., Hal H. Harrison, "Life Afield: Sportsmen Do Not Want Free Licenses," *Pittsburgh Post-Gazette*, March 31, 1959, 18; Johnny Mock, "All Outdoors," *Pittsburgh Press*, January 20, 1952, 42; "Pending Legislation Affecting Sportsmen Called 'Screwball,'" *Potter (Pa.) Enterprise*, March 22, 1951, 8; Johnny Mock, "All Outdoors: Firearms Legislation to Require Registration of Firearms Sought," *Pittsburgh Press*, December 22, 1946, 21; Michael Seaman, "Sportsmen Oppose Firearms Bill," *Harrisburg (Pa.) Telegraph*, March 15, 1941, 17; "Sportsmen Oppose Attempt to Hamper Firearms Use," *Connellsville (Pa.) Daily Courier*, February 17, 1941, 7; "Listing of Arms Is Opposed by State Sportsmen," *Harrisburg (Pa.) Evening News*, February 13, 1941, 5; John G. Mock, "Firearms Measure Same Old Tune," *Pittsburgh Press*, January 19, 1941, sec. 3, p. 10; Boynton and Coal Run and Gun Club of Boynton, "Sportsmen Issue Warning!," *Meyersdale (Pa.) Republic*, May 4, 1939, 8; John G. Mock, "Solution for 'Gun-Toting' Is Law Enforcement," *Pittsburgh Press*, April 26, 1936, S2.

12. Jim Varner, "Sportsmen, Help Crush Anti-Firearms Propaganda," PGN, July 1963, 61, 64.

13. See Charles, *Armed in America*, 195, 197, 231–40, 245–46.

14. For examples of sportsmen, hunters, and gun owners writing in opposition to Philadelphia's law, see Jerry Kenney, "Fishing and Hunting," *New York Daily News*, April 26, 1965, C27; Thomas Wolfgang, "Gun Laws Seen as Threat to Our National Security," *Pottsville (Pa.) Republican and Herald*, March 27, 1965, 8; Thomas Wolfgang,

"Gordon Man Presents Views on Controversial Gun Laws," *Pottsville Republican and Herald*, March 26, 1965, 14.

15. Television interview transcript, June 1965, RPSP, Press Room File 1963–71, carton 4, folder 12, Gun Control Law 1965–68.

16. Memorandum from Robert McCormick to Raymond P. Shafer, September 22, 1965, RPSP, Press Room File 1963–71, carton 4, folder 12, Gun Control Law 1965–68.

17. "Staisey Expects Greatest Year in Conservation," *Pittsburgh Press*, October 16, 1966, sec. 1, p. 20; "Sportsmen Split Ticket: Shafer-Staisey," *Pittsburgh Press*, October 2, 1966, sec. 2, p. 5.

18. Unsigned memorandum to Robert McCormick, [March] 1967, RPSP, Press Room File 1963–71, carton 4, folder 12, Gun Control Law 1965–68.

19. "Shafer Urges Strong Support for $500 Million Bond Issue," *Oil City (Pa.) Derrick*, March 20, 1967, 9.

20. "Shafer Opposes Gun Restrictions, Sportsmen Told," *Franklin (Pa.) News-Herald*, March 22, 1967, 28.

21. "Gun Law Discussed at Stoystown Meeting," *Somerset (Pa.) Daily American*, April 7, 167, 8.

22. "Shafer Against Firearms' Ban on Sportsmen," *Pottsville (Pa.) Republican and Herald*, March 22, 1967, 1.

23. See, e.g., letter from Alan S. Krug, Pennsylvania Rifle and Pistol Club legislative director, to Raymond P. Shafer, March 2, 1967, RPSP, Subject Files 1964–71, carton 36, folder 3, Firearms Control.

24. Patrick Boyle, "Shafer Seeks Tough State Gun Law," *Pittsburgh Press*, March 12, 1967, sec. 1, p. 28; Saul Kohler, "Shafer Backing Stronger Law to Control Guns," *Philadelphia Inquirer*, March 12, 1967, sec. 2, p. 1.

25. Letter from Leonard A. Green, Pennsylvania Federal of Sportsmen's Clubs vice president, to Raymond P. Shafer, March 13, 1967, RPSP, Subject Files 1964–71, carton 36, folder 3, Firearms Control.

26. Telegram from Leonard A. Green, Pennsylvania Federal of Sportsmen's Clubs vice president, to Raymond P. Shafer, March 12, 1967, RPSP, Subject Files 1964–71, carton 36, folder 3, Firearms Control.

27. Letter from Alan S. Krug, Pennsylvania Rifle and Pistol Club legislative director, to William C. Sennett, March 13, 1967, RPSP, Subject Files 1964–71, carton 36, folder 3, Firearms Control; letter from James N. Spicer, Pennsylvania Rifle and Pistol Club legislative director, to William C. Sennett, March 14, 1967, RPSP, Subject Files 1964–71, carton 36, folder 3, Firearms Control.

28. Letter from Krug to Sennett, March 13, 1967.

29. Copies of some of the letters can be found in RPSP, Subject Files 1964–71, carton 36, folder 1, Firearms Control.

30. "Shafer Against Firearms' Ban on Sportsmen," *Shenandoah (Pa.) Evening Herald*, March 22, 1967, 1.

31. "Gov. Shafer Denies News Reports; Reaffirms Support for Sportsmen," *GW*, April 7, 1967, 1; letter from Neal Knox, editor of *Gun Week*, to Robert McCormick, March 24,

1967, RPSP, Press Room File 1963–71, carton 4, folder 12, Gun Law 1965–68; letter from L. James Bashline, assistant managing editor of *Field and Stream*, to Robert McCormick, March 30, 1967, RPSP, carton 4, folder 12, Gun Law 1965–68.

32. Shafer's form letter responses on gun control essentially mirrored the position of gun rights organizations. See, e.g., letter from Raymond P. Shafer to Gerald J. Porter, January 17, 1968, RPSP, Subject Files 1964–71, carton 36, folder 3, Firearms Control; letter from Raymond P. Shafer to Glenn O. Baker, July 19, 1967, RPSP, Subject Files 1964–71, carton 36, folder 1, Firearms Control.

33. Interoffice Note to Robert McCormick, [May] 1967, RPSP, Press Room File 1963–71, carton 4, folder 12, Gun Control Law 1965–68; letter from George McCann, Pennsylvania Federation of Sportsmen's Clubs, to Raymond P. Shafer, May 18, 1967, RPSP, Subject Files 1964–71, carton 36, folder 3, Firearms Control.

34. In the wake of Martin Luther King, Jr.'s assassination, Democratic Pennsylvania state representative Herbert Fineman introduced firearms legislation. See, e.g., Bill Fidati, "Fineman to Introduce New Gun Control Bill," *Philadelphia Daily News*, April 16, 1968, 5; Mason Denison, "Gun Control," *Somerset (Pa.) Daily American*, April 16, 1968, 4; "New Gun Control Bill 'Goes Out of the Way' to Help Owners," *Lock Haven (Pa.) Express*, April 15, 1968, 4. The Pennsylvania Rifle and Pistol Association denounced Fineman's legislation as "28 pages of the worst legislative mess ever produced in this Commonwealth" and the "first step toward a police state." See James N. Spicer, "On the Legislative Scene," *Pennsylvania Rifle and Pistol Association Newsletter*, Spring 1968.

35. Herbert Fineman, "State House Leader Explains Proposed Gun-Control Bill," *Pittsburgh Press*, May 24, 1968, 26; "Tougher Road Laws Urged in Shafer's 4th Message," *Allentown (Pa.) Morning Call*, May 1, 1968, 2; letter from James R. Doran, editor of the *Patriot Evening News*, to Raymond P. Shafer, September 18, 1967, RPSP, Press Room File 1963–71, carton 4, folder 12, Gun Law 1965–68.

36. William E. Deibler, "Gun Law Not Answer—Shafer," *Pittsburgh Post-Gazette*, June 6, 1968, 6; "Shooting of Bobby Kennedy an 'Unconscionable Tragedy,'" *Hazelton (Pa.) Standard-Speaker*, June 6, 1968, 2; "State Leaders Shocked, Saddened by Shooting," *Latrobe (Pa.) Bulletin*, June 5, 1968, 27. See also "The Right Approach," *PGN*, April 1968, 43. Shafer's view was undoubtedly in accordance with the gun rights community. See, e.g., Bob Bell, "Do We Need 35,000,001," *PGN*, April 1968, 1.

37. Shafer would later claim that he never changed his position. Rather, he "advanced" his existing position. See "Gov. Shafer Denies Gun Curb Reversal," *Pittsburgh Press*, July 1, 1968, 7; "Shafer Reports Mail Favors Gun Controls," *Pottsville (Pa.) Republican and Herald*, July 1, 1968, 1; "Shafer Denies Reversing Gun Control Stand," *Philadelphia Daily News*, July 1, 1968, 6.

38. "County Legislators Split on New Gun Control Law," *York (Pa.) Gazette and Daily*, June 14, 1968, 1, 43. At this press conference, Shafer rebuked the Pennsylvania Game Commission's recommendation. See memorandum from Glenn L. Bowers, executive director Pennsylvania Game Commission, to William C. Sennett, June 11, 1968, RPSP, Press Room File 1963–71, carton 4, folder 12, Gun Law 1965–68.

39. Rowland Evans and Robert Novak, "Dirksen as Platform Chief Riles Governors," *Moline (Ill.) Dispatch*, June 24, 1968, 4; "GOP Governors Urge Gun Curbs," *San Bernardino County (Calif.) Sun*, June 16, 1968, 3; "GOP Governors May Differ on Gun Control in Platform," *Shreveport (La.) Times*, June 15, 1968, 4A; "Governors Shy Off Guns," *Pittsburgh Post-Gazette*, June 15, 1968, 5; Walter R. Mears, "Rocky Says He'll Overtake Nixon," *Moline Dispatch*, June 15, 1968, 18; "Weapon Issue Promises GOP Fight," *Pottstown (Pa.) Mercury*, June 15, 1968, 2; "Gun Control Laws Topic of Governors," *Hazleton (Pa.) Standard-Speaker*, June 15, 1968, 2. The Republican Party ultimately included gun control in the "crime" section of their plank in 1968. See "Excerpts from Text of Republican Party Platform as Approved at Miami Convention," *Baltimore (Md.) Sun*, August 5, 1968, A4.

40. Rowland Evans and Robert Novak, "Dirksen as Platform Chief Riles Governors," *Moline (Ill.) Dispatch*, June 24, 1968, 4. Pressure was also brought to bear by the National Association of Attorneys General, which adopted a resolution urging the state to enact strict gun controls. See "Attorney General Urges State Gun Control Laws," *Fort Lauderdale (Fla.) News*, June 11, 1968, 12A.

41. Thomas L. Kimball, "Firearms and Control Legislation," June 11, 1968, WEGP, box 6, folder 11.

42. See, e.g., letter from John R. Charles to Raymond P. Shafer, June 27, 1968, RPSP, Subject Files 1964–71, carton 36, folder 1, Firearms Control; memorandum from Glenn L. Bowers to Robert McCormick, "Gun Control Legislation," June 23, 1968, RPSP, Press Room File 1963–71, carton 4, folder 12, Gun Law 1965–68. The letters Shafer received were on par with those letters received by State Representative Herbert Fineman after having introduced firearms legislation a year earlier. See William Ecenbarger, "Angry Mail Pours Down on Gun Control Author," *Simpson's Leader-Times* (Kittanning, Pa.), May 18, 1968, 6 (detailing letters sent to Fineman accusing him of being a Nazi and Communist).

43. See, e.g., "Gun Control Opponents 'Pot Shot' Gov. Shafer," *New Castle (Pa.) News*, June 27, 1968, 2; "Sportsmen Leader Calls Gun Control Proposal Ridiculous," *Kane (Pa.) Republican*, June 26, 1968, 1; "Spokesman for State Sportsmen Raps Bill," *Wilkes-Barre (Pa.) Times Leader*, June 25, 1968, 20.

44. Memorandum from William C. Sennett to Hugh E. Flaherty, secretary of legislation and public affairs, June 27, 1968, RPSP, Subject Files 1964–71, carton 36, folder 2, Firearms Control. See also memorandum from Glenn L. Bowers, Pennsylvania Game Commission executive director, to Raymond P. Shafer, July 3, 1968, RPSP, Press Room File 1963–71, carton 4, folder 12, Gun Law 1965–68. By 1968 it had become common practice for sporting, hunting, and shooting organizations to draft model firearms legislation. See Pennsylvania Rifle and Pistol Association, P.R.&P.A. Bill No. 66-3, "Firearms Ownership, Safety and Lawful Transport Bill," January 1, 1967, WEGP, box 6, folder 10; Pennsylvania Rifle and Pistol Association, P.R.&P.A. Bill No. 66-4, "An Act to Consolidate, Amend and Revise the Penal Laws of the Commonwealth," September 1966, WEGP, box 6, folder 10; Pennsylvania Rifle and Pistol Association, P.R.&P.A. Bill No. 66-1, "An Act Regulating the Issuance of

Hunting Licenses to Persons Under the Age of 16 Years and Providing for the Giving of Instruction in the Safe Handling and Use of Firearms and Bow and Arrow to Such Persons; and Fixing Effective Date," August 1966, WEGP, box 6, folder 10; Pennsylvania Rifle and Pistol Association, P.R.&P.A. Bill No. 66-2, "An Act to Consolidate, Amend and Revise the Penal Laws of the Commonwealth," August 1966, WEGP, box 6, folder 10. For some background as to why sporting, hunting, and shooting organizations, particularly in Pennsylvania, drafted such legislation, see Alan S. Krug, keynote address before the 1966 Convention of the Pennsylvania Sportsmen's Clubs, "Firearms Legislation: A Perspective," March 25, 1966, WEGP, box 6, folder 10; Franklin L. Orth, address before the Northeast Fish and Wildlife Conference, "The Sportsman and the Law," January 18, 1965, WEGP, box 6, folder 10.

45. See, e.g., letter from Hugh Flaherty, secretary of legislation and public affairs, to James N. Spicer, Pennsylvania Rifle and Pistol Association legislative chairman, July 12, 1968, RPSP, Subject Files 1964–71, carton 36, folder 3, Firearms Control; press release, Commonwealth of Pennsylvania Governor's Office, June 21, 1968, RPSP, Subject Files 1964–71, carton 36, folder 1, Firearms Control.

46. "Gun Register Law Sought for State," *Pittsburgh Press*, July 30, 1967, sec. 1, p. 11.

47. Press release, Commonwealth of Pennsylvania Governor's Office, July 13, 1968, RPSP, Subject Files 1964–71, carton 36, folder 1, Firearms Control.

48. "Gun Bill Opponents Slate Rally," *Latrobe (Pa.) Bulletin*, July 16, 1968, 5; "Group at Rally Protests Gun Control Laws," *Canonsburg (Pa.) Daily Notes*, July 3, 1968, 10; "Rally Protests Gun Controls," *Franklin (Pa.) News-Herald*, July 3, 1968.

49. "900 Persons Attend Gun Control Rally," *Franklin (Pa.) News-Herald*, July 17, 1968, 14.

50. "3,500 Protest Gun Control at Johnstown," *Monongahela (Pa.) Daily Republican*, July 18, 1968, 2.

51. "Battle Lines Drawn on Congress Fight Over Gun Control," *Kane (Pa.) Republican*, July 18, 1968, 1 (emphasis added); "NRA Spokesman Says Battle Lines Drawn on Gun Control," *Clearfield (Pa.) Progress*, July 18, 1968, 3 (emphasis added).

52. See, e.g., "Opposition Increases in Final Tabulation of Gun Control Bill," *Potter (Pa.) Enterprise*, July 24, 1968, 1.

53. See, e.g., "House Defeats Stiffer Gun Bill," *Hazleton (Pa.) Standard-Speaker*, July 17, 1968, 1.

54. "Senate Oks Stiffer Gun Crime Bill," *Pittsburgh Post-Gazette*, July 18, 1968, 7.

55. Press release, Commonwealth of Pennsylvania Governor's Office, July 30, 1968, RPSP, Subject Files 1964–71, carton 36, folder 1, Firearms Control; "Assembly Approves Firearms Measure Dealing with Crimes," *Franklin (Pa.) News-Herald*, July 20, 1968, 3; "6 L.V. Legislators Reverse Stand on Gun-Control Bill," *Allentown (Pa.) Morning Call*, July 20, 1968, 16; "On Gun Bill, L.V. Legislators Cast Identical Votes," *Allentown Morning Call*, July 18, 1968, 7.

56. "Gun Controls Are Still Needed," *Philadelphia Inquirer*, July 20, 1968, editorial section, p. 1; "Veto Threatened on Bill Exempting Teachers Struck from Pay Penalty," *York (Pa.) Gazette and Daily*, July 18, 1968, 36.

57. Saul Kohler, "Shafer Signs Bills to Increase Gun Penalties," *Philadelphia Inquirer*, July 31, 1968, 1.

58. In the case of State Representative Herbert Fineman, the warnings escalated to death threats. See, e.g., Saul Kohler, "Police Guard Fineman After Phone Threats Over Gun Control Bill," *Philadelphia Inquirer*, July 22, 1968, 1; "Fineman's House Under Guard," *Pittsburgh Post-Gazette*, July 22, 1968, 1.

59. Letter from Roger M. Latham, outdoor editor of *Pittsburgh Press*, to Raymond P. Shafer, July 8, 1968, RPSP, Subject Files 1964–71, carton 36, folder 2, Firearms Control.

60. Letter from Raymond P. Shafer to Roger M. Latham, outdoor editor of *Pittsburgh Press*, July 17, 1968, RPSP, Subject Files 1964–71, carton 36, folder 2, Firearms Control.

61. "Pennsylvania Sportsmen to Oppose Clark," *GW*, February 23, 1968, 2; "Sportsmen of State Oppose Clark," *Pittsburgh Press*, January 30, 1968, 39; "State Sportsmen Oppose Sen. Clark," *Hazleton (Pa.) Standard-Speaker*, January 30, 1968, 5; "Federation Hits Clark," *Pittsburgh Post-Gazette*, January 30, 1968, 15.

62. Memorandum from Bernard E. Norwitch to Senator Joseph S. Clark, January 9, 1968, JSCP, box 114, folder Schweiker File.

63. Memorandum from Norwitch to Clark, January 9, 1968.

64. Thomas P. Snyder, "Enmity of Various Groups Cited: Shapp Predicts 'Uphill Fight' for Sen. Clark," *Pittsburgh Post-Gazette*, February 26, 1968, 19; Thomas P. Snyder, "Dent Making Rounds: Clark Facing Rough Primary," *Pittsburgh Post-Gazette*, February 23, 1968, 5.

65. See, e.g., "Clark's Stand on Firearms Irks Sportsmen," *Allentown (Pa.) Morning Call*, February 29, 1968, 26.

66. James N. Spicer, "The Political Scene and How It Affects Your," *Pennsylvania Rifle and Pistol Association Newsletter*, Winter 1968; "Sportsmen Oppose Clark's Firearms Bill," *Stroudsburg (Pa.) Pocono Record* (, April 17, 1968, 4.

67. Robert A. Dobkin, "Dent Promises Strong Fight Against Clark," *Hazleton (Pa.) Standard-Speaker*, February 14, 1968, 12. See also Robert A. Dobkin, "Congressman Filed as Clark Opponent in Dems' Primary," *Kane (Pa.) Republican*, February 14, 1968, 1.

68. See, e.g., "Democrats . . . Nominate John H. Dent for U.S. Senate," *McConnellsburg (Pa.) Fulton Democrat*, April 18, 1968, 2.

69. "Democrats. . . ."

70. Memorandum to Harry Schwartz, February 27, 1968, JSCP, box 114, folder Schweiker File.

71. Letter from Edward T. Balderston, Pennsylvania Federation of Sportsmen's Clubs president, to Joseph S. Clark, March 28, 1968, JSCP, box 173, folder Gun Control File.

72. "Sportsmen Get Letter: Sen. Clark Explains President's Gun Bill," *Pittsburgh Post-Gazette*, March 22, 1968, 22.

73. After receiving a letter from an NRA member supporting his position on firearms controls, Clark believed most NRA members felt the same way and it was the NRA's proliferation of false and misleading propaganda that was the

problem. See "Sen. Clark Claims NRA Members Don't Agree with Leaders' Politics," *GW*, April 12, 1968, 5.

74. Press Release from Senator Joseph S. Clark, March 22, 1968, JSCP, box 173, folder Gun Control File.

75. "Sportsmen Get Letter: Sen. Clark Explains President's Gun Bill," *Pittsburgh Post-Gazette*, March 22, 1968, 22.

76. "Your Senators Report" transcript, July 17, 1967, RPSP, Press Room File 1963–71, carton 4, folder 12, Gun Law 1965–68. See also "Dent Making Rounds: Clark Facing Rough Primary," *Pittsburgh Post-Gazette*, February 23, 1968, 5; "Sen. Clark Proposes National Gun Curbs," *Philadelphia Inquirer*, July 11, 1967, 5.

77. Press release from Senator Joseph S. Clark, March 22, 1968, JSCP, box 173, folder Gun Control File.

78. Prepared statement to the editors of *Pennsylvania's Outdoor People*, March 24, 1968, JSCP, box 271, folder S.1. Clark also ran several radio advertisements across Pennsylvania outlining his moderate gun control position. See Jerome S. Cahill, "Clark's Support of Gun Curbs Threatens His Political Future," *Philadelphia Inquirer*, April 15, 1968, 17.

79. For sources supporting the content within this paragraph, see "Sen. Clark Seeks Gun Control Law," *Hazleton (Pa.) Standard-Speaker*, April 6, 1968, p. 2; "Emotionalism on Gun Controls," *Pittsburgh Post-Gazette*, April 2, 1968, 10; Steve Szalewicz, "Local Sportsmen Oppose Oil Drilling In Lake Erie," *Franklin (Pa.) News-Herald*, March 26, 1968, 12; "Parley Bugged, Sportsmen Say," *Pittsburgh Press*, March 24, 1968, 2; speech of John Dent before the Pennsylvania Federation of Sportsmen's Clubs, March 22, 1968, JSCP, box 173, folder Gun Control File; speech of Richard S. Schweiker before the Pennsylvania Federation of Sportsmen's Clubs, March 22, 1968, JSCP, box 173, folder Gun Control File; "Rizzo Supports Johnson Bill on Gun Control," *Philadelphia Inquirer*, March 22, 1968, 8.

80. "Clark Charges 'Gun-Sellers' Try to Beat Him," *Philadelphia Inquirer*, April 18, 1968, 5.

81. Fred Jones, "Hunters Rip Clark at Polls," *Pittsburgh Press*, April 29, 1968, 18.

82. The final primary election tally was 442,135 votes for Clark and 383,946 votes for Dent. Despite the closer than expected primary race, Clark won fifty-four out of the sixty-seven Pennsylvania counties. For the full county-by-county breakdown of votes, see "Clark-Dent Senate Vote," *Philadelphia Inquirer*, April 25, 1968, 6.

83. Press release from Senator Joseph S. Clark, undated 1968, JSCP, box 174, folder Gun Control File.

84. Ingrid Jewell, "Clark Win Pleases Schweiker," *Pittsburgh Post-Gazette*, April 25, 1968, 4.

85. "People Back Gun Control, Clark Says," *Pittsburgh Press*, May 1, 1968, 5; press release from Senator Joseph S. Clark, May 1, 1968, JSCP, box 271, folder News Releases.

86. Memorandum to AFS, May 14, 1968, JSCP, box 100, folder Schweiker File 1968. This plan was initially devised in February 1968 but was not actually executed until

May. See memorandum from Harry Schwartz to MJB, February 13, 1968, JSCP, box 114, folder Schweiker File.

87. Jay Sharbutt, "Clark Swaps Barbs with Schweiker," *Hazleton (Pa.) Standard-Speaker*, May 2, 1968, 22.

88. Letter from Richard S. Schweiker to Mrs. Del DiFeo, May 17, 1968, JSCP, box 173, folder Gun Control File; letter from Richard S. Schweiker to S. Wilkins, May 17, 1968, JSCP, box 173, folder Gun Control File (same).

89. News release from Congressman Dick Schweiker, June 4, 1968, JSCP, box 114, folder Schweiker File.

90. It is worth noting that Clark also briefly called out Schweiker for flip-flopping on gun control in the first debate. See Joseph H. Miller, "Clark-Schweiker Friendly Debate Winds Up in a Draw," *Philadelphia Inquirer*, June 22, 1968, 5; "Clark, Schweiker Swap 'Flip-Flop' Charges," *Delaware County Daily Times* (Chester, Pa.), June 22, 1968, 2; Ted Mellin, "Clark, Schweiker Argue—On Means, Not Ends," *Allentown (Pa.) Morning Call*, June 22, 1968, 5, 9.

91. James Helbert, "Schweiker Asks Ballot for 18s, Gun Controls," *Pittsburgh Press*, June 29, 1968, 8; "Schweiker Backs Tough Gun Bill," *Hazleton (Pa.) Standard-Speaker*, June 21, 1968, 6; Jerome S. Cahill, "Sustained Support for Gun Controls," *Philadelphia Inquirer*, June 13, 1968, 26.

92. "Clark, Schweiker to Debate on Radio, TV," *Pittsburgh Press*, June 15, 1968, 3.

93. Transcript of debate between Richard S. Schweiker and Senator Joseph Clark, July 2, 1968, RSSP, box 34, folder 34, 11.

94. Transcript, July 2, 1968, 11–12. For some newspaper reports on this debate, see "Schweiker, Clark Exchange TV Barbs," *Philadelphia Inquirer*, July 3, 1968, 12; "Clark-Schweiker Debates Opened," *Pittsburgh Post-Gazette*, July 3, 1968, 2; "Clark Thinks He Won First Debate with Schweiker," *Sayre (Pa.) Evening Times*, July 3, 1968, 5; Lee Linder, "Clark Claims Victory in First Debate with Schweiker," *Indiana (Pa.) Gazette*, July 3, 1968, 3.

95. It appears Clark first flip-flopped on firearms registration nearly a month earlier. See Douglas Smith, "Clark Joins Dodd Fight on Gun Bill," *Pittsburgh Press*, June 12, 1968, 44.

96. Gerald L. Lichty, "Firearms Registration Is Communist Program," *Meyersdale (Pa.) Republic*, June 27, 1968, 4.

97. Citizens Opposed to Further Firearms Legislation, "Necessity Is the Plea for Every Infringement of Human Liberties . . . It Is the Argument of Tyrants," *Stroudsburg (Pa.) Pocono Record*, July 5, 1968, 19.

98. Venango County Federation of Sportsmen's Clubs, "Quotations from People Whose Names You Will Remember," *Franklin (Pa.) News-Herald*, August 3, 1968, 8.

99. Citizens Committee for Sane Gun Legislation, "Has Registration Stopped This Killing?," *Clearfield (Pa.) Progress*, July 27, 1968, 6.

100. See Joseph S. Clark, "Eighteen Points for Democrats: A Proposal for the Democratic Platform," August 13, 1968, JSCP, box 116, folder News Releases; transcript,

"Television Spot for Senator Clark on Gun Control," undated, JSCP, box 98, folder Joseph S. Clark Campaign Literature; Joseph S. Clark, "Clark Defends Position on Guns," *Pittsburgh Post-Gazette*, August 3, 1968, 6; Fran Fry, Jr., "Sen. Clark Visits Franklin, Discusses Gun-Bill, War," *Franklin (Pa.) News-Herald*, July 18, 1968, 2; Frank M. Matthews, "Clark to Stay Neutral in Pick for President," *Pittsburgh Post-Gazette*, July 13, 1968, 4; "Clark 'Scared' in Reelection Race," *Franklin News-Herald*, July 13, 1968, 2; "Stiffer Gun Law Seen by Scott," *Pittsburgh Post-Gazette*, July 5, 1968, 5.

101. "Sportsmen Say TV, Movies Lead to Gun Violence," *Shamokin (Pa.) News-Dispatch*, July 18, 1968, 13.

102. Black Forest Conservation Association, "Think-Act," *Coudersport (Pa.) Potter Enterprise*, September 25, 1968, 3.

103. See letter from Michael J. Byrne, Joseph S. Clark executive assistant, to Edward F. Cooke, September 17, 1968, JSCP, box 98, folder Joseph S. Clark Campaign Literature; "Scott, Clark Back Gun-Control Bill," *Pittsburgh Press*, September 17, 1968, 28; Talking Points, "Questions and Answers on Senator Clark's Views on Gun Control," September 12, 1968, JSCP, box 98, folder Joseph S. Clark Campaign Literature; memorandum from Edward Cooke to Fred Frank, "Senator Clark's Gun Control Position," September 9, 1968, JSCP, box 98, folder Joseph S. Clark Campaign Literature.

104. See "Clark Says Opponent Zig-Zags," *Franklin (Pa.) News-Herald*, September 17, 1968, 2; James Helbert, "Clark Makes Pitch to Democrats Here," *Pittsburgh Press*, September 13, 1968, 14; "Clark Fires Barrels at Schweiker," *Pittsburgh Post-Gazette*, September 13, 1968, 7; "Clark Blasts Richard Nixon, Schweiker," *Kane (Pa.) Republican*, September 13, 1968, 6.

105. "Statement of Senator Joseph S. Clark on the Senate Campaign," [September 13, 1968,] JSCP, box 116, folder News Releases.

106. See, e.g., press release from Richard S. Schweiker, September 9, 1968, JSCP, box 100, folder Schweiker File; "Your Next Senator Speaks on Gun Control," *Pennsylvania Rifle and Pistol Association Newsletter*, fall 1968, 11.

107. "Schweiker Raps Clark," *Pittsburgh Post-Gazette*, September 14, 1968, 6.

108. Memorandum from Michael J. Byrne to Harry K. Schwartz, "Re: Anti-Clark Ad in 'Outdoor People,'" October 1, 1968, JSCP, box 99, folder Election—Public Relations 1968.

109. See "Clark Defends Gun Controls," *Pittsburgh Press*, October 24, 1968, 18; Remarks of "Clark Asks Schweiker for 'Gun' Stand," *Hanover (Pa.) Evening Sun*, October 22, 1968, 18; "Clarify Stand on Gun Control, Clark Asks Foe," *Clearfield (Pa.) Progress*, October 22, 1968, 5; press release from Senator Joseph S. Clark before Pennsylvania Newspaper Publishers Association, October 23, 1968, JSCP, box 116, folder News Releases; Senator Joseph S. Clark, "Senator Clark Challenges Schweiker to Clarify His Gun Control Stand," October 21, 1968, JSCP, box 98, folder Campaign Releases 1968; "Keep Clark in the Senate," *Frankline (Pa.) News-Herald*, October 18, 1968, 4; Television Spots for Senator Clark on Gun Control, undated, JSCP, box 98, folder Campaign TV and Radio 1968. Here, Schweiker called out Clark for "deliberately

disguising his gun control record." See "Gun Control Record Disguised," *Indiana (Pa.) Gazette*, November 2, 1968, 20.

110. Black Forest Conservation Association, "Prevent Gun Registration!," undated, JSCP, box 173, folder Firearms; Outdoorsman for Schweiker of Venango County, "Prevent Gun Registration!," *Oil City (Pa.) Derrick*, November 2, 1968, 6; Outdoorsman for Schweiker of Venango County, "Prevent Gun Registration!," *Franklin (Pa.) News-Herald*, November 2, 1968, 16.

111. See "The Truth About the Gun Control Law," *Uniontown (Pa.) Morning Herald*, November 4, 1968, 23; "The Truth About the Gun Control Law," *Simpson's Leader-Times* (Kittanning, Pa.), November 2, 1968, 11; "The Truth About the Gun Control Law," *Clearfield (Pa.) Progress*, November 1, 1968, 14; "The Truth About the Gun Control Law," *Sayre (Pa.) Evening Times*, November 1, 1968, 15.

112. "Sportsmen," *Oil City (Pa.) Derrick*, November 4, 1968, 5.

113. "Both Clark, Schweiker Winners," *Indiana (Pa.) Gazette*, November 5, 1968, 5.

114. James Helbert, "Clark Lost Touch, Staisey Says," *Pittsburgh Press*, November 8, 1968, 34; Ingrid Jewell, "Maverick Ways Fatal in Clark's Third Try," *Pittsburgh Post-Gazette*, November 7, 1968, 12; "Clark Was Own Enemy—Foerster," *Pittsburgh Post-Gazette*, November 7, 1968, 5.

115. Letter from Waynard Stahl to Joseph S. Clark, November 7, 1968, JSCP, box 173, folder Firearms.

116. Letter from Richard Zawacki to Joseph S. Clark, November 8, 1968, JSCP, box 173, folder Firearms.

117. *Statistics of the Presidential and Congressional Election of November 5, 1968*, 38.

118. Transcript of debate between Richard S. Schweiker and Senator Joseph Clark, July 2, 1968, RSSP, box 34, folder 34.

119. Transcript of domestic affairs debate between Senator Joseph S. Clark and Congressman Richard S. Schweiker, October 20, 1968, RSSP, box 34, folder 34; transcript, third TV debate between Senator Joseph S. Clark and Congressman Richard S. Schweiker, held at WCAU-TV, Philadelphia, October 1, 1968, RSSP, box 34, folder 34; transcript, WTAE Television and Radio in Pittsburgh Presents the Second in a Series of Four Live Debates Between Senator Joseph S. Clark and Congressman Richard S. Schweiker, July 27, 1968, RSSP, box 34, folder 34.

120. See, e.g., "About Face," *Pennsylvania Rifle and Pistol Association Newsletter*, fall 1968, 10; "GOP Speaker Says Team Effort Needed for GOP Team Victory," *Warren (Pa.) Times-Mirror and Observer*, September 9, 1968, 3.

121. Mary Walton, "Once Again, Gun Lobby Rolls Out the Big Guns," *Philadelphia Inquirer*, October 19, 1975, 1A, 14A; "Sportsmen Unite Against Sen. Clark," *Pittsburgh Post-Gazette*, October 18, 1968, 5.

122. Interview with Joseph Tydings by Patrick J. Charles, July 12, 2018, part 2, 7:55–10:21 (on file with author) (acknowledging that Clark's defeat made advocating for firearms controls on Capitol Hill "much more difficult," for if "Clark could be defeated, anybody could be defeated").

2. The Rise of the "Gun Lobby"

1. See, e.g., NRA, *Americans and Their Guns*, ed. James E. Serven (Harrisburg, Pa.: Stackpole Books, 1967); Louis F. Lucas, "This Very Day," *AR*, August 1959, 16.

2. See, e.g., "Words of Wisdom," *AR*, March 1967, 14; Merritt A. Edson, "As Allowed by Law," *AR*, November 1953, 16.

3. "A Paul Revere Organization," *AR*, March 1958, 14.

4. "1974 Oral History of Milton Reckord," undated, Milton Reckord Papers, series 5, box 14, folder 10 (College Park: University of Maryland Library) (hereafter Reckord Papers), A1–37, B1–22, C1–25.

5. See, e.g., Richard Harris, "Annals of Legislation: If You Love Your Guns," *New Yorker*, April 20, 1968, 56, 57; "Aimless," *Time Magazine*, September 9, 1966; "A Paul Revere Organization," *AR*, March 1958, 14.

6. See M. A. Reckord, NRA executive vice president, to W. F. Roper, Smith & Wesson advertising manager, April 16, 1929, S&WR, box 3, folder 9, NRA; M. A. Reckord, NRA executive vice president, to W. F. Roper, Smith & Wesson advertising manager, April 12, 1929, S&WR, box 3, folder 9, NRA; letter from M. A. Reckord, NRA executive vice president, to W. F. Roper, Smith & Wesson advertising manager, October 10, 1928, S&WR, box 3, folder 9, NRA; M. A. Reckord, NRA executive vice president, to W. F. Roper, Smith & Wesson advertising manager, March 19, 1927, S&WR, box 3, folder 9, NRA; letter from M. A. Reckord, NRA executive vice president, to W. F. Roper, Smith & Wesson advertising manager, December 7, 1926, S&WR, box 3, folder 9, NRA.

7. See, e.g., "Firearms Bill Passed in House Is Favored Here," *Fitchburg (Mass.) Sentinel*, December 18, 1924, 1; "Firearms Legislation Defeated in Pennsylvania Legislature," *American Artisan*, July 7, 1917, 28.

8. See, e.g., letter from Smith & Wesson to George F. Brooks, Harrington & Richardson Arms Co., December 8, 1927, S&WR, box 1, folder 16, Gun Legislation; letter from John W. Harrington, Harrington & Richardson Arms Co. treasurer, to Smith & Wesson, November 9, 1926, S&WR, box 1, folder 15, Gun Legislation; letter from George F. Brooks, Harrington & Richardson Arms Co., to Smith & Wesson, February 2, 1926, S&WR, box 1, folder 15, Gun Legislation.

9. Patrick J. Charles, *Armed in America: A History of Gun Rights from Colonial Militias to Concealed Carry* (Amherst, N.Y.: Prometheus Books, 2018), 179–91.

10. For a useful example of this cooperation, see "Pistol Protection vs. Pistol Prohibition," *Adventure*, September 30, 1923, 178–80. For articles and editorials in sporting, hunting, and shooting magazines supporting the USRA's gun rights advocacy efforts, see Peter P. Carney, "Regarding Uniform Revolver Law," *OL*, March 1925, 175; Henry Morris, "Will Anti-Pistol Laws Decrease Crime?," *OL*, July 1924, 71–72; Joe Taylor, "The Price of Murder," *F&S*, May 1924, 28–29; "The Anti Anti-Pistol Situation," *F&S*, September 1923, 28–29; J. A. McGuire, "That Proposed Revolver Law," *OL*, April 1923, 249; George M. Dudley, "An Appeal to Sportsmen," *OL*, February 1923, 93; Eltinge F. Warner, "The Anti Anti-Pistol Fight," *F&S*, October 1922, 640.

11. Although USRA was the first to advocate for model firearms legislation affecting all firearms owners, the editors of *Field and Stream* were seemingly the first to advocate for "sane" and "uniform" legislation as it pertained to hunting and conservation. See E. T. Warner, "Field and Stream's Platform," *F&S*, December 1907, 2; "The Sportsman and Politics," *F&S*, July 1902, 244; "To Beat the Legislators," *F&S*, July 1897, 78–79; "Uniform Game Laws," *F&S*, September 1896, 114. It was not until 1916, four years after the USRA began advocating for model firearms legislation, that the organization's efforts received regular exposure in sporting, hunting, and shooting magazines. The first mention of the USRA's role in combatting restrictive firearms legislation appeared in a 1912 edition of *Field and Stream*. See "National Disarmament," *F&S*, August 1912, 360–61.
12. Charles, *Armed in America*, 192–93.
13. "States Are Asked to Pass Uniform Revolver Laws," *Albuquerque (N.M.) Morning Journal*, May 19, 1912, 6.
14. "The U.S. Revolver Association to Take Hand in Law Making," *Miami (Fla.) Herald*, March 20, 1912, 9.
15. "States Are Asked to Pass Uniform Revolver Laws."
16. Memorandum accompanying January 11, 1925, letter from Frank H. Hanson to Smith & Wesson, "Why Is This Thus?," undated, S&WR, box 1, folder 14, Gun Legislation.
17. USRA, "Sane Regulation of Revolver Sales: Why Revolver Sales Should Be Uniform," Bulletin no. 2, January 24, 1923, CLGP, box 2, folder Gun Law Correspondence, 1.
18. Charles, *Armed in America*, 156–61, 172. See USRA, "Sane Regulation of Revolver Sales: Why Revolver Sales Should be Uniform," 2; "A Bill to Provide for Uniform Revolver Sales: Based Upon Senate Bill 4012 Introduced in the U.S. Senate," September 22, 1922, § 8, CLGP, box 2, folder Gun Law Correspondence.
19. The USRA claimed that if their model firearms legislation was "passed nationally," it "would do away with the flood of 'Thou Shall Nots' which is nullifying our title of the land of liberty and home of the brave." *U.S.R.A. Bulletin* 11, no. 11 (August 1926): 4, MFP, box 5, folder 53.
20. USRA, "Sane Regulation of Revolver Sales."
21. USRA, "Disarming the Criminal," Bulletin no. 3, January 31, 1923, MFP, box 5, folder 53.
22. Adam Winkler, *Gunfight: The Battle Over the Right to Bear Arms in America* (New York: Norton, 2011), 208; "Criminals Don't Like It," *Reading (Pa.) Times*, January 23, 1924, 4; "Concealed Weapons," *Arizona Republic* (Phoenix), August 18, 1923, 4; "A Tightening Up of Crime Laws," *Arizona Republic*, April 4, 1923, 4; "Wants Pistols Sold Here Under License," *NYT*, February 14, 1923, 5; "Asks Regulation of Pistol Sale," *Gettysburg (Pa.) Times*, November 4, 1922, 1.
23. In the February 1, 1926, edition of *American Rifleman*, the NRA stated it was prompted to join the movement after the USRA's annual meeting in 1926, which was held a month earlier. The NRA also stated that there had been some interorganizational

jealousies with the USRA, but they quickly "vanished" upon the NRA offering to join forces. See "All Together Fellows! Pull!," *AR*, February 1, 1926, 21.

24. The cooperation between the two groups came following the National Conference of Commissioners (NCC) decision to explore model firearms legislation of its own. See "N.R.A. Directors Hold Sixty-First Annual Meeting," *AR*, March 1932, 7–9; C. B. Lister, "N.R.A. Policies for '28 Outlined at Meetings," *AR*, March 1928, 5–6; Henry Morris, "The National Crime Commission Anti-Gun Bill," *OL*, June 1927, 28–29, 80–81; Jack Rohan, "N.R.A. Directors Meet," *AR*, March 1927, 5; "Urges Control of Traffic in Machine Guns," *Rochester (N.Y.) Democrat and Chronicle*, February 6, 1927, 9; "To Ask All States for Ban on Pistols," *NYT*, January 30, 1927, 4; "Uniform Statute on Firearms Planned," *Reno (Nev.) Gazette-Journal*, January 14, 1927, 8; Charles V. Imlay, "The Uniform Firearms Act," *American Bar Association Journal* 12 (1926): 767–69; "Pistol Law Another on Program of National Conference on Uniform State Laws," *Battle Creek (Mich.) Enquirer*, August 25, 1925, 17.

25. It seems this takeover began on March 26, 1932, in the wake of New York governor Franklin D. Roosevelt having vetoed the USRA's and NRA's attempt at repealing and replacing the Sullivan Law with the USRA's model firearms legislation. See Charles, *Armed in America*, 194–203.

26. Charles, *Armed in America*, 204–5.

27. In most cases, these so-called reformers or do-gooders were merely advocating for firearms restrictions because they believed such restrictions would be in the best interest of public safety. See, e.g., Nicholas Albano, *Good Morning Judge!* (Newark, N.J.: Colyer, 1932), 189–211; John R. Thomson, "Put the Revolver Away!," *Continent*, October 6, 1921, 1121; Matthew J. Eder, "The Urgent Need of Anti-Pistol Legislation," *National Police Journal*, November 1917, 6, 26–27; Frederick L. Hoffman, "The Increase in Murder," *Annals of the American Academy of Political and Social Science* 125 (May 1926): 20–29; George P. Le Brun, "Fatalities in Manhattan," *World Almanac and Encyclopedia* (N.p.: Press Publishing, 1916), 844; Frederick L. Hoffman, "The Homicide of American Cities for 1914," *Spectator*, December 23, 1915, 388–90; Frederick L. Hoffman, "The Suicide Record of 1914," *Spectator*, November 25, 1915, 327–29; Edward Marshall, "Guarding New York Against Death by Violence," *NYT*, March 1, 1914, 44; Frederick L. Hoffman, "Homicide Records of American Cities," *Spectator*, November 6, 1913, 204–6; "Is the Pistol Responsible for Crime?," *Journal of American Institute of Criminal Law and Criminology* 1 (1911): 793–94; "Homicide and the Carrying of Concealed Weapons," *Journal of American Institute of Criminal Law and Criminology* 2 (1911): 92; William McAdoo, "The Concealed Weapon: How to Prevent Fifty Thousand Crimes a Year," *New-York Tribune*, July 2, 1905, B11.

28. See, e.g., Henry Morris, "The Folly of Anti-Gun Laws," *OL*, November 1922, 337–38; Horace Kephart, "The Right to Bear Arms," *Outing*, May 1922, 70–71.

29. See, e.g., "Make This Another Banner Shooting Year . . .," *AR*, March 1938, insert, 1; "How Will They Vote?," *AR*, November 1932, 6; "Practical 'Peace Conference,'" *AR*, March 1931, 6; "Resisting the Anti-Gun Crank," *AR*, April 1, 1927, 10; "Watch the Anti-Firearm Laws," *A&M*, December 15, 1919, 8.

30. See, e.g., Otto R. Keiter, "Anti-Legislation Plaint," *AR*, October 1939, 36.

31. This was partly because the NRA did not shy away from referring to antifirearms laws as "un-American." See, e.g., "Anti-Firearm Laws," *A&M*, October 1, 1922, 14; "Firearms and Crime Prevention," *A&M*, February 8, 1919, 318.

32. Sheldon served as the editor of the Guns and Game Department of the *Sportsman*, and subsequently for *Country Life* and *Outdoors Magazine*. He also wrote articles for several sporting, hunting, and shooting publications, including *Forest and Stream*, *Field and Stream*, *Shooting Times*, and the NRA's flagship magazine, *American Rifleman*.

33. "A Nation of Riflemen," undated 1944, HPSP, doc. 303, folder 13 (written for *American Legion Magazine* but, due to budget constraints was never published); "Un-American Activities," undated, HPSP, doc. 303, folder 26; "[Untitled Writing]," undated, HPSP, doc. 303, folder 37.

34. See, e.g., Karl T. Frederick, "Are You Men or Mutton?," *F&S*, February 1932, 13; Archibald Rutledge, "What Sportsmen Bring Home," *F&S*, October 1936, 17.

35. In 1927 the motto read, "America—Once Again—A Nation of Riflemen"; in 1947 it motto read, "Make American Again a Nation of Riflemen." See "Barriers Burned Away!," *AR*, November 15, 1926, back cover; and "Target for 1947," *AR*, January 1947, 3.

36. See, e.g., "Fight!," *AR*, August 1932, 4.

37. See "NRA Head Scoffs at Gun License Law in New York," *Albuquerque (N.M.) Journal*, January 7, 1955, 14; C. B. Lister, "Invasion," *AR*, February 1943, 11; "Suggest Training in Use of Small Arms By Citizens," *Oshkosh (Wis.) Daily Northwestern*, June 25, 1940, 9; "C. B. Lister Assails Cummings Speech," *Wilmington (Del.) Morning News*, November 29, 1935, 3; "The Sinister Influence," *AR*, April 1935, 6; "Stick to the Issue, Mr. Alco!," *AR*, November 1934, 6; "Powder Smoke," *AR*, October 1934, 4; "Shades of the Pioneers!," *AR*, September 1934, 4; "Gun Registration," *AR*, April 1934, 4; Karl T. Frederick, "Are You Men or Mutton?," *F&S*, February 1932, 13.

38. See William Fulton, "Sullivan Law, Boon to Thugs, 40 Years Old," *Chicago Tribune*, November 1, 1951, 6F; C. B. Lister, "A Soldier Speaks," *AR*, December 1949, 8; C. B. Lister, "Simple Arithmetic," *AR*, November 1949, 10; C. B. Lister, "Matter of Proportion," *AR*, October 1948, 10; C. B. Lister, "Optimist—Or Sucker?," *AR*, September 1948, 12; C. B. Lister, "State of Mind," *AR*, June 1948, 8; C. B. Lister, "Pattern in Red," *AR*, April 1948, 10; C. B. Lister, "Passion for Crisis," *AR*, March 1948, 10; C. B. Lister, "The Opium Eaters," *AR*, September 1947, 10; C. B. Lister, "War and Peace," *AR*, June 1947, 6; C. B. Lister, "Straightening the Record," *AR*, March 1947, 6; C. B. Lister, "For Disarming the Bourgeoisie," *AR*, January 1947, 7; C. B. Lister, "The History of Liberty," *AR*, May 1946, 9; C. B. Lister, "Pious Subterfuge," *AR*, January 1946, 9; C. B. Lister, "Invasion," *AR*, February 1943, 11; "Zero Hour," *AR*, December 1940, 4; "'National Defense' Decoy," *AR*, August 1940, 4; "Why Firearms Control," *AR*, November 1939, 36; "Gun Editor Sharpe on Anti-Gun Laws," *AR*, December 1934, 36; "The Clearing Picture," *AR*, December 1933, 4; "Why Gun Laws?," *AR*, November 1933, 4; "The Senate Sets an Example," *AR*, February 1929, 6; "Practical 'Peace Conference,'" *AR*, March 1934,

6; "Winter Sports," *AR*, December 1928, 6; "Everybody's Business," *AR*, November 1928, 6.

39. "Lawless (?) America," *AR*, April 1931, 6.

40. See, e.g., "Tyros on the Hill," *AR*, December 1932, 6; "The Best Defense," *AR*, April 1932, 6; "Bandit Menace Is Best Ended with Bullets," *Connellsville (Pa.) Daily Courier*, November 18, 1931, 3; F. Theodore Dexter, "Facing an Armed Crook," *AR*, January 1930, 24, 38; "—And They Thought He Wouldn't Fight!," *AR*, March 1928, 18; Allyn H. Tedmon, "Boys and Rifles," *AR*, November 1927, 8–9; "Opposes Firearms Laws," *Akron (Ohio) Beacon Journal*, April 6, 1927, 4; "Page Magistrate McAdoo," *AR*, August 1, 1926, 8.

41. See, e.g., Calvin Goddard, "The Pistol Bogey," *American Journal of Police Science* 1 (1930): 178–87; Frederick, "Pistol Regulation, Part 1," 450–51.

42. See "Russia Is Learning to Shoot," *AR*, August 1935, 38; "Another Phase of the Gun Problem," *AR*, June 1932, 48; C. B. Lister, "Governor Roosevelt Upholds Sullivan Law," *AR*, May 1932, 20–21; "Bandits Fear Armed Resistance," *AR*, December 1931, 36; "Who Says Armed Resistance Is Futile?," *AR*, December 1931, 34; "One More Instance of Armed Resistance," *AR*, November 1931, 30; "A Lesson for America," *AR*, September 1930, 39; Calvin Goddard, "Gang Guns," *AR*, January 1930, 16, 38; "A 'Big' Newspaper Makes a Discovery," *AR*, March 1929, 6, 28; Jack Rohan, "No Freedom for Crooks," *AR*, January 1, 1927, 9–11; Philip B. Sharpe, "Thug Medicine," *AR*, November 15, 1926, 5–6; "A Day in Chicago," *AR*, October 15, 1926, 8; A. Dumbell, "Reactions to an Editorial," *AR*, September 1, 1926, 11; C. B. Lister, "The Remedy," *Du Pont Magazine*, March 1924, 10–11.

43. The NRA also pushed this message when promoting itself and the shooting sports. See, e.g., William S. Dutton, "Why Not Become a Crack Shot?," *Elks Magazine*, August 1924, 16–17, 80.

44. See, e.g., "Shades of the Pioneers!," *AR*, September 1934, 4; "The Best Defense," *AR*, April 1932, 6; E. V. Menefee, "Indiana Vigilantes Alert," *AR*, March 1932, 43; "Talks Value of Training With Pistol, Rifle," *Wilmington (Del.) Evening Journal*, March 23, 1932, 25; Major W. D. Frazer, "The Future of American Pistol Shooting," *AR*, November 15, 1926, 3, 5.

45. "Vigilante Method Short and to the Point," *AR*, August 1928, 30.

46. "The Attorney General Is Inconsistent," *AR*, January 1934, 4.

47. "Guns vs. Bandits," *AR*, November 1939, 36.

48. For the column's final appearance, see "Guns vs. Bandits," *AR*, March 1941, 36.

49. Walter J. Howe, "The Armed Citizen," *AR*, September 1958, 32.

50. "The Silent Protectors," *AR*, January 1971, 28.

51. See, e.g., Merritt A. Edson, "The Right to Bear Arms," *AR*, July 1955, 14; Merritt A. Edson, "The Right to Bear Arms," *Maryland Conservationist*, March 1956, 14–17.

52. See, e.g., *National Firearms Act: Hearing Before the Committee on Ways and Means House Resolution*, 73rd Congressional Record (Washington, D.C., 1934), 59; Goddard, "The Pistol Bogey," 187; "Our Friends—the Policemen," *AR*, July 1930, 6; "A Day in Chicago," *AR*, October 15, 1926, 8; "You Can't Fool the Editors All the Time," *AR*, May 15,

1925, 14; "The Question of Intent," *AR*, March 15, 1925, 13; "The Police Panacea," *A&M*, May 15, 1923, 10; "The Gun-Toting Criminal," *A&M*, November 1, 1922, 12.

53. See, e.g., "NRA Basic Policy," *AR*, July 1964, 31; "NRA Policy Statement on . . . Firearms Legislation," *AR*, July 1958, 35; Frank C. Daniel, "The Gun Law Problem," *AR*, February 1953, 18, 46; Merritt A. Edson, "To Keep and Bear Arms," *AR*, August 1952, 6.

54. This provision was contained in both the USRA's and NRA's model state firearms legislation. See "A Bill to Provide for Uniform Revolver Sales," § 7; *Uniform Firearms Act: Drafted by the National Conference of Commissioners on Uniform State Laws* (Chicago, 1930), 4, § 6n.

55. See "Merry Christmas—and Gun Laws," *AR*, December 1929, 6.

56. See "A New Spring Song," *AR*, May 1940, 4; "Winter Sports," *AR*, December 1928, 6; "There Ought to Be a Law," *Albuquerque (N.M.) Journal*, December 30, 1928, 26; "Editorial Points to Peril of Anti-Pistol Bills Before Congress," *Franklin (Pa.) News-Herald*, December 13, 1928, 3; Karl T. Frederick, "The Outlook as Regards Anti-Firearms Legislation," *AR*, January 1928, 7; John Edwin Hoag, "There Ought to Be a Law," *OL*, September 1926, 242.

57. C. B. Lister, "The Remedy," *Du Pont Magazine*, March 1924, 10.

58. "The Sinister Influence," *AR*, April 1935, 6.

59. Given this modest circulation, tracking down copies of the USRA's bulletins proved rather difficult. However, I was able to locate a handful in the private papers of two early twentieth-century gun rights advocates. For copies, see MFP, box 5, folder 53; CLGP, box 2, folder Gun Law Correspondence.

60. Charles, *Armed in America*, 198–203.

61. Despite advertising itself as a lobby intent on fighting antifirearms legislation, the NRA did not change its mission statement to reflect it. See, e.g., NRA, *Shooting Rules* (Washington, D.C., 1933), 1.

62. Beginning with the June 1932 issue of *American Rifleman*, the NRA listed ten organizational objectives on the cover page. The first objective was providing "assistance to legislators in drafting laws discouraging the use of firearms for criminal purposes." The second was the "prevention of the passage of legislation unnecessarily restricting the use of firearms by honest citizens." The remaining eight objectives related to firearms safety and education. See "Why?," *AR*, June 1932, 3.

63. Indeed, as early as 1926, the NRA began advertising its role in fighting anti-gun legislation. These advertisements, however, were far less extreme than those published from 1932 onward. See, e.g., NRA, *The National Matches: August 26 to September 16* (Camp Perry, Ohio, 1928), 11; NRA, *Program of the Gallery Outdoor Rifle and Pistol Competitions* (Washington, D.C., 1928), 6; *The National Matches: August 21 to September 18* (Camp Perry, Ohio, 1927), 7; "7 Reasons Why Your Friends Should Be Members of the Association," *AR*, April 1927, 147.

64. "Wanted—Another 50,000 Sportsmen," *AR*, July 1932, 54.

65. "This Service Warrants the Support of Every Gun-Loving Sportsman," *AR*, June 1933, 2.

66. "Tyros on the Hill," *AR*, December 1932, 6.

67. "The Clearing Picture," *AR*, December 1933, 4.

68. "N.R.A. Service," *AR*, January 1934, 3.

69. The NRA first began reporting in detail on state and local firearms legislation in 1933. See "Roll Call of 1933 Firearms Legislation," *AR*, May 1933, 30; "Roll Call of 1933 Firearms Legislation," *AR*, April 1933, 38; "The Roll Call of 1933 Firearms Legislation," *AR*, March 1933, 20–21.

70. For some of the earliest examples of these bulletins and press releases, see *To Regulate Firearms in Commerce: Hearings Before a Subcommittee of the Committee on Commerce United States Senate* (Washington, D.C.: Government Printing Office, 1934), 65–75; NRA, *The Story of the Alco Bill* (1934), MFP, box 5, folder 52.

71. See, e.g., letter from C. B. Lister, NRA secretary-treasurer, to Mr. Kasper, June 15, 1934 (on file with author): "Besides these and other tangible benefits you will have the satisfaction of knowing that you are an active member of the only national organization in America which is successfully fighting those gun laws which seek to disarm the honest citizen. At the same time we are constantly assisting the authorities to frame sensible fire-arm laws."

72. For a brief account of this history published by the NRA in 1940, see NRA, *The Pro and Con of Firearms Legislation*, 9. For a brief account published by the NRA in 1968, see NRA, *The Gun Law Problem* (Washington, D.C., 1968), 4–6. For useful accounts of this history, see Alexander DeConde, *Gun Violence in America: The Struggle for Control* (Boston: Northeastern University Press, 2001), 140–45; and Lee Kennett and James L. Anderson, *The Gun in America: The Origins of a National Dilemma* (Westport, Conn.: Greenwood Press, 1975), 206–11.

73. The first attempt at federal firearms legislation occurred in the 1920s with the introduction of the Capper Bill and continued with the spread of UFA. See, e.g., "Curb Gangsters Buying Guns Is Object of Bill," *Chicago Daily Tribune*, April 12, 1930, 7; "Tight Ban on Gun Buying Is Proposed in Senate," *Baltimore (Md.) Sun*, April 12, 1930, 6; "'Anti-Crook' Gun Bill Up; 'Hit Honest Citizens!' Is Plaint," *Cincinnati (Ohio) Enquirer*, April 12, 1930, 10; "A 'Big' Newspaper Makes a Discovery," *AR*, March 1929, 6.

74. Charles, *Armed in America*, 212–13.

75. See "Firearms for Criminals," *Wilkes-Barre (Pa.) Record*, January 11, 1934, 6; "Seeks Tightening Up on Criminals," *Gazette and Daily York (Pa.)*, January 6, 1934, 4; "Tighten Law's Grasp on Crime, Cummings' Plea," *Des Moines (Iowa) Register*, January 6, 1934, 2; "Broaden Anti-Crime Powers Is Plea of Atty. Gen. Cummings," *Ludington (Mich.) Daily News*, January 5, 1934, 3.

76. "The Attorney General Is Inconsistent," *AR*, January 1934, 4.

77. Senator's Copeland early attempts at federal firearms legislation ultimately went nowhere, in large part to the organized opposition of sportsmen. See "That Non-Sensical Gun Bill," *OL*, May 1926, 363; Charles L. Gilman, "Forest, Stream and Target," *Minneapolis Daily Star*, September 12, 1925, 11; E. L. Stevenson, "The Copeland Anti-Pistol Bill," *OL*, October 1924, 292–94; "The Sawed-Off Gun in Lieu of Pistol,"

Minneapolis Star Tribune, August 16, 1924, 10; Henry Morris, "Will Anti-Pistol Laws Decrease Crime?," *OL*, July 1924, 71–73; "A Challenge to the Author of the Copeland Anti-Pistol Bill," *OL*, June 1924, 492; Joel Shomaker, "Shall We Legislate American-ism Out of Americans?," *OL*, May 1924, 345; Edward A. Leonard, "Anti-Pistol Toting Law," *Shreveport (La.) Times*, May 24, 1924, 6; A. W. Payne, "Anti-Firearm Menace Renewed," *OL*, March 1924, 178; "Wild Lifers Give $25 to Campaign of Women's Club," *Franklin (Pa.) News-Herald*, March 20, 1924, 2. It appears that Copeland's early attempts at federal firearms legislation were at the request of—and drafted by—then New York City chief magistrate William McAdoo. See William McAdoo, *When the Court Takes a Recess* (New York: Dutton, 1924), 131–32.

78. "U.S. Control of Firearms Plan to Check Crime," *Wilkes-Barre (Pa.) Evening News*, December 29, 1933, 2; "Copeland Bill to Ask Control Firearms Sale," *Lebanon (Pa.) Evening Report*, December 28, 1933, 7; "Laws to Fight Crime Drafted: Copeland Offers 21-Point Program," *Detroit (Mich.) Free Press*, December 23, 1933, 7; "President Hears Congress' Plan to Battle Crime," *Battle Creek (Mich.) Inquirer*, December 17, 1933, 1, 2.

79. See, e.g., "1974 Oral History of Milton Reckord," undated, MRP, series 5, box 14, folder 10, A23–31; "Will We Stay in High?," *AR*, October 1927, 22; "$100,000 for Civil-ian Clubs," *AR*, February 1927, 8; "The Budget and You," *AR*, December 15, 1926, 12.

80. NRA, press release, "Sportsmen Assail Anti-Pistol Laws as Help to Crime," Janu-ary 19, 1934, *To Regulate Commerce in Firearms*, 66 (emphasis added).

81. NRA, press release, untitled, January 24, 1934, *To Regulate Commerce in Firearms*, 68.

82. NRA, press release, January 24, 1934, 69.

83. NRA, "Sportsmen Assail Anti-Pistol Laws as Help to Crime," 66.

84. For examples of the NRA's press releases, or modified versions of them written by outdoors editors in newspapers across the country, see Ray P. Holland, "Guns," *F&S*, May 1934, 15; Eltinge F. Warner, "Senators, We Ask You!," *F&S*, May 1934, 32; "War-ner Decries Firearms Bill," *Detroit (Mich.) Free Press*, April 22, 1924, sports section, 6; Ollie Baus, "In the Big Outdoors," *Indianapolis (Ind.) Star*, February 11, 1934, part 5, 2; "Sportsmen Oppose Bill to Disarm All Citizens," *Sayre (Pa.) Evening Times*, Feb-ruary 9, 1934, 7; "Sports of All Sorts," *Bradford (Pa.) Evening Star and Daily Record*, February 9, 1934, 8; "The Right to Own Guns," *Newark (Ohio) Advocate*, February 8, 1934, 4; "Firearms in the Senate," *Carlsbad (N.M.) Daily Current-Argus*, February 7, 1934, 2; Stuart Cameron, "Sportsmen Map Fight to Defeat U.S. Firearms Bill," *Oakland (Calif.) Tribune*, January 31, 1934, 17; "American Sportsmen Fight Copeland's Fire-arms Bill," *Green Bay (Wis.) Press-Gazette*, January 31, 1934, 9; "Sportsmen Assail Anti-Pistol Laws as Help to Crime," *Monmouth Democrat* (Freehold, N.J.), January 25, 1934, 6. For some examples of the Pennsylvania Game Commission redistributing the NRA's message, see "Attention Sportsmen!," *Elizabethville (Pa.) Echo*, February 15, 1934, 2; "Firearms Bill Big Handicap to Sportsmen," *Brooksville (Pa.) Jeffersonian-Democrat*, February 8, 1934, 1, 3. For examples of the Izaak Walton League oppos-ing federal firearm legislation, see letter from Kenneth A. Reid, Izaak Walton League executive secretary, to Lyle H. Boren, April 13, 1942, LHBP, box 21, folder 17, Gun Control; Bert Claflin, "Izaak Waltons Foremost in Conservation Program,"

Appleton (Wis.) Post-Crescent, May 8, 1934, 2; Bert Claflin, "Blazed Trails for Sportsmen," *Green Bay (Wis.) Press-Gazette*, May 5, 1934, 14; "Anti-Firearms Bills Opposed at Convention," *Sheboygan (Wis.) Press*, April 21, 1934, 17. For opinion editorials written by sportsmen, hunters, and firearms owners opposing federal firearms legislation, see "Left-Handed Wisdom Disclosed in Copeland Firearms Measure," *Salt Lake (Utah) Telegram*, March 23, 1934, 4; Sherley C. Hulsen, "Files and Hacksaw Blades," *Pittsburgh Post-Gazette*, March 20, 1934, 12; Iver T. Henricksen, "Arm Every Descent Citizen," *Sioux City (Iowa) Journal*, March 16, 1934, 4; Marksman, "The Copeland Firearms Bill . . .," *Fremont (Ohio) News-Messenger*, March 15, 1934, 3.

85. See "Gun Registration," *AR*, April 1934, 4; "Keep Those Telegrams Coming," *AR*, March 1934, 6; "Firearms in the Senate," *AR*, February 1934, 5.
86. "Keep Those Telegrams Coming," 6.
87. For the full bill, see "H.R. 9066," undated, *National Firearms Act: Hearings Before the Committee on Ways and Means* (Washington, D.C.: Government Printing Office, 1934), 1–3.
88. "Statement of Honorable Homer S. Cummings, Attorney General of the United States," April 16, 1968, *National Firearms Act*, 5.
89. Statement of Adjutant General Milton Reckord, Adjutant General of the State of Maryland, Executive Vice President of the National Rifle Association," April 18, 1934, *National Firearms Act*, 36–38.
90. "Statement of Joseph B. Keenan, Assistant Attorney General," April 18, 1934, *National Firearms Act*, 64–66.
91. "Statement of Karl T. Frederick, President National Rifle Association," April 18, 1934, *National Firearms Act*, 38–50.
92. "1974 Oral History of Milton Reckord," undated, MRP, series 5, box 14, folder 10, B15–19.
93. "Statement of Karl T. Frederick," 51–62.
94. "Statement of Karl T. Frederick," 62–64, 81–82.
95. "Disarmament by Subterfuge," *AR*, May 1934, 4.
96. See C. B. Lister, "Firearms Laws in the 73d Congress," *AR*, July 1934, 5, 17.
97. See generally *National Firearms Act*, 83–166.
98. "Keenan Clashes with Reckord at Gun Hearing," *Baltimore (Md.) Evening Sun*, May 14, 1934, 30.
99. Copies of S. 885, S. 2285, and S. 3680 can be found in the committee hearings. See *To Regulate Commerce in Firearms*, 1 8.
100. *To Regulate Commerce in Firearms*, 8.
101. For a contemporaneous account of the contentious nature of the hearing, see Frederick R. Barkley, "Reckord Again Hits Firearms Control Plan," *Baltimore (Md.) Evening Sun*, May 28, 1934, 4, 30.
102. *To Regulate Commerce in Firearms*, 10.
103. In one newsletter, the NRA not only celebrated the tabling of Copeland's firearms bills but also criticized Copeland as having little to no knowledge of firearms. See

NRA, "The Proposed Federal Firearms Law, H.R. 9066," undated, *National Firearms Act*, 72.

104. *To Regulate Commerce in Firearms*, 10–12.

105. *To Regulate Commerce in Firearms*, 16

106. *To Regulate Commerce in Firearms*, 17–22.

107. *To Regulate Commerce in Firearms*, 22–31.

108. *To Regulate Commerce in Firearms*, 57–60, 63.

109. *To Regulate Commerce in Firearms*, 64.

110. *To Regulate Commerce in Firearms*, 84–104.

111. C. B. Lister, "Firearms Laws in the 73d Congress," *AR*, July 1934, 18.

112. M. A. Reckord, "Senate 3," *AR*, August 1938, 10–11; *Firearms: Hearing Before a Subcommittee of the Committee on Interstate and Foreign Commerce House of Representatives* (Washington, D.C.: Government Printing Office, 1937), 4 (hereafter *Firearms House Hearing*); *To Regulate Commerce of Firearms: Hearing Before the Committee on Commerce United States Senate* (Washington, D.C.: Government Printing Office, 1935), 1.

113. 48 U.S. Stat. 1236 (1934).

114. "Random Shots," *AR*, August 1934, 2.

115. See NRA, *The Story of the Alco Bill* (1934), MFP, box 5, folder 5; "Stick to the Issue Mr. Alco!," *AR*, November 1934, 6; "Powder Smoke," *AR*, October 1934, 4; "Shades of Pioneers!," *AR*, September 1934, 5.

116. As early as mid-December 1934, in a press release, the NRA expressed support for Senator Copeland's bill, which had not yet been introduced to Congress. See "Arms Possession Ban Advocated: Rifle Association Asks Severe Penalty for Toting by Criminals," *Washington, D.C., Evening Star*, December 16, 1934, E14.

117. "Congress Must Choose," *AR*, January 1935, 4.

118. See "Third Progress Report on Firearms Legislation for 1935," *AR*, April 1935, 30–31; "Annual Meetings Open Association's New Year," *AR*, March 1935, 13, 17; "Progress Report on Firearms Legislation for 1935, 20–21; "S. 3," *AR*, February 1935, 5; "Recently Proposed Firearms Legislation," *AR*, February 1935, 26; "S. 3," *AR*, February 1935, 5; "Congress Must Choose," *AR*, January 1935, 4.

119. See, e.g., *To Regulate Commerce of Firearms*, 8–9; "Sportsmen Want to Disarm Criminals," *Piqua (Ohio) Daily Call*, January 2, 1935, 8.

120. See Charles, *Armed in America*, 222–25.

121. Very few of these letters and telegrams have survived. Fortunately, examples can be found in the papers of Charles W. Tobey. See, e.g., letter from Nashua Rifle and Revolver Club to Charles W. Tobey, March 4, 1935, CWTP, box 5, folder 6, Firearms Legislation 1935; letter from Belknap County Sportsmen's Association, Inc. to Charles W. Tobey, March 1, 1935, CWTP, box 5, folder 6, Firearms Legislation 1935; letter from Merrimack County Fish and Game Club to Charles W. Tobey, February 14, 1935, CWTP, box 5, folder 6, Firearms Legislation 1935; letter from Edward R. Stanley, Jr., to Charles W. Tobey, January 11, 1935, CWTP, box 5, folder 6, Firearms Legislation 1935.

122. One letter went so far as to call S. 3 a "radical firearms bill" that undoubtedly contained a few "jokers" meant to disarm law-abiding citizens. See letter from Erwin A. Rowe to Charles W. Tobey, March 7, 1935, CWTP, box 5, folder 6, Firearms Legislation 1935.
123. See, e.g., *To Regulate Commerce of Firearms*, 4, 22; "U.S. Firearms Control Sought," *Reading (Pa.) Times*, January 3, 1935, 18.
124. See *To Regulate Commerce of Firearms*, 4, 22. The NRA defended repealing these laws on the grounds that they were "drastic." *To Regulate Commerce of Firearms*, 45–46. The NRA's argument proved unavailing, and the provision was subsequently removed. See *Firearms House Hearing*, 3.
125. *To Regulate Commerce of Firearms*, 8–16, 44–46.
126. *To Regulate Commerce of Firearms*, 23–24, 20.
127. Homer Cummings, *Firearms and the Crime Problem* (Washington, D.C.: Government Printing Office, 1938), 1–5. For an example of how the press reported on Cummings's speech, see "Cummings Asks Registration of All Firearms," *Baltimore (Md.) Evening Sun*, October 5, 1937, 36.
128. Cummings, *Firearms and the Crime Problem*, 9. The NRA often recited the Department of Justice's admission that criminals would not immediately register their firearms as an argument against any firearms registration law. See, e.g., "Federal Firearms Registration," *AR*, February 1937, 4; "Disarmament by Subterfuge," *AR*, May 1934, 4. What the NRA omitted, however, was that registration would make it somewhat more difficult for criminals to acquire firearms. See, e.g., Brien McMahon, Milton A. Reckord, and Sydney R. Montague, "How Can We Stop the March of Crime?," *Bulletin of America's Town Meeting of the Air* 3, no. 22 (April 4, 1938): 1, 9; J. Weston Allen, *Government Control of Firearms* (1937), 36.
129. See, e.g., "Wanted! 2,000 Members This Month," *AR*, April 1938, insert; "Make This Another Banner Shooting Year . . .," *AR*, March 1938, insert.
130. "What Will the Next Congress Say About Anti-Firearms Legislation?," *AR*, November 1937, insert, f-g.
131. "Congress Convenes This Month," *AR*, January 1938, insert, 1.
132. C. B. Lister, "Federal Firearms Registration," *AR*, January 1938, 27.
133. "Progress Report of Firearms Legislation," *AR*, April 1938, 8.
134. "An End to Innuendo!," *AR*, May 1938, 4.
135. See, e.g., H. R. Baukhage, "Cummings Gets Set for Fight on His Gun Bill," *Baltimore (Md.) Evening Sun*, February 28, 1938, 3, H. R. Baukhage, "Cummings Pushes Drive for Arms Registration Bill," *Minneapolis Star Tribune*, February 27, 1938, part 2, p. 5.
136. McMahon, Reckord, and Montague, "How Can We Stop the March of Crime?," 10–11 (statement of Milton A. Reckord).
137. McMahon, Reckord, and Montague, 29.
138. C. B. Lister, "Problems as Well as Progress Expected in 1937," *AR*, January 1937, 5, 6.
139. See letter from J. Edgar Hoover to Joseph B. Keenan, "Re: Further Suggested Changes in the National Firearms Act," May 14, 1935, HCPS4C, box 103; letter from J. Edgar Hoover to Harold M. Stephens, September 10, 1935, HCPS4, box 103; letter from J.

Edgar Hoover to Joseph B. Keenan, October 8, 1935, HCPS4C, box 103; letter from Gordon Dean to Joseph B. Keenan, October 28, 1935, HCPS4, box 103; letter from Homer Cummings to J. Edgar Hoover, November 7, 1935, HCPS4C, box 103; letter from J. Edgar Hoover to Homer Cummings, November 9, 1935, HCPS4C, box 103; letter from Gordon Dean to Joseph B. Keenan, November 20, 1935, HCPS4C, box 103; letter from Joseph B. Keenan to Homer Cummings, "In re: National Firearms Act," November 20, 1935, HCPS4C, box 103.

140. See letter from J. Edgar Hoover to Homer Cummings, "Re: Recent Developments in Highly-Powered Pistols and Revolvers," March 19, 1936, HCPS4C, box 103, 1–3; letter from J. Edgar Hoover to Homer Cummings, February 5, 1936, HCPS4C, box 103; letter from J. Edgar Hoover to Brian McMahon, April 4, 1936, HCPS4C, box 103.

141. See, e.g., Rex Collier, "An Interview of the Honorable Homer Cummings Attorney General of the United States," April 25, 1968, HCPS4S, box 215, 4; Department of Justice, "A Statement Concerning the Proposed National Small Arms Act," March 23, 1938, HCPS4C, box 103; Homer Cummings, "Firearms and the Crime Problem," October 5, 1937, HCPS4S, box 215, 6.

142. See McMahon, Reckord, and Montague, "How Can We Stop the March of Crime?," 5–29; letter from Gordon Dean to Homer Cummings, February 14, 1938, HCPS4C, box 103; letter from Homer Cummings to Gordon Dean, February 21, 1938, HCPS4C, box 103; letter from Alexander Holtzoff to Homer Cummings, February 14, 1938, HCPS4C, box 103; Department of Justice, "A Statement Concerning the Proposed National Small Arms Act," March 23, 1938, HCPS4C, box 103; letter from Gordon Dean to Homer Cummings, "Re: Firearms," April 2, 1938, HCPS4C, box 103; letter from J. Weston Allen to Homer Cummings, "Re: Conference with Eugene Meyer," April 5, 1938, HCPS4C, box 103.

143. See letter from J. Weston Allen to Homer Cummings, April 5, 1938, HCPS4C, box 103; letter from Alexander Holtzoff to Homer Cummings, April 26, 1938, HCPS4C, box 103; letter from Homer Cummings to John Tibby, May 2, 1938, HCPS4C, box 103.

144. Neal Peirce, "Gun Control: The Issue That's a Non-Issue," *Philadelphia Inquirer*, October 6, 1980, 9A.

145. The findings of the survey were printed across the United States. See, e.g., Institute of Public Opinion, "Pistol Registration Approved by 4 to 1 Majority in Survey," *Altoona (Pa.) Tribune*, May 2, 1938, 11; Institute of Public Opinion, "Pistol Registration Approved by 4 to 1 Majority in Survey," *Rochester (N.Y.) Democrat and Chronicle*, May 1, 1938, F1; Institute of Public Opinion, "Pistol Registration Approved by 4 to 1 Majority in Survey," *Tampa Bay (Fla.) Times*, May 1, 1938, 29; Institute of Public Opinion, "Pistol Registration Approved by 4 to 1 Majority in Survey," *Lincoln (Neb.) Star*, May 1, 1938, 13; "Public Willing to List Pistols," *Louisville (Ky.) Courier-Journal*, May 1, 1938, 70; Institute of Public Opinion, "Registration of Guns Approved by 4 to 1 Survey," *Pittsburgh Press*, May 1, 1938, Society Section, 2.

146. See, e.g., J. Weston Allen to *New York Herald Tribune*, May 10, 1938, reprinted in *Congressional Record* 83, part 10 (1938), 1948; letter from Homer Cummings to Robert L. Doughton, April 11, 1938, RLDP; "Guns and the Law," *Boston Globe*, May 13, 1938, 22.

147. "Sportsmen's Victory," AR, August 1938, 4.

148. 53 U.S. Stat. 1250 (1938).

149. The Federal Firearms Act did nothing to supersede state and local laws requiring a permit to purchase a firearm. See "Pistol Permit Laws," AR, November 1938, 29–31, 34; "Questions and Answers on the Federal Firearms Act," AR, October 1938, 64.

150. "Directors Meeting, 1939," AR, March 1939, 9, 11.

151. See "Sportsmen! Up in Arms to Protect Your Arms!!," Harrisburg (Pa.) Telegraph, April 15, 1939, supplement, 3; "Gun-Owning," Miami (Fla.) News, April 10, 1939, 3B; "Firearms Legislation 1939," AR, March 1939, 31.

152. See, e.g., C. B. Lister, "Just Grass Roots Stuff!," AR, April 1947, 6; "Progress Report: Legislation," AR, March 1947, 29; NRA, The Pro and Con of Firearms Legislation, 2–4, 9–15.

153. See, e.g., C. B. Lister, "The Backdoor Approach," AR, November 1945, 5.

154. For a short post–World War II summary of the NRA's view on fighting firearms legislation during this period, see C. B. Lister, "Mission Accomplished!," AR, December 1945, 9.

155. See "Politics and Propaganda," AR, September 1940, 4; " 'National Defense' Decoy," AR, August 1940, 4.

156. See "Rifle Club," Los Angeles Times, June 29, 1940, part 1, 10; "Will Sell No More Rifles," Wisconsin State Journal, June 25, 1940, 4; "Denies Selling Rifles to Bunds," York (Pa.) Gazette and Daily, June 14, 1940, 20; "Rifle Association Membership Eyed," Salem (Ore.) Statesman Journal, May 22, 1940, 1.

157. The War Department program was crucial in expanding the NRA's membership from the early to mid-twentieth century. The NRA often touted the program to enlist new members. See, e.g., "Every Club Member Should Read the Rifleman," undated 1938, CRCNYP ("Club members who desire the privilege of purchasing government rifles from the War Department . . . should join the Association"); NRA, The Typical American Sport (Washington, D.C.: 1935), 15 (outlining the benefits associated with becoming a NRA rifle club, including the "privilege of purchasing from the War Department through the Director of Civilian Marksmanship the Service Springfield, the .22 caliber Springfield, ammunition, and such other items of equipment as my become available from time to time"). For an NRA member to purchase surplus military rifles or ammunition, all that was required was proof of NRA membership and that said member be in "good standing." NRA-affiliated rifle clubs could not purchase the surplus military rifles. They were, however, able to loan rifles from the War Department. All that was required was that the affiliated rifle club "promptly" submit an Annual Return of United States Property report to the War Department. Letter from Major R. H. Lord, Office of the Director of Civilian Marksmanship, to Sylvester E. Walker, Canaan Rifle Club secretary, December 10, 1937, CRCNYP; letter from Captain R.H. Lord, Office of the Director of Civilian Marksmanship, to Sylvester E. Walker, Canaan Rifle Club secretary, December 10, 1934, CRCNYP; Canaan Rifle Club, Annual Return of United States Property, December 31, 1938, CRCNYP; Canaan Rifle Club,

Annual Return of United States Property, December 31, 1937, CRCNYP; Canaan Rifle Club, Annual Return of United States Property, December 31, 1936, CRCNYP; Canaan Rifle Club, Annual Return of United States Property, December 31, 1934, CRCNYP; Canaan Rifle Club, Annual Return of United States Property, December 31, 1933, CRCNYP.

158. See Steven J. Ross, *Hitler in Los Angeles: How Jews Foiled Nazi Plots Against Hollywood and America* (New York: Bloomsbury, 2017), 230, 241, 270; Laura B. Rosenzweig, *Hollywood's Spies: The Undercover Surveillance of Nazis in Los Angeles* (New York: New York University Press, 2017), 126–27.

159. See "German Born Defendant Vows He'd Die for U.S.," *Brooklyn Daily Eagle*, May 7, 1940, 1, 8; "Fr. Coughlin Backs 'Front' Men Accused of Revolt Conspiracy," *Boston Globe*, January 22, 1940, 1, 9; "U.S. to Sift Alleged Coughlin Link to 'Front,'" Washington Indicates," *Brooklyn (N.Y.) Daily Eagle*, January 19, 1940, 1, 3; "Reveal Probe of Front Recruiting Among Cops," *New York Daily News*, January 17, 1940, 4.

160. C. B. Lister, *Facts or Innuendo? An Answer to an Unjust Attack by Congressman Dickstein* (Washington, D.C.: NRA, June 1940), 3, MFP, box 5, folder 52.

161. Prior to this, the NRA issued a separate special bulletin cautioning NRA-affiliated rifle clubs to "be sure of the men you admit to membership in your clubs." "Fifth Column Drive Spreads," *New Philadelphia (Ohio) Daily Times*, June 7, 1940, 1.

162. "Important Decisions," *AR*, August 1940, 22.

163. See Herbert W. Slater," *Rod and Gun,*" *Santa Rosa (Calif.) Press Democrat*, March 6, 1941, 9; "Medina Club Opposes Bill on Firearms," *Rochester (N.Y.) Democrat and Chronicle*, March 3, 1941, 13; Howard Kemp, "Sportsmen in the Area Aim to Halt Impending 'Gun' Legislation," *Rochester Democrat and Chronicle*, February 23, 1941, 2B; "Listing of Arms Is Opposed by Sportsmen," *Harrisburg (Pa.) Evening News*, February 13, 1941, 5; John G. Mock, "Firearms Measure Same Old Tune," *Pittsburgh Press*, January 19, 1941, sec. 3, 10; "Victor Sportsmen to Fight Gun Registration Measures," *Rochester Democrat and Chronicle*, December 5, 1940, 21; Phil Sharpe, "Watch Out! Mr. Sportsman: Anti-Firearms Fanatics Are Trying to Put Something Over on You," *National Sportsman*, December 1940, 12–14; Bill Backus, "Rod and Gun: Watch for Attempt to Snatch Guns," *Hackensack (N.J.) Record*, September 17, 1940, 17; "Checking of Guns Fought at Redlands," *Los Angeles Times*, September 17, 1940, part 2, 20; "Ordinance Proposed to Make Registration of Firearms Compulsory," *San Bernardino County (Calif.) Sun*, September 8, 1940, 15.

164. "Important Decisions," 22.

165. "Zero Hour," *AR*, December 1940, 4.

166. "Suggest Training in Use of Small Arms by Citizens," *Oshkosh (Wis.) Northwestern*, June 25, 1940, 9.

167. C. B. Lister, "An Open Letter: To the Chairman of Local Civilian Councils," *AR*, February 1942, 29.

168. See, e.g., "The Nazi Deadline," *PGN*, May 1942, 24–25; Eltinge F. Warner, "Gun Registration?," *F&S*, April 1941, 21; Francis A. Marvin, Jr., "The Latest Plot to Take Your Guns Away," *OL*, April 1941, 20–22.

169. See, e.g., Bruce Catton, "The Spotlight on Fifth Column Diplomacy!," *Akron (Ohio) Beacon Journal*, November 24, 1940, 4D; "Has the Dies Committee Inquiry Been of Benefit to the U.S.?," *Detroit (Mich.) Free Press*, June 9, 1940, 5; "The American Forum: Has the Dies Committee Inquiry Been of Benefit to the U.S.?," *Pittsburgh Sun-Telegraph*, June 2, 1940, part 4, 2.

170. "Fifth Column Activities," *Foreign Service Magazine*, October 1940, 42.

171. Not every gun rights advocate made this switch right away. See, e.g., Bob Nichols, "In Times Like These," *F&S*, March 1941, 19. Despite having embraced the fifth column sensationalism, at times the NRA still made sure to distribute "common-sense" arguments against firearms controls. See, e.g., C. B. Lister, "Awakening," *AR*, September 1941, 6; "The Most Uncommon Thing," *AR*, March 1941, 4.

172. See, e.g., "Outdoors," *St. Louis (Mo.) Dispatch*, January 12, 1941, 4A; "Lent Tells Rifle League About Pending Bills," *Kingston (N.Y.) Daily Freeman*, December 5, 1940, 9.

173. See, e.g., NRA, *The Pro and Con of Firearms Legislation*, 14.

174. *Let's Fight the Fifth Column Trap*, reprinted in Al Seidler, "The Outdoor Sportsman," *Brooklyn Citizen*, December 23, 1940, 11. An original copy of *Let's Fight the Fifth Column Trap* does not appear to have survived—at least not that I could find after years of searching. Fortunately, the newspaper *Brooklyn Citizen* reprinted the entire special bulletin in two parts, on December 23 and 24, 1940.

175. *Let's Fight the Fifth Column Trap*, December 23, 1940, 11.

176. *Let's Fight the Fifth Column Trap*, December 24, 1940, 11.

177. C. B. Lister, "The Nazi Deadline," *American Rifleman*, February 1942, 7.

178. "Untitled," undated, HPSP, document 303, folder 41.

179. Letter from E. E. Torbett to John William "Elmer" Thomas, March 21, 1941, JWTP, box LG 48, Folder 63, Firearms Control Act; letter from Walter J. Seeliger to John William "Elmer" Thomas, March 21, 1941, JWTP, box LG 48, folder 63, Firearms Control Act.

180. Letter from Arthur G. Baraw, Los Angeles City Council secretary, to Los Angeles City Council, April 17, 1940, LACCMV1, folder Firearms-Small.

181. Letter from Walter C. Peterson, Los Angeles City Council clerk, to Los Angeles City Council Police and Fire Committee, November 8, 1940, LACCMV1, folder Firearms-Small; report from Los Angeles City Council Police and Fire Committee, April 30, 1940, LACCMV1, folder Firearms-Small; Letter from R. E. Davis, Los Angeles City Council clerk, to Los Angeles City Council, undated, LACCMV1, folder Firearms-Small.

182. Letter from C. B. Lister, NRA secretary-treasurer, to Los Angeles City Council, November 4, 1940, LACCMV1, folder Firearms-Small Registration.

183. Letter from Walter C. Peterson, Los Angeles City Council clerk, to Los Angeles City Council Legislative Committee, November 23, 1940, LACCMV1, folder Firearms-Small.

184. Letter from Walter C. Peterson, Los Angeles City Council clerk, to Los Angeles City Council Legislative Committee, March 26, 1941, LACCMV1, folder Firearms-Small.

185. See, e.g., J. R. Stewart, "Right to Bear Arms," *Oakland (Calif.) Tribune*, April 24, 1941, 44; "Game Association Opposes Bills to Restrict Firearms," *Bakersfield Californian*, March 27, 1941, 4; "Petitions Hit Proposed Bills Regulating Guns," *Santa Clarita (Calif.) Signal*, March 14, 1941, 1; Gun Owner, "Firearms Restrictions," *Santa Rosa (Calif.) Press Democrat*, March 12, 1941, 12; E. B. Anderson, "Arming Our People," *Oakland Tribune*, February 17, 1941, 24.

186. For a useful history of the Zoot Suit Riots, see Eduardo Obregon Pagan, *Murder at the Sleepy Lagoon: Zoot Suits, Race, & Riot in Wartime L.A.* (Chapel Hill: University of North Carolina Press, 2003), 145–90.

187. Memorandum from C. B. Horrall, Los Angeles chief of police, to Los Angeles Board of Police Commissioners, "Registration, Regulation and Control of Firearms," undated, LACCMV1, folder Firearms.

188. Letter from Arthur G. Baraw, Los Angeles City Council secretary, to Los Angeles City Council, August 4, 1943, LACCMV1, folder Firearms; "New Law Would Curb Gun Traffic," *Los Angeles Times*, July 21, 1943, part 2, p. 12.

189. Report of Los Angeles City Council Public Safety Committee, September 21, 1943, LACCMV1, folder Firearms.

190. "Gun Owners Protest Curb," *Los Angeles Times*, September 16, 1943, part 2, p. 1.

191. See, e.g., Jim Day, "Pipefuls," *Bakersfield Californian*, October 30, 1943, 7; "Can't Be Done," *Van Nuys (Calif.) News*, October 15, 1943, 1; "Red Raider?," *Van Nuys News*, October 1, 1943, 1; "Kill Proposed Gun Ordinance," *Van Nuys News*, September 28, 1943, 2; "Council Kills Plan Involving Firearms Owners," *Los Angeles Times*, September 24, 1943, part 2, p. 10.

192. Richard Griswold del Castillo, "The Los Angeles 'Zoot Suit Riots' Revisited: Mexican and Latin American Perspectives, *Mexican Studies* 16 (2000): 367, 382–85.

193. Carl Winter, "Registering Firearms," *Van Nuys (Calif.) News*, October 15, 1943, part 2, p. 10.

194. See, e.g., C. B. Lister, "For Disarming the Bourgeoisie," *AR*, January 1947, 6; C. B. Lister, "Mission Accomplished!," *AR*, December 1945, 6, 9.

195. Walter Frank, "Outdoor Sportsmen: Sportsmen Protest Arms Registration," *Central New Jersey Home News* (Brunswick, N.J.), March 14, 1948, 21.

196. NRA, *Annual Report of the Executive Director and Secretary to the Board of Directors for the Calendar Year* (Washington, D.C., 1947), 20.

197. *Biennial Report of the Attorney General of the State of Vermont: Sesquicentennial Issue for the Two Years Ending June 30, 1940* (Springfield, Vt.: Springfield Printing Co., 1940), 13; "Bar Is for Registration of Foreign Political Party Members," *Burlington (Vt.) Free Press*, October 3, 1940, 2; "Changing Constitution," *Burlington Free Press*, September 19, 1940, 6.

198. Vermont Bar Association, *Report of the Proceedings of the Sixty-Fourth Annual Meeting October 7 and 8, 1941*, vol. 35 (1942): 94.

199. "No Amendments," *Burlington (Vt.) Free Press*, March 27, 1941, 6; "Four Suggested Changes Buried Under Big Vote," *Burlington Free Press*, March 26, 1941, 3.

200. See, e.g., *To Regulate Commerce in Firearms*, 19–20, 22–23, 59, 66, 69; *National Firearms Act*, 54–55, 81.
201. As it pertained to immigrant restrictions, the NRA was piggybacking on the recommendations of the Department of Justice and the Joint Federal-State Conference on Law Enforcement Problems of National Defense. See "To Head Session on Defense Laws," *Baltimore Sun*, July 29, 1940, 20; *Proceedings of the Federal-State Conference on Law Enforcement Problems of National Defense*, vii, 4–5, 14, 16–17, 29.
202. NRA, *The Pro and Con of Firearms Legislation*, 14.
203. NRA, *From Tyro to Master* (Washington, D.C., 1946), 63; NRA, *How to Obtain N.R.A. Rifle and Pistol Instructors' Ratings* (Washington, D.C., 1945), 3, MFP, box 4, folder 51.
204. See "300,000 in Rifle Association Told to Watch 5th Columnists," *Binghamton (N.Y.) Press and Sun-Bulletin*, June 7, 1940, 1; "U.S. Closes Canadian and Mexican Border to Passage of Aliens," *Kane (Pa.) Republican*, June 7, 1940, 1.
205. NRA, *Annual Report of the Executive Director and Secretary to the Board of Directors*, 20.
206. Charles, *Armed in America*, 232–34. The NRA made sure to tout its involvement World War II. See, e.g., C. B. Lister, "Important and Urgent," *AR*, October 1945, 1.
207. NRA, *Annual Report of the Executive Director and Secretary to the Board of Directors*, 21.
208. See, e.g., W. H. B. Smith, "Souvenir Firearms of World War II," *AR*, October 1945, 26–29.
209. See, e.g., "Theft of Pistol Prompts Plea on Souvenirs," *Binghamton (N.Y.) Press and Sun-Bulletin*, December 27, 1945, 3; Anne LoPresti, "List Automatic Weapon Souvenirs, U.S. Warns," *Dayton (Ohio) Herald*, December 15, 1945, 14; Robert C. Ruark, "Death in the Duffle Bags—Souvenir War Guns Give Police Headache as Crime Increases," *Pittsburgh Press*, December 9, 1945, 18; "U.S. Seizing Enemy Weapons in This Area," *Binghamton Press and Sun-Bulletin*, December 3, 1945, 5; "Chiefs Urge Close Check on Firearms," *Hartford (Conn.) Courant*, October 31, 1945, 1; "State Police Push Gun Registry to Check Crime Wave as Watchman Dies of Injuries," *Indianapolis (Ind.) News*, September 18, 1945, 1; Elmer Gaede, "Guns: War Souvenirs Can Run You Afoul of the Law," *Detroit (Mich.) Free Press*, August 12, 1945, 12.
210. Harry S. Truman, President's News Conference, January 15, 1946, Public Papers of Harry S. Truman 1945–1953, https://www.trumanlibrary.org/publicpapers/index.php?pid=1457.
211. See, e.g., Anne LoPresti, "List Automatic Weapon Souvenirs, U.S. Warns," *Dayton (Ohio) Herald*, December 15, 1945, 14; "U.S. Seizing Enemy Weapons in This Area," *Binghamton (N.Y.) Press and Sun Bulletin*, December 3, 1945, 5.
212. "Proposed Registration of Firearms Opposed," *Louisville (Ky.) Courier-Journal*, January 12, 1946, 13; "Bill for Arms Registration Rouses Anger of Sportsmen," *Baltimore (Md.) Sun*, January 12, 1946, 9; "Hawkes Firearms Bill Awaits Action," *Bridgewater (N.J.) Courier-News*, January 4, 1946, 2.
213. C. B. Lister, "Pious Subterfuge," *AR*, January 1946, 9. Even before President Truman addressed the issue or a bill was proposed, the NRA railed against it as a "Gestapo" idea, built on the "legislative dictum on which Mussolini, Hitler, and every dictator before rode into power." See C. B. Lister, "The Backdoor Approach,"

AR, November 1945, 5. The NRA characterized contemporaneous state attempts at firearms registration in the same vein. See, e.g., "Bailey Urged to Veto Firearms Registration," *Jackson (Miss.) Clarion-Ledger*, February 19, 1946, 8 (summarizing and quoting letter from NRA secretary-treasurer C. B. Lister to Mississippi governor Thomas L. Bailey).

214. Lister, "Pious Subterfuge," 9.

215. For the quotations, see Mike Dwyer, "Line on the Sportsman," *Oakland (Calif.) Tribune*, February 12, 1946, 11; Milford K. Smith," Stray Shots and Short Casts," *Rutland (Vt.) Daily Herald*, February 4, 1946, 8; Rudolph O. Prosser, "Gun Registration," *Passaic (N.J.) Herald-News*, January 30, 1946, 10; Johnny Mock, "New Firearms Bill Recalls Drive in 1940 Which Failed," *Pittsburgh Press*, January 15, 1946, 28; "Proposed Law Would Classify Sportsmen as Criminals," *Bridgewater (N.J.) Courier-News*, January 15, 1946, 4.

216. See, e.g., Letter from Lyle H. Boren to B. R. Elliott, February 15, 1946, LHBP, box 21, folder 17, Gun Control; "One More Restriction," *Portsmouth (N.H.) Herald*, February 12, 1946, 4; form letter from Bourke Hickenlooper to constituents, January 17, 1946, BHP, box 20, folder Gun Control 1946.

217. "Firearms Registration," *Detroit Free Press*, January 25, 1947, 3.

218. "Clark Will Seek Tighter Firearms Laws," *Louisville (Ky.) Courier-Journal*, December 8, 1946, 12.

219. See, e.g., Ted Trueblood, "Mid-Summer Miscellany," PGN, June 1947, 14, 38.

220. For NRA literature opposing Senator Wiley's bill, see "Progress Report: Legislation," *AR*, March 1947, 29; C. B. Lister, "Straightening the Record," *AR*, March 1947, 6; C. B. Lister, "For Disarming the Bourgeoisie," *AR*, January 1947, 7.

221. Tubby Toms, "Out in the Open," *Indianapolis (Ind.) News*, February 21, 1947, part 2, 20. For the NRA's memorandum announcing this development, see C. B. Lister, memorandum to NRA Directors, Referees and Club Secretaries, undated 1947, MFP, box 5, folder 52.

222. C. B. Lister, "A Gun-Shy Texan," *AR*, February 1947, 6.

223. Lister, 231–35.

224. "Opinions on the Sale of Guns," *New York Herald Tribune*, May 18, 1958, 24.

225. See letter from Irving Perlmeter, head of Public Relations, Department of Treasury, to Charles W. Jackson, director of advertising liaison, Office of Government Reports, July 23, 1947, JTGP, box 4, folder War Trophies; circular from Carroll E. Mealey, deputy commissioner, Department of Treasury, "Registration of Machine Pistols and Machine Guns Imported by Members of the Armed Forces," July 10, 1947, JTGP, box 4, folder War Trophies; circular from G. F. Hussey, Jr., chief of Bureau of Ordnance, "Public Safety in Handling Explosive-Type War Trophies," July 1, 1947, JTGP, box 4, folder War Trophies; circular from Dwight D. Eisenhower, chief of staff, War Department, "War Trophies: Explosive Type," June 20, 1947, JTGP, box 4, folder War Trophies; press release, Department of Treasury, no. S-332, May 18, 1947, JTGP, box 4, folder War Trophies; circular from R. J. Stann, director of public relations, NRA, untitled, undated, JTGP, box 4, folder War Trophies.

226. Enclosure to circular from Carroll E. Mealey, deputy commissioner, Department of Treasury, untitled, April 30, 1947, JTGP, box 4, folder War Trophies; memorandum from Henry Schneider, War Trophy Safety Committee, to President Harry S. Truman, July 24, 1947, HSTP/WHCF/PPF, box 630, folder 2177, NRA.

227. "Battlefield Trophies," AR, November 1947, 42; "Drive Under Way to 'Pull Teeth' of Wartime Trophies," White Plains (N.Y.) Journal News, June 18, 1947, 7; "Government Cracks Down on Weapons," Shreveport (La.) Times, May 19, 1947, 8.

228. In a circular on the NWTSP, the NRA informed affiliated clubs that participation was highly encouraged because "from an NRA standpoint even a few unfortunate accidents due to the carelessness in the handling and use of an explosive-type weapons have a profound adverse effect on public opinion." Circular from R. J. Stann, director of Public Relations, NRA, untitled, undated, JTGP, box 4, folder War Trophies.

229. For the history of Oswald's rifle, see Keith Wheeler, " 'Cursed Gun'—the Track of C2766," Life, August 27, 1965, 62–65; Report of the President's Commission on the Assassination of President Kennedy (Washington, D.C.: U.S. Government Printing Office, 1964), 118–21.

3. The Great "Gun Lobby" Awakening

1. Oscar Godbout, "Shooters and Legislative Group Will Zero in on Sullivan Law Thursday," NYT, November 17, 1963, S17.

2. Patrick J. Charles, Armed in America: A History AR of Gun Rights from Colonial Militias to Concealed Carry (Amherst, N.Y.: Prometheus Books, 2018), 234–36. This is not to say, however, that several lawmakers and government officials were unaware of the NRA's opposition. See, e.g., memorandum from James V. Bennett to attorney general William P. Rogers, "Re: Proposal for Gun Registration," October 19, 1959, JVBPP, Subject Files, 1933–1966, box 10, folder 6; letter from James V. Bennett to Paul H. Douglas, March 12, 1958, JVBPP, Subject Files, 1933–1966, box 10, folder 6.

3. McCandlish Phillips, "Legislators Ask Arms Law Change," NYT, November 23, 1963, 30.

4. See "Guns in the City," NYT, June 26, 1964, 28; "Rockefeller Signs Bill on Firearms," NYT, April 7, 1964, 27; "New Restrictions on Firearms Quickly Voted by State Senate," NYT, February 20, 1964, 31.

5. See, e.g., Nicholas Kristof, "It's Time to Talk About the N.R.A.," NYT, October 29, 2018; Michael S. Rosenwald, "The NRA Once Believed in Gun Control and Had a Leader Who Pushed for It," Washington Post, February 22, 2018; Arica L. Coleman, "When the NRA Supported Gun Control," Time, July 29, 2016; Steven Rosenfeld, "The NRA Once Supported Gun Control," Salon, January 14, 2013; Adam Winkler, "The Secret History of Guns," Atlantic, September 2011.

6. See, e.g., memorandum from C. B. Lister, NRA executive director, to NRA board of directors, "Keeping 'On the Beam,' " September 19, 1949, MAEP, box 27.

7. See Jennifer Carlson, *Citizen-Protectors: The Everyday Politics of Guns in an Age of Decline* (New York: Oxford University Press, 2015), 61–62; Michael Waldman, *The Second Amendment: A Biography* (New York: Simon & Schuster, 2014), 87–107; Adam Winkler, *Gunfight: The Battle Over the Right to Bear Arms in America* (New York: Norton, 2011), 8–9, 63–68; Joan Burbick, *Gun Show Nation: Gun Culture and American Democracy* (New York: New Press, 2006), 67–84; Kristin A. Goss, *Disarmed: The Missing Movement for Gun Control* (Princeton, N.J.: Princeton University Press, 2006), 172–73. But also see Matthew J. Lacombe, *Firepower: How the NRA Turned Gun Owners Into a Political Force* (Princeton, N.J.: Princeton University Press, 2021) (properly demonstrating how the NRA gradually grew its political power from the 1930s through the early 1970s).
8. Tim Mak, *Misfire: Inside the Downfall of the NRA* (New York: Penguin Books, 2021), 43–45.
9. See, e.g., "The Illegal Use of Guns," *AR*, December 1964, 16; "Realistic Firearms Controls," *AR*, January 1964, 14; "There Ought to Be a Law!," *AR*, October 1956, 16; "This Is Our Stand," *AR*, May 1965, 16; Merritt A. Edson, "As Allowed by Law," *AR*, November 1953, 16; Merritt A. Edson, "Education Versus Legislation," *AR*, March 1955, 16; Merritt A. Edson, "Education Versus Legislation," *AR*, April 1953, 12; "Congratulations, Gentlemen," *AR*, May 1930, 6.
10. See, e.g., NRA, *The Story of the National Rifle Association* (Washington, D.C., 1961), 4.
11. "Minutes of the Meeting of Directors of the National Rifle Association of America," February 1, 1946, MAEP, box 7.
12. "A Busy Legislative Year Ahead," *AR*, January 1955, 47. At times, however, the original five-part test periodically appeared in post-1961 literature. See, e.g., NRA, *Standing Firm: Against Efforts to Disarm American Sportsmen by Restrictive Legislation* (Washington, D.C., 1968); "Test of a Gun Law," *AR*, February 1963, 13. If an NRA member or gun rights supporter was unsure whether a law was "reasonable," they were advised to reach out to their local NRA representative, state shooting representative or local shooting representative. See, e.g., Tom Siatos, "Editorially Speaking," *G&A*, June 1961, 6.
13. See, e.g., NRA, *"Be It Enacted" May Mean Goodbye Guns!* (Washington, D.C., 1961), 6; NRA, *"Be It Enacted" May Mean Goodbye Guns* (Washington, D.C., 1953), 2; Merritt A. Edson, NRA executive director, "National Rifle Association's 1951 Annual Convention Executive Director's Message," October 8, 1951, MAEP, box 15.
14. See, e.g., "Rifleman Spokesmen Refute New Control," *Arizona Republic* (Phoenix), May 5, 1963, 10C; Floyd L. Parks, NRA executive director, "Appreciate Support of Firearms Views," *Indianapolis (Ind.) Star*, May 8, 1958, 16; Floyd L. Parks, NRA executive director, "Controlling Firearms," *Minneapolis Star*, January 21, 1958, 8A; Merritt A. Edson, NRA executive director, "Asks: Why Blame Gun?," *Rock Island (Ill.) Argus*, October 31, 1953, 4.
15. See, e.g., Earl Shelsby, "Outdoor Living," *Baltimore (Md.) Sun*, January 18, 1965, S16; Robert Charles, "Review Gun Laws Already on Books," *Boston Globe*, February 8, 1964, 6; "Proposed Firearms Laws Must Be Effective, Necessary," *Stroudsburg (Pa.)*

Pocono Record, December 14, 1963, 18; Jerry W. Perkins, "Anti-Gun Law Proposals Hit," *Tulare (Calif.) Advance Register*, December 10, 1963, 10; "Protect What Makes Us Strong!," *GM*, March 1963, 40, 61–62; "Propose Action Against Use, Not Possession of Firearms," *Hazelton (Pa.) Standard-Speaker*, July 10, 1962, 20; Bob Walsh, "Observations: Outlaw Guns?," *Warren County (Pa.) Observer*, December 7, 1960, 4; "A Gun Law Test," *Great Falls (Mont.) Tribune*, December 4, 1960, 6; C. Richard Rogers, "Rifleman Asks Questions About Any Legislation to Restrict Firearms," *Indianapolis (Ind.) Star*, October 11, 1959, 22; Howard J. Smith Jr., "Guns and the Law," *New York Herald Tribune*, September 28, 1959, 20; "Statement of C. R. Gutermuth, director Wildlife Management Institute, Relating to Interstate Traffic in Firearms and Ammunition, Alcohol and Tobacco Tax Division," August 27, 1957, LMP, box 154, folder 5, Firearms; William Daniel Dalton, "Letter to the Editor: Anti-Gun Bill Before State Legislature Called Ridiculous by Rifle Association Member," *Bedford (Ind.) Daily-Times Mail*, January 28, 1957, 10.

16. "National Rifle Association Convention Supplement," *AR*, December 1948, 24, 30.
17. See, e.g., memorandum from C. B. Lister, NRA executive director, to NRA board of directors, "Keeping 'On the Beam,'" September 19, 1949, MAEP, box 27.
18. Charles, *Armed in America*, 207.
19. See, e.g., Louis F. Lucas, "This Very Day," *AR*, August 1959, 16; Merritt A. Edson, "The Greatest Dangers," *AR*, June 1955, 16; Merritt A. Edson, "Education Versus Legislation," *AR*, March 1955, 16; "A Busy Legislative Year Ahead," *AR*, January 1955, 47, 80.
20. John D. Dingell, "Criminals, Guns and the Gun Law Controversy!," *G&A*, April 1964, 22, 23.
21. See, e.g., C. B. Lister, "A Solider Speaks," *AR*, December 1949, 8; C. B. Lister, "Number One Problem," *AR*, July 1948, 8; C. B. Lister, "State of Mind," *AR*, June 1948, 8; C. B. Lister, "For Disarming the Bourgeoisie," *AR*, January 1947, 7; C. B. Lister, "As Ye Think," *AR*, June 1944, 7.
22. See, e.g., NRA, *Americans and Their Guns*, ed. James E. Serven (Harrisburg, Pa.: Stackpole Books, 1967); NRA, *Your NRA: Information for Members of the National Rifle Association of America* (1959) (on file with author); NRA, *Questions and Answers: Facts About the N.R.A.* (1946); letter from C. B. Lister, NRA secretary-treasurer, to NRA members, August 26, 1941, MFP, box 5, folder 52; NRA, *I Am the N.R.A.* (1936) (on file with author).
23. See, e.g., "The NRA of America," *AR*, June 1961, 16; memorandum from C. B. Lister, NRA secretary-treasurer, to NRA members, "Important and Urgent!," undated, reprinted in *AR*, October 1945, 1; NRA, *The Pro and Con of Firearms Legislation*, 16–17; "He Profits Most Who Serves Best," *AR*, February 1938, 4.
24. Charles, *Armed in America*, 231–38, 195–97, 254.
25. See, e.g., "Directors Meeting, 1939," *AR*, March 1939, 9, 11.
26. Daniel K. Stern, "Tell the People!," *AR*, March 1955, 39, 40.
27. See "NRA 'Mission Accomplished,'" *AR*, December 1945, 6–9.
28. See, e.g., "The National Rifle Ass'n," *Sports Afield*, January 1920, 44. By 1961 the NRA stated in its annual operating report that its relationship with the Department of

Defense was "on a most friendly and cooperative basis" and working with the NBPRP "closer . . . than ever before." NRA, *1961 Operating Reports*, 4.

29. For background on the information contained in this paragraph, see *Americans and Their Guns*, 102–227; Robert M. Ujevich, legislative attorney, Library of Congress Legislative Reference Service, "Legislative History of 10 U.S.C. 4308," April 21, 1965, CSJP, box 187, folder Firearms; Grover S. Williams, legislative attorney, Library of Congress Legislative Reference Service, "Federal Assistance to Rifle Clubs," June 22, 1964, CSJP, box 187, folder Firearms; Frank C. Daniel, NRA secretary, "Civilian Marksmanship in Countries Other than the United States," October 31, 1960, CTHP, box 433, folder NRA; Frank C. Daniel, NRA secretary, "Legislative History—National Board for the Promotion of Rifle Practice," October 31, 1960, CTHP, box 433, folder NRA; legislative bulletin from Merritt A. Edson, NRA executive director, to NRA members, "[Appropriations for the National Board for the Promotion of Rifle Prac-tice]," April 14, 1952, CTHP, box 433, folder 10, NRA; C. B. Lister, "You Ought to Know . . . the Director of Civilian Marksmanship, the National Board for the Pro-motion of Rifle Practice," AR, March 1950, 32–33.

30. See, e.g., "The National Rifle Association of America," *AR*, October 1940, 64; "The Committee Cooperates," *AR*, April 1938, 4; NRA, *The Typical American Sport* (Wash-ington, D.C., 1935), 15; "Merry Christmas—And Gun Laws," *AR*, December 1929, 6; "7 Reasons Why Your Friends Should Be Members of the Association," *AR*, April 1927, 147; "$100,000 for Civilian Clubs," *AR*, February 1927, 56; "The Budget and You," *AR*, December 15, 1926, 376; "National Board Drafts Regulations for Rifle Practice Fund," *A&M*, January 25, 1917, 343–44; "The Civilian Rifle Practice Appro-priation," *A&M*, August 17, 1916, 409. In 1928, with inclusion of an amendment to the NDA codifying the National Matches, the NRA was confident that appropriations for said matches would be budgeted annually. For more background on this, see Milton A. Reckord, "National Matches Secured Annually," *AR*, July 1928, 14; "A Victory," *AR*, July 1928, 6; Milton A. Reckord, "National Matches Definitely Secured for Fall of 1928," *AR*, April 1928, 19, 32; "Tell Them!," *AR*, April 1928, 6; "The Les-son of the National Match Fight," *AR*, March 1928, 22; "Time for a Show-Down," *AR*, February 1928, 74; Milton A. Reckord, "To Members of the National Rifle Asso-ciation," *AR*, January 1928, 8; "Shall the National Matches Be Held Each Year?," *AR*, August 1927, 355. However, the events of the Great Depression awakened the NRA to the reality that even though federal law required the War Department to budget appropriations for the National Matches, there was no guarantee that said appropriations would be forthcoming. It was not until the mid-twentieth century, following the lessons learned from the congressional appropriations process during the Great Depression, as well as the Franklin D. Roosevelt adminis-tration's decision to pause the sale of surplus military equipment to NRA affili-ated clubs and members after news reports of said equipment falling into the hands of Nazi sympathizers, that the NRA changed the manner in which it described the appropriations or "government aid" that ultimately benefited the NRA, its affiliated clubs, and members. "Regional Matches to Take Place of National

Matches," *AR*, July 1932, 14–15; *Americans and Their Guns*, 231–32. Therein NRA officials began consistently messaging that the organization did not at all benefit financially from defense appropriations or the continued existence of the NBPRP. See, e.g., NRA, *Bylaws of the National Rifle Association of America* (Washington, D.C., March 29, 1957), i; Merritt A. Edson, "Tis Education Forms the Common Mind," *AR*, October 1952, 20; "Congress Votes Funds for National Board," *AR*, August 1952, 20, 34; Merritt A. Edson, "Hangman or Healer!," *AR*, May 1952, 12. While the NRA was not wrong in denying a *direct* financial benefit, the truth was it materially benefited, whether measured via the continued growth in NRA membership rolls, the NRA maintaining its connections and affiliation with the U.S. military, or the NRA using the NBPRP as a political springboard for other lobbying efforts. See, e.g., C. Richard Rogers, "The NRA Story," *GM*, April 1962, 16, 47; "Rifle Club Boondoggle," *AR*, January 1958, 14; J. A. Harper, "Can't We Awaken the National Board?," *AR*, April 1952, 13–15.

31. "Modern Minute Men Proposed as Guard Against Red Threat," *Jefferson City (Mo.) Post-Tribune*, October 21, 1942, 1; "Home Guard of Sportsmen Receives Additional Support," *Willmington (Del.) News Journal*, June 3, 1942, 1.

32. "U.S. Home Defense Need Cited: Rifleman Training Urged," *Indianapolis (Ind.) Star*, June 14, 1961, 40.

33. See, e.g., August P. Beilmann, "For Gun Enthusiasts," *Washington (Mo.) Citizen*, March 27, 1961, 6; Bill Allen, "Outdoor Georgia: NRA Firearm Instruction Program Eases Parental Anxiety Over Children's Guns," *Atlanta Constitution*, July 25, 1953, 8; "Rifle Training Pays Dividends for Teenagers," *Waco (Tex.) Tribune-Herald*, April 27, 1952, sec. 4, 8; C. B. Lister, "You Ought to Know . . . the Director of Civilian Marksmanship, the National Board for the Promotion of Rifle Practice," *AR*, March 1950, 32–33; memorandum from C. B. Lister, NRA executive director, to Major General Merritt A. Edson, "Notes Regarding the National Rifle Association of America," January 3, 1950, MAEP, box 27; "Pistol and Rifle Shooting Popular American Sport," *Paterson (N.J.) Morning Call*, April 4, 1944, 16.

34. NRA, *1963 Operating Report* (Washington, D.C., 1964), 22.

35. See, e.g., "Outdoors Questions," *Pittsburgh Press*, March 31, 1963, sec. VI, p. 4; Al Bennett, "Outdoor Life," *Bridgeport (Conn.) Post*, February 17, 1963, D5.

36. NRA and Department of the Army, *The Right to Keep and Bear Arms* (Washington, D.C.: Army Pictorial Center, 1962) (the film can be found on YouTube).

37. The coproduction of films with the U.S. military was in part driven by the NRA's congressional allies. See letter from Carl T. Hayden to Robert S. McNamara, secretary of defense, September 24, 1962, CTHP, box 422, folder 10, NRA (requesting that appropriations be used to "publicize and document in motion pictures and by all other means of communication" the NRA-sponsored national matches).

38. See, e.g., "88th Annual Meetings," *AR*, May 1959, 18; John Scofield, "Armed, Alert, and Peaceful," *AR*, October 1950, 10; C. B. Lister, "It Is Good—for a Free America," *AR*, November 1947, 10.

39. Often the NRA offered free memberships to military officers who served in either presidential administrations or in other high-ranking capacities to gain access. See RLSP, box 88, folder NRA; RBAP, box 47, folder NRA Speech; CELP, box B122, folder NRA.

40. Letter from Milton A. Reckord, NRA executive vice president, to Colonel James Roosevelt, January 4, 1938, FDRPP, Personal Files, part 11, folder NRA.

41. Memorandum from William D. Hassett, White House Assistant, to Secretary of War Harry H. Woodring, January 25, 1938, FDRPP, Personal Files, part 11, folder NRA.

42. Letter from President Franklin D. Roosevelt to Milton A. Reckord, NRA executive vice president, February 1, 1938, FDRPP, Personal Files, part 11, folder NRA; letter from Secretary of War Harry H. Woodring to William D. Hassett, White House Assistant, January 29, 1938, FDRPP, Personal Files, part 11, folder NRA.

43. "President Commends Association at Annual Meeting," *AR*, March 1938, 22.

44. Letter from Jim Berryman, *American Rifleman* editor, to Charles G. Ross, secretary to President Harry S. Truman, October 19, 1945, HSTPF, box 630, folder NRA.

45. "The President of the United States," *AR*, December 1945, 10; letter from President Harry S. Truman to C. B. Lister, NRA secretary-treasurer, November 14, 1945, HSTPF, box 630, folder NRA; letter from Jim Berryman, *American Rifleman* editor, to Eben Ayers, press secretary to President Harry S. Truman, HSTPF, box 630, folder NRA.

46. See HSTPF, Official File, box 339, folder War Trophies; JTGP, box 4, folder War Trophies.

47. See DDEPP, Personal Files, box 845, folder NRA.

48. Letter from President Dwight D. Eisenhower to Floyd L. Parks, NRA executive director, May 18, 1956, DDEPP, Personal Files, box 845, folder NRA; letter from President Dwight D. Eisenhower to Floyd L. Parks, NRA executive director, May 7, 1956, DDEPP, Personal Files, box 845, folder NRA; letter from Floyd L. Parks, NRA executive director, to President Dwight D. Eisenhower, May 4, 1956, DDEPP, Personal Files, box 845, folder NRA; memorandum from Colonel Robert L. Schulz to Ann Whitman, May 1, 1956, DDEPP, Personal Files, box 845, folder NRA; letter from Floyd L. Parks, NRA executive director, to Colonel Robert L. Schulz, military aide to President Dwight D. Eisenhower, April 25, 1956, DDEPP, Personal Files, box 845, folder NRA.

49. On Kennedy, see ". . . An Important Role in Our National Defense," *AR*, May 1961, 26–27; letter from Frank C. Daniel, NRA official, to President John F. Kennedy, April 19, 1961, JFKPP, President's Office Files, Personal Secretary's Files, Memberships, December 1960–April 1961; letter from President John F. Kennedy to Franklin L. Orth, NRA executive vice president, March 20, 1961, JFKPP, President's Office Files, Personal Secretary's Files, Memberships, December 1960–April 1961; letter from Franklin L. Orth, NRA executive vice president, to President John F. Kennedy, March 7, 1961, JFKPP, President's Office Files, Personal Secretary's Files, Memberships, December 1960–April 1961; Charles, *Armed in America*, 242–44. Nixon disavowed his gifted NRA life membership upon assuming the presidency. See

"Concerning President Nixon," AR, April 1969, 16; "Rifle Unit Membership Is Disavowed by Nixon," NYT, February 23, 1969, 48.

50. See generally DDEPP, Personal Files, box 7, book 6.

51. Message of the President to be Read by the Honorable Bryce N. Harlow at the Annual Banquet of the NRA, March 23, 1960, DDEPP, Personal Files, box 845, folder NRA; markup of NRA drafted letter, undated, DDEPP, Personal Files, box 845, folder NRA; letter from Franklin L. Orth, NRA executive vice president, to Bryce N. Harlow, deputy assistant to President Dwight D. Eisenhower, February 15, 1960, DDEPP, Personal Files, box 845, folder NRA.

52. See, e.g., Milton Reckord, "Speech #1," undated 1967, MRP, series 5, box 14, folder 6 ("Among the many outstanding public personages who have been members of the National Rifle Association are five Presidents and two Chief Justices of the United States Supreme Court.").

53. Letter from Floyd L. Parks, NRA executive director, to Colonel Robert L. Schulz, April 25, 1956, DDEPP, Personal Files, box 845, folder NRA.

54. The principal evidence against the NRA's assertion can be found in Chief Justice Earl Warren's papers, which detail the various organizations in which Warren was truly active. See generally Earl Warren Papers, boxes 754–86 (Washington, D.C.: Library of Congress Manuscripts Division). The NRA is not listed.

55. See, e.g., C. B. Lister, "Well, Well!," AR, November 1948, 10; NRA, The Story of the Alco Bill (1934), 4–5, MFP, box 5, folder.

56. See, e.g., "The Positive Approach," AR, August 1961, 16; "Telling Our Story," AR, January 1961, 16; "Gallup Poll Hits Gun Owners," AR, October 1959, 12; "Let's Take the Offensive," AR, September 1958, 16.

57. "Let's Sound Off!," AR, July 1956, 16.

58. Louis F. Lucas, "This Very Day," AR, August 1959, 16.

59. See, e.g., John F. Soubier, "Before It's Too Late . . .," AR, September 1958, 17–19; "A Busy Legislative Year Ahead," AR, January 1955, 47, 80; Frank C. Daniel, "The Gun Law Problem," AR, February 1953, 16–18; "Second Annual NRA Convention," AR, December 1949, 21, 22. The earliest instance I could find in which sportsmen, hunters, and gun owners were provided with express talking points and guidance in defeating restrictive firearms legislation was written by Nathaniel C. Nash in 1916, who would go on to serve as a USRA official and later as NRA president. See Nathaniel C. Nash, Jr., "Anti-Revolver Legislation: Part 3," A&M, November 30, 1916, 104, 107; Nathaniel C. Nash, Jr., "Anti-Revolver Legislation: Part 2," A&M, November 23, 1916, 165–66; Nathaniel C. Nash, Jr., "Anti-Revolver Legislation: Part 1," A&M, November 16, 1916, 145–46.

60. "A Paul Revere Organization," AR, March 1958, 14.

61. The first proposal was an amendment to the 1938 Federal Firearms Act (FFA) prohibiting the shipment, transportation, or receipt in interstate or international commerce of any firearm by any person who was convicted or under indictment for a crime punishable for a term exceeding one year. See United States Treasury Department Internal Revenue Service, "News Release: IR-404," October 4, 1961,

JVBPP, Subject Matter Files, 1933–1966, box 11, folder 8; "Crime Legislation Sent to the White House," *Los Angeles Times*, September 20, 1961, 4; "Senate Broadens Federal Firearms Act," *Louisville (Ky.) Courier-Journal*, June 14, 1961, 6; "Tough Laws to Battle Crime Urged," *Santa Rosa (Calif.) Press Democrat*, April 7, 1961, 11. The second proposal was also an amendment to the FFA that repealed and replaced the phrase "crime of violence" with "crime punishable by imprisonment for a term exceeding one year." See An Act to Strengthen the Federal Firearms Act, Public Law 87–342, October 3, 1961; "New Public Law Amends Arms Shipment Regulations," *Van Nuys (Calif.) Valley News*, October 15, 1961, 19A. The NRA-sponsored UFA had defined the phrase "crime of violence" as the crimes of "murder, manslaughter, rape, mayhem, assault to do great bodily harm, robbery, burglary [housebreaking, breaking and entering, kidnapping and larceny]." *Uniform Firearms Act: Drafted by the National Conference of Commissioners on Uniform State Laws* (Chicago, 1930), 3, § 1. Although the NRA was behind the amended language and intended it to define more narrowly who was prohibited from receiving, shipping, or transporting a firearm in interstate or foreign commerce, some gun rights supporters expressed concern that it could be used to disarm more people, not less. See, e.g., Ben Avery, "Rod and Gun: New Anti-Gun Law Could Disarm U.S.," *Arizona Republic* (Phoenix), April 8, 1962, C9.

62. See, e.g., "Getting Tougher with Criminals," *Camden (N.J.) Courier-Post*, March 1, 1960, 12; Roscoe Drummond, "'Easy Acquisition' of Firearms Helps Juvenile Criminals?," *San Bernardino County (Calif.) Sun*, December 31, 1959, 32; Roscoe Drummond, "Juvenile Problem: Weapons in the Wrong Hands," *Cincinnati (Ohio) Enquirer*, December 30, 1959, 8; Roscoe Drummond, "Firearms Possession Law Is Problem for Congress," *New York Herald Tribune*, December 28, 1959, 15; "Juvenile Gangs and Firearms Control," *Asheville (N.C.) Citizen-Times*, November 14, 1959, 5; Peter Kihss, "US Urged to Curb Flow of Weapons to Street Gangs," *NYT*, September 24, 1959, 1; George Gallup, "Public Would Deny Teenagers Guns," *Arizona Republic* (Phoenix), September 4, 1959, 7.

63. This prohibition was a key provision in the NRA-sponsored Uniform Firearms Act (UFA) and the USRA-sponsored Capper Bill. See *Uniform Firearms Act*, 5, § 8; "A Bill to Provide for Uniform Revolver Sales: Based Upon Senate Bill 4012 Introduced in the U.S. Senate," September 22, 1922, §§ 9–10, CLGP, box 2, folder Gun Law Correspondence.

64. "Riflemen Spokesmen Refute New Control," *Arizona Republic* (Phoenix), May 5, 1963, 15C; "Right to Own Gun Warmly Defended," *Pittsburgh Post-Gazette*, May 3, 1963, 4; "Curb on Weapons for Law-Abiding Persons Opposed," *St. Louis (Mo.) Post-Dispatch*, May 2, 1963, 2; "Crime and Punishment," *AR*, April 1963, 16; "A Knowledge of Existing Gun Laws," *AR*, March 1963, 12.

65. See, e.g., E. B. Mann, "The Editor's Corner," *GM*, December 1961, 6. It is worth noting that—much like it leveraged its involvement in both the UFA and the 1934 National Firearms Act (NFA) to obtain political credibility—the NRA leveraged its cooperation with Dodd to lobby for beneficial defense appropriations. See

Statement of Franklin L. Orth, executive vice president National Rifle Association of America, to the Defense Subcommittee of the Appropriations Committee of the United States Senate, May 23, 1962, 8, BHP, box 15, folder NRA Correspondence, 1957–1963. Months later, after President Kennedy's assassination, the NRA claimed that it cooperated with Dodd to stop the "relative ease" with which "unscrupulous dealers" sold and minors purchased handguns "through advertisements in cheap, pulp magazines and their subsequent delivery by common carrier." See letter from Franklin L. Orth, NRA executive vice president, to Hugh Scott, December 7, 1963, HSP, box 78.

66. "Mail-Order Guns," AR, August 1963, 16.

67. Carl Bakal, The Right to Bear Arms (New York: McGraw-Hill, 1966), 194–95. This is not to say, however, that the NRA did not maintain reservations about proceeding with Dodd's S. 1975 as written. See letter from Franklin L. Orth, NRA executive vice president, to Robert F. Sikes, November 20, 1963, RFSP, box 197, folder Firearms (outlining the NRA's policy on firearms controls and stating formal objections to Dodd's S. 1975).

68. Kenneth G. Brown, "Is Control Over Guns Needed?," La Crosse (Wis.) Tribune, February 23, 1964, 24; "Gun Control Law Planned," Albany (Ore.) Democrat-Herald, December 5, 1963.

69. See J. J. Basil and Daniel J. Moutin, "Firearms Legislation and the Gun Owner," AR, July 1964, 30–32; "Reasonable and Informed Citizens," AR, June 1964, 16; Misuse of Firearms," AR, March 1964, 16; "Basic Facts of Firearms Control," AR, February 1964, 14; "Realistic Firearms Controls," AR, January 1964, 14; letter from Franklin L. Orth, NRA executive vice president, and Louis F. Lucas, NRA executive director, to NRA members, [January] 1964, JGOP, box 2, folder Gun Control; E. B. Mann, "The Second Amendment Is NOT Enough!," GM, January 1964, 16–18. Franklin L. Orth, "Right Upheld to Bear Arms," NYT, December 3, 1963, 42.

70. "Law and Order," AR, July 1964, 16.

71. For details on the NRA's agitation with the media, see Charles, Armed in America, 250–54.

72. See, e.g., David Willis, "Kennedy Death Reveals Laxity in Most States," Orlando (Fla.) Sentinel, January 28, 1964, 13A; Daniel Rapoport, "Was Rep. Anfuso's Bill Really a Ridiculous One?," Murfreesboro (Tenn.) Daily News-Journal, January 20, 1964, 8; Josephine Ripley, "The Case for Gun Controls," Honolulu (Hawaii) Advertiser, December 29, 1963, A10, Tom Nolan, "Pressure Is On to Make It Harder to Pull Trigger," Doylestown (Pa.) Daily Intelligencer, December 5, 1963, 10; "Murder by Mail Order," Lansing (Mich.) State Journal, December 1, 1963, C4; Clarke Ash, "Spotlight on Lax Gun Laws," Miami (Fla.) News, November 26, 1963, 6A.

73. See Franklin L. Orth, "The Sportsman and the Law," Northeast Fish and Wildlife Conference, January 18, 1965, WEGP, box 6, folder 10 (speech detailing the NRA's position on firearms controls); Drew Pearson, "Tip on Telephones, Teen-Agers from LBJ," Fort Myers (Fla.) News-Press, December 8, 1963, 10; James Deakin, "Ease with Which Oswald Bought Gun Stirs Demand for New Law," St. Louis (Mo.) Post-Dispatch,

December 8, 1963, 73; "Here Is the Story of Rifle Used by Assassin," *Chicago Tribune*, December 8, 1963, 5; Drew Pearson, "Gun Lobby Killed Arms Import Bill," *Anniston (Ala.) Star*, December 8, 1963, 4; Drew Pearson, "Lax Laws Abet Mail-Order Crime," *Detroit Free Press*, December 8, 1963, B3; Frank A. White, "The Hoosier Day," *Rushville (Ind.) Republican*, December 2, 1963, 3.

74. See "Rifle Association Opposes Gun Registration, but Favors Control of Sales," *Cincinnati (Ohio) Enquirer*, December 12, 1963, 18; "Doesn't Oppose Legislation: National Rifle Group Voices Disapproval of Gun Licensing," *Ogden (Utah) Standard-Examiner*, December 12, 1963, 22; "Covering Gun Misuse: NRA Favors Some Curbs," *Tucson (Ariz.) Daily Citizen*, December 11, 1963, 24; NRA, "Where Does the NRA Stand on Firearms Legislation?," undated, JVBPP, Subject File, 1933–1966, box 11, folder 3; NRA, "Where Does the NRA Stand on Firearms Legislation?," HBP, box 445, folder Firearms Legislation 1964.

75. See, e.g., NRA, *1963 Operating Report*, 8–9.

76. "The Clearing Picture," *AR*, December 1933, 4; "Roll Call of 1933 Firearms Legislation," *AR*, May 1933, 30; "Roll Call of 1933 Firearms Legislation," *AR*, April 1933, 38; "Quiet Efficiency," *AR*, April 1933, 6; "Our Business Is Everybody's Business," *AR*, March 1933, 6; "The Roll Call of 1933 Firearms Legislation," *AR*, March 1933, 20–21.

77. "Why?," *AR*, November 1932, 3.

78. See, e.g., NRA, *The Typical American Sport*, 5, 15.

79. Letter from C. B. Lister, NRA secretary-treasurer, to NRA members, August 26, 1941, MFP, box 5, folder 52.

80. See, e.g., NRA, *From Tyro to Master* (Washington, D.C., 1946), 62, and the back covers of the following NRA publications: *Pistol Rules* (Washington, D.C., 1946); *Pistol Classification 1946* (Washington, D.C., 1945); *Pistol Classification 1942* (Washington, D.C., 1941); *Small-Bore Rifle Rules 1941* (Washington, D.C., 1939).

81. "A Matter of Personal Pride," *AR*, November 1956, 16; Floyd L. Parks, "Realizing Our Opportunities," *AR*, June 1956, 16; "For Everyone Interested in Guns . . . Membership in the NRA," *Muzzle Blasts*, April 1954, 12; "Your First Line of Defense Against BAD GUN LAWS Begins Here," *AR*, February 1954, 43; Merritt A. Edson, "As Allowed by Law," *AR*, November 1953, 16; Merritt A. Edson, "Think Big, Be Big," *AR*, January 1953, 12; "Current Firearms Legislation," *AR*, April 1952, 34; Merritt A. Edson, "The National Rifle Association and a Happy New Year!," *AR*, January 1952, 12; John Scofield, "The Voice, the Pen, the Vote . . . ," *AR*, January 1951, 10; NRA, *1950 Annual Meetings Program* (San Francisco, October 1950), 15; "Yours—Only One!," *AR*, October 1941, 2; "You May Well Be Proud!," *AR*, March 1941, 1; "Time to Vote—and to Invest," *AR*, November 1940, 5; "Why N.R.A. Membership?," *AR*, March 1940, 2; "The Job of the Year," *AR*, June 1939, 3; "We Have Just Begun—to Go Places," *AR*, February 1939, front insert; "Let's Raise Our Sights!," *AR*, January 1939, front insert; "Double the Power!," *AR*, May 1929, front insert.

82. "This Modern Sentry Duty Is Part of Your Membership Benefits," *AR*, July 1958, 14 (emphasis added).

83. John M. Schooley, "An Address by the Retiring President," *AR*, May 1963, 27–28 (emphasis added).

84. See, e.g., C. Richard Rogers, "The NRA Story," *GM*, April 1962, 16, 46; NRA, *1961 Operating Reports*, 11; Jim Varner, "New Year—Old Problems," PGN, January 1961, 45, 47; "Louis F. Lucas, "Build NRA," *AR*, January 1960, 14. It is worth noting that the NRA sometimes lowered or elevated its role in fighting firearms controls depending on the audience. See Merritt A. Edson, "Think Big, Be Big," *AR*, January 1953, 12; Merritt A. Edson, "Target for Tomorrow," *AR*, December 1952, 6, 8, 12; Merritt A. Edson, "The Convention Target, 1952," *AR*, November 1952, 4, 12; John Scofield, "Back to First Principles," *AR*, February 1951, 10.

85. Federal Regulation of Lobbying Act, Title III of the Legislative Reorganization Act of 1946, Pub. L. No. 601, c. 753, 79th Cong., 2nd Sess., August 2, 1946. For a useful legislative history and analysis of the FRLA, see Belle Zeller, "American Government and Politics: The Federal Regulation of Lobbying Act," *American Political Science Review* 42 (April 1948): 239–71; "The Federal Lobbying Act of 1946," *Columbia Law Review* 47 (January 1947): 98–109.

86. Senate Report No. 1400, 79th Cong., 2nd Sess., May 31, 1946, 27 (emphasis added).

87. For the quotes, see NRA, *Questions and Answers*; NRA, *Fundamentals of Scope Sights* (Washington, D.C., 1952), inside cover. For a useful summary of NRA's legal argument against being classified as a lobby, see James Deakin, *The Lobbyists* (Washington, D.C.: Public Affairs Press, 1966), 201–19.

88. *United States v. Harriss*, 347 U.S. 612, 621–23 (1954).

89. In 1968, while under investigation by the FBI for illegal lobbying, the NRA asserted that its collection of membership dues—even though a portion was directly used to influence legislation—did not qualify as receiving lobbying contributions under *Harriss*. And to further shield itself, the NRA made sure that any monetary contributions made by its members in addition to their regular dues, even if done so voluntarily, was promptly returned. The NRA came up with a legal work-around, however, where the respective member could make an additional contribution so long as it was associated with new membership enrollment. See letter from Harold W. Glassen, NRA president, to J. W. Moddelsee, August 14, 1968, HWGP, box 1.

90. On the NRA's role and influence in defeating legislation, see, e.g., Merritt A. Edson, "An Open Letter to the Membership," *AR*, September 1951, 12; "It Always Seems There's Gonna Be a Fight," *AR*, January 1949, 3; NRA, *How . . . to Get the Maximum Enjoyment Out of Your Gun* (Washington, D.C.: Montgomery Ward, 1932–1935). On its legislative service as an essential benefit, see, e.g., "What's the Biggest Single Advantage of NRA Membership?," *AR*, July 1956, 14; "Now's the Time to Double-Up," *AR*, April 1947, 98; "He Profits Most Who Serves Best," *Am AR*, February 1938, 4.

91. Letter from J. H. Fauntleroy, NRA membership division director, to NRA members, [January 1964], JJFJP, series 3, box 247, folder 5, NRA. Although this letter does not have a date stamped on it, the date can be verified by comparing the letter's cited membership total of 612,000 with January 1964 newspaper articles citing the same

number. See, e.g., Jay Mc Alear, "Rod and Gun: N.R.A. Stand on Firearms Legislation," *Hackensack (N.J.) Record*, January 17, 1964, 52.

92. See, e.g., "86th Annual Meetings," *AR*, May 1957, 22, 23 (noting that only $22,278 of
the NRA's total $1,798,992 budget went to legislative bulletins); "Annual Report
Highlights," *AR*, May 1956, 22, 23 (noting that only $30,583 of the total $1,839,479
budget went to such bulletins).

93. In 1961, for instance, the NRA's flagship magazine, *American Rifleman*, accounted
for forty-four percent of the NRA's annual operating expenses. NRA, *1961 Operating Reports*, 8–9. Not only did virtually every monthly edition of the *AR* in 1961
contain columns like "What the Lawmakers Are Doing" and "The Armed Citizen,"
but more often they contained some type of article or editorial highlighting the
need for NRA members to fight anti-firearms legislation. See "The Positive
Approach," *AR*, August 1961, 16; "Legislative Activity in 1961," *AR*, August 1961, 22;
Report of the Executive Vice President for 1961," June 1961, 26; Bartlett Rummel,
"Pistol Licensing Laws: Do They Deny Your Right to Self-Defense?," *AR*, April 1961,
23–24; "What the Lawmakers Are Doing," *AR*, March 1961, 21; "Inform Your Legisla-
tor," *AR*, January 1961, 8. In addition to using the pages of *AR* as a sounding board
against antifirearms legislation, the NRA also sent legislative bulletins to affected
members, as well as corresponding and coordinating with state and local NRA-
affiliated rifle clubs to fight antifirearms legislation. See NRA, *1961 Operating Reports*,
11; for a full breakdown of how the NRA allocated its 1961 expenses, see 23–24.

94. NRA, *Your NRA*, 4 (1959 ed.).

95. For the quote, see "A Paul Revere Organization," *AR*, March 1958, 14. On the NRA
using its First Amendment freedoms, see, e.g., NRA, *Your NRA: Information for Members of the National Rifle Association* (Washington, D.C.: 1962), 5; J. J. Basil, Jr., NRA
Legislative Service, "Are Firearms Control Laws Adequate?," *Akron (Ohio) Beacon
Journal*, June 17, 1956, 2D.

96. See, e.g., transcript of WABC Radio press conference, Harold W. Glassen, NRA president, June 22, 1968, HWGP, box; Donald M. Rothberg, "Federal Gun Control Battle
Waxes Hot," *Elmira (N.Y.) Star-Gazette*, June 18, 1968, 6; remarks of Harold W. Glassen,
NRA president, before the Annual Meeting of the National Society of State Legislators, Chicago, July 27, 1967, HWGP, box 1; speech of Harold W. Glassen, NRA president, before the National Press Club, Washington, D.C., June 29, 1967, HWGP, box 1.

97. *Federal Firearms Act: Hearings Before the Subcommittee to Investigate Juvenile Delinquency
of the Committee on the Judiciary United States Senate* (Washington, D.C.: U.S. Government Printing Office 1967), 563 (emphasis added).

98. For instance, in a post–Kennedy assassination letter addressed to all NRA members, Executive Vice President Franklin L. Orth and Executive Director Louis F.
Lucas wrote: "This may be the most important letter you have received form your
Association. It pertains to the wave of anti-firearms feeling in American and what
we can do to combat it." Letter from Franklin L. Orth and Louis F. Lucas to NRA
members, [January] 1964, JGOP, box 2, folder Gun Control. Orth and Lucas went on
to add that both the NRA's and the shooting fraternity's "number one problem"

was fighting the "avalanche of proposed restrictive firearms legislation at the national, state and local levels." A copy of this letter can also be found in JJFPJ, series 3, box 247, folder 5, NRA.

99. See, e.g., letter from David M. Byrne to Page H. Belcher, November 29, 1963, PBP, box 74, folder 12a, Commerce Committee-Gun Control; letter from Mrs. J. L. Wheeler, Jr., to Carl Albert, undated 1962, CAP, box LG 52, folder 44, Judiciary Gun-Control; letter from Chas P. Fields to Lee Metcalf, March 9, 1960, LMP, box 154, folder 5, Firearms.

100. Letter from Robert H. Kirkwood to Wayne Morse, May 29, 1957, WEMP, box 14, folder 14.

101. Letter from D. C. Besley to Lee Metcalf, October 21, 1957, LMP, box 154, folder 5, Firearms.

102. For Anfuso's bill, see Federal Pistol Registration Act, H.R. 613, 87th Cong., 1st Sess., January 3, 1961. For examples of conspiracy letters, see letter from S. A. Davis to Carl Hayden, March 21, 1962, CTHP, box 285, folder 10, Firearms Registration 1959–1963; letter from James S. Wilkinson to Carl Hayden, June 6, 1962, CTHP, box 285, folder 10, Firearms Registration 1959–1963; letter from Hoyt H. Nave to Carl Albert, April 25, 1962, CAP, box LG 52, folder 44, Judiciary-Gun Control.

103. Letter from Semion Barto Hendrix, Jr. to Robert L. Sikes, February 10, 1961, RFSP, box 137, folder Firearms.

104. Letter from Virgil Tapps to Bourke Hickenlooper, September 18, 1961, BHP, box 20, folder 9, Gun Control 1962.

105. See, e.g., Miles S. Vaughn, "Voice of the People," *Tucson Arizona Daily Star*, September 6, 1959, 12D; Roy Fair, "Americans Need Rifle Training," *Rochester (N.Y.) Democrat and Chronicle*, August 28, 1956, 18; W. T. Burnette, "The Constitutional Right to Bear Arms," *Chicago Tribune*, February 13, 1955, part 1, 24; Arlington H. Kirk, "Letters to the Editor," *Stroudsburg (Pa.) Pocono Record*, March 12, 1951, 7; Walter Frank, "With the Outdoor Sportsmen," *Central New Jersey Home News* (New Brunswick), January 24, 1950, 13.

106. See, e.g., C. B. Lister, "Simple Arithmetic," *AR*, November 1949, 10; C. B. Lister, "Matter of Proportion," *AR*, October 1948, 10; C. B. Lister, "Optimist—or Sucker?," *AR*, September 1948, 12; C. B. Lister, "Pattern in Red," *AR*, April 1948, 10; C. B. Lister, "Passion for Crisis," *AR*, March 1948, 10.

107. NRA, *The Pro and Con of Firearms Registration* (Washington, D.C., 1968), 5, 10. The pamphlet was published and distributed as early as 1960. See J. M. Laing, "Now Is Time to Feed Birds," *Beckley (W.Va.) Post-Herald*, February 21, 1960, 15 (urging readers to acquire the NRA pamphlet to remove "any doubt about the firearms registration issue").

108. NRA, *The Pro and Con of Firearms Registration*, 10. The NRA had advanced this impromptu claim several times over the previous decade. See, e.g., Grant Loftin, "NRA Head Scoffs at Gun License in New York," *Albuquerque (N.M.) Journal*, January 7, 1955, 14; F. C. Daniel, "Registration of Private Guns Branded Usual Step Toward Imposition of Dictatorship," *Tampa Bay (Fla.) Times*, May 14, 1950, 19.

3. THE GREAT "GUN LOBBY" AWAKENING

109. For the Library of Congress's findings, see Robert Sherrill, *The Saturday Night Special* (New York: Charterhouse, 1973), 179–80.
110. See, e.g., "Rules for Revolution," *Escondido (Calif.) Times-Advocate*, November 9, 1954, 2; "Master Plan," *American Legion Magazine*, November 1954, 6.
111. See "Revolution Rules," *Kane (Pa.) Republican*, January 12, 1942, 4.
112. See, e.g., "Federal Firearms Legislation," *Dan Smoot Report* 10, no. 11, (March 16, 1964): 81, 84.
113. James J. Kilpatrick, "Rules for Revolution Reprinted Many Times," *Spokane (Wash.) Chronicle*, July 2, 1970, 4.
114. In the September 1970 edition of *American Rifleman*, the NRA acknowledged the questionable authenticity of the "Communist Rules for Revolution." But the NRA refused to acknowledge having made a historical mistake, nor did it ever concede the document was fake. See Ashley Halsey, Jr., "Those Irrepressible 'Rules for Revolution,'" *AR*, September 1970, 10. It was not until the January 1973 edition of *AR* that the NRA begrudgingly acknowledged there were some historical errors in its reporting. However, the NRA refused to apologize for claiming that communists wanted to register and confiscate all firearms. See Ashley Halsey, Jr., "Ending the Mystery of the 'Rules,'" *AR*, January 1973, 15–16.
115. See, e.g., Robert J. Kukla, *Gun Control: A Written Record of Efforts to Eliminate the Private Possession of Firearms in America* (Harrisburg, Pa.: Stackpole Books, 1973), 218–19 (written by an NRA official, edited by former NRA president Harlon B. Carter, and paid for and distributed with NRA funding); Henry W. Bravo, "Antis Fear Disarming," *Tampa Bay (Fla.) Times*, May 31, 1959, 3D; F. C. Daniel, "Registration of Private Guns Branded Usual Step Toward Imposition of Dictatorship," *Tampa Bay Times*, May 14, 1950, 19; C. B. Lister, "Simple Arithmetic," *AR*, November 1949, 10; "Charge Reds Back Tighter U.S. Gun Laws: Sportsmen Flay 'Leftist Move,'" *Chicago Tribune*, January 28, 1948, 14; "Rules for Revolution," *Lexington (Miss.) Advertiser*, August 15, 1946, 4 (entire reprint of the rules via *AR*).
116. See "A Report from Shooters Club of America," *GM*, October 1963, 6; Tom Siatos, "Editorially Speaking," *G&A*, May 1962, 6.
117. See, e.g., "Register Communists—Not Guns," *Bob Sikes Reports*, June 25, 1968, RFSP; Drew Pearson, "Firearms Bill Remains in Committee; Los Angeles Riots Spurred Gun Sales," *Reno (Nev.) State Journal*, September 9, 1965, 4; Tom Foust, "Rod and Gun," *Arizona Daily Star* (Tucson), May 6, 1965, D3; Lynn Ludlow, "S.F. Recruiter for Minutemen," *San Francisco Examiner*, February 12, 1965, 8; R. C. Wagner, "Registration," *Oakland (Calif.) Tribune*, December 31, 1964, 10. This gun rights mantra was also in response to President's Kennedy assassination, where some in the gun rights community thought that Kennedy might not have been assassinated by Lee Harvey Oswald if the registration laws against communists would have been enforced. See, e.g., Anita Jacobs, "Registering Firearms," *Green Bay (Wis.) Press-Gazette*, April 21, 1964, 5; "Too Soft on Communism," *Bob Sikes Reports*, December 17, 1963, RFSP.
118. See, e.g., Neal Knox, "Abusive Letters Cause Harm to Gun Fraternity," *GW*, March 3, 1967, 2; B. Fritz Samuels, "Where Do We Stand on Anti-Gun Laws?," *G&A*, May 1965,

22; "Firearms Defenders Getting Frenzied," *Binghamton (N.Y.) Press and Sun-Bulletin*, March 7, 1965, 12A; Charles Nicodemus, "Dissemination and Misinformation: Barrage Against Gun Bill," *Philadelphia Inquirer*, March 4, 1965, 7; C. B. Lister, "Optimist—Or Sucker?," *AR*, September 1948, 12.

119. See, e.g., Thomas J. Dodd, news release, October 31, 1966, TJDP, box 205, folder 5414; Fulton Lewis, Jr., "Dodd Target of Ultra-Rightists," *Baytown (Tex.) Sun*, July 14, 1965, 8; Thomas J. Dodd, news release, March 28, 1965, TJDP, box 201, folder 5185; "Charge of Critics, Answers," *Binghamton (N.Y.) Press and Sun-Bulletin*, March 7, 1965, 12A.

120. See, e.g., letter from E. L. Jenks to Carl Albert, June 8, 1968, CAP, box GN 47, folder 4, Gun Control 1968; George Richardson, "Writes About Warren Commission," *El Paso (Tex.) Times*, February 24, 1964, 4; memorandum from George E. Hiscott, chairman of the Counter-Subversive Committee, American Legion Post 738, to all Legionnaires, "Personal Disarmament: 'Johnny, Get Your Gun' Is Going to Be the Order to Turn It In!," undated 1963, BC, box 63L.

121. I found a copy of Fred C. Koch's letter in the papers of two congressmen, representing different states. This suggests that Koch sent the letter to several members of Congress. See letter from Fred C. Koch to Weston Vivian, May 4, 1965, WVP, box 4, folder Gun Control; letter from Fred C. Koch to Carl Albert, May 3, 1965, CAP, box LG 92, folder 39, Gun Control.

122. In addition to the NRA's own admissions within the pages of *American Rifleman*, evidence of its direct lobbying for appropriations can be found by researching congressional papers. For some examples, see letter from Bourke B. Hickenlooper to Carl T. Hayden, May 18, 1962, BHP, box 15, folder 3, Gun Correspondence, 1954–1968; statement of Franklin L. Orth, NRA executive vice president, to the Defense Subcommittee of the Appropriations Committee, March 28, 1962, BHP, box 15, folder 8, NRA Correspondence, 1957–1963; letter from Marion Ewers, Prescott Sportsmen's Club president, to Carl T. Hayden, March 8, 1962, CTHP, box 285, folder 10, Firearms Registration, 1959–1963; letter from Roy L. Elson, aide to Carl T. Hayden, to Francis S. Hewitt, Senate Committee on Appropriations assistant clerk, March 5, 1962, CTHP, box 433, folder 9, NRA; letter from Ben Avery, NRA board member, to Carl T. Hayden, August 6, 1960, CTHP, box 433, folder 10, NRA; letter from Paul R. Eaton, administrative assistant to Carl T. Hayden, to Ben Avery, NRA board member, July 8, 1960, CTHP, box 433, folder 10, NRA; letter from Ben Avery, NRA board member, to Carl T. Hayden, May 17, 1960, CTHP, box 433, folder 10, NRA; letter from Floyd L. Parks, NRA executive director, to NRA board of directors, April 3, 1957, CTHP, box 433, folder 10, NRA; letter from Irvine C. Porter, NRA executive committee, to Carl T. Hayden, December 6, 1956, CTHP, box 433, folder 10, NRA; letter from Irvine C. Porter, NRA executive committee, to Lister Hill, December 13, 1955, CTHP, box 433, folder 10, NRA; letter from Carl T. Hayden to Irvine C. Porter, NRA executive committee, September 1, 1955, CTHP, box 433, folder 10, NRA; letter from Merritt A. Edson, NRA executive director, to Carl T. Hayden, August 12, 1955, CTHP, box 433, folder 10, NRA; letter from Irvine C. Porter, NRA executive

committee, to Carl T. Hayden, May 28, 1955, CTHP, box 433, folder 10, NRA; legislative bulletin from Merritt A. Edson, NRA executive director, to NRA members, ["Appropriations for the National Board for the Promotion of Rifle Practice"], April 14, 1952, CTHP, box 433, folder 10, NRA; F. L. Wyman, NRA secretary, to John William Thomas, December 21, 1949, JWTP, box LG 77, folder 10, Appropriations Committee; letter from John William Thomas to Milton A. Reckord, NRA executive vice president, June 9, 1948, JWTP, box LG 66, folder 23, Appropriations Committee in Military Establishment.

123. In addition to the NRA's own admissions within the pages of *American Rifleman*, evidence of the NRA's lobbying for appropriations can be found by researching congressional papers. For examples, see letter from Franklin L. Orth, NRA executive vice president, to Wilbur D. Mills, October 14, 1963, RFSP, box 171, folder H.R. 8065; letter from Robert F. Sikes to Wilbur D. Mills, August 15, 1963, RFSP, box 171, folder H.R. 8065; letter from Robert F. Sikes to Frank C. Daniel, NRA secretary, August 15, 1963, RFSP, box 171, folder H.R. 8065; letter from Robert F. Sikes to Frank C. Daniel, NRA secretary, August 13, 1963, RFSP, box 171, folder H.R. 8065; letter from Frank C. Daniel, NRA secretary, to Robert F. Sikes, August 9, 1962, RFSP, box 171, folder H.R. 8065; letter from Franklin L. Orth, NRA executive vice president, to Bourke T. Hickenlooper, March 31, 1962, BHP, box 15, folder 3, Gun Correspondence, 1954–1968; letter from Frank C. Daniel, NRA secretary, to Thomas E. Morgan, April 28, 1958, RFSP, box 68, folder Firearms 1958; letter from Floyd L. Parks, NRA president, to Bourke B. Hickenlooper, October 2, 1957, BHP, box 15, folder 8, NRA Correspondence, 1957–1963; letter from Floyd L. Parks, NRA president, to Robert S. Kerr, February 27, 1958, RSKP, box LG 9, folder 11, Gun Control, 1958, 1961–1962.

124. There were instances where NRA officials went from congressional office to congressional office to convey the group's point of view on firearms controls, but this was infrequent. See, e.g., ESMP, box 312, folder 6, Firearms Control.

125. Robert Sherrill, "A Lobby on Target," *New York Times Magazine*, October 15, 1966, 246, 250.

126. For documentary support for the information in this paragraph, see "Argue Strict U.S. Control of Mail Guns: Dodd Asks Support; Iowan Opposed," *Des Moines (Iowa) Register*, December 14, 1963, 1; "Federal Aid for Shooting Ranges," *AR*, December 1963, 33; "Important Bills in Congress," *AR*, September 1963, 31; "A Sullivan Law for DC," *AR*, June 1963, 23; Tommy Seward, "Nat'l Riflemen Oppose Anti-Gun Law; Recreation User Fee 'Liked,'" *Newport News (Va.) Daily Press*, March 31, 1963, 5C; Ben Avery, "'Mr. Arizona' Will be Honored at Home," *Arizona Days and Ways Magazine* (Phoenix), November 12, 1961, 7; N. F. McNaughton, "Reader Reports Gun Law Changed," *Duncan (Okla.) Banner*, February 14, 1961, 5; "Amendments Passed . . . National Firearms Act," *AR*, July 1960, 4; "Legislative Activity in 1960," *AR*, July 1960, 20; "What the Lawmakers Are Doing," *AR*, June 1960, 4; letter from Cecil R. King to John James Flynt, Jr., June 19, 1959, JJFJP, series 3, box 247, folder 5, NRA; letter from Louis F. Lucas, NRA executive director, to Bruce Alger, June 2, 1959, JJFJP, series 3,

box 247, folder 5, NRA; letter from Cecil R. King to Bourke B. Hickenlooper, June 19, 1959, BHP, box 15, folder 8, NRA Correspondence, 1957–1963; "Annual Award," *Mason City (Iowa) Globe-Gazette*, April 2, 1959, 17; letter from Louis F. Lucas, NRA deputy executive director, to Bourke B. Hickenlooper, April 30, 1958, BHP, box 15, folder 8, NRA Correspondence, 1957–1963; letter from Louis F. Lucas, NRA deputy executive director, to John James Flynt, Jr., April 9, 1958, JJFJP, series 3, box 247, folder 5, NRA; letter from Floyd L. Parks, NRA executive director, to Robert S. Kerr, February 27, 1958, RSKP, box LG 9, folder 11, Gun Control 1958, 1961–1962; Douglas Larsen and Kenneth O. Gilmore, "Washington Sidelights," *Hazleton (Pa.) Plain Speaker*, March 30, 1956, 8; "Familiar Ground," *Anderson (Ind.) Herald*, May 14, 1955, 11; "News & Notes from the Office of Congressman Cecil R. King," *Wilmington (Calif.) Daily Press Journal*, April 16, 1953, 13; "U.S. Rifle Group Selects Officers," *Des Moines (Iowa) Register*, March 20, 1953, 4.

127. The term *official family* can be found in several internal NRA documents. See, e.g., C. R. Gutermuth, "A Yuletide Message from the President," NRA, News Letter Official Family, December 16, 1974, MRP, series 5, box 14, folder 3; memorandum from Irvine W. Reynolds, NRA chairman of public affairs committee, to NRA executive committee, "Report of the Public Affairs Committee," January 10, 1975, MRP, series 5, box 14, folder 2; NRA, "Weekly Legislative Report Nos. 27 and 28," July 26, 1967, RHP, box 249, folder 6.

128. See generally *Federal Firearms Act: Hearings Before the United States Senate Committee on the Judiciary to Investigate Juvenile Delinquency*, 88th Cong., 1st Sess. (Washington, D.C.: U.S. Government Printing Office, 1965).

129. Charles, *Armed in America*, 275–78.

130. Letter from Harold W. Glassen, NRA president, to Jon D. Charleston, March 5, 1968, HWGP, box 1; memorandum from Louis A. Benton, NRA public relations committee chairman, to Robert F. Sikes, "NRA PUBLIC RELATIONS PROGRAM—IMPORTANT!," May 10, 1967, RFSP, box 310, Folder NRA 1967.

131. One of the initiatives to come out of this was an internally written organizational history. See generally NRA, *Americans and Their Guns*.

132. See letter from Harold W. Glassen, NRA president, to J. W. Moddelsee, August 14, 1968, HWGP, box 1; letter from Harold W. Glassen, NRA president, to Dwain L. Fritz, August 7, 1968, HWGP, box 1; memorandum from John R. Hess, NRA director of public relations, to NRA board of directors, February 21, 1968, HWGP, box 1; letter from Franklin L. Orth, NRA executive vice president, to Paul M. Beard, January 5, 1968, HWGP, box 1; letter from Franklin L. Orth, NRA executive vice president, to G.W.K. King, December 26, 1967, HWGP, box 1; Ben A. Franklin, "Gun Curb Fight Opens in Capitol," NYT, April 9, 1967, 96.

133. See "UN Attack Prompts Massive Probe," *Binghamton (N.Y.) Press and Sun-Bulletin*, December 12, 1964, 1; "UN Building Bazooka Target; Anti-Castro Cubans Suspected," *Bridgewater (N.J.) Courier-News*, December 12, 1964, 1; "Claims Army Aids Rightists," *Des Moines (Iowa) Register*, August 14, 1964, 2; Drew Pearson, "Demonstrations Will

Continue," *Sheboygan (Wis.) Press*, June 23, 1964, 22; "Minutemen Said to Be Getting Free Arms from Defense Dept.," *St. Louis (Mo.) Post-Dispatch*, May 27, 1964, 3A; "Says Rightist Letter 'Call to Anarchy,'" *Santa Cruz (Calif.) Sentinel*, May 1, 1964, 11; "Gun-Happy Fanatics: A Growing Menace," *Boston Globe*, January 12, 1964, B22.

134. In 1973 the NRA published its version of the events leading up to the Gun Control Act of 1968 in part to demonize the national media as having an "anti-gun" bias. See Robert J. Kukla, *Gun Control: A Written Record of Efforts to Eliminate the Private Possession of Firearms in America* (Harrisburg, Pa.: Stackpole Books, 1973).

135. See, e.g., "The Latest Twist in Anti-Gun Propaganda," *AR*, December 1968, 16; "Getting Away With Statistical Murder?," *AR*, November 1968, 17; "Gun Registration: The Myths and Facts," *AR*, October 1968, 69; Harold W. Glassen, "Another Opinion: The Right to Bear Arms," *NYT*, June 16, 1968, E17; John W. Finney, "Senators Predict Strict Gun Curbs as Pressure Rises," *NYT*, June 13, 1968, 1; "Whose Right to Be Biased? Gun Owners Ask TV Network," *AR*, May 1967, 38–39; "In the Interests of Accuracy," *AR*, January 1967, 106; "The Big Half-Truth and Smear by Association," *AR*, December 1966, 16. Journalist Carl Bakal particularly drew the ire of the NRA, which claimed he was both biased and unqualified to be a journalist. See "Dodd Blessed Anti-Gun Book Bears New Title, Little Else," *AR*, September 1968, 54–56; "The U.S. Justice Department Investia, and *New Yorker*," *AR*, June 1968, 16; "The NRA Is Up to Its Old Tricks," *Louisville (Ky.) Courier-Journal*, August 26, 1966, A10; "Rifle Group Head Refutes Antagonist's Views," *Arizona Republic* (Phoenix), August 19, 1966, 23.

136. Harold W. Glassen, "Vice-President's Report 1967: First Board of Directors Meeting," undated 1967, HWGP, box 1.

137. Oscar Godbout, "Wood, Field and Stream: National Rifle Association Is Called Target of Antifirearms Crusade," *NYT*, November 29, 1964, S7.

138. This concession was made even though the IRS issued a June 1968 public release stating that the NRA qualified as a tax exempt 501(c)(4) organization. See Internal Revenue Service, Public Information, "Tax Exempt Status of the National Rifle Association," June 13, 1968, JSCP, box 173, folder Firearms.

139. See Franklin L. Orth, "A Special Message: Sportsmen and Gun Laws," *AR*, August 1969, 46–47; "NRA Official Registers as U.S. Lobbyist," *AR*, February 1969, 29; "NRA's Orth Registers as Agent," *GW*, January 3, 1969, 1. "FBI Investigating NRA," *GW*, December 20, 1968, 1; "Rifle Group Registers as Lobbyist in Capital," *NYT*, December 13, 1968, 20; "FBI Probing Rifle Group," *Baltimore (Md.) Sun*, December 7, 1968, A8; "Unregistered NRA Probed, FBI Admits," *Indianapolis (Ind.) Journal*, December 7, 1968, 38; "Tax Write-Offs Lost By Donors to Sierra Club," *Baltimore (Md.) Sun*, August 23, 1968, A5; "Rifle Association Holds a Tax-Exempt Status," *NYT*, June 15, 1968, 18; "Review of Rifle Group's Tax Exemption Is Urged," *NYT*, May 16, 1967, 28.

140. Letter from John J. Wilson, Law Offices of Whiteford, Hart, Garmody and Wilson, to Harold W. Glassen, NRA president, November 29, 1968, Minutes of the Executive Committee of the NRA, December 6–7, 1968, HWGP, box 1.

4. A Political Synopsis of the Great "Gun Lobby" Awakening

1. Edward M. Kennedy, "First in Guns, Last in Controls," *NYT*, August 24, 1972.

2. For more information on how the legislative reporting service worked, see National Rifle Association, *Your NRA: Information for Members of the National Rifle Association of America* (1959) (on file with author); "Opinions on the Sale of Guns," *New York Herald Tribune*, May 18, 1958, 24; Calvin Goddard, "How Illinois Organized to Fight Anti-Firearms Legislation," *AR*, November 1934, 9, 19; "Random Shots," *AR*, July 1934, 4; "Keep Those Telegrams Coming," *AR*, March 1934, 6. The editors of *Guns & Ammo* and *Guns Magazine* also educated readers on the importance of being politically active. See, e.g., "Shooters' Club of America," *GM*, July 1965, 12; George W. North, "The 'Pen' Can Protect the 'Sword,'" *G&A*, September 1964, 26–27; Donald Martin, "The Fight Against Bad 'Gun Laws' Must Be Made at the Grass Roots Level," *G&A*, June 1963, 18–19; George W. North, "Here's What You Can Do!," *G&A*, March 1963, 18–20; James E. Serven, "Protect What Makes Us Strong!," *GM*, March 1963, 40–42.

3. See, e.g., Neal Knox, "Abusive Letters Cause Harm to Gun Fraternity," *GW*, March 3, 1967, 2.

4. For a useful example, see generally CWTP, box 52, folder 18, Firearms Bills 1947.

5. For examples, see letter from Joyce Hancock, Yuma Women's Reel & Rifle Club president, to Carl T. Hayden, December 8, 1959, CTHP, box 285, folder Firearms Registration, 1959–1963; letter from Russell B. Juckett, Mount Vernon Rifle and Pistol Club president, to Warren Magnuson, August 21, 1957, WNMP, box 97, folder 19, Treasury-IRS-Firearms Regulations; letter from Northern Colorado Rod and Gun Club to Wayne Morse, August 9, 1957, WEMP, box 14, folder 14; letter from Agnes L. Nelson, Park Gun Club secretary, to George E. MacKinnon, February 20, 1947, GEMP, box 4, folder Firearms Bill 1947; letter from Juliet A. Lerat, Mercury Rifle and Pistol Club secretary, to Lyle H. Boren, October 9, 1941, LHBP, box 21, folder 17, Gun Control.

6. For examples, see letter from Powder River Sportsmen's Club to Wayne Morse, August 21, 1957, WEMP, box 14, folder 14; petition from William J. Krieg and Minnesota sportsmen to George E. MacKinnon, February 7, 1947, GEMP, box 4, folder Firearms Bill 1947; letter from Thomas Wann, Minnesota Game Protective League second vice president, to George E. MacKinnon, February 7, 1947, GEMP, box 4, folder Firearms Bill 1947; letter from T. R. Watson, Poteau Sportsmen's Club secretary, to John William Thomas, February 6, 1946, JWTP, box LG 62, folder 25, Firearms Registration-Hawkes; letter from L. R. Larson, Fayette County Sportsman Club, to Bourke B. Hickenlooper, January 23, 1946, BHP, box 20, folder 9, Gun Control 1946; letter from B. J. Heber, United Sportsmen vice president, January 15, 1946, BHP, box 20, folder 9, Gun Control 1946; letter from Raleigh Bearbower, Lime Creek Fish & Game Club secretary, to Bourke B. Hickenlooper, January 15, 1946, BHP, box 20, folder 9, Gun Control 1946; letter from J. W. Chambers, Osceola County Conservation League president, to Bourke B. Hickenlooper, January 9, 1946, BHP, box 20, folder 9, Gun Control 1946; letter from David C. Ermoud, Secretary Greenville

Sportsmen's Club, to Charles W. Tobey, April 2, 1938, CWTP, box 6, folder 35, Firearms Legislation 1938; letter from P. S. Glasson, Secretary White Mountain Sportsman's Club, to Charles W. Tobey, March 26, 1938, CWTP, box 6, folder 35, Firearms Legislation 1938.

7. For examples, see letter from J. E. Mountjoy, Izaak Walton League, to Carl Albert, February 13, 1947, CAP, box LG 4, folder 28, Firearms Registration; Kenneth A. Reid, Izaak Walton League of America executive secretary, to Lyle H. Boren, April 13, 1942, LHBP, box 21, folder 17, Gun Control.

8. See, e.g., "Aimless: Opponents of Federal Legislation to Control Firearms," *Time*, September 9, 1966, 25.

9. Richard Harris, "Annals of Legislation: If You Love Your Guns," *New Yorker*, April 20, 1968, 56, 57. Another common feature of many gun rights supporters who took part in letter-writing campaigns was the intensity of their involvement. It was common for the supporter not only to write frequently, but also to write a wide array of politicians on the same firearms control. The constituent letters contained in the political papers housed at the University of Michigan's Bentley Historical Library and the Carl Albert Congressional Research and Studies Center at the University of Oklahoma bear this out.

10. For examples, see letter from Warren Magnuson to W. A. Kindler, August 29, 1957, WNMP, box 97, folder 19, Treasury-IRS-Firearms Regulations; letter from Wayne Morse to Mildred Comfort, Roseburg Rifle Club secretary, August 23, 1957, WEMP, box 14, folder 14; letter from Lyle H. Boren to B. R. Elliott, February 15, 1946, LHBP, box 21, folder 17, Gun Control; letter from John William Thomas to B. F. Bohling, February 5, 1946, JWTP, box LG 62, folder 25, Firearms Registration-Hawkes; letter from Lyle H. Boren to J. C. Berger, April 11, 1938, LHBP, box 21, folder 17, Gun Control.

11. For examples, see letter from Carl T. Hayden to D. Zaffe, July 17, 1962, CTHP, box 285, folder 10, Firearms Registration, 1959–1963; letter from Toby Morris to W. T. Webb, March 24, 1947, TMP, box 3, folder 95, Gun Control; form letter from George E. MacKinnon, "Re: Firearms Bill H.R. 1061," undated 1947, GEMP, box 4, folder Firearms Bill 1947; letter from John William Thomas to James G. Boden, February 11, 1946, JWTP, box LG 62, folder 25, Firearms Registration-Hawkes; letter from John William Thomas to Walter J. Seeliger, April 2, 1941, JWTP, box LG 48, folder 63, Firearms Control Act; letter from John William Thomas to Daniel E. Bird, Jr., February 7, 1941, JWTP, box LG 48, folder 63, Firearms Control Act; letter from John William Thomas to Hollie Lee Mason, May 25, 1937, JWTP, box LG 48, folder 41, Commerce Committee on Gun Control.

12. Letter from Carl Albert to J. E. Mountjoy, February 16, 1947, CAP, box LG 4, folder 28, Firearms Registration. For other examples, see letter from Clare E. Hoffman to Albert Behnke, February 27, 1947, CEHP, box 29, folder Firearms; letter from Clare E. Hoffman to Wendell A. Ball, February 26, 1947, CEHP, box 29, folder Firearms; letter from Bourke B. Hickenlooper to B. J. Heber, United Sportsmen vice president, January 15, 1946, BHP, box 20, folder 9, Gun Control 1946.

13. Letter from Montana delegation to Dwight E. Avis, Internal Revenue Service, Alcohol and Tobacco Division director, May 29, 1957, LMP, box 154, folder 5, Firearms.

14. For information pertaining to the 1938 public opinion poll, see Institute of Public Opinion, "Pistol Registration Approved by 4 to 1 Majority in Survey," *Altoona (Pa.) Tribune*, May 2, 1938, 11; Institute of Public Opinion, "Pistol Registration Approved by 4 to 1 Majority in Survey," *Rochester (N.Y.) Democrat and Chronicle*, May 1, 1938, F1; Institute of Public Opinion, "Pistol Registration Approved by 4 to 1 Majority in Survey," *Tampa Bay (Fla.) Times*, May 1, 1938, 29; Institute of Public Opinion, "Pistol Registration Approved by 4 to 1 Majority in Survey," *Lincoln (Neb.) Star*, May 1, 1938, 13; "Public Willing to List Pistols," *Louisville (Ky.) Courier-Journal*, May 1, 1938, 70; Institute of Public Opinion, "Registration of Guns Approved by 4 to 1 Survey," *Pittsburgh Press*, May 1, 1938, Society Section, 2.

15. See George Gallup, "Public for Curb on Sale of Guns," *Los Angeles Times*, August 30, 1959, 31; George Gallup, "Permits for All Firearms?," *Daily Boston Globe*, August 30, 1959, 1, 20.

16. "Gallup Poll Hits Gun Owners," *AR*, October 1959, 8.

17. Louis F. Lucas, "Individual Preparedness," *AR*, October 1959, 16.

18. See "Well-Meaning, But Without Understanding," *AR*, January 1957, 14; "There Ought to be a Law!," *AR*, October 1956, 16; "Let's Sound Off!," *AR*, July 1956, 16; Merritt A. Edson, "The Greatest Danger," *AR*, June 1955, 16; Merritt A. Edson, "Education Versus Legislation," *AR*, April 1953, 12; Frank C. Daniel, "The Gun Law Problem," *AR*, February 1953, 16–18, 46; Merritt A. Edson, "A Realistic Approach," *AR*, October 1951, 16; C. B. Lister, "Number One Problem," *AR*, July 1948, 8; C. B. Lister, "Just Grass Roots Stuff," *AR*, April 1947, 6. For the quotes, see "Gallup Poll Hits Gun Owners," *AR*, October 1959, 8.

19. For the "unthinking public" quote, see W. I. Bowman, "Anti-Gun," *Muzzle Blasts*, February 1960, 3.

20. Copies of the *Guns Magazine* letters can be found in several congressional archives. For some examples, see letter from E. B. Mann to Carl Hayden, June 10, 1963, CTHP, box 285, folder 12, Firearms Registration 1963; letter from E. B. Mann to Bourke B. Hickenlooper, June 10, 1963, BHP, box 15, folder 3, Gun Correspondence; letter from E. B. Mann to Page Belcher, June 4, 1963, PBP, box 79, folder 8, Gun Control; letter from E. B. Mann to Carl Albert, June 4, 1963, CAP, box GL 69, folder 37, Judiciary-Gun Control; letter from William B. Edwards to Thomas Jefferson Steed, January 14, 1960, TJSP, box 20, folder 14, Miscellaneous 1960; letter from William B. Edwards to Herman Talmadge, January 11, 1960, HTP, box 296, folder 34, Second Amendment.

21. "Know Your Lawmakers," *GM*, June 1959, 17.

22. I previously tallied the number of congressional responses at 118. This was a minor miscalculation, but it does not change the conclusion that by the "1960s substantially more members of Congress supported an individualized interpretation of the Second amendment than opposed it." It also does not change the conclusion that at that time "very few members of Congress were versed in the historical

antecedents of the Second Amendment." See Patrick J. Charles, *Armed in America: A History of Gun Rights from Colonial Militias to Concealed Carry* (Amherst, N.Y.: Prometheus Books, 2018), 229, 230.

23. These evidentiary biases appear to have affected the second iteration of responses from September 1963 through May 1966. See, e.g., "Political Candidates and the Pro-Gun Issue," *GM*, October 1964, 19; "Pro-Gun Law Takes Shape," *GM*, August 1964; "Know Your Lawmakers," *GM*, August 1963, 8.

24. The columns can be found in "Know Your Lawmakers," *GM*, June 1959, 17, through "Know Your Lawmakers," *GM*, February 1962, 4.

25. The columns can be found in "Know Your Lawmakers," *GM*, September 1963, 6, through May 1966, 4.

26. The thirty-two lawmakers' responses were published in the following chronological order: Senator Frank Church (Idaho), Representative James F. Bottin (Mont.), Representative John Brademas (Ind.), Senator J. W. Fulbright (Ark.), Senator Paul H. Douglas (Ill.), Senator Peter H. Dominick (Colo.), Representative Donald C. Bruce (Ind.ana), Representative Frank J. Becker (N.Y.), Representative Charles E. Bennett (Fla.), Senator E. L. Bartlett (Alaska), Representative J. Caleb Boggs (Del.), Senator George D. Aiken (Vt.), Senator Joseph S. Clark (Pa.), Representative Paul Findley (Ill.), Representative Ralph Harvey (Ind.), Representative William Henry Harrison (Wyo.), Representative Ralph Harding (Idaho), Representative William Jennings Bryan Dorn (S.C.), Senator Gale McGee (Wyo.), Representative Melvin R. Laird (Wis.), Representative Daniel J. Flood (Pa.), Representative John Dowdy (Tex.), Representative John D. Dingell (Mich.), Senator Absalom W. Robertson (Va.), Senator Edward V. Long (Mo.), Representative Arnold Olsen (Mont.), Representative Howard W. Robinson (N.Y.), Representative Robert F. Sikes (Fla.), Representative Richard L. Roudebush (Ind.), Senator Paul J. Fannin (Ariz.), Governor Frank B. Morrison (Neb.), and Governor John H. Reed (Me.).

27. See, e.g., "Know Your Lawmakers" articles in *GM*, December 1965, 4 (New Jersey representative Frank Thompson, Jr.); April 1965, 4 (New York representative Howard W. Robison); February 1965, 4 (Montana senator Lee Metcalf); December 1964, 4 (California senator Thomas H. Kuchel); August 1964, 4 (Wisconsin representative Melvin R. Laird); and January 1964, 4 (Alaska senator E. L. Bartlett).

28. See, e.g., "Know Your Lawmakers" articles in *GM*, March 1965, 4 (Texas representative O. C. Fisher); January 1965, 4 (Illinois representative Roland V. Libonati); November 1964, 4 (New Mexico senator E. L. Mechem); September 1964, 4 (California representative Craig Hosmer); August 1964, 4 (Illinois representative Edward J. Derwinski); May 1964, 4 (Wyoming representative William Henry Harrison); March 1964, 4 (Utah representative Laurence J. Burton and Ohio representative John M. Ashbrook); February 1964, 45 (Texas representative Bruce Alger).

29. For Sikes, see "Know Your Lawmakers," *GM*, May 1965, 4; August 1960, 4). For Dingle, see "Know Your Lawmakers," *GM*, October 1964, 4; November 1959, 4. For Fannin, see "Know Your Lawmakers," *GM*, October 1965, 4 (as senator; February 1961, 4 (as governor).

30. See, e.g., Bill Nye, "JFK and Gun Rights," *Longview (Wash.) Daily News*, November 27, 2013, A5; David B. Kopel, "The Great Gun Control War of the Twentieth Century— and Its Lessons for Gun Laws Today," *Fordham Urban Law Journal* 39 (2012): 1528, 1536–37.

31. Carl Hilliard, "Kennedy Quoted as Being Supporter of 'Right to Bear Arms': Guns' Editor Recalls Views of Late Chief," *Albuquerque (N.M.) Journal*, December 13, 1963, H1.

32. "Kennedy and Guns," *New Haven (Mo.) Leader*, January 16, 1964, 6.

33. "Know Your Lawmakers," *GM*, April 1960, 4 (Massachusetts senator John F. Kennedy).

34. For the full speech, see John F. Kennedy, Commemorative Message on Roosevelt Day, January 29, 1961, JFKPP, White House Central Subject Files, box 111, FDR. For news coverage of Kennedy's speech, see "New Minute Men Urged by Kennedy," *NYT*, January 30, 1961, 13; "Kennedy Says US Needs Minute Men," *Los Angeles Times*, January 30, 1961, 4; "Kennedy Calls for Minute Men," *Nashville Tennessean*, January 30, 1961, 2; "Minute Men: Needed for Nation," *Cincinnati (Ohio) Enquirer*, January 30, 1961, 1.

35. Letter from Franklin L. Orth to President John F. Kennedy, March 7, 1961, JFKPP, President's Office Files, Personal Secretary's Files, Memberships, December 1960-April 1961.

36. Letter from President John F. Kennedy to Franklin L. Orth, March 20, 1961, JFKPP, President's Office Files, Personal Secretary's Files, Memberships, December 1960-April 1961.

37. Letter from Frank Daniel to President John F. Kennedy, April 19, 1961, JFKPP, President's Office Files, Personal Secretary's Files, Memberships, December 1960-April 1961.

38. See generally John F. Kennedy Papers, Pre-Presidential, Senate Files, folder JFK-SEN-066612, Boston, John F. Kennedy Presidential Library and Museum.

39. There are several examples over the past half century where a gun rights advocate and supporters have claimed that John F. Kennedy was an ardent supporter of gun rights. See, e.g., Awr Hawkins, "JFK: Lifetime NRA Member, Second Amendment Supporter," *Breitbart*, November 18, 2013, https://www.breitbart.com/politics/2013/11/18/jfk-lifetime-member-of-the-nra-defender-of-the-second-amendment/; Mike Fuljenz, "Guns, Silver and John F. Kennedy," *AR*, November 17, 2013, https://www.americanrifleman.org/articles/2013/11/17/guns-silver-and-john-f-kennedy/; Michael P. Timko, "Gun Control People Mislead Public," *Hazleton (Pa.) Standard Speaker*, April 12, 1993, 17; Ralph Sheets, "All About Guns," *Newark (Ohio) Advocate*, December 18, 1980, 4. Take, for instance, the Republican National Convention in 1988, where Charlton Heston, who was speaking at an NRA-sponsored event, told the attending audience, "[If] John Kennedy were alive today he'd probably be here [at this NRA-sponsored event]." See Anne Groer, "Parties, Protests Mix Well in Big Easy," *Orlando (Fla.) Sentinel*, August 18, 1988, A6.

40. "Know Your Lawmakers," *GM*, October 1963, 6 (Illinois senator Everett M. Dirksen).

41. See EMDP, Remarks, Releases, and Interviews, folder "Is Gun Control a Myth?," 1966; EMDP, Remarks, Releases, and Interviews, folder *Meet the Press*, NBC, August 6, 1967; "GOP Senators to Act Today on Gun Control," *Los Angeles Times*, August 9, 1966, part

1, 7; Jack Bell, "Senators Move Cautiously on Gun Control Legislation," *Moline (Ill.) Dispatch*, August 3, 1966, 15.

42. EMDP, Remarks, Releases, and Interviews, folder *Face the Nation*, CBS, August 6, 1967.

43. "Know Your Lawmakers," *GM*, December 1960, 4 (Montana representative Lee Metcalf).

44. "Know Your Lawmakers," *GM*, August 1961, 4 (Montana representative Lee Metcalf).

45. Metcalf's third response was written line-by-line verbatim from his second response. See "Know Your Lawmakers," *GM*, February 1965, 4 (Montana representative Lee Metcalf).

46. See "Montana Lawmakers Reply on Firearms Legislation," *Helena (Mont.) Independent-Record*, September 2, 1966, 4; John Kamps, "Delegation Opposes Arms Control," *Missoulian* (Mont.), June 6, 1965, 16; LMP, box 659, folder Speech on Gun Control, May 5, 1965; LMP, box 661, folder 5, Speech and Announcement on Firearms, May 1, 1965; Kenneth Scheibel, "Gun-Toters Have Fire in Eyes," *Missoulian*, February 16, 1964, 10; statement of Senator Lee Metcalf of Montana on Gun Control Legislation before the Senate Subcommittee to Investigate Juvenile Delinquency, July 11, 1967, FEMP, box 196, folder 18.

47. "Sportsmen's Stand on Firearms Supported by Metcalf, Olsen," *Butte Montana Standard-Post*, August 1, 1965, 10; "Congressmen Give View on Firearms Law," *Butte Montana Standard*, July 30, 1965, 14; John Camps, "Proposed Gun Curbs Find Few Friends in Montana," *Billings (Mont.) Gazette*, June 6, 1965, 1; Lee Metcalf, [speech on Firearms Controls,] May 1, 1965, LMP, box 661, folder 5, Speech and Announcement on Firearms, May 1, 1965.

48. See, e.g., letter from Lee Metcalf to Maude Hunt, November 4, 1963, LMP, box 154, folder 5, Firearms; letter from Maude Hunt to Lee Metcalf, October 31, 1963, LMP, box 154, folder 5, Firearms; letter from Lee Metcalf to Colonel Dave Hantelman, October 17, 1963, LMP, box 154, folder 5, Firearms; letter from Colonel Dave Hantelman to Lee Metcalf, October 14, 1963, LMP, box 154, folder 5, Firearms.

49. Letter from Franklin L. Orth, NRA vice president, to Lee Metcalf, October 20, 1965, LMP, box 652, folder 7, Campaign Materials-Gun Control, 1968–1972.

50. 114 Cong. Rec. 16482 (June 10, 1968) (statement of Montana representative Lee Metcalf).

51. See, e.g., Joe DeSave, "Registration, Confiscation," *Great Falls (Mont.) Tribune*, July 1, 1968, 6. The pressure placed on Metcalf would ultimately lead to him to walk back his support. See H. W. C. Newberry, "Outdoors with Doc," *Kalispell (Mont.) Daily Inter Lake*, July 28, 1968, 8; "Sen. Metcalf Opposes Firearms Registration," *Kalispell Daily Inter Lake*, July 7, 1968, 1.

52. Compare letter from Mike Mansfield to Riley Johnson, Fishing and Hunting News editor, March 9, 1964, LMP, box 154, folder 5, Firearms, with 114 Cong. Rec. 16481 (June 10, 1968) (statement of Montana senator Mike Mansfield).

53. Letter from Mike Mansfield to Leo Lesnik, June 26, 1968, MMP, box 85, folder 2.

54. U.S. Const., Art. I, Sec. 8, Cl. 3 (that Congress has the power "to regulate Commerce with foreign Nations, and among the several States, and with the Indian Tribes").

55. See, e.g., Cleve Corlett, "Hart Hits Gun Control Legislation," *Lansing (Mich.) State Journal*, October 6, 1967, C3.

56. See, e.g., Saul Friedman, "Also Wants Change in Gun Control Plan: Hart to Seek New Rights Bill," *Detroit (Mich.) Free Press*, September 30, 1967, 15A; "Proper Firearm Use Defended: 'Fair' Gun Control Laws Backed," *Lansing (Mich.) State Journal*, August 28, 1966.

57. Letter from Philip A. Hart to Lawrence Powers, September 10, 1968, PAHP, box 186, folder Gun Control.

58. McGovern was opposed to federal firearms controls well before 1967. See, e.g., George McGovern, press release, September 23, 1965, GMP, box 482, folder S.14, Federal Firearms Act; memorandum to George McGovern, June 8, 1965, GMP, box 482, folder S.14, Federal Firearms Act.

59. Associated Press, "McGovern Against Dodd Firearms Control Bill," *Rapid City (S.D.) Journal*, August 5, 1967, 3.

60. "Know Your Lawmakers," *GM*, October 1960, 4 (South Dakota representative George McGovern).

61. Letter from George McGovern to South Dakota constituents, June 14, 1968, GMP, box 608, folder Firearms Miscellaneous Correspondence.

62. "No Disagreement on Gun Control McGovern Says," *Rapid City (S.D.) Journal*, October 25, 1968, 13; Associated Press, "Republicans Repeat Chant; McGovern Questions Foes," *Sioux Falls (S.D.) Argus-Leader*, October 23, 1968, 34.

63. See, e.g., Letter from James G. O'Hara to Theodore R. Goodwin, July 26, 1968, JGOP, box 10, folder Gun Control; James G. O'Hara et al., "Dear Colleague" [letter for "Strong and Effective Gun Control Legislation"], June 20, 1968, JGOP, box 10, folder Gun Control; letter from James G. O'Hara to Wallace J. Klewicki, April 18, 1966, JGOP, box 6, folder Dodd Bill; letter from James G. O'Hara to Thomas P. Handlon, Jr., March 31, 1964, JGOP, box 2, folder Gun Control. As a historical aside, O'Hara maintained a narrow view of the Second Amendment. See "Know Your Lawmakers," *GM*, September 1960, 4 (Michigan representative James G. O'Hara).

64. See, e.g., "Boggs Votes for Mail Order Gun Sales Bill," *Shreveport (La.) Journal*, July 25, 1968, 4A; letter from Hale Boggs to E. J. Murphy, Louisiana Shooting Association, Inc., president, February 22, 1967, HBP, box 460, folder Firearms Legislation 1967; letter from Hale Boggs to Louise Jennings, September 15, 1967, HBP, box 454, Firearms Legislation 1966; letter from Hale Boggs to Anthony J. Deckelmann, July 16, 1965, HDP, box 447, folder Firearms Legislation 1965; letter from Hale Boggs to Richard H. Nelson, January 14, 1964, HBP, box 445, folder Firearms Legislation 1964.

65. "Know Your Lawmakers," *GM*, December 1964, 4 (Maine senator Edmund S. Muskie).

66. See, e.g., letter from Edmund S. Muskie to Sumner L. Thompson, September 8, 1964, ESMP, box 312, folder 6, Firearms Control; letter from Edmund S. Muskie to Helen K. Bachrach, August 13, 1964, Muskie Papers, box 312, folder 6, Firearms Control; letter from Edmund S. Muskie to Grace C. Saunders, March 25, 1964, ESMP, box 312, folder 6, Firearms Control.

67. See, e.g., letter from Edmund S. Muskie to Don B. Kates, March 18, 1970, ESMP, box 940, folder 2, Gun Control; letter from Edmund S. Muskie to Roberta J. Feller, November 18, 1969, ESMP, box 785, folder 4, Firearms Control; form letter from Edmund S. Muskie on Gun Control, August 5, 1969, ESMP, box 785, folder 4, Firearms Control.

68. Edmund S. Muskie, [Question-Answer Session in Brewer, Maine,] October 4, 1970, ESMP, box SC94, 22:04–26:30.

69. See, e.g., letter from Wallace F. Bennett to Maynard M. Sorenson, April 27, 1965, WFBP, box 316, folder 4, Firearms 1965–1966; letter from Wallace F. Bennett to Robert L. Bradley, March 26, 1965, WFBP, box 316, folder 4, Firearms 1965–1966; letter from Wallace F. Bennett to John D. Stewart, February 17, 1965, WFBP, box 316, folder 4, Firearms 1965–1966; letter from Wallace F. Bennett to Judge Sterling R. Bossard, October 5, 1965, WFBP, box 316, folder 4, Firearms 1965–1966.

70. Letter from Wallace F. Bennett to Mr. Owen's history class, March 18, 1965, WFBP, box 316, folder 4, Firearms 1965–1966.

71. Letter from Cecil R. King and Robert F. Sikes to Wallace F. Bennett, January 10, 1966, WFBP, box 322, folder 6, Firearms 1965–1966.

72. See, e.g., Letter from Wallace F. Bennett to Walter G. Koplin, October 12, 1967, WFBP, box 333, folder 9, Firearms 1967; letter from Wallace F. Bennett to Lee A. Wankier, September 29, 1967, WFBP, box 333, folder 8, Firearms 1967; letter from Wallace F. Bennett to Franklin L. Orth, NRA executive vice president, September 11, 1967, WFBP, box 333, folder 8, Firearms 1967; letter from Wallace F. Bennett to Ralph R. Dyment, February 14, 1967, WFBP, box 333, folder 8, Firearms 1967; letter from Wallace F. Bennett to P. O. Ackley, September 16, 1966, WFBP, box 316, folder 6, Firearms 1965–1966; letter from Tom C. Korologos, administrative assistant to Wallace F. Bennett, to Franklin L. Orth, NRA executive vice president, August 16, 1966, WFBP, box 316, folder 6, Firearms 1965–1966; letter from Franklin L. Orth, NRA executive vice president, to Wallace F. Bennett, August 12, 1966, WFBP, box 322, folder 6, Firearms 1965–1966; letter from Wallace F. Bennett to Alden E. Roylance, May 3, 1966, WFBP, box 322, folder 6, Firearms 1965–1966.

73. Bennett noted as much in a letter to Milton S. Eisenhower, who was appointed by President Lyndon B. Johnson to head the National Commission on the Causes and Prevention of Violence. See letter from Wallace F. Bennett to Milton S. Eisenhower, June 13, 1968, WFBP, box 227, folder 86.

5. The Evolution of the NRA and Firearms Control Politics

1. Compare "NRA's Growth Encouraging," *GW*, January 19, 1968, 4, with "Operations in 1963," *AR*, June 1964, 26.

2. Compare NRA, *Operating Report '69* (Washington, D.C., 1970), 14, RNP, Personal Papers, box 9, folder NRA, with "Operations in 1963," *AR*, June 1964, 26.

3. Compare "Table of Contents," AR, December 1967, 2; with "Table of Contents," AR, January 1964, 2.

4. Franklin L. Orth, "NRA 'Thrives on Adversity,'" AR, January 1968, 15.

5. As it pertains to the Dodd Bill, the NRA informed lawmakers and the media that the organization had long supported reasonable firearms legislation. It claimed this was evidenced by the organization's willingness to work "closely with Senator Dodd . . . in drafting the original bill, which was introduced on August 2, 1963." See NRA, "Where Does the NRA Stand on Firearms Legislation?," HBP, box 445, folder Firearms Legislation 1964. Additionally, the NRA noted: "The Dodd Bill, as it stands today, is not being opposed by the NRA, as its provisions are in accordance with the long-standing policy of NRA."

6. For some examples in the wake of President Kennedy's assassination, see NRA, The Gun Law Problem (Washington, D.C., 1965), 14–16; J. J. Basil, Jr., and Daniel J. Mountin, "Firearms Legislation and the Gun Owner," AR, July 1964, 30–31; "Basic Facts of Firearms Control," AR, February 1964, 14; "What the Lawmakers Are Doing," AR, February 1964, 28.

7. Patrick J. Charles, Armed in America: A History of Gun Rights from Colonial Militias to Concealed Carry (Amherst, N.Y.: Prometheus Books, 2018), 212–18. It was through affiliated rifle clubs that the NRA accomplished most of its lobbying and advocacy efforts. See letter from Harold W. Glassen to Dwain L. Fritz, August 7, 1968, HWGP, box 1; "Maryland Sportsmen Rally to Fight Bills," GW, March 8, 1968, 2; Jack J. Basil, "What the Lawmakers Are Doing: Illinois, California, Connecticut Enact Gun Laws with Sportsmen's Cooperation," AR, August 1967, 54; J. J. Basil and Daniel J. Moutin, "Firearms Legislation and the Gun Owner," AR, July 1964, 30–32.

8. "Current Federal Gun Legislation," AR, May 1965, 17–19; Bill Davidson, "NRA Still Waits to Make Decision on Gun Proposal," Tucson (Ariz.) Citizen, February 4, 1965, 44; Bill Davidson, "Papagos Could Help Selves by Taking Off Coyote's Halo," Tucson Citizen, January 29, 1965, 30; Bill Hunter, "Outdoor Almanac," Burlington (N.C.) Daily Times-News, January 20, 1965, 6B, 8B; Bill Davidson, "Phoenix' Spillman Has Game-Fist Candidacy Going," Tucson Daily Citizen, January 8, 1965, 30.

9. See, e.g., "United We Stand," AR, January 1965, 16–18; "The Illegal Use of Guns," AR, December 1964, 16.

10. See "The Misuse of Firearms," AR, March 1964, 16; letter from Franklin L. Orth, NRA executive vice president, et al. to NRA members, January 30, 1964, JJFJP, series 3, box 247, folder 5, NRA.

11. See "Lawmakers to Consider Firearms Restrictions," Reno Nevada State Journal, December 31, 1964, 4; "The Gun Problem," St. Louis (Mo.) Post-Dispatch, December 17, 1964, 2D; "A Starter Needed Toward Curbing the Gun Traffic," Louisville (Ky.) Courier-Journal, December 10, 1964, 16; "Sensible Gun Control," Bridgeport (Conn.) Post, December 10, 1964, 34; "Rifle Group Bides Time on Mail-Order Gun Ban Bill," Fresno (Calif.) Bee, December 9, 1964, 7; Uncle Dudley, "Guns Too Easy to Get," Boston Globe, December 8, 1964, 14; Ben A. Franklin, "Rifle Unit Split Over Gun Curbs," NYT,

December 7, 1964, 1, 29; "Battle Rages on 2 Fronts Over Gun Law," *Rochester (N.Y.) Democrat and Chronicle*, December 7, 1964, 2.

12. See, e.g., Bob Rankin, "Outdoors: New Gun Laws," *Cincinnati (Ohio) Enquirer*, February 16, 1965, 29; "NRA Still Waits to Make Decision on Gun Proposal," *Tucson (Ariz.) Daily Citizen*, February 4, 1965, 44; "Firearms Bill Deserves Support," *Arizona Daily Star*, February 4, 1965, 12D; "No Guns for the Reckless," *Hagerstown (Md.) Daily Mail*, January 29, 1965, 4; John D. Ewing, "News Analyst Says Dodd Bill Will Be Pushed for Passage," *Shreveport (La.) Times*, January 10, 1965, 6D.

13. See Russell Tinsley, "Outdoor Scene: New Gun Law Is Proposed," *Austin (Tex.) American*, March 4, 1965, 59; Charles Nicodemus, "Dissemination of Misinformation: Barrage Against Gun Bill," *Philadelphia Inquirer*, March 4, 1965, 7; George Kellam, "Bill to Protect Legal Gun Owners Set for Congress," *Fort Worth (Tex.) Star-Telegram*, March 3, 1965, sec. 2, p. 3; Bill Davidson, "Dodd Wants His Bill but Isn't Bullheaded," *Tucson (Ariz.) Citizen*, March 2, 1965, 17; Bill Davidson, "Sen. Dodd Seeks Sportsman Support," *Tucson Citizen*, March 1, 1965, 37.

14. "Statement of Senator Thomas J. Dodd, Section of Criminal Law, Americana Hotel, New York," August 12, 1964, JVBPP, Subject Files, 1933–1966, box 10, folder American Bar Foundation-Panel Discussion.

15. See Joseph Hearst, "Curbs Sought on Mail Order Gun Traffic," *Chicago Tribune*, January 7, 1965, 2A; "'Minority' Barred Gun Bill—Dodd," *Tucson (Ariz.) Daily Citizen*, January 6, 1965, 15.

16. "Mail-Order Gun Control," *AR*, March 1965, 16 (emphasis added).

17. Lyndon B. Johnson, "Special Message to Congress on Law Enforcement and Administration of Justice," March 8, 1965, 1 *Public Papers of the Presidents of the United States: Lyndon B. Johnson: 1965* (Washington, D.C.: U.S. Government Printing Office, 1966), 263–71.

18. This was second time in two years that Dodd had failed to proceed with an NRA compromise bill. See Carl Bakal, *The Right to Bear Arms* (New York: McGraw-Hill, 1966), 194–95 (detailing the NRA's early cooperation with Dodd); "A Report on Federal Gun Legislation," *AR*, March 1964, 24–27.

19. Immediately after President Johnson announced his firearms proposal, Dodd "vigorously applauded" it. See "Mail Order Gun Ban Among Johnson's Anticrime Aims," *Burlington (Vt.) Free Press*, March 9, 1965, 1; "Johnson Asks New Laws to Fight Crime," *Tampa (Fla.) Tribune*, March 9, 1965, A1, A6.

20. Thomas J. Dodd, news release, March 28, 1965, TJDP, box 201, folder 5184; "Dodd Seeking New Controls on Firearms," *Asbury Park (N.J.) Press*, March 22, 1965, 15.

21. "Why Penalize?," *Pensacola (Fla.) News Journal*, March 19, 1965, 4A.

22. "Federal Gun Legislation," *AR*, January 1966, 15.

23. "Gun Bill Praised by National Rifle Group," *Minneapolis Star Tribune*, March 25, 1965, 38.

24. "Gun Bill Praised by National Rifle Group."

25. See, e.g., Karl T. Frederick, *Pistol Regulation: Its Principles and History* (Washington, D.C.: NRA 1946), 42–49, MFP, box 5, folder 52; C. B. Lister, "The Shooter's No. 1

Problem," *Official Gun Book*, ed. Charles R. Jacobs (New York: Crown, 1950), 4, 6; NRA, *The Pro and Con of Firearms Legislation* (Washington, D.C., 1940), 1.

26. United States Revolver Association, "Criminals Not Made by Pistols," Bulletin no. 5, February 15, 1923, MFP, box 5, folder 53.

27. Charles Nicodemus, "Launches Million-Letter Drive: Rifle Association Hits Gun Proposal," *Tampa (Fla.) Times*, March 30, 1965, 3.

28. Remarks of Senator Thomas J. Dodd before Ford Hall Forum, Boston, Mass., "The Use of Firearms: Right or Privilege?," March 28, 1965, TJDP, box 201, folder 5185.

29. Bill Davidson, "Sportsmen Can Back House Bill 7472," *Tucson (Ariz.) Citizen*, May 7, 1965, 34. See also National Wildlife Federation, "King Introduces New Measure to Control Mail-Order Handgun Sales," *Conservation Report*, Report no. 18, April 23, 1965, BHP, box 20, folder 13, Gun Control 1965; letter from Bourke B. Hickenlooper to Melvin Tudor, April 15, 1965, BHP, box 20, folder 13, Gun Control 1965; letter from Bourke B. Hickenlooper to Jim Scott, April 15, 1965, BHP, box 20, folder 13, Gun Control 1965.

30. See "Gun Control Confusion," *AR*, June 1965, 16; "This Is Our Stand," *AR*, May 1965, 16; "Current Federal Gun Legislation," *AR*, May 1965, 17–19; NRA, *The Gun Law Problem*, 12–13; "NRA Basic Policy," *AR*, July 1964, 31.

31. Letter from Franklin L. Orth, NRA executive vice president, to NRA Membership, April 9, 1965, JVBPP, Subject File, 1933–1966, box 11, NRA Literature.

32. *Federal Firearms Act: Hearings Before the Subcommittee to Investigate Juvenile Delinquency of the Committee on the Judiciary United States Senate*, 89th Congress, 1st Session (Washington, D.C.: Government Printing Office, 1965), 195–97. For newspaper coverage of Orth's testimony, see "Gun Curb Bill Hit by Riflemen," *Boston Globe*, May 22, 1965, 2; Jerry T. Baulch, "Riflemen Protest Mail-Order Ban," *Pittsburgh Post-Gazette*, May 22, 1965, 2; "National Rifle Association Official Fires at Gun Bill," *Cincinnati (Ohio) Enquirer*, May 22, 1965, 36.

33. *Federal Firearms Act*, 197–206.

34. *Federal Firearms Act*, 206.

35. *Federal Firearms Act*, 207.

36. *Federal Firearms Act*, 207–11.

37. It is worth noting that despite Dodd having dispelled several of the NRA's claims, the organization continued to assert them to rally its members and the wider gun rights community. See, e.g., Harlon B. Carter, "The NRA . . . What It Is and Does," *AR*, November 1965, 17–20; "The Power to Legislate," *AR*, August 1965, 16.

38. Statement of Senator Warren G. Magnuson before the Senate Committee on Commerce, December 10, 1963, WNMP, box 193, folder 73.

39. See, e.g., remarks of Harold W. Glassen, president National Rifle Association of America, before the Annual Meeting of the National Society of State Legislatures, Chicago, Illinois, July 27, 1967, HWGP, box 1; "Existing Federal Gun Controls," *AR*, April 1966, 16; NRA, *Basic Facts of Firearms Control* (Washington, D.C., 1965); J. Basil, Jr., and Daniel J. Mountin, "Firearms Legislation and the Gun Owner," *AR*, July 1964, 30–31; "Basic Facts of Firearms Control," *AR*, February 1964, 14.

40. "95th NRA Annual Meetings and Sessions," *AR*, June 1966, 28, 29; "A Suggestion to Congress," *AR*, January 1966, 14.
41. "Federal Gun Legislation," *AR*, January 1966, 15–16.
42. *To Regulate Firearms in Commerce: Hearings Before a Subcommittee of the Committee on Commerce United States Senate* (Washington, D.C.: Government Printing Office, 1934), 22–23.
43. NRA congressional surrogates, Florida representative Robert F. Sikes and Arizona senator Carl Hayden, ultimately put forward the proposal. See Franklin L. Orth, "Where the NRA Stands . . .," *AR*, September 1966, 21–22; "What the Lawmakers Are Doing," *AR*, July 1966, 21; "What the Lawmakers Are Doing," *AR*, June 1966, 39.
44. Herbert Sandusky, "Outdoor Mississippi: Eastland Against Firearms Bill," *Jackson (Miss.) Clarion-Ledger*, August 1, 1965, 6E.
45. Just prior to the mass shooting, gun rights supporters expressed confidence that Dodd's bill would not be considered. See, e.g., Carl Wolff, "Our Man in Washington, *GM*, August 1966, 19–20.
46. Jack Bell, "Gun Control Action Faces Maze of Roadblocks," *Davenport (Iowa) Quad-City Times*, August 3, 1966, 26.
47. James W. Canan, "Gun Control Bill Stymied," *Binghamton (N.Y.) Press and Sun-Bulletin*, September 2, 19566, 8; "Lawmaker Sees Need for Local Gun Controls," *Northwest Arkansas Times* (Fayetteville), August 4, 1966, 26; "Dodd Bill Doesn't Go Far Enough: Magnuson Says States Must Act," *Saint Joseph (Mich.) Herald-Press*, August 4, 1966, 28.
48. See, e.g., Everett Dirksen, form letter on gun control, September 8, 1966, EMDP, Form Letters, folder Firearms 1966; NBC's *Meet the Press* transcript, August 7, 1966, EMDP, Remarks, Releases, and Interviews, folder Meet the Press, NBC.
49. See, e.g., letter from Thomas J. Dodd to Edward Kennedy, August 18, 1966, TJDP, box 73, folder 2109; letter from Thomas J. Dodd to Joseph Tydings, August 18, 1966, TJDP, box 77, folder 2212.
50. Letter from Harlon B. Carter, NRA president, to Carl Albert, August 5, 1966, CAP, box LG 89, folder 37, Gun Control.
51. Letter from Carl Albert to Harlon B. Carter, NRA president, August 10, 1966, box LG 89, folder 37, Gun Control.
52. "What the Lawmakers Are Doing: Senators 'Unload' on Dodd Gun Bill," *AR*, November 1966, 40.
53. "Chances Dim for Gun Bill; Dodd Angry," *Rochester (N.Y.) Democrat and Chronicle*, September 1, 1966, 9A.
54. Letter from Thomas J. Dodd to Joseph Tydings, October 3, 1966, TJDP, box 77, folder 2212; letter from Thomas J. Dodd to Edward Kennedy, October 3, 1966, TJDP, box 73, folder 2109.
55. Letter from Bourke B. Hickenlooper to Bob Brownwell, October 20, 1966, BHP, box 15, folder 4, Bob Brownwell Correspondence 1957–1968.
56. Lyndon B. Johnson, "Annual Message to the Congress on the State of the Union," January 10, 1967, 1 *Public Papers of the Presidents of the United States: Lyndon B. Johnson: 1967* (Washington, D.C.: U.S. Government Printing Office, 1968), 2, 7.

57. Lyndon B. Johnson, "Special Message to the Congress on Crime in America," February 6, 1967, 1 *Public Papers of the Presidents of the United States: Lyndon B. Johnson: 1968*, pp. 134, 142, 143.

58. "Firearms Legislation—a Recurring Fever," AR, March 1967, 8. For a detailed analysis of the NRA's objections to Dodd's S. 1, see NRA Legislative Service, "Principal Objections to S.1 . . . First Session, 90th Congress," November 1967, MRP, series 5, box 14, folder 6.

59. See, e.g., "What the Lawmakers Are Doing: Drive to Pass Celler Bill Begins," AR, April 1967, 17–19; "What the Lawmakers Are Doing: Celler Creates Gun Bill Crisis in Congress," AR, March 1967, 15–17; "What the Lawmakers Are Doing: Dodd Bill Back; More State Gun Curbs Sought," AR, February 1967, 20–21. To punctuate this point, as well as the talking point that firearms control ultimately lead to firearms confiscation, the NRA ran a two-part series on the history of Soviet firearms laws. See Will N. Graves, Jr., "How the Soviet Controls Guns: Part 2," AR, February 1967, 38–41; Will N. Graves, Jr., "How the Soviet Controls Guns: Part 1," AR, January 1967, 42–45.

60. "Crime Control for Non-Criminals?," AR, April 1967, 16.

61. "New Fact Sheet Available: The Truth About Guns," AR, February 1967, 8.

62. See, e.g., Donald Martin, "The Gun Law Crisis—Now!," G&A, June 1965, 24–25, 62–63; Pete Brown, "A Threat to Gun Ownership?," *Sports Afield*, August 1963, 19–21, 72, 74.

63. "The Austin Affair," G&A, October 1966, 6.

64. "Who Is Emanuel Celler?," *Association to Preserve Our Right to Keep and Bear Arms Newsletter*, March 1967, 3.

65. "Technique for Take-Over," *Association to Preserve Our Right to Keep and Bear Arms Newsletter*, June–July 1967, 2–5 (reprinted from the *Herald of Freedom*, May 19, 1967).

66. The NRA helped in playing up this belief. See, e.g., "The Faces of the Opposition," AR, November 1967, 18.

67. E. B. Mann, "Politics Is Your Business," January 23, 1967, EBMP, box 7, folder 16 (article submitted for publication for *Shooting Industry* magazine).

68. Carl Wolff, "Our Man in Washington: Will the Real 'Gun Lobby' Please Stand Up?," GM, February 1966, 16–17.

69. See, e.g., "Rep. Casey Raps 'Anti-Gun Lobby'; Pushes Bill to 'Strike at Criminal,'" GW, March 24, 1967, 1, 3.

70. Letter from Bourke B. Hickenlooper to Bob Brownwell, March 31, 1966, BHP, box 15, folder 4, Gun Correspondence, 1957–1968.

71. See, e.g., "NRA Chief Hears Hruska, Kennedy; Open Legislative Session Canceled," GW, April 14, 1967, 1, 6; "Firearms Industry Association Backs Hruska-Type Legislation," GW, January 20, 1967, pp. 1–2; Neal Knox, "The Rifleman—Its 'New Look,'" GW, December 16, 1966, 4.

72. See, e.g., "Changing NRA's Image," GW, May 3, 1968, 4.

73. "NRA Intensifies Campaign to Air Gun Control Laws," *Salt Lake (Utah) Tribune*, April 1, 1967, 2.

74. Letter from Edward M. Kennedy to Franklin L. Orth, NRA executive vice president, March 17, 1967, RHP, box 248, folder 8.
75. Letter from Franklin L. Orth, NRA executive vice president, to Edward M. Kennedy, March 21, 1967, RHP, box 248, folder 8.
76. Letter from Edward M. Kennedy to Franklin L. Orth, NRA executive vice president, March 28, 1967, RHP, box 248, folder 8.
77. See "Rifle Association Hears Senator: Teddy Seeks Backing on Gun Controls," *Indianapolis (Ind.) Star*, April 3, 1967, 2; "Ted Kennedy Tells Rifle Group Gun Control Regulations Are Due Soon," *Sacramento (Calif.) Bee*, April 3, 1967, A9; "Ted Kennedy Challenges Rifle Group," *Tampa (Fla.) Tribune*, April 3, 1967, 15A; "Gun Curbs Sure, Rifle Group Told by Sen. Ted Kennedy," *Cincinnati (Ohio) Enquirer*, April 3, 1967, 16.
78. "Defensive Tactics Fail," *GW*, April 21, 1967, 4.
79. Letter from Harold W. Glassen to Neal Knox, April 25, 1967, HWGP, box 1, folder Crack Pot File.
80. Harold W. Glassen, "Senator Kennedy's Invitation to Address Open Committee Meeting in Boston," [March or April 1967,] HWGP, box 1.
81. "Who Guards America's Homes?," *AR*, May 1967, 16.
82. "Rifle Association Checking Extremists," *La Crosse (Wis.) Tribune*, April 20, 1965, 6.
83. Lister, "The Shooter's No. 1 Problem," *Official Gun Book*, 6.
84. See, e.g., "Black Panthers and Blind Kittens," *AR*, September 1970, 20. According to NRA officials, in 1967 only 16 percent of NRA-affiliated clubs were integrated. See Robert Sherill, "A Lobby on Target," *NYT Magazine*, October 15, 1966, 246, 249. Based on my research, the March 1968 edition of *AR* seems to be the first instance where the NRA published an opinion from the Black community. See William J. White, "Why Anti-Gun Laws 'Hit Hardest at the Negro,'" March 1968, 21.
85. See, e.g., Earl Sherwood, "Slaying Spurs Propaganda for Federal Firearms Controls," *Armed Eagle*, September 1968, 4 (building off the NRA's "Can Three Assassins Kill a Civil Right" editorial to advance the conspiracy theory that the assassination of Senator Robert F. Kennedy was a communist plot); Clark L. Bradley, press release, "Need for More Gun Laws—Fact or Hysteria?," June 12, 1968, DMP, series 3, Subject Files, folder Gun Control 1967–1970 (noting how the Second Amendment allows Californians to "acquire and bear arms for protection," including against the "rising number of militant minority and left-wing organizations"); "Technique for Take-Over," *Association to Preserve Our Right to Bear Arms Newsletter*, June–July 1967, 2 (reprinted from the *Herald of Freedom*, May 19, 1967) (building off the NRA's "Who Guards America's Homes?" editorial to advance the conspiracy theory that firearms control supporters were being influenced or co-opted by the Soviet Union).
86. See, e.g., "U.S. Has 'Moral Pollution,' Dick Gregory Warns Students," *York (Pa.) Daily Record*, September 29, 1967, 1–2; "Congressional 'Hearing' on Firearms," *Des Moines (Iowa) Tribune*, July 19, 1965, 4; "Slow Death for the Hooded Terrorists," *Dayton (Ohio) Journal Herald*, June 23, 1965, 4; "Solon Says Extremists Get Ammo," *Austin-American Statesman* (Tex.), August 13, 1964, B19; Warren Berry, "Is U.S. Arming Race Fanatics?," *Salina (Kans.) Journal*, May 24, 1964, 20.

87. "Rifle Group Urges Members to Form Anti-Riot Posses," *Tampa (Fla.) Tribune*, May 7, 1967, 9A (reprinted from the *New York Times*); Ben A. Franklin, "Armed Civilian Posses Urged as Riot Defense," *Louisville (Ky.) Courier-Journal*, May 7, 1967, 18A.

88. Joseph D. Tydings, "Senator Scores NRA Opposition to Gun Control," *York (Pa.) Daily Record*, March 24, 1969, 17.

89. "Sportsmen All," *Redlands (Calif.) Daily Facts*, May 11, 1967, 20.

90. "What We Want Now! What We Believe," *Black Panther: Black Community News Service*, November 23, 1967, 3.

91. In response to the criticism of the "Who Guards America's Homes?" editorial, the NRA issued several press releases refuting that the organization endorsed vigilantism: "The NRA does not approve or support any group activities that properly belong to the national defense or police. The NRA does not approve or support any group that by force, violence, or subversion seeks to overthrow the Government and take the law into its hands, or that endorses or espouses doctrines of operation in an extralegal manner." Ashley Halsey, Jr., "Rifleman Fire Back," *Miami (Fla.) News*, May 20, 1967, 2.

92. See, e.g., letter from Franklin C. Daniel, NRA secretary, to Thomas E. Wessel, October 10, 1968, TEWP ("I agree with you, if more people were armed and determined to protect themselves, there would be much less of this open street crime"); "Merry Christmas—and Gun Laws," *AR*, December 1929, 6.

93. The NRA's preference for having more citizens armed appeared frequently in *American Rifleman* going back to the 1920s. Beginning in 1932 it conveyed its preference for arming more citizens in a reoccurring column titled "Guns vs. Bandits." The column started off monthly and then appeared sporadically. See chapter 2. In 1958 the NRA once more advanced this view in a column titled "The Armed Citizen." See Walter J. Howe, "The Armed Citizen," *AR*, September 1958, 32. The organization felt the column showed that "law enforcement officers cannot at all times be where they are needed to protect life or property in danger of serious violation," and thus there were "many instances" where "the citizen has no choice but to defend himself with a gun." Years later it slightly modified its defense of "The Armed Citizen" column on the grounds that there are "instances in which the mere presence of a firearm in the hands of a resolute citizen prevented crime without bloodshed." "The Silent Protectors," *AR*, January 1971, 28.

94. See, e.g., *National Firearms Act: Hearing Before the Committee on Ways and Means House Resolution*, 73rd Congressional Record (Washington, D.C., 1934), 59; Calvin Goddard, "The Pistol Bogey," *American Journal of Police Science* 1 (1930): 178, 187; "Our Friends— the Policemen," *AR*, July 1930, 6 ("Regulate the sale of arms, and license those who wish to carry them"); "A Day in Chicago," *AR*, October 15, 1926, 8; "You Can't Fool the Editors All the Time," *AR*, May 15, 1925, 14 ("The *AR* does not oppose wise regulatory measures with regard to powerful weapons in crowded communities. No body of men in the country understands the need for wise regulation better than this staff"); "The Question of Intent," *AR*, March 15, 1925, 13; "The Police Panacea," *A&M*, May 15, 1923, 10; "The Gun-Toting Criminal," *A&M*, November 1, 1922, 12.

95. David Conover, "To Keep and Bear Arms," *AR*, September 1985, 40–41. See, e.g., Merritt A. Edson, "The Right to Bear Arms," *AR*, July 1955, 14; Merritt A. Edson, "The Right to Bear Arms," *Maryland Conservationist*, March 1956, 14–17; Lister, "The Shooter's No. 1 Problem," *Official Gun Book*, 4–6.

96. Adam Winkler, *Gunfight: The Battle Over the Right to Bear Arms in America* (New York: Norton, 2011), 237–45.

97. See, e.g., Thaddeus Morgan, "The NRA Supported Gun Control When the Black Panthers Had the Weapons," *History.com*, March 22, 2018, https://www.history.com /news/black-panthers-gun-control-nra-support-mulford-act; Adam Winkler, "The Secret History of Guns," *Atlantic* (September 2011), https://www.theatlantic.com /magazine/archive/2011/09/the-secret-history-of-guns/308608/.

98. Carol Anderson, *The Second: Race and Guns in a Fatally Unequal America* (New York: Bloomsbury, 2021), 138, 135–36 (emphasis added). Anderson cites a law review article as support. See Cynthia Deitle Leonardatos, "California's Attempts to Disarm the Black Panthers," *San Diego Law Review* 36 (1999), 947, 973. This article cites the newspaper article from 1967, which was widely published by local California newspapers. See, e.g., Jerry Rankin, "Heavily Armed Negro Group Walks Into Assembly Chamber," *Los Angeles Times*, May 3, 1967, part 1, pp. 3, 28.

99. Rankin, "Heavily Armed Negro Group," 28.

100. The same is true for Anderson's other claim that the Second Amendment is racist. Compare Anderson, *The Second*, 26–39, with Charles, *Armed in America*, 70–121 (outlining the constitutional origins of the Second Amendment); Patrick J. Charles, "Racist History and the Second Amendment: A Critical Commentary," 43 *Cardozo Law Review* (2022): 1343, 1368–75 (rebutting the Second Amendment is racist claim). In advancing this claim, Anderson uncovered nothing new. She relied primarily on a law review article written in 1998 by Carl T. Bogus—an article in which Bogus admits that the "Second Amendment is racist" claim is based on "circumstantial" evidence. See Carl T. Bogus, "The Hidden History of the Second Amendment," *U.C. Davis Law Review* 31 (1998): 309, 544, 371–72.

101. This includes the often-stated historical claim that the push to regulate Saturday Night Specials (cheap handguns) in the 1970s was a means to "control" Blacks. See, e.g., Anderson, *The Second*, 140. The historical claim stems from a 1973 book, Robert Sherrill, *The Saturday Night Special* (New York: Charterhouse, 1973), 280. What does Sherrill provide in the way of historical evidence for his conclusion? Nothing. The same holds true for several other historical claims he makes; Sherrill was not a historian but a news reporter. Yet, despite his lack of evidence, his racist claim regarding Saturday Night Special legislation in the 1970s lives on. Sadly, it has been repeated by many respectable writers in articles, law reviews, and books—none of which has provided a shred of historical evidence that proves it.

102. The bill's primary appeal to California lawmakers was that it closed an armed carriage loophole in California law. There was particular concern about the ability of anyone to carry a firearm openly on government property (except for prisons). See memorandum from George H. Murphy, legislative counsel of California, to

Jesse M. Unruh, "Firearms-#18777," May 3, 1967, JMUP, Speaker's Office Files, Series 2, Correspondence Files, 1959–1970, folder 503, Political-Gun Control.

103. See letter from Jack Lindsay, legislative secretary to Ronald Reagan, to Don Mulford, May 19, 1967, DMP, series 1, Bill Files, folder A.B. 1591; letter from Don Mulford to Ronald Reagan, April 21, 1967, DMP, series 1, Bill Files, folder A.B. 1591; letter from John A. Nejedly, Contra Costa County district attorney, to Ronald Reagan, April 20, 1967, DMP, series 1, Bill Files, folder A.B. 1591; "Peace Gradually Returning to the Community of Clyde," *Redlands (Calif.) Daily Facts*, September 23, 1966, 12; "Shots Boost Bay Tension on Vigilantes," *San Francisco Examiner*, September 21, 1966, 3. In the years that followed, the problem of "open carry" armed patrols played out in other jurisdictions, including Denver, Colorado, and Toledo, Ohio. See, e.g., "Gun Control Law Is Given Okay," *Marion (Ohio) Star*, May 30, 1970, 9; "Toledo Council Approves Gun Control Law," *Fremont (Ohio) News-Messenger*, May 29, 1970, 3; "Gun Control Bill Opposed in Toledo," *Circleville (Ohio) Herald*, April 27, 1970, 5; "Council Air Gun Control for Toledo," *East Liverpool (Ohio) Evening Review*, April 27, 1970, 10; "Denver Council OK's Gun Control," *Gettysburg (Pa.) Times*, July 11, 1968, 5; "Denver Council Votes for Gun Controls," *Colorado Springs (Colo.) Gazette-Telegraph*, July 4, 1968, 1.

104. Notes of Don Mulford meeting with E. F. Tod Sloan, NRA field representative, on A.B. 1591, undated 1967, DMP, series 1, Bill Files, folder A.B. 1591.

105. There is no question that the Black Panther Party was a strong factor in Mulford initially drafting A.B. 1591. See letter from Don Mulford to Ronald Reagan, April 21, 1967, DMP, series 1, Bill Files, folder A.B. 1591. Mulford's bill was initially to apply only in populated cities. See "Protection of Capitol Written Into State Gun Control Plans," *Eureka (Calif.) Humboldt Standard*, May 10, 1967, 15.

106. See, e.g., Remarks of Harold W. Glassen, president of the National Rifle Association of America, before the Annual Meeting of the National Society of State Legislatures, Chicago, Illinois, July 27, 1967, HWGP, box 1; "More Amendments Are Due: Assembly Unit Holds Fire on Gun Control Bill," *Sacramento (Calif.) Bee*, May 27, 1967, A5; "Assembly Unit Okays Gun Control Bills; Another Is Deferred After Intrusion," *Sacramento Bee*, May 3, 1967, A12.

107. Letter from Don Mulford to John W. Bader, June 22, 1967, DMP, series 1, Bill Files, folder A.B. 1591.

108. Richard Bergholz, "Reagan Will Fight for Gun Ownership," *Los Angeles Times*, August 3, 1966, part 1, 3; letter from Ronald Reagan to Ernest Henrique, October 19, 1966, RRGCF, box C34, folder Legal Affairs; Gun Control; "Reagan Gets Firearms Bill," *Reno (Nev.) Gazette-Journal*, July 28, 1967, 14; "Gun Control Law on Reagan's Desk," *Santa Cruz (Calif.) Sentinel*, July 28, 1967, 14; "Gun Control Bill Signed by Reagan," *Eureka (Calif.) Times Standard*, July 28, 1967, 1; Jack Welter, "New Gun Controls Sent to Reagan," *San Francisco Examiner*, July 27, 1967, 1.

109. "Heavier Guard Set to Protect Reagan," *Los Angeles Times*, May 10, 1967, 13, 17.

110. Letter from Harold W. Glassen to William L. Kleinpaste, October 10, 1967, HWGP, box 1, folder Crack Pot File.

111. Letter from Franklin L. Orth, NRA executive vice president, to Theodore Webb, May 23, 1967, HWGP, box 1, folder Crack Pot File.
112. See, e.g., NRA Office of Public Relations, news release, "NRA Membership Tops 900,000," January 5, 1968, MRP, series 5, box 14, folder 5.
113. Opening Remarks of Harold W. Glassen, NRA president, High Power Opening Ceremony, August 21, 1967, HWGP, box 1.
114. "The Faces of the Opposition," *AR*, November 1967, 18.
115. Text of statement by Harold W. Glassen, National Rifle Association president, at National Press Club, Washington, D.C., June 29, 1967, HWGP, box 1.
116. "Glassen Elected New President," *GW*, April 21, 1967, 1, 3; "Alternative Offered Congress: Glassen Raps Gun Bill," *Lansing (Mich.) State Journal*, April 7, 1967, 1B. For NRA president Harlon B. Carter's outgoing speech before the April 1967 NRA annual meeting, see "Outgoing President Urges Rededication to Principles," *AR*, June 1967, 41.
117. Harold W. Glassen, "Vice-President's Report 1967: First Board of Directors Meeting," undated 1967, HWGP, box 1.
118. Harold W. Glassen, "Acceptance Speech," [April] 1967, HWGP, box 1.
119. For some restatements of the "twenty thousand" firearms laws by the NRA, it's "official family," and the wider gun rights community, see Bob Bell, "35,000,001 . . . And Then?," *PGN*, March 1969, 1; letter from Ken Carrell, Josephine County Sportsmen Association secretary, to Robert Packwood, February 14, 1969, RWPP, box 6, folder 10, Legislation-Judiciary, Gun Control 1969; letter from Don Holm, *Oregonian* wildlife editor, to Robert Packwood, January 28, 1969, RWPP, box 6, folder 10, Legislation-Judiciary, Gun Control 1969; Bill Riviere and Edward Kennedy, "The Great Gun Debate," *Boston Sunday Globe*, April 7, 1968, 8, 13; Bob Bell, "Do We Need 35,000,001?," *PGN*, April 1968, 1; Alan S. Krug, "Firearms Legislation: A Scientist's Perspective," March 1, 1968, reprinted in *Fact Pack II on Firearms Ownership* (Riverside, Conn.: National Shooting Sports Foundation, 1970), 57–59; Ken Gookins, "In the Great Outdoors," *Zanesville (Ohio) Times Recorder*, August 19, 1967, 3B. The fabricated twenty thousand firearms laws claim continued into the 1970s. See, e.g., letter from Lew H. Sarchet, Oklahoma Rifle Association secretary, to Thomas Jefferson Steed, TJSP, box 80, folder 16, Judiciary-Gun Control; letter from John D. Dingell to Karl S. Klicka, July 8, 1975, WDFP, box 18, folder Gun Control; Nancy Jackson, "Handgun Debate Ends in Standoff," *Battle Creek (Mich.) Enquirer*, November 5, 1971, B1.
120. The hypocrisy of the fabricated twenty thousand estimate was seemingly lost on the NRA. See, e.g., "Wanted: The Real Facts on Gun Fatalities," *AR*, October 1967, 20 (criticizing firearms control supporters for relying on what the NRA believed were fabricated and misleading statistics); NRA, *The Truth About Guns*, 1–10.
121. The NRA must have known the twenty thousand estimate was a farce. For in 1975 it published a book titled *Firearms and Laws Review*, which was a digest of the principal provisions of the firearms laws throughout the United States. The digest

included nowhere close to the twenty thousand estimate. At most, it contained a few thousand legal provisions—not necessarily laws—from federal, state, and local governments. See NRA, *Firearms and Laws Review* (Washington, D.C., 1975), 99–138.

122. NRA Office of Public Relations, news release, "NRA Offers Program on Gun Control Legislation," April 7, 1967, MRP, series 5, box 14, folder 6. Yet in a speech before the Ohio Gun Collectors Association in June 1965, Glassen gave the impression that the NRA's "four-point plan" was not all that different from its legislation stance in 1963. See "NRA Legislative Policy Unchanged President Tells Ohio Gun Collectors," *GW*, June 9, 1967, 1, 6.

123. Milton Reckord, "Speech #1," undated 1967, MRP, series 5, box 14, folder 6.

124. Compare "NRA Position on Gun Legislation," *AR*, May 1967, 17, with "What the Lawmakers Are Doing: Senators 'Unload' Dodd Gun Bill," *AR*, November 1966, 40; Franklin L. Orth, "Where the NRA Stands . . .," *AR*, September 1966, 21–22.

125. Wayne L. Morse, firearms control form letter, June 15, 1967, WEMP, box 19, folder 12.

126. See, e.g., "Anti-Gun Bill Tactics Protested," *AR*, April 1967, 20.

127. See letter from Harlon B. Carter, former NRA president, to Roman Hruska, April 25, 1967, RHP, box 39, folder 98; John M. Schooley, NRA Firearms Legislation Committee chairman, "National Rifle Association of America Report of the Firearms Legislation Committee," April 5, 1967, RHP, box 249, folder 8; letter from Woodson D. Scott, NRA Subcommittee on Firearms Legislation chairman, to NRA Committee on Firearms Legislation, April 2, 1967, RHP, box 249, folder 8; memorandum from Daniel J. Mountin, NRA secretary, to NRA Committee on Firearms Legislation, November 2, 1966, RHP, box 249, folder 8.

128. See NRA Legislative Service, *Weekly Legislate Report Nos. 20 and 21*, June 5, 1967, RHP, box 249, folder 8.

129. NRA Office of Public Relations, news release, "Hruska Introduces Gun Bill, Gains Rifle Assn. Support," May 25, 1967, MRP, series 5, box 14, folder 6. Through California representative Cecil R. King, the NRA was able to introduce a companion bill to S. 1852 in the House of Representatives. See "Support for King's Bill," *GW*, May 26, 1967, 4; "NRA-Endorsed Mail Order Control Bill Introduced by Rep. Cecil King: Proposal Similar to Sen. Hruksa's," *GW*, May 5, 1967, 1–2.

130. See "Drive to Pass Dodd-Celler Bills Stepped Up," *AR*, November 1967, 34–35; "Dodd Moves S. 1 Out! LBJ Calls for Gun Law," *GW*, September 29, 1967, 1, 3.

131. See "What the Lawmakers Are Doing: Celler Bill Given Slight Push," *AR*, December 1967, 24–25; Robert S. McNeill, "The Pro and Cons of Gun Control," *San Bernardino County (Calif.) Sun*, November 26, 1967, B15–B16; "Celler Bill Vote Unlikely This Session," *GW*, November 24, 1967, 1, 3; "Gun Bill Goes to Full Committee," *Arizona Republic* (Phoenix), November 9, 1967, 53; Dan Thomasson, "Gun-Control Compromise Sought," *Pittsburgh Press*, September 27, 1967, 10; "Celler Plan: Less Strict Gun Bill Is Proposed," *Fort Worth (Tex.) Star-Telegram*, September 26, 1967, 3C; "Firearms Proposal Is Cut to Cover Only Handguns," *Sacramento (Calif.) Bee*, September 27, 1967, A4.

132. "Do Americans *Really* Want New Gun Laws?," *AR*, April 1968, 16.

133. See, e.g., Harold W. Glassen, opening remarks in debate with Sen. Thomas J. Dodd, WGBH-TV, Boston, March 12, 1968, HWGP, box 1; Milton Reckord, "Speech #1," undated 1967, MRP, series 5, box 14, folder 6; transcript of Face to Face, a Confrontation on Gun Control Legislation Between Senator Joseph D. Tydings and Harold W. Glassen, Moderated by Mark Evans, October 29, 1967, 28, HWGP, box 1 (statement of NRA president Harold W. Glassen) ("There's no question that a government has a right to restrict who shall use arms. . . . It is an individual right but that does not mean that there cannot be reasonable restrictions upon that right.").

134. See, e.g., "Gun Control Fight Crystalizes Pressure Groups," *Group Research Report* 7, no. 12 (June 28, 1968), WDFP, box 3, folder Gun Control; "Your Gun Is Their Target," *Armed Eagle*, March–April 1968, 1; "Report on Association Activities," *Armed Eagle*, January–February 1968, 1.

135. Harold W. Glassen, opening remarks in debate with Sen. Thomas J. Dodd, WGBH-TV, Boston, March 12, 1968, HWGP, box 1.

136. Harold W. Glassen, Speech Before the 97th Annual NRA Meetings, April 6, 1968, HWGP, box 1.

137. Harold W. Glassen, statement before the Rotary Club, Los Angeles, February 9, 1968, HWGP, box 1.

138. Glassen, speech before the 97th Annual NRA Meetings.

6. 1968

1. "NRA's Growth Encouraging," *GW*, January 19, 1968, 4.

2. For the NRA's membership numbers, see NRA, *Operating Report '69* (Washington, D.C., 1970), 14, RNP, Personal Papers, box 9, folder NRA; NRA, *1966 Operating Report* (Washington, D.C., 1967), 4.

3. Gene Washer, "Around the Circuit: National Rifle Association Chides Robert Kennedy," *Clarksville (Tenn.) Leaf-Chronicle*, January 24, 1968, 9.

4. "Rifle Association VP Sees Compromise Bill," *Lancaster (Pa.) Sunday News*, March 31, 1968, 46.

5. "Are We Really So Violent?," *AR*, February 1968, 16.

6. "Non-Violence Begins at Home—On the TV," *AR*, July 1968, 18.

7. See generally Report of the National Advisory Commission on Civil Disorders (Washington, D.C.: National Institute of Justice, 1968).

8. See, e.g., memorandum to Thomas J. Dodd, "Gun Bill and the Anti-Rioting Bill," August 10, 1967, TJDP, box 81, folder 2345; memorandum to Thomas J. Dodd, untitled, July 28, 1967, TJDP, box 81, folder 2345; David J. McIntyre, News from Senator Joseph D. Tydings, July 28, 1967, JTP, series 6, box 22, folder 22, Statements on Gun Control 1967–1970.

9. "Orth Wants Reasonable Gun Legislation Passed," *GW*, January 5, 1968, 1; "NRA Unhappy with Congress," *Tyler (Tex.) Morning Telegraph*, January 4, 1968, sec. 3, p. 2.

10. *Congressional Record* 114, part 7 (Washington, D.C.: U.S. Government Printing Office, 1968), 8522–25, 8530, 8579, 8584–89.

11. See "Senate Unit Turns Down Gun Control Proposals," *Sacramento (Calif.) Bee*, April 5, 1968, A2; "Senate Kills Gun Control Proposals," *Sioux City (Iowa) Journal*, April 5, 1968, A2; "Senate Judiciary Committee Rejects LBJ Gun-Control Bill," *Montgomery (Ala.) Advertiser*, April 5, 1968, 20; "Gun Control Proposals Are Rejected," *Indianapolis (Ind.) News*, April 5, 1968, 4.

12. There were also calls at the state and local levels. See, e.g., "Legislators Have Been Busy," *GW*, April 19, 1968, 4.

13. See, e.g., Thomas J. Dodd, "Statement on Martin Luther King," April 4, 1968, TJDP, box 209, folder 5618; Bill Riviere and Edward M. Kennedy, "The Great Gun Debate," *Boston Sunday Globe*, April 7, 1968, 8–13; Hubert H. Humphrey, "Remarks After the Assassination of Dr. Martin Luther King, Jr.," undated, WWWPP, box 114, folder 1.

14. "Senate Unit Turns Down Gun Control Proposals," *Sacramento (Calif.) Bee*, April 5, 1968, A2.

15. Thomas J. Dodd, Press Release, "A Single Gun in the Wrong Hands Could Change the World, Dodd Says," April 8, 1968, TJDP, box 209, folder 5619.

16. For some other gun rights views of the post-King assassination riots, see Rex Applegate, "Guns and the Law: Some Thoughts on Riots and Gun Laws," *GM*, August 1968, 32–33, 72–73; Carl Wolff, "Our Man in Washington," *GM*, July 1968, 17.

17. "Rifle Group's View of Death," *Des Moines (Iowa) Register*, April 7, 1868, 2.

18. Peter Laine, "Pressure Committee to Reverse Self on Gun Bill," *Akron (Ohio) Beacon Journal*, April 12, 1968, 3.

19. "Kennedys, Dodd Urge to Back Workable Gun Bills," *AR*, May 1968, 43.

20. "Do Americans *Really* Want New Gun Laws?," *AR*, April 1968, 16; John M. Snyder, "Why Anti-Gun Polls Are Open to Doubt," *AR*, April 1968, 20–21.

21. "Senate Panel Approves Curb on Gun Sales," *Louisville (Ky.) Courier-Journal*, April 6, 1968, A3

22. "97th Annual Meetings," *AR*, June 1968, 21, 22.

23. "Rifle Group Head Asks Defeat of Gun Proposal," *Hartford (Conn.) Courant*, April 12, 1968, 31.

24. Letter from Ben Avery to Paul J. Fannin, April 16, 1968, PJFP, box 139, folder 8, Firearms Control Correspondence, January 1967–April 1968.

25. "Who's Distorting the Facts?," *GW*, April 12, 1968, 4.

26. "National Rifle Body Head Scores Rigid Gun Controls," *Sacramento (Calif.) Bee*, April 16, 1968, B2; "[Image and Caption of Harold W. Glassen,]" *Sacramento Bee*, April 14, 1968, A16.

27. "Gun Laws Don't Deter Assassins," *Rochester (N.Y.) Democrat and Chronicle*, April 17, 1968, 16A; "Gun Bill Can't Stop Killing, Rifle Association Head Says," *Miami (Fla.) Herald*, April 17, 1968, 15A; "Doubts Effects on Gun Curbs," *Des Moines (Iowa) Tribune*, April 16, 1968, 5.

28. Letter from Thomas J. Dodd to Roman Hruska, April 17, 1968, TJDP, box 209, folder 5619.

29. Memorandum from Bob Perry to Thomas J. Dodd, "Conference with Senator Hruska Regarding Gun Bill," April 17, 1968, TJDP, box 209, folder 5619.

30. Thomas J. Dodd, speech before Georgetown University, Washington, D.C., Untitled, April 30, 1968, TJDP, box 209, folder 5623.

31. "Senate Debate Begins on Firearms Measure," *GW*, May 17, 1968, 1, 2; "Senate Begins Debate on Gun Control Bill," *Lincoln (Neb.) Star Journal*, May 15, 1968, 2; "Hruska Versus Ted Kennedy: Sharp Gun Control Debate in Senate," *San Francisco Examiner*, May 15, 1968, 7.

32. *Congressional Record* 114, part 11, p. 14798.

33. Letter from Thomas J. Dodd to Roman Hruska, May 24, 1968, TJDP, box 87, folder 2500.

34. "Senate Passes Crime Bill; Would Undo Court Rulings," *Bridgeport (Conn.) Post*, May 24, 1968, 12; "Senate-Passed Crime Bill Hits Supreme Court Rulings," *Boston Globe*, May 24, 1968, 10.

35. "Senate Okays Crime Bill," *Tampa Bay (Fla.) Times*, May 24, 1968, 1.

36. For a detailed history, see Lawrence O'Donnell, *Playing with Fire: The 1968 Election and the Transformation of American Politics* (New York: Penguin Press, 2017).

37. Hubert H. Humphrey, form letter on firearms controls, March 21, 1967, HHHP, Vice Presidential Legislation Files, 1964–1968, box 1006, folder January–April 1967.

38. Memorandum from Gerry Bush to John G. Stewart, May 23, 1968, HHHP, 1968 Presidential Campaign Files, John G. Stewart Research Files, box 1, folder Gun Control.

39. Letter from Neal Knox to Hubert H. Humphrey, April 29, 1968, HHHP, 1968 Presidential Campaign Files, John G. Stewart Research Files, box 1, folder Gun Control.

40. "HHH: 'Must Require Registration, Licenses,'" *GW*, July 26, 1968, 1, 2.

41. This story was reported in newspapers across the country through the Associated Press. See, e.g., "Gun Controls Opposed," *NYT*, June 6, 1968, 22; John Herbers, "Kennedy Heckled in Oregon Over Controls," *NYT*, May 28, 1968, 10; "Kennedy Debates Gun Controls in Oregon; Two Planes Nearly Collide," *Sacramento (Calif.) Bee*, May 28, 1968, A3; "Planes Carrying Kennedy, Party in Near Collision," *Orangeburg (S.C.) Times and Democrat*, May 28, 1968, 2; "RFK, Press Planes in Near Miss," *Boston Globe*, May 28, 1968, 28.

42. For more details on the events leading up to and after Robert F. Kennedy's assassination, see O'Donnell, *Playing with Fire*, 269–72.

43. See, e.g. "The Gun Under Fire," *Time*, June 21, 1968, 13–18.

44. It is worth noting that this was not the first time that businesses reacted this way in response to the death of a Kennedy. See, e.g., "Sears Halts Mail, Store Pistol Sales," *Atlanta Journal Constitution*, December 1, 1963, 41.

45. "Montgomery Ward, Sears Has Gun Policy," *Johnson City (Tenn.) Press*, June 20, 1968, 21; John Chamberlain, "We Need Something More than Gun Laws," *Lebanon (Pa.) Daily News*, June 14, 1968, 4.

46. Joseph D. Tydings, press release, June 5, 1968, JTP, series 6, box 22, folder 22, Statements on Gun Control 1967–1970. Tydings's response was understandable given how close he was to Senator Kennedy. In fact, Tydings had been on the campaign trail

with Kennedy for sixty days and only flew back to Maryland to vote in his state's primary election. Audio interview with Joseph D. Tydings by Patrick J. Charles, July 12, 2018, part 1, 16:50–17:10 (on file with author).

47. Thomas J. Dodd, news release, "Statement on Shooting of Senator Kennedy," June 5, 1968, TJDP, box 210, folder 5651. The following day, after Kennedy succumbed to his wounds, Dodd issued a much less political statement, with no mention of firearms controls. See Statement of Thomas J. Dodd on the Floor of the Senate, June 6, 1968, TJDP, box 89, folder 2551.

48. Jack Miller, "Congress Moves on Gun Control," *Springfield (Mo.) News-Leader*, June 6, 1968, 30.

49. "Letter to the President of the Senate and to the Speaker of the House Urging Passage of an Effective Gun Control Law," June 6, 1968, *Public Papers of the President of the United States: Lyndon B. Johnson: Containing the Public Messages, Speeches, and Statements of the President 1968-69*, vol. 1 (Washington, D.C.: U.S. Government Printing Office, 1970), 296–97.

50. CBS TV, Special Report, "Gun Bill Debated in House, Harold Glassen Comments," June 6, 1968, HWGP, box 1.

51. See, e.g., Clark Mollenhoff, "House Passes Gun Controls in Crime Bill," *Des Moines (Iowa) Register*, June 7, 1968, 1, 8.

52. See Robert W. Lucas, "LBJ Charges Panel to Look Under All Rugs," *Binghamton (N.Y.) Press and Sun-Bulletin*, June 11, 1968, 6C; "Commission to Study Violence," *Cincinnati (Ohio) Enquirer*, June 7, 1968, 15.

53. United States Postal Office, General Release No. 109, June 12, 1968, CAP, box LG 112, Folder 14, Majority Leader Files, Special Files, Summary of Pending Gun Control Legislation.

54. Thomas L. Kimball, "Firearms Control Legislation," June 11, 1968, WEGP, box 6, folder 11.

55. Harold W. Glassen, "Another Opinion: The Right to Bear Arms," *NYT*, June 16, 1968, E17. A speech that parrots this editorial can be found in Glassen's personal papers but reads a bit differently. See Harold W. Glassen, press release, undated 1968, HWGP, box 1 ("It is reminiscent of the 1930's before and during World War II when the Goebel's propaganda machine worked so well on the German people using the principle of the big lie.").

56. Harold W. Glassen, "Another Opinion: The Right to Bear Arms," *NYT*, June 16, 1968, E17.

57. "Gun Law Lobby Formed," *Boston Globe*, June 25, 1968, 13; "DC Bracing for Marchers; Gun Curbs Notch New Gain," *Pittsburgh Press*, June 18, 1968, 1.

58. Emergency Committee on Gun Control, "All Those Working for More Effective Gun Control Legislation," undated, 1, 3, JHGA, Senate Papers, Personal/Political Series, box 53, folder.

59. For behind-the-scenes documentation on the ECGC's tactics, see generally WLDPP, box 15, folder 17.

60. See, e.g., "Ad 37," *NYT*, June 15, 1968, 21.

61. "Ad 48," *NYT*, June 17, 1968, 27. For gun rights advocates' response to the ECGC's advertising, see "A Special Report: Anti-Gun Ad Campaign Lacks Boom," *AR*, August 1968, 24–25; "Anti-Gun Lobby Hits with Well-Organized Campaign," *GW*, July 19, 1968, 6.

62. See statement by Senator Thomas J. Dodd on the floor of the Senate, June 11, 1968, TJDP, box 210, folder 5655; letter from Ramsey Clark, attorney general of the United States, to Hubert H. Humphrey, vice president of the United States Senate, June 10, 1968, TJDP, box 210, folder 5655; letter from Ramsey Clark, attorney general of the United States, to James O. Eastland, Senate Judiciary Committee chairman, June 10, 1968, TJDP, box 210, folder 5655.

63. Thomas J. Dodd, news release, untitled, June 18, 1968, TJDP, box 210, folder 5661.

64. On June 11, 1968, the House Judiciary Committee conducted its first vote on President Johnson's firearms bill proposal, which resulted in a 16 to 16 tie. See Philip Dodd, "House Group's Tie Vote Hits Gun Curb Bill," *Chicago Tribune*, June 12, 1968, 1B.

65. "Judiciary Committee Clears Tight Gun-Control Measure," *Allentown (Pa.) Morning Call*, June 21, 1968, 6.

66. See Thomas J. Dodd, news release, untitled, June 10, 1968, TJDP, box 210, folder 5652; letter from Ramsey Clark, attorney general of the United States, to Hubert H. Humphrey, vice president of the United States Senate, June 10, 1968, TJDP, box 210, folder 5655 (includes bill titled "An Act to Require the Registration of Firearms"). However, President Johnson's firearms registration and licensing bill, S. 3691, was officially introduced weeks later.

67. Memorandum from Bob Perry to Thomas J. Dodd, "Prospects for the Various Gun Bills," June 17, 1968, TJDP, box 89, folder 2531. It was questionable for Dodd's staff to label Tydings's firearms registration and licensing bill as the "most extreme." This was because the bill placed the onus on state governments to resolve the issue. See letter from Joseph D. Tydings to Bourke B. Hickenlooper, June 10, 1968, BHP, box 21, folder 3, Gun Control 1968 ("The bill will place primary responsibility on each state to enact a strong gun law, but will provide Federal government protection to the extent any state fails to act.").

68. Memorandum from Bob Perry to Thomas J. Dodd, "Prospects for the Various Gun Bills," June 17, 1968, TJDP, box 89, folder 2531.

69. The account of this conversation was taken from the University of Virginia's secret White House tapes project. See Conversation Between Lyndon B. Johnson and Joseph Tydings, June 19, 1968, Secret White House Tapes: Lyndon Johnson Presidency, University of Virginia Miller Center, https://millercenter.org/the-presidency/secret-white-house-tapes/conversation-joseph-tydings-june-19-1968. For a much different recollection of this conversation, see Joseph D. Tydings and John W. Frece, *My Life in Progressive Politics: Against the Grain* (College Station: Texas A&M University Press, 2018), 298.

70. Audio interview with Joseph D. Tydings by Patrick J. Charles, July 12, 2018, part 2, 5:15–6:00 (on file with author).

71. "LBJ Asks Rifle-Shotgun Sales Ban; Dodd Introduces Registration Bill," *GW*, June 21, 1968, 1, 2.
72. "Johnson Demands Gun Registration, Owner Licensing; Backlash Building," *GW*, July 5, 1968, 1, 2; John Chadwick, "Senate Group Postpones Gun Control Law Action," *Sacramento (Calif.) Bee*, June 28, 1968, A2.
73. Letter from Harold W. Glassen, NRA president, to all NRA members, June 14, 1968, reprinted in *Bangor (Me.) Daily News*, July 1, 1968, 20.
74. See, e.g., Bob Neal, "Panic on the Hill," *G&A*, September 1968, 36–37, 105; E. B. Mann, "Tilting at Windmills," *GM*, August 1968, 28–29, 54–56.
75. See, e.g., Martin Stoffel, "Firearms Registration," *McHenry (Ill.) Plaindealer*, July 3, 1968, sec. 2, p. 2; E. T., "Takes Issue with Views in Editorial on Gun Laws," *Bridgeport (Conn.) Post*, July 1, 1968, 26; Eric E. Shawver, "Firearms Registration a Threat," *Tampa Bay (Fla.) Times*, July 1, 1968, 16A; Robert E. Schulz, "Suggests Registering Ropes Besides Guns," *Oshkosh (Wis.) Northwestern*, July 1, 1968, 8; J. H. Dupuy, "Gun Registration Dangerous Precedent," *Orlando (Fla.) Sentinel*, June 24, 1968, 4. But see "Half a Loaf Is Better than None," *Montgomery (Ala.) Advertiser*, July 23, 1968, 4 (editorial stating that firearms registration will lead to firearms confiscation as much as vehicle registration leads to vehicle confiscation); "Gun Confiscation—Can It Happen?," *San Francisco Examiner*, July 21, 1968, 2B (editorial responding to sportsmen's claim that firearms registration leads to firearms confiscation).
76. See, e.g., "Registration Raises Issue of Confiscation, NRA Holds," *AR*, August 1968, 42–43; "Truths to Remember: Part 2," *AR*, August 1968, 23; Letter from Harold W. Glassen to Robert J. Martin, July 8, 1968, HWGP, box 1; "Why Gun Controls?," *Des Moines (Iowa) Register*, June 27, 1968, 8; "Dodd, NRA Head Debate Gun Law," *St. Louis (Mo.) Post-Dispatch*, June 24, 1968, 6C; Richard H. Stewart, " 'Panic' Gun Laws Feared by McCarthy," *Boston Globe*, June 24, 1968, 2; "President of NRA Fears 'Confiscation,' " *Greenville (S.C.) News*, June 24, 1968, 11.
77. "Gun Control Makes Strange Bedfellows," *AR*, September 1968, 18.
78. Anti-Defamation League, "Research and Evaluation Report: Extremism, Violence and Guns," June 26, 1968, BHP, box 21, folder 4, Gun Control July 1968 (listing the political positions of several gun rights advocacy groups); "Gun Control Fight Crystalizes Pressure Groups," *Group Research Report*, June 28, 1967, WDFP, box 3, folder Gun Control (same); Everett C. Lerch, *Don't Let Them Take Away Your Gun!* (Bristol, Tenn.: Urgent Publications, 1968), 6–7, BHP, box 21, folder 4, Gun Control July 1968); "Gun Control Will Be Final Move Before Takeover," *Common Sense*, July 1968, 1, BHP, box 21, folder 4, Gun Control July 1968.
79. *Wake Up, America! Before the "Liberals" Take Away Your Guns!* (Phoenix, Ariz.: July 1, 1968), GWRP, box 219, folder Gun Control.
80. Earl Sherwood, "Slaying Spurs Propaganda for Federal Gun Controls," *Armed Eagle*, September 1968, 4.
81. See, e.g., "Opposition to Gun Laws Building as Delays Slow 'Mail Order' Bill," *GW*, July 12, 1968, 1.

82. Letter from Thomas J. Dodd to Lyndon B. Johnson, July 5, 1968, TJDP, box 89, folder 2551.

83. For reporting on the hearing, see "Dodd Loses 'Cool' at Hearing; California May Vote on Gun Bill," *GW*, August 9, 1968, 12; Alan E. Schoenhaus, "Dodd Is Booed at Hearing on Gun Controls," *Bridgeport (Conn.) Post*, July 17, 1968, 1, 26; Charles F. J. Morse, "Sportsmen Boo Dodd at Gun Bill Hearing," *Hartford (Conn.) Courant*, July 17, 1968, 1, 4.

84. The day after the hearing, Dodd issued a press release referring to the actions of the attending sportsmen, hunters, and gun owners as "hysterical mob rule." Thomas J. Dodd, news release, "Senator Dodd Assails 'Mob Rule' at State Legislative Hearing on Guns," July 17, 1968, TJDP, box 211, folder 5682.

85. Tydings and Frece, *My Life in Progressive Politics*, 299. Prior to Senator Kennedy's assassination, Mansfield would be best described as a cautious moderate on firearms controls. See "Montana Lawmakers Reply on Firearms Legislation," *Helena (Mont.) Independent-Record*, September 2, 1966, 4; John Kamps, "Delegation Opposes Arms Control," *Missoulian* (Missoula, Mont.), June 6, 1965, 16; letter from Mike Mansfield to Riley Johnson, Fishing and Hunting News editor, March 9, 1964, LMP, box 154, folder 5, Firearms.

86. See John Kamps, "After Kennedy's Death . . . Rocky Mountains Ease Gun Control Objections," *Great Falls (Mont.) Tribune*, June 18, 1968, 7; "Mansfield Favors Tydings Bill," *Billings (Mont.) Gazette*, June 18, 1968, 2; Kenneth Scheibel, "Why Did Mike Switch on Guns?," *Billings Gazette*, June 16, 1968, 2; "Pressure Builds for Tougher Gun Controls," *Kalispell (Mont.) Daily Inter Lake*, June 17, 1968, 1; "Mike Backs 'Toughest' Gun Registration Bill," *Billings Gazette*, June 16, 1968, 1, 10; "Mansfield Favors Gun Registration," *Billings Gazette*, June 11, 1968, 1, 2.

87. See, e.g., Gene S. Goldenberg, "'Peoples Lobby' Backs Gun Control," *Oneonta (N.Y.) Star*, June 12, 1968, 3.

88. "Our Readers' Opinions . . . About Gun Controls and Senator's Stand," *Great Falls (Mont.) Tribune*, July 6, 1968, 6; "Proposed Gun Controls Arouse Readers," *Billings (Mont.) Gazette*, June 30, 1968, 5; "Mike and Gun Control," *Kalispell (Mont.) Daily Inter Lake*, June 28, 1968, 4; "Anti-Gun Bill Mail Deluging Mike," *Missoulian* (Missoula, Mont.), June 26, 1968, 10; "Our Readers' Opinions . . . Aim Gun Control Law at Criminal Element," *Great Falls Tribune*, June 24, 1968, 6; Kenneth Scheibel, "Montana Blistering Mike for Gun Stand," *Billings Gazette*, June 20, 1968, 1; "Petitions Seek to Block Gun Control," *Missoulian*, June 19, 1968, 1. But see "Mansfield Shows His Courage," *Helena (Mont.) Independent-Record*, June 28, 1968, 4 (defending Mansfield's decision to cosponsor and back firearms registration and licensing); "Time for Sound Thinking About . . . Gun Control Legislation," *Great Falls Tribune*, June 23, 1968, 6; "Change of Heart on Gun Controls," *Missoulian*, June 20, 1968, 6.

89. Mike Mansfield, press release, "Remarks of Senator Mike Mansfield at the Annual Dinner of the American Advisory Committee, European Institute of Business Administration," June 27, 1968, MMP, box 44, folder 42.

90. "Sen. Mansfield Gives Views on Anti-Gun Legislation," *Kalispell (Mont.) Daily Inter Lake*, June 19, 1968, 10.

91. See, e.g., letter from Mike Mansfield to Steve Rapkoch, June 27, 1968, MMP, box 85, folder 2; letter from Mike Mansfield to Hugh W. Dresser, June 19, 1968, MMP, box 85, folder 2.

92. "Mike Opposing Gun Registration," *Billings (Mont.) Gazette*, July 4, 1968, 1; "Mike Opposes Johnson's Gun Measure," *Missoulian* (Missoula, Mont.), July 4, 1968, 3; "Speaks Out Against Administration Bill," *Great Falls (Mont.) Tribune*, July 4, 1968, 2; "Mansfield Says 'No' to LBJ Gun Proposal," *Billings Gazette*, June 27, 1968, 1.

93. "LBJ Cites N.Y. Ambush in Appeal," *Fremont (Calif.) Argus*, July 4, 1968, 5; John Kamps, "Shooting of Young Montanan Changed Mansfield," *Missoulian* (Missoula, Mont.), July 4, 1968, 3; "Fishtail Marine Shot in Washington," *Billings (Mont.) Gazette*, June 6, 1968, 1.

94. Letter from Mike Mansfield to Mrs. Leo Lesnik, June 26, 1968, MMP, box 85, folder 2.

95. Gun count as of August 3, 1968, MMP, box 85, folder 1.

96. "By Opposing Gun Registration . . . Rep. Olsen Riddles 'Mike and Me' Image," *Great Falls (Mont.) Tribune*, July 10, 1968, 1, 2.

97. John Morrison, "Gun Law Battle Rages," *Butte Montana Standard*, July 30, 1968, 9; "Olsen Favors State Control for Firearms," *Helena (Mont.) Independent-Record*, July 9, 1968, 8; "Olsen's Mail Is Running 10–1 Against Gun Laws," *Butte Montana Standard*, July 8, 1968, 5.

98. "Olsen Will Vote Against Gun Control Legislation," *Helena (Mont.) Independent-Record*, July 18, 1968, 8; "Olsen to Vote No on Gun Law," *Billings (Mont.) Gazette*, July 18, 1968, 12.

99. See, e.g., Daniel J. Foley, "Smiley Dislikes 'Politician' Image," *Billings (Mont.) Gazette*, October 23, 1968, 23; "Dick Smiley Attacks Arnold Olsen," *Great Falls (Mont.) Tribune*, July 28, 1968, 7; "Smiley Questions Olsen on Guns," *Billings Gazette*, July 21, 1968, 12; "Crime Control, Says Smiley, Not Gun Control," *Missoulian* (Missoula, Mont.), July 2, 1968, 2.

100. "Anderson Wins by Biggest Majority Since 1920," *Helena (Mont.) Independent Record*, November 22, 1968, 12.

101. "Anderson Wins by Biggest Majority Since 1920."

102. John Morrison, "Congressional Race a Matter of Record," *Helena (Mont.) Independent-Record*, October 30, 1968, 18; "'Poor' Gun Law—Battin," *Billings (Mont.) Gazette*, July 29, 1968, 3; Kenneth Schiebel, "Gun Proposals 'Loaded'—Battin," *Billings Gazette*, July 10, 1968, 18.

103. Letter from James F. Battin to Robert Ellsworth, Nixon Headquarters executive director, October 2, 1967, RNPP, White House Central Files, box 26, Staff Member Office Files, folder Martin Anderson, Gun Control Legislation.

104. Letter from Richard M. Nixon to James F. Battin, October 17, 1967, RNPP, White House Central Files, box 26, Staff Member Office Files, folder Martin Anderson, Gun Control Legislation; letter from Robert Ellsworth, Nixon Headquarters executive director, to James F. Battin, October 12, 1967, RNPP, White House

Central Files, box 26, Staff Member Office Files, folder Martin Anderson, Gun Control Legislation.

105. See, e.g., Richard M. Nixon, *Toward Freedom from Fear* (May 8, 1968) (making no mention of firearms controls in a five-point plan to stop crime).

106. Memorandum from William H. Webster to Alan Greenspan, June 10, 1968, RNPP, White House Central Files, box 26, Staff Member Office Files, folder Martin Anderson, Gun Control.

107. Memorandum from Marty Pollner to Leonard Garment et al., "Re: RMN's Statement Gun Control Legislation," June 13, 1968, RNPP, White House Central Files, box 26, Staff Member Office Files, folder Martin Anderson, Gun Control.

108. Memorandum from Marty Pollner to Richard M. Nixon et al., "Re: Gun Registration Legislation," June 15, 1968, RNPP, White House Central Files, box 74, Staff Member Office Files, folder Len Garment, 1968 Political Campaign File, Gun Control.

109. Statement of Richard M. Nixon, June 17, 1968, RNPP, White House Central Files, box 26, Staff Member Office Files, folder Martin Anderson, Gun Control.

110. Richard M. Nixon, *Disarming the Criminal Class* (July 9, 1968), HHHP, 1968 Presidential Campaign Files, John G. Stewart Research Files, box 1, folder Gun Control. The firearms-control statements within the Nixon campaign's July 1968 brochure were reprinted in *Gun Week*. See "Humphrey Allegation Ires Nixon Supporters," *GW*, September 27, 1968, 6.

111. William L. Wallace, "The Gun Legislation Issue," [June–July] 1968, RNPP, White House Central Files, box 26, Staff Member Office Files, folder Martin Anderson, Gun Control Legislation.

112. William L. Wallace, "A Recommended Policy Position on the Gun Issue," July 22, 1968, RNPP, White House Central Files, box 26, Staff Member Office Files, folder Martin Anderson, Gun Control Legislation.

113. See, e.g., "Wallace Opposed to Gun Controls," *Chicago Tribune*, October 19, 1968, sec. 1, 10; "Wallace Calls Gun Control Bill 'Silly,'" *GW*, October 4, 1968, 9; "Shrewd Political Move," *GW*, September 20, 1968, 4.

114. Wallace, "The Gun Legislation Issue."

115. Wallace, "A Recommended Policy Position on the Gun Issue."

116. See the discussion later in this chapter and accompanying notes.

117. Adam Spiegel, "All Md. Congressmen Favor Stricter Law," *Baltimore (Md.) Evening Sun*, June 7, 1968, C24.

118. "Sen. Brewster Drops Support of Tydings Bill," *GW*, September 6, 1968, 2; "Gun Views Clarified," *Baltimore (Md.) Sun*, August 21, 1966, C6.

119. Gardner L. Bridge, "Sign or Veto Gun Control Bill, Ford Tells LBJ," *Shreveport (La.) Times*, June 14, 1968, 9A; "People of the Times," *Corpus Christi (Tex.) Caller-Times*, June 14, 1968, B1.

120. See, e.g., "Nelson Clarifies Gun Control Position," *Capital Times* (Wis.), June 24, 1968, 34.

121. "Foes on Gun Control Step Up Campaign," *Eau Claire (Wis.) Daily Telegram*, June 19, 1968, 5A.

122. Frank M. Matthews, "Shafer to Seek Gun Curb Plank," *Pittsburgh Post-Gazette*, June 14, 1968, 8.

123. "Governors Shy Off Guns," *Pittsburgh Post-Gazette*, June 15, 1968, 5; "GOP Governors May Differ on Gun Control in Platform," *Shreveport (La.) Times*, June 15, 1968, 4A; "Babcock Aligns Himself Against Gun Controls," *Great Falls (Mont.) Tribune*, June 15, 1968, 7; James Ragsdale, "Republicans Worry About Gun Controls," *South Idaho Press* (Burley), June 14, 1968, 1.

124. See, e.g., "State Opponents Use Same Tired Arguments vs. Gun Control," *Long Beach (Calif.) Independent Press-Telegram*, June 23, 1968, B3; "Babcock and Hundreds of Montanans Oppose 'Emotion' Gun Control Bills," *Kalispell (Mont.) Daily Inter Lake*, June 20, 1968, 12; "Deluge of Letters on Gun Controls," *Oakland (Calif.) Tribune*, June 14, 1968, 1, 8; "State Gun Control Bill Killed," *Oakland Tribune*, June 12, 1968, 17.

125. Walter R. Mears, "Rocky Says He'll Overtake Nixon," *Moline (Ill.) Dispatch*, June 15, 1968, 18; Walter R. Mears, "Governors Advise GOP Listen to Advice," *Rapid City (S.D.) Journal*, June 15, 1968, 2.

126. "GOP Governors Urge Gun Curbs," *San Bernardino County (Calif.) Sun*, June 16, 1968, A3 (emphasis added); Charles Whiteford, "GOP Leaders Say Integrity Is Main Issue," *Baltimore (Md.) Sun*, June 16, 1968, 3 (emphasis added).

127. Don McKee, "Governors: States Should Control Guns," *Charlotte (N.C.) News*, June 19, 1968, 3A; "Governors Argue Anti-Crime Plans," *Alabama Journal* (Montgomery), June 18, 1968, 1; Bob Webb, "South's Governors Divided on Gun Law," *Cincinnati (Ohio) Enquirer*, June 18, 1968, 21" Southern Governors Favor Gun Control?," *Orlando (Fla.) Evening Star*, June 17, 1968, 3A. The resolution was opposed by Georgia governor Lester Maddox, who wanted the conference to agree to one opposing all firearms controls. See Remer Tyson, "Maddox Is Snubbed on Guns, Court," *Atlanta Constitution*, June 19, 1968, 7.

128. "Governors OK Gun Control," *San Francisco Examiner*, July 24, 1968, 4.

129. Letter from Phillip H. Hoff to James L. Oakes, Vermont attorney general, June 10, 1968, PHHP, drawer 11–2, folder 28.

130. Letter from James L. Oakes, Vermont attorney general, to Phillip H. Hoff, June 19, 1968, PHHP, drawer 11–2, folder 29.

131. "Free Port Urged by N.E. Governors," *Bennington (Vt.) Banner*, June 28, 1968, 1; "NE Governors, at Stowe, Talk Guns, Power, Crime," *Brattleboro (Vt.) Reformer*, June 28, 1968, 1; "Oakes Wants Gun Owners to Register," *Bennington Banner*, June 20, 1968, 3; "Vt. Gun Controls Pushed by Chittenden County DA," *Brattleboro Reformer*, June 18, 1968, 2.

132. Joe Fisher, "Governors' Confab Winds Up with Gun Control Fight," *Bridgewater (N.J.) Courier-News*, July 25, 1968, 3; "Governors OK Gun Control," *San Francisco Examiner*, July 24, 1968, 4.

133. "Dirksen Alters Position on Stiffer Gun Controls," *De Kalb (Ill.) Daily Chronicle*, June 14, 1968, 6.

134. Philip Dodd, "Maneuvering Slows Senate Action on Guns," *Chicago Tribune*, July 11, 1968, sec. 1A, p. 7; "Senate Waters Down Gun Control," *Decatur (Ill.) Herald and Review*, July 11, 1968, 1.

135. Republican Party Platform of 1968, August 5, 1968.
136. Harold W. Glassen, NRA president, to F. W. Rutherford, August 13, 1968, HWGP, box 1.
137. Glassen to Rutherford.
138. See, e.g., National Council for a Responsible Firearms Policy, Press Release, "Poor Progress Toward Strict Gun Controls Called 'Massive Negligence, Campaign Issue,'" August 23, 1968, HBP, box 156, folder 1968 Platform Committee, National Council for a Responsible Firearms Policy; Joseph S. Clark, "Eighteen Points for Democrats: A Proposal for the Democratic Platform," August 13, 1968, JSCP, box 116, folder News Releases (urging the party to adopt a platform that supported a "strong Federal gun control law, providing for registration and licensing").
139. Statement of Senator Joseph D. Tydings on crime and law enforcement before the 1968 Democratic Platform Committee, August 22, 1968, HBP, box 156, folder 1968 Platform Committee, Joseph Tydings, Re: Crime.
140. Testimony of Dr. J. Elliott Corbett, National Council for Responsible Firearms Policy, before Panel I of the Platform Committee Democratic National Convention, August 23, 1968, HBP, box 156, folder 1968 Platform Committee, National Council for a Responsible Firearms Policy.
141. Thomas J. Dodd, news release, "Senator Dodd Calls for Strong Gun Control Plank in Democratic Party Platform," August 18, 1968, TJDP, box 211, folder 5697.
142. Statement of Senator Thomas Dodd before the Platform Committee of the Democratic Party's National Convention, August 21, 1968, HBP, box 155, folder 1968 Platform Committee, Thomas Dodd, Re: Gun Control.
143. Democratic Party Platform of 1968, August 26, 1968.
144. See, e.g., Hubert H. Humphrey, remarks after the assassination of Dr. Martin Luther King, Jr., [April 1968], WWWPP, box 115, folder 1 (making no mention of firearms control).
145. See, e.g., statement of Vice President Hubert H. Humphrey on gun control legislation, July 17, 1968, HHHP, 1968 Presidential Campaign Files, John G. Stewart Research Files, box 1, folder Gun Control.
146. See, e.g., Harold W. Glassen, NRA president, to F. W. Rutherford, August 13, 1968, HWGP, box 1.
147. "Dems Will Hear Plea for Guns," *Saint Joseph (Mich.) Herald-Press*, July 30, 1968, sec. 2, p. 1.
148. Letter from Harold W. Glassen to Paul E. Jurgens, August 26, 1968, HWGP, box 1.
149. E. B. Mann, "The Mann Says," *Gun World*, [November] 1968, EBMP, box 8, folder 22.
150. Platform of the Democratic Party of Texas (Austin: September 17, 1968) (on file with author).
151. "Delaware Democratic Platform Text," *Wilmington (Del.) Morning News*, August 24, 1968, 28; "Delaware Democratic Platform Text," *Wilmington (Del.) News Journal*, August 24, 1968, 4.
152. Bill Severin, "Iowa Demo Platform Backs Gun Controls," *Waterloo (Iowa) Courier*, June 30, 1968, 1, 2.

153. "Vermont Dems and Republicans Meeting Today on Their 1968 Platform Planks," *Brattleboro (Vt.) Reformer*, September 21, 1968, 2; "Oakes Renews Plan to License Gun Owners," *Barre (Vt.) Times Argus*, September 19, 1968, 11; "Vermont Republicans Begin to Construct Campaign Platform," *Rutland (Vt.) Daily Herald*, September 13, 1968, 18; "GOP Moves Cautiously on Gun Control," *Burlington (Vt.) Free Press*, September 13, 1968, 3.

154. "Comparison of Platforms Shows Parties Close in Vermont," *Burlington (Vt.) Free Press*, October 23, 1968, 19; "Democrats Take Gun Stand," *Burlington Free Press*, September 23, 1968, pp. 1, 3; "Vermont GOP Platform Drafting Group Rejects Gun Registration," *Burlington Free Press*, September 18, 1968, 8.

155. John Wyngaard, "LAX UW Student Discipline Attacked in GOP Platform," *Appleton (Wis.) Post-Crescent*, October 3, 1968, B7; John Wyngaard, "State GOP Planks Censure UW Discipline, Drug Traffic," *Green Bay (Wis.) Post-Gazette*, October 2, 1968, A11; "Wisconsin Platform Widens Split in Democratic Party," *Chippewa (Wis.) Herald-Telegram*, October 2, 1968, 4.

156. Patrick J. Charles, *Armed in America: A History of Gun Rights from Colonial Militias to Concealed Carry* (Amherst, N.Y.: Prometheus Books, 2018), 25–26.

157. Dale Pullen, "Sikes Hits LBJ Gun Plea," *Palm Beach (Fla.) Post*, June 30, 1968, E11.

158. "Mail Order Gun Ban Slowed by House Rules Chairman," *Boston Globe*, June 26, 1968, 9; John F. Finney, "Gun Registration Demand May Kill Control Passage," *San Bernardino County (Calif.) Sun*, June 26, 1968, A4; "Colmer Fears Emotional Vote; Delays House Action on Guns," *St. Joseph (Mo.) Gazette*, June 26, 1968, 1.

159. Joseph R. L. Sterne, "One Gun Bill Sacrificed to Aid Other," *Baltimore (Md.) Sun*, July 9, 1968, 1.

160. "Administration 'Mail Order' Bill, Casey Bill Cleared for House Vote," *GW*, July 19, 1968, 1, 2; John H. Averill, "Bill Curbing Mail Gun Sales Cleared for Action in House," *Philadelphia Inquirer*, July 10, 1968, 1, 3.

161. "House Kills Registration of All Guns," *Philadelphia Inquirer*, July 20, 1968, 1 (noting "wide" opposition to the mandatory minimum provision).

162. "Collector License Helps," *GW*, August 9, 1968, 4; "House Approves 'Mail Order' Bill, Rejects Licensing and Registration," *GW*, August 2, 1968, 1, 2; "Claims of House Support for Gun Control Disputed," *Tampa Bay (Fla.) Times*, July 18, 1968, 6A.

163. Harold Rummel, "Sikes Resigns as Director of Rifle Group," *Tampa Bay (Fla.) Times*, July 1, 1967, 2B.

164. "House Approves Limited Controls on Sales of Guns," *Miami (Fla.) Herald*, July 25, 1968, 1.

165. Lee Hickling, "Weaker Gun Bill Gets OK," *Rochester (N.Y.) Democrat and Chronicle*, July 25, 1968, 1A, 2A; "Gun Control Bill Goes to Senate," *Shreveport (La.) Journal*, July 25, 1968, 4.

166. "Senate Gets Watered Gun Bill; No Final Action Till September," *Boston Globe*, July 25, 1968, 24; "Celler Threatens Probe of Rifle Group: List of Provisions of House-Passed Gun-Control Bill," *Des Moines (Iowa) Tribune*, July 25, 1968, 9.

167. "What the Lawmakers Are Doing: Gun Issue Livens Up; Probe Threatened," *AR*, September 1968, 28–29.

168. "Rep. Smith and Gun Controls," *Los Angeles Times*, July 27, 1968, part 3, p. 4.

169. Ann Wood, "Celler Threatens Probe of Rifle Association: NRA 'Exemption' Is Charged in Amendment to Gun Bill," *Philadelphia Inquirer*, July 26, 1968, 3.

170. Don Stephen Cupps, "Bullets, Ballots, and Politics: The National Rifle Association Fights Gun Control," Ph.D. diss., Princeton University, 1970, 199–200.

171. For Tydings's reasons for supporting the amendment, see Joseph D. Tydings, "Gun Crime and the Prosecutor," address before the Practicing Law Institutes Seminar, New York, July 31, 1968, JTP, series 6, box 27, folder 23, Writings on Gun Control, 1967–1970.

172. Thomas J. Dodd, news release, "Senator Dodd Hails Judiciary Committee Approval of Longarm Bill," July 24, 1968, TJDP, box 211, folder 5687.

173. "Congressional Action on 'Mail Order' Bill Expected After Recess," *GW*, August 9, 1968, 1–2.

174. See, e.g., "Truths to Remember: Part 2," *AR*, August 1968, 23; "Half-Truths, Confusion, Misinformation Cloud National Debate on Gun Controls," *Wilkes-Barre (Pa.) Times Leader*, August 3, 1968, 11; "Local Opinion on Guns," *Bridgewater (N.J.) Courier-News*, July 31, 1968, 26.

175. "Gun Law Smokescreen," *GW*, September 27, 1968, 4; "NRA Chief Ridicules Case for Gun Laws," *Fresno (Calif.) Bee*, August 25, 1968, 6A; "Dodd Debates NRA President on Gun Laws," *Hartford (Conn.) Courant*, August 25, 1968, 27.

176. E. B. Mann, "Tilting at Windmills," *GM*, August 1968, 28, 56.

177. "Senate Back to Work, Gun Bill Hassle Begins," *GW*, September 20, 1968, 1, 2.

178. See, e.g., William Kling, "Senate OK's Gun-Control Legislation," *Chicago Tribune*, September 19, 1968, 1, 4; Roy McGhee, "Senate Votes 70–17 OK of Gun Control Measure," *Santa Rosa (Calif.) Press Democrat*, September 19, 1968, 1.

179. "Foes of Firearms Measure Hold Hope for House-Senate Conference Action," *GW*, October 4, 1968, 1, 2; Isabell Hall, "Gun Control Bill: The Two Versions," *Fort Lauderdale (Fla.) News*, September 22, 1968, 5H.

180. "House Accepts Conference Committee Draft of Firearms Control Measure," *GW*, October 25, 1968, 1, 2; "Conference Committee Toughens Gun Control Bill; Adds All Ammunition," *GW*, October 18, 1968, 1, 2; "The Gun Curb Bill," *Boston Globe*, October 10, 1968, 26; James R. Polk, "Senate Approves Gun Control Bill," *Atlanta Constitution*, October 10, 1968, 2; "Accord Reached on Gun Control," *Charlotte (N.C.) Observer*, October 9, 1968, 1.

181. Public Law 90–618, An Act to Amend Title 18, United States Code, to Provide for Better Control of the Interstate Traffic in Firearms, October 22, 1968, 82 Stat. 1213.

182. "Gun Control Still an Issue in Congress," *AR*, October 1968, 74–75; Harold W. Glassen, address before Salt Lake City Chamber of Commerce, October 8, 1968, HWGP, box 1; Harold W. Glassen, "Gun Registration and How it Affects the Sportsman," prepared remarks in Rochester, N.Y., September 28, 1968, HWGP, box 1;

Woodson D. Scott, "Report of the Committee on Firearms Legislation," September 16, 1968, HWGP, box 1.

183. "The Answer Is Simply Law Enforcement," *AR*, July 1968, 16.

184. "Senate Passes Gun Control Bill Somewhere Between NRA, LBJ," *Rapid City (S.D.) Journal*, September 19, 1968, 1; "Senate Passes Gun Law; Sends it to House Unit," *Salisbury (Md.) Daily Times*, September 19, 1968, 1, 20.

185. "NRA Chief: 'Minority, Hell, 50 Million Behind Us," *Rochester (N.Y.) Democrat and Chronicle*, September 28, 1968, B1.

186. "Guns vs. Votes," *Association to Preserve Our Right to Keep and Bear Arms Newsletter*, May 1968, 1, 12.

187. "Even with Us—It's Ballots Before Bullets," *AR*, October 1952, 63.

188. "Hysteria in High Places," *AR*, January 1932, 4.

189. Association to Preserve Our Right to Keep and Bear Arms, "Let's *DO* Keep the Record Straight About OUR GUNS!!," *Longview (Wash.) Daily News*, November 2, 1963, 24.

190. "Burton: Enjoy This Year's Hunt?," *Provo (Utah) Daily Herald*, November 3, 1968, 2.

191. The four incumbent representives to vote for the House version of the State Firearms Control Assistance Act and lose reelection were Porter Hardy (Virginia), Donald Irwin (Connecticut), Harvey Machen (Maryland), and John G. Dow (New York).

192. The two incumbents to vote for the Gun Control Act of 1968 and lose reelection were Donald Irwin (Connecticut) and John G. Dow (New York).

193. Dow's challenger, Republican Martin B. McKneally, came out in opposition to firearms registration, but only after the Senate passed its version of the State Firearms Control Assistance Act. See Janet Fisch, "Gun Registration Hit by District Attorney," *White Plains (N.Y.) Journal News*, October 23, 1968, 17; "McKneally Against More Gun Controls," *Hackensack (N.J.) Record*, October 7, 1968, C1. For McKneally's coming out late against firearms controls, one commentator referred to him as a "poacher" who "waits until he sees which issues are popular." "McKneally Steals Show in PBA Appearance," *White Plains (N.Y.) Journal News*, October 17, 1968, 13. It is also worth noting that Dow did not vote either for or against the Gun Control Act of 1968 when it came up for a final vote before the House.

194. Tom Siatos, editor-in-chief of *Guns & Ammo*, claimed a much larger victory. See his "Editorial," G&A, January 1969, 6. The editors of Association to Preserve Our Right to Keep and Bear Arms (APORKBA) newsletter *Armed Eagle* also claimed a large victory. See "Gun Control Issue Elects Senators," *Armed Eagle*, January–February 1969, 4.

195. "Effect of Gun Control Issue Seen in Vote Results," *AR*, January 1969, 28–29.

196. "Gun Owners Heard During '68 Elections," *GW*, November 15, 1968, 1–2.

197. Carl Wolff, "What the Kennedy Election Means," *GM*, April 1968, 8.

198. Steve Szalewicz, "One Touch of Nature: Throw Him Out!," *Franklin (Pa.) News-Herald*, November 21, 1968, 20.

199. Gene Coleman, "The Inside on Outdoors: Sportsmen Zapped Clark," *Scranton (Pa.) Times-Tribune*, November 17, 1968, D6.

200. See, e.g., Glenn Titus, "Brooke Urges Registration of All Guns," *Oklahoma City Daily Oklahoman*, May 12, 1968, sports section, 6.

201. "Monroney, 5 Others Switch on Gun Curbs," *Oklahoma City Times*, June 15, 1968, 8; "10 Senators Seek Tougher Gun Controls," *Oklahoma City Daily Oklahoman*, June 13, 1968, 1–2; "Mail Favoring Gun Control Swamps State Congressmen," *Oklahoma City Daily Oklahoman*, June 12, 1968, 13 (quoting Monroney as stating, "For the first time in all the years that we have been receiving mail on this subject, the people who favor strict control substantially outnumber those who don't.").

202. "Mike Backs Gun Control by States," *Oklahoma City Daily Oklahoman*, July 4, 1968, 36.

203. Compare "Mike Monroney Is Important to Oklahoma," *Stillwell (Okla.) Democrat-Journal*, October 10, 1968, 5, with "Who Can Best Represent Oklahoma?," *McIntosh County Democrat* (Checotah, Okla.), October 31, 1968, 8.

204. See, e.g., "Hatfield For, Morse Against Gun Control," *Salem (Ore.) Statesmen Journal*, October 1, 1968, 4; "Senate Oks Ammo Sale Ban," *Salem (Ore.) Capital Journal*, September 17, 1968, 16.

205. Floyd McKay, "Packwood Doubts Bomb Halt Will 'Save' Morse from Upset," *Salem (Ore.) Statesmen Journal*, November 2, 1968, 5; "Comparing Morse, Packwood," *Salem (Ore.) Capital Journal*, October 29, 1968, 4; Floyd McKay, "Morse, Packwood Quizzed," *Salem Statesmen Journal*, October 20, 1968, 5; Floyd McKay, "Young Bob Packwood Running Hard to Score Victory Over Veteran Senator," *Salem Statesmen Journal*, October 16, 1968, 23; "Public Forum: Double Talk Charged," *Coos Bay (Ore.) World*, September 17, 1968, 4 (editorial calling out Packwood for supporting the Omnibus Crime Control and Safe Streets Act).

206. "Packwood Flays Controls on Guns," *Salem (Ore.) Capitol Journal*, May 6, 1968, 8.

207. During the Republican primary, Packwood is quoted as stating: "Guns don't kill. People kill and a gun control bill will not change this fact." See "McCarthy Offers to Debate RFK in Oregon; Opponent Yet Mum," *Corvallis (Ore.) Gazette-Times*, May 15, 1968, 20.

208. "Nelson Holds Firm in Debate with Leonard," *Madison (Wis.) Capital Times*, November 1, 1968, 8; "Reprehensible Smear Tactics," *Racine (Wis.) Journal Times*, November 2, 1968, 12; James D. Selk, "Leonard Shows His Mettle in Stretch Run," *Wisconsin State Journal* (Madison), October 31, 1968, sec. 1, 6; "LaFollette Urges More Pollution Action," *Janesville (Wis.) Daily Gazette*, October 29, 1968, 7; "Need Advisers on Resources, Candidate Says," *Manitowoc (Wis.) Herald-Times*, October 29, 1968, 10; "Nelson, Proxmire Voted for Gun Control Law," *Appleton (Wis.) Post-Crescent*, October 11, 1968, 3; "Leonard Opposes Registration of Hunting Firearms," *Wisconsin Rapids Daily Tribune*, October 11, 1968, 11.

209. "Optimistic Ervin Hits Campaign Trail," *Charlotte (N.C.) News*, October 17, 1968, 4A; "Ervin Favors State Gun Controls; Says He Can't OK Fortas' Nomination," *Charlotte (N.C.) Observer*, July 6, 1968, 4B; Edward Cody, "Mail Pours In: State Gun Controls Needed, Says Ervin," *Charlotte Observer*, July 6, 1968, 20B; James K. Batten, "Please for Gun Controls Flooding Congressmen," *Charlotte Observer*, June 16, 1968, 3B; Roy Parker, Jr., "Ervin's Mail Favors Gun Controls; Other Solons Get Mixed Reaction," *Raleigh (N.C.) News and Observer*, June 13, 1968, 1, 13. Prior to the assassination of Senator Robert F. Kennedy, North Carolina senator Sam Ervin was opposed to

firearms controls. See "Ervin Against Gun Controls," *Rocky Mount (N.C.) Telegram*, April 7, 1968, 4A.

210. "Ervin Not Taking GOP Foe Lightly," *Raleigh (N.C.) News and Observer*, October 18, 1968, 38; "Somers Offers Ervin Free Time on TV," *Charlotte (N.C.) Observer*, October 18, 1968, 28A; "Somers Opposes Gun Controls," *Charlotte Observer*, October 10, 1968, 4A; Bill Stancil, "Somers Raps Scott, Attacks Ervin Vote on Gun Controls," *Rocky Mount (N.C.) Telegram*, September 21, 1968, 1; "Somers Attacks Ervin's Record," *Asheville (N.C.) Citizen-Times*, September 15, 1968, 7D; "Somers Against Federal Gun Control Bill," *Raleigh News and Observer*, July 3, 1968, 16.

211. "Control Guns or Die, Aiken Says," *Rutland (Vt.) Daily Herald*, September 10, 1968, 12; "Outdoors with Ed Keenan on Gun Control," *Burlington (Vt.) Free Press* (VT), August 24, 1968, 9; "Aiken Says Vermont Should Enact Its Own Gun Control Legislation," *Burlington Free Press*, August 22, 1968, 20; "Aiken Sure St. Albans Will Get Federal Funds for Water Project," *Burlington Free Press*, August 14, 1968, 1; Vonda Bergman, "Vermonter in Washington," *Brattleboro (Vt.) Reformer*, July 3, 1968, 9; "Senators, Safford Cool to Gun Laws," *Rutland Daily Herald*, June 12, 1968, 1, 6.

212. "These Are the Major Candidates for State Office in Vermont," *Rutland (Vt.) Daily Herald* (VT), September 6, 1968, 6; "Tufts, Kelley Speak Out Against Gun Registration," *Burlington (Vt.) Free Press*, September 3, 1968, 7; "Gun Club Backs Tufts," *Rutland Daily Herald*, August 22, 1968, 16; 'Gun Club for Tufts," *Rutland Daily Herald*, August 27, 1968, 5; "Legislative Gun Control Group Named," *Barre (Vt.) Times Argus*, August 15, 1968, 16; Daniel A. Neary, Jr., "Bill Tufts: The Man and His Candidacy," *Brattleboro (Vt.) Reformer*, August 13, 1968, 12; "Debate or Face Defeat, Challenger Tells Aiken," *Brattleboro Reformer*, July 19, 1968, 2; Stephen C. Terry, "'Giant Killer' Stalking Aiken," *Rutland Daily Herald*, June 25, 1968, 2; "Tufts Predicts He Will Defeat Senator Aiken," *Burlington Free Press*, June 25, 1968, 10; Vic Maerki, "Aiken to Seek Reelection to Senate," *Burlington Free Press*, June 18, 1968, 1.

213. "Candidates, Incumbents Strongly Oppose Further Gun-Control Legislation," *Douglas County Herald* (Ava, Mo.), October 24, 1968, 8; "Washington Observer Gives Predictions of State Races," *Jefferson City (Mo.) Post-Tribune*, October 23, 1968, 1A; Fred W. Lindecke, "Party Label Helps Eagleton," *St. Louis (Mo.) Post-Dispatch*, October 13, 1968, 1B; Eagleton Urges Tougher Curbs," *St. Louis Post-Dispatch*, June 21, 1968, 3A; "Missouri Campaigns Bids in Gear Again," *Kansas City (Mo.) Times*, June 11, 1968, 4; "Eagleton Renews Gun Law Support," *Jefferson City Post-Tribune*, May 16, 1968, 13; "Gun Laws Have Eagleton's Support," *Chillicothe (Mo.) Constitution-Tribune*, May 16, 1968, 3; "Eagleton Sees a Close Race in Clay County," *Kansas City (Mo.) Star*, May 7, 1968, 4.

214. "GIs Riot at Army Stockade," *St. Joseph (Mo.) Gazette*, August 30, 1968, 1A, 2A.

215. "No Disagreement on Gun Control McGovern Says," *Rapid City (S.D.) Journal*, October 25, 1968, 12; "GOP Urges Straight Tickets; McGovern Talks Education," *Mitchell (S.D.) Daily Republic*, October 24, 1968, 13; "Republicans Repeat Chant; McGovern Questions Foes," *Sioux Falls (S.D.) Argus-Leader*, October 23, 1968, 34; "GOP Continues Gun Law Attack," *Rapid City Journal*, October 18, 1968, 1; "Gubbrud Points Fish Lake Talk to Democrats," *Sioux Falls Argus-Leader*, July 20, 1968, 6; "Gun Registration

Difficulty Cited," *Sioux Falls Argus-Leader*, July 5, 1968, 1; "Appeal Made for Support of Gun Control," *Sioux Falls Argus-Leader*, June 16, 1968, 2; "McGovern for Limited Gun Controls," *Mitchell Daily Republic*, June 15, 1968, 2; letter from George McGovern to South Dakota constituents, June 14, 1968, GMP, box 608, folder Firearms Miscellaneous Correspondence.

216. "Ford Questions Humphrey's Stand on Debates," *Rapid City (S.D.) Journal*, October 17, 1968, 1.

217. Tom Siatos, "Editorial," *G&A*, January 1969, 6.

218. See, e.g., Franklin L. Orth, "Senate Debating Controversial Issue: Gun Control," *Muscatine (Iowa) Journal and New-Tribune*, May 22, 1968, 12 (noting that Javits proposed a "middle ground" amendment to the Omnibus Crime Control and Safe Streets Act).

219. Jacob K. Javits, "Law, Order and Justice," speech before the Borough of Queens, New York City, October 12, 1968, JKJP, box 42, folder Law, Order and Justice; "Gun Curb Versions Similar," *Binghamton (N.Y.) Press and Sun-Bulletin*, September 19, 1968, 1; Jacob K. Javits, "Gun Control: Recognition That U.S. Is Now 70% Urban," remarks before Senate floor, September 17, 1968, JKJP, box 41, folder Gun Control, September 17, 1968; Jacob K. Javits, "For Gun Controls," *Canandaigua (N.Y.) Daily Messenger*, July 17, 1968, 4; "New Voice on Guns," *Allentown (Pa.) Morning Call*, June 13, 1968, 18; Gene S. Goldenberg, " 'Peoples Lobby' Backs Gun Control," *Oneonta (N.Y.) Star*, June 12, 1968, 3; "Three Democrats Vying for Senate Nomination Ask Stiffer Gun Laws," *Oneonta Star*, June 12, 1968, 2.

220. "Javits Urges Viet Peace with Honor," *Glens Falls (N.Y.) Times*, September 21, 1968, 7; Gene S. Goldenberg, "Javits Defends Gun Law," *Oneonta (N.Y.) Star*, September 18, 1968, 1; "Churches Ask All to Observe Guns Deadline," *New York Daily News*, August 12, 1968, 18; "Javits Won't OK Ticket Now," *Binghamton (N.Y.) Press and Sun-Bulletin*, August 12, 1968, 10A; Jacob K. Javits, news release, "Sen. Javits to Appear at Community Rallies for Gun Control Sunday Afternoon," August 11, 1968, JKJP, box 41, folder Gun Control, August 11, 1968; "Javits Denies Storming Out of Platform Hearing," *Scranton (Pa.) Tribune*, August 2, 1968, 1; Jacob K. Javits, "The Congress and Gun Control," remarks before Kiwanis Club of Ithaca, N.Y., July 22, 1968, JKJP, box 41, folder Kiwanis Club of Ithaca, Gun Control.

221. Shane Crosby, "Sen. Javits Is 'Sticking to His Guns,' " *Kingston (N.Y.) Daily Freeman*, October 1, 1968, 5; "Federation Passes 'Dump Javits' Motion," *Kingston Daily Freeman*, September 13, 1968, 19; "Area Sportsmen Clubs Want Javits—OUT," *Kingston Daily Freeman*, August 22, 1968, 26; "Final SASC Poll—No Gun Legislation," *Kingston Daily Freeman*, August 20, 1968, 21.

222. Frank M. Mauro and Art Sperl, "Dump Javits" cochairs, "Freeman Readers Write the Editor," *Kingston (N.Y.) Daily Freeman*, September 25, 1968, 5.

223. Jacob K. Javits, news release, "Local Gun Lobby Seeking to 'Dump Javits' for Influential Backing of Firearms Bills," JKJP, box 41, folder Gun Lobby Dump Javits Campaign.

224. "Javits Will Face Fire of State's Sportsmen," *Rochester (N.Y.) Democrat and Chronicle*, September 25, 1968, 4C.

225. Mike Power, "Javits Defends Gun Controls," *Rochester (N.Y.) Democrat and Chronicle*, September 28, 1968, B1; "Gun Control Misreads—Javits," *Binghamton (N.Y.) Press and Sun-Bulletin*, September 28, 1968, 9.

226. Jacob K. Javits, "Federal Gun Control Laws: Facts and Illusions," speech before New York State Conservation Council, September 27, 1968, JKJP, box 42, folder New York State Conservation Council, Gun Control.

227. Bill Roden, "Adirondack Sportsman," *Glens Falls (N.Y.) Post-Star*, October 3, 1968, 20, 22.

228. The NRA understood its "strength" and "ability to accomplish its object and purposes" depended "entirely upon the support of loyal Americans who believe in the right to keep and bear arms." See NRA, *Operating Report '69*, 11, RNP, Pre-Presidential Collection, Personal Papers, box 9, folder NRA. The NRA also thought it important to use its platform to fight against antifirearms legislation. See Harold W. Glassen, "Vice-President's Report 1967: First Board of Directors Meeting," undated 1967, HWGP, box 1 (outlining best practices for the NRA in opposing antifirearms legislation).

229. "Effect of Gun Issue Seen in Vote Results," *AR*, January 1969, 28, 29. In July 1968 Gurney introduced a bill that would have imposed a ten-year mandatory minimum for a first felony committed with a firearm, and a twenty-five-year mandatory minimum for a second. See "Gurney Tips Off the Voters," *Fort Myers (Fla.) News-Press*, July 10, 1968, 4.

230. Pete Laine, "LBJ Bats .390 with Florida Delegation," *Miami (Fla.) Herald*, October 25, 1968, 6A; Charles Stafford, "Florida Delegation Split Over Gun Legislation," *Tampa (Fla.) Tribune*, June 16, 1968, 1A, 8A; Peter Laine, "Gurney: Head Start Fails, Too," *Miami Herald*, April 26, 1968, 8A. However, Gurney did oppose federal firearms registration. See Daile Pullen, "Gurney, Collins Differ in Senate Race Viewpoints," *Palm Beach (Fla.) Post*, July 21, 1968, A9.

231. "Gun Owners Heard During '68 Elections," *GW*, November 15, 1968, 1.

232. "Sen. Brewster Drops Support of Tydings Bill," *GW*, September 6, 1968, 2.

233. See, e.g., Michael Parks, "TV Image Aids Mathias Bid," *Baltimore (Md.) Sun*, November 2, 1968, B7; "Mahoney Hits Hard on Gun Curb Issue," *Salisbury (Md.) Daily Times*, October 20, 1968, A8; "Mahoney, Mathias on Offensive," *Baltimore Sun*, October 12, 1968, B6, B20; "Mahoney Scores Gun Law, Terms It 'Communist Idea,'" *Baltimore Sun*, October 10, 1968, C20; "Candidates View War, Gun Control," *Cumberland (Md.) Evening Times*, September 3, 1968, 13; "Mac Votes for Gun Control," *Frederick (Md.) News*, June 12, 1968, 1.

7. 1969–1970

1. "An NRA Life Member in the White House," *AR*, January 1969, 14.

2. Letter from Franklin L. Orth, NRA executive vice president, to NRA lifetime members, January 29, 1969, TEWP (owned by author).

3. E. B. Mann, "In Focus," *Shooting Industry*, January 1969, 6.

4. Tom Siatos, "Editorial," *G&A*, January 1969, 6.

5. S. J. Schoon, "The Nixon Position???," *Armed Eagle*, March 1969, 7.

6. American Independent Party Platform of 1968, October 13, 1968.

7. See, e.g., "Humphrey Allegation Ires Nixon Supporters," *GW*, September 27, 1968, 6.

8. Compare Statement of Richard M. Nixon, June 17, 1968, RNPP, White House Central Files, box 26, Staff Member Office Files, folder Martin Anderson, Gun Control; Richard M. Nixon, *Disarming the Criminal Class* (July 9, 1968), HHHP, 1968 Presidential Campaign Files, John G. Stewart Research Files, box 1, folder Gun Control, with Alan C. Webber, "Where the NRA Stands on Gun Legislation," *AR*, March 1968, 22; Franklin L. Orth, "Where the NRA Stands . . .," *AR*, September 1966, 21–22; "NRA Policy Statement on Firearms Legislation," *AR*, July 1958, 35.

9. "Nixon Urged to Resign NRA Life Membership," *GW*, January 31, 1969, 1.

10. Daniel Rapoport, "National Rifle Association: Nixon Belongs to Club Opposing Gun Controls," *Shreveport (La.) Times*, January 13, 1969, 4C; "Rifle Club Says Nixon Is Member," *Raleigh (N.C.) News and Observer*, January 13, 1969, 5; "Rifle Group Notes Nixon Is a Member," *Indianapolis (Ind.) Star*, January 13, 1969, 2.

11. "President Quits Rifle Association," *Detroit (Mich.) Free Press*, February 23, 1969, 6A; "No NRA Membership—Nixon," *Binghamton (N.Y.) Press and Sun-Bulletin*, February 23, 1969, 2A; "Membership Disavowed," *Tallahassee (Fla.) Democrat*, February 22, 1969, 12A; Daniel Rapoport, "Nixon Shuns Link to NRA," *Alexandria (Va.) Town Talk*, February 23, 1969, 1.

12. "Executive Director's Report," *AR*, May 1954, 34–37.

13. "Executive Director's Report," *AR*, May 1954, 37. Nixon could not have maintained and owned these handguns even if he wanted to. As required by law, such honorary gifts are not kept by the recipients but are rather cataloged and stored by the federal government. See Jack Maskell, *Gifts to the President of the United States* (Washington, D.C.: Congressional Research Service, August 16, 2012).

14. "83 Years of Public Service," *AR*, May 1954, 38–39.

15. See, e.g., "A Statement Concerning President Nixon," *AR*, April 1969, 16; "President Nixon Resigns Honorary Membership in NRA," *GW*, March 21, 1969, 5. For the "double-crosser" accusation, see letter from William Loeb to Pat Buchanan, July 18, 1972, White House Central Files, box 35, Staff Member Office Files, folder Michael P. Balzano, Gun Control; letter from William Loeb to Ashely Halsey, Jr., *AR* editor, June 30, 1971, RFSP, box 444, folder Ballew Shooting.

16. See Bob Neal, "Washington Report: Nixon Backs Sport Shooters!," *G&A*, November 1969, 8, 73; "What the Lawmakers Are Doing: Administration Opposes Registration," *AR*, September 1969, 32–34; "Administration Officials Oppose Federal Gun Registration-Licensing," *GW*, August 8, 1969, 1–2.

17. Statement of Donald E. Santarelli, Associate Deputy Attorney General Department of Justice, Before the Subcommittee to Investigate Juvenile Delinquency Committee on the Judiciary United States Senate on S. 100, S. 849, S. 8977, S. 2433,

July 24, 2019, RNPP, White House Special Files, Egil Krogh, box 65, folder Gun Control 1969, 1–2.

18. Santarelli statement, July 24, 2019, 3–5. Santerelli's proposed ban on Saturday Night Specials quickly became a political flashpoint for many within the gun rights community. This was primarily due to the recently published findings for the National Commission on the Causes and Prevention of Violence, which was commissioned by President Lyndon B. Johnson in the wake of Senator Robert F. Kennedy's assassination. The commission called for the strict handgun controls, including licensing. See, e.g., Willis L. Hobart, "Violence Commission Says . . . Confiscate Handguns," *G&A*, November 1969, 28–29, 85–87; "Gun Legislation Report," *Muzzle Blasts*, November 1969, 4; Bob Bell, "Handgunfiscation?," *PGN*, October 1969, 1; "The 'Violence Report' Explodes," *AR*, September 1968, 31; "Conclusion of Commission Report," *GW*, September 5, 1969, 19; "Knowledge of Violence Commission Report Important to Sportsmen," *GW*, August 29, 1969, 7, 15; "Handgun Ban Proposal Draws Mixed Reaction," *GW*, August 15, 1969, 1–2; "Panel Says Turn 'Turn Them In,'" *GW*, August 15, 1969, 4; Wallace F. Bennett, news release, "Bennett Calls Violence Commission Report Unrealistic, Unreasonable," July 28, 1969, WFBP, MSS 20, box 228, folder 18. However, it was an idea that the NRA had repeatedly endorsed. See, e.g., "Let's See Who Backs This Handgun Control," *AR*, July 1969, 10; "Restraint on TV, Cheap Handguns Wins Favor," *AR*, March 1968, 15; NRA Office of Public Relations, News Release, "NRA Offers Program on Gun Control Legislation," April 7, 1967, MRP, series 5, box 14, folder 6; "Mail-Order Guns," *AR*, August 1963, 16.

19. "What the Lawmakers Are Doing: Ammo Bill Hits 'Backdoor' Registration," *AR*, March 1969, 34–38.

20. "What the Lawmakers Are Doing."

21. Memorandum from Paul W. Eggers to Egil Krogh, "Memorandum to Mr. Egil Krogh, Jr. Staff Assistant to the Counsel," April 29, 1969, RNPP, White House Special Files, Egil Krogh, box 65, folder Gun Control 1969, 2.

22. "Senate Support Grows for Ammo Removal Bill," *GW*, March 7, 1969, 1–2.

23. See, e.g., "Senator Bennett Asks Ammo Rule Revision," *GW*, February 21, 1969, 1, 3; "Bennett Urges Elimination of Ammunition Registration," *Toole (Utah) Transcript-Bulletin*, January 31, 1969, 6; "Bennett Moves to Change Ammunition Registration," *Richfield (Utah) Reaper*, January 30, 1969, 3; "Ammunition Licensing Draws Denunciation by Sen. Bennett," *Ogden (Utah) Standard-Examiner*, January 15, 1969, 13A; Frank Hewlett, "Bennett Seeking to Repeal Ammo Registration Law," *Salt Lake City (Utah) Tribune*, January 12, 1969, A3.

24. See, e.g., "Action on Ammunition," *AR*, March 1969, 18.

25. "What the Lawmakers Are Doing: Ammo Bill Hits 'Backdoor' Registration," *AR*, March 1969, 34; National Shooting Sports Foundation, News Release, "Back-Door Registration," March 1969, WFBP, MSS 20, box 265, folder 8; "Demos Back Bennett Bill," *Tooele (Utah) Transcript-Bulletin*, March 4, 1969, 4; Thomas Jefferson Steed, news release, February 27, 1969, TJSP, box 46, folder 16, Judiciary-Gun Control 1969.

26. "Attempts to Redraft Gun Control Act Get Added Push," *Sacramento (Calif.) Bee*, July 30, 1969, 1; "Gun Control Foe Is Given New 'Ammo,'" *Des Moines (Iowa) Tribune*, July 30, 1968, 43; "Most Federal Gun Bills Would Aid Firearms Owners," *AR*, June 1969, 62; "What the Lawmakers Are Doing: Easing of Ammunition Rules Seems Likely," *AR*, May 1969, 38.

27. "Senate Ammo Bill Reported Favorably in Senate; Dodd Pushes Handgun Bill," *GW*, October 10, 1969, 1–2; "What the Lawmakers Are Doing: Fresh Moves Made on Ammo," *AR*, October 1969, 52–53, 55.

28. See chapter 6.

29. Letter from the Montana Arms Collectors Association to Sportsmen/Gun Owners, October 23, 1968, MMP, box 85, folder 2; "Mike Is Target of Firing Line," *Billings (Mont.) Gazette*, June 26, 1968, 1; "Mail Heaviest in 25 Years . . . Mike Standing Firm on Gun Control Legislation," *Great Falls (Mont.) Tribune*, June 26, 1968, 7.

30. Henry Moore, "Rod and Gun: Senators Ask Change in Gun Control Act," *Boston Globe*, March 25, 1969, 32; Bob Hood, "Senators Rewrite Gun Control Bill," *Fort Worth (Tex.) Star-Telegram*, March 7, 1969, 3C; "Bill Seeks to Ease Ammunition Guides," *Minneapolis Star Tribune*, March 16, 1969, H12; Robert A. Barnes, "Members of Congress Charge 'Backdoor' Gun Registration," *Port Huron (Mich.) Times Herald*, March 13, 1969, 12; "'Backdoor' Gun Registration Rules Charged," *Louisville (Ky.) Courier-Journal*, March 5, 1969, A9. Mansfield was well aware that he was mischaracterizing the provisions within the Gun Control Act. See "Facts About the Gun Crime Law," undated [1969], MMP, box 85, folder 1 (noting that the Gun Control Act "does *not* compile or make gun owner lists available").

31. Mike Mansfield, press release, "Remarks of Senator Mike Mansfield at the Annual Dinner of the American Advisory Committee, European Institute of Business Administration," June 27, 1968, MMP, box 44, folder 42.

32. "Gun Misuse Penalties Asked in Senate Bills," *GW*, February 21, 1969, 1 (noting how sportsmen are aware that Mansfield changed positions).

33. Statement of Mike Mansfield, July 23, 1969, MMP, box 45, folder 5.

34. Although both Democrats and Republicans presented similar bills in previous Congresses, for the 91st Congress the mandatory minimum proposal proffered by Mansfield was first considered by Republicans. See "GOP Seeks Gun Misuse Sentences," *GW*, December 13, 1968, 1.

35. Statement of Mike Mansfield, July 23, 1969.

36. "Fishtail Marine Shot in Washington," *Billings (Mont.) Gazette*, June 6, 1968, 1; "LBJ Cites N.Y. Ambush in Appeal," *Fremont (Calif.) Argus*, July 4, 1968, 5; John Kamps, "Shooting of Young Montanan Changed Mansfield," *Missoulian* (Missoula, Mont.), July 4, 1968, 3; letter from Mike Mansfield to Mrs. Leo Lesnik, June 26, 1968, MMP, box 85, folder 2.

37. "Explanation of Lesnik Mandatory Sentencing Bill," undated 1969, MMP, box 85, folder 3; "Senate Bill Sets Jail for Gun Use: Montana Marine's Murder Sparks Mansfield Motion," *Baltimore (Md.) Sun*, November 20, 1969, A1.

38. "Senators Say Yes: Lesnik Gun Bill Passes," *Spokane (Wash.) Spokesman-Review*, November 20, 1969, 5.

39. See generally HSP, box 78.

40. "How the U.S. Senate Voted on Registration, Licensing," *AR*, November 1968, 23–24.

41. See, e.g., "Scott Urges Senate Reject Gun Law Curbs," *Lebanon (Pa.) Daily News*, September 16, 1968, 15; "Scott Fights Weakening of Gun Controls," *Lancaster (Pa.) New Era*, September 16, 1968, 34; "Tydings Pushes for Senate Action on Gun Control Law," *Canonsburg (Pa.) Daily Notes*, July 10, 1968, 10; "Senate Support for Gun Control Law Builds Up," *Tyrone (Pa.) Daily Herald*, June 17, 1968, 4.

42. "Gun Control Act to Be Softened?," *Ithaca (N.Y.) Journal*, July 30, 1969, 2; "Attempts to Ease Gun Control Act Get Boost," *Waterloo (Iowa) Courier*, July 30, 1969, 28.

43. "Scott, Schweiker Back Gun Control," *Clearfield (Pa.) Progress*, November 10, 1969, 10; "Scott Supported by 38 Other Senators in Ammunition Bill," *Lock Haven (Pa.) Express*, July 1, 1969, 11; letter from Hugh Scott to Zehnder H. Confair, March 27, 1969, reprinted in Del Kerr, "Outdoors in Potter County," *Potter (Pa.) Enterprise*, April 16, 1969, 5.

44. Email from Kenneth E. Davis, former staffer for Hugh Scott, to Patrick J. Charles, "Re: Hugh Scott and Sportsmen," February 28, 2018 (on file with author).

45. Letter from Jack L. Conmy, Richard S. Schweiker press secretary, to Gene Cowan, Hugh Scott administrative assistant, March 26, 1969, RSSP, box 20, folder 58.

46. Email from Davis to Charles, February 28, 2018.

47. "Lest We Forgive & Forget!," *GW*, October 10, 1969, 4.

48. "Scott Continues Fence Mending in Pennsylvania," *GW*, October 24, 1969, 2.

49. "Scott Speaks Out on Final Ammo Repeal," *Schuylkill Haven (Pa.) Call*, December 4, 1969, 9; "Sportsmen Will Welcome: Bennett-Scott Anti-Gun Control Bill Cleared for Senate Action," *Elizabethtown (Pa.) Chronicle*, September 25, 1969, 1; "Bennett-Scott Anti-Gun Bill Sent to Senate," *Benton (Pa.) Argus*, September 25, 1969, 8; "Senator Scott Visits County in Effort to Align with Sportsmen," *Potter (Pa.) Enterprise*, August 20, 1969, 1; "Scott Supported by 38 Other Senators in Ammunition Bill," *Lock Haven (Pa.) Express*, July 1, 1969, 11; "Scott Hearing Set to Help Sportsmen," *Hazleton (Pa.) Standard-Speaker*, July 15, 1969, 14.

50. For a list of S. 849's original cosponsors, see "What the Lawmakers Are Doing: Ammo Bill Hits 'Backdoor' Registration," *AR*, March 1969, 34.

51. "Scott Admits Gun Act 'Mistake'; Challenges *Gun Week* Editorial," *GW*, December 5, 1969, 3.

52. "G & A Exclusive Report: Leading Senator Admits Gun Law Mistake!," *G&A*, March 1970, 46–47.

53. "Scott Admits Gun Act 'Mistake,'" December 5, 1969, 3.

54. Memorandum from Donald E. Santarelli to Egil Krogh, "Gun Control," March 16, 1970, RNPP, White House Special Files, Textual Materials, Box 3, Folder Geoffrey Shepard, Guns and Ammunition.

55. "Washington Whispers," *U.S. News & World Report*, July 6, 1970, 7. A similar political shift was taking place at the state level. See, e.g., Bill Davidson, "Few Governors Favor New State Gun Control Laws," *AR*, May 1969, 42–43.

56. For a copy of Sikes's speech, see Robert F. Sikes, speech before the National Rifle Association's 1969 Annual Meetings, March 30, 1969, CAP, box BI 8, folder 48, Robert Sikes; "Our Man in Washington," *GM*, July 1969, 12–15.

57. "So Gun Laws Work—It Says There," *AR*, March 1969, 18.

58. Harold W. Glassen, remarks before the Duke Law Forum, Duke University, February 18, 1969, HWGP, box 1, 7.

59. *Annual Meeting of the Board of Directors of the National Rifle Association, April 9-10, 1968* (Washington, D.C., 1968), HWGP, box 1, 17.

60. Letter from National Shooting Sports Foundation to [Philip H. Hoff], June 21, 1968, PHHP, drawer 11–2, folder 29.

61. On the NRA, see Woodson D. Scott, "A Statement by the President of the National Rifle Association," *AR*, March 1970, 16. It is worth noting that the NRA did give serious consideration to both a data-retrieval system and model firearms purchaser identification cards legislation. See Harold W. Glassen, "Remarks of the President at the NRA Annual Members Meeting," March 29, 1969, *Minutes of the Members Meeting of the NRA, March 29, 1969*, HWGP, box 1, 4; Harold W. Glassen, address before the Salt Lake City Chamber of Commerce, October 8, 1968, HWGP, box 1, 20; Woodson D. Scott, "Report of the Committee on Firearms Legislation," September 16, 1968, *Minutes of the Meeting of the Executive Committee of the National Rifle Association of America, December 7-8, 1968* (Washington, D.C., 1968), HWGP, box 1. The NSSF approach is discussed in George Skelton, "License Firearm Owner, Gun Lobby Says," *Indianapolis (Ind.) Star*, December 25, 1968, 33. The editors of *Gun Week* took the lead in bringing the issue to the attention of the gun rights proponents. See "Should We Compromise?" *GW*, February 7, 1969, 4. Of the *Gun Week* readers to respond, seventy-four out of seventy-nine gave a resounding "no compromise" answer. See "'No Compromise'—Readers," *GW*, March 7, 1969, 4, 7.

62. See, e.g., E. B. Mann, "Has Industry Betrayed Us?" *GM*, June 1969, 28–30, 64; John Stetson, "Outdoors," *Alton (Ill.) Evening Telegraph*, April 28, 1969, 17; Robert M. Price, "Rebuttal: Yes, Industry Has Betrayed Us," *GM*, October 1969, 18–20, 51.

63. National Shooting Sports Foundation, "Policy on Firearms Legislation," *GW*, April 4, 1969, 16.

64. See, e.g., "Shooting Sports Prepares Model for Contiguous State Measures," *GW*, March 14, 1969, 1–2.

65. "Compromise Cart Upset!" *GW*, June 20, 1969, 4; "Model Firearms Legislation," *Fact Pack II on Firearms Ownership* (Riverside, Conn.: National Shooting Sports Foundation, 1970), 17–42.

66. "No Compromise" was later adopted as the slogan of the gun rights extremist organization NAKBA. See NAKBA, *What Is the National Association to Keep and Bear Arms?* (Medford, Ore., 1972), BC, box 7L, folder NAKBA.

67. "'Never Yield' Carter Says: NRA Past President Challenges Sportsmen to Grass Roots Action," *GW*, March 21, 1969, 7. Carter was not the first prominent NRA official to embrace the idea of no compromise. Writing in 1950, Executive Director C. B. Lister espoused a similar opinion. See C. B. Lister, "The Shooter's No. 1 Problem," *Official Gun Book*, ed. Charles R. Jacobs (New York: Crown, 1950), 4–6.

68. See, e.g., "United We Stand—Divided?," *GW*, January 24, 1969, 4 (claiming a lack of coordination and cooperation among the "firearms fraternity").

69. See, e.g., letter from Ken Carrell, Josephine County Sportsman Association secretary, to Robert W. Packwood, February 14, 1969, RWPP, box 6, folder 10, Legislation-Judiciary, Gun Control 1969; letter from N. Douglas Yeager, APORKBA chairman, to Robert W. Packwood, January 23, 1969, RWPP, box 6, folder 10, Legislation-Judiciary, Gun Control 1969. Such political action groups included the recently founded Allied Pennsylvania Sportsmen, The Right to Bear Arms, and Firearms and Individual Rights (FAIR). See, e.g., "Pro-Gun Group Info Sought," *GW*, October 17, 1969, 4.

70. "Sportsmen's Groups Forming," *GW*, November 28, 1969, 4.

71. "Minnesota Candidates Switch Election Goals," *GW*, March 13, 1970, 1, 5; "Bun Lobby Seeks Head's Political Head," *Minneapolis Star Tribune*, February 10, 1970, 23; "Minnesota Sportsmen Lead Anti-Head Drive," *GW*, February 6, 1970, 1–2; Ted Smebakken, "Gun Lobby Zeroes in on Head," *Minneapolis Star*, February 9, 1970, 14B; "Bill Limiting Gun Controls Shelved," *Minneapolis Star Tribune*, May 7, 1969, 11; "Minnesota Group Forms to Fight Bad Gun Proposals," *GW*, May 2, 1969, 18; "Backers Outgunned in Permit Battle," *St. Cloud (Minn.) Times*, April 2, 1969, 13; "LeVander's Gun Control Proposals Termed 'Harsh,'" *Bemidji (Minn.) Pioneer*, March 31, 1969, 1.

72. "Virginia Sportsmen Chalk Up Election Wins," *GW*, December 5, 1968, 2; "Virginia Sportsmen Establish Organization to Fight Anti-Gun Legislation at All Levels," *GW*, November 7, 1969, 3; "Virginia Alliance Tops 900 Members," *GW*, April 18, 1969, 16; "Will Fight Laws Against Guns," *Petersburg (Va.) Progress-Index*, August 19, 1968, 8.

73. "Ohio Sportsmen's Group Opposes Five, Supports Three in Primary," *GW*, May 1, 1970, 1–2; "Lukens Firms Law-Order Stand," *Cincinnati (Ohio) Enquirer*, April 6, 1970, 27; "Ohio Alliance Starts Drive for Members," *GW*, April 3, 1970, 3; "Ohio Sportsmen Form Statewide Lobbying, Political Organization," *GW*, November 15, 1969, 1–2; "Sportsmen Eye Fight on Firearms," *Logan (Ohio) Daily News* (OH), October 30, 1969, 3; "Ohio Gunmen Set Meeting to Organize," *Marion (Ohio) Star*, October 30, 1969, 20; "Gun Control Bill in Trouble," *Akron (Ohio) Beacon Journal*, March 29, 1967, C6.

74. See "West Virginia Site of New Organization," *GW*, April 24, 1970, 3; "SCOPE Issues Resolution Opposing Goodell, McCarthy," *GW*, March 13, 1970, 10; "Michigan Sportsmen Form New Organization," *GW*, February 20, 1970, 1–2; "Pro-Gun Group Directory Adds Names," *GW*, January 30, 1970, 2; "Missouri-Kansas Firearms Group Works for Sportsmen's Causes," *GW*, January 23, 1970, 5; "State Pro-Gun Organization Forms in North Carolina," *GW*, January 23, 1970, 2; "Directory of Pro-Gun Organizations," *GW*, January 2, 1970, 2; "Michigan Group Plans to Fight Anti-Gunners,"

GW, December 19, 1969, 7; "Utah Sportsmen United to Form Intermountain Gun Owners Group," *GW*, December 5, 1969, 5; "Group Forms to Combat Bad Gun Laws," *GW*, April 25, 1969, 9; "United Firearms Owners Oppose Gun Compromise," *GW*, April 4, 1969, 6; "Kansas Sportsmen United to Promote Common Goals," *GW*, November 28, 1968, 2; "California Organization Provides Information on Anti-Gun Proposals Via Phone Network," *GW*, November 7, 1969, 9; "Connecticut to Organize," *GW*, September 19, 1969, 3.

75. NRA, *Operating Report '69* (Washington, D.C., 1970), 11, RNPP, Pre-Presidential Collection, Personal Papers, box 9, folder NRA.

76. Compare "Table of Contents," *AR*, December 1968, 2, with "Table of Contents," *AR*, December 1969, 2. For all of 1969, circulation of *AR* dropped as low as 1,069,000. "Table of Contents," *AR*, October 1969, 2. On costs, see NRA, *Operating Report '69*, 17.

77. "Time to Stand Up and Be Counted," *AR*, October 1969, 16. To maintain its current operating budget, the NRA needed to grow by 100,000 to 120,000 members by the close of 1969. See "Report of the Executive Vice President Franklin L. Orth to NRA Executive Committee Meeting," December 7, 1968, *Minutes of the Executive Committee of the National Rifle Association of America, December 7-8, 1968* (Washington, D.C., 1968), HWGP, box 1.

78. Franklin L. Orth, "A Special Message: Sportsmen and Gun Laws," *AR*, August 1969, 46–47.

79. Orth, "A Special Message."

80. This can be seen in the continued drop in circulation of *AR*. "Table of Contents," *AR*, January 1970, 2 (stating an *American Rifleman* circulation of 1,080,000, which was down 12,000 from December 1969).

81. See chapter 6.

82. Compare "Total Net Subscriptions Paid," *GW*, January 31, 1969, 1, with "Total Net Subscriptions Paid," *GW*, January 30, 1970, 1 (showing a 70 percent increase in *Gun Week* circulation from 35,878 to 51,114).

83. NRA, "Mr. Gun Owner," *GW*, February 13, 1970, 3.

84. NRA, "Shooters Beware!," *GW*, March 13, 1970, 3.

85. See, e.g., Otto R. Keiter, "Anti-Legislation Plaint," *AR*, October 1939, 36; C. B. Lister, "The Remedy," *Du Pont Magazine*, March 1924, 10.

86. See, e.g., C. B. Lister, "The Nazi Deadline," *AR*, February 1942, 7; "Danger Ahead!! Help!!" *AR*, April 1941, insert, 2; "Zero Hour," *AR*, December 1940, 4; "Important Decisions," *AR*, August 1940, 22; " 'National Defense' Decoy," *AR*, August 1940, 4.

87. See, e.g., Harold W. Glassen, Remarks Before Stetson University, Deland, Florida, April 14, 1969, HWGP, box 1, 2.

88. "What the Lawmakers Are Doing: Congress Threshes Out the Gun Law Issue," *AR*, November 1968, 22–23.

89. Copies of the letter can be found in several congressional papers. See letter from Ashley Halsey, Jr., *American Rifleman* editor, to Mike Mansfield, July 29, 1970, MMP, box 85, folder 1; to Winston L. Prouty, July 29, 1970, WLPP, carton A112, folder 26; to George D. Aiken, July 29, 1970, GDAP, crate 19, folder 1; to Thomas Jefferson Steed,

July 29, 1970, TJSP, box BL 7, folder 19, Steed Bill-Repeal Gun Control Act 1969; to Page Belcher, July 29, 1970, PBP, box 138, folder 13A, Firearms Legislation; to Fred R. Harris, July 29, 1970, FHP, box 183, folder 16b, Crime-Firearms Control. Not every member of Congress replied to the letter.

90. See Patrick J. Charles, "The 'Reasonable Regulation' Right to Arms: The Gun Rights Second Amendment Before the Standard Model," in *A Right to Bear Arms? The Contested Role of History in Contemporary Debates on the Second Amendment*, ed. Jennifer Tucker, Barton C. Hacker, and Margaret Vining (Washington, D.C.: Smithsonian Press, 2019), 167–84.

91. "New Constitution Ok'd," *Chicago Tribune*, December 16, 1970, sec. 1, pp. 1, 8.

92. "Illinois' Right or Fright?," *GW*, April 10, 1970, 4.

93. "Illinois Sportsmen Scorn Constitutional Provision," *GW*, December 4, 1970, 1.

94. The NRA had long acknowledged the existence of the "police power" as a regulatory check on the right to arms. See, e.g., Harold W. Glassen, "Right to Bear Arms Is Older than the Second Amendment," *AR*, April 1973, 22; Harold W. Glassen, Remarks Before the Duke Law Forum, Duke University, February 18, 1969, HWGP, box 1, 8; Judge Bartlett Rummel, "To Have and Bear Arms," *AR*, June 1964, 41; "Basic Facts of Firearms Control," *AR*, February 1964, 14; NRA, *The Pro and Con of Firearms Legislation* (Washington, D.C., 1940), 4; Karl T. Frederick, *Pistol Regulation: Its Principles and History* (Washington, D.C.: NRA, 1932), 26–27.

95. Raymond F. Hamel, "Con-Con Protects Gun Owners," *Chicago Tribune*, December 8, 1970, sec. 1, p. 20.

96. "NRA Official Supports Illinois Constitution," *GW*, December 18, 1970, 1–2. On Kukla's views, see, e.g., Robert J. Kukla, *Gun Control* (Harrisburg, Pa.: Stackpole Books, 1973); Thomas Gregory, "Support Increases for Gun Law," *Decatur (Ill.) Herald and Review*, August 17, 1969, sec. 4, p. 1; "Gun Support Assailed," *Chicago Tribune*, June 15, 1968, 5.

97. See, e.g., "Tydings Reelection Bid Attacks NRA," *AR*, August 1970, 52.

98. See, e.g., NRA, *Some Questions and Answers on Firearms Controls* (Washington, D.C., 1970); NRA, *The Gun Law Problem* (Washington, D.C., 1968); NRA, *The Pro and Con of Firearms Registration* (Washington, D.C., 1968).

99. Publius & Associates, *Firearms and Freedom* (1968), https://youtu.be/OyxlV-RWNOk. For specific quotes, see 5:15–5:32 (emphasis added) and 5:15–6:32.

100. For video, see "Mayor Daley of Chicago-1968," *Associated Press*, April 15, 1968, https://www.youtube.com/watch?v=olNN2iT41S4.

101. Daley later revised his order by having Chicago police limit themselves to "minimum force." "Return to Reason," *Battle Creek (Mich.) Enquirer*, April 21, 1968, sec. 2, p. 2; "Chicago Mayor Clarifies Order to 'Shoot to Kill,'" *Port Huron (Mich.) Times Herald*, April 18, 1968, 6A.

102. E. E. Schmitz, "Proclamation of the Mayor," April 18, 1906 (San Francisco: Museum of the City of San Francisco). What was unusual was that law enforcement was able to disarm anyone seen carrying a weapon, as well as "shoot without warning any person acting suspiciously." See "Among the Dead," *San Bernardino County (Calif.)*

Sun, April 19, 1906, 2. According to one report, on the first day of the shooting order, law enforcement "did not hesitate to shoot anyone suspected of looting" and killed twenty such persons. "College Boys Join the Gun Brigade: Twenty Looter Shot Dead Amid Ruins," *San Bernardino County Sun*, April 20, 1906, 4. Despite the harshness of the order, looting continued to ravage San Francisco for weeks. See, e.g., "Making Looters Clear the Street," *Bakersfield (Calif.) Morning Echo*, May 13, 1906, 4; "Oakland Landlords Overreach Themselves," *Santa Cruz (Calif.) Sentinel*, April 29, 1906, 1; "Searching in Ruins for Loot," *Los Angeles Evening Express*, April 28, 1906, 1; "Looting in the City," *Sacramento (Calif.) Bee*, April 28, 1906, 1; "Bullets Will Await Looting Sightseers," *San Francisco Chronicle*, April 28, 1906, 4; "Men Shoot Fiends Who Try to Rob," *San Francisco Call*, April 22, 1906, 1–2.

103. See, e.g., "Wanton Murder by the Guards," *San Francisco Chronicle*, April 24, 1906, 8; "Bullet Ends Life of Millionaire," *Los Angeles Herald*, April 24, 1906, 6.

104. "Blame Militia for Looting," *Santa Cruz (Calif.) Evening Sentinel*, May 1, 1906, 2.

105. Publius & Associates, *Firearms and Freedom*, 0:36–2:10.

106. For a detailed history and legal analysis, see Patrick J. Charles, *Armed in America: A History of Gun Rights from Colonial Militias to Concealed Carry* (Amherst, N.Y.: Prometheus Books, 2018), 70–120.

107. See, e.g., Captain Charles S. Wheatley, "The People, the Constitution, and Firearms," *OL*, June 1930, 104; Eltinge F. Warner, "You Have No Constitutional Rights!" *F&S*, March 1932, 15; "Constitutional Provision on Arms," *OL*, August 1921, 148.

108. United States Revolver Association, "Criminals Not Made by Pistols," *Bulletin* no. 5, February 15, 1923, MFP, box 5, folder 53.

109. "Guns vs. Bandits," *AR*, November 1939, 36.

110. "Guns vs. Bandits," *AR*, March 1941, 36; Walter J. Howe, "The Armed Citizen," *AR*, September 1958, 32.

111. See, e.g., Connecticut Sportsmen's Alliance, "The Right to Keep and Bear Arms—Crime Control," undated 1970, LPWP, box 1785, folder 15, 1969–1970 Research Files-Gun Control (stating that the "safety of the United States depends upon a responsible citizenry, skilled in the safe and effective use of firearms," and the "right of each citizen to own firearms is the strongest deterrent to crime. Almost 200 years of experience has proven that our faith in an open society is not misplaced, provided we do not chip away at the basic freedoms in our Bill of Rights."); "The Answer is Simply Law Enforcement," *AR*, July 1968, 16; "Law and Order," *AR*, July 1964, 16.

112. "Loeb Calls for Arming Citizens for Protection," *GW*, January 23, 1970, 7.

113. On arming citizens, see, e.g., John E. Osborn, "Guns, Crime, and Self-Defense," *AR*, September 1967, 143; Paul L. Shumaker, "Sportsmen Must Educate Public on Defending Home with Firearms," *GW*, February 13, 1970, 18; "Who Guards America's Homes?," *AR*, May 1967, 16; Bill Clede, "Gun Safety Begins at Home," *GM*, June 1963, 28–30, 38, 40. C. Richard Rogers, "The NRA Story," *GM*, April 1962, 16, 46. On average citizens performing law enforcement roles, see, e.g., "Creating 'Vigilantism' Where None Exists," *AR*, June 1967, 16; Ashley Halsey, Jr., "Rifleman Fire Back," *Miami (Fla.) News*, May 20, 1967, 2; "The Private Army Hoax," *AR*, September 1965, 20. But

see "The Attorney General Is Inconsistent," *AR*, January 1934, 4 (stating that crime could be effectively "stamped out by an aroused *armed* citizenry, either called to the aid of the police as possemen, or, as in the days of the Old West, disgusted with corrupt police officials and organized into their own law-enforcement groups— the Vigilantes").

114. Bill R. Davidson *To Keep and Bear Arms* (New Rochelle, N.Y.: Arlington House, 1969), 23–57; Rex Applegate, "Guns and the Law: Some Thoughts on Riots and Gun Laws," *GM*, August 1968, 32–33, 72–73.

115. James B. Whisker, *Our Vanishing Freedom: The Right to Keep and Bear Arms* (McLean, Va.: Heritage House, 1972), 55–57. It is worth mentioning that right-wing gun rights extremists often pulled their ideas from material in the NRA's *American Rifleman*. See, e.g., Jac Weller, "A Nation of Armed Citizens," *AR*, September 1970, 48–51; "Communism Versus Gun Ownership," *AR*, August 1970, 16.

116. Before the view was edited for public consumption, some in the gun rights community were worried that the film would depict anti-gun propaganda. See Carl Wolff, "Our Man in Washington," *GM*, August 1969, 12–14; "Gun Legislation," *Muzzle Blasts*, August 1969, 3, 25.

117. See Department of Treasury, *That's What It's All About* (1970), https://catalog.archives .gov/id/11904.

118. See, e.g., "Why Senator Dodd Is Unfit to Conduct an Impartial Investigation of Treasury's Gun Control Film," *Aim & Fire: The Official Publication of Firearms Lobby of America*, no. 4, undated 1970, 1 (criticizing the film as "nothing more than a grade 'c' Hollywood gangster movie embellished with bikini-clad girls and symbols of sex and violence"); Carl Wolff, "Anti-Gun Movie Marked for Death," *GM*, April 1970, 16–17 (describing the final film as having "removed" any pertinent information related to the Gun Control Act, thus leaving "only the sex and violence"); Del Kerr, "Outdoors in Potter County," *Coudersport (Pa.) Potter Enterprise*, March 4, 1970, 7; "Lobby Force Gun Film Ban," *Tampa Bay (Fla.) Times*, February 21, 1970, 4A; Jimmy Jordan, "IRS Gets It Coming and Going," *Pittsburgh Post-Gazette*, February 3, 1970, 18.

119. Saul Friedman, "Sportsmen Lobby Gets Gun-Law Film Killed as 'Too Violent,'" *Detroit (Mich.) Free Press*, February 23, 1970, 10C.

120. Carl Wolff, "Our Man in Washington," *GM*, October 1968, 21, 64; "Non-Violence Begins at Home—on the TV," *AR*, July 1968, 18; "Are We Really So Violent?," *AR*, February 1968, 16.

121. "Congressman, Sportsmen Blast ATFD Movie 'Explaining Gun Law,'" *GW*, February 13, 1969, 1–2.

122. Memorandum from the White House to Eugene Rossides, January 21, 1970, RNPP, White House Special Files, Textual Materials, Box 3, Folder Geoffrey Shepard, Guns and Ammunition.

123. "Congressman, Sportsmen Blast ATFD Movie 'Explaining Gun Law.'"

124. "CBS Airs Special Report on ATFD's Gun Act Movie," *GW*, March 6, 1970, 1–2; "CBS Shows ATFD Movie," *GW*, February 27, 1960, 1.

125. "What the Lawmakers Are Doing: U.S. Drops Firearms Mail Label," *AR*, March 1970, 34–37.

126. For examples of contiguous firearms bills, see Model Firearms Legislation," *Fact Pack II on Firearms Ownership*, 24–27.

127. On the two cities' registration ordinances, see "Optimism Still Held for San Francisco Law," *GW*, September 5, 1969, 1–2; "San Francisco Begins Gun Registration," *GW*, July 25, 1969, 1, 6; "State Supreme Court Upholds SF Gun Law," *GW*, May 9, 1969, 1–2; "The 'Wrong' of Bearing Arms," *Los Angeles Times*, April 30, 1969, part 2, 6; Gene Blake, "State High Court Opens Door to Gun Controls," *Los Angeles Times*, April 28, 1969, part 1, p. 3. On the state preemption law, see E. B. Mann, "In Focus," *Shooting Industry*, January 1970, 4; "Another Anti-Gun Setback" *GW*, September 26, 1969, 4; "Reagan Signs California Bill Barring Local Laws," *GW*, September 19, 1969, 1, 3; Gerald Faris, "3 Councilmen to Fight for B. H. Firearms Law," *Los Angeles Times*, September 18, 1969, part 7, pp. 1, 10; "Reagan Signs Flood of Bills, Including Gun Law, Tax Break," *San Bernardino County (Calif.) Sun*, September 5, 1969, A1, A2; "SF Mayor Rips New Measure on Gun Registration," *Chico (Calif.) Enterprise-Record*, September 5, 1969, 1B; "Police Ask for Veto of Gun Bill," *San Francisco Examiner*, August 11, 1969, 8; "Alioto Raps Gun Control Bill by Sen. Richardson," *Monrovia (Calif.) Daily News-Post*, August 8, 1969, 1; "Gun Control Bill Worries S.F. Mayor," *San Mateo (Calif.) Times*, August 8, 1969, 1; "City Gun-Control Ban Gains," *Long Beach (Calif.) Independent*, August 7, 1969, A7; "Gun Control Bill Goes to Senate," *Oakland (Calif.) Tribune*, August 7, 1968, F7. A similar firearms preemption bill was offered in Kentucky. See "Pre-emption Bill Offered in Kentucky," *GW*, April 10, 1970, 1.

128. E. B. Mann, "The Mann Says," *Gun World*, [June] 1970, 14, 57, EBMP, box 9, folder 33.

129. "Preparing for the Primary," *Armed Eagle*, February 1970, 9.

130. See, e.g., John Lachuk, "Sportsmen's Organized Might . . .," *G&A*, October 1970, 32–33, 86–87; "Americans Take Action," *Armed Eagle*, April 1970, 1, 5.

131. "A Middle Ground," *Casper (Wyo.) Star-Tribune*, September 18, 1967, 4; "Know Your Lawmakers," *GM*, August 1964, 4; "Know Your Lawmakers," *GM*, July 1960, 4 (statement of Wyoming senator Gale McGee).

132. "McGee Adds Opposition to Gun Bill," *Casper (Wyo.) Star-Tribune*, May 17, 1968, 12.

133. "McGee Says He Will Vote for Control of Firearms," *Casper (Wyo.) Star-Tribune*, June 24, 1968, 12.

134. "McGee Insists on Gun Registration," *Casper (Wyo.) Star-Tribune*, July 12, 1968, 2.

135. "Wants Sports Ammo Removed from List," *Casper (Wyo.) Star-Tribune*, February 2, 1969, 22.

136. Chuck Morrison, "Hunting and Fishing: Sen. McGee and the Gun Control Act," *Casper (Wyo.) Star-Tribune*, March 30, 1969, 18.

137. "McGee Says Dr. Eisenhower Gun Law Is 'Unacceptable,'" *Casper (Wyo.) Star-Tribune*, July 31, 1969, 3.

138. "Gun Club Lauds McGee's Stand on Gun Control," *Casper (Wyo.) Star-Tribune*, September 30, 1969, 2.

139. James E. Billings, "Press Release 'Smells,'" *Casper (Wyo.) Star-Tribune*, April 6, 1969, 7.

140. "McGee Reports on Budget, Post Office Reorganizing," *Casper (Wyo.) Star-Tribune*, February 24, 1970, 2. The reason McGee took credit was that he had just introduced a bill that would have overridden the Johnson administration's rule. See "McGee Offers Firearms Bill," *Billings (Mont.) Gazette*, January 24, 1970, 9.

141. "Saddle Burr in the Senate?," *GW*, March 6, 1970, 4.

142. Ann Kormylo, "Wold Raps Proposed Federal Gun Control," *Casper (Wyo.) Star-Tribune*, October 30, 1968, 15; "Gun Control Waste of Time: Wold," *Casper Star-Tribune*, August 13, 1968, 2; "Wold Continues Attack on WHH," *Casper Star-Tribune*, July 30, 1969, 12.

143. "Wold Says Alexander Falls for McGee's 'Propaganda,'" *Casper (Wyo.) Star-Tribune*, April 22, 1970, 2; "Wold Decides He'll Run for Senate Seat," *Casper Star-Tribune*, April 7, 1970, 1.

144. "What the Lawmakers Are Doing: Anti-Bomb Bills Pile Up in Congress," *AR*, June 1970, 50, 51, 67; "McGee Moves to Free .22 Ammo from Curb," *Casper (Wyo.) Star-Tribune*, April 18, 1970, 2.

145. Heidi Norskog, "NRA Endorses Senator McGee," *Casper (Wyo.) Star-Tribune*, October 3, 1970, 1.

146. "Stone Says McGee 'Deceives' Public on NRA Endorsement," *Casper (Wyo.) Star-Tribune*, October 10, 1970, 5; "Tydings Reelection Bid Attacks NRA," *AR*, August 1970, 52 ("Any NRA members supporting [Citizens Against Tydings] do so personally and on an individual basis. The NRA, which is non-partisan and non-political, has taken no position in this or other State campaigns.").

147. "Report of NRA Backing Sen. McGee Called Untrue," *GW*, October 30, 1970, 1–2; "Stone Says McGee 'Deceives' Public on NRA Endorsement," October 10, 1970.

148. John Wold, "Time to Put Wyoming First," *Casper (Wyo.) Star-Tribune*, November 1, 1970, 37–44; "Time for the Whole Truth!" *Casper Star-Tribune*, October 10, 1970, 19; "Time for the Whole Truth!," *Jackson Hole (Wyo.) Guide*, October 10, 1970, 19.

149. Michael Frome, "Rate Your Candidate," *F&S*, September 1970, 60–65.

150. See, e.g., "Let's Shoot Straight," *Casper (Wyo.) Star-Tribune*, October 21, 1970, 15.

151. See chapter 6.

152. David Scribner, "Hoff Answers GOP 'Baloney,' Comments on 'Vile Whispers' in North Shire," *Burlington (Vt.) Free Press*, October 6, 1970, 1, 14; Charles Bonenti, "Hoff Answers GOP 'Baloney,' Comments on 'Vile Whispers' at Burr & Burton," *Burlington Free Press*, October 6, 1970, 1, 14.

153. "Hoff," *Barre (Vt.) Times Argus*, October 27, 1970, 1, 2; "Hoff," *Rutland (Vt.) Daily Herald*, October 27, 1970, 1, 20.

154. Re-Elect Senator Prouty Committee, "Compare These Statements on Gun Control," *Rutland (Vt.) Daily Herald*, October 29, 1970, 14; Re-Elect Senator Prouty Committee, "Compare These Statements on Gun Control," *Brattleboro (Vt.) Reformer*, October 29, 1970, 13; Re-Elect Senator Prouty Committee, "Compare These Statements on Gun Control," *Bennington (Vt.) Banner*, October 29, 1970, 7.

155. Mike Rosenberg, "Gun Control Conspiracy?" *Rutland (Vt.) Daily Herald*, August 22, 1968, 16; Pat Slattery, "Vermont's Largest Gun Dealer in Favor of Stringent Controls," *Barre (Vt.) Times Argus*, June 19, 1968, 13; "Senators, Stafford Cool to Gun Laws," *Rutland Daily Herald*, June 13, 1968, 1, 6.

156. Hoff merely accused Prouty of distorting his firearms control position. "Prouty-Hoff Arbitration Said to be 'Impossible,'" *Bennington (Vt.) Banner*, October 31, 1970, 1.

157. The apology came in the form of a newspaper advertisement and was taken from a speech Hoff delivered on October 7 before the Vermont Federation of Sportsmen's Clubs. See "Phil Hoff Speaks Out on Gun Control," *Burlington (Vt.) Free Press*, October 31, 1970, 13.

158. See, e.g., "Hale Mt. Club Endorses 'Sportsmen's' Candidates," *Bennington (Vt.) Banner*, October 28, 1970, 3; Re-Elect Senator Prouty Committee, "Prouty News," October 14, 1970, WLPP, carton D13, folder 67; Winston L. Prouty, press release, [Vermont Sportsmen's Clubs], undated 1970, WLPP, carton A112, folder 26; draft letter from Winston L. Prouty to Vermont Federation of Sportsmen Clubs, Inc., October 5, 1970, WLPP, carton A112, folder 26; Hugh Barron, "The World Outdoors," *Brattleboro (Vt.) Reformer*, September 15, 1970, 6; "Speech of Sen. Prouty Heard by Sportsmen," *Brattleboro Reformer*, September 12, 1970, 5; Frank Dion, speech given on behalf of Winston L. Prouty to sportsmen, September 10, 1870, WLPP, carton A115, folder 29. The Prouty campaign knew firearms controls was an "emotional" issue that "unites 1 of 4; *a large group of firearms people.*" [Election report from field], September 29, 1970, WLPP, carton A112, folder 26.

159. "Congress Finds Quorum Difficult," *South Bend (Ind.) Tribune*, September 24, 1968, 5; "Gun-Control Bill Passed By Senate," *Indianapolis (Ind.) News*, September 19, 1968, 2; "Hartke Votes with Majority," *Terre Haute (Ind.) Tribune*, September 17, 1968, 10; "Senate OK's Gun Mail Ban," *South Bend Tribune*, September 17, 1968, 6.

160. Jack Alikire, "Black Powder Restriction Bill Considered by Congress," *Lafayette (Ind.) Journal and Courier*, July 24, 1970, 14; "Law Protects Muzzle Loaders," *Columbus (Ind.) Republic*, July 10, 1970, 15; "Hartke Sponsors Bill to Protect Sport Shooting," *Anderson (Ind.) Daily Bulletin*, July 9, 1970, 11; "Hartke Proposes Amendment to Gun Control Act," *Greenfield (Ind.) Daily Reporter*, September 11, 1969, 2.

161. Republican State Central Committee, "A Review of the Actions in the United States Senate by Senator Vance Hartke," *Indianapolis (Ind.) Star*, November 1, 1970, sec. 2, 17; Republican State Central Committee, "A Review of the Actions in the United States Senate by Senator Vance Hartke," *Munster (Ind.) Times*, November 1, 1970, 8C; Republican State Central Committee, "A Review of the Actions in the United States Senate by Senator Vance Hartke," *Terre Haute (Ind.) Tribune-Star*, November 1, 1970, 22; Republican State Central Committee, "A Review of the Actions in the United States Senate by Senator Vance Hartke," *Bedford (Ind.) Daily-Times Mail*, November 1, 1970, 9; Rowland Evans and Robert Novak, "Will Strike by GM Doom GOP Hopes in the Middle West," *Philadelphia Inquirer*, October 26, 1970, 9; "Sportsmen's Council to Back Rep. Roudebush," *Noblesville (Ind.) Ledger*, August 25, 1970, 4; Robert Mooney, "Roudebush Lauds Nixon's Viet Policy, Issues Blast at Hartke," *Indianapolis Star*,

August 2, 1970, sec. 2, p. 4; Robert J. Miller, "Sen. Hartke Has a Sorry Record," *Indianapolis News*, February 24, 1970, 7; Right to Bear Arms, "We Need Your Help!," undated, HHHP, 1970 Senate Campaign Files, box 13, folder Gun Control.

162. Committee of Concerned New Mexicans, "Attention New Mexicans," *Santa Fe New Mexican*, November 1, 1970, D12; Sportsmen Against Montoya, "Attention Sportsmen," *Albuquerque (N.Mex.) Journal*, November 1, 1970, C16; "Montoya Is Deceiving New Mexicans," *Santa Fe New Mexican*, November 1, 1970, B5; Truth or Consequences, "Attention Sportsmen," *Deming (N.Mex.) Headlight*, October 29, 1970, 3B.

163. See, e.g., "What the Lawmakers Are Doing: 'Backdoor Registration' of Ammo Partly Ended," *AR*, January 1970, 34–36.

164. "State Political Briefs," *Las Vegas (N.Mex.) Optic*, October 27, 1970, 6 (noting that Montoya voted against firearms registration four times in 1968); Joe Montoya for Senator Club, "The Truth About Senator Montoya's Stand on Gun Control," *Clovis (N.Mex.) News-Journal*, October 23, 1870, 3.

165. "Sen. Would Exclude Ammunition Clause," *Clovis (N.Mex.) News-Journal*, August 12, 1969, 12; "Montoya Backs Bill," *Carlsbad (N.Mex.) Current-Argus*, August 12, 1969, 1.

166. "Montoya Retraces Gun Control Stand," *Clovis (N.Mex.) News-Journal*, October 26, 1970, 8; "Montoya Considers Gun Repeal," *Santa Fe New Mexican*, October 25, 1970, A6.

167. "Moss Addresses Utah Sportsman Association," *Roy (Utah) Sun Chronicle*, July 30, 1970, sec. 2, 1; "Moss Sees No Repeal of Gun Control Laws," *Provo (Utah) Daily Herald*, July 13, 1970, 4; "Environmental Cleanliness Stressed at Sportsman Convention," *Utah Sun-Advocate*, May 7, 1970, 6; Dave Kadleck, "Pollution? Touch and Go!" *Salt Lake City (Utah) Deseret News*, April 29, 1970, 4C; "Burton Asks Firearms Bill Repeal," *San Juan Record* (Monticello, Utah), March 19, 1970, 2;

168. See "One Small Slip Hurt Burton's Chances?," *Ogden (Utah) Standard-Examiner*, October 15, 1970, 11A; "Campaign '70: Analyst on Moss-Burton Race: 'Both Are Good Men,'" *Provo (Utah) Daily Herald*, October 16, 1970, 5.

169. Lee Byrd, "An Outsider Views Utah's Election," *Salt Lake City (Utah) Deseret News*, October 20, 1970, A17. The fact that both Moss and Burton adamantly opposed firearms controls is not to say there was not any campaign drama related to the issue. In the September 1970 issue of *Guns Magazine* appeared an advertisement accusing Moss of supporting federal firearms controls. Moss demanded an immediate retraction given the "irreparable harm" that such an accusation could have on his reelection campaign. "Magazine Ad Angers Sen. Moss," *Ogden (Utah) Standard-Examiner*, September 3, 1970, 11A.

170. See, e.g., "The Flap About Gun Control," *Longview (Tex.) News-Journal*, October 26, 1970, 4A; "Senate Rivals Are Political Look-Alikes," *Fort Worth (Tex.) Star-Telegram*, August 16, 1970, 10E.

171. Lloyd Bensten, "Attention Sportsmen!," *Marshall (Tex.) News Messenger*, November 1, 1970, 2B; Lloyd Bentsen, "Would You Have Voted for the 1968 Gun Control Act," *Gilmer (Tex.) Mirror*, October 29, 1970, 8.

172. See, e.g., Lloyd Bentsen, "The Truth About Gun Control," *Kilgore (Tex.) News Herald*, November 2, 1970, 9; Lloyd Bentsen, "The Truth About Gun Control," *Longview (Tex.) News-Journal*, October 31, 1970, 4A.

173. Roger Summers and Jim Vachule, "Credentials of Bush, Bentsen Too Similar for Many," *Fort Worth (Tex.) Star-Telegram*, November 1, 1970, 12A; "Bush Supporters Retract Ad," *Fort Worth Star-Telegram*, October 31, 1970, 16A; Ben Sargent, "Senatorial Hopefuls Take Issue on Gun Control Legislation," *Marshall (Tex.) News Messenger*, October 25, 1970, A9.

174. Lloyd Bentsen, press release on repeal of Gun Control Act, October 7, 1970, LBP, box 2, folder Press Releases-Gun Control.

175. See, e.g., Bush for Senate Committee, "George Bush," *Victoria (Tex.) Advocate*, November 3, 1970, 7A; Bush for Senate Committee, "George Bush Doesn't Believe in Hight Behind a Party Label," *Austin (Tex.) American*, November 2, 1970, 21.

176. U.S. Const., Art. I, Sec. 8, Cl. 3 (that Congress has the power to "regulate Commerce with foreign Nations, and among the several States, and with the Indian Tribes").

177. See, e.g., Cleve Corlett, "Hart Hits Gun Control Legislation," *Lansing (Mich.) State Journal*, October 6, 1967, C3.

178. See, e.g., Saul Friedman, "Also Wants Change in Gun Control Plan: Hart to Seek New Rights Bill," *Detroit (Mich.) Free Press*, September 30, 1967, 15A; "Proper Firearm Use Defended: 'Fair' Gun Control Laws Backed," *Lansing (Mich.) State Journal*, August 28, 1966, G9.

179. Letter from Philip A. Hart to Lawrence Powers, September 10, 1968, PAHP, box 186, folder Gun Control; "Controls on Guns Heating Up," *Detroit (Mich.) American*, June 18, 1968, 2; "Hart May Switch Sides on Gun Issue," *Petoskey (Mich.) News-Review*, June 17, 1968, 7.

180. Letter from Philip A. Hart to Denis Lessard, May 24, 1969, PAHP, box 177, folder Firearms Registration; letter from Philip A. Hart to William G. Emmer, March 1, 1969, PAHP, box 177, folder Firearms Registration; "Hart, Griffin Split Votes," *Lansing (Mich.) State Journal*, September 19, 1968, A9; "Congressional Support Growing for Tougher Gun Control Measures," *Traverse City (Mich.) Record-Eagle*, June 17, 1968, 1; "Hart May Back LBJ's Gun Plan," *Holland (Mich.) Evening Journal*, June 16, 1968, 13.

181. Letter from Philip A. Hart to Elliott E. Parrish, September 13, 1968, PAHP, box 186, folder Gun Control.

182. Memorandum from John M. Cornman to Philip A. Hart et al, "Guns (Shudder)," undated 1969, PAHP, box 177, folder Firearms.

183. Letter from Philip A. Hart to R. G. Harvey, December 11, 1969, PAHP, box 177, folder Firearms; letter from Philip A. Hart to X. B. Shaffer, October 16, 1969, PAHP, box 177, folder Firearms.

184. Letter from Philip A. Hart to Charles William Moll, December 30, 1969, PAHP, box 177, folder Firearms.

185. SAM was established "to engage in legislation, political and educational activities to preserve the right of the law-abiding citizen to keep and bear arms, to assist in

formulating properly directed crime control legislation, and to uphold the Constitutions of the United States and the State of Michigan." See "Sportsmen, SAM Is Here!," *SAM Newsletter No. 2*, August 1, 1970, 4; "Sportsmen . . . SAM is Here!," *GW*, May 8, 1970, 5.

186. Tom Opre, "Politicians Beware . . . SAM Is on Move," *Detroit Free Press*, May 24, 1970, 6F; "Defeat of Sen. Philip Hart Number One Target of SAM," *GW*, March 27, 1970, 2; "Local Man Heads State Group," *Traverse City (Mich.) Record-Eagle*, March 9, 1970, 10; Frank Mainville, "500 Hunters Join Forces," *Lansing (Mich.) State Journal*, March 1, 1970, A3.

187. See, e.g., memorandum from John B. Martin, chairman, Michigan Commission on Crime, Delinquency and Criminal Administration, to George W. Romney, on reexamination of Michigan firearms control laws, December 2, 1968, GWRP, box 420, folder Firearms; letter from George W. Romney to W. A. Cole, July 31, 1968, GWRP, box 219, folder Gun Control; "Romney Asks Gun Controls," *Ludington (Mich.) Daily News*, July 23, 1968, 1; "Romney Asks State Gun Control Plan," *Traverse City (Mich.) Record-Eagle*, July 23, 1968, 19; letter from George W. Romney to Price Daniel, assistant to the president for federal-state relations, June 26, 1968, GWRP, box 219, folder Gun Control Law.

188. "SAM to Hear Mrs. Romney," *Traverse City (Mich.) Record-Eagle*, September 9, 1970, 10; "Lenore to Explain Gun Stand to SAM," *Lansing (Mich.) State Journal*, September 5, 1970, C3; "Mrs. Romney to Meet with SAM," *SAM Newsletter No. 3*, September 1, 1970, 1; Frank Mainville, "Lenore Reiterates Arms Control Belief," *Lansing State Journal*, September 13, 1970, A3.

189. See, e.g., Sportsmen's Alliance of Michigan, "Sportsmen!," *Lansing (Mich.) State Journal*, November 2, 1970, D2; Sportsmen's Alliance of Michigan, "Sportsmen!," *Lansing State Journal*, November 2, 1970, C4; Sportsmen's Alliance of Michigan, "Sportsmen!," *Traverse City (Mich.) Record-Eagle*, October 31, 1970, 24.

190. Clark Hoyt, "Underground Campaigning: Smear Leaflets Appear as Vote Nears," *Detroit (Mich.) Free Press*, October 31, 1970, 3A.

191. "WANTED," *SAM Newsletter No. 4*, November 1, 1970, 3–4.

192. "Citizens Against Mansfield Group Forming in Montana," *GW*, February 6, 1970, 6; "Group Organizes to Oppose Mansfield," *Billings (Mont.) Gazette*, January 23, 1969, 19; David O. McKay, "Editor's Outlook," *Southern Utah Free Press* (Hurricane), January 22, 1970, 2–3; "Association on the Move," *Armed Eagle*, December 1969, 4. On February 15, 1970, CAM ran an advertisement officially rescinding "ALL AFFILIATION with any other organized body" "due to legal complications," Daniel J. Masse, *Missoulian* (Missoula, Mont.), February 15, 1970, 27.

193. Letter from Daniel J. Masse to Mike Mansfield, [December 9, 1969], MMP, box 85, folder 1.

194. Citizens Against Mansfield, "Firearms Legislation Can Disarm Only You, Mr. Citizen," April 16, 1970, Benedict Collection, box 45, folder Citizens Against Mansfield.

195. Citizens Against Mansfield, "Citizens of Montana: Do You Know Sen. Mansfield's Voting Record?," February 28, 1970, Benedict Collection, box 45, folder Citizens Against Mansfield.

196. "Clinton Bar Owner After Mike," *Great Falls (Mont.) Tribune*, June 22, 1970, 9; "Mike's Stand on Guns Leading to Headaches," *Havre (Mont.) Daily News*, June 23, 1970, 5; Citizens Against Mansfield, "Taxpayers and Gunowners of Montana," *Billings (Mont.) Gazette*, June 1, 1970, H14; Citizens Against Mansfield, "Attention Gun Owners!" *Butte Montana Standard*, May 31, 1970, 6; Citizens Against Mansfield, "Taxpayers and Gunowners of Montana," *Missoulian* (Missoula, Mont.), May 24, 1970, 14; "Gun Control Repeal Urged," *Kalispell (Mont.) Daily Inter Lake*, May 21, 1970, 12; letter from John Wight to Mike Mansfield, March 6, 1970, MMP, box 85, folder 1; letter from John L. McKeon to Peggy DeMichael, Mike Mansfield assistant, March 4, 1970, MMP, box 85, folder 1; H. W. C. Newberry, "Outdoors with Doc," *Kalispell Daily Inter Lake*, March 1, 1970, 7; H. W. C. Newberry, "Gun Owners Set Goals," *Kalispell Daily Inter Lake*, February 1, 1970, 7; letter from Rudy Kienle to Mike Mansfield, January 21, 1970, MMP, box 85, folder 2.
197. "Mansfield Has New Opponent," *Butte Montana Standard*, June 22, 1970, 12; letter from D. Roscoe Nickerson to Joseph Meglen, May 21, 1970, MMP, box 85, folder 2.
198. Letter from Ashley Halsey, Jr., *American Rifleman* editor, to Daniel J. Masse, June 4, 1970, MMP, box 85, folder 2.
199. Letter from Ashley Halsey, Jr., *American Rifleman* editor, to Mike Mansfield, June 5, 1970, MMP, box 85, folder 2 ("In order to avoid any misunderstanding on the part of anyone, I have written to Mr. Daniel J. Masse as enclosed, and wish you to know of it.").
200. It is worth noting that Ashley Halsey, Jr., refused to step in when the Connecticut Sportsmen's Alliance used editorials and quotes from the *American Rifleman*, in its campaign to defeat Emilio Q. Daddario, Democratic candidate for Connecticut governor. Letter from Emilio Q. Daddario to Ashley Halsey, Jr., *American Rifleman* editor, September 18, 1970, EQDP, box 28, folder Firearms; letter from Emilio Q. Daddario to Ashley Halsey, Jr., *American Rifleman* editor, August 14, 1970, EQDP, box 28, folder Firearms; letter from Ashley Halsey, Jr., *American Rifleman* editor, to Emilio Q. Daddario, August 7, 1970, EQDP, box 28, folder Firearms; letter from Emilio Q. Daddario to Ashley Halsey, Jr., *American Rifleman* editor, July 30, 1970, EQDP, box 28, folder Firearms.
201. See, e.g., "Show Your Voter Registration Card," *AR*, February 1970, 14; "Can Three Assassins Kill a Civil Right?," *AR*, July 1968, 16–18; "Law and Order," *AR*, July 1964, 16; "A Man and His Gun," *AR*, March 1959, 14. It is also worth noting that prior to including this disclaimer, the NRA did not object to persons, organizations, publishers, or news outlets reprinting their editorials in part or in full.
202. Charles, *Armed in America*, 274–75.
203. See, e.g., "Black Panthers and Blind Kittens," *AR*, September 1970, 20; Merritt A. Edson, "In Their Own Keeping," *AR*, November 1952, 16.
204. See, e.g., "Why Gun Laws?," *AR*, November 1933, 4; "How Will They Vote?," *AR*, November 1932, 6; "High Hats and Riding Breeches," *AR*, October 1932, 4; "Hysteria in High Places," *AR*, January 1932, 4. It is worth noting that less than a year prior, NRA executive vice president Franklin L. Orth had applauded the efforts of those

political action groups that sought to affect the outcome of the 1970 "Senatorial elections and local races" as representing *all* the legitimate firearms owners in their areas." See Franklin L. Orth, "A Special Message: Sportsmen and Gun Laws," *AR*, August 1969, 46, 47.

205. "Show Your Voter Registration Card," *AR*, February 1970, 14; Citizens Against Mansfield, "Show Your Voter Registration Card," April 16, 1970, Benedict Collection, box 45, folder Citizens Against Mansfield.

206. See "Tydings Reelection Bid Attacks NRA," *AR*, August 1970, 52 (unofficially endorsing the political advocacy of Citizens Against Tydings). It is also worth noting that CAM advertised itself as a nonpartisan organization. See Citizens Against Mansfield Newsletter, February 5, 1970, Benedict Collection, box 45, folder Citizens Against Mansfield ("C.A.M. . . . a non-partisan political organization, whose very existence is to REPEAL THE GUN CONTROL ACT OF 1968 . . . and to defeat Senator Mike Mansfield"). At no point in CAM's literature did it hint or imply it supported one political party over another.

207. See, e.g., letter from Mike Mansfield to Ashley Halsey, Jr., *American Rifleman* editor, September 11, 1970, MMP, box 85, folder 2; letter from Ashley Halsey, Jr., *American Rifleman* editor, September 3, 1970, MMP, box 85, folder 2.

208. See letter from Allen Martin to Mike Mansfield, October 17, 1970, MMP, box 85, folder 2; letter from Richard J. Conklin to Mike Mansfield, August 11, 1970, MMP, box 85, folder 2; letter from John Staigmiller to Mike Mansfield, August 10, 1970, MMP, box 85, folder 2; memorandum to Mike Mansfield, "Re; Critical Advertisement Appearing in, Among Others 'The Daily Inter Lake,'" July 14, 1970, MMP, box 85, folder 2; letter from John L. McKeon to Peggy DeMichael, Mike Mansfield assistant, March 4, 1970, MMP, box 85, folder 1; [internal Mansfield campaign notes], undated 1970, MMP, box 85, folder 1.

209. Letter from Mike Mansfield to Stewart Ford, October 20, 1970, MMP, box 85, folder 2; letter from Mike Mansfield to Maxine L. Blickenstaff, October 19, 1970, MMP, box 85, folder 2; letter from Mike Mansfield to John Wight, October 14, 1970, MMP, box 85, folder 2; letter from Harry B. Mitchell to Mike Mansfield, September 28, 1970, MMP, box 85, folder 2.

210. See "Mansfield Issues Call to Get Nation Moving," *Butte Montana Standard*, October 18, 1970, 8.

211. See, e.g., letter from Mike Mansfield to M. D. Farnsworth, August 13, 1970, MMP, box 85, folder 2; letter from Mike Mansfield to John W. Bartlett, April 6, 1970, MMP, box 85, folder 2; letter from Mike Mansfield to Barbara Lindquist, March 13, 1970, MMP, box 85, folder 2.

212. "Scott Continues Fence Mending in Pennsylvania," *GW*, October 24, 1969, 2.

213. "Pro-Scott Group Wants Ban on 'Mud-Slinging,'" *GW*, April 3, 1970, 3; Mason Denison, "Sesler's Candidacy," *Wilkes-Barre (Pa.) Times Leader*, March 4, 1970, 10; Ben Callaway, "Politics Splits Sportsmen," *Philadelphia Daily News*, February 24, 1970, 53; "Sesler Rips Scott on Conservation," *Pittsburgh Press*, February 22, 1970, sec. 1, 27; "Sportsmen Choosing Sides in Scott's Election Bid," *GW*, February 20, 1970,

1–2; "Scott Meets Outdoorsmen," *New Castle (Pa.) News*, February 19, 1970, 2; "Senator Scott Will Meet With 'Outdoorsmen for Scott' Group," *Elizabethtown (Pa.) Chronicle*, February 12, 1970, sec. 1, p. 6.

214. See "Republicans Form Group to Retire Sen. Hugh Scott," *GW*, January 23, 1970, 3; "Group Opposes Hugh Scott's Re-Election," *GW*, October 3, 1969, 3.

215. Del Kerr, "Outdoors in Potter County," *Coudersport (PA) Potter Enterprise*, February 25, 1970, 11.

216. "Scott Election Hopes Dimming, Clark Claims," *GW*, June 12, 1970, 1–2.

217. "Sportsmen Choosing Sides in Scott's Election Bid," *GW*, February 20, 1970, 1–2.

218. "Sen. Scott Found Wanting on Gun Control Matters," *GW*, March 27, 1970, 1, 7, 10.

219. Gene Harris, "Sesler's Campaign to Unseat Scott Is Mired in Obscurity," *Philadelphia Inquirer*, September 13, 1970, 22; William G. Sesler, "Debate: A Senate Voice for Pennsylvania," *Connellsville (Pa.) Daily Courier*, September 4, 1970, 16; Del Ker, "Outdoors in Potter County," *Coudersport (Pa.) Potter Enterprise*, April 29, 1970, 12; "Sesler Appears at Demo Rally; Gives Stand on Leading Issues," *Coudersport Potter Enterprise*, April 22, 1970, 14; Jack Moore, "Sesler Raps Sen. Scott," *Lancaster (Pa.) New Era*, April 21, 1970, 17; "Sesler, Casey, Kline Campaign Starts," *Chambersburg (Pa.) Public Opinion*, April 8, 1970, 1.

220. Ford Burkhart, "Shapp Says State Moves Toward Serious Depression," *Hanover (Pa.) Evening Sun*, September 22, 1970, 12.

221. "Anti-Scott," *Pittsburgh Press*, May 10, 1970, sec. 3, 2; "Another Group Forms to Oppose Sen. Scott," *GW*, April 3, 1970, 1–2; "Register Now—Vote Later!" *GW*, March 13, 1970, 3; letter from George Alderson, Citizens Against Scott chairman, to Citizens Against Scott members, undated 1970, Benedict Collection, box 45, folder Citizens Against Scott.

222. "Only Against," *Baltimore (Md.) Sun*, October 8, 1969, A12; "Anti-Tydings Political Party Is Registered," *Cumberland (Md.) News*, October 7, 1969, 3; Jerry Stilkind, "Anti-Tydings Group Tries to Register—and Fails Again," *Baltimore Sun*, September 30, 1969, C8; Bill Burton, "Water and Woods," *Baltimore Evening Sun*, October 7, 1969, D13; "Sportsmen Oppose Tydings," *Annapolis (Md.) Capital*, October 7, 1969, 8.

223. "Anti-Tydings Group Gathers," *Baltimore (Md.) Sun*, December 10, 1969, A19; " 'Citizens Against Tydings' Oppose Gun Control," *Hagerstown (Md.) Morning Herald*, November 20, 1969, 14; "From Our Reporter's Notebooks," *Hagerstown Daily Mail*, November 8, 1969, 1; "Club Hears from Tydings Opponents," *Salisbury (Md.) Daily Times*, November 6, 1969, 14; Alice S. Vlach, "CAT and Guns," *Baltimore Evening Sun*, October 23, 1969, A10.

224. "State Wildlife Group Seeks to Block Nuclear Plant," *Hagerstown (Md.) Morning Herald*, January 27, 1970, 6; "Maryland Sportsmen's Clubs Join to Form 'Citizens Against Tydings,' " *GW*, September 26, 1969, 1.

225. See, e.g., "Tydings Asks Mandatory ID Card to Purchase Guns," *Hagerstown (Md.) Morning Herald*, November 6, 1969, 7.

226. Joseph Tydings, "American and the Gun," *Playboy*, March 1969, 80–82, 207–9.

227. "Anti-Tydings Forces Give Senator 'Welcome' at Fair," *GW*, August 15, 1969, 3; Jerome Kelly, "Tydings Girds for Tough Senate Race, Predicts Another Mahoney

Candidacy," *Baltimore (Md.) Evening Sun*, April 15, 1969, C1; Naomi S. Rovner, "Two Stickers Aimed at Tydings," *Baltimore Sun*, April 1, 1969, C20.

228. Michael Parker, "Sen. Tydings Attempting to Impersonate 'Sportsman,'" *GW*, October 10, 1969, 3.

229. Report from W. B. Doner & Company to Joseph D. Tydings, "Senator Tydings Qualitative Research," May 1970, JTP, series 5, box 4, folder 8, Tydings for Senate '70—Media, 1969–1970.

230. This was also made clear to Tydings in a letter from Fifth District Democratic Club. See letter from Stanley L. Harrison, Fifth District Democratic Club president, to Joseph Tydings, series 5, box 3, folder Tydings for Senate '70—Howard County, 1968–1970.

231. Thomas J. Dodd, *The Dodd Gun Rights Act* (1970), RFSP, box 376, folder Firearms 1970.

232. W. B. Doner & Company, "The Tydings Bill Guarantees Your Constitutional Rights," undated, JTP, series 5, box 4, folder Tydings for Senate '70—Media, 1969–1970; Joseph D. Tydings, news release from Tydings for Senate in 70, July 18, 1970, JTP, series 5, box 4, folder Tydings for Senate '70—Mahoney, 1968–1970; form letter from Bert I. Hickman, Jr. to shooters, July 10, 1970, JTP, series 5, box 3, folder Tydings for Senate '70—Hickman Letter, 1970; "Gun Control," undated, JTP, series 5, box 1, folder Tydings for Senate '70—Crime, Labor, HEW, 1970.

233. Dictated letter from Eleanor Tydings Ditzen to Joseph D. Tydings, undated, JTP, series 5, box 2, folder Tydings for Senate '70—Campaign Statements, Interviews, Questions, and Answers 1970.

234. For copies of these advertisements, see Citizens Against Tydings, "IF YOU THINK . . .," *GW*, August 28, 1970, 9; Citizens Against Tydings, "If Tydings Wins . . . YOU LOSE!" *GW*, May 1, 1970, 8; Citizens Against Tydings, "If Tydings Wins . . . YOU LOSE!" *GW*, April 24, 1970, 14.

235. "Tydings: 'I Need Your Support,'" *Hagerstown (Md.) Daily Mail*, July 1, 1970, 3. For other estimates of the mailing list, see "Junk Mail . . . Those Unwanted Letters Might Have Started With Uncle Sam," *Mansfield (Ohio) News-Journal*, April 28, 1970, 1, 6 (estimating CAT's mailing list to be around 140,000 people); "Legal but Smelly," *Camden (N.J.) Courier-Post*, April 13, 1970, 14 (estimating CAT's mailing list to be around 142,000 people); Bentley Orrick, "Lowe 'Seriously' Considers Opposing Senator Tydings," *Baltimore (Md.) Sun*, April 8, 1970, C24 (estimating CAT's mailing list to be around 200,000 people). According to news reports, CAT bought a mailing list of 142,000 firearms dealers and collectors from the IRS. "Washington Round Up . . . Nixon Sees Growing Opposition to Carswell," *Bridgewater (N.J.) Courier-News*, March 28, 1970, 14; "Won't Sell List of Gun Collectors," *Ithaca (N.Y.) Journal*, March 26, 1970, 15.

236. APORKBA and Firearms and Individual Rights (FAIR) held such raffles. See Jack Anderson, "'Defeat Tydings' Raffle," *Santa Rosa (Calif.) Press Democrat*, July 28, 1970, 4; Marquis Childs, "Tydings Caught in Crime, Gun Crossfire," *Baltimore (Md.) Sun*, July 22, 1970, A13. Another group to get involved in raising money for CAT was the Frederick County Sportsmen's Council. See "Gun Show to Provide Funds for Anti-Tydings Campaign," *GW*, August 14, 1970, 3.

237. "Joe Tydings Threatens NRA If Re-Elected," *GW*, October 16, 1970, 1; "Tydings: 'I Need your Support,'" *Hagerstown (Md.) Daily Mail*, July 1, 1970, 3; "Tydings Cites Campaign Issue Over Gun Control," *Cumberland (Md.) News*, June 30, 1970, 3; "Tydings Blasts Gun Interests," *Baltimore (Md.) Evening Sun*, June 29, 1970, C20, C28.

238. "Tydings Warns Against 'Gun Lobby Smear Sheet,'" *Hagerstown (Md.) Daily Mail*, October 27, 1970, 17; "Gun Lobby Issue Arises," *Annapolis (Md.) Capital*, October 26, 1970, 3; Thomas B. Edsall, "'Gun Lobby Donates to Foe's Campaign' Tydings Charges," *Baltimore (Md.) Evening Sun*, October 23, 1970, C26; Joseph D. Tydings, remarks at an open meeting sponsored by Frederick County Committee for Tydings, September 12, 1970, JTP, series 6, box 27, folder Writings Gun Control, 1967–1070.

239. Phil Ebersole, "Senate Candidates Hear Each Other on Issues," *Hagerstown (Md.) Daily Mail*, October 6, 1970, 18; "Tydings Wins Primary in Very Close Contest," *GW*, October 2, 1970, 1–2; "Sportsmen Back Beall," *Hagerstown Morning Herald*, September 26, 1970, 16; "Beal Opposes Gun Licensing," *Baltimore (Md.) Sun*, August 28, 1970, A12; "Rep. Glenn Beall to Oppose Tydings In Maryland Senate Race," *GW*, July 3, 1970, 1–2.

240. "Tydings Wins Primary in Very Close Contest," *GW*, October 2, 1970, 1–2.

241. See, e.g., "Election Showdown Near!" *GW*, October 16, 1970, 4; "Tydings Reelection Bid Attacks NRA," *AR*, August 1970, 52.

242. J. Robert Esher, "Sportsmen Against Tydings," *Baltimore (Md.) Sun*, June 30, 1970, A14.

243. For copies of the advertisements see Citizens Against Tydings, "Tydings Calls This Ad 'Political Pornography,'" *Annapolis (Md.) Capital*, November 2, 1970, 15; Citizens Against Tydings, "REAL CRIMINALS ARE LAUGHING AT TYDINGS . . .," *Frederick (Md.) News*, October 31, 1970, A12; Citizens Against Tydings, "REAL CRIMINALS ARE LAUGHING AT TYDINGS . . .," *Salisbury (Md.) Daily Times*, October 30, 1970, 19; Citizens Against Tydings, "Tydings Calls This Ad 'Political Pornography,'" *Hagerstown (Md.) Morning Herald*, October 30, 1970, 16; Citizens Against Tydings, "Tydings Calls This Ad 'Political Pornography,'" *Hagerstown Daily Mail*, October 30, 1970, 19; Citizens Against Tydings, "SENATOR TYDINGS SENDS HIS SINCERE THANKS . . .," *GW*, October 9, 1970, 20; Citizens Against Tydings, "The Truth About Tydings and Guns," *Annapolis Capital*, September 14, 1970, 26; Citizens Against Tydings, "The Truth About Tydings and Guns," *Hagerstown Morning Herald*, September 14, 1970, 21; Citizens Against Tydings, "The Truth About Tydings and Guns," *Hagerstown Daily Mail*, September 12, 1970, 11; Citizens Against Tydings, "The Truth About Tydings and Guns," *Salisbury Daily Times*, September 11, 1970, 9.

244. Lou Panos, "Gun Lobby Went After, Got Tydings," *Baltimore (Md.) Evening Sun*, November 4, 1970, A23.

245. "Sportsmen Dump Tydings, Dodd from Senate Seats," *GW*, November 20, 1970, 1–2.

246. Ashely Halsey, Jr., and J. M. Snyder, "Anti-Gun Leaders Toppled," *AR*, December 1970, 22–23.

247. "Beal Gives His Thanks to Voters Around State," *Baltimore (Md.) Evening Sun*, November 6, 1970, C2, C24.

248. "Beall Pledges Support for Nixon Viet Policy," *Frederick (Md.) News*, December 4, 1970, A3.

249. "White House Tactics Hurt Him, Tydings Says," *Baltimore (Md.) Evening Sun*, December 7, 1970, C4.

250. See, e.g., Joseph D. Tydings and John W. Frece, *My Life in Progressive Politics: Against the Grain* (College Station: Texas A&M University Press, 2018, 303, 317; audio interview with Joseph D. Tydings by Patrick J. Charles, July 12, 2018, part 2, 13:30–14:30 (on file with author).

251. Tydings and Frece, *My Life in Progressive Politics*, 316–18.

252. See, e.g., Nelson Poynter, "Sen. Tydings: Was He 'Smeared?'" *Tampa Bay (Fla.) Times*, August 30, 1970, D1; "Ethics Rules for Congress," *Pittsburgh (Pa.) Post-Gazette*, August 27, 1970, 12; " 'Ill Tydings' Part of Maryland Scene," *Indianapolis (Ind.) News*, August 27, 1970, 47.

253. Audio interview with Joseph D. Tydings by Patrick J. Charles, July 12, 2018, part 2, 15:50–16:30 (on file with author); "Tydings Ponders Defeat," *Kansas City (Mo.) Star*, December 9, 1970, 1F; "White House Tactics Hurt Him, Tydings Says," *Baltimore (Md.) Evening Sun*, December 7, 1970.

254. Sam Roberts, "Joseph Tydings, Ex-Democratic Senator and Nixon Target, Dies at 90," *NYT*, October 12, 2018 (available online); "What Timing," *Wilmington (Del.) Morning News*, November 19, 1970, 18; " 'Conflict of Interest' Denied by Sen. Tydings," *GW*, September 18, 1970, 1, 6.

255. C. E. Clayton, "Election '70—Mandate for Repeal!," *G&A*, April 1971, 24–25, 63–64.

256. See, e.g., Barbara Carlson, "Daddario, Duffey, Dodd Rapped on Handgun Control Backing," *Harford (Conn.) Courant*, October 10, 1970, 31; "Election Showdown Near!" *GW*, October 16, 1970, 4; "Connecticut Sportsmen's Alliance Aims to Defeat Sen. Dodd, Duffy," *GW*, September 18, 1970, 3; "Dodd Bill Would Put U.S. in Gun Business," *GW*, July 11, 1969, 1–2.

257. Jack Zaiman, "State Democrats: Sen. Dodd Starts Moving Up," *Hartford (Conn.) Courant*, March 8, 1970, 3B; Jack Zaiman, "State Democrats: Senate Donnybrook Explodes," *Hartford Courant*, February 22, 1970, 3B; "Dodd Announces Bid for New Senate Term," *Bridgeport (Conn.) Telegram*, January 7, 1970, 2; "Senator Dodd Under Scrutiny by Tax Agency," *GW*, January 10, 1969, 1–2.

258. Sally Jo Restivo, "Joe Duffey: A Candidate Democrats Don't Mention," *Meriden (Conn.) Journal*, October 28, 1970, 22; Jack Zaiman, "Senate Race: Dodd Really Shakes Up Things," *Hartford (Conn.) Courant*, October 11, 1970, 3B; Jack Zaiman, "The Senate: Don't Sell Anybody Short Yet," *Hartford Courant*, August 23, 1970, 3B; "Dodd Enters Senate Race as Independent Candidate," *GW*, August 7, 1970, 1–2; Jack Zaiman, "Can Senator Dodd Do the Impossible," *Hartford Courant*, July 27, 1970, 18; "Dodd's Decision Awaited on Race as Independent," *Bridgeport Post*, July 19, 1970, 4.

259. H. C. Weisbrod, "Record Set Straight on Weicker's Votes," *Bridgeport (Conn.) Post*, October 9, 1970, 24.

260. See E. B. Mann, "In Focus," *Shooting Industry*, December 1970, 6; Ashely Halsey, Jr., and J. M. Snyder, "Anti-Gun Leaders Toppled," *AR*, December 1970, 22–23; "Two of

the Big Three Defeated!," *GW*, November 20, 1970, 4; John O. Ainos, "CAT Officials Modest in Victory; Give Credit to Those Who Helped," *GW*, November 20, 1970, 3; "Sportsmen Dump Tydings, Dodd from Senate Seats," *GW*, November 20, 1970, 1–2; "Dodd and Tydings Dumped," *Armed Citizen News*, November–December 1970, 1.

261. See, e.g., "Register All Firearms Says Goodell," *GW*, October 30, 1970, 1–2; "How Area Congress Bloc Voted," *Binghamton (N.Y.) Press and Sun-Bulletin*, September 23, 1968, 6B; "Tennessee Vote Told," *Clarksville (Tenn.) Leaf-Chronicle*, September 22, 1968, 6; "Tennessee Vote Record," *Jackson (Tenn.) Sun*, September 22, 1968, 2; "Gore Supports Ban on Mail Order Guns," *Nashville Tennessean*, July 23, 1968, 4.

262. Gore and Goodell were, however, criticized from time to time by their political opponents for having supported firearms controls. See, e.g., "Sportsmen for Brock Take Aim at Gore in Tennessee," *GW*, October 16, 1970, 2; John Parish, "Bill Brock Gives Warning of 'Tidal Wave of Crime,'" *Jackson (Tenn.) Sun*, October 11, 1970, 11; "Bixby Answers Goldberg on Drug Charges," *Kingston (N.Y.) Daily Freeman*, October 8, 1970, 4; Alex Bontemps, "Gore Inactive While Crime Rises: Brock," *Nashville Tennessean*, October 7, 1970, 14; Charles Holcomb, "3 Senate Hopefuls Clash, but Debate Has No Victor," *Rochester (N.Y.) Democrat and Chronicle*, October 12, 1970, 8B; Charles E. Holcomb, "Praise Buckley," *Ithaca (N.Y.) Journal*, September 25, 1970, 8; Andrew Schlesinger, "Gore Claims GOP Funds 'Onslaught,'" *Nashville Tennessean*, September 24, 1970, 1; Tom Ingram, "Brock Says Inflation May Hurt Campaign," *Nashville Tennessean*, July 10, 1970, 11; Tom Ingram, "Brock Stresses Role of Negroes," *Nashville Tennessean*, April 21, 1970, 9.

263. See, e.g., James C. Free, "Why Southern Democrats 'Returned to the Fold,'" *Nashville Tennessean*, December 12, 1982, 3B; "Bill Brock's Ups and Downs in Politics," *Johnson City (Tenn.) Press*, December 9, 1970, 4; Elaine Shannon, "Gores Says He Won't Run Again," *Nashville Tennessean*, November 5, 1970, 1A, 3A; John Parish, "That's Politics," *Jackson (Tenn.) Sun*, November 2, 1970, 1, 13; Lyndell Jeffers, "National Eye Focused on State's Senate Combat," *Johnson City Press*, October 19, 1970, 15.

264. "Nixon Will Support Rocky, Avoid Senate," *Kingston (N.Y.) Daily Freeman*, September 25, 1970, 4; Woodie Fichette, "Goodell's Prospects Grow Dimmer in Broome," *Binghamton (N.Y.) Press and Sun-Bulletin*, September 24, 1970, 3A.

265. Bart Barnes, "Charles E. Goodell, Ex-Senator from New York, Dies at 60," *Washington Post*, January 22, 1987; "Nixon Stops Short of Endorsing Buckley," *Chicago Tribune*, October 22, 1970, sec. 1, p. 5; Andrew Tulley, "Capital Fare," *Montgomery (Ala.) Advertiser*, August 3, 1979, 4.

266. See, e.g., Richard S. Schweiker, press release, "Schweiker Urges Scott Support by Pennsylvania Sportsmen," October 1970, RSSP, box 20, folder 58.

267. See, e.g., "Election Showdown Near!" *GW*, October 16, 1970, 4; "Sportsmen and the Press," *GW*, August 28, 1970, 4.

268. "20 Gun Clubs Join in Political Alliance," *Dayton (Ohio) Daily News*, November 5, 1969, 29; "Sports in Brief," *Akron (Ohio) Beacon Journal*, November 3, 1969, C4; "Sportsmen Eye Fight on Firearms," *Logan (Ohio) Daily News*, October 30, 1969, 3; "Ohio Gunmen Set Meeting to Organize," *Marion (Ohio) Star*, October 30, 1969, 28.

269. Gun rights advocates made Glenn a political target early on. See, e.g., "Glenn Must Not Make It!," *GW*, December 26, 1969, 4; "Glenn 'Won't Make It' Ohio Sportsmen Claim," *GW*, December 26, 1969, 1–2; Jim Robey, "All Outdoors: Ex-Astronaut Glenn Draws OSA Blast," *Dayton (Ohio) Journal Herald*, December 12, 1969, 33; "Ohio Sportsmen Form Statewide Lobbying, Political Organization," *GW*, November 14, 1969, 1–2; "Glenn Expected to Enter Senate Race," *GW*, August 8, 1969, 2; "John Glenn May Seek Senate Seat," *GW*, January 24, 1969, 1–2.

270. John Thomas, "Group to Fight Gun-Law candidates," *Dayton (Ohio) Daily News*, January 29, 1970, 31.

271. "Ohio Sportsmen's Group Opposes Five, Support Three in Primary," *GW*, May 1, 1970, 1–2; "Ohio Alliance Starts Drive for Members," *GW*, April 3, 1970, 3; John Thomas, "Left Over Notes Give Insight to Campaigning," *Dayton (Ohio) Daily News*, March 19, 1970, 29; Jim Robey, "All Outdoors: Peppermint vs. Mosher," *Dayton Journal Herald*, December 30, 1969, 10; Jim Robey, "All Outdoors: Ex-Astronaut Glenn Draws OSA Blast," *Dayton Journal Herald*, December 12, 1969, 33.

272. Arnold Jeffcoat, "Glenn Says Sportsmen Not Told His Real Views," *GW*, May 8, 1970, 1, 3.

273. Arnold Jeffcoat, "Glenn Says Sportsmen Not Told His Real Views," *GW*, May 8, 1970, 3, 14; Harold Barr, "Youth of Today Top Challenge, Declares Glenn," *Fremont (Ohio) News-Messenger*, April 6, 1970, 1.

274. Arnold Jeffcoat, "Glenn Says Ramsey Clark, LBJ Got Him to Head Anti-Gun Lobby Committee," *GW*, May 15, 1970, 14–15.

275. "The Sportsmen's Splashdown," *GW*, May 15, 1970, 4.

276. "Political Demise of John Glenn," *Armed Eagle*, June 1970, 7.

277. Jack W. Germond, "From Space to Senate Orbit Goal of Glenn," *Binghamton (N.Y.) Press and Sun-Bulletin*, May 3, 1970, B1; Rowland Evans and Robert Novak, "Inside Report: Glenn's Campaign in Low Key," *Casper (Wyo.) Star-Tribune*, April 18, 1970, 4.

278. Joseph Kraft, "Age of the Militants Plutocrat in Politics," *Louisville (Ky.) Courier-Journal*, June 26, 1970, 14; "This Week's Primaries Revealed No Onrushing Political Tide," *Louisville Courier-Journal*, May 7, 1970, 10; "Glenn Inconsistent, Metzenbaum Claims," *Dayton (Ohio) Journal Herald*, March 14, 1970, 15.

279. See, e.g., "Ohio Sportsmen's Group Opposes Five, Support Three in Primary," *GW*, May 1, 1970, 1–2; "Gun Group Takes Aim at Lukens," *Dayton (Ohio) Daily News*, April 29, 1970, 25. The OSA ran a full-page advertisement in *Gun Week* opposing Robert Taft, Jr.'s candidacy. The advertisement outlined in detail how Taft voted for both the Gun Control Act and the Omnibus Crime Control and Safe Streets Act. See Ohio Sportsmen's Alliance, "Notice to All Sportsmen Who Plan to Vote for Taft," *GW*, May 8, 1970, 24; "Ohio Primary Senate Races: Rhodes, Taft Offer Opposing Gun Control Views in Close Race," *GW*, May 1, 1970, 2; Ken Gookins, "Outdoor Notes: How Big Do Ohio Groundhogs Grow?" *Newark (Ohio) Advocate*, April 25, 1970, 13; "Rhodes Backs Fair Gun Law," *Lancaster (Ohio) Eagle-Gazette*, January 29, 1970, 19; "Rhodes Supports Sportsmen's Position," *Wilmington (Ohio) News-Journal*, January 29, 1970, 9; Richard E. Lightner, "Inside the Statehouse," *Mansfield (Ohio) News-Journal*,

January 11, 1970, D5; "Rhodes to Speak at Killdeer: Area Sportsmen's Spot Dedication Is Set Friday," *Marion (Ohio) Star*, October 9, 1969, 1, 19.

280. "Ohio Candidates Offer Views on Gun Legislation," *GW*, October 2, 1970, 1, 10 (outlining the political differences between Taft and Metzenbaum on the firearms control issue).

281. "HHH: 'Must Require Registration, Licenses,'" *GW*, July 26, 1968, 1, 2.

282. For the 600,000 number, see "Minnesota Sportsmen Lead Anti-Head Drive," *GW*,
February 6, 1970, 1–2.

283. Bernie Shellum, "Spannaus Tells Police: Gun Controls Needed," *Minneapolis Star Tri-
bune*, August 11, 1970, 18; "Spannaus Feels Gun Issue 'Inflammatory,'" *Minneapolis
Star*, July 2, 1970, 13B; Bruce Nelson, "Spannaus' 5-Point Urban Proposal Includes
Tight Gun Control Plan," *St. Cloud (Minn.) Times*, January 12, 1970, 4.

284. "State Table," *Minneapolis Star*, November 4, 1970, 5A; Bruce Nelson, "Some DFLers
Back Away from Party's Gun Control Plank," *St. Cloud (Minn.) Times*, September 5,
1970, 5; Bruce Nelson, "Forsythe Claims Lawyers Backing Him for Office," *St. Cloud
Times*, August 22, 1970, 4; "Forsythe Against Gun Control Legislation," *Winona (Minn.)
Daily News*, August 13, 1970, 17.

285. "Fraser, Enroth Disagree on Gun Control, Crime," *Minneapolis Star Tribune*, October 21, 1970, 22; Finlay Lewis, "Elderly Tell Fraser They Fear to Go Out at Night,"
Minneapolis Star Tribune, September 9, 1970, 1, 6.

286. "Latest State Return," *St. Cloud (Minn.) Times*, November 6, 1970, 13; Finlay Lewis,
"DFL Again Holds State Power," *Minneapolis Star Tribune*, November 5, 1970, 1.

287. "Anderson Repudiates DFL Gun-Permit Plank," *Minneapolis Star Tribune*, September 5, 1970, 1.

288. Letter from Hubert H. Humphrey to Ted Van Dyk, October 13, 1970, HHHP, Interim
Files, box 14, folder Gun Control. Van Dyk had privately inquired about Humphrey's
change in position. See memorandum from Ted Van Dyk to Hubert H. Humphrey,
"Re: Gun Control," September 23, 1970, HHHP, Interim Files, box 14, folder Gun
Control.

289. Letter from Humphrey to Van Dyk, October 13, 1970.

8. 1971–1974

1. Memorandum from Donald E. Santarelli to Egil Krogh, "Gun Control," March 16,
1970, RNPP, White House Special Files, Textual Materials, Box 3, Folder Geoffrey
Shepard, Guns and Ammunition.

2. Memorandum from Geoffrey Shephard to Richard M. Nixon, "Gun Control Legislation," August 17, 1973, GCSF, box 5, folder Gun Control.

3. See, e.g., "Claims No Effect on Crime: Gun Bill Can't Stop Killing, Rifle Association
Head Says," *Miami (Fla.) Herald*, April 17, 1968, 15A; "Restraint on TV, Cheap Handguns Wins Favor," *AR*, March 1968, 15.

4. C. B. Lister, "All in a Day's Work," *AR*, December 1928, 31.

5. "Mail-Order Guns," *AR*, August 1963, 16.
6. NRA Office of Public Relations, News Release, "NRA Offers Program on Gun Control Legislation," April 7, 1967, MRP, series 5, box 14, folder 6.
7. "Let's See Who Backs This Handgun Control," *AR*, July 1969, 10.
8. Frank Murray, "Loophole Allows Firms to Assemble Cheap Guns," *Bridgeport (Conn.) Post*, December 17, 1969, 18; "Many Guns Still Available Through Loophole in Gun Law," *Bridgeport Telegram*, December 17, 1969, 13; "Senate Group Says OK: Buy Ammunition but Not Tell the Name?," *Cincinnati (Ohio) Enquirer*, September 20, 1969, 25; "Gun Law Bill Called Loophole," *Binghamton (N.Y.) Press and Sun-Bulletin*, September 20, 1969, 7.
9. "Bennett Ammo Bill Reported Favorably in Senate; Dodd Pushes Handgun Bill," *GW*, October 10, 1969, 1–2; "What the Lawmakers Are Doing: Dodd Seeks New Handgun Restrictions," *AR*, November 1969, 44; "IRS Standards Set for Handgun Imports," *AR*, May 1969, 39.
10. L. R. Kershner, "Sabotage from Within Precedes Loss of Right to Possess Guns," *GW*, May 29, 1970, 14.
11. "No Sabotage from Within," *GW*, June 19, 1970, 4.
12. Memorandum from Egil Krogh, Jr., to John D. Ehrlichman, "Saturday Night Special Gun Legislation," November 16, 1971, RNPP, White House Special Files, box 3, folder Geoffrey Shepard, Saturday Night Specials.
13. Memorandum from G. Gordon Liddy to Henry Cashan et al., "Meeting with Members of the Shooting Sports Fraternity," January 18, 1971, RNPP, White House Special Files, box 3, folder Geoffrey Shepard, Guns and Ammunition.
14. Memorandum from Egil Krogh, Jr., to Chuck Colson, "Support from Gun Enthusiasts," March 27, 1971, JDEP, box 22, folder Guns; memorandum from G. Gordon Liddy to Eglis Krogh, Jr., March 26, 1971, RNPP, White House Special Files, box 3, folder Geoffrey Shepard, Guns and Ammunition.
15. Memorandum from G. Gordon Liddy to Henry Cashan et al., "Meeting with Members of the Shooting Sports Fraternity," January 18, 1971, RNPP, White House Special Files, box 3, folder Geoffrey Shepard, Guns and Ammunition. Nixon's advisors deemed such an assurance necessary given the recent reports of the administration considering putting together legislation that aligned with some of the NCCPV's recommendations. See, e.g., "White House Frowns on Sweeping New Gun Laws," *AR*, March 1971, 19; "Nixon Administration Gun Policy Unchanged by Commission Report," *GW*, February 12, 1971, 1 2; "Federal Law Reform Urged by President," *GW*, February 5, 1971, 1–2; "Handguns First; Then?," *Armed Citizen News*, February 1971, 1.
16. See Ashley Halsey, Jr., "150 Handguns Given Hazard Tests," *AR*, May 1971, 19; "Gun Talks at White House!" *GW*, April 9, 1971, 4; "Friendly White House a Startling Change," *Rifle Magazine*, March 1971, n.p.p., RNPP, White House Special Files, box 3, folder Geoffrey Shepard, Guns and Ammunition; "White House Frowns on Sweeping New Gun Laws," *AR*, March 1971, 19; "Speak Out on Gun Laws!" *GW*, February 12, 1971, 4.

17. Memorandum from G. Gordon Liddy to Egil Krogh, Jr., et al., June 2, 1971, RNPP, White House Special Files, box 3, folder Geoffrey Shepard, Saturday Night Specials; memorandum from Egil Krogh, Jr., to G. Gordon Liddy, "*Gun Week* Editorial," April 8, 1971, JDEP, box 22, folder Guns; memorandum from G. Gordon Liddy to Egil Krogh, Jr., et al., April 7, 1971, RNPP, White House Special Files, box 3, folder Geoffrey Shepard, Guns and Ammunition; memorandum from G. Gordon Liddy to Egil Krogh, Jr., et al., March 29, 1971, RNPP, White House Special Files, box 3, folder Geoffrey Shepard, Guns and Ammunition; memorandum from G. Gordon Liddy to Egil Krogh, Jr., et al., March 26, 1971, RNPP, White House Special Files, box 3, folder Geoffrey Shepard, Guns and Ammunition.
18. "Gun Talks at White House!," *GW*, April 9, 1971, 4.
19. "Editorial," *Handloader Magazine*, March–April 1971, n.p.p., RNPP, White House Special Files, box 3, folder Geoffrey Shepard, Guns and Ammunition.
20. "Trigger Talk," *GM*, July 1971, 1.
21. See Ashley Halsey, Jr., "Handgun Torture Tests: How Much Can They Stand?" *AR*, July 1971, 17; Ashley Halsey, Jr., "150 Handguns Given Hazard Tests," *AR*, May 1971, 19.
22. Memorandum from Egil Krogh, Jr., to Donald Santarelli, "Carl Stern and NBC Coverage of Saturday Night Special Testing," April 19, 1971, JDEP, box 22, folder Guns.
23. Memorandum from G. Gordon Liddy to Egil Krogh, Jr., et al., April 19, 1971, RNPP, White House Special Files, box 3, folder Geoffrey Shepard, Guns and Ammunition.
24. John N. Mitchell, transcript of interview on *David Frost Show*, April 1, 1971, RNPP, White House Special Files, box 3, folder Geoffrey Shepard, Guns and Ammunition.
25. G. Gordon Liddy, transcript of remarks before the legislative session of the Annual Meeting of the National Rifle Association, April 4, 1971, RNPP, White House Special Files, box 3, folder Geoffrey Shepard, Guns and Ammunition, 2, 3–4.
26. Louis Harris, "Public Opinion Analysis: Gun Curbs, Yes; Own Firearms, Also Yes," *Fresno (Calif.) Bee*, June 3, 1971, A10.
27. Richard M. Nixon Tapes, Conversation No. 4–2, Telephone Call with H.R. Haldeman, June 1, 1971, 4:19 p.m.–4:21 p.m., nixontapeaudio.org/chron1/rmn_e004a.mp3.
28. Richard M. Nixon Tapes, Conversation No. 66–2, Cabinet Room Meeting, July 23, 1971, 3:11 p.m.–6:45 p.m., nixontapeaudio.org/cab/rmn_e066a.mp3. Nixon was subsequently briefed that the NRA had supported the "outlawing" of Saturday Night Specials in the past, the organization was being "kept informed of [the] Administration's development of tests seeking objective standards for handguns, and that they will be consulted in the development of legislation if we find such legislation feasible." See memorandum from Egil Krogh, Jr., to John Ehrlichman, "Saturday Night Specials," July 28, 1971, RNPP, White House Special Files, box 3, folder Geoffrey Shephard, Saturday Night Specials.
29. Memorandum from Egil Krogh, Jr., to John Ehrlichman, "Saturday Night Specials," July 28, 1971.
30. Memorandum from Donald E. Santarelli to John Mitchell, "Gun Control—Saturday Night Specials," October 6, 1971, RNPP, White House Special Files, box 3, folder Geoffrey Shephard, Saturday Night Specials ("We should have been the first on this

issue. Birch Bayh has now stolen it from us by setting hearing and introducing his own bill before we were ready.").

31. "Unhappy Birthday for GCA!," *GW*, October 22, 1971, 4; "Ban on Cheap Handguns Supported by Nixon Administration's Spokesman," *GW*, October 1, 1971, 1–2; "Bayh Bill Would Prohibit Sale of U.S. Produced Cheap Handguns," *GW*, August 27, 1971, 1–2.

32. See, e.g., "Handgun Sales Endanger Policemen, Lindsay Says," *St. Louis (Mo.) Post-Dispatch*, September 15, 1971, 10A; "Hruska to Push Gun Control Bill," *Beatrice (Neb.) Daily Sun*, September 15, 1971, 15.

33. Memorandum from Charles Colson to Egil Krogh, Jr., October 7, 1971, RNPP, White House Special Files, box 3, folder Geoffrey Shephard, Saturday Night Specials.

34. There was a plan in place to hold another White House meeting with the NRA and other gun rights representatives on October 18, 1971. See memorandum from Egil Krogh, Jr., to Charles Colson, "Gun Lobby Meeting," October 5, 1971, RNPP, White House Special Files, box 3, folder Geoffrey Shephard, Saturday Night Specials; memorandum from Geoffrey Shepard to William Dickey, "Gun Control Meeting," October 5, 1971, RNPP, White House Special Files, box 3, folder Geoffrey Shephard, Saturday Night Specials. However, the meeting was nixed to avoid "severe political attack." Memorandum from Charles Colson to Egil Krogh, Jr., October 7, 1971, RNPP, White House Special Files, box 3, folder Geoffrey Shephard, Saturday Night Specials.

35. "Cat Is Out of the Bag!," *GW*, October 1, 1971, 4.

36. "Watch Nixon on the 'Saturday Night Specials,'" *Armed Citizen News*, December 1971, 1.

37. "Bayh Hearings Reveal Agreement of NRA with 'Cheap' Handgun Ban," *GW*, October 22, 1971, 1–2.

38. Memorandum from Egil Krogh, Jr., to Geoffrey Shepard, October [19–28], 1971, RNPP, White House Special Files, box 3, folder Geoffrey Shephard, Saturday Night Specials.

39. Memorandum from Egil Krogh, Jr., to William Timmons, "Saturday Night Special Legislation," October 28, 1971, RNPP, White House Special Files, box 3, folder Geoffrey Shephard, Saturday Night Specials.

40. Memorandum from Egil Krogh, Jr., to Geoffrey Shepard, October [19–28], 1971.

41. Memorandum from Egil Krogh, Jr., to John D. Ehrlichman, "Saturday Night Special Gun Legislation," November 16, 1971, White House Special Files, box 3, folder Geoffrey Shephard, Saturday Night Specials.

42. Memorandum from Geoffrey Shepard to Egil Krogh, Jr., "Saturday Night Special Gun Legislation," November 18, 1971, White House Special Files, box 3, folder Geoffrey Shephard, Saturday Night Specials.

43. See, e.g., C. B. Lister, "A Foot in the Door," *AR*, April 1946, 13; C. B. Lister, "Registration—Confiscation," *AR*, March 1946, 9; C. B. Lister, "Pious Subterfuge," *AR*, January 1946, 9; "Random Shots," *AR*, August 1934, 2.

44. See, e.g., "Are Treasury Agents the Gestapo?" *Appleton (Wis.) Post-Crescent*, September 20, 1971, 4; "Gestapo-Like Raid Has No Place in Society," *Columbus (Neb.) Telegram*, October 8, 1971, 4; Art Reid, "Outdoors," *Southern Illinoisan* (Carbondale),

August 22, 1971, 13; "A.T.F.D.'s Substitute for a Phone," *Armed Citizen News*, August 1971, 1, 8; letter from Daniel J. Masse, To Keep and Bear Arms, Inc. director, to Robert F. Sikes, July 8, 1971, RFSP, box 444, folder Ballew Shooting; "Letter from Raymond Reeder to Robert W. Packwood, July 7, 1971, RWPP, box 18, folder 23, Legislation-Judiciary, Gun Control 1971; "ATFD Guns Down Collector," *Armed Citizen News*, July 1971, 1, 8.

45. William Loeb, "Treasury Gestapo at Work," *Manchester (N.H.) Union Leader*, July 8, 1971, 1, 10.

46. "Official Report Defends Raids, Admits Errors," *AR*, September 1971, 26–27; Arnold Jeffcoat, "Continuing Investigation Uncovers More ATFD Errors Made During Raid," *GW*, July 23, 1971, 1–2, 7.

47. "Whitewash Won't Cover All Dirt!," *GW*, May 11, 1973, 4; "Ballew Leaves Hospital; $5 Million Claim Filed," *GW*, October 15, 1971, 1, 5; "Ballew Shooting Report Described as 'Whitewash,'" *Alliance*, October 1971, 1; "Dingell Seeking Additional Information on Shooting," *GW*, September 17, 1971, 1, 6; "More Study Needed in Ballew Case!" *GW*, September 3, 1971, 4; "Ballew Shooting Report Described as 'Whitewash,'" *GW*, August 20, 1971, 1–2. For a copy of the Department of Treasury report on the Ballew Shooting, as well as a summary of the report's findings, see letter from John B. Connally to Robert F. Sikes, August 2, 1971, RFSP, box 444, folder Ballew Shooting; Department of Treasury, Report of the Investigation Regarding Execution of Search Warrants at 1014 Quebec Terrace, Silver Spring (June 7, 1971), undated, RFSP, box 444, folder Ballew Shooting.

48. "ATFD Denies Harassment Charles in Arrest of 27 Texas Gun Dealers," *GW*, April 28, 1972, 1; "Fresh Proof That the 1968 Gun Act Is Faulty," *AR*, March 1972, 16–17; "Ballew-Type Shooting in Detroit Stirs Dispute Over FBI Tactics," *GW*, December 10, 1971, 1–2; "FBI Follows ATFD Steps!" *GW*, December 10, 1971, 4; "How the Gun Control Act 'Creates Criminals,'" *AR*, October 1971, 20.

49. A. H. Pickles, "Why Some View the 1968 Gun Control Act as a National Affliction," *AR*, November 1971, 24–25.

50. "Rep. Gude Asks for Supplemental Report on Shooting of Ballew," *GW*, August 27, 1971, 1, 3.

51. "Ballew Case to Verse by Reader," *GW*, September 17, 1971, 14.

52. "Bayh Hearings Reveal Agreement of NRA with 'Cheap' Handgun Ban," *GW*, October 22, 1971, 1–2.

53. See "NRA Activities in 1972," *AR*, July 1973, 60; "NRA Activities in 1971, *AR*, September 1972, 61; "What They Heard," *AR*, June 1972, 46, 47; remarks of NRA president Fred M. Hakenjos before the Members Meeting, April 22, 1972, *Minutes of the Members Meeting of the National Rifle Association* (Washington, D.C.: NRA, 1972), RFSP, box 488, folder NRA 1972; "NRA Activities in 1971," *AR*, June 1971, 62.

54. "Table of Contents," *AR*, December 1968, 2.

55. See, e.g., "Table of Contents," *AR*, September 1974, 2 (circulation of 1,058,000); "Table of Contents," *AR*, June 1974, 2 (circulation of 1,081,000); "Table of Contents," *AR*, June 1973, 2 (circulation of 1,075,000); "Table of Contents," *AR*, June 1972, 2

(circulation of 1,026,000); "Table of Contents," *AR*, January 1972, 2 (circulation of 1,027,000); "Table of Contents," *AR*, December 1971, 2 (circulation of 1,035,000); "Table of Contents," *AR*, March 1971, 2 (circulation of 1,080,000).

56. Compare "Total Distributed," *GW*, December 28, 1973, 1, with "Total Distribution," *GW*, February 27, 1970, 1.

57. See "NRA Activities in 1971," *AR*, September 1972, 61; form letter from Maxwell E. Rich, NRA executive vice president, to all NRA members, October 3, 1971, BC, box 45, folder NRA.

58. NRA, "Daddy, What Was a Hunter?" *AR*, January 1972, 99.

59. "Why a Hunting Magazine," *AR*, June 1973, 18. The first edition of *American Hunter* appeared as an insert in the July 1973 edition of *AR*.

60. This stagnation or decline occurred even though the NRA and other gun rights advocates both urged political action and provided supporters with the tools to achieve it. See Keith M. Gaffaney, "CRPA Fights Good Fight for Firearms," *AR*, May 1973, 53–54; James N. Spicer and Richard H. Poff, "How to Write Your Congressman," *Alliance*, May 1972, 10; Elliott L. Minor, "State Associations Play Vital Role," *AR*, April 1972, 26–27; George T. Lonergan, "Your Voice in the State House," *AR*, January 1971, 51.

61. See memorandum from Geoffrey Shepard to Egil Krogh, Jr., "Saturday Night Special Gun Legislation," November 18, 1971, White House Special Files, box 3, folder Geoffrey Shephard, Saturday Night Specials; memorandum from Egil Krogh, Jr., to John D. Ehrlichman, "Saturday Night Special Gun Legislation," November 16, 1971, RNPP, White House Special Files, box 3, folder Geoffrey Shepard, Saturday Night Specials; memorandum from John D. Ehrlichman to Richard M. Nixon, October 30, 1971, RNPP, White House Special Files, box 3, folder Geoffrey Shephard, Saturday Night Specials.

62. "Administration 'Softening' Stand on Handgun Control Legislation," *GW*, December 17, 1971, 1–2.

63. See "What the Lawmakers Are Doing: Nixon Handgun Bill Final," *AR*, March 1972, 48–49 (showing the NRA obtained a draft of the bill for comment well before public release).

64. Letter from John D. Dingell to Donald E. Santarelli, December 23, 1971, RNPP, White House Special Files, box 3, folder Geoffrey Shephard, Saturday Night Specials.

65. See Elliot L. Minor, "What They Saw," *AR*, June 1872, 43, 49–50; "What the Lawmakers Are Doing: Nixon Handgun Bill Final," *AR*, March 1972, 48–49; "What's Going on Over Handguns," *AR*, January 1972, 46.

66. Bruce Nelson, "Some DFLers Back Away from Party's Gun Control Plank," *St. Cloud (Minn.) Times*, September 5, 1970, 5.

67. "Humphrey 'Flip-Flops' Again," *GW*, June 16, 1972, 4; Carl Greenberg and John Kumbula, "Handgun Curbs Long Overdue—Humphrey," *Los Angeles Times*, May 27, 1972, part 2, pp. 3, 6.

68. Letter from Fred R. Harris to Ashley Halsey, Jr., *American Rifleman* editor, August 25, 1970, FHP, box 18, folder 16B, Crime-Firearms Control; Fred R. Harris, Capitol Report,

December 4, 1969, FHP, box 183, folder 16B, Crime-Firearms Control; letter from Fred R. Harris to Charles A. North, August 11, 1966, FHP, box 40, folder 3, Firearms; letter from Fred R. Harris to M. M. Alexander, April 21, 1965, FHP, box 9, folder Firearms.

69. Letter from Fred R. Harris to William O. Morse, October 22, 1968, FHP, box 103, folder 17, Crime and Criminals, Constituent Correspondence; letter from Fred R. Harris to Elvin M. Amen, March 13, 1969, FHP, box 143, folder 27, Crime-Firearms Control; letter from Fred R. Harris to Linda Talbutt, August 8, 1968, FHP, box 103, folder 18, Crime and Criminals, Constituent Correspondence.

70. Memorandum from Marjorie Mosburg to Fred R. Harris, undated 1971, FHP, box 253, folder 21, Public Relations Gun Control Information.

71. Memorandum to Fred R. Harris, "Re: Gun Control Position," October 27, 1971, FHP, box 224, folder 5, Firearms Control 1971.

72. David S. Broder, "Cost of Office," *Dayton (Ohio) Journal Herald*, November 18, 1971, 5; " 'I'm Broke,' Harris Says in Quitting Race," *Oklahoma City Daily Oklahoman*, November 11, 1971, 1, 2.

73. "Sportsmen's Conference's Recommends Federation of State Associations," *GW*, May 5, 1972, 1.

74. "Bremer Reported at Other Rallies by Wallace Aides, Policemen," *Baltimore (Md.) Sun*, May 17, 1972, A1, A6; Stephen J. Lynton, "Wallace Shot and Critically Wounded in Laurel; Suspect Arraigned Here; Two Guards, Woman Spectator Also Hit," *Baltimore Sun*, May 16, 1972, A1, A8.

75. "Gun in Wallace Shooting Traced by U.S. in 10 Minutes," *Baltimore (Md.) Sun*, May 17, 1972, A6.

76. Richard M. Nixon Tapes, Conversation No. 725–11, Oval Office Meeting with H. R. Haldeman et al., May 16, 1972, 8:43 p.m.–9:47 p.m., nixontapeaudio.org/chron3/rmn _e725a.mp3.

77. "Nixon Opposes Federal Gun Laws," *GW*, May 12, 1972, 1, 2, 8.

78. "NRA Warns Congress on Gun Control Acts," *Hartford (Conn.) Courant*, May 20, 1972, 12; "NRA Chief: Gun Control No Solution," *Streator (Ill.) Times*, May 18, 1972, 11; George Monaghan, "Gun Controls Still Opposed by NRA, Majka," *Wilmington (Del.) News Journal*, May 16, 1972, 35.

79. Letter from Robert F. Sikes to Maxwell E. Rich, NRA executive vice president, June 19, 1972, RFSP, box 462, folder Firearms 1972.

80. NRA, statement on Bayh bill, S. 2507, undated 1972, RFSP, box 462, folder Firearms 1972.

81. *Gun Week* editors primarily blamed the NRA's policy position on Saturday Night Specials for this. See, e.g., "Nixon Needs Our Support," *GW*, August 4, 1972, 4; "S. 2507—A 'Sticky' Bill!," *GW*, July 21, 1972, 4.

82. Hruska was, however, able to advance several pro-gun "features" in S. 2507. See memorandum from Frank C. Daniel, NRA secretary, to NRA Official Family, June 30, 1972, RFSP, box 462, folder Firearms 1972. On passage in the committee, see "Senate Panel Okays Bayh Measure; Celler Committee Starts Hearings," *GW*, July 14, 1972,

1–2; NRA Legislative Information Service, "Weekly Legislative Report," June 30, 1972, RFSP, box 462, folder Firearms 1972; Muriel Dobbin, "Anti-Gun Bill Approved by Senate Unit," *Baltimore (Md.) Sun*, June 28, 1972, A1, A5; "Senate Unit Oks Bayh's Gun Bill Banning 'Saturday Night Specials,'" *Indianapolis (Ind.) Star*, June 27, 1972, 13; "Senate Panel Oks Gun Control," *Hagerstown (Md.) Morning Herald*, June 28, 1972, 1.

83. See memorandum from Geoffrey Shephard to Richard M. Nixon, "Gun Control Legislation," August 17, 1973, GCSF, box 5, folder Gun Control; John M. Snyder, "The Nixon Position on Handguns," *AR*, August 1972, 54–55; "U.S. Officials Oppose Broad Gun Controls," *Los Angeles Times*, June 30, 1972, part 1, p. 15; "The Text of President Nixon's White House Press Conference," *Baltimore (Md.) Sun*, June 30, 1972, A6; "Transcript of President Nixon's News Conference Emphasizing Foreign Affairs," *NYT*, June 30, 1972, https://www.nytimes.com/1972/06/30/archives/transcript-of-president-nixons-news-conference-emphasizing-foreign.html; Richard M. Nixon Tapes, Conversation No. 138–8, Camp David Conversation with John D. Ehrlichman, June 29, 1972, 1:33 p.m.–1:43 p.m., nixontapeaudio.org/chron3/rmn_e135a.mp3.

84. "NRA Reverses Stand on Handgun Legislation," *GW*, August 4, 1972, 1–2.

85. "NRA Outlines 5-Point Anti-Crime Program," *AR*, August 1972, 57.

86. Arnold Jeffcoat, "Senate Passes Bayh Bill; Could Stop Interstate Trade in Handguns," *GW*, August 25, 1972, 1–2; "Californians' Votes on Issues in Congress," *Los Angeles Times*, August 16, 1972, part 2, p. 5; "Senate Passes Gun Bill," *Baltimore (Md.) Sun*, August 10, 1972, A1, A7; "Senate Passes Ban on Selling of Easily Concealable Guns," *Los Angeles Times*, August 10, 1972, part 1, pp. 1, 27; Albert Sehlstedt, Jr., "Senate Kills Bills to Ban, License Guns," *Baltimore Sun*, August 8, 1972, A5.

87. "Gun Controls Too Hot for Most Politicians," *Chicago Tribune*, June 29, 1972, sec. 1, pp. 1, 4.

88. See memorandum from Geoffrey Shephard to Richard M. Nixon, "Gun Control Legislation," August 17, 1973, GCSF, box 5, folder Gun Control.

89. Republican Party Platform of 1972, August 21, 1972, *American Presidency Project*, https://www.presidency.ucsb.edu/documents/republican-party-platform-1972 (emphasis added).

90. Democratic Party Platform of 1972, July 11, 1972, *American Presidency Project*, https://www.presidency.ucsb.edu/documents/1972-democratic-party-platform. There was an attempt by several Democratic mayors, most notably New York mayor John V. Lindsay, to have the 1972 Democratic Party Platform advocate for "banning the sale and private ownership of handguns." See "Democrats Hear Mayors Tell Needs of U.S. Cities," *Des Moines (Iowa) Register*, June 20, 1972, 4.

91. NRA Legislative Information Service, "Weekly Legislative Report," July 21, 1972, RFSP, box 462, folder Firearms 1972.

92. Marquis Childs, "Democrats' Talk Is Irrelevant to Nation's Ills," *Baltimore (Md.) Sun*, July 10, 1972, A13.

93. See McGovern for President, "McGovern Issues Position Paper on Crime Control," June 9, 1972, GMP, box 97, folder Gun Control 1972; Carl Greenberg and John Kumbula, "Handgun Curbs Long Overdue—Humphrey," *Los Angeles Times*, May 27, 1972,

part 2, p. 1; John Kumbula, "Curb on Sales of Handguns Long Overdue, Humphrey Says," *Los Angeles Times*, May 26, 1972, part 1, p. 3; John Rawlinson, "McGovern Says He'll Aid Minority," *Arizona Daily Star* (Tucson), May 25, 1972, A5.

94. Louis Harris, "Open Campaigning Favored," *Bismarck (N.D.) Tribune*, July 20, 1972, 8; George Gallup, "71% Urges Tighter Gun Control," *Nashville Tennessean*, July 2, 1972, 5B.

95. See "Attention Sportsmen: Which One Will You Vote For?," *Alliance*, November 1972, 1; "Platforms and Views on Gun Control," *AR*, October 1972, 63 (providing Nixon with more favorable coverage than McGovern); E. B. Mann, "Mann Says: It Can Happen Here," *Gun World*, [September] 1972, 16, 74, EBMP, box 11, folder 4; "McGovern Seeks Ban on Handguns," *GW*, August 18, 1972, 1; "Nixon Needs Our Support," *GW*, August 4, 1972, 4; Peyton Autrey, "Great Gun Grab Is *Your* Fault!," *G&A*, August 1972, 34–35; John M. Snyder, "The Nixon Position on Handguns," *AR*, August 1972, 54–55 (by and large defending President Nixon's position on Saturday Night Specials without officially endorsing him).

96. Harlon B. Carter, "Nixon—The Shooters' Man for '72!," *G&A*, October 1972, 40–41, 94, 96.

97. See A. J. Hollowell, "What Gives?," *Armed Citizen News*, November 1972, 1 (criticizing the editors of *Gun Week* and *Guns & Ammo* for endorsing Nixon, not AIP presidential candidate John G. Schmitz); A. J. Hollowell, "No Compromise," *Armed Citizen News*, October 1972, 1 (endorsing AIP presidential candidate John G. Schmitz). On Schmitz's views, see, e.g., Lee Fremstad, "Schmitz: Opponents All Back Socialism," *Sacramento (Calif.) Bee*, October 26, 1972, A3; "Presidential Candidate Against Gun Controls," *GW*, October 6, 1972, 1–2; "Platforms and Views on Gun Control," *AR*, October 1972, 63; "What the Lawmakers Are Doing: House Committees May Decide Bayh Bill Fate," *AR*, October 1972, 64–65; John Schmitz, "State Roundup," *Tustin (Calif.) News*, June 27, 1968, 2; "Gun Control Bill Is Under Fire in Senate," *Sacramento (Calif.) Bee*, July 1, 1967, A7; Henry C. MacArthur, "Senator Schmitz Sees No Need for Stricter Control of Guns," *San Rafael (Calif.) Daily Independent Journal*, June 29, 1967, 22.

98. "Nixon Needs Our Support," *GW*, November 3, 1972, 4.

99. "President Quits Rifle Association," *Detroit (Mich.) Free Press*, February 23, 1969, 6A; "No NRA Membership—Nixon," *Binghamton (N.Y.) Press and Sun-Bulletin*, February 23, 1969, 2A; "Membership Disavowed," *Tallahassee (Fla.) Democrat*, February 22, 1969, 12A; Daniel Rapoport, "Nixon Shuns Link to NRA," *Alexandria (Va.) Town Talk*, February 23, 1969, 1.

100. George McGovern, "The Environment . . . Now and Future," *F&S*, November 1972, 14, 16, 122.

101. See "Reigner—Reel No. 2," October 28, 1972, GMP, box 97, folder Gun Control 1972; "McGovern on the Issues," *Cleveland (Ohio) Plain Dealer*, September 24, 1972, AA1, AA2; McGovern for President, "McGovern Issues Position Paper on Crime Control," June 9, 1972, GMP, box 97, folder Gun Control 1972; McGovern for President, "McGovern Calls for Control of Small Weapons and Anniversary of RFK Death," June 6, 1972,

GMP, box 97, folder Gun Control 1972; response by Senator George McGovern to Women's International League for Peace and Freedom Questionnaire, April 7, 1972, GMP, box 97, folder Gun Control 1972; [McGovern Policies on Crime and Justice,] undated, RNPP, 1972 Election File—George McGovern Gun Control.

102. "President Quits Rifle Association," *Detroit (Mich.) Free Press*, February 23, 1969, 6A; "No NRA Membership—Nixon," *Binghamton (N.Y.) Press and Sun-Bulletin*, February 23, 1969, 2A; "Membership Disavowed," *Tallahassee (Fla.) Democrat*, February 22, 1969, 12A; Daniel Rapoport, "Nixon Shuns Link to NRA," *Alexandria (Va.) Town Talk*, February 23, 1969, 1.

103. These numbers were compiled by analyzing the FBI's Uniform Crime Rates.

104. Jack C. Landau, "Law 'n' Order View," *Billings (Mont.) Gazette*, November 6, 1972, 4; "Liberals Adopt Law and Order," *Philadelphia Inquirer*, September 1, 1972, 7; Henry J. Taylor, "Law and Order Is an Issue," *Napa Valley (Calif.) Register*, July 31, 1972, 4A; McGovern for President, "McGovern Issues Position Paper on Crime Control," June 9, 1972, GMP, box 97, folder Gun Control 1972; Dan Lynch, "McGovern: Cut Fat, Leave Muscle in Military," *Philadelphia Inquirer*, April 16, 1972, 16A.

105. For the sources relative to this paragraph, see John M. Snyder, "Gun Foes Lose Out at Polls," *AR*, January 1973, 44; "Celler and Mikva Dumped," *Armed Citizen News*, December 1972, 1; "No Rest for Gun Owners," *GW*, November 24, 1972, 4.

106. See, e.g., People for Haskell Committee, "When Senator Allott," *Greely (Colo.) Daily Tribune*, November 3, 1972, 9; Evan Barrett, "Metcalf on Guns," *Great Falls (Mont.) Tribune*, November 2, 1972, 7; "Lawmen Support Sheehy," *Billings (Mont.) Gazette*, October 31, 1972, 9.

107. The only notable gun rights political advocacy group formed leading into the 1972 elections was Society Against Mikva. See generally AMP, box 16, folder 11, Society Against Mikva. While Mikva ultimately lost his 1972 reelection campaign, it was not due to the sportsmen's vote. The Election Day loss was primarily due to Mikva running for reelection in a redistricted, largely rural congressional district. See John A. Jenkins, "The Man the Gun Lobby Couldn't Shoot Down," *Chicago Tribune Magazine*, February 14, 1982, 19–20, 22, 26, 28, 30; Bob Lahey, "Long Campaign: A Time to Settle Political Accounts," *Chicago Daily Herald*, October 16, 1972 sec. 1, p. 5; Al Messerschmidt, "Young, Mikva Woo New 10th District," *Roselle (Ill.) Register*, September 5, 1972, sec. 1, p. 2. Furthermore, Mikva's opponent for the 1972 election, Sam Young, also supported handgun controls. See "Mikva, Young Square Off in Non-Debate," *Des Plaines (Ill.) Herald*, September 14, 1972, 1.

108. James T. Wooten, "Stennis Is Shot in Robbery in Front of Home in Capital," *NYT*, January 31, 1973, https://www.nytimes.com/1973/01/31/archives/stennis-is-shot-in-robbery-in-front-of-home-in-capital-stennis-shot.html; "Senator Stennis' Vital Signs Reported 'Stable,'" *Greenwood (Miss.) Commonwealth*, January 31, 1973, 1.

109. Richard M. Nixon, President's News Conference, January 31, 1973, *American Presidency Project*, https://www.presidency.ucsb.edu/documents/the-presidents-news-conference-86.

110. Richard M. Nixon, State of the Union Message to the Congress on Law Enforcement and Drug Abuse Prevention, March 14, 1973, *American Presidency Project*, https://www.presidency.ucsb.edu/documents/state-the-union-message-the-congress-law-enforcement-and-drug-abuse-prevention.

111. "The Presidential Oath and Richard Nixon," *Armed Citizen News*, April 1973, 4.

112. "NRA Reverses Stand on Handgun Legislation," *GW*, August 4, 1972, 1–2.

113. Bob Barnes, "After the Ball: NRA Offers Reward in Stennis Shooting," *Muncie (Ind.) Star Press*, February 14, 1973, 13; Jeanette Kliejunas, "Self-Defense Is Kohler Program Topic," *Sheboygan (Wis.) Press*, February 8, 1973, 26.

114. "NRA Officials Says Stennis Attack Shows Gun Control Not the Answer," *Hazleton (Pa.) Standard-Speaker*, February 12, 1973, 4.

115. "Government Asks Court to Dismiss Challenge of '68 Gun Control Act," *GW*, January 26, 1973, 1, 2.

116. See Ashley Halsey, Jr., "Can the Second Amendment Survive?," *AR*, March 1973, 17–19; "How to Kill a Republic," *AR*, March 1973, 16.

117. Senate Subcommittee on Constitutional Rights of the Committee on the Judiciary, *Layman's Guide to Individual Rights Under the United States Constitution* (Washington, D.C.: U.S. Government Printing Office, 1973), 8. The 1973 *Layman's Guide*'s portion on the Second Amendment was identical to previous editions. See p. 6 of the 1966 edition and pp. 4–5 of the 1962 edition.

118. "More Anti-Gun Propaganda," *GW*, May 4, 1973, 4.

119. Patrick J. Charles, *Armed in America: A History of Gun Rights from Colonial Militias to Concealed Carry* (Amherst, N.Y.: Prometheus Books, 2018), 279–95.

120. See, e.g., John Brabner-Smith, "Firearm Regulation," *Law and Contemporary Problems* 1 (1934): 400–414; Daniel J. McKenna, "The Right to Keep and Bear Arms," *Marquette Law Review* 12 (1928): 138–49; Lucilius A. Emery, "The Constitutional Right to Keep and Bear Arms," *Harvard Law Review* 28 (1915): 473–77.

121. See Judge Bartlett Rummel, "To Have and Bear Arms," *AR*, June 1964, 38–41.

122. "Statement of Senator Thomas J. Dodd, Section of Criminal Law, Americana Hotel, New York," August 12, 1964, JVBPP, Subject File, 1933–1966, box 10, American Bar Foundation-Panel Discussion.

123. See, e.g., Department of Justice Memorandum, "Re: Federal Firearms Control and the Second Amendment," undated 1965, *Federal Firearms Act: Hearings Before the Subcommittee to Investigate Juvenile Delinquency on the Committee on the Judiciary United States Senate* (Washington, D.C.: U.S. Government Printing Office, 1965), 41–48; statement by Attorney General Nicholas Katzenbach before the Subcommittee on Juvenile Delinquency of the Senate Committee on the Judiciary on S. 1592, a Bill to Amend the Federal Firearms Act," Department of Justice, May 19, 1965, 7.

124. Statement of Richard M. Nixon, June 17, 1968, RNPP, White House Central Files, box 26, Staff Member Office Files, folder Martin Anderson, Gun Control.

125. E. B. Mann, "In Focus," *Shooting Industry*, September 1973, 4–5; letter from E. B. Mann to Jerry [Unknown], "Re: Robert M. Price Article 'The 2nd Amendment . . .'," June 26,

1973, EBMP, box 41; Harold W. Glassen, "Right to Bear Arms Is Older than the Second Amendment," *AR*, April 1973, 22–23.

126. Robert A. Sprecher, "The Lost Amendment," *American Bar Association Journal* 51 (1965): 554–57, 665–69. This was Sprecher's second time winning an ABA writing competition. In 1945 he won the ABA's annual Ross Essay Competition for best legal short fiction article. See "Robert A. Sprecher Dies at 64; Judge on U.S. Court of Appeals," *Chicago Tribune*, May 17, 1982, sec. 5, p. 7.

127. See, e.g., William L. Garrison, Jr., *Bibliography of Pro-Gun Literature, 1960-1978* (Bellevue, Wash.: Second Amendment Foundation, 1979); *1975 NRA Firearms and Laws Review*, 33–38; NRA Legislative Reporting Service, "Notes and Sources on the Right to Keep and Bear Arms," June 13, 1967, RHP, box 249, folder 8.

128. See "Minutes of the Annual Meeting of the NRA Board of Directors," April 9–10, 1968, HWGP, box 1.

129. Memorandum from Geoffrey Shephard to Richard M. Nixon, "Gun Control Legislation," August 17, 1973, GCSF, box 5, folder Gun Control.

130. See memorandum from William E. Timmons to Geoffrey Shepard, "Gun Control Legislation," September 4, 1973, WETP, box 30, folder Crime-Gun Control Ammunition; memorandum from Tom C. Korolgos to William E. Timmons, "Shepard's Gun Memo," August 31, 1973, WETP, box 30, folder Crime-Gun Control Ammunition; memorandum from Geoffrey Shepard to Mel Laird, "Gun Control," August 20, 1970, WETP, box 30, folder Crime-Gun Control Ammunition.

131. "Backwash from Watergate: New U.S. Attorney General Turns Out to Be Kennedy Anti-Gun Pal," *AR*, July 1973, 21.

132. "An Injustice to Handgun Owners," *AR*, October 1973, 24–25; "New Problems for Nixon!," *GW*, October 5, 1973, 4.

133. Memorandum from Jack Marsh to Jim Cannon, March 10, 1975, JCP, box 21, folder Dick Parsons.

134. See, e.g., press conference transcript, "The Republican Leadership of the Congress," June 13, 1968, RTHP, box 51, folder Eve and Jerry Show, June 13, 1968; Carl Wolff, "Our Man in Washington: The Cry for Gun Laws," *GM*, November 1966, 18–19; "LBJ Calls for Gun Control Measure Passage," *Traverse City (Mich.) Record-Eagle*, August 3, 1966, sec. 2, 1; Gerald R. Ford, press release, "Statement by House minority leader Gerald R. Ford-Michigan," August 2, 1966, GRFCP, box D7, folder Ford Press Releases.

135. "Ford Replacing Agnew," *GW*, October 26, 1973, 4.

136. "Anti-Rockefeller Stand Brings Nationwide Publicity," *PB*, November 1974, 6; "Anti-Gun Rockefeller to Be Vice-President," *Armed Citizens News*, September 1974, 1; "Citizens Committee . . . Opposes Rockefeller," *PB*, September 1974, 1, 4.

137. Letter from Gerald R. Ford to Maxwell E. Rich, NRA executive vice president, August 28, 1974, GRFPP, White House Central Files, box 2300, folder NRA.

138. Memorandum from Kenneth Cole to Gerald R. Ford, "Firearms," September 6, 1974, GCSF, box 5, folder Gun Control.

9. 1974–1980

1. "NRA Outlines Position on Lobbying Controls," *GW*, June 29, 1973, 5; "The Knight in Rusty Armor Tackles an Imaginary Dragon," *AR*, May 1973, 16.
2. John M. Snyder, "Committee to Conduct Lobbying Study," *AR*, June 1973, 36.
3. "NRA to Step Up Legislative Action," *AR*, December 1973, 15.
4. "Snyder Selected for National Council," *Kingston (N.Y.) Daily Freeman*, November 28, 1971, 3.
5. "Right to Bear Arms Political Action Fund," *Citizens Committee for the Right to Keep and Bear Arms Newsletter* 3, no. 4 (1973): 1.
6. John M. Snyder, "NRA Registers as Lobby to Uphold Gun Ownership," *AR*, April 1974, 16–17.
7. "Act Before It Is Too Late," *AR*, September 1974, 22.
8. "The Terrible Thirty: Do We Need Them?" *PB*, June 1974, 8; "The Terrible Thirty: Do We Need Them?" *PB*, April 1974, 8.
9. "What the Lawmaker's Are Doing: Risk of Anti-Gun Laws," *AR*, January 1975, 56.
10. "Election Results Threaten Right to Keep & Bear Arms: Demonstrated Need for Politicization of 50,000,000 Gun Owners," *PB*, November 1974, 1.
11. "1975: The Outlook," *PB*, January 1975, 5.
12. NRA, "Executive Committee Action Report," January 11–12, 1975, MRP, series 5, box 14, folder 4, 6–7.
13. "1975 Seen Year for Gun Controls," *Allentown (Pa) Morning Call*, September 28, 1975, A10; "Carter Ready to Tackle NRA's Foes," *AR*, June 1975, 17; "NRA Establishes Institute for Legislative Action," *NRA Unified Sportsmen of America Reports from Washington*, May 5, 1975, 1.
14. " 'Never Yield' Carter Says: NRA Past President Challenges Sportsmen to Grass Roots Action," *GW*, March 21, 1969, 7.
15. Harlon B. Carter, "Saturday Night Special," *G&A*, June 1974, 24–25.
16. Harlon B. Carter, "Anti-Gun Hysteria Prelude to a Police State," *G&A*, December 1974, 24–25; Harlon B. Carter, "The Issue Is Crime Not Guns!," *G&A*, August 1974, 30–31, 86.
17. Harlon B. Carter, "Gun Control: Denial of Free Men's Rights!," *G&A*, February 1975, 26, 27.
18. Harlon B. Carter, "Liberalism and Gun Control: JUST WHERE DO YOU DRAW THE LINE?," *G&A*, March 1975, 28, 76. For more on Carter's view of race, racism, and firearms controls, see Harlon B. Carter, "Crime Control = Gun Control = Race Control???," *G&A*, February 1974, 26–27, 76–78.
19. See, e.g., Barry M. Goldwater, speech before the 100th Anniversary Banquet of the National Rifle Association, Washington, D.C., April 7, 1971, BMGP, series 6, box 58, folder 36.
20. See, e.g., "More Amendments Are Due: Assembly Unit Holds Fire on Gun Control Bill," *Sacramento (Calif.) Bee*, May 27, 1967, A5; "Assembly Unit Okays Gun Control Bills; Another Is Deferred After Intrusion," *Sacramento Bee*, May 3, 1967, A12.

21. "Heavier Guard Set to Protect Reagan," *Los Angeles Times*, May 10, 1967, 13, 17.
22. "[Bottom of Page]," *PB*, June 1975, 2.
23. Ronald Reagan, "Ronald Reagan Champions Gun Ownership," *G&A*, September 1975, 34–35.
24. See, e.g., Harlon B. Carter, "The Hidden Dangers in Gun Control," *AR*, September 1976, 49; Harlon B. Carter, "How to Oppose Unfair Firearms Legislation," *AR*, July 1976, 47–48; Mike Barnicle, "An End to Fear: Rent-A-Gun!," *Boston Globe*, February 1, 1976, C5; John J. Fialka, "Anti-Gun Control Lobby Loads Its Artillery," *Nashville Tennessean*, December 28, 1975, 7B; letter from Harlon B. Carter, NRA-ILA executive director, to NRA members, [undated] 1975, TJSP, box 75, folder 2, Judiciary-Gun Control 1975; "NRA Stand: No Compromise on Gun Laws," *AR*, November 1975, 44; "A Loaded Handgun," *Boston Globe*, November 18, 1975, 24; Jim Klobuchar, "Is the Public a 'Radical' on Gun Controls?" *Minneapolis Star*, October 30, 1975, 17B.
25. Letter from Harlon B. Carter, NRA-ILA executive director, to NRA members, [January] 1976, DMFP, box 151, folder Gun Control 1976.
26. See, e.g., Rowland Evans and Robert Novak, "The Grave Challenge to Ford," *Boston Globe*, November 8, 1974, 27; James M. Naughton, "Senate and House Margins Are Substantially Enlarged," *NYT*, November 6, 1974, https://www.nytimes.com/1974/11 /06/archives/senate-and-house-margins-are-substantially-enlarged-democrats -widen.html; Christopher Lydon, "The Coming Congress Will Be Both Younger and More Liberal," *NYT*, October 13, 1974, https://www.nytimes.com/1974/10/13/archives /democrats-await-a-flood-of-votes-exceptions-to-the-rule.html.
27. "NRA Stand: No Compromise on Gun Laws," *AR*, November 1975, 44.
28. Memorandum from Jim Cavanaugh to Gerald R. Ford, "Gun Control," February 25, 1975, GRFPP, Geoffrey C. Shepard Files, box 5, folder Gun Control.
29. "Your Chance to Speak Up," *AR*, March 1975, 15; memorandum from Warren Hendriks to Geoffrey C. Shepard, "National Rifle Association Correspondence," February 24, 1975, GRFPP, Geoffrey C. Shepard Files, box 5, folder Gun Control; letter from Maxwell E. Rich, NRA executive vice president, to John O. Marsh, Jr., February 18, 1975, GRFPP, Geoffrey C. Shepard Files, box 5, folder Gun Control.
30. "President Ford Says Registration Is Wrong," *AR*, May 1975, 54; memorandum from Jack Marsh to Jim Cannon, "[Gun Control Legislation]," March 10, 1975, GRFPP, James Cannon Papers, box 21, folder Dick Parsons; memorandum from Jim Cannon to Richard D. Parsons, "Gun Control Legislation," March 10, 1975, GRFPP, Richard D. Parsons Files, box 7, folder Gun Control Act Amendments of 1975; letter from John O. Marsh, Jr., to Maxwell E. Rich, NRA executive vice president, March 4, 1974, GRFPP, Geoffrey C. Shepard Files, box 5, folder Gun Control (noting that the Ford administration was still putting together a formal position on firearms controls); "What the Lawmakers Are Doing: Administration Out to Get Criminals, Not Firearms," *AR*, November 1974, 44–46.
31. Edward H. Levi, transcript of speech before the International Association of Chiefs of Police, April 6, 1975, GRFPP, Philip Buchen Files, box 18, folder Gun Control, 5–6, 11–15.

32. Memorandum from David R. MacDonald to Edward H. Levi, "Gun Control," May 12, 1975, GRFPP, Richard D. Parsons Files, box 8, folder Gun Control General.

33. Gerald R. Ford, Special Message to the Congress on Crime, June 19, 1975, *American Presidency Project*, https://www.presidency.ucsb.edu/documents/special-message-the-congress-crime.

34. Letter from Richard L. Corrigan, NRA legislative liaison, to Theodore Marrs, June 18, 1975, GRFPP, Theodore Marrs Files, box 52, folder NRA.

35. "Citizens Committee Blasts Ford's Anti-Gun Statement," *PB*, August 1975, 1, 5; Ashley Halsey, Jr., "The President's Stand on Guns," *AR*, August 1975, 23.

36. Memorandum from Kenneth Lazarus to Richard D. Parsons, July 11, 1975, GRFPP, Kenneth A. Lazarus Files, box 27, folder Gun Control.

37. "Sen. Fong Introduces Ford's Anti-Gun Bill," *PB*, September 1975, 2; "Administration's Gun Bill in Trouble," *NRA Unified Sportsmen of America Reports from Washington*, August 11, 1975, 1; letter from Neta Messersmith to Charles Leppert, July 29, 1975, GRFPP, Vernon C. Loen and Charles Leppert Files, box 12, folder Handgun Legislation.

38. "Administration Bill Sponsors to Push Gun Registration," *AR*, October 1975, 54; "What the Lawmakers Are Doing: NRA Legislative Efforts Succeed," *AR*, September 1975, 53–54; Merrill W. Wright, "The True 'Saturday Night Special,'" *AR*, September 1975, 31; "Administration Gun Bill Outlined," *NRA Unified Sportsmen of America Reports from Washington*, July 28, 1975, 1.

39. See, e.g., letter from Harlon B. Carter, NRA-ILA executive director, to NRA Members, [January] 1976, DMFP, box 151, folder Gun Control 1976; letter from Harlon B. Carter, NRA-ILA executive director, to NRA Members, [undated] 1975, TJSP, box 75, folder 2, Judiciary-Gun Control 1975; "What the Lawmakers Are Doing: Hard Fight Centers on Handguns," *AR*, December 1975, 47–48; "NRA Stand: Not Compromise on Gun Laws," *AR*, November 1975, 44–45; Harlon B. Carter, "Carter's Column," *NRA-ILA Reports from Washington*, October 21, 1975, 3; "Ford Position Zapped in CCRKBA Resolution," *PB*, October 1975, 1.

40. Memorandum from Roland Elliott to Gerald R. Ford, "Incoming Mail for the Week of September 29–October 3, 1975," GRFPP, Ron Nessen Papers, box 128, folder Roland Elliott.

41. Memorandum from Roland Elliott to Gerald R. Ford, "Incoming Mail for the Week of November 17–21, 1975," GRFPP, Ron Nessen Papers, box 12, folder Roland Elliott.

42. Memorandum from Ronald L. Elliott to Gerald R. Ford, "Incoming Mail for the Week of November 24–28, 1975," December 18, 1975, GRFPP, Ron Nessen Papers, box 128, folder Roland Elliott.

43. See, e.g., "Big News That All News Media Missed or So Much (and No More) For Polls," *AR*, August 1975, 22; "Do Americans *Really* Want New Gun Laws?," *AR*, April 1968, 16; John M. Snyder, "Why Anti-Gun Polls Are Open to Doubt," *AR*, April 1968, 20–21.

44. Letter from Maxwell E. Rich, NRA executive vice president, to Heather D. Rinker, April 5, 1975, PAHP, box 52, folder NRA.

45. *Firearms Legislation: Hearings Before the Subcommittee on Crime of the Committee on the Judiciary, House of Representatives, Ninety-Fourth Congress, First Session on Legislation* (Washington, D.C.: U.S. Government Printing Office, 1976), 2880.

46. "Pro-Gun Poll Comes as Revelation," *AR*, February 1976, 16–17.

47. Decision Making Information, *Attitudes Toward Gun Control: Overview of a National Survey of the American Electorate* (October 1975), 1–56, GRFPP, John C. Vickerman Papers, box 9, folder Firearms Organizations.

48. "Public Overwhelmingly Favors Private Ownership of Guns," *Coudersport (Pa.) Potter Enterprise*, February 4, 1976, 8.

49. See, e.g., "Harris Survey: 73% Support Gun Control," *Ithaca (N.Y.) Journal*, October 27, 1975, 10.

50. Decision Making Information, *Attitudes Toward Gun Control*, 32. After having identified several objectivity concerns with the DMI survey, I reached out to the Duke Center for Firearms Law for a second set of eyes. I was referred to Alex Jakubow, associate director for empirical research and data services at the Goodson Law Library, who was able to confirm that the survey indeed contained several methodological and objectivity concerns.

51. Press release, [DMI Survey Supported by 39 Members of Congress,] December 18, 1975, GRFPP, Rogers C.B. Morton Files, box 1, folder Gun Control.

52. Letter from Roman L. Hruska et al. to members of Congress, December 18, 1975, GRFPP, Rogers C. B. Morton Files, box 1, folder Gun Control; letter from Roman L. Hruska et al. to members of Congress, December 18, 1975, GANP, box 165, folder 13, Gun Control Background, 1968, 1974–1976.

53. Harlon B. Carter, "Carter's Column," *NRA-ILA Reports from Washington*, December 31, 1975, 3.

54. See, e.g., John O'Dell, "GOP Women Give Reagan Standing Ovation at Newport," *Santa Ana (Calif.) Register*, December 12, 1975, A15; Ronald Reagan, "Ronald Reagan Champions Gun Ownership," *G&A*, September 1975, 34–35.

55. Gerald R. Ford, Address Before a Joint Session of the Congress Reporting on the Statue of the Union, January 19, 1976, *American Presidency Project*, https://www .presidency.ucsb.edu/documents/address-before-joint-session-the-congress -reporting-the-state-the-union.

56. Appointments, January 20, 1976, GRFPP, David R. MacDonald Papers, folder White House Meeting on Firearms.

57. Memorandum from John C. Vickerman to William E. Simon et al., "Firearms Meeting," January 23, 1976, GRFPP, David R. MacDonald Papers, folder White House Meeting on Firearms.

58. See Charles Askins, "The White House Conference on Gun Control," *G&A*, May 1976, 28–29, 105; "White House Hears Pro-Gun Side," *AR*, March 1976, 16, 19; "Alan Gottlieb Represents Citizens Committee at White House Summit Conference on Gun Control," *PB*, February 1976, 4–5.

59. Memorandum from Rex D. Davis, BATF director, to David R. MacDonald, "National Rifle Association," March 12, 1976, GRFPP, David R. MacDonald Papers, folder White House Meeting on Firearms.

60. Letter from Harry L. Tennison, Game Conservation International president, to John C. Vickerman, February 2, 1976, GRFPP, John C. Vickerman Papers, box 9, folder Firearms Organizations.

61. Citizens for Reagan, news release, "Text of Governor Ronald Reagan's Nationwide Television Address, NBC Network," March 31, 1976, GRFPP, Ron Nessen Papers, box 39, folder Reagan—Nationwide TV Address, March 31, 1976.

62. "Urgent! Emergency! Bulletin!," *PB*, May 1976, 1.

63. Memorandum from Ken Lazarus to Philip Buchen, "Gun Control," April 19, 1976, GRFPP, Philip Buchen Files, box 18, folder Gun Control ("The NRA is reacting predictably to the action of the House Judiciary Committee on the subject of gun control.").

64. Memorandum from Ken Lazarus to Philip Buchen, April 14, 1976, GRFPP, Philip Buchen Files, box 18, folder Gun Control.

65. "Ford Against Gun Registration," *Paris (Tex.) News*, April 20, 1976, 1.

66. "Ford Against Gun Registration."

67. Memorandum for Record, "Reagan Activities in Michigan," May 13, 1976, GRFPP, Ron Nessen Papers, box 39, folder Reagan.

68. Memorandum from Mike Duval to Richard Cheney, "Gun Control Legislation," June 4, 1976, GRFPP, Michael Raoul-Duval Files, box 16, folder Gun Control.

69. Memorandum from Peter J. Wallison to Nelson Rockefeller, "Convention Matters," June 9, 1976, GRFPP, Presidential Handwriting File, box 37, folder Political Affairs.

70. Letter from H. L. Richardson, Gun Owners of American Campaign Committee '76 chairman, to Stuart Spencer, July 30, 1976, GRFPP, Michael Raoul-Duval Files, box 16, folder Gun Control.

71. "22. Gun Control," GRFPP, Michael Raoul-Duval Files, box 26, folder Republican Party Platform—Domestic Policy Planks—Contested Issues Analyses.

72. Republican Party Platform of 1976, August 18, 1976, *American Presidency Project*, https://www.presidency.ucsb.edu/documents/republican-party-platform-1976.

73. Democratic Party Platform of 1976, July 12, 1976, *American Presidency Project*, https://www.presidency.ucsb.edu/documents/1976-democratic-party-platform.

74. See, e.g., Jimmy Carter Presidential Campaign, press release, "The Hand-Gun Issue," January 16, 1976, JCPPP, 1976 Presidential Campaign, Sam Bleicher Subject Files, box 34, folder Gun Control.

75. See, e.g., "Ford-Carter Views on Guns," *AR*, October 1976, 24; "What the Lawmakers Are Doing: Ford Signs NRA-Backed Measure," *AR*, October 1976, 52–53; Harlon B. Carter, "Anti-Gunners Surround Jimmy Carter," *AR*, October 1976, 51; "Rifle Association Chief Hails Ford Pro-Gun Stance," *Oklahoma City Daily Oklahoman*, September 16, 1976, 54; "What the Lawmakers Are Doing: New Gun Curbs Urged by Party," *AR*, September 1976, 50; NRA-ILA, ews release, "President Gives Strong Pro-Firearms Statement," September 16, 1976, GRFPP, White House Central Files, box 2300, folder NRA.

76. See, e.g., "What the Lawmakers Are Doing: Two Gun Control Bills Still Loom as Threat," *AR*, July 1976, 46; "Sen. Mansfield Says '76 Action Unlikely on Gun Bill," *Arizona Republic* (Phoenix), May 22, 1976, A23.

77. Letter from Gerald R. Ford to Ashley Halsey, Jr., *American Rifleman* editor, September 14, 1976, GRFPP, Wayne Valis Files, box 5, folder Gun Control Meeting; "Ford-Carter Views on Guns," *AR*, October 1976, 24.

78. James Deakin, "Ford Promises Crusade Against Crime," *St. Louis (Mo.) Post-Dispatch*, September 27, 1976, 1A, 4A (emphasis added).

79. See letter from Lindsey Henderson, Jr., Georgia Wildlife Federation president, to Jimmy Carter, July 20, 1976, CNP, box 20, folder Gun Control.

80. Memorandum from Conservationists for Cater to Stu Eizenstat, "Possible NRA-Gun Control Problem," July 8, 1976, JCPPP, 1976 Presidential Campaign, Sam Bleicher Subject Files, box 34, folder Gun Control.

81. Memorandum from Jane Yarn to Stu Eizenstat, "Registration of Handguns," August 6, 1976, JCPPP, Sam Bleicher Subject Files, box 34, folder Gun Control.

82. Memorandum from Thomas Kimball, Jimmy Carter for President Task Force, "Sportsmen's Concern with Gun Control," August 6, 1976, JCPPP, Sam Bleicher Subject Files, box 34, folder Gun Control; memorandum from Stu Eizenstat to Jimmy Carter, "Re: Gun Control," August 3, 1976, CNP, box 20, folder Gun Control.

83. Form letter from Tom Lowndes to "Shooting Enthusiast," undated 1976, JCPPP, 1976 Presidential Campaign, Jane Yarn Subject Files, box 253, folder Gun Control.

84. Form letter from Jim Morrison, Conservationists for Carter, to sportsmen, undated 1976, JCPPP, 1976 Presidential Campaign, Jane Yarn Subject Files, box 253, folder Gun Control.

85. Jimmy Carter Presidential Campaign, flyer, "Jimmy Carter on Guns and Hunting," undated 1976, JCPPP, 1976 Presidential Campaign, Jane Yarn Subject Files, box 253, folder Gun Control.

86. Jimmy Carter for President, press release, "Gerald Ford's Record on Gun Control," undated 1976, JCPPP, Sam Bleicher Subject Files, box 34, folder Gun Control.

87. See, e.g., "President Issues Pro-Gun Statement," *PB*, October 1976, 8, 10; Jeffrey S. John, "Carter's Secret Stand on Firearms," *G&A*, October 1976, 33–34, 130–34; "What the Lawmakers Are Doing: New Gun Curbs Urged by Party," *AR*, September 1976, 50; "Jimmy Carter Is Anti-Gun," *Armed Citizen News*, September 1976, 3–4; "Democratic Convention Indulges in Anti-Gun Lust as Candidates, Platform, Fund Raiser Call for Gun Ban," *PB*, August 1976, 6–7; Ted Lattanzio, "National Democratic Platform Has Anti-Gun Plank," *NRA-ILA Reports from Washington*, July 7, 1976, 1; "Carter's Suspicious Cronies," *GW*, July 2, 1976, 1; "Carter Fund-Raiser Mounts Attack on NRA," *AR*, June 1976, 39.

88. Form letter from P. M. Goldman, Georgia Outdoor Sportsmen's Club, to firearms owners, undated 1976, JCPPP, 1976 Presidential Campaign, Thomas Lowndes, Jr., Subject File, box 302, folder Gun Control.

89. Harlon B. Carter, "Carter's Column," *NRA-ILA Reports from Washington*, September 20, 1976, 2.

90. Memorandum from Sam Bleicher to Carlton Neville, "Attached Paper on Ford Position on Gun Control," October 1, 1976, JCPPP, 1976 Presidential Campaign, Jane Yarn Subject Files, box 253, folder Gun Control.

91. See letter from Jim Morrison, Conservationists for Carter executive director, to Seward Eber, Vermont Natural Resources Council executive director, JCPPP, 1976 Presidential Campaign, Jane Yarn Subject Files, box 253, folder Gun Control; letter from Jim Morrison, Conservationists for Carter executive director, to Carlton Neville, September 30, 1976, JCPPP, 1976 Presidential Campaign, Thomas Lowndes, Jr. Subject File, box 302, folder Guns and Hunting.

92. George Reiger, "*Field & Stream* Interviews Jimmy Carter," *F&S*, November 1976, 102–5; Charles Elliott, "Ford, Carter on the Issues," *OL*, November 1976, 82–83, 157.

93. E. B. Mann, "Our Endangered Tradition: The Record Speaks," *F&S*, November 1976, 14, 20.

94. Letter from Ashley Halsey, Jr., *American Rifleman* editor, to John M. Carlin, Democratic Presidential Committee southwest regional coordinator, October 5, 1976, JCPPP, Sam Bleicher Subject Files, box 34, folder Gun Control.

95. Compare "Table of Contents," *AR*, November 1976, 4 (showing a circulation of 1,125,000), with "Table of Contents," *AH*, November 1974, 4 (showing the last publicized *American Hunter* circulation at 165,000).

96. From the first, October 1973 issue of *American Hunter* through the October 1976 issue, not one article or editorial appeared that remotely resembled the politically charged articles and editorials in the pages of *American Rifleman*. The November 1976 issue of *American Hunter* was notably the first and only issue until November 1977. Subsequently, following infamous Cincinnati Revolt of 1977, where the NRA's voting members reformed the organization to oppose any and all firearms controls, issues of *American Hunter* contained a reoccurring segment titled "Your NRA Update," which frequently contained politically charged articles and editorials. See, e.g., "Hunters Stunned by F.W.S. Study," *AH*, March 1978, 9–10; "Gun Owners Score Wings in Off Year Elections," *AH*, February 1978, 12; "NRA Opposes Alaskan Bill," *AH*, January 1978, 12; "Field Rep Program Increased by NRA," *AH*, December 1977, 10, 12.

97. "Why a Hunting Magazine," *AR*, June 1973, 18.

98. Letter from Gerald R. Ford to Ashley Halsey, Jr., *American Rifleman* editor, September 14, 1976, GRFPP, Wayne Valis Files, box 5, folder Gun Control Meeting; "Ford-Carter Views on Guns," *AR*, October 1976, 24.

99. Letter from Ashley Halsey, Jr., *American Rifleman* editor, to John M. Carlin, Democratic Presidential Committee southwest regional coordinator, October 5, 1976, JCPPP, Sam Bleicher Subject Files, box 34, folder Gun Control.

100. "Mr. Carter's Position Paper on Guns, Hunting," *AH*, November 1976, 12–13.

101. Ashley Halsey, Jr., "The Election vs. You as a Hunter," *AH*, November 1976, 11–13.

102. "Transcript of the Final Debate Between 2 Presidential Candidates," *NYT*, October 23, 1976, https://www.nytimes.com/1976/10/23/archives/transcript-of-the-final-debate-between-2-presidential-candidates.html.

103. "Gallup Presidential Election Trial-Heat Trends, 1936–2008," undated, *Gallup*, https://web.archive.org/web/20170630070844/http://www.gallup.com/poll/110548/gallup-presidential-election-trialheat-trends-19362004.aspx#4.

104. See, e.g., "Carter Victor Raises Hope for National Law (Despite Pro-Gun Lobby)," *Washington Report*, November 1976, DNFP, box 151, folder Gun Control 1976.

105. Eric Rohrbach, "Victory Fund Helps Pro-Gun Candidates," *PB*, July 1976, 2.

106. "Target 66," *PB*, August 1976, 10.

107. Form letter from Gun Owners of America Target '76 to Robert F. Sikes, undated 1976, RFSP, box 627, folder Firearms 1976.

108. Harlon B. Carter, "Why We Must Fight on Against Gun Controls," *AR*, November 1976, 18.

109. See, e.g., Michael Frome, "Rate Your Candidate," *F&S*, September 1970, 60–65.

110. But see E. B. Mann, "Our Endangered Tradition: The Elections," *F&S*, March 1977, 108 (asserting that the "score [was] about even: some wins, some losses," but a "far cry from the upheaval of pro-gun voting strength we hoped for and tried to engender").

111. See, e.g., Ashely Halsey, Jr., and J. M. Snyder, "Anti-Gun Leaders Toppled," *AR*, December 1970, 22–23; "Sportsmen Dump Tydings, Dodd from Senate Seats," *GW*, November 20, 1970, 1–2; Lou Panos, "Gun Lobby Went After, Got Tydings," *Baltimore (Md.) Evening Sun*, November 4, 1970, A23.

112. "White House Tactics Hurt Him, Tydings Says," *Baltimore (Md.) Evening Sun*, December 7, 1970, C4.

113. Letter from Joseph D. Tydings to Don C. Matchan, May 9, 1974, JTP, series 8, box 1, folder Gun Control 1965–1983.

114. See Kay Mills, "It's Who You Coalesce," *Arizona Daily Star* (Tucson), May 3, 1976, A11; Norman Wilson, "Tydings Issues Major Paper Repeating Stands on Crime," *Baltimore (Md.) Evening Sun*, April 20, 1976, pp. C1–C2; Joseph D. Tydings, "Tydings Responds to Questions on Conservation, Handguns," *Frederick (Md.) News*, March 24, 1976, A4.

115. Bill Burton, "Tydings and Guns—Again," *Baltimore (Md.) Sun*, May 16, 1976, H2; "Group Again Will Oppose Tydings Bid," *Cumberland (Md.) Sunday Times*, April 25, 1976, 14.

116. Joseph D. Tydings, "Mr. Tydings Explains His New Stand on Guns," *Baltimore (Md.) Sun*, May 12, 1976, A14; "Tydings Labels Criticism by Sarbanes as 'Personal,'" *Hagerstown (Md.) Daily Mail*, May 6, 1976, 5; "Tydings Trying to Defuse Gun Control Support Issue," *Cumberland (Md.) News*, May 6, 1976, 2; Barry C. Rascovar, "Tydings Admits 'Mistake' in Seeking Curb on Rifles," *Baltimore Sun*, May 5, 1976, C1; Robert Timberg, "Tydings: Major Effort Set to Win Over Old Gun-Control Adversaries," *Baltimore Evening Sun*, May 4, 1976, C2; Barry C. Rascovar, "Gun Issue Continues to Dog Tydings," *Baltimore Sun*, May 4, 1976, C1–C2.

117. Robert Timberg, "Tydings Favors Mandatory Jail Terms," *Baltimore (Md.) Evening Sun*, May 11, 1976, C2.

118. David Goeller, "Sarbanes Trounces Tydings in Maryland Race for U.S. Senate Seat," *Cumberland (Md.) News*, May 19, 1976, 1.

119. "Tydings, Sarbanes Clash Over Jobs," *Cumberland (Md.) Evening Times*, May 17, 1976, 3; Paul Bertorelli, "Sarbanes Favors Gun Control, 'Gradle to Grave' Health Plan," *Hagerstown (Md.) Daily Mail*, May 13, 1976, 8.

120. "Candidates Rated on Stands for Right to Gun Ownership," *Hagerstown (Md.) Daily Mail*, October 29, 1976, 4.

121. Ralph Nader Congress Project, *The Judiciary Committees: A Study of the House and Judiciary Committees* (New York: Grossman, 1975), 326.

122. "Streamlined NRA Staff Offers More Activities Within Balanced Budget," *AR*, January 1977, 18.

123. "Carter Resigns as Head of ILA," *AR*, January 1977, 42.

124. Craig G. Mader, "Editor's Mailbag: Rifle Association Infiltrated, He Says," *Benton Harbor (Mich.) News-Palladium*, February 2, 1977, 2.

125. "Progress Made Toward New NRA Headquarters," *AR*, August 1976, 14. The decision to move the NRA headquarters was not really a surprise. The organization announced the possibility of such a move as early as 1971. See "National Shooting Center Proposed," *AR*, May 1971, 42.

126. See John F. McManus, "NRA Being Subverted?" *Del Rio (Tex.) News Herald*, May 15, 1977, 7; John F. McManus, "Open Revolt Threatened," *Centralia (Wash.) Daily Chronicle*, May 14, 1977, 6.

127. In 1975 alone, the NRA-ILA raised over $4,000,000 for operations in its first year—eight times its annual budget of $500,000. See "NRA Stand: No Compromise on Gun Laws," *AR*, November 1975, 44.

128. A creative memorandum for the National Rifle Association on the National Outdoors Center, May 1977, EDP, box 121, folder Report 2867B.

129. "Membership Drive, Survey Help NRA," *AR*, May 1977, 50.

130. E. B. Mann, "Our Endangered Tradition: For the NRA: A Mandate," *F&S*, August 1977, 14–15.

131. "The First Job: Protecting the Second Amendment," *AR*, May 1977, 54

132. "NRA Unwelcome in Washington: Annual Meeting Switched to Cincinnati," *Kingston (N.Y.) Daily Freeman*, May 20, 1977, 5.

133. Harlon B. Carter, "This Is Your NRA," *AR*, March 1978, 60.

134. See, e.g., "Institute Reports: Carter White House Gets Taste of Gun Lobby Might," *AR*, July 1978, 78; "Your Check on Congress!," *AR*, January 1978, 64.

135. Harlon B. Carter quote taken from "Guns: A Rare Look at the NRA," *60 Minutes*, September 18, 1977, available at https://www.youtube.com/watch?v=cKWhZofa2BU.

136. See, e.g., E. B. Mann, "Our Endangered Tradition: The NRA: Bigger, Better, Bolder," *F&S*, September 1979, 10, 28; E. B. Mann, "Our Endangered Tradition: The NRA: An Update," *F&S*, November 1978, 8, 10, 67; "Mailroom Problems at NRA Headquarters Will Be Corrected," *AR*, October 1977, 8; "By Laws Available," *AR*, October 1977, 60–68; Jim Carmichael, "The NRA Revolution," *OL*, September 1977, 102–5; "Your NRA Update: Executive Committee Meets," *AR*, September 1977, 8, 10; E. B. Mann, "Our Endangered Tradition: For the NRA: A Mandate," *F&S*, August 1977, 14–15; "Concerned NRA Members Redirect Their Association," *AR*, July 1977, 16–17.

137. The circulation numbers of AR weigh this out. At the time of the Cincinnati Revolt in 1977, circulation was at 1,242,000. "Table of Contents," AR, June 1977, 4. A year later, it dropped as low as 1,040,000. "Table of Contents," AR, May 1977, 4.
138. "Membership Hits New High of More than 1.3 Million," NRA Official Journal, reprinted in AR, December 1979, 1.
139. Memorandum from Robert Lipshutz et al. to Jimmy Carter, "Draft Handgun Control Legislation," June 13, 1977, JCPP, Stuart Eizenstat Subject File, box 165, folder Gun Control.
140. For an accurate summary of the draft bill's contents, see memorandum from Stuart Eizenstat to Annie M. Gutierrez, "Summary of Draft Handgun Legislation," July 18, 1977, JCPP, Stuart Eizenstat Subject File, box 165, folder Gun Control.
141. "Possible Move Seen on BATF/Justice Dept Bill," Weekly Bullet, June 27, 1977, JCPP, Annie Gutierrez's Subject File, box 20, folder Gun Control.
142. See "CCRKBA Leads Fight in Nation's Capital for Gun Owners' Rights as Snyder Moves to Thwart White House-Congressional Anti-Gun Gang Up," PB, September 1977, 4–5.
143. The memorandum was stapled to a CCRKBA letter dated September 13, 1977, which denotes the memorandum was written not long after the letter's receipt. See "Reasons for Proceeding Expeditiously with an Administration Handgun Control Proposal," [mid-to-late September 1977,] JCPP, Annie Gutierrez's Subject File, box 20, folder Gun Control; letter from John M. Snyder, CCRKBA, to Annie M. Gutierrez, September 13, 1977, JCPP, Annie Gutierrez's Subject File, box 20, folder Gun Control.
144. "Reasons for Proceeding Expeditiously with an Administration Handgun Control Proposal."
145. See memorandum to media liaison staff, "Gun Control," July 29, 1977, JCPP, Press Files, box 76, folder Handgun Control; memorandum from Stuart Eizenstat to Jimmy Carter, "Gun Control Bill," July 22, 1977, JCPP, Stuart Eizenstat Subject File, box 165, folder Gun Control.
146. "Worst Firearms Bill Yet Has White House Okay," AR, February 1978, 47.
147. Memorandum from Stuart Eizenstat to Annie M. Gutierrez, "Summary of Draft Handgun Legislation," July 18, 1977, JCPP, Stuart Eizenstat Subject File, box 165, folder Gun Control.
148. Memorandum from WBJ to Stuart Eizenstat and Bert Carp, "Crime Message and Gun Control," March 1, 1978, JCPP, Annie Gutierrez's Subject File, box 20, folder Gun Control.
149. Firearms control proponents in Congress frequently requested that President Carter be more forthright on the issue. See, e.g., letter from Donald M. Fraser et al. to Jimmy Carter, July 31, 1977, DMFP, box 151, folder Gun Control 1977.
150. See Memorandum from Annie Gutierrez to [Franklin White], "[Handguns]," July 2, 1978, JCPP, Franklin White Subject File, box 9, folder Handgun Working File; memorandum from Stuart Eizenstat and Annie Gutierrez to Jimmy Carter, "Handgun Policy," May 23, 1978, JCPP, Stuart Eizenstat Subject File, box 165, folder Gun

Control; memorandum to media liaison, [Gun Control,] April 27, 1978, JCPP, White House Press Office, box 16, folder Gun Control.

151. See "Firearms," *Federal Register* 43 (March 21, 1978): 11803–10.

152. Memorandum from Annie Gutierrez to [Franklin White], "[Handguns]," July 2, 1978, JCPP, Franklin White Subject File, box 9, folder Handgun Working File.

153. Paul Stone, "Battle Lines Are Drawn in News Gun Control Fight," *Boston Globe*, July 23, 1978, A3.

154. "DeConcini Says Ad Was Wrong," *Arizona Daily Sun* (Flagstaff), July 30, 1978, 5; "Congressman Ashbrook Skewers U.S. Treasury Department Officials as CCRKBA and NRA Unite to Battle Proposed BATF Firearms Regulations," PB, June 1978, 4–5, 7; Tom Fegely, "Outdoors: Rifle Association, Sen. Schweiker Take Aim at Treasury Dept. Firearms Registration Proposal," *Allentown (Pa.) Morning Call*, April 18, 1978, C3.

155. "Looking Back on the 95th Congress," AR, December 1978, 81, 82; "Carter White House Gets Taste of Gun Lobby Might," AR, July 1978, 78.

156. See, e.g., Charles Stafford, "The Rifle Lobby Takes Aim and Again Hits a Bull's-Eye," *St. Petersburg (Fla.) Times*, June 12, 1978, pp. 1A, 5A; "Bauman Blasts BATF 'Honored' to Be CCRKBA Advisor," PB, June 1978, 1, 3.

157. "Carter White House Gets Taste of Gun Lobby Might," AR, July 1978, 78–80.

158. "BATF Budget Cut by Senate 61–31," AR, September 1978, 100–101; "Congress Vetoes BATF Reg Funds," AR, August 1978, 75–76.

159. Memorandum from Annie Gutierrez to [Franklin White], "[Handguns,]" July 2, 1978, JCPP, Franklin White Subject File, box 9, folder Handgun Working File.

160. Neal Knox, "The Front Line: Choosing Political Candidates," AR, October 1978, 83–84. Conversely, in line with previous election cycles, the CCRKBA published their political grades in full. See "Citizens Committee for the Right to Keep and Bear Arms Compiles Congressional Votes on Firearms Legislation," PB, September 1978, 1, 3–5.

161. Federal Election Commission, "Leading PACs in 1978 Elections," *The Washington Lobby* (Washington, D.C.: Congressional Quarterly, 1979), 75; E. B. Mann, "Our Endangered Tradition: Let's Not Fight Each Other!," *F&S*, February 1979, 14, 16; "Gun Lobby's Mixed Record," *Lincoln (Neb.) Star Journal*, January 17, 1979, 8; "Pro-Gun Voters Shape 96th Congress," AR, January 1979, 66–68; "NRA Expects Attacks but Not from Friends," AR, November 1978, 80–82.

162. "Pro-Gun Voters Shape 96th Congress." According to the NRA, the 83 percent number was up from 72 percent for the elections in 1976. See Neal Knox, "Knox On: The Upcoming Congressional Elections," AR, September 1978, 99.

163. Short and Durenberger maintained a similar firearms control policy position. See "Durenberger and Short on the Issues," *Minneapolis Star*, November 3, 1978, 6A.

164. See Neal Peirce, "Gun Control: The Issue That's a Non-Issue," *Philadelphia Inquirer*, October 6, 1980, 9A; Louis Harris, "78% Now Favoring Handgun Controls," *Arizona Daily Star* (Tucson), August 19, 1979, 3E; Louis Harris, "Big Majority Favors Controls on Handguns," *St. Petersburg (Fla.) Times*, August 16, 1979, 17A; "Pollster's Opinion: Americans Back Gun Controls," *Arizona Daily Star*, October 25, 1975, 5A.

165. "The Two Faces of Birch Bayh," *PB*, October 1980, 7.
166. Birch Bayh, "Bayh Lines: Right to Bear Arms," *Bedford (Ind.) Times-Mail*, September 24, 1980, 2.
167. Despite denying having endorsed Bayh, the NRA did publish a positive article on the Indiana senator going into the 1980 election. See "Institute Reports: Bayh Questions BATF 'Reforms,'" *AR*, November 1980, 50.
168. "Bayh NRA Letter Just a 'Thank You,'" *Indianapolis (Ind.) News*, October 22, 1980, 8.
169. See memorandum from Franklin White and Mark Cunha to Stuart Eizenstat, "Policy on Handgun Legislation," December 12, 1979, JCPP, Franklin White Subject File, box 9, folder Handgun Working File; letter from Franklin White to David J. Steinberg, National Council for Responsible Firearms Policy, June 15, 1979, JCPP, Franklin White Subject File, box 10, folder Handgun Working File; letter from Stuart E. Eizenstat to R. T. Stern, May 15, 1979, JCPP, Franklin White Subject File, box 10, folder Handgun Working File; Jimmy Carter, "The President's News Conference," April 10, 1979, *American Presidency Project*, https://www.presidency.ucsb.edu/documents/the-presidents-news-conference-981; letter from Stuart E. Eizenstat to Abner J. Mikva, February 15, 1979, JCPP, Stuart Eizenstat Form Letters, box 108, folder Gun Control; memorandum from W. Michael Blumenthal, Department of Treasury, to Jimmy Carter, February 1, 1979, JCPP, Franklin White Subject File, box 10, folder Handgun Working File.
170. "Reagan, Connally, Crane Big Winners in Nation's First Presidential Preference Poll of Firearms Owners, Conducted by Citizens Committee," *PB*, February 1980, 4–5.
171. For some different accounts of the forum, see E. B. Mann, "Our Endangered Tradition: Gun Ownership Views," *F&S*, July 1980, 22–23; "Institute Reports: N.H. Rally Draws Presidential Hopefuls," *AR*, April 1980, 59–60; Mark Nelson, "Anderson Hopes Plain Talk, Liberal Bent Aid Him in NH," *Fort Worth (Tex.) Star-Telegram*, February 24, 1980, 2A; "Gun Supporters' Boos Shoot Down Anderson's Speech," *Morristown (N.J.) Daily Record*, February 19, 1980, 3; "Rep. Anderson Draws Fire for Favoring Gun Control," *St. Louis (Mo.) Dispatch*, February 19, 1980, 4A; "N.H. Crowd Hits Licensing: Gun Control Fans Boo Anderson," *Lancaster (Pa.) New Era*, February 19, 1980, 7.
172. The CCRKBA was also very critical of Kennedy. See, e.g., "Kennedy Measure Would Establish Justice Department Dictatorship," *PB*, December 1979, 1, 4–5, 8; "Ted Kennedy: A Man Whose Time Has Come . . . and Gone," *PB*, November 1979, 2, 7.
173. The first NRA-ILA advertisement against Kennedy appeared in the September 1979 edition of AR, wherein the group used the possibility of a Kennedy run for president to fundraise for the Political Victory Fund. See "The Next President?," *AR*, September 1980, 59.
174. Neal Knox, "Will the Real Kennedy Please Stand Up?" *Sioux City (Iowa) Journal*, January 20, 1980, C9.
175. Neal Knox, "Seventeen Good Reasons for Sportsmen to Vote Against Senator Ted Kennedy on April 22 in the Democratic Primary," *Allentown (Pa.) Morning Call*, April 13, 1980, C11.

176. "Close the Door on Kennedy!" *Allentown (Pa.) Morning Call*, April 18, 1980, C7.

177. "Four Years of the Carter Administration: An Affront to the Rights of Gun Owners," *AR*, October 1980, 59.

178. "Institute Reports: NRA Endorses Reagan: A Reagan Victory Equals Gun Owner Victory," *AR*, October 1980, 58.

179. "Gallup Presidential Election Trial-Heat Trends, 1936–2008," undated, *Gallup*, https://web.archive.org/web/20170630070844/http://www.gallup.com/poll/110548/gallup-presidential-election-trialheat-trends-19362004.aspx#4.

180. "Institute Reports: Sportsmen Key to November Victories," *AR*, January 1981, 62.

181. See, e.g., Jack Samson, "Reagan on Guns, Hunting," *F&S*, October 1980, 56–57, 131–35; Rich Kirkpatrick, "Reagan, Bush Woo Sportsmen," *Hazleton (Pa.) Standard-Speaker*, September 25, 1980, 20; Scott Macleod, "Bush Addresses Sportsmen: Freedom for Gun Owners Promised by Candidate," *Tyrone (Pa.) Daily Herald*, September 20, 1980, 1; Ronald Hawkins, "Bush Speaks to Sportsmen in Carlisle," *Carlisle (Pa.) Sentinel*, September 20, 1980, 1; "Reagan Runs on Pro-Gun Platform," *PB*, September 1980, 4–5; John D. Lofton, Jr., "Reagan-Bush Views Compared," *Clarksdale (Miss.) Press Register*, August 3, 1980, 5A. When Bush and Reagan were both vying for the Republican nomination, the latter hit the former for having voting for the Gun Control Act. See David Nyhan, "Right Wing Comes to Reagan's Aid," *Boston Globe*, May 3, 1980, 3.

182. "Reagan Gets Gun Owners' Endorsement," *Miami (Fla.) Herald*, October 30, 1980, 8A.

183. David Rossie, "Reagan Uses a Fake Lure to Troll for the Votes of Sportsmen," *Binghamton (N.Y.) Press and Sun-Bulletin*, September 19, 1980, 3A; Bill Quimby, "Outdoor Leaders Ride Reagan Wagon," *Tucson (Ariz.) Citizen*, September 19, 1980, 3D; "Metaksa Named ILA Deputy Director," *AR*, April 1980, 60. Metaksa would go on to conduct a pro-gun interview with Reagan and publish it in the November 1980 issue of *Guns & Ammo*. See "Reagan Speaks Out on Gun Control," *G&A*, November 1980, 28, 112–13.

184. George Reiger, "Carter on Gun Laws and the Environment," *F&S*, September 1980, 92, 94, 96–98; "What Is Your View on Gun Control," undated 1980, JCPP, Franklin White Subject File, box 9, folder Handguns.

185. See, e.g., "I Will Never Lie to You," *PB*, October 1980, 1; "Four Years of the Carter Administration: An Affront to the Rights of Gun Owners," *AR*, October 1980, 59; "CCRKBA Attacks: Carter Record Hit During Pro-Gun Rally," *PB*, June 1980, 1, 3, 7–8.

186. See, e.g., Institute Reports: Emotionalism Ignores Facts," *AR*, February 1981, 58; John M. Snyder, "John Lennon and Gun Law Inanity," *PB*, January 1981, 1; "America's Hunters: Sickest of the Sick," *Bridgewater (N.J.) Courier-News*, December 27, 1980, 6; "NRA Prepares Gun Control Fight," *Rutland (Vt.) Daily Herald*, December 14, 1980, 2; "Loading Up . . . NRA Defensive After Lennon Death," *Sacramento (Calif.) Bee*, December 14, 1980, A3.

187. "Reagan's Position Against Gun Control Remains Firm," *Owensboro (Ky.) Messenger-Inquirer*, December 10, 1980, 6B.

188. "The Diplomatic Rifle," *PB*, February 1981, 3.

Epilogue

1. C. B. Lister, "Beware Wing and Mirage," *AR*, August 1944, 5.
2. See, e.g., NRA, *The Pro and Con of Firearms Registration* (Washington, D.C., 1968), 10; F. C. Daniel, "Registration of Private Guns Branded Usual Step Toward Imposition of Dictatorship," *Tampa Bay (Fla.) Times*, May 14, 1950, 19.
3. See, e.g., Daniel K. Stern, "Tell the People!," *AR*, March 1955, 39, 40.
4. "Freedom!," *Armed Citizen News*, January 1971, 1.
5. Barry Goldwater, "A Proper Balance," *G&A*, November 1964, 26.
6. Republican Party Platform of 1980, *American Presidency Project*, July 15, 1980, https://www.presidency.ucsb.edu/documents/republican-party-platform-1980.

Index

GPSR Authorized Representative: Easy Access System Europe, Mustamäe tee
50, 10621 Tallinn, Estonia, gpsr.requests@easproject.com

www.ingramcontent.com/pod-product-compliance
Lightning Source LLC
Chambersburg PA
CBHW021952090426
42811CB00041B/2415/J